# HOUGHTON MIFFLIN

# The Mathematics Experience

## Senior Authors

**Mary Ann Haubner**
Mount St. Joseph College
Cincinnati, Ohio

**Edward Rathmell**
University of Northern Iowa
Cedar Falls, Iowa

**Douglas Super**
Vancouver School Board
Vancouver, Canada

## Senior Consulting Author

**Lelon R. Capps**
University of Kansas
Lawrence, Kansas

## Authors

**Harold Asturias**
Norwood Street School
Los Angeles, California

**Harry Bohan**
Sam Houston State
University
Huntsville, Texas

**William L. Cole**
Michigan State University
East Lansing, Michigan

**Portia C. Elliott**
University of Massachusetts
Amherst, Massachusetts

**Francis J. Gardella**
East Brunswick Public Schools
East Brunswick, New Jersey

**Ana María Golán**
Santa Ana Unified
School District
Santa Ana, California

**Edwin McClintock**
Florida International
University
Miami, Florida

**Jean M. Shaw**
University of Mississippi
University, Mississippi

**Charles Thompson**
University of Louisville
Louisville, Kentucky

**Leland Webb**
California State University
Bakersfield, California

**Barbara Elder Weller**
Montclair Public Schools
Montclair, New Jersey

**Alma Wright**
Trotter Elementary School
Roxbury, Massachusetts

**Judith S. Zawojewski**
National-Louis University
Evanston, Illinois

## Houghton Mifflin Company   Boston

Atlanta       Dallas       Geneva, Illinois
Palo Alto     Princeton    Toronto

# Critical Readers

**Dennis Anderson**
Canyon Park Junior High School
Bothell, Washington

**Mary Buck**
C. R. Anderson Middle School
Helena, Montana

**Lorraine Cooke**
Jefferson Elementary School
Bath, South Carolina

**Janice Grashel**
Instructional Skills Coordinator
Lawrence, Kansas

**Lee Hoagland**
Westlawn Elementary School
Mobile, Alabama

**Charlotte Hughes**
Marbrook Elementary School
Wilmington, Delaware

**Terell Kaiser**
Valley Elementary School
East Grand Forks, Minnesota

**Rebecca Kirkland**
Highland Elementary School
Dothan, Alabama

**Charlene Little**
Whitney Young Middle School
Detroit, Michigan

**Rebecca Manning**
Brant Elementary School
Brant, New York

**Mark Medina**
King Elementary School
Colorado Springs, Colorado

**Michael Monaghan**
Emerson Elementary School
Wichita, Kansas

**Jill Moore**
Yolanda Elementary School
Springfield, Oregon

**Betty Pugh**
Paris Intermediate School
Paris, Arkansas

**Peter Scarano**
Elijah Elementary School
Clinton, Iowa

**Kathryn Scott**
Sandpiper Elementary School
Scottsdale, Arizona

**Calvin Shilt**
Shroder Middle School
Cincinnati, Ohio

**Jeanie Sisson**
Red Oak Elementary School
Oklahoma City, Oklahoma

**Susan Stonebraker**
South Central Elementary School
Canonsburg, Pennsylvania

**Donald J. Sweeney**
Silverhill School
Silverhill, Alabama

**Robert Tate**
Thomas Middle School
Philadelphia, Pennsylvania

**Ann Watson**
Rockefeller Elementary School
Little Rock, Arkansas

**Carol Wood**
Elma Elementary School
Elma, New York

# Multicultural Reviewers

**Gail Christopher**
Americans All
Chicago, Illinois

**Jane Horii**
Former Master Teacher
San Francisco Unified
School District
San Francisco, California

**Christella D. Moody**
Eastern Michigan Universit
Ypsilanti, Michigan

# Field Test Teachers

**Adam Artis**
Trotter Elementary School
Roxbury, Massachusetts

**Julie Book**
Edison Elementary School
Waterloo, Iowa

**Barbara Costa**
St. Teresa School
Cincinnati, Ohio

**Carolyn Donahue**
Patrick J. Kennedy School
East Boston, Massachusetts

**Ruben P. Guzman**
William Howard Taft
Middle School
Brighton, Massachusetts

**Ann G. Hill**
Nishuane School
Montclair, New Jersey

**Michael R. Johnson**
Wayne Van Horn School
Bakersfield, California

**Terry Kawas**
Forrestdale School
Rumson, New Jersey

**Mary E. Leydon**
William Howard Taft
Middle School
Brighton, Massachusetts

**Emma Louie**
Wayne Van Horn School
Bakersfield, California

**Kelly J. Martin**
Waverly Middle School
Lansing, Michigan

**Trudy Olson**
Irving Elementary School
Waterloo, Iowa

**Elaine Randolph-Jacobs**
Patrick J. Kennedy School
East Boston, Massachusetts

**Janet Reinhart**
Patrick J. Kennedy School
East Boston, Massachusetts

**William J. Rudder**
William Howard Taft
Middle School
Brighton, Massachusetts

**Mary Sue Salzarulo**
St. Teresa School
Cincinnati, Ohio

**Louise Scanlon-Oberg**
Trotter Elementary School
Roxbury, Massachusetts

**Sally Schneider**
St. Raphael School
Louisville, Kentucky

**Kathleen Schweer**
St. Teresa School
Cincinnati, Ohio

**Henry Smith**
William Howard Taft
Middle School
Brighton, Massachusetts

**Jo Ann Smithmeyer**
St. Teresa School
Cincinnati, Ohio

**Frances M. Stuart**
Patrick J. Kennedy School
East Boston, Massachusetts

**Kathleen Harris Sullivan**
William Howard Taft
Middle School
Brighton, Massachusetts

**Susan Thompson**
Sam Houston Elementary
School
Huntsville, Texas

**Willard Vredenburg**
South Miami Middle School
Miami, Florida

**Robert Walsh**
Patrick J. Kennedy School
East Boston, Massachusetts

**Julie Weseman**
Blackhawk Elementary School
Waterloo, Iowa

**Polly Wing**
Trotter Elementary School
Roxbury, Massachusetts

# Contents

# 3 Multiplication and Division: Whole Numbers and Decimals

# 4 Variables, Expressions, and Equations

# 5 Number Theory and Fraction Concepts

# 6 Fractions: Addition and Subtraction

# 7 Fractions: Multiplication and Division

# 8 Geometry and Measurement

# 9 Ratio, Proportion, and Applications

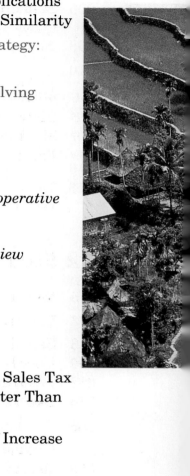

# 10 Percent

# 11 Percent Applications

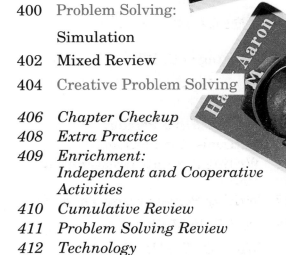

# 12 Statistics and Probability

# 13 Integers and Coordinate Graphing

# 14 Geometry and Measurement

# 15 Statistics and Probability

# DISCOVERY

Superstar producer, Quentin Blake is organizing a mega-concert for Earth Day. Rock bands are arriving from around the world. Quentin manages the production from his telecommunications console.

A number of bands are midjourney on their way to the stadium. Quentin's computer gives him a readout of the travel plans of each group and their current distance from O'Hare Airport in Chicago. Copy and complete the computer display and readout.

**Air travel for all five bands**

Total distance: 16,026 mi

Still to travel: 5,083 mi

Miles traveled: ▨

**Air Travel Budget**

Planned: $700,000

Expenses to date: $576,908

Difference: ▨

| MILEAGE | Dallas | Paris | New York | Moscow | London |
|---|---|---|---|---|---|
| Chicago | 784 | 4,517 | 736 | 5,598 | 4,391 |
| Dallas | — | 5,023 | 1,354 | 6,083 | 4,865 |
| Paris | 5,023 | — | 3,791 | 1,657 | 240 |
| New York | 1,354 | 3,791 | — | 4,970 | 3,696 |
| Moscow | | | | | 1,714 |
| L | | | | | |

| Group | Coming From | Miles Away | Miles Flown |
|---|---|---|---|
| Hawks | New York | 17 | ▨ |
| Dogies | Dallas | 309 | ▨ |
| M3R | Moscow | 1,258 | ▨ |
| Royals | London | 1,091 | ▨ |
| Zowies | Paris | 2,408 | ▨ |

A. $50.05 − 37.95

**1** ◫

B. $14.06 + $3 + 84¢ + $8

**2** ◫

C. $64.46 3.13 + 32.65

D. $9.57 − 6.44

**3** ◫

E. $1.45 + 3.75

**4** ◫

F. $9.05 − $2.33

G. 72.7 − 0.138

**5** ◫

H. 864 + 67

**6** ◫

I. 43,957 216,368 + 682,783

J. 27.295 − 5.195

**7** ◫

K. 27 + 6.3

**8** ◫

L. 43.627 + 37.932

M. 7.0005 − 4.3456

**9** ◫

N. 7.045 − 2.65

**10** ◫

O. 0.04 5.2 16 + 0.616

Help Julia to wire the sound stage for the concert. The number on the correct plug is between the answers to the problems on each side of the outlet. Compute. Then write the plug numbers for outlets 1–10.

$5  $20  $6  $50  15  30  40  100  1,000  3

# DISCOVERY

How many people attended the Live Aid concerts? To find out, multiply. Then add the answers to Exercises 1, 3, and 4.

1.  37
   × 8

2.  58
   × 60

3.  43
   × 68

4.  871 × 180

5.  4,070 × 67

6.  35.73 × 1,000

7.  2.604 × 3.9

8.  0.072 × 0.06

9.  3.74 × 3.5

Divide. Round to the nearest tenth. The fastest route to the stadium follows a path of quotients between 5 and 500. Write the quotients for the rock bands to follow.

6)636

820 ÷ 8

6.79 ÷ 2.4

90)360

32)509

42,078 ÷ 64

6,732 ÷ 16

396 ÷ 24

6.2596 ÷ 0.11

39.98 ÷ 2.5

0.4)16.8

1.302 ÷ 0.31

AIRPORT

STADIUM

Quentin has ordered promotional items to sell at the benefit concert. Find the cost of each item. (*Hint:* Divide the cost of a box by the quantity in a box.)

| ITEM | COST OF 1 BOX | QUANTITY IN 1 BOX | COST FOR 1 ITEM | SELLING PRICE |
|---|---|---|---|---|
| Q. mug | $6.09 | 6 | $6.09 ÷ 6 | $3.00 |
| R. T-shirt | $86.70 | 7 | $86.70 ÷ 7 | $15.00 |
| S. buttons | $5.29 | 17 | $5.29 ÷ 17 | $.75 |
| T. programs | $16.66 | 32 | $16.66 ÷ 32 | $2.00 |

Many fans buy one of each of these four items.

10. How much does Quentin pay for one each of these four items?

11. How much does a fan pay for one each of these four items?

12. How much profit is made on a sale of one each of these four items?

# Table of Numbers

| | O | P | Q | R | S | T | U | V | W |
|---|---|---|---|---|---|---|---|---|---|
| **A** | 65 | 38 | 82 | 49 | 19 | 77 | 91 | 24 | 56 |
| **B** | 436 | 903 | 150 | 539 | 828 | 671 | 295 | 747 | 361 |
| **C** | 108 | 94 | 699 | 75 | 470 | 274 | 86 | 562 | 316 |
| **D** | 5,239 | 2,430 | 6,771 | 1,121 | 9,036 | 7,329 | 3,615 | 8,484 | 4,418 |
| **E** | 1,045 | 6,616 | 789 | 2,318 | 989 | 5,231 | 3,251 | 832 | 4,119 |
| **F** | 0.3 | 0.80 | 0.9 | 0.71 | 0.6 | 0.34 | 0.79 | 0.2 | 0.65 |
| **G** | 4.8 | 9.7 | 5.3 | 1.1 | 3.5 | 1.6 | 7.2 | 2.9 | 2.4 |
| **H** | 1.25 | 2.7 | 8 | 9.58 | 3.9 | 4.5 | 7 | 4.63 | 8.6 |
| **I** | $\frac{2}{3}$ | $\frac{1}{2}$ | $\frac{6}{12}$ | $\frac{5}{6}$ | $\frac{1}{4}$ | $\frac{7}{12}$ | $\frac{1}{6}$ | $\frac{3}{4}$ | $\frac{1}{3}$ |
| **J** | $4\frac{1}{2}$ | $3\frac{3}{10}$ | $2\frac{3}{5}$ | $1\frac{1}{10}$ | 7 | $3\frac{2}{5}$ | $4\frac{8}{10}$ | 5 | $2\frac{4}{5}$ |
| **K** | $\frac{5}{16}$ | $2\frac{5}{8}$ | $2\frac{1}{2}$ | $\frac{7}{8}$ | $4\frac{1}{16}$ | $1\frac{1}{4}$ | $1\frac{3}{8}$ | $3\frac{3}{4}$ | $4\frac{7}{16}$ |
| **L** | 0.2 | 1.5 | $4\frac{3}{4}$ | 0.25 | $\frac{3}{10}$ | $\frac{1}{2}$ | 0.75 | $2\frac{1}{4}$ | $1\frac{4}{5}$ |
| **M** | 50% | 1% | 100% | 25% | 5% | 75% | 30% | 200% | 80% |
| **N** | -3 | -5 | 8 | 0 | -2 | 3 | -1 | 6 | -4 |

Ideas for using this table for estimation, mental math, and for calculator activities are found periodically in the Two Minute Math sections of the Teacher's Edition.

**DID YOU KNOW . . . ?**

The fastest pitch recorded was thrown by Nolan Ryan in 1974. His record speed was 100.9 mi/h.

The ERA (earned run average) is the average number of runs a pitcher allows per 9-inning game. The graph below compares the ERAs of pitchers in the 1910s with those in the 1980s.

## ERA Leaders 1917-1919 and 1987-1989

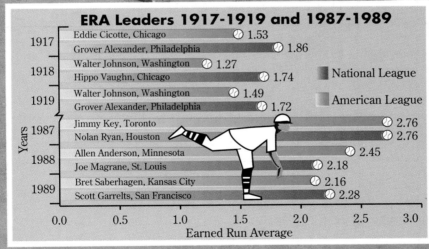

| Years | Pitcher | ERA |
|-------|---------|-----|
| 1917 | Eddie Cicotte, Chicago | 1.53 |
| 1917 | Grover Alexander, Philadelphia | 1.86 |
| 1918 | Walter Johnson, Washington | 1.27 |
| 1918 | Hippo Vaughn, Chicago | 1.74 |
| 1919 | Walter Johnson, Washington | 1.49 |
| 1919 | Grover Alexander, Philadelphia | 1.72 |
| 1987 | Jimmy Key, Toronto | 2.76 |
| 1987 | Nolan Ryan, Houston | 2.76 |
| 1988 | Allen Anderson, Minnesota | 2.45 |
| 1988 | Joe Magrane, St. Louis | 2.18 |
| 1989 | Bret Saberhagen, Kansas City | 2.16 |
| 1989 | Scott Garrelts, San Francisco | 2.28 |

■ National League
■ American League

Earned Run Average: 0.0   0.5   1.0   1.5   2.0   2.5   3.0

**USING DATA**

Collect
Organize
**Describe**
Predict

Who has the best ERA of all pitchers in the bar graph?

Which league had more top ERAs?

Why do you think ERAs are higher in more recent years?

# I *Knew* That!

## What Is Number Sense?

It is important that we develop a sense for understanding and using numbers in our everyday lives.

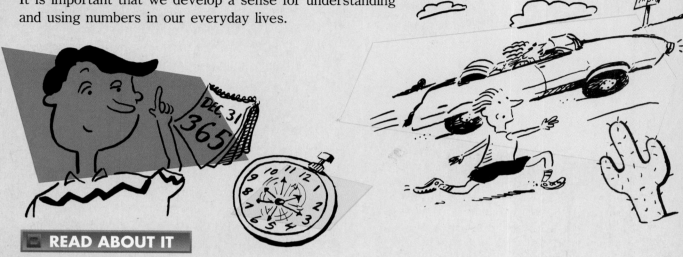

**READ ABOUT IT**

### If you have number sense:

You know that 365 days (d) is 1 year (yr),  365 hours (h) has to be less than 1 yr.

You know that 78 miles (mi) is more than 72 mi,  a golf score of 72 is better than one of 78.

You know that 100 is a large number when it describes the number of years a person has lived,  100 is small when it describes the number of minutes a person has lived.

You know that the product of 0.5 and 50 is half of 50,  the product of 5 and 50 is five times greater than 50.

You know that a car can travel greater than 50 mi in 1 h,  a person cannot run 50 mi in 1 h.

Use your number sense to write *true* or *false* for each statement about 12,164.

The number **12,164** is:

1. the number of dollars you might pay for a new car.

2. the distance in miles from New York City to Boston.

3. close to the product of $2 \times 600$.

4. close to the number of stars in the sky.

5. less than half of 25 thousand.

6. close to the number of minutes in $9\frac{1}{2}$ d.

7. 2,164 more than 10,000.

8. closer to 12,000 than to 13,000.

9. 2,100 less than 14,264.

10. the next counting number after 12,263.

11. a number you can easily count to in $\frac{1}{2}$ h.

Use your number sense to find a number in the box that matches the description.

12. the shoe size of an adult male

13. the amount left after you have eaten some pizza

14. the number of weeks in most Februarys

15. the number of pages read in $1\frac{1}{2}$ h

■ **WRITE ABOUT IT**

16. Write a sentence explaining what you think number sense is.

# Exponents

The Great Pyramid at Giza, built for King Cheops, is more than 4,500 yr old. About 100,000 workers built the pyramid. You can write the number of workers in **exponential form**.

$$100{,}000 = 10 \times 10 \times 10 \times 10 \times 10 = 10^5 \text{ workers.}$$

The **exponent**, 5, below tells how many times the **base**, 10, is used as a **factor**.

$$\text{base} \longrightarrow 10^5 \longleftarrow \text{exponent}$$

What patterns can you find with other powers of 10 below?

$$
\begin{aligned}
10{,}000 &= 10 \times 10 \times 10 \times 10 &&= 10^4 \\
1{,}000 &= 10 \times 10 \times 10 &&= 10^3 \\
100 &= 10 \times 10 &&= 10^2 \\
10 &= 10 &&= 10^1 \\
1 &= &&= 10^0
\end{aligned}
$$

> **Any nonzero number with an exponent of 0 is 1.**
> **Any number with an exponent of 1 is the number itself.**

Other examples:

| Exponential Form | | Factors | Standard Form |
|---|---|---|---|
| $7^2$ | *seven to the second power, or seven squared* | $7 \times 7$ | 49 |
| $6^3$ | *six to the third power, or six cubed* | $6 \times 6 \times 6$ | 216 |
| $3^4$ | *three to the fourth power* | $3 \times 3 \times 3 \times 3$ | 81 |

**THINK ALOUD** Can you write 81 another way using an exponent?

## GUIDED PRACTICE

Give the exponent if the factors are written in exponential form.

1. $2 \times 2 \times 2 \times 2 \times 2$

2. $12 \times 12 \times 12 \times 12 \times 12 \times 12 \times 12$

3. **THINK ALOUD** Does $2^4$ equal $4^2$? Does interchanging the base and the exponent always work? Explain your answer.

4   LESSON 1–2

The early Egyptians knew many principles of geometry, such as the right triangle relationships, and used them to construct the pyramids.

## PRACTICE

Write in exponential form.

**4.** $2 \times 2 \times 2 \times 2$ $2^4$  **5.** $3 \times 3 \times 3 \times 3 \times 3$ $3^5$

**6.** $8 \times 8 \times 8$ $8^3$   $4^3$   **7.** five squared $5$

**8.** four to the third power   **9.** two to the sixth power

**10.** seven cubed   **11.** nine squared $9^2$

**12.** six to the zero power $6^0 = 1$

Write in standard form and as a product of factors when possible.

**13.** $5^2$       **14.** $12^2$       **15.** $4^2$       **16.** $9^2$

**17.** $7^3$       **18.** $10^3$       **19.** $15^2$       **20.** $16^0 = 1$

**21.** $2^1$       **22.** $15^1$       **23.** $6^2$       **24.** $2^3$

**CALCULATOR**  Write in standard form.

**25.** $35^5$           **26.** $29^4$           **27.** $9^6$

**28.** $12^5$           **29.** $17^4$           **30.** $55^3$

## PROBLEM SOLVING

**NUMBER SENSE**  Choose the correct answer.

**31.** Was the Great Pyramid originally 8 ft, 481 ft, or 4,810 ft tall?

**32.** Does the Great Pyramid contain about 20, 200, or 2,000,000 stone blocks?

---

## *Critical Thinking*

Work with a partner to discover the patterns for multiplying and dividing numbers with exponents.

$3^2 \times 3^4 = (3 \times 3) \times (3 \times 3 \times 3 \times 3) = 3^6$

$2^5 \div 2^2 = \dfrac{2 \times 2 \times 2 \times 2 \times 2}{2 \times 2} = 2 \times 2 \times 2 = 2^3$

Are the bases the same? Compare the exponents.

**1. IN YOUR WORDS**  Write rules for the product and quotient of numbers with exponents.

**2.**  Write the product or quotient as a number with an exponent.

**a.** $6^2 \times 6^3$       **b.** $7^4 \times 7^2$       **c.** $5^2 \times 5^6$       **d.** $2^3 \times 2^4 \times 2^5$

**e.** $5^7 \div 5^3$       **f.** $8^9 \div 8^5$       **g.** $10^{12} \div 10^3$       **h.** $256^5 \div 256^2$

# Place Value: Whole Numbers, Decimals

The largest publication in the world is the 1,112-volume set of *British Parliamentary Papers* of 1800–1900. The publication has a mass of 3,303.15 kilograms (kg).

Our number system is based on powers of ten. The value of each digit in a number depends on its place. The place value table helps you understand the different ways this mass can be written.

| ten-thousands | thousands | hundreds | tens | ones | | tenths | hundredths | thousandths |
|---|---|---|---|---|---|---|---|---|
| $10^4$ | $10^3$ | $10^2$ | $10^1$ | $10^0$ | | $\frac{1}{10^1}$ | $\frac{1}{10^2}$ | $\frac{1}{10^3}$ |
| 10,000 | 1,000 | 100 | 10 | 1 | | 0.1 | 0.01 | 0.001 |
| | 3 | 3 | 0 | 3 | . | 1 | 5 | |

**Standard form:** 3,303.15

**Word form:** three thousand, three hundred three, and fifteen hundredths

**Short word form:** 3 thousand, 3 hundred 3, and 15 hundredths

**Expanded form:** $(3 \times 1{,}000) + (3 \times 100) + (3 \times 1) + \left(1 \times \frac{1}{10}\right) + \left(5 \times \frac{1}{100}\right)$

**Expanded form with exponents:** $\left(3 \times 10^3\right) + \left(3 \times 10^2\right) + \left(3 \times 10^0\right) + \left(1 \times \frac{1}{10^1}\right) + \left(5 \times \frac{1}{10^2}\right)$

**THINK ALOUD** One million is $10^6$, or 1,000,000. Explain how you would write 1 billion in standard form and in expanded form with exponents.

---
### GUIDED PRACTICE
---

1. **THINK ALOUD** Write 2,015 in expanded form with exponents. Why do you not need to write $0 \times 10^2$?

Write the number in short word form and with exponents.

2. 4,053
3. 43,000,005
4. 20.103
5. 873.52

6. **CRITICAL THINKING** Explain why 1.5 million and 1,500,000 are the same number.

Write in standard form.

**7.** 27 thousand, 583

**8.** 12 and 4 tenths

**9.** 751 thousand, 23

**10.** 17 and 3 hundredths

**11.** 399 and 5 tenths

**12.** 59 and 13 thousandths

**13.** 73 and 824 thousandths

**14.** 32 million, 352 thousand, and 6 tenths

**15.** $600 + 90 + 6 + 0.8$

**16.** $30,000 + 100 + 60 + 3 + 0.3$

**17.** $40 + 7 + 0.1 + 0.05$

**18.** $50,000 + 4,000 + 300 + 80 + 9 + 0.3$

**19.** a half million

**20.** a thousand thousand

**21.** six thousand million

**22.** $(6 \times 10^3) + (5 \times 10^2) + (7 \times 10^1)$

**23.** $(3 \times 10^2) + (5 \times 10^0) + \left(2 \times \frac{1}{10^1}\right)$

**24.** $(9 \times 10^2) + (5 \times 10^1) + \left(4 \times \frac{1}{10^2}\right)$

**25.** 2.5 thousand

**26.** 34.2 thousand

**27.** 6.8 million

**28.** 42.51 million

Write the number in expanded form with exponents.

**29.** 7,854

**30.** 45.42

**31.** 1.083

**32.** 8,382.35

**33.** ten million

**34.** one hundred million

**35.** ten billion

**NUMBER SENSE** Match the description with the number in word form.

**36.** the number of words in the world's longest personal letter

**a.** one hundred eighty-two

**37.** the width of *Super Book*, the world's largest book, in meters

**b.** one million, four hundred two thousand, three hundred forty-four

**38.** the number of letters in the longest word ever to appear in literature

**c.** two and seventy-four hundredths

# Comparing and Ordering Numbers

Two birds common to many parts of the United States are the cardinal and the red-winged blackbird. These birds have similar average lengths. Which bird's average length is greater?

The number line below shows how the two lengths compare.

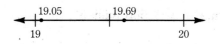

The cardinal has the greater length because 19.69 > 19.05.

You can compare numbers by looking at the farthest place to the left that has different digits.

cardinal
19.69 cm

Compare   68,532   and   68,919.
We know        5      <        9,
    so   68,532   <   68,919.

Compare   51.321   and   51.32.
              51.321              51.320 ⇐ Annex zeros as needed.
We know           1      >           0,
      so   51.321   >   51.32.

Compare   18.39   and   18.36   and   18.30. ⇐ Annex a zero.
We know        9      >      6      >      0,
    so   18.39   >   18.36   >   18.3. ⇐ 18.36 is between 18.39 and 18.3.

---

## GUIDED PRACTICE

Compare. Choose >, <, or = .

**1.** 17.3 is less than 17.36       **2.** 571 ▓ 5107

**3.** 0.001 ▓ 0.0001

Order from the greatest to the least.

**4.** 4.25; 4.2; 4.3             **5.** 9.051; 9.057; 9.05

**6.** 598,200; 59,820; 5,982

**7. THINK ALOUD** Are there *less than, exactly,* or *more than* nine numbers between 1 and 2? Explain.

red-winged blackbird
19.05 cm

MATH AND SCIENCE

Compare. Choose $>$, $<$, or $=$ .

**8.** 456 ▤ 546

**9.** 935 ▤ 594

**10.** 1,490 ▤ 1,409

**11.** 0.51 ▤ 0.512

**12.** 0.483 ▤ 0.48

**13.** 0.87 ▤ 0.087

**14.** 10.26 ▤ 10.260

**15.** 192.15 ▤ 193.02

**16.** 43.51 ▤ 17.871

**17.** 0.999 ▤ 1.000

**18.** 0.99 ▤ 0.1

**19.** 658.362 ▤ 658.359

**20.** $3^3$ ▤ $4^2$

**21.** $27^0$ ▤ $5^1$

**22.** $3^4$ ▤ $9^2$

**23.** 1 billion ▤ 987 million

**24.** 1 billion ▤ 1,500 million

Order from the least to the greatest.

**25.** 3,835; 3,560; 3,480

**26.** 0.514; 0.541; 0.554

**27.** 0.01; 0.001; 0.1

**28.** 5.384; 5.348; 5.843

**29.** $12^2$; $21^2$; $13^2$

**30.** $17^1$; $27^1$; $30^1$

**NUMBER SENSE** Match the letter with the number.

**31.** 0.1

**32.** 0.75

**33.** 1.3

**34.** 1.09

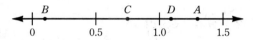

**CRITICAL THINKING** Give two numbers between the given pair of numbers.

**35.** 351 and 354

**36.** 99 and 100

**37.** 0.004 and 0.009

**38.** 9.528 and 9.531

Use the table below to solve.

**39.** Which birds are smaller in average length than the Baltimore oriole?

**40.** Outlines of a chickadee, robin, and woodpecker are drawn to scale below. Match the outlines to the kind of bird.

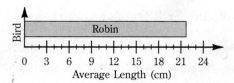

A    B    C

**41.** Copy and complete the bar graph. Show all birds mentioned on pages 8 and 9.

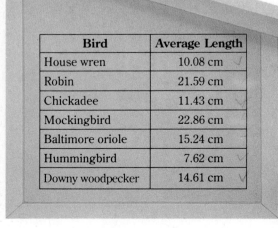

| Bird | Average Length |
|------|----------------|
| House wren | 10.08 cm |
| Robin | 21.59 cm |
| Chickadee | 11.43 cm |
| Mockingbird | 22.86 cm |
| Baltimore oriole | 15.24 cm |
| Hummingbird | 7.62 cm |
| Downy woodpecker | 14.61 cm |

## Problem Solving:
## Four-Part Process

There are 100 floors in Chicago's John Hancock building. The elevator takes about 15 seconds (s) to go to the next floor and stop. If you stopped at each floor, about how many minutes would it take to get to the 100th floor?

### Understand the problem.

| | |
|---|---|
| Know what to find. | What is the question? |
| Read for information. | How many floors are there?<br>How long does it take to travel and stop at each floor? |

### Make a plan.

| | |
|---|---|
| Ask questions. | Would it take *more* or *less* than 100 minutes (min)? |
| Decide what to do. | Find how far the elevator goes in 1 min.<br>15 s ⇨ 1 floor<br>60 s, or 1 min ⇨ 4 floors<br>If the elevator takes 1 min to stop at 4 floors, how many minutes for 100 floors?<br>100 ÷ 4 = ? |

### Carry out the plan.

| | |
|---|---|
| Work through the plan. | 100 ÷ 4 = 25<br>The elevator takes 25 min to stop at 100 floors. |

### Look back.

| | |
|---|---|
| Is your answer reasonable? | The answer is reasonable. In each of the 25 min, the elevator has stopped at 4 floors. |
| Did you answer the question? | Reread the question.<br>Check your labels. |

Can you think of another way to solve the problem?

**CRITICAL THINKING**   Why do tall buildings have express elevators that go only to the top floors?

MATH AND SOCIAL STUDIES

Use the four-part process to solve.

1. In 1812, about 100 people lived in the Chicago area. Today, the population is about 30,000 times greater.

   a. When did about 100 people live in Chicago?

   b. What operation would you use to find today's population?

   c. About how many people live in Chicago today?

2. Greg got on a Sears Tower elevator at the 1st floor. He went up 10 floors, up 5 more floors, down 8 floors, up 12 floors, down 4 floors, and got off. On which floor did Greg get off the elevator?

Solve.

3. The Sears Tower is 1,454 ft tall. Is that *more than* or *less than* a quarter mile? (1 mi = 5,280 ft)

4. The Great Chicago Fire destroyed much of the city in 1871. How many years ago was that?

5. There are 7,000 fish and other water animals in the John G. Shedd Aquarium. Do you think that is an exact number or an estimate?

6. Jean Baptiste Pointe du Sable, an African American, built a trading post on the Chicago River in the 1770s. The Du Sable Museum of African-American History is named for him. Chicago has 16 other ethnic history museums. How many ethnic history museums are in Chicago?

7. Each different letter in *CHICAGO* has a different number value. If the sum of the numbers is 40, what number value does each letter have?

8. Chicago's Hispanic population was 247,343 in 1970, 422,061 in 1980, and 545,852 in 1990. Did it grow more from 1970 to 1980 or from 1980 to 1990?

# OUR SOLAR SYSTEM

**D** id you know that the Sun is about 5,000,000,000 yr old? This medium-sized star is now only at the halfway point of its life. As the center of our Solar System, the Sun is our nearest star. The Sun is about 93,000,000 mi away from Earth.

1. Of 500 million, 5 billion, and 5,000 million, which are short word forms of 5,000,000,000?

2. Is 9.3 million, 93 million, or 93 hundred thousand a short word form of 93,000,000?

3. How long is the Sun expected to live?

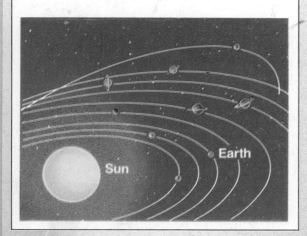

**O** ur Solar System spans vast distances. Use the table to solve.

| Planet | Average Distance from the Sun (in million miles) |
|---|---|
| Pluto | 3,675.3 |
| Earth | 93.0 |
| Jupiter | 483.8 |
| Mercury | 36.0 |
| Saturn | 887.1 |
| Venus | 67.3 |
| Uranus | 1,783.9 |
| Mars | 141.7 |
| Neptune | 2,795.5 |

4. Explain why it is correct to use the number 67,300,000 to describe the distance in miles between Venus and the Sun.

5. About how far away is Saturn from the Sun in standard form?

6. How much closer is Mars to the Sun than Neptune is?

7. List the planets by their distances from the Sun in order from the least to the greatest.

The Sun and its planets are part of the Milky Way galaxy. The Milky Way has more than 100 billion stars. There are more than 1 billion galaxies found in the universe.

8. Rewrite the numbers in the paragraph about the Milky Way in standard form.

9. Ten thousand stars are represented by each star below. How many stars are represented in all?

10. Each star in the miniature galaxy below represents 10 million stars. How many stars are represented in all?

Comets are very common in our Solar System. The nucleus of a comet may be up to 10 thousand miles in diameter and its tail can be as long as 28 million miles.

Halley's comet is now traveling in its orbit away from the Sun. The greatest distance the comet travels from the Sun is about 3.28 billion miles.

11. Rewrite in standard form the three large numbers in the paragraphs about comets.

12. Is the comet's tail longer than the distance between Earth and the Sun?

# Rounding Whole Numbers and Decimals

Which of these facts is easier to remember?

The Boston Marathon is 26.218 mi long.
The Boston Marathon is about 26 mi long.

Most people find it easier to remember a number like 26 than a number like 26.218.

The number line shows that 26.218 is close to 26.

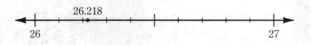

Here's how you round 26.218 to the nearest whole number, 26.

- Mark the digit in the ones' place.
- Look at the digit to the right.    26.218
  Is it 5 or greater?
- Round down to 26, since 2 is less than 5.

**THINK ALOUD**  What would you do if the digit to the right were 5 or greater?

Other examples:

Round 34,568 to hundreds.  ⇨ 34,600      Round 39.963 to tens.  ⇨ 40

Round 7.0834 to hundredths.  ⇨ 7.08      Round 0.1543 to tenths.  ⇨ 0.2

━━━━━━━━━━━━━━━━ **GUIDED PRACTICE** ━━━━━━━━━━━━━━━━

Round each number to the given place.

1. 55,789; hundreds, thousands

2. 0.539; tenths, hundredths

3. **NUMBER SENSE**  Is 38.39 closer to 38 or 39? To which whole number would it be rounded?

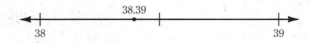

4. **CRITICAL THINKING**  What is the greatest whole number that rounds to 500?

Round to the nearest ~~ten~~ and hundred.

| | | | | | |
|---|---|---|---|---|---|
| **5.** | 483 | **6.** | 1,907 | **7.** | 5,864 |
| **8.** | 9,485 | **9.** | 10,079 | **10.** | 67,279 |
| **11.** | 8,006 | **12.** | 54,637 | **13.** | 100,741 |
| **14.** | 750,013 | **15.** | 995,329 | **16.** | 667,555 |

Round to the nearest ~~tenth~~, hundredth, and whole number.

| | | | | | |
|---|---|---|---|---|---|
| **17.** | 3.736 | **18.** | 382.426 | **19.** | 12.996 |
| **20.** | 6.328 | **21.** | 42.4563 | **22.** | 18.358 |
| **23.** | 0.039 | **24.** | 0.997 | **25.** | 6.003 |
| **26.** | 5,176.15 | **27.** | 185.476 | **28.** | 8.7298 |

**NUMBER SENSE**  Match each number with a letter on the number line.

| | | | | | |
|---|---|---|---|---|---|
| **29.** | 1,650 | **30.** | 1,111 | **31.** | 1,875 |
| **32.** | 591 | **33.** | 738.99 | **34.** | 2,311.51 |

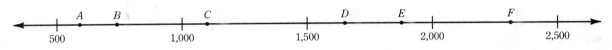

A    B         C              D    E              F

500        1,000        1,500        2,000        2,500

**PROBLEM SOLVING**

Solve.

**35.** What is the greatest number of runners that could have entered the Bermuda Marathon?

**36.** Which marathon had about 1,000 fewer runners than the Moscow Marathon? about 2,000 more?

**37.** What is the least number of runners that could have run in Detroit? in Moscow?

APPROXIMATELY 1,200 RUNNERS START THE BERMUDA MARATHON

Nearly 13,000 run the Kawaguchi - Ko Marathon

Close to 10,250 start the Detroit Marathon

About 11,000 begin in the Moscow Marathon

## When Do We Estimate?

Many times you do not need to use your math skills to calculate an exact answer. Instead you estimate. An **estimate** is a number close enough to an exact number that permits you to make a correct decision.

### 🔲 READ ABOUT IT

We use estimates when . . .

• an estimate is as good as an exact number.

How slow should a car be going to be driving safely in foggy conditions?

How far is it to the next town?

• there is no way of knowing the exact number.

Milk is rich in calcium. How much calcium goes into your system when you drink a glass of milk?

How much Vitamin C is in your diet each day?

• we could get the exact number but it is too difficult.

How many people used a ferryboat to go to work in New York City last Tuesday?

How many people were in New York City at 8:00 this morning?

• we want to check whether an exact computation is reasonable.

The **perimeter** is the total distance around.
Our backyard has a perimeter of 120 yards (yd).

$36\frac{3}{4}$ yd

$36\frac{3}{4}$ yd

$23\frac{1}{4}$ yd

$23 + 37 + 23 + 37 = 120$ yd

## 🔲 TALK ABOUT IT

**1.** Find each number below in the airport scene above. Decide whether it is used as an *exact number* or an *estimate*. Explain.

   **a.** $495.17      **b.** $900      **c.** 846 mi      **d.** 2nd

   **e.** $2.95      **f.** 9 runs      **g.** $1,200      **h.** $1\frac{1}{2}$ d

**2.** Is the number of people standing at the New York ticket counter exact or estimated? Why?

**3.** Mr. Rivera figures the cost of two tickets to Dallas would be $495.17 + $495.17 = $990.34. Is his computation reasonable?

**4.** Would the manager of Chicago's O'Hare airport report the number of passengers inside all terminal buildings at a given time as an exact or estimated number? Why?

**5.** Would the number of airplane takeoffs in one day at Seattle's Sea-Tac airport be an exact number or an estimate? Why?

## 🔲 WRITE ABOUT IT

**6.** Think of an exact number not already mentioned on this page that you might see or use at an airport. Now name a number that is an estimate.

## LANGUAGE & VOCABULARY

Tell whether you think the statement uses an *estimate* or an *exact number*. Explain your decision.

1. There are 45,000 people in the stadium today watching the Boston Red Sox play the Cleveland Indians.

2. My aunt lives 12 blocks from my house.

3. On a recent diet, Roberto lost 22 lb.

4. The school cafeteria served 328 lunches yesterday.

## QUICK QUIZ ✓

Write in standard form. *(pages 4–7)*

1. $4^3$

2. $(1 \times 10^2) + (7 \times 10^1) + (9 \times 10^0) + \left(3 \times \frac{1}{10^2}\right)$

3. 7 million, 1 thousand, and 4 tenths

4. 9.8 million

Compare. Choose >, <, or =. *(pages 8–9, 12–13)*

5. 2.5 billion ▨ 3 million

6. $3^4$ ▨ $9^2$

7. 0.666 ▨ 1.000

Round the number to the given places. *(pages 14–15)*

8. 97,801; hundreds, thousands

9. 21.059; tenths, hundredths

Solve. *(pages 10–11)*

10. The Empire State Building in New York City is 1,472 ft tall. The Gateway Arch in St. Louis, Missouri, is 842 ft shorter than the Empire State Building. The Eiffel Tower in Paris, France, is 1,052 ft tall.

    a. Which of the three structures is 1,472 ft tall?

    b. How does the Eiffel Tower compare in size to the Empire State Building?

    c. How much taller is the Eiffel Tower than the Gateway Arch?

Write the answers in your learning log.

**1.** What do you know about a number with an exponent?

**2.** How are exponents and multiplication related? Include an example in your explanation.

**3.** Your friend thinks decimals with two places are always smaller than decimals with three places. Explain what is wrong with this thinking.

**DID YOU KNOW . . . ?** The highest temperature ever recorded in the United States was 134°F. The lowest temperature was ⁻80°F. How do the highest and lowest temperatures ever recorded in your town compare with these temperatures?

In the first round of a hopscotch game, Ellie jumped in box 1. In the second round, she jumped in boxes 1 and 2. In the third round, she jumped in boxes 1, 2, and 3, and so on. How many boxes will she have jumped in at the end of eight rounds?

# Metric Units: Length

The metric system has standard units of measure. The **meter** (**m**) is the basic unit of length in the metric system.

A doorknob is about 1 m above the floor. A letter is about 1 millimeter (mm) thick. A mail carrier's little finger is about 1 centimeter (cm) wide.

The metric system is based on powers of ten. Each metric unit is ten times as great as the unit to its right and one-tenth as great as the unit to its left.

| kilometer | hectometer | dekameter | meter | decimeter | centimeter | millimeter |
|---|---|---|---|---|---|---|
| km | hm | dam | m | dm | cm | mm |
| 1,000 m | 100 m | 10 m | 1 m | 0.1 m | 0.01 m | 0.001 m |

These rules are used to change metric units.

1. To change from a *larger* unit to a *smaller* unit, *multiply* by a power of ten.

2. To change from a *smaller* unit to a *larger* unit, *divide* by a power of ten.

3.258 km = 3,258 m

Which rule was used? By which number was 3.258 multiplied? Why?

437.3 cm = 4.373 m

Which rule was used? By which number was 437.3 divided? Why?

## GUIDED PRACTICE

1. **NUMBER SENSE**  Choose the appropriate metric unit. Use *km, m, cm,* or *mm.*

   a. the length of a thumbtack

   b. the distance between towns

2. Change 352.73 m into kilometers, centimeters, and millimeters.

3. **THINK ALOUD**  Suppose you were asked to measure the length of a hall in your school. Would you rather measure in meters or decimeters? Explain.

**NUMBER SENSE**  Name an appropriate unit for measuring the item.
Choose *km*, *m*, *cm*, or *mm*.

**4.** the height of a mountain

**5.** the distance from Denver to Detroit

**6.** your height

**7.** the length of a fly

Copy and complete.

**8.** 7 m = ▦ cm

**9.** 10 km = ▦ m

**10.** 14 m = ▦ mm

**11.** 2 m = ▦ cm

**12.** 5 km = ▦ m

**13.** 4 m = ▦ km

**14.** 5.9 m = ▦ km

**15.** 3.4 cm = ▦ mm

**16.** 0.035 km = ▦ cm

**17.** 425 m = ▦ km

**18.** 1.4 km = ▦ mm

**19.** 1 mm = ▦ km

**MIXED REVIEW**  Compare. Choose
>, <, or = .

**20.** 0.5 million ▦ a half million

**21.** $7^2$ ▦ $4 \times 10^1$

**22.** $6^4$ ▦ $10^3$

**23.** 7.9 cm ▦ 3 m

**24.** 1,800 mm ▦ 18 m

**25.** 350 km ▦ 1,000 m

Find two endpoints on the rule for each line segment length.

**26.** 55 mm

**27.** 3 cm

**28.** 0.9 cm

**29.** 1.8 cm

**30.** 0.003 m

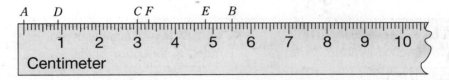

Work with a partner to solve.

**31.** A swimming pool
company sells three
different shapes of pools.
Find the perimeter of
(the total distance
around) each pool.

**32.** **IN YOUR WORDS**  Draw
a pool that represents
a perimeter of 30 m.
Label the dimensions.
Compare your diagram
with a classmate's. Are the
pools the same shape?
Explain.

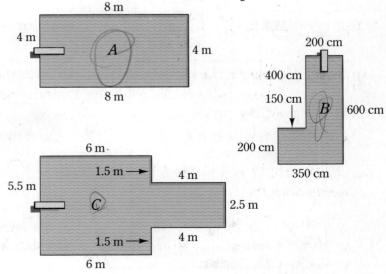

## Metric Units: Capacity

It is interesting to know that at peak times close to 169,800 kiloliters (kL) of water flow over Niagara Falls in 1 min.

This is the same as 169,800,000 L of water per minute.

Four glasses of water is about 1 L.

A drop of water is about 1 mL.

The **liter (L)** is the basic unit of capacity in the metric system.

**Capacity** is a measure of how much a container holds.

| kiloliter | hectoliter | dekaliter | liter | deciliter | centiliter | milliliter |
|-----------|-----------|-----------|-------|-----------|------------|------------|
| kL | hL | daL | L | dL | cL | mL |
| 1,000 L | 100 L | 10 L | 1 L | 0.1 L | 0.01 L | 0.001 L |

These rules are used to change metric units.

1. To change from a *larger* unit to a *smaller* unit, *multiply* by a power of ten.

2. To change from a *smaller* unit to a *larger* unit, *divide* by a power of ten.

54 mL = 0.054 L

Which rule was used? By which number was 54 divided? Explain?

4.5 kL = 4,500 L

Which rule was used? By which number was 4.5 multiplied? Explain.

Estimate the capacity of the container.

**1.** a small measuring cup    **2.** a toothpaste tube    **3.** a large paint can

**4.** a kitchen sink    **5.** an aquarium    **6.** the gas tank of a car

Copy and complete.

**7.** 20 L = ▦ mL    **8.** 25 L = ▦ mL    **9.** 27 L = ▦ mL

**10.** 1.500 L = ▦ mL    **11.** 2.600 L = ▦ mL    **12.** 7.210 L = ▦ mL

**13.** 0.123 L = ▦ mL    **14.** 0.251 L = ▦ mL    **15.** 0.278 L = ▦ mL

**16.** 14.5 L = ▦ mL    **17.** 9.2 L = ▦ mL    **18.** 0.1L = ▦ mL

**19.** 3,000 mL = ▦ L    **20.** 4,000 mL = ▦ L    **21.** 7,000 mL = ▦ L

**22.** 1,200 mL = ▦ L    **23.** 1,803 mL = ▦ L    **24.** 2,315 mL = ▦ L

**25.** 700 mL = ▦ L    **26.** 634 mL = ▦ L    **27.** 815 mL = ▦ L

Compare. Choose >, <, or =.

**28.** 5 L ▦ 50 mL    **29.** 300.5 mL ▦ 200 L    **30.** 0.05 L ▦ 0.005 kL

**31.** 0.992 mL ▦ 9 cL    **32.** 125 mL ▦ 1.25 L    **33.** 1,000 L ▦ 1 kL

**MIXED REVIEW** Copy and complete. Are the units measures of *length* or *capacity*?

**34.** 7.5 km = ▦ m    **35.** 27 mL = ▦ L    **36.** 16 mm = ▦ cm

**37.** 33 cL = ▦ L    **38.** 0.2 m = ▦ mm    **39.** 9.1 kL = ▦ L

**NUMBER SENSE** Match the example with the numerical expression.

**40.** the capacity in liters of the world's tallest water tower in New Jersey

**a.** $2.260922 \times 10^{19}$

**41.** the capacity in kiloliters of the Pacific Ocean

**b.** $7 \times 10^{23}$

**42.** the capacity in liters of a pelican's pouch

**c.** $946,250$

**43.** the capacity in kiloliters of Lake Baikal, the lake with the largest amount of fresh water

**d.** $(1 \times 10^1) + (1 \times 10^0) + (4 \times \frac{1}{10})$

# Metric Units: Mass

Did you know that the mass of an adult male polar bear can be more than 454 kg?

**A polar bear at birth is just under 1 kg. A horsefly has a mass close to 1g.**

> The **kilogram** (**kg**) is the basic unit of mass in the metric system.

> **Mass** is a measure of the quantity of matter in an object.

When you use something you know to figure out something you do not know, you make a MATH CONNECTION.

To change units of mass, make a MATH CONNECTION using powers of ten as you did with metric units of length and capacity.

1.4 kg = 1,400 g ← Did you multiply or divide by a power of ten? Explain. What power of ten was used? → 45 mg = 0.045 g

═══ GUIDED PRACTICE ═══

1. Write the word for each abbreviation. Then copy and complete the chart.

| kg | hg | dag | g | dg | cg | mg |
|----|----|-----|---|----|----|----|
| ▦ g | ▦ g | ▦ g | 1 g | 0.1 g | ▦ g | ▦ g |

**NUMBER SENSE**  Which unit is appropriate to measure the mass? Choose *kg*, *g*, or *mg*.

2. an orange    3. a seventh grader    4. a sheet of paper    5. a box of cereal

═══ PRACTICE ═══

About how many horseflies do you need to equal the given mass?

6. 50 g    7. 3 kg    8. 4,000 mg

MATH AND SCIENCE

Copy and complete.

**9.** 14 kg = ▦ g

**10.** 21 kg = ▦ g

**11.** 35 kg = ▦ g

**12.** 1 kg = ▦ mg

**13.** 1 kg = ▦ g

**14.** 10 kg = ▦ g

**15.** 9 kg = ▦ g

**16.** 11 g = ▦ mg

**17.** 17 g = ▦ mg

**18.** 4,600 kg = ▦ mg

**19.** 1,672 g = ▦ kg

**20.** 2,137 g = ▦ kg

**21.** 800 mg = ▦ g

**22.** 6 kg = ▦ mg

**23.** 2 mg = ▦ g

**24.** 9.15 g = ▦ mg

**25.** 7 g = ▦ kg

**26.** 2.5 kg = ▦ mg

**MIXED REVIEW** Write two equivalent quantities for each.

**27.** 7 m   **28.** 0.2 g   **29.** 6.2 L   **30.** 12 cL   **31.** 0.5 km   **32.** 4,500 mg

---

**PROBLEM SOLVING**

**33.** **NUMBER SENSE** Read carefully. Then change the inappropriate units to something more commonly used.

The length of the adult male polar bear averages between 2,400 mm and 3,400 mm. The adult female measures about 1,800 mm in length and has a mass ranging from 181,000 g to 227,000 g. Polar bear families stay together for about 730 d. Newborn polar bears have a mass of about 680,000 mg and are about 254 mm long.

Polar bears can smell food as far away as 16,000,000 mm. They can run short distances at speeds of up to 56,300 m/h.

---

## Critical Thinking

Volume, capacity, and mass in the metric system are related for water at 4°C. The **centimeter cube (cm$^3$)** below shows this relationship. Work with a partner to answer the questions.

**1.** If the capacity is 8 mL, what is the mass?

**2.** If the volume is 15 cm$^3$, what is the capacity?

**3.** If the mass is 50 mg, what is the volume?

volume = 1 cm$^3$
capacity = 1 mL
mass = 1 g

## Problem Solving Strategy: Using a Pattern

On an airline flight from Traverse City to Detroit, there was 1 empty seat for every 3 passengers. The seating capacity on the small plane is 36. How many passengers were on the flight?

This problem can be solved by finding and continuing a pattern. A table, like the one below, makes the pattern easier to see.

| Empty seats | 1 | 2 | 3 | 4 | | | | | |
|---|---|---|---|---|---|---|---|---|---|
| Passengers | 3 | 6 | 9 | 12 | | | | | |
| Total seats | 4 | 8 | 12 | 16 | | | | | |

**THINK ALOUD** Describe the pattern for the number of passengers. Describe the pattern for the total number of seats.

Now continue the patterns to solve the problem on your own. How many passengers were on the flight from Traverse City to Detroit?

### GUIDED PRACTICE

Use a pattern to solve the problem.

1. On a Lansing-Chicago flight, there were 2 empty seats for every 5 passengers. The plane can seat 42 people. How many empty seats were there? How many passengers were on board?

2. A Grand Rapids–Cleveland flight had 3 empty seats for every 4 passengers. Of the 154 seats, 66 were empty. Could there have been 98 passengers on that flight?

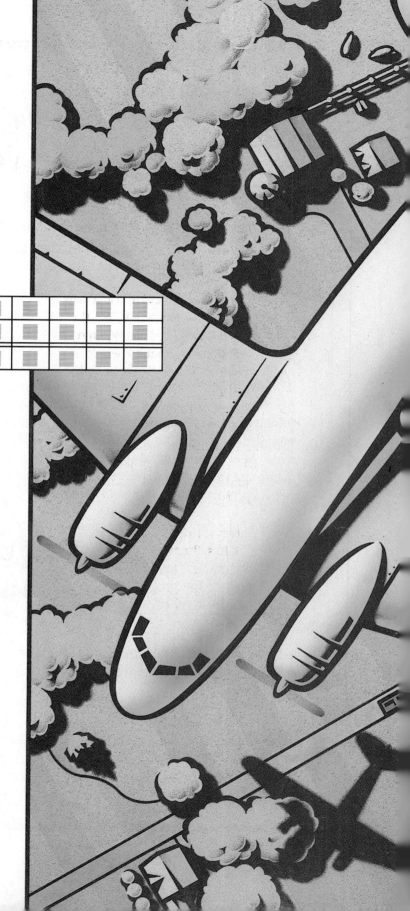

Find a pattern to help you solve the problem.

3. An airport cafeteria has square tables that seat 4 people. When 2 tables are side by side, 6 people can be seated. How many people can be seated if 8 tables are side by side?

4. On Monday, Sally tells 3 friends her travel plans. On Tuesday, each of her 3 friends tells 3 people. If this pattern continues, how many people other than Sally will know her travel plans after 4 d?

5. Suppose you start saving for a trip. You save $1 the 1st week, $2 the 2nd week, $4 the 3rd week, and so on. How much money would you have saved after 6 weeks (wk)?

 Choose a strategy to solve.

6. The sum of the first 2 odd numbers (1 + 3) is 4, the first 3 is 9, the first 4 is 16, and so on. What is the sum of the first 12 odd numbers?

7. The display of cereal boxes at the right has 3 rows. If the display pattern were continued for 15 rows, how many boxes would there be altogether?

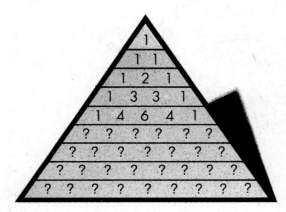

8. **IN YOUR WORDS** The number pattern at the left is called Pascal's Triangle. Write the next four rows of the pattern. Describe a few patterns you see.

---

**LANGUAGE & VOCABULARY**

Give the prefix. Be sure the sentence makes sense.

*kilo- deci- milli- deka-*

1. Ramon's fish tank holds three _____ liters.

2. Laurie measured her pencil and found it to be a little less than two _____ meters.

3. Chartia weighs about one _____ gram more when she weighs herself holding her math book than when she weighs herself without holding it.

4. Douglas estimates the thickness of a nickel to be three _____ meters.

---

**TEST ✔**

---

**CONCEPTS**

Write in standard form. *(pages 4–7)*

1. 3 thousand, 80
2. $5^3$
3. 3.7 million
4. 7 and 183 thousandths
5. $(1 \times 10^2) + \left(3 \times \dfrac{1}{10^2}\right)$
6. $5{,}000 + 80 + 3 + 0.2$

Order from the least to the greatest. *(pages 8–9)*

7. 1.03; 1.30; 1.33
8. 0.803; 0.083; 0.830
9. 9.9; 0.99; 9.09

Copy and complete. *(pages 20–25)*

10. 20 cm = ▦ m
11. 3,500 g = ▦ kg
12. 8 L = ▦ mL

Compare. Use >, <, or =. *(pages 20–25)*

13. 100 cm ▦ 1,000 mm
14. 5.7 g ▦ 570 mg
15. 300 mL ▦ 0.3 L

**SKILLS**

Round to the given place. *(pages 14–15)*

16. 384.49; ones' place
17. 3,102; hundreds' place
18. 6.94; tenths' place
19. 0.187; hundredths' place

Solve. *(pages 10–15, 26–27)*

**20.** Scientists believe that the last ice age began about 2 million years ago. The earliest ice age is believed to have begun about 2.3 billion years ago.

    **a.** About how many years ago did the first ice age begin?

    **b.** How is 2.3 billion written in standard form?

    **c.** How many years passed between the beginnings of the first ice age and the last ice age?

**21.** On an obstacle course, a runner must jump over water holes. The first hole is 3 in. across. If each hole is double the width of the previous one, how wide is the fifth hole?

**22.** The Internal Revenue Service allows taxpayers to round the amount they owe to the nearest dollar. Mr. Benitez owes $384.49. For what amount can he write the check?

**LEARNING LOG**

Write the answers in your learning log.

  **1.** What connection can you make between the metric system and place value?

  **2.** Explain why, when you change from a larger unit of measure to a smaller unit of measure, you get a greater number for an answer.

Write in standard form. *(pages 4–7)*

**1.** $2^0$      **2.** $9^2$      **3.** $10^1$      **4.** $12^2$      **5.** $5^3$

**6.** $1,000 + 30 + 0.1 + 0.02$      **7.** $(4 \times 10^0) + \left(6 \times \frac{1}{10^1}\right)$

Compare. Choose $>$, $<$, or $=$. *(pages 8–9, 12–13)*

**8.** $35{,}874$ ▧ $35{,}784$      **9.** $1.000$ ▧ $6^0$      **10.** $93$ billion ▧ $9.3$ million

Order from the least to the greatest. *(pages 8–9)*

**11.** $96{,}094$; $96{,}904$; $96{,}409$      **12.** $4.001$; $4.010$; $3.999$

Round to the nearest hundredth, tenth, and whole number. *(pages 14–15)*

**13.** $2.157$      **14.** $13.092$      **15.** $456.117$      **16.** $10.351$

Copy and complete. *(pages 20–25)*

**17.** $3 \text{ cm} = $ ▧ $\text{ mm}$      **18.** $3{,}000 \text{ m} = $ ▧ $\text{ km}$      **19.** $157 \text{ cm} = $ ▧ $\text{ m}$

**20.** $2.4 \text{ L} = $ ▧ $\text{ mL}$      **21.** $1{,}500 \text{ mL} = $ ▧ $\text{ L}$      **22.** $0.3 \text{ L} = $ ▧ $\text{ mL}$

**23.** $2.3 \text{ kg} = $ ▧ $\text{ g}$      **24.** $10 \text{ mg} = $ ▧ $\text{ g}$      **25.** $1{,}805 \text{ g} = $ ▧ $\text{ kg}$

Solve. *(pages 10–11, 26–27)*

**26.** During one month, it rained four times. The following amounts of rain fell: 0.92 in., 1.31 in., 1.02 in., and 2.4 in. If the normal amount of rainfall for the month is 4.75 in., how much more rain than the normal amount fell?

**27.** A square yard has been fenced using 2 fence posts on each side. Another has been fenced using 3 posts on each side. How many posts would be needed for a fence with 6 posts on each side?

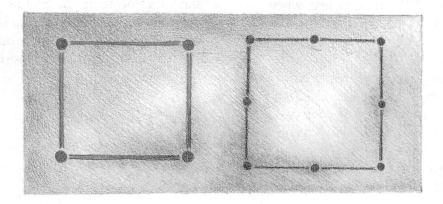

# WORLD RECORDS

Select a record that interests you. It may come from the world of sports, science, music or any other field you enjoy. Try to find the following information about the record you choose:

- what the record is today and who holds it
- when the record was first set
- how many times the record has been broken
- the difference between the original record and today's record
- possible explanations for the old record being broken

For example, the world record for depth of underwater dives in a machine increased from 245 ft in 1865 to 35,802 ft in 1990. The original record was officially broken 14 times during those years.

## Measure for Measure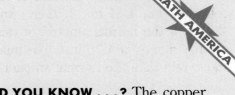

Work with a partner. Together write a short story of several paragraphs in which you use metric or customary measures. For example, in a story about a walk in the woods, you might write, "We froze in fear when we saw a bear just 2,000 cm to our left."

Use as many different measures as possible. You may want to read the story aloud to the rest of your class. Then ask your classmates to name the measures using other metric or customary units. For example, the bear would be 20 m away.

MATH AMERICA

**DID YOU KNOW . . . ?** The copper "skin" that protects the Statue of Liberty is about 0.2 cm thick. Is your outer layer of skin thicker or thinner than that of the Statue of Liberty?

## ODD TIMES 🔢

Play this game with a partner. You will need a calculator and a number cube labeled 1–6. After entering the number 2 on your calculator, take turns rolling a number cube.

- If the number on the cube is odd, multiply by 10.
- If the number on the cube is even, divide by 10.

Continue rolling the number cube and multiplying or dividing the number on the calculator display by 10. The first player to reach 20,000 wins the game.

## HOW OLD? 🔢

Mike likes to do things differently. Yesterday, he told everyone that his baby sister Amanda was about 18,489,600 s old. If Amanda was born at midnight on May 1, what was yesterday's date and how old was she? Use your calculator to find out.

How old are you in seconds?

## LAST MOVE 💻

In the computer activity *The Last Move,* you compare decimal numbers. Play this pencil and paper game with another person to sharpen your skills.

Player 1 begins with the number 0.8426 and must write a number that is greater with each turn. Player 2 begins with the number 5,791 and must write a number that is less with each turn.

You are allowed two ways to write a new number:

1.  exchange two digits                                         $5,791 \longrightarrow 5,719$

2.  multiply or divide the number by 10              $5,791 \div 10 = 579.1$

Play continues until Player 1 can no longer write a greater number obeying the rules *or* Player 2 can no longer write a number that is less obeying the rules. The player who takes the last move wins.

**DID YOU KNOW . . . ?**

In January 1984, the Queen Elizabeth 2, a luxury passenger ship, paid a toll of $97,696.38 to pass through the Panama Canal. What a bargain this was! It would have cost the ship ten times as much in fuel and salaries to sail around South America.

The red lines show the length of trips from New York to Acapulco, San Francisco, and Honolulu via the Panama Canal.

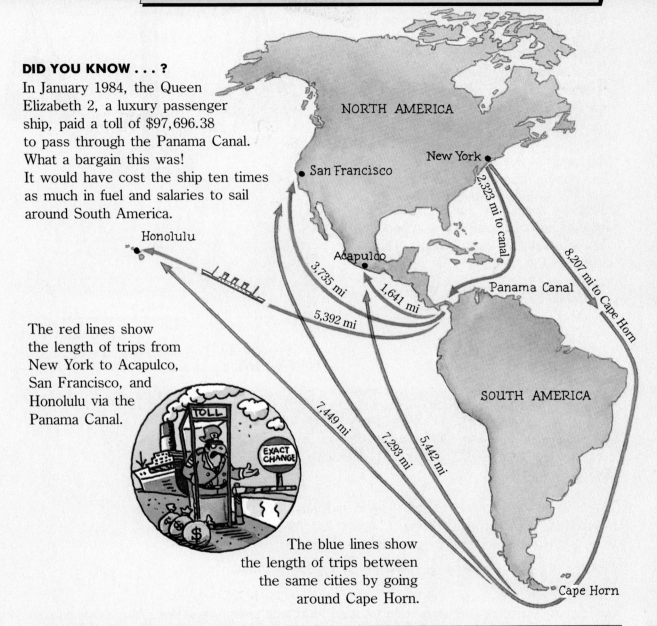

The blue lines show the length of trips between the same cities by going around Cape Horn.

**USING DATA**

| Collect |
| **Organize** |
| Describe |
| Predict |

How many miles are saved by using the canal?

List the distances for both kinds of trips in a table. Include the number of miles saved for each of the three trips by using the Panama Canal.

# Variables and Equations

The scales at the right are balanced. An unknown mass called a **variable** is represented by the letter $n$. What is the mass in grams?

The **equation** below represents the problem.

What number added to 57 equals 95?

$$n \quad + \quad 57 \quad = \quad 95$$

You can find the **solution** to this equation by substituting different values for $n$ until you find one that makes the equation true.

Try 35 as a solution to the equation.
$n + 57 = 95$
$35 + 57 = 92$

$92 \neq 95$   The two quantities are not equal.

35 is not a solution.

Try 38 as a solution.
$n + 57 = 95$
$38 + 57 = 95$

$95 = 95$   The two quantities are equal.

So, $n = 38$. The unknown mass is 38 g. The solution to the equation is 38.

**An equation is a mathematical sentence stating that two quantities are equal.**

**The unknown number $n$ is called the variable.**

Other examples:

4 times what number equals 36?
$4 \times k = 36$
$k = 9$   The solution is 9.

What number divided by 6 equals 8?
$b \div 6 = 8$
$b = 48$   The solution is 48.

---

**GUIDED PRACTICE**

Solve the equation.

**1.** What number minus 22 equals 11?
$x \; 33 \; - \quad 22 \quad = \quad 11$

**2.** 35 divided by what number equals 5?
$35 \quad \div \quad 7 \quad p \quad = \quad 5$

Is 4 the solution to the equation? Write *yes* or *no*.

**3.** $17 - x = 13$
    Yes

**4.** $b \times 6 = 21$
    No

**5.** $8 - n = 12$
    No

**PRACTICE**

Is 7, 8, 9, 10, 11, or 12 a solution to the equation?

**6.** $24 + n = 33$ _9_

**7.** $5 \times w = 45$ _9_

**8.** $56 \div z = 8$ _7_

**9.** $x - 9 = 3$ _12_

**10.** $n + 14 = 25$ _11_

**11.** $90 \div y = 9$ _10_

Is the number in parentheses a solution? Write *yes* or *no*.

**12.** $17 + k = 35$ (18) _yes_

**13.** $y - 13 = 28$ (15) _no_

**14.** $12 \times n = 60$ (4) _no_

**15.** $51 \div n = 3$ (17) _yes_ _107_

**16.** $n \times 3 = 58$ (16) _no_

**17.** $d - 34 = 19$ (53) _yes_

Solve the equation.

**18.** $p - 14 = 6$ _20_

**19.** $7 \times m = 28$ _4_

**20.** $g + 15 = 23$ _8_

**21.** $x \div 8 = 6$ _48_

**22.** $r - 7 = 11$ _18_

**23.** $88 = 8 \times t$ _11_

**24.** $23 + 7 + w = 42$ _12_

**25.** $4 \times n = 17 + 11$ _7_ _28_

**26.** $w \div 2 = 17 - 9$ _16_ _=18_

**27. CRITICAL THINKING** The scales are *not* balanced. Name four numbers for *n* that allow you to keep $<$ or $>$ in the statement.

**a.** $n + 5 < 8$

**b.** $n + 5 > 8$

_12 5 15c_

_10 20 300 800,000_

**PROBLEM SOLVING**

Work with a partner to solve.

**28.** Find a figure in one of the three diagrams at the right that has the same shape and direction as each of the following: $\vee$, $\triangle$, and $\sqsubset$.

  **a.** What number is inside each figure?

  **b.** Substituting these figures with their numbers, is the puzzle-equation $\vee + \triangle = \sqsubset$ true?

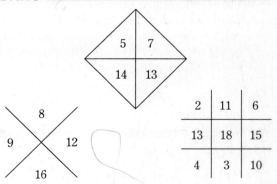

Find the unknown number using the three diagrams.

**29.** $> + n = <$

**30.** $r \times \triangle = \sqsubset$

**31.** $z \div \sqcap = \sqsupset$

**32.** $a - \triangledown = \lrcorner$

**33.** $q + \triangleright = \wedge$

**34.** $m \div \sqcup = \sqcap$

## Mental Math and Properties of Addition

Suppose you drive 74 mi from Baltimore to Harrisburg, 57 mi from Harrisburg to Reading, and then 43 mi from Reading to Allentown. What would be the total length of the trip?

You can find the sum mentally.

$57 + 43 = 100$ — Look for easy combinations to add.

$74 + 100 = 174$ — Add the rest.

The total trip is 174 mi.

Knowing the properties of addition can help you compute mentally.

**THINK ALOUD** Which property was used above?

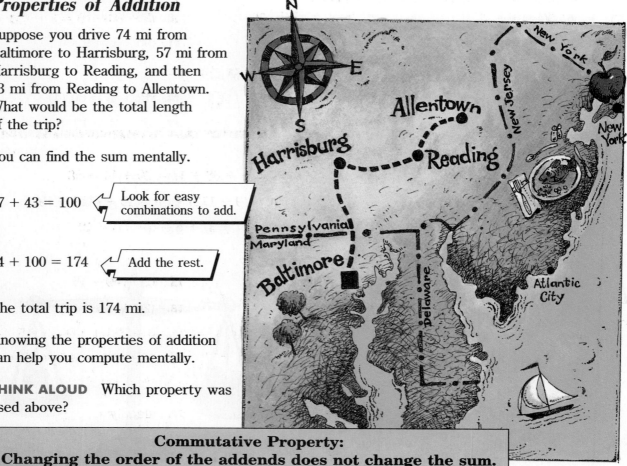

---

### Commutative Property:
**Changing the order of the addends does not change the sum.**

In arithmetic:  $74 + 57 = 57 + 74$
$131 = 131$

In algebra:  $a + b = b + a$

---

### Associative Property:
**Changing the grouping of the addends does not change the sum.**

In arithmetic:
$(74 + 57) + 43 = 74 + (57 + 43)$
$174 = 174$

In algebra:
$(a + b) + c = a + (b + c)$

---

### Identity Property:
**The sum of zero and any other number is that number.**

In arithmetic:  $74 + 0 = 74$

In algebra:  $a + 0 = a$

**MATH AND GEOGRAPHY**

Name the property shown by the equation.

**1.** $39 + 0 = 39$      **2.** $39 + 3 = 3 + 39$      **3.** $(3 + 30) + 9 = 3 + (30 + 9)$

Look for tens as you add mentally. Name the property you used.

**4.** $13 + 19 + 17$      **5.** $(58 + 16) + 14$      **6.** $23 + 17 + 0$

Name the property shown by the equation.

**7.** $(125 + 84) + 16 = 125 + (84 + 16)$      **8.** $29 + 68 + 11 = 29 + 11 + 68$

**9.** $0 + 1,225 = 1,225$      **10.** $(19 + 112) + 18 = 19 + (112 + 18)$

**11.** $64 + 48 + 16 = 64 + 16 + 48$      **12.** $(17 + 3) + 6 = 6 + (17 + 3)$

Use the properties to look for tens and add mentally.

**13.** $98 + 25 + 2$      **14.** $17 + 18 + 3 + 2$      **15.** $65 + 89 + 15$

**16.** $28 + (2 + 59)$      **17.** $(146 + 83) + 17$      **18.** $(26 + 91) + 9$

**19.** $22 + 0 + 36 + 8$      **20.** $(77 + 94) + 16 + 0$      **21.** $0 + 235 + 1,000 + 15$

**22.** $1,008 + (12 + 56)$      **23.** $164 + 119 + 106$      **24.** $72 + (18 + 135) + 0$

Write an equation to illustrate each addition property.

**25.** commutative      **26.** associative      **27.** identity

**28. CRITICAL THINKING** Evaluate the expressions.
$(a - b) - c$ and $a - (b - c)$. Use $a = 10$, $b = 6$, and $c = 4$.
What conclusion can you draw?

Use the mileage table. Find the total distance
of each Pennsylvania driving tour mentally.

**29.** Reading to Philadelphia
to Allentown to Hazelton

**30.** Scranton to Lebanon to
Philadelphia to Allentown

**31.** Philadelphia to Allentown
to Hazelton to Scranton

**32.** Lancaster to Reading to Allentown
to Philadelphia to Lancaster

| | Allentown | Philadelphia | Reading | Scranton |
|---|---|---|---|---|
| Allentown | | 54 | 43 | 74 |
| Hazelton | 48 | 99 | 53 | 42 |
| Lancaster | 76 | 66 | 32 | 127 |
| Lebanon | 63 | 87 | 31 | 106 |
| Reading | 43 | 62 | | 95 |

# Pick and Choose

*Problem Solving: Choosing Mental Math, Paper and Pencil, or Calculator*

### ☐ READ ABOUT IT

Rainbow Bridge is the highest natural arch in the world. It is located on the Navajo Reservation in southern Utah.

In solving the problems in this lesson, you can use mental math, paper and pencil, or a calculator. You decide.

### ☐ TALK ABOUT IT

What method would you choose? Solve.

**THINK ABOUT USING**

**MENTAL MATH**  when you know an easy way to compute in your head;

**CALCULATOR**  when the computation is complex;

**PAPER AND PENCIL**  when the computation is too hard for mental math and too easy for a calculator.

Rainbow Bridge spans 278 ft across a canyon. The highest point of the arch is 309 ft. The arch is 42 ft thick at the highest point.

1. What is the height of the tallest object that could fit under the bridge?

2. How many times higher is the highest point of the arch than a 5 ft child?

3. How many times longer is the bridge's span than the longest side of your classroom? Measure to the nearest foot.

4. Is it reasonable to say that the span of Rainbow Bridge is about 6 times longer than the 78 ft length of a tennis court? If *no*, explain.

On May 30, 1910, President William Taft declared Rainbow Bridge and the 160 acres of land around it as a national monument.

5. How many years ago was this?

6. How many days ago was this? (*Hint:* 1912 was a leap year.)

You can walk across the top of Rainbow Bridge, since the arch is 33 ft wide.

7. A Ping-Pong table is 5 ft wide. How many Ping-Pong tables would safely fit side-by-side across the top of the bridge? Explain.

MATH AND GEOGRAPHY

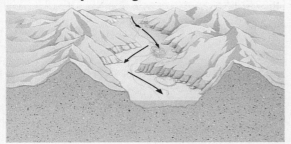

**Millions of years ago:**

**Now:**

Bridge Creek

Rainbow Bridge is in southern Utah, about 150 mi north of Flagstaff, Arizona. Flowing water, wind, and changes in temperature over time have shaped the arch we call Rainbow Bridge. Although the bridge is easily spotted, it is located in rough country. You can get to within a quarter mile of Rainbow Bridge via a 50-mi, or 2-h, boat ride on Bridge Creek. This creek is very small as it passes under the bridge.

### ▣ WRITE ABOUT IT

**8.** Use the information given on these two pages to write a math problem about Rainbow Bridge that can be solved using either mental math, paper and pencil, or calculator. Explain which method you chose and why.

## Adding Whole Numbers and Decimals

The human body needs riboflavin for growth and for healthy skin and eyes. The Recommended Daily Allowance (RDA) for riboflavin for 11- to 14-year-old boys is 1.6 mg.

Does the food listed at the right provide the daily amount of riboflavin recommended for 12-year-old boys?

| Food | Riboflavin (mg) | Calories |
|---|---|---|
| Hamburger (3 oz) | 0.17 | 185 |
| Spinach (1 c) | 0.25 | 45 |
| Asparagus ($\frac{2}{3}$ c) | 0.22 | 40 |
| White Bread (1 slice) | 0.05 | 70 |
| Milk (8 oz) | 0.41 | 150 |

| Add. Line up the decimal points. | Estimate to check your sum. Round to tenths. |
|---|---|
| $\begin{array}{r} {}^{1\ 2} \\ 0.17 \\ 0.25 \\ 0.22 \\ 0.05 \\ +\ \ 0.41 \\ \hline 1.10 \end{array}$ | $\begin{array}{r} 0.2 \\ 0.3 \\ 0.2 \\ 0.1 \\ +\ 0.4 \\ \hline 1.2 \end{array}$ |

The estimate shows that the sum, 1.10, is reasonable.

Twelve-year-old boys need more than 1.10 mg of riboflavin each day.

Other examples:

5,338 + 64 + 889:

$$\begin{array}{r} 5{,}338 \\ 64 \\ +\ \ \ 889 \\ \hline 6{,}291 \end{array}$$

5.8 + 7.623 + 2:

$$\begin{array}{r} 5.800 \\ 7.623 \\ +\ 2.000 \\ \hline 15.423 \end{array}$$

You may need to annex zeros.

$15 + 28¢ + $33.93:

$$\begin{array}{r} \$15.00 \\ .28 \\ +\ \ 33.93 \\ \hline \$49.21 \end{array}$$

**THINK ALOUD**  How is adding whole numbers the same as adding decimals? How is it different?

### GUIDED PRACTICE

1. **THINK ALOUD**  Explain how you would estimate to check the sum.

   **a.** 6,847 + 513

   **b.** 5.8 + 3.57.

Add. Check your answer.

2. $\begin{array}{r} 537 \\ +\ 489 \\ \hline \end{array}$

3. $\begin{array}{r} 5.348 \\ +\ 2.769 \\ \hline \end{array}$

4. 72,265 + 4,892

5. 16.007 + 0.19 + 30.118

Add. Use a calculator, mental math, or pencil and paper. Check your answer.

**6.**   5.6
    + 2.3

**7.**   12.7
    + 3.2

**8.**   253
    + 78

**9.**   18
    + 7.9

**10.**   $1.34
    + 2.86

**11.**   8,516
    + 4,067

**12.**   38.527
    + 5.964

**13.**   $58.48
    + 95.37

**14.**   7,530
    + 3,738

**15.**   0.3
    + 2.373

**16.**   5.8
    2.38
    + 4

**17.**   2.136
    0.87
    + 2.64

**18.**   73,591
    263,468
    + 793,244

**19.**   $32.62
    5.18
    + 21.63

**20.**   $27.15
    .67
    + .52

**21.** 0.05 + 6.3 + 18 + 0.724

**22.** $13.07 + $6 + 72¢ + 45¢

**23.** $14.34 + $17.90 + 4¢ + $20

**24.** 0.0004 + 1.3 + 48.02 + 6.0006

**25.** a half million + 400 thousand

**26.** 3.4 million − 1.5 thousand

**CALCULATOR**   Use a calculator to find the sum.

**27.** $44.25 + $6.50 + 78¢ + $154.10

**28.** $670 + $7.95 + $375.98 + $94 + 35¢

**NUMBER SENSE**   Place decimal points
in the addends to make each equation true.

**29.** 398 + 136 = 5.34

**30.** 155 + 121 = 12.255

**31. MENTAL MATH**   Which is greater:
   $(4.2 + 3.8) + 9.7$ or $9.7 + (4.1 + 3.8)$?

**32. CRITICAL THINKING**   What is the value of $m$
   in the equation $3.2 + 6.9 = 6 + 0.9 + m$?

 Choose estimation
or a calculator to solve.

**33.** In a recent year, each person in the
United States ate an average of 41.32 kg
fresh vegetables, 37.29 kg canned
vegetables, and 7,980 g frozen vegetables.
How many kilograms of vegetables did
each person average per year?

**34.** An 11- to 14-year-old girl needs
2,200 calories daily. If a 12-year-
old girl ate all the food in the table
on page 40, about how many more
calories would she need that day?

## Front-End Estimation

| Super Sale! | Video Tape Recorder $219.45 | Video Tapes $7.69 each |
|---|---|---|
| Double Cassette Portable Stereo $47.49 | AM/FM Pocket Radios $16.29 each | Electronic Portable Typewriter $99.99 |
| Answering Machine $59.29 | Touch-Tone Phone $26.79 | Compact Disc $14.95 each |

Is $45 enough to buy a compact disc, a blank video tape, and an AM/FM pocket radio?

You can use **front-end estimation** to decide.

| Add the front-end digits, the dollars. | Look at the cents. Find sums close to one dollar. | Add the dollars and cents. |
|---|---|---|
| $14.95<br>7.69<br>+ 16.29<br>$37 | $14.95} about $1<br>7.69<br>+ 16.29} about $1<br>about $2 | $37<br>+  2<br>$39 |

**THINK ALOUD**   Can you tell if $45 is enough?

Other examples:

$4.58<br>  .39 } about $1

2.16<br>+ 1.91 } about $1<br>$7   + about $2 ≈ $9

≈ means is about.

$42.00<br>16.89 } about $1

2.29<br>+ .69 } about $1<br>$60   + about $2 ≈ $62

═══════════════ GUIDED PRACTICE ═══════════════

Use front-end estimation to decide if the answer is reasonable.
Write *yes* or *no*.

1. Answer: $42.81
   $37.98
     2.88
   +  1.95

2. Answer: $10.89
   $1.36
    .42
   7.49
   + 3.62

3. Answer: $91.78
   $74.41
     3.55
     .95
   + 2.87

Use the front-end method to estimate.

| 4. | 5. | 6. | 7. | 8. |
|---|---|---|---|---|
| $6.24 | $3.26 | $50.93 | $39.58 | $8.44 |
| 4.81 | .71 | 8.71 | 2.96 | 4.39 |
| + .98 | + 4.89 | + 30.29 | + .29 | + 5.21 |

| 9. | 10. | 11. | 12. | 13. |
|---|---|---|---|---|
| $32.19 | $47.92 | $20.87 | $73.52 | $11.89 |
| .98 | 31.03 | 6.21 | 3.74 | 7.02 |
| 6.01 | .75 | 21.49 | 10.45 | 2.98 |
| + 12.76 | + 5.26 | + 4.52 | + .28 | + 28.01 |

**14.** $4.12 + $8.79 + $8.94 + $.84

**15.** $.48 + $.39 + $.67 + $.35

**16.** $8.39 + $1.09 + $9.24 + $1.39

**17.** $74.99 + $8.98 + $2.34 + $6.67

**18. CRITICAL THINKING**  Round $8.45, $6.24, and $2.29 to the nearest dollar and estimate the sum. Now find the sum using the front-end method. Which answer is closer to the actual sum?

Estimate. Use the prices on page 42.

**19.** Is $180 enough to buy 10 compact discs and 3 AM/FM pocket radios?

**20.** What is the total cost of one each of the eight items on sale?

**21.** You have $200 with which to buy an electronic typewriter, an answering machine, and a touch-tone phone. After purchasing these three items, do you have enough money left for a double cassette portable stereo?

## Mental Math

You can mentally check your change from the money you gave for a purchase by **counting on.** Suppose you buy a book for $7.75 and pay for it with a $10 bill:

$7.75 → $8.00    → $9; $10

 +    *Your change: $2.25*

Use the counting-on method to find the change. What bills and coins would you use?

**1.** $10 − $5.25    **2.** $8.00 − $7.62    **3.** $50 − $6.98

# MIDCHAPTER CHECKUP

## LANGUAGE & VOCABULARY

Decide whether the equation is always true. Write *yes* or *no*. If *yes*, tell whether the *Commutative Property*, the *Associative Property*, or the *Identity Property* proves it. If *no*, give an example that shows the equation is not true.

1. $x + 73 = 73 + x$

2. $r - 18 = 18 - r$

3. $0 + m = m$

4. $(21 + b) + 97 = 21 + (b + 97)$

## QUICK QUIZ

Solve. *(pages 34–35)*

1. $18 + n = 25$

2. $34 - c = 19$

3. $y - 9 = 8$

Use the properties to look for tens and add mentally. *(pages 36–37)*

4. $11 + 49 + 16 = \blacksquare$

5. $2,608 + (64 + 12) = \blacksquare$

Add. Check your answer. *(pages 40–41)*

6. $62.37 + .055 + 1.679 = \blacksquare$

7. $49,365 + 4,936 + 493 = \blacksquare$

Use the front-end method to estimate. *(pages 42–43)*

8. $29.23 + 2.65 + 11.08$

9. $109.39 + 70.70 + 21.98$

Solve. *(pages 38–39)*

10. The Grand Canyon in Arizona took about 8 million years to form. It is 217 mi long. The first recorded boat trip through the canyon took place in 1869.

    a. In what year did the first recorded boat trip through the Grand Canyon take place?

    b. What operation would you use to find the length of time between 1869 and any other year?

    c. How many years ago did the first recorded boat trip through the Grand Canyon take place?

44 MIDCHAPTER CHECKUP

Write the answers in your learning log.

1. Describe three kinds of mistakes students might make when adding decimals.

2. Which do you think is the more accurate method for estimating sums of money—rounding to the nearest dollar or front-end estimation? Explain.

**MATH AMERICA**

**DID YOU KNOW . . .?** The population of the American colonies in 1620 was 350. Compare that number with the number of people who live in your city or town.

**BONUS**

The symbols (in parentheses) and some spaces have been left out of the equation. Insert the symbols and add some spaces to make the equation true.

Example: 28213 = 17 (+,−)
        28 + 2 − 13 = 17

1. 92813 = 24 (+,−)

2. 15311 = 56 ( × , + )

3. 10527 = 110 (−,+)

4. 426134 = 16 (÷,+,−)

*[handwritten notes:]*

There is 7 days in a week
There are 365 days in a year
There are 30 day in most months
There are 10 years in a decade

How many
weeks in a month = 4-5
weeks in a year = 50 52
Weeks in a decade = 480 500

28   4 280
    50350
    R15

12 × 10
120

## Subtracting Whole Numbers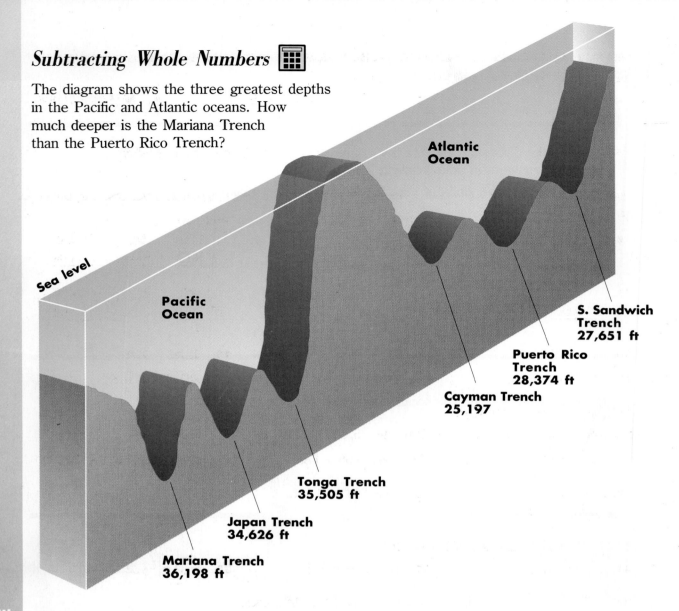

The diagram shows the three greatest depths in the Pacific and Atlantic oceans. How much deeper is the Mariana Trench than the Puerto Rico Trench?

**Atlantic Ocean**

Sea level

**Pacific Ocean**

**S. Sandwich Trench 27,651 ft**

**Puerto Rico Trench 28,374 ft**

**Cayman Trench 25,197**

**Tonga Trench 35,505 ft**

**Japan Trench 34,626 ft**

**Mariana Trench 36,198 ft**

Subtract to find the difference.

$$
\begin{array}{r}
{}^{2}\,{}^{15}\quad{}^{11}\\
\cancel{3}\,\cancel{6},\,\cancel{1}\,9\,8\\
-\,2\,8\,,\,3\,7\,4\\
\hline
7\,,\,8\,2\,4
\end{array}
$$

Add to check.

$$
\begin{array}{r}
28{,}374\\
+\ \ 7{,}824\\
\hline
36{,}198
\end{array}
$$

The Mariana Trench is 7,824 ft deeper than the Puerto Rico Trench.

**THINK ALOUD** Explain how you would estimate the difference above.

Other examples:

$3{,}000 - 111$:

$$
\begin{array}{r}
{}^{2}\ {}^{9}\ {}^{9}\ {}^{10}\\
\cancel{3{,}000}\\
-\ \ \ 1\,1\,1\\
\hline
2\,,\,8\,8\,9
\end{array}
$$

Check:

$$
\begin{array}{r}
2{,}889\\
+\ \ \ 111\\
\hline
3{,}000
\end{array}
$$

$7{,}901 - 5{,}832$:

$$
\begin{array}{r}
{}^{8}\ {}^{9}\ {}^{11}\\
7{,}\cancel{9}\cancel{0}\cancel{1}\\
-\ 5{,}8\,3\,2\\
\hline
2{,}0\,6\,9
\end{array}
$$

Check:

$$
\begin{array}{r}
2{,}069\\
+\ 5{,}832\\
\hline
7{,}901
\end{array}
$$

MATH AND SCIENCE

Find the difference. Check your answer.

**1.**  4,387
  −   159

**2.**  16,000
  − 2,729

**3.** 8,751 − 5,326

**4.** 10,002 − 3,908

**5.** What is the difference if 4 thousands and 5 tens are subtracted from 83,456?

PRACTICE

Subtract and check. Use a calculator, mental math, or pencil and paper.

**6.**  874
  − 58

**7.**  754
  − 86

**8.**  930
  − 483

**9.**  530
  − 207

**10.**  6,482
  − 3,294

**11.**  4,002
  − 3,581

**12.**  5,306
  − 3,094

**13.**  17,352
  − 5,795

**14.**  52,003
  − 15,265

**15.**  800,000
  − 752,804

**16.** 415 − 98

**17.** 700 − 289

**18.** 4,052 − 208

**19.** 21,014 − 9,038

**20.** 8,009 − 4,968

**21.** 287,351 − 9,882

**MIXED REVIEW** Compute.

**22.** 45 + 3.55

**23.** 2,456 + 398

**24.** 5,006 − 359

**25.** 0.7 + 95.6

**26.** 0.93 + 4.2

**27.** 85 + 699

**28.** 3,214 − 78

**29.** 956 + 788

**30.** 2.3 + 4.78

**31.** 872 − 345

**32. CRITICAL THINKING** If 6,482 − 3,294 is 3,188, what is 7,482 − 4,294?

**ESTIMATE** Estimate the difference.

**33.** 2,148 − 966

**34.** 18,253 − 6,836

**35.** 45,238 − 32,657

**36. CALCULATOR** Explain how you can find the difference between 38,320,574,731 and 24,879,397,856 with a calculator.

PROBLEM SOLVING

 Use the graph on page 46.
Choose estimation or a calculator to solve.

**37.** There are 5,280 ft in 1 mi. Is the Mariana Trench about 6 mi or 7 mi deep?

**38.** How many feet deeper is the Tonga Trench than the Sandwich Trench?

**39.** Mt: Everest is 29,028 ft high. If it were on the bottom of the Puerto Rico Trench, would its peak be above the ocean's surface? If so, by how much?

**40.** Which is farther away from sea level, Mt. McKinley or the Cayman Trench? by how much? (Mt. McKinley is 20,320 ft high.)

# Subtracting Decimals 🔢

The amounts of silver mined by six countries in a recent year is represented in the bar graph. How many more kilograms of silver did Mexico mine than Canada?

If you know how to subtract whole numbers, you can make a **MATH CONNECTION** to subtract decimals.

| Line up the decimal points. | Add to check. |
|---|---|
| $$\begin{array}{r} \overset{1}{2}.146 \\ -\ 1.210 \\ \hline 0.936 \end{array}$$ | $$\begin{array}{r} 0.936 \\ +\ 1.210 \\ \hline 2.146 \end{array}$$ |

Mexico mined 0.936 million kilograms, or 936,000 kg, more than Canada.

**THINK ALOUD** Explain how to estimate the difference above.

Other examples:

Subtract 0.774 from 34.

| Annex zeros. | Check: |
|---|---|
| $$\begin{array}{r} \overset{3}{}\overset{9}{}\overset{9}{}\overset{10}{} \\ 34.000 \\ -\ \ 0.774 \\ \hline 33.226 \end{array}$$ | $$\begin{array}{r} 33.226 \\ +\ \ 0.774 \\ \hline 34.000 \end{array}$$ |

$59.08 - 40.29$:

| | Check: |
|---|---|
| $$\begin{array}{r} \overset{8}{}\ \ \overset{9}{}\overset{18}{} \\ 59.08 \\ -\ 40.29 \\ \hline 18.79 \end{array}$$ | $$\begin{array}{r} 18.79 \\ +\ 40.29 \\ \hline 59.08 \end{array}$$ |

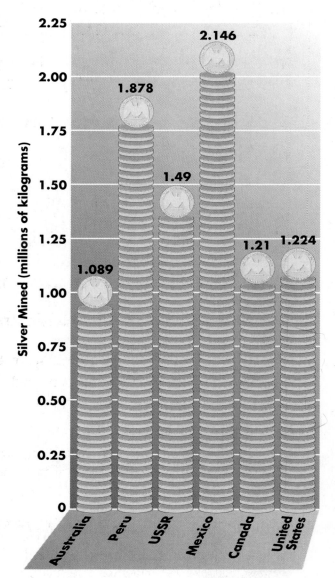

**Leading Silver Mining Countries**

Silver Mined (millions of kilograms)

Australia 1.089, Peru 1.878, USSR 1.49, Mexico 2.146, Canada 1.21, United States 1.224

---

## GUIDED PRACTICE

Subtract and check.

**1.**  $$\begin{array}{r} 7.64 \\ -\ 5.32 \end{array}$$

**2.**  $$\begin{array}{r} \$15.68 \\ -\ \ 3.92 \end{array}$$

**3.** $89.35 - 34.5$

**4.** $47 - 0.513$

**5. THINK ALOUD** Explain why 52 and 52.000 are the same number.

MATH AND SOCIAL STUDIES

Subtract and check. Use a calculator, mental math, or pencil and paper.

| | | | | | | | | | |
|---|---|---|---|---|---|---|---|---|---|
| **6.** | 8.94 − 4.33 | **7.** | 18.678 − 4.378 | **8.** | 74 − 0.664 | **9.** | 800.34 − 427.48 | **10.** | 8.072 − 2.685 |
| **11.** | 53.7 − 0.159 | **12.** | $73.60 − 38.80 | **13.** | 3.058 − 0.64 | **14.** | 21.7 − 8.52 | **15.** | 7.9 − 6.05 |
| **16.** | 0.546 − 0.159 | **17.** | 9 − 7.293 | **18.** | $60.02 − 46.79 | **19.** | 3,500 − 873.24 | **20.** | 3.00064 − 2.38476 |

**21.** 5.7 − 2.852   **22.** 8.064 − 3.79   **23.** $7.05 − $3.28

**24.** 2 million − 1.2 million   **25.** 5 million − 2.25 million

**MIXED REVIEW**   Compute.

**26.** 423.8 + 1.75   **27.** 513 − 245   **28.** 99 + 864   **29.** 0.7 − 0.09

**30.** 0.04 − 0.006   **31.** 5,246 + 999   **32.** 12.76 + 295   **33.** 12 − 3.7

**ESTIMATE**   Estimate the difference.

**34.** 41.852 − 3.798   **35.** 54.6 − 0.809   **36.** 0.14 − 0.12881

 **CHOOSE**   Use the graph on page 48.
Choose estimation or a calculator to solve.

**37.** Which country mined about one and a half million kilograms of silver?

**38.** What was the total number of million kilograms of silver mined by the six countries?

**39.** **CREATE YOUR OWN**   Write a math problem about the leading silver mining countries. Give it to a friend to solve.

## *Critical Thinking*

With a partner, think of a strategy to identify which decimals in the box were subtracted from which to obtain each difference below.

| | | |
|---|---|---|
| 0.624 | | 0.906 |
| | 0.83 | |
| 0.468 | | 0.682 |

**1.** 0.438   **2.** 0.148   **3.** 0.362   **4.** 0.282   **5.** 0.058

**6.** Can you name other strategies that would work? Explain.

## Problem Solving: Reading for Understanding

You may need to read a passage several times before you can solve a problem.

### ☐ READ AND TALK ABOUT IT

**First read the passage quickly.**

- What is it about?

**Now reread it carefully to solve these problems.**

- In what year did the Wright Brothers invent the airplane?
- Can you tell whether the *Spirit of St. Louis* is a more popular exhibit than the *Kitty Hawk*?
- Can you tell when the National Air and Space Museum opened?

Read the passage as often as necessary to answer the question.

1. Did James Smithson donate about 5 million or 0.5 million dollars?

2. How long ago did the Wright Brothers invent the airplane?

3. How long ago did Lindbergh make his famous solo flight?

4. In what year did the Smithsonian open?

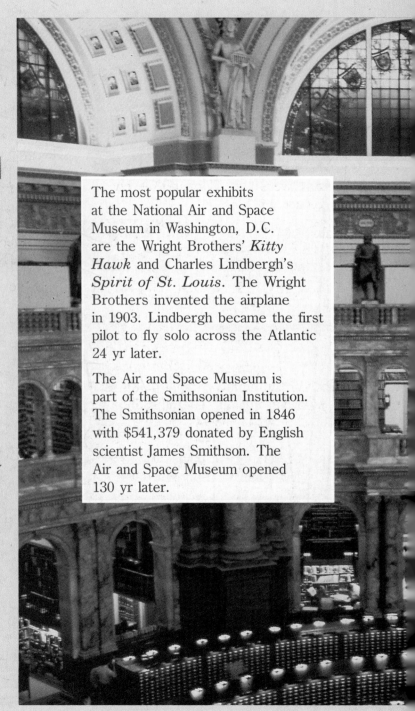

The most popular exhibits at the National Air and Space Museum in Washington, D.C. are the Wright Brothers' *Kitty Hawk* and Charles Lindbergh's *Spirit of St. Louis*. The Wright Brothers invented the airplane in 1903. Lindbergh became the first pilot to fly solo across the Atlantic 24 yr later.

The Air and Space Museum is part of the Smithsonian Institution. The Smithsonian opened in 1846 with $541,379 donated by English scientist James Smithson. The Air and Space Museum opened 130 yr later.

MATH AND SOCIAL STUDIES

The Library of Congress in Washington, D.C., is the national library of the United States.
The library was established in 1800. Fifteen years later, Congress purchased the 6,000 books in the private library of Thomas Jefferson for the Library of Congress.

Today, the library has 84 million items, including more than 20 million books and pamphlets.
Of special value are the 5,600 books that were printed after 1450 but before 1501.

## READ AND WRITE ABOUT IT

Read the passage as often as necessary to answer the question.

5. How long ago was the Library of Congress established?

6. Which is a good estimate of the age of the library's oldest books?

   **a.** 440 yr          **b.** 540 yr

7. In what year were books bought from the library of Thomas Jefferson?

8. Can you tell the exact number of books in the Library of Congress? Explain.

Solve. Use the graph below.

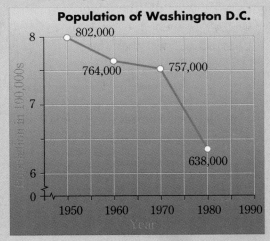

**Population of Washington D.C.**

9. What is the population for each year?

10. Do you think the population increased or decreased in 1990? Explain.

11. When looking at the graph, what did you
    **a.** read quickly?
    **b.** read first?
    **c.** read slowly?

**LANGUAGE & VOCABULARY**

Explain how the first problem in the pair can help you find the difference in the second problem. Use math vocabulary in your explanation.

**1.**
```
    2,943
  + 8,607
   11,550
```
```
   11,550
  - 2,943
```

**2.**
```
    6,000
  - 1,975
    4,025
```
```
    6,110
  - 1,975
```

**TEST ✓**

**CONCEPTS**

Use the properties of addition to look for tens and compute mentally. *(pages 36 – 37)*

**1.** $23 + 89 + 77$

**2.** $108 + 35 + 65$

**3.** $(93 + 0 + 7) + 259$

Is the number in parentheses the solution? Write *yes* or *no*. *(pages 34–35)*

**4.** $n \times 4 = 96$ (14)

**5.** $3 \times r = 13 + 86 + 2$ (7)

**6.** $w - 43 = 64$ (22)

**SKILLS**

Add. *(pages 40–41)*

**7.**
```
    1.8
  + 4.7
```

**8.**
```
   135.02
  + 89.19
```

**9.**
```
  $203.98
  + 67.17
```

**10.**
```
   76,809
      395
  + 1,782
```

**11.** $0.82 + 13.7 + 15.309$

**12.** 3 million + 4.7 thousand

Subtract. *(pages 46–49)*

**13.**
```
   42,258
  - 13,379
```

**14.**
```
    2,101
  -   912
```

**15.** $308 - 194$

**16.**
```
  $40.00
  - 18.53
```

**17.**
```
   76.84
  - 9.679
```

**18.** $8.001 - 2.15$

Use the front-end method to estimate. *(pages 42–43)*

**19.**   $42.15
        + 16.89

**20.**   $139.08
           50.89
         + 25.98

**21.**  $4.32 + $8.17 + $1.53

---

**PROBLEM SOLVING**

Solve. *(pages 38–39, 46–49)*

**22.** The flying distance between Los Angeles and Paris, France, is 5,601 mi. The flying distance from Los Angeles to Tokyo, Japan, is 5,470 mi.

   **a.** What is the flying distance from Los Angeles to Paris?

   **b.** Would a flight from Paris to Los Angeles be *more than* or *less than* 11,000 mi?

   **c.** What is the total distance of a flight from Paris to Los Angeles to Tokyo?

**23.** An 11- to 14-year-old girl needs 2,200 calories from her daily food. How many more calories does a 13-year-old girl need to eat today if she has already eaten 1,785 calories?

**24.** Ri has $40 to spend on clothes. She spends $18.53 for a shirt. How much does she have left to spend?

---

**LEARNING LOG**

Write the answers in your learning log.

**1.** Explain how two decimals can have different numbers of places and still represent the same number. Give an example.

**2.** Is it more difficult for you to estimate answers to addition problems or to subtraction problems? Why do you think you answered the way you did?

Solve the equation. *(pages 34–35)*

**1.** $12 + a = 21$      **2.** $53 - m = 29$      **3.** $c + 45 = 81$

**4.** $64 \div d = 16$      **5.** $n \div 8 = 11$      **6.** $3 \times e = 27$

Use the properties of addition to look for tens and compute mentally.
*(pages 36–37)*

**7.** $94 + 28 + 6$      **8.** $171 + 203 + 29$      **9.** $15 + 40 + 46$

**10.** $(17 + 23) + 82$      **11.** $(72 + 32) + 128$      **12.** $36 + (0 + 44)$

Use the front-end method to estimate. *(pages 42–43)*

**13.**
$$\begin{array}{r} \$16.71 \\ + 25.42 \\ \hline \end{array}$$

**14.**
$$\begin{array}{r} \$115.35 \\ 20.57 \\ + 89.03 \\ \hline \end{array}$$

**15.**
$$\begin{array}{r} \$150.18 \\ 37.35 \\ + 42.44 \\ \hline \end{array}$$

Write the answer. *(pages 40–41, 46–49)*

**16.**
$$\begin{array}{r} 3.8 \\ + 1.9 \\ \hline \end{array}$$

**17.**
$$\begin{array}{r} 18.5 \\ + 13.7 \\ \hline \end{array}$$

**18.**
$$\begin{array}{r} 108.3 \\ + 62.9 \\ \hline \end{array}$$

**19.**
$$\begin{array}{r} 4.9 \\ + 28 \\ \hline \end{array}$$

**20.**
$$\begin{array}{r} 0.6 \\ 17.8 \\ + 9.65 \\ \hline \end{array}$$

**21.**
$$\begin{array}{r} 8,012 \\ - 5,731 \\ \hline \end{array}$$

**22.**
$$\begin{array}{r} 96,000 \\ - 52,351 \\ \hline \end{array}$$

**23.**
$$\begin{array}{r} 67,312 \\ - 9,876 \\ \hline \end{array}$$

**24.**
$$\begin{array}{r} 103,000 \\ - 25,671 \\ \hline \end{array}$$

**25.**
$$\begin{array}{r} 9.83 \\ - 5.41 \\ \hline \end{array}$$

**26.**
$$\begin{array}{r} 60.25 \\ - 29.37 \\ \hline \end{array}$$

**27.**
$$\begin{array}{r} 14.15 \\ - 6.803 \\ \hline \end{array}$$

**28.**
$$\begin{array}{r} 81 \\ - 3.92 \\ \hline \end{array}$$

Solve. *(pages 38–39, 50–51)*

**29.** Auto Mart and Car World are selling the same model of car. If Auto Mart is asking $15,879 and Car World is asking $15,495 for the same model, how much money can you save if you buy the car at Car World?

**30.** Scientists believe that the Sun's core may reach temperatures as high as 15 million degrees Celsius. The Sun's outer atmosphere, the corona, reaches temperatures close to 3 million degrees Celsius. About what is the difference in temperature between the Sun's core and its corona?

## Plan For The Future

Work with a group. Decide on a business that you could start. Try to find answers to the kinds of questions you would face if you really were starting a business. Among the questions you need to consider are the following:

- What will you sell?
- How much do you want to earn?
- How many items do you need to sell?
- How much will you charge per item?
- Will you advertise? If so, where?
- What expenses will you have?

Once you decide on the type of business, there are many places to obtain information. You can try the following:

- business people in your community
- local manufacturers' associations
- magazines and newspapers (to find out about advertising rates and rental costs)

When you have completed your research, share your information with the rest of the class.

## The Bells Are Ringing

Each day you are in school, you spend most of your time doing schoolwork. However, you may be surprised to learn how much time you spend on other activities. These may include eating lunch and moving between classes. To estimate the amount of school time you spend on other activities, keep a record for several days of the number of minutes that you spend on these other activities. Then answer these questions:

- Does the number of minutes spent on other activities remain constant from day to day?
- What type of activity takes the most time away from schoolwork? Were you surprised by the results?
- Were you surprised by the results?

## Population Information

The United States Census is taken every 10 years. The most recent one was taken in 1990. Perhaps you helped complete a census form. You can find information on the census either in the official report at the library or in an almanac. Find the data and compare the 1980 and 1990 populations of

- the United States
- your state
- your city
- your age group

What is the equivalent value?

**1.** $6^3$

   **a.** 18

   **b.** 63

   **c.** 216

   **d.** none of these

**2.** 13.8 million

   **a.** 1,380,000

   **b.** 13,800,000

   **c.** 130,000,000

   **d.** none of these

**3.** $(2 \times 10^3) + (8 \times 10^0)$

   **a.** 2,800

   **b.** 2,080

   **c.** 2,008

   **d.** none of these

**4.** 1,800 mL

   **a.** 1.8 L

   **b.** 0.18 L

   **c.** 18 L

   **d.** none of these

**5.** 49 cm

   **a.** 4.9 m

   **b.** 490 mm

   **c.** 0.049 m

   **d.** none of these

**6.** 326 g

   **a.** 3,260 mg

   **b.** 3.26 kg

   **c.** 0.326 kg

   **d.** none of these

What is the value of $n$?

**7.** $n + 14 = 73$

   **a.** 59

   **b.** 87

   **c.** 69

   **d.** none of these

**8.** $82 - n = 37$

   **a.** 55

   **b.** 45

   **c.** 119

   **d.** none of these

**9.** $n + 18 = 50$

   **a.** 900

   **b.** 1,000

   **c.** 800

   **d.** none of these

Find the answer.

**10.** Which number is greater than 39,763?

   **a.** 39,673

   **b.** 39,367

   **c.** 39,759

   **d.** none of these

**11.** Between which two numbers is 8.04?

   **a.** 8.05 and 8.09

   **b.** 7.95 and 8.03

   **c.** 7.99 and 8.10

   **d.** none of these

**12.** $0.08 + 9.79 =$

   **a.** 9.77

   **b.** 9.87

   **c.** 10.59

   **d.** none of these

**13.**
$$\begin{array}{r} \$205.69 \\ +\ \ 18.93 \\ \hline \end{array}$$

   **a.** $224.62

   **b.** $224.52

   **c.** $212.62

   **d.** none of these

**14.**
$$\begin{array}{r} 3,000 \\ -\ \ 682 \\ \hline \end{array}$$

   **a.** 2,418

   **b.** 3,682

   **c.** 2,428

   **d.** none of these

**15.** $3.5 - 1.96 =$

   **a.** 1.54

   **b.** 2.46

   **c.** 1.64

   **d.** none of these

## PROBLEM SOLVING REVIEW

Remember the strategies and types of problems you've had so far. Solve, if possible.

1. A service telephone call costs $.40 for the first 3 min and $.10 for each additional 2 min.

   **a.** How much does a 3-min call cost?

   **b.** Are the first 3 min of a telephone call *cheaper* or *more expensive* than the additional minutes?

   **c.** How much would a 21-min telephone call cost?

2. Every time a certain ball hits the ground, it bounces back one-half the distance of the drop. If the ball is dropped from a height of 32 ft, how high will it bounce after it hits the ground the fourth time?

3. A driver sees a road sign after driving 1 mi, another after 3 mi, another after 6 mi, and another after 10 mi. If the pattern continues, how many miles will the driver travel between the fifth and sixth road signs?

4. Will earns $25/wk after school. He always spends $18 of this money and saves the rest. One week he earned an extra $12 for overtime work. If he saved the entire $12, how much did he put in the bank that week?

5. On her vacation, Sondra spent $479 on airfare and $83/d for each of the 6 d she was away. If she left on her vacation with exactly $1,000, how much money did she have left when she returned?

6. The year after Rosa's class graduated, the school's population fell to 729 students. How many of the 729 students were boys?

7. Jet fuel costs $1.85/gal. If a jet's tank can hold 350 gal of fuel, how much does it cost to fly the jet 500 mi?

8. Compact disks (CDs), which usually cost $11.99, are on sale for $8.99 each. Tapes, which usually cost $6.99, are selling for $5.50 each. What is the total cost of 1 CD and 1 tape on sale?

9. The number of students in Rosa's school increased from 684 to 743. Originally, there were 362 girls. With the increase there are 391 girls. How many new students are girls?

## SHOPPING FOR THREE

Ask a friend to try this activity.

You must buy three items. You can buy more than one of an item, but you can't spend more than $10. How many different combinations of items can you buy? The person who can list the most in three minutes wins.

| Notebook | Pen | Record |
|----------|-----|--------|
| $.79 | $1.29 | $6.89 |

| Book | Puzzle |
|------|--------|
| $3.65 | $2.89 |

## IT ADDS UP

Copy and complete the magic square so that when you add across, down, or diagonally, the sums will always be the same.

| 2.70 | 9.45 | 8.10 |
|------|------|------|
|      |      |      |
| 5.40 |      |      |

## LIGHTNING ADDITION

In the computer activity *Decimal Dispatch,* you estimate decimal sums. Sharpen your number sense skills with this game. Work in pairs. You do not need a computer.

Write the addition problems on a set of cards and the answers on another set. Shuffle the answer cards. With one player acting as a timer, the other player must match each problem with the correct answer card as quickly as possible. The timer records the time and checks the answers with a calculator. Players then switch roles. Who had the faster time? Who had more correct matches?

Problems:

| A | B | C | D | E |
|---|---|---|---|---|
| 3.467 | 2.314 | 2.813 | 2.749 | 2.047 |
| + 2.519 | + 3.146 | + 2.784 | + 2.856 | + 3.689 |

Answer cards:  5.460   5.605   5.736   5.986   5.597

**DID YOU KNOW . . . ?**

Americans buy a total of 50,000 television sets every day. If you spread the sets evenly along the roads between New York and Los Angeles, they would be about 100 yd apart—the length of a football field.

The sign below tells how many items Americans buy each day.

**Buy Buy Buy**

Radios
**120,000**

Cars
**25,000**

Books
**5,000,000**

Wristwatches
**190,000**

Pencils
**4,000,000**

Running shoes
**52,000**

**USING DATA**

Collect

**Organize**

**Describe**

Predict

Which of the above items do Americans buy more than 50 million of in 1 yr?

Organize the facts in a table. Show how many yards apart pencils, books, etc., would be from each other if they were spread evenly on the 2,800 mi from New York to Los Angeles.

# Mental Math and Properties of Multiplication

A helicopter tour of Manhattan Island costs about $50
plus $3 tax per person. About how much
would the tour cost for 6 passengers?

You can compute this mentally.

$6 \times 50 = 300$

$6 \times 3 = 18$     The tour would cost about $318.

The multiplication properties can help you compute mentally.

**THINK ALOUD**   Explain which property was used above.

| **Commutative Property: Changing the order of the factors does not change the product.** |
|---|

In arithmetic:   $50 \times 6 = 6 \times 50$          In algebra:   $a \times b = b \times a$

$300 = 300$

| **Associative Property: Changing the grouping of the factors does not change the product.** |
|---|

In arithmetic:                          In algebra:

$(50 \times 3) \times 6 = 50 \times (3 \times 6)$          $(a \times b) \times c = a \times (b \times c)$

$150 \times 6 = 50 \times 18$

$900 = 900$

| **Distributive Property: The product of a factor and a sum is equal to the sum of the products.** |
|---|

In arithmetic:                          In algebra:

$6 \times (50 + 3) = (6 \times 50) + (6 \times 3)$          $a \times (b + c) = (a \times b) + (a \times c)$

$6(53) = 300 + 18$

$318 = 318$

| **Identity Property: The product of one and any other number is that number.** |
|---|

In arithmetic:   $50 \times 1 = 50$          In algebra:   $a \times 1 = a$

| **Zero Property: The product of zero and any other number is zero.** |
|---|

In arithmetic:   $53 \times 0 = 0$          In algebra:   $a \times 0 = 0$

**THINK ALOUD** Explain which multiplication property
is used in each equation.

**1.** $34 \times 19 = 19 \times 34$  **2.** $0 \times x = 0$

**3.** $1 \times m = m$  **4.** $8 \times 18 = (8 \times 10) + (8 \times 8)$

Use the multiplication properties to simplify mentally.

**5.** $150 \times 1 \times 4$  **6.** $1{,}432 \times 0 \times 54$  **7.** $20 \times 70 \times 5$

**8.** $(30 + 7) \times 2$  **9.** $(13 \times 25) \times 4$  **10.** $6 \times (20 + 5)$

**11.** $90 \times 1 \times 60$  **12.** $250 \times 7 \times 2$  **13.** $20 \times (5 \times 23)$

**14.** $(9 \times 35) \times 2$  **15.** $25 \times 83 \times 4$  **16.** $92 \times 8 \times 0 \times 53$

**17.** $(9 \times 125) \times 4$  **18.** $25 \times (13 \times 4)$  **19.** $(250 \times 11) \times 4$

**NUMBER SENSE** Find a match that makes an equation.

**20.** $16 \times (35 + 16) =$  **a.** $(88 + 35) \times 16$

**21.** $16 \times (35 \times 88) =$  **b.** $(16 \times 35) \times 88$

**22.** $16 \times (88 + 35) =$  **c.** $(16 \times 35) + (16 \times 16)$

Use a property to solve mentally.

**23.** The water shuttle from Manhattan Island to
La Guardia Airport costs about $20 per person.
What is the total cost for 75 passengers?

**24.** The bus from Manhattan to JFK Airport costs
about $11 per person. If the bus makes 8 trips
in one day, how much money is collected if
25 seats are bought for each trip?

### Estimate

You can use **compatible numbers** to estimate a product.
Compatible numbers are close to original numbers but
easier to use.

$$247 \Rightarrow 250$$
$$\underline{\times\, 4} \quad\quad \underline{\times\, 4}$$

*250 is close to 247, but is easier to multiply.*

Use a compatible number to help you estimate the product.

**1.** $495 \times 7$  **2.** $117 \times 6$  **3.** $838 \times 2$  **4.** $2{,}968 \times 8$

## Order of Operations

Michelle won a contest at her local grocery store. When she collected her prize, she correctly answered the skill-test question below. Which way did Michelle simplify the expression?

$$5 + 8 \times (2 + 6) \div 4$$
$$13 \times (2 + 6) \div 4$$
$$13 \times 8 \div 4$$
$$104 \div 4$$
$$26$$

$$5 + 8 \times (2 + 6) \div 4$$
$$5 + 8 \times (8) \div 4$$
$$5 + 64 \div 4$$
$$5 + 16$$
$$21$$

Which one is correct?

**THINK ALOUD** Use the **order of operations** rules below to explain why 26 is not correct and 21 is.

Simplify in this order:

1. Do all operations within parentheses first.

2. Simplify all numbers with exponents.

3. Multiply and divide in order from left to right.

4. Add and subtract in order from left to right.

**THINK ALOUD** Explain the steps used to simplify.

$$6 \times (10 + 4) \div 2^2$$
$$6 \times 14 \div 2^2$$
$$6 \times 14 \div 4$$
$$84 \div 4$$
$$21$$

$$(6 \times 10) + 4 \div 2^2$$
$$60 + 4 \div 2^2$$
$$60 + 4 \div 4$$
$$60 + 1$$
$$61$$

$$(6 \times 10 + 4) \div 2^2$$
$$(60 + 4) \div 2^2$$
$$64 \div 2^2$$
$$64 \div 4$$
$$16$$

━━━━━━━━━━━━━━ **GUIDED PRACTICE** ━━━━━━━━━━━━━━

Name the operation to be done first.

**1.** $8 + 7 \times 3$      **2.** $6^2 \div (5 - 2)$      **3.** $13 + 9^2 - 6$      **4.** $(18 - 7) \times 3$

Follow the order of operations to simplify.

**5.** $9 + 3 \times 6$      **6.** $(7 + 3) \times 4$      **7.** $8 - 9 \div 3^2$

**8.** $25 \times 2 + 4^2$      **9.** $25 \times (2 + 4)$      **10.** $9 + 2 - 6 \div 3$

---

## PRACTICE

Simplify the expression. Use a calculator, mental math, or pencil and paper.

**11.** $42 \times 2 - 16$     **12.** $13 + 8 \times 4$     **13.** $(10 - 1) \div 3$

**14.** $4 \times 2 + 5 - 3$     **15.** $14 - 6 \times 2 - 1$     **16.** $72 - 6 \times 1$

**17.** $14 - 6 \times (2 - 1)$     **18.** $15 \div 5 \times 9 + 2$     **19.** $2 + 2 \times 2 \div 2 - 2$

**20.** $1 \times 40 + 3$     **21.** $50 \times (9 - 6) \div 3$     **22.** $10 + 0 \div 2^2$

**23.** $9 + 6 \times 4 - 5 \times 3$     **24.** $17 + 20 \div 2 \div 2 \div 5$     **25.** $20 \times 4 \div 5 + 0 \times 1$

**26.** $(8 + 4) \div 2^2$     **27.** $3^2 \times (16 \div 4) \div 4$

**28.** $42 + 58 + (60 - 40 \div 5)$     **29.** $5^2 \times 1^3 \times (7 \div 1)$

**30.** $2^2 \times 5 \div 4 + 3$     **31.** $(99 \div 9 - 3 \times 2) - (7 - 4)$

**CRITICAL THINKING**   Insert parentheses to make the mathematical sentence true.

**32.** $19 - 16 \div 3 = 1$     **33.** $6 \times 4 + 8 = 72$     **34.** $23 + 5 \times 4 = 112$

**35.** $6 \times 4 + 8 \div 2 = 36$     **36.** $18 - 14 \times 20 \div 5 = 16$

---

## PROBLEM SOLVING

 Choose mental math, paper and pencil, or calculator to solve.

**37.** Tim won $1,000 in a local contest. To claim his prize, he had to find the product of:
$5 + 12 \div 3$ and $15 - (3 \times 4)$.
What is the product?

**38.** The answer to the skill-test question for the Spanish Club contest is 93. What is the question:
$(42 - 36 \div 4) \times 3$ or
$78 - 44 \div 2^2 + (4 + 22)$?

**39.** **CREATE YOUR OWN**   Write a skill-test question with five numbers and at least three different operations that has an answer of 79.

# Multiplying Whole Numbers

Chicago's O'Hare Airport averages about 2,150 flights a day. At this rate, about how many flights would there be in February during a non-leap year?

Multiply the 2,150 flights by the 28 d (days) in February.

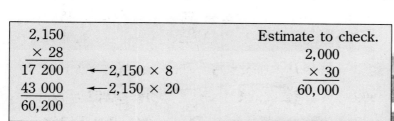

```
  2,150                    Estimate to check.
×    28                         2,000
 17 200  ←2,150 × 8            ×   30
 43 000  ←2,150 × 20          60,000
 60,200
```

There would be about 60,200 flights in February.

**THINK ALOUD** Without computing, decide whether O'Hare averages about 785,000 or 785,000,000 flights in a year. Explain.

Other examples:

```
     529        Estimate to check.        1,406       Estimate to check.
×    390               500           ×       58             1,400
  47 610             ×   400          11 248              ×    60
 158 700           200,000            70 300             84,000
 206,310                              81,548
```

---

Choose the best estimate.

**1.** 38 × 22 is about:
   **a.** 800   **b.** 8,000  **c.** 900

**2.** 63 × 793 is about:
   **a.** 40,000  **b.** 48,000  **c.** 4,800

Find the product. Check your answer.

**3.**     38
    × 25

**4.**     63
    × 80

**5.**  3,281 × 8

**6.**  508 × 83

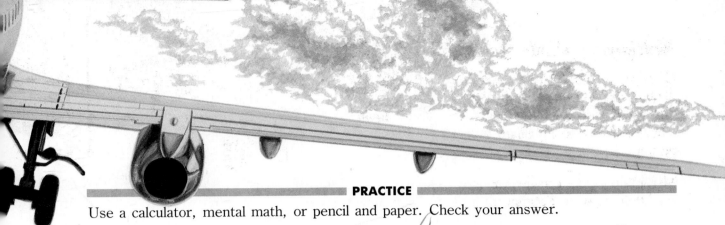

Use a calculator, mental math, or pencil and paper. Check your answer.

**7.**  58
    $\times$ 7

**8.**  81
    $\times$ 30

**9.**  76
    $\times$ 43

**10.**  90
    $\times$ 28

**11.**  46
    $\times$ 14

**12.** $34 \times 9$

**13.** $32 \times 79$

**14.** $16 \times 225$

**15.** $637 \times 21$

**16.** $205 \times 70$

**17.** $718 \times 899$

**18.** $3,060 \times 83$

**19.** $2,956 \times 740$

**20.** $2,005 \times 507$

**21.** $\$504 \times 288$

**22.** $\$6,308 \times 326$

**23.** $31 \times \$5,163$

**MIXED REVIEW**   Compute.

**24.** $12.4 + 3.75$

**25.** $16 \times 29$

**26.** $45 - 9.2$

**27.** $185 + 46$

**28.** $721 - 345$

**29.** $0.4 - 0.25$

**30.** $5 \times 743$

**31.** $3.7 + 0.5$

**MENTAL MATH**   Simplify mentally.

**32.** $50 \times (40 \times 90)$

**33.** $(47 \times 250) \times 8$

**34.** $(3 \times 25) \times 4,000$

**CHOOSE**   Choose estimation or paper and pencil to solve.

| Speedair Flights | | | | | |
|---|---|---|---|---|---|
| Detroit to: | Plane | Seating Capacity | Departure Time | Arrival Time | Frequency |
| New York | 757 | 224 | 9:50 P.M. | 11:27 P.M. | Daily |
| Miami | DC10 | 325 | 8:00 A.M. | 10:42 A.M. | Daily |
| Nassau | DC9 | 118 | 9:05 A.M. | 2:00 P.M. | MTWTHF |

**35.** Name two exact numbers and two estimates in the table.

**36.** All Speedair flights are in the same time zone. About how many hours and minutes does each flight last?

**37.** Represent the seating capacities of the three kinds of airplanes with a pictograph. Use the symbol ◆ to represent 25 seats.

## *Multiplying Decimals*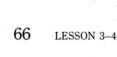

After his trip to Canada, Brian came home with $9.89 in Canadian money. What was the value of Brian's money in U.S. dollars? At that time, the exchange rate was:

$1 Canadian = $.85 U.S.

- Multiply the Canadian money ($9.89) by the U.S. exchange rate ($.85). Note how the decimal point is placed in the product.

$$
\begin{array}{r}
9.89 \quad \leftarrow\text{2 decimal places} \\
\times \ 0.85 \quad \leftarrow\text{2 decimal places} \\
\hline
4945 \\
7912 \phantom{0} \\
\hline
8.4065 \quad \leftarrow\text{4 decimal places}
\end{array}
$$

To the nearest cent, Brian's Canadian money was worth $8.41 in U.S. funds.

- Estimate to check the answer.
$10 \times 0.85 = $8.50
$8.50 is close to $8.41.

---

Other examples:

What is $0.28 \times 0.4$?

$$
\begin{array}{r}
0.28 \quad \leftarrow\text{2 decimal places} \\
\times \ 0.4 \quad \leftarrow\text{1 decimal place} \\
\hline
0.112 \quad \leftarrow\text{3 decimal places}
\end{array}
$$

Estimate to check: $0.3 \times 0.4 = 0.12$

---

**THINK ALOUD** Why is the product, 0.112, smaller than 0.28 and 0.4?

Find the product of 2.69 and 16. On a calculator:

2.69 ⨯ 16 = 43.04

Estimate to check: $3 \times 16 = 48$

---

**GUIDED PRACTICE**

**NUMBER SENSE** Choose the correct product. Do not calculate.

**1.** $2.7 \times 8$    2.16, 21.6, 216

**2.** $2.37 \times 14$    331.8, 3.318, 33.18

Is the product *reasonable* or *unreasonable*? If *unreasonable*, find the correct product.

**3.** $20.5 \times 3.1$    635.5

**4.** $4.6 \times 0.05$    0.23

Use a calculator, mental math, or pencil and paper. Check your answer.

5.　2.73
　　× 2.3

6.　5.307
　　× 5.8

7.　30.241
　　× 0.72

8.　　0.05
　　× 0.03

9.　　0.0053
　　× 0.046

10. $3.25 × 0.04

11. $21.15 × 0.8

12. $70.00 × 0.004

13. 16.78 × 1,000

14. 495.2 × 10

15. 56 × 100

16. 4.5 × 3.8

17. 4.3 × 0.253

18. 7.2 × 2.42

19. 0.42 × 0.12

20. 0.2 × (6 − 0.8)

**MIXED REVIEW** Compute.

21. 542 − 16

22. $6 + 5^3$

23. 0.009 × 0

24. 7,002 ÷ 9

25. $8.45 × 1^3$

26. 40 − 3.7

27. 9.5 × 100

28. $3^3 + 2^3$

**ESTIMATE** Estimate the product.

29. $5.29 × 1.3

30. $698.95 × 0.6

31. 40¢ × 0.28

**CHOOSE** Choose paper and pencil or calculator to solve. Round to cents.

32. Bonnie changed 12,750 Mexican pesos to U.S. dollars. If 1 peso at that time was equal to $.0038 U.S., how much U.S. money did she get?

33. If 1 peso exchanges for $.0041 U.S., how much U.S. money can Bonnie get for 125,000 pesos?

## Critical Thinking

The [M+] key on a calculator enters a number into memory. The [MR] key recalls the number.

Discuss how you would use a calculator's memory keys to change the Japanese yen to U.S. dollars.
Use 1 Japanese yen = $.0065 U.S.

1. 80 yen　　2. 560 yen　　3. 4,000 yen　　4. 94,000 yen　　5. 896,200 yen

# Dividing Whole Numbers

A year is the number of days a planet takes to orbit the Sun. One year on Mercury is equal to about 2,112 Earth hours. How many Earth days is that?

There are 24 h in 1 d. So, divide 2,112 by 24 to find the number of Earth days.

| Divide 2,112 by 24. | Multiply to check. |
|---|---|
| $\begin{array}{r} 88 \\ 24\overline{)2,112} \\ -192 \\ \hline 192 \\ -192 \\ \hline 0 \end{array}$ | $\begin{array}{r} 88 \\ \times\ 24 \\ \hline 352 \\ 176 \\ \hline 2,112 \end{array}$ |

One year on Mercury is equal to about 88 Earth days.

**THINK ALOUD**  About how many days longer is a year on Earth than a year on Mercury?

Another example:

What is $1,483 \div 37$?    Check:

$$\begin{array}{r} 40\ R3 \\ 37\overline{)1,483} \\ -148 \\ \hline 03 \end{array} \qquad \begin{array}{r} 40 \\ \times\ 37 \\ \hline 1,480 \\ +\quad 3 \\ \hline 1,483 \end{array}$$

Add the remainder.

---

======== **GUIDED PRACTICE** ========

**NUMBER SENSE**  Choose the correct quotient. Do not calculate.

1.  $39\overline{)351}$    9, 90

2.  $62\overline{)3,100}$    5, 50

3.  $25\overline{)1,750}$    7, 70

4.  $192\overline{)11,520}$    6, 60

Divide. Check your answer.

5.  $42\overline{)812}$

6.  $19\overline{)288}$

7.  $4,056 \div 78$

Mercury

Divide. Check your answer.

**8.** $50\overline{)250}$  **9.** $8\overline{)828}$  **10.** $4\overline{)804}$  **11.** $9\overline{)210}$

**12.** $21\overline{)357}$  **13.** $3\overline{)369}$  **14.** $43\overline{)603}$  **15.** $21\overline{)2,121}$

**16.** $382 \div 48$  **17.** $823 \div 24$  **18.** $750 \div 25$  **19.** $265 \div 53$

**20.** $85\overline{)5,149}$  **21.** $36\overline{)180}$  **22.** $107\overline{)8,495}$  **23.** $231\overline{)3,812}$

**24.** $5,400 \div 54$  **25.** $4,294 \div 38$  **26.** $491 \div 415$  **27.** $35,030 \div 62$

**MIXED REVIEW**   Simplify.

**28.** $0.04 + 0.086$  **29.** $500 - 7.39$  **30.** $58 \times 0.4$  **31.** $468 \div 9$

**32.** $0.2 - 0.19$  **33.** $234 \div 13$  **34.** $3.7 + 29.98$  **35.** $0.6 \times 0.07$

**MENTAL MATH**   Compare the quotients mentally. Use >, <, or =.

**36.** $480 \div 12 \ \blacksquare\ 4,800 \div 120$  **37.** $180 \div 30 \ \blacksquare\ 1,800 \div 30$

**38.** **CALCULATOR**   Find each quotient. Then write the next three divisions in the pattern.

$111,111 \div 3 \Rightarrow 222,222 \div 6 \Rightarrow 333,333 \div 9 \Rightarrow$

**CHOOSE**   Choose paper and pencil or calculator to solve.

**39.** About how many hours are in 1 Earth year? Assume 1 yr is equal to 365 d.

**40.** One year on Venus is about 5,400 Earth hours. How many Earth days are there in 5,400 h?

**41.** Order from least to greatest: 25 d, 40,000 s, 34,800 min.

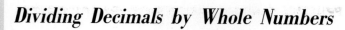

# Dividing Decimals by Whole Numbers

A **fathom** is a unit of length that measures water depth. One fathom is 6 ft. About how many fathoms deep is Lake Erie? Round to whole numbers.

Divide 209.9 by 6 to find the depth of Lake Erie in fathoms.

If you can divide whole numbers, you can use a **MATH CONNECTION** to divide a decimal by a whole number.

```
      34.9   is about 35
  6)209.9
   - 18
     ———
      29
    - 24
     ———
      59
    - 54
     ———
       5
```

Line up the decimal points. To round to a whole number, divide until there is a number in the tenths' place.

Lake Erie is about 35 fathoms deep.

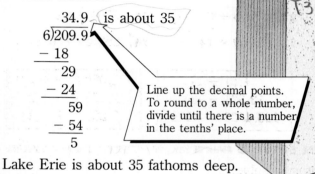

Lake Erie
209.9 ft

Lake Huron
751.6 ft

Lake Ontario
800.9 ft

Lake Michigan
922.2 ft

Lake Superior
1,332.5 ft

Canada

Lake Superior

Lake Huron

Lake Ontario

Lake Michigan

Lake Erie

---

**THINK ALOUD** Use the examples below to explain how far you divide when you round to hundredths.

```
      2.888  is about 2.89
  27)78.000
    - 54
     ———
      240
    - 216
     ———
      240
    - 216
     ———
      240
    - 216
     ———
       24
```

Add zeros after the decimal point to continue dividing.

```
      0.012  is about 0.01
   7)0.084
    - 7
     ———
      14
    - 14
     ———
       0
```

---

Divide. Round to tenths.

1. 338.4 ÷ 8

2. 35.2 ÷ 14

3. 7.93 ÷ 32

MATH AND GEOGRAPHY

Divide until there is no remainder.

**4.** $5\overline{)7.25}$ **5.** $2\overline{)7.012}$ **6.** $8\overline{)10.01}$ **7.** $60\overline{)37.68}$ **8.** $66\overline{)6.27}$

Divide. Round to tenths.

**9.** $19.12 \div 3$ **10.** $93.5 \div 8$ **11.** $2.3 \div 6$ **12.** $25.49 \div 9$

Divide. Round to hundredths.

**13.** $33.52 \div 7$ **14.** $4.32 \div 3$ **15.** $3.17 \div 28$ **16.** $12.98 \div 31$

Divide. Round to cents.

**17.** $\$45.07 \div 12$ **18.** $\$6.50 \div 53$ **19.** $\$2.88 \div 17$ **20.** $\$18.74 \div 36$

**MIXED REVIEW** Compute. Round to cents.

**21.** $\$352 \div 9$ **22.** $\$6.79 \times 0.5$ **23.** $\$2.05 \div 6$ **24.** $\$704 \div 12$

**25.** $\$87.60 \div 21$ **26.** $\$36.28 \times 0.3$ **27.** $\$9.60 \div 14$ **28.** $\$82.59 \times 0.1$

**29.** **CALCULATOR** Find each quotient.
Then write two more divisions
for the pattern.

| |
|---|
| $1.21 \div 11$ |
| $12.321 \div 111$ |
| $123.4321 \div 1{,}111$ |

| |
|---|
| $1.089 \times 9 \div 1$ |
| $2.178 \times 8 \div 2$ |
| $3.267 \times 7 \div 3$ |

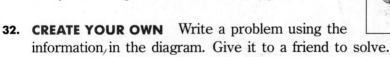

**CHOOSE** Choose paper and pencil or calculator to solve.
Use the diagram on page 70. Round to tenths.

**30.** What are the depths in fathoms of Lake Superior,
Lake Michigan, Lake Huron, and Lake Ontario?

**31.** Lake Baikal, in the USSR, is the deepest lake
in the world, at about 886 fathoms. About how
many feet deeper is it than Lake Superior?

**32.** **CREATE YOUR OWN** Write a problem using the
information in the diagram. Give it to a friend to solve.

USSR

Lake Baikal

---

*Estimate*

You can use **clustering** to estimate a sum.

$19 + 22 + 17 + 21 + 18 + 23$
$6 \times 20 = 120$

All numbers cluster around 20.
The sum is about 120.

Estimate the sum using the cluster method.

**1.** $28 + 31 + 29 + 32 + 27$ **2.** $12 + 9 + 11 + 8 + 13 + 7$

# Think Again!

## Problem Solving:
## Look Back

Sequoia and Kings Canyon national parks in central California are the home of some of the oldest living things on Earth today—the giant Sequoia trees.

When solving the problems about the giant Sequoia trees, use the data on page 73 and the check list to ensure that you have reasonable answers.

**REASONABLE ANSWER CHECK LIST**

✔ Did you answer the question?

✔ Did you calculate correctly?

✔ Is your answer labeled with the right units?

✔ Does the answer need to be rounded to a whole number to make sense?

### TALK ABOUT IT

Work with your group. Is the answer *reasonable* or *unreasonable*?
If *unreasonable,* explain why and find a reasonable answer.

1. What is the approximate height of the General Sherman Tree in yards?
   (Hint: Recall that 3 ft = 1 yd)
   Answer:          about 825 yd

2. How long ago was Sequoia National Park established?
   Answer:          102 ft

3. Since about what year do scientists think the General Sherman Tree has been alive?
   Answer:          about 300 B.C.

4. About how many 6-ft adults would equal the height of the General Sherman Tree?
   Answer:          45.817 adults

5. What is the height of the General Grant Tree?
   Answer:          267.9 yd

6. If your arm span is 5 ft, about how many would it take to encircle the base of the General Sherman Tree?
   Answer:          30 yd

7. Yellowstone became a national park 18 yr earlier than Sequoia National Park. In what year was Yellowstone established?
   Answer: 1872

MATH AND GEOGRAPHY

Sequoia and Kings Canyon national parks are side by side in central California. The two parks are often considered as one. Sequoia became our second national park in 1890. Kings Canyon became a national park in 1940.

The oldest and most magnificent trees in the two parks are named for American generals. The General Sherman Tree, the world's biggest tree in volume of wood, is found in Sequoia National Park. It is 274.9 ft high and has a circumference at its base of 102.6 ft. Scientists estimate the tree to be between 2,000 and 2,500 yr old.

The General Grant Tree is 7 ft shorter than the General Sherman Tree but 5 ft larger in circumference.

## ▢ WRITE ABOUT IT

8. Work with your group. Estimate how many feet of growth the General Sherman Tree has averaged each year since it has been alive. Look back to see whether your answer is reasonable.

# MIDCHAPTER CHECKUP

Choose the correct answer for the exercise. Explain your choice.

1. $7 \times (40 + 8) =$    336 or 288

2. $108 \times 1 =$    109 or 108

3. $65 \times 0 =$    65 or 0

4. $3 + 9 \times 5 =$    48 or 60

5. $3 \times 2^2 - 6 + 5 =$ 11 or 7

## QUICK QUIZ ✓

Simplify. *(pages 60–63)*

1. $(80 + 3) \times 7$
2. $9 \times (8 \times 4)$
3. $4 + 3^2 \times 2 - (6 - 4)$

Multiply. *(pages 64–67)*

4. $\$3,756 \times 24$
5. $8.06 \times 3.42$

Divide. Write the answer, including the remainder. *(pages 68–69)*

6. $36\overline{)2,053}$
7. $22\overline{)2,373}$

Divide. Round to hundredths. *(pages 70–71)*

8. $16\overline{)48.8}$
9. $35.6 \div 22$

Solve.

10. Dana bought 8 paper plates and 8 napkins for a party. Each plate cost $.20, and each napkin cost $.09.

    a. How much did Dana pay for each paper plate?

    b. What multiplication property would help you find the total amount Dana spent?

    c. How much did Dana spend altogether?

Write the answers in your learning log.

1. Explain how the multiplication properties in arithmetic are related to the same properties in algebra.

2. On a test Mark worked out the problem $\frac{16}{2} \times 4$ and got an answer of 2. His teacher marked it wrong. Explain Mark's mistake.

MATH AMERICA

**DID YOU KNOW . . . ?** The part of Niagara Falls that is in New York State is called the American Falls. About 2.5 cm of the ledge of the falls wear away each year. About how much have the American Falls worn away in your lifetime?

BONUS

Use your knowledge of the order-of-operations rules and number properties to solve this problem.

How many expressions having a value from 0 to 5 can you create using only 4's and any operation signs you need? Here is one way to create an expression with a value of 1.

$$\frac{4 \times 4}{4 \times 4}$$

## Exploring Multiplying and Dividing Decimals

You can multiply a number by a power of 10 mentally because it follows a pattern.

Look for a pattern as you find the product.

**1.** $5 \times 10$        **2.** $0.4 \times 10$        **3.** $4.23 \times 10$

    $5 \times 100$             $0.4 \times 100$           $4.23 \times 100$

    $5 \times 1,000$         $0.4 \times 1,000$        $4.23 \times 1,000$

    $5 \times 10,000$      $0.4 \times 10,000$      $4.23 \times 10,000$

**4.** When you multiply a number by a whole-number power of 10, is the product *greater than* or *lesser than* the original number?

**5.** **IN YOUR WORDS** What do you notice about the movement of the decimal point when multiplying by a whole-number power of 10? Describe the relation between the movement of the decimal point and the number of zeros in the power of 10.

**6.** **IN YOUR WORDS** Write a rule for mentally multiplying a number by a whole-number power of 10.

Mentally multiply the number by 10, 100, and 1,000.

**7.** 58                **8.** 6,238              **9.** 7.4

**10.** 0.04           **11.** 6,047             **12.** 32.08

You can also mentally divide a number by a power of 10 by using a pattern.

Look for a pattern as you find the quotient.

**13.** $8 \div 10$       **14.** $0.3 \div 10$        **15.** $56.4 \div 10$

     $8 \div 100$            $0.3 \div 100$          $56.4 \div 100$

     $8 \div 1,000$         $0.3 \div 1,000$       $56.4 \div 1,000$

     $8 \div 10,000$      $0.3 \div 10,000$      $56.4 \div 10,000$

**16.** When you divide a number by a whole-number power of 10, is the quotient *greater than* or *lesser than* the original number?

**17.** **IN YOUR WORDS** What do you notice about the movement of the decimal point when dividing by a whole-number power of 10?

**18.** **IN YOUR WORDS** Write a rule for mentally dividing a number by a whole-number power of 10.

Mentally divide the number by 10, 100, and 1,000.

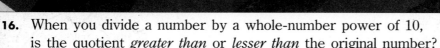

**19.** 6          **20.** 530          **21.** 42,185          **22.** 12.83          **23.** 0.7

What number multiplied by 100 results in the given product?

**24.** 10          **25.** 64.4          **26.** 0.054          **27.** $10^3$

What number divided by 1,000 results in the given quotient?

**28.** 2,509          **29.** 0.083          **30.** 97.5          **31.** $10^2$

**32.** What operation is the same as multiplying by 1,000 and then dividing by 100?

Mentally divide the number by 10. Write down the quotient. Then mentally multiply the original number by 0.1 (a decimal power of 10) and write down the product.

**33.** 765          **34.** 43.4          **35.** 1,323          **36.** 6,670.5

**37.** **IN YOUR WORDS** What can you conclude as you compare your quotients and products in Exercises 33–36?

**38.** **IN YOUR WORDS** Divide any four numbers by 100 and write down the quotients. Now multiply each quotient by 0.01 and write down the product. What do you conclude?

**39.** **IN YOUR WORDS** Explain the relationship between dividing by 1,000 and multiplying by 0.001.

# Scientific Notation

Scientists have developed a method for writing very large numbers. This method, called **scientific notation**, allows you to write very large numbers in an easier way. The area of the USSR is large. Scientists would write $22,402,000$ as $2.2402 \times 10^7$ in scientific notation.

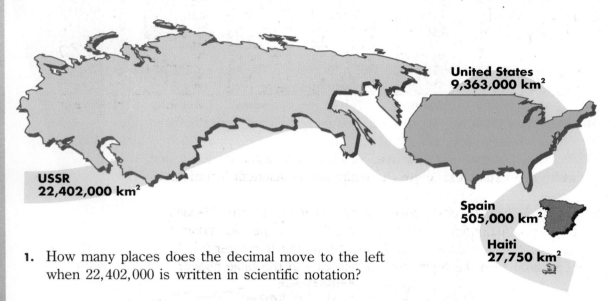

**United States**
**9,363,000 km²**

**USSR**
**22,402,000 km²**

**Spain**
**505,000 km²**

**Haiti**
**27,750 km²**

1.  How many places does the decimal move to the left when $22,402,000$ is written in scientific notation?

2.  What is $10^7$ in standard form?

There is an easy way to remember how to write numbers in scientific notation.

$$22,402,000 = 2.2402 \times 10^7$$

a number from 1 to 10 $\qquad$ a power of 10

The decimal moved 7 places.

> **A number written in scientific notation has two factors. One factor is a number greater than or equal to 1 but less than 10. The other factor is a power of 10.**

3.  Written in scientific notation, what is $450,000,000$? $4,500,000,000$? $45,000,000$?

4.  What are the areas of the United States, Spain, and Haiti in scientific notation?

5.  **IN YOUR WORDS** Explain what happens when you change $5.3 \times 10^5$ to standard form.

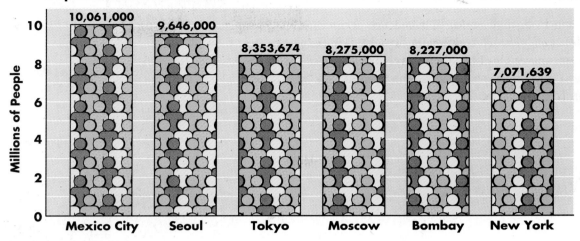

**Population of World Cities**

Mexico City 10,061,000
Seoul 9,646,000
Tokyo 8,353,674
Moscow 8,275,000
Bombay 8,227,000
New York 7,071,639

(y-axis: Millions of People, 0, 2, 4, 6, 8, 10)

6. Of the populations listed above, which do you think are exact and which are estimates? Write the estimates in scientific notation.

7. If you include the city's surrounding metropolitan area, Mexico City's population increases to about $1.55 \times 10^7$ people. What is this number in standard form? About how much greater is this population than the figure for Mexico City in the table above?

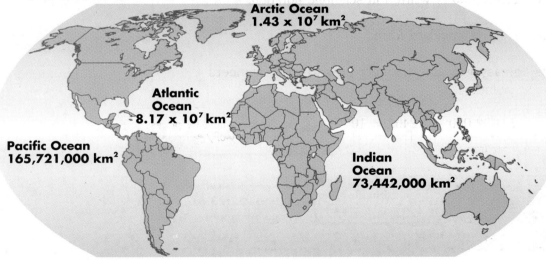

Arctic Ocean
$1.43 \times 10^7 \, km^2$

Atlantic Ocean
$8.17 \times 10^7 \, km^2$

Pacific Ocean
165,721,000 km²

Indian Ocean
73,442,000 km²

8. In scientific notation, list the areas of the oceans in order from smallest to largest.

9. Copy and complete the bar graph at the right representing the areas of the oceans.

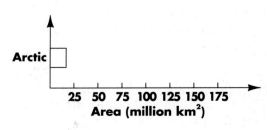

Arctic

25  50  75  100  125  150  175
Area (million km²)

# Dividing Decimals by Decimals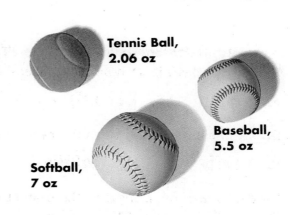

Tennis Ball, 2.06 oz

A Ping-Pong ball and a golf ball are about the same size, but have different weights. A Ping-Pong ball weighs only 0.09 oz. How many Ping-Pong balls would equal the weight of 1 1.62-oz golf ball?

Baseball, 5.5 oz

Softball, 7 oz

How many times does 0.09 divide into 1.62?

To change the divisor to a whole number, multiply it by 100. Multiply the dividend by the same power of 10.

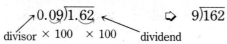

$$0.09\overline{)1.62} \quad \Rightarrow \quad 9\overline{)162}$$

divisor × 100    × 100   dividend

| Divide. | Check using the original divisor. |
|---|---|
| $\begin{array}{r} 18 \\ 9\overline{)162} \\ -\ 9 \\ \hline 72 \\ -\ 72 \\ \hline 0 \end{array}$ | $\begin{array}{r} 18 \\ \times\ 0.09 \\ \hline 1.62 \end{array}$ |

Volleyball, 9.88 oz

Football, 15 oz

Eighteen Ping-Pong balls equal the weight of one golf ball.

Another example:
What is $1.57 \div 0.4$ to the nearest tenth?

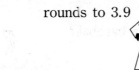

$$\begin{array}{r} 3.92 \\ 0.4\overline{)1.5.70} \\ -\ 12 \\ \hline 37 \\ -\ 36 \\ \hline 10 \\ -\ 8 \\ \hline 2 \end{array}$$

rounds to 3.9

Multiply the divisor and dividend by 10 so the divisor is a whole number.

Why is the division worked to the hundredths' place?

Basketball, 22.93 oz

---

## GUIDED PRACTICE

**THINK ALOUD** Explain how you would change the divisor to a whole number. What would you do to the dividend?

**1.** $0.7\overline{)4.9}$   **2.** $0.65\overline{)1.82}$   **3.** $84.21 \div 0.802$   **4.** $24 \div 0.4$

Find the quotient. Round to tenths when necessary.

**5.** $0.6\overline{)8.4}$   **6.** $1.5\overline{)47.5}$   **7.** $0.50 \div 0.12$   **8.** $3.6 \div 0.09$

Divide until there is no remainder. Check your answer.

**9.** $0.8\overline{)7.2}$     **10.** $0.2\overline{)14.4}$     **11.** $5.5\overline{)82.5}$     **12.** $1.2\overline{)13.68}$

Divide. Round the quotient to the nearest tenth.

**13.** $2.3\overline{)3.78}$     **14.** $1.9\overline{)4.83}$     **15.** $1.7\overline{)140}$     **16.** $1.67\overline{)4.771}$

Divide. Round the quotient to the nearest cent.

**17.** $47.35 \div 6.1$     **18.** $36.82 \div 0.83$     **19.** $6.73 \div 3.9$     **20.** $15.37 \div 6.4$

Divide. Round the quotient to the nearest thousandth.

**21.** $8 \div 0.53$     **22.** $7.836 \div 2.7$     **23.** $0.249 \div 0.08$     **24.** $481 \div 3.5$

**MIXED REVIEW**   Compute.

**25.** $89.7 + 128.63$     **26.** $1.14 \div 0.06$     **27.** $45.6 - 7.95$     **28.** $105.6 \times 4.8$

**29.** $50 - 38.75$     **30.** $0.9 + 0.75$     **31.** $67.9 \div 9.7$     **32.** $85.3 \times 0.8$

**33.** **CREATE YOUR OWN**   Find the quotients. Then find the next three quotients in the pattern. Now make up a similar division pattern.

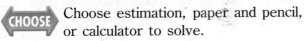

$50 \div 5$    ⇨    $50 \div 0.5$    ⇨    $50 \div 0.05$    ⇨

**CHOOSE** Choose estimation, paper and pencil, or calculator to solve.

**34.** Estimate the number of tennis balls that would equal the weight of a basketball.

**35.** How much more does a basketball weigh than a baseball?

**36.** Make a pictograph representing the weights of the balls shown on page 80. Use the symbol • for 1 oz.

---

**Mental Math**

The three apples were cut in half, or 3 was divided by 0.5. Study how dividing by 0.5 can be done mentally.

$3 \div 0.5$ is the same as $3 \times 2$ ⇨ $6$

Now try to divide mentally.

**1.** $16 \div 0.5$     **2.** $75 \div 0.5$     **3.** $1.4 \div 0.5$     **4.** $1.9 \div 0.5$

# Estimating Quotients

Montezuma Castle and Walnut Canyon are two national monuments in central Arizona. Montezuma Castle contains a 5-story prehistoric Native American cliff dwelling. Walnut Canyon has ancient Native American cliff dwellings built in shallow caves.

About how many times larger is the site of the Walnut Canyon National Monument than the site of the Montezuma Castle National Monument?

How many times does 858 divide into 2,249?

**Montezuma Castle, 858 acres
The Sinagua people built these dwellings and lived here from 1125 to 1400.**

Use compatible numbers to estimate this quotient.

Pick two numbers that are close to these numbers and divide easily. Estimate.

$$858\overline{)2{,}249}$$   ⇨   $$\overset{3}{900\overline{)2{,}700}}$$   ⟵ 2,700 is easy to divide by 900.

Walnut Canyon National Monument is about 3 times larger.

Notice that there can be more than one choice of compatible numbers when you estimate a quotient.

$$4.2\overline{)46.6}$$   ⇨   $$\overset{12}{4\overline{)48}}\quad\overset{11}{4\overline{)44}}\quad\overset{10}{4\overline{)40}}$$

**THINK ALOUD**   Which estimate would you choose for the example above? Why?

━━━━━━━━━━━━━━━━━━━━━━ GUIDED PRACTICE ━━━━━━━━━━━━━━━━━━━━━━

Choose a compatible number. Estimate the quotient.

**1.** $92\overline{)371}$   $90\overline{)\phantom{00}}$

**2.** $31\overline{)335}$   $\phantom{00}\overline{)330}$

**3.** $7.8\overline{)76}$   $8\overline{)\phantom{00}}$

**Walnut Canyon, 2,249 acres**

Use compatible numbers to estimate the quotient.

**4.** $21\overline{)83}$    **5.** $32\overline{)891}$    **6.** $37\overline{)835}$    **7.** $18\overline{)583}$

**8.** $73\overline{)63.8}$    **9.** $98\overline{)72.6}$    **10.** $27\overline{)48.3}$    **11.** $81\overline{)329.3}$

**12.** $2.2\overline{)86}$    **13.** $3.7\overline{)803}$    **14.** $6.3\overline{)582}$    **15.** $1.9\overline{)1,623}$

**16.** $473 \div 46$    **17.** $382 \div 63$    **18.** $1,115 \div 42$    **19.** $8,237 \div 19$

**20.** $89.4 \div 27$    **21.** $41.2 \div 51$    **22.** $528.3 \div 51$    **23.** $639.2 \div 98$

**24.** $149 \div 2.7$    **25.** $9,578 \div 5.2$    **26.** $7,914 \div 1.8$    **27.** $4,821 \div 3.3$

**PROBLEM SOLVING**

 Choose estimation or calculator to solve.

**28.** About how many times smaller is the land occupied by the Statue of Liberty than by the Devil's Tower?

**29.** The Timpanogos Cave and the Oregon Caves, formed in limestone, are both known for their great beauty.
About how many times more area do the Oregon Caves cover than does the Timpanogos Cave?

| Sites of National Monuments | |
|---|---|
| Devil's Tower, WY | 1,347 acres |
| Statue of Liberty, NY | 58 acres |
| Oregon Caves, OR | 488 acres |
| Timpanogos Cave, UT | 250 acres |
| Organ Pipe Cactus, AZ | 330,689 acres |

**30.** One square mile is 640 acres. About how many square miles is the Organ Pipe Cactus National Monument?

**31.** **CREATE YOUR OWN** Write a question of your own that can be solved using the facts in the table.

# Problem Solving: Too Much or Too Little Information

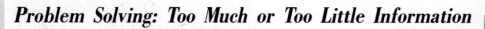

Sometimes in problem solving there are more facts than you need. Other times there are not enough facts.

October 26, 1861. St Joseph, Missouri. The Pony Express closed today, due to the opening two days ago of the new transcontinental telegraph. The Pony Express began on April 3, 1860. Since then, 34,753 letters were delivered. The Pony Express charged $10 an ounce to deliver mail but never made a profit.

Along the 1,966-mi Pony Express route between here and Sacramento, California, riders changed horses in 2 min at stations spread about 10 mi apart. Going night and day, riders delivered the mail to Sacramento in about 10 days. Each rider rode about 75 mi, then relayed the mail to the next rider. Riders earned from $100 to $150 per month.

For about how many months was the Pony Express in operation?

• Reread the passage carefully.
• What information would you use to solve the problem?
• What information is not needed to solve the problem?

Now solve the problem.

---

## GUIDED PRACTICE

**1.** Which question do you have enough information to answer?

   **a.** How long did it take to deliver Lincoln's speech?

   **b.** If a rider reached a station at 9:23, when would he be ready to leave?

   **c.** What did a rider's mailbag weigh?

**2.** What information do you need to find the value of the mail in a Pony Express mailbag?

   **a.** The Pony Express started on April 3, 1860.

   **b.** Each rider had 2 min at each stop.

   **c.** A mailbag carried 15 lb and mail cost $10/oz.

MATH AND HISTORY

## PRACTICE

Use the information on page 84. If enough is given, solve the problem. Otherwise, state what information is needed.

**3.** On what date did the transcontinental telegraph open?

**4.** About how many stops might a rider make in 75 mi?

**5.** How much money did the Pony Express lose?

**6.** What was the most money a Pony Express rider could make in 1 yr?

**7.** How much did it cost to send a letter by telegraph?

**8.** About how many Pony Express stations could there have been?

**9.** About how many miles did the mail travel in 24 h?

**10.** **CREATE YOUR OWN** Use the information on page 84 to write a question for a friend to solve.

**CHOOSE** Choose a strategy to solve.

**11.** On the average, about 350 letters were delivered on each trip. Use the total number of letters delivered to find about how many trips were made in all.

**12.** Before the Pony Express, it took 25 d to deliver mail by stagecoach to California. How many days less did the Pony Express take?

# Investigating Exercise ⊹

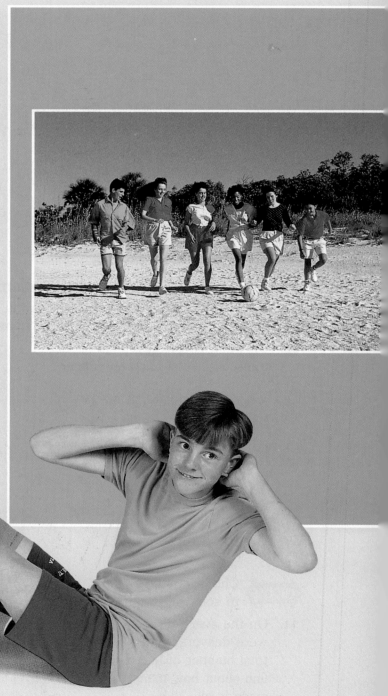

Running, jogging, dancing, rowing, and playing basketball or other sports are all examples of aerobic exercise. Aerobic exercise is continuous exercise for an extended period of time that makes you breathe faster. It increases the amount of oxygen your body needs.

Everyone knows that it is important to get enough exercise. But how much exercise is enough? Can there be such a thing as *too much* exercise? Get ready to find out what your heartbeat has to do with it.

Work in a small group.

1. Think of as many kinds of exercises as you can and make a list. Then write whether each kind is aerobic exercise.

2. After 30 min of aerobic exercise, most people are breathing faster than normal. Their hearts are beating faster than normal. Find out why aerobic exercise causes this to happen.

MATH AND HEALTH

3. Place the three middle fingers of one hand on the inside of your wrist close to the base of the thumb. Wait until you can feel your pulse and count the beats.

4. Use a stopwatch or watch with a second hand to find out how many times your heart beats in 10 s. Record the results of all members of your group.

5. Convert the 10-s information into heartbeats per minute. Discuss with your group how to do this.

6. In what other ways can the heartbeat be measured?

7. Predict the effect of 30 min of aerobic exercise on the rate of your heartbeat. Would the rate increase, decrease, or stay the same? Discuss some other effects that aerobic exercises could have.

8. Record your heartbeat rate just before and just after exercising. Report and discuss your findings with classmates.

9. Why is it important to know how fast your heart beats at rest and during or after exercise? Is there value in increasing the heartbeat? What is the value of knowing your maximum heartbeat?

10. Prepare a simple weekly exercise plan that a healthy student your age could follow. Should an exercise plan be checked with a doctor? Give some reasons.

---

### LANGUAGE & VOCABULARY

---

Write *true* or *false*. If the statement is false, prove that it is false by giving an example.

1. When you evaluate an expression using the order of operations rules, you always add first.

2. When you divide, the quotient is always smaller than the dividend.

3. Multiplying a number by 100 and then dividing it by 1,000 is the same as dividing the number by 10.

---

### TEST ✔

---

#### CONCEPTS

Simplify. *(pages 60–63)*

1. $2 \times (50 \times 8)$

2. $3 \times (27 + 3)$

3. $29 \times 0 \times 7$

4. $70 \times 1 \times 3$

5. $15 \times (2 \times 5)$

6. $35 \times 1 \times 8 \times 0$

7. $3 + 9 \times 4$

8. $25 - 3^2 + 2 \times 5$

9. $6 + (2 \times 3^2) - 8$

Write in scientific notation. *(pages 78–79)*

10. 3,800,000

11. 36,700,000

12. 129,000

#### SKILLS

Multiply. *(pages 64–67)*

13. 
$$\begin{array}{r} 63 \\ \times\ 7 \\ \hline \end{array}$$

14. 
$$\begin{array}{r} 95 \\ \times\ 6 \\ \hline \end{array}$$

15. 
$$\begin{array}{r} 748 \\ \times\ 23 \\ \hline \end{array}$$

16. 
$$\begin{array}{r} 608 \\ \times\ 59 \\ \hline \end{array}$$

17. $35.6 \times 21$

18. $40.09 \times 3.7$

19. $6,024 \times 375$

20. $\$4.95 \times 100$

21. $2.75 \times 0.9$

22. $87.65 \times 3.2$

*Put in remainder form*

Divide. *(pages 68–69)*

**23.** $15\overline{)371}$     **24.** $76\overline{)805}$     **25.** $44\overline{)3,099}$     **26.** $109\overline{)2,716}$

Divide. Round to tenths. *(pages 70–71, 80–81)*

**27.** $23\overline{)35.61}$     **28.** $56.08 \div 95$     **29.** $3.2\overline{)82.63}$

Use compatible numbers to estimate the quotient. *(pages 82–83)*

**30.** $23\overline{)409}$     **31.** $49\overline{)2,487}$     **32.** $83\overline{)71.6}$

## PROBLEM SOLVING

Solve. *(pages 60–61, 84–85)*

**33.** A pottery shop has 6 large shelves that hold 60 mugs each. There are also 6 smaller display shelves with 7 mugs on each.

  **a.** How many mugs does each large shelf hold?

  **b.** Since the number of large and small shelves are the same, which property can you use to solve the problem?

  **c.** How many mugs altogether do the shelves hold?

**34.** Mrs. Jackson earns $18.75 per hour as a part-time accountant. After 3 wk she has earned $1,125.00 and has deposited $875.00 in her checking account. How many hours has she worked in the past 3 wk?

**35.** A school group went on a picnic. If 371 students went on minibuses that held 15 students each, how many buses were needed?

## LEARNING LOG

Write the answers in your learning log.

  **1.** Explain how to multiply and divide decimals by powers of ten.

  **2.** Explain how to decide how many zeros to add when converting from scientific notation to standard form.

Simplify. *(pages 60–63)*

**1.** $60 \times (1 \times 3)$     **2.** $18 \times 0 \times 5$     **3.** $4 \times (23 + 2)$     **4.** $(5 \times 3) \times 6$

**5.** $74 \times 0 \times 1$     **6.** $(97 + 3) \times 5$     **7.** $(8 \times 30) \times 2$     **8.** $5 \times 16 \times 20$

**9.** $4 + 10 \times 6$     **10.** $23 - 7 \times (3 - 1)$     **11.** $25 \div 5 \times 3^2$

**12.** $10^2 + 3 \times 8 - 4$     **13.** $2^2 + (4 + 5) - 12$

**14.** $17 + 0 - (10 - 1)$     **15.** $(2^3 - 4) \div 2$

Write the answer. *(pages 64–67)*

| **16.** | **17.** | **18.** | **19.** | **20.** |
|---|---|---|---|---|
| 84 | 307 | 39 | 567 | 986 |
| $\times\ 7$ | $\times\ 6$ | $\times 23$ | $\times\ 45$ | $\times\ 78$ |

| **21.** | **22.** | **23.** | **24.** | **25.** |
|---|---|---|---|---|
| 3.45 | 7.081 | 16.684 | $.84 | 0.007 |
| $\times\ 2.5$ | $\times\ 100$ | $\times\ 56$ | $\times 0.63$ | $\times\ 1.35$ |

Divide. Write the answer, including the remainder. *(pages 68–69)*

**26.** $6\overline{)735}$     **27.** $21\overline{)809}$     **28.** $29\overline{)3,099}$     **29.** $84\overline{)7,961}$

Divide. Round to hundredths. *(pages 70–71, 80–81)*

**30.** $4\overline{)27.63}$     **31.** $16\overline{)35.92}$     **32.** $1.7\overline{)58.08}$     **33.** $9.8\overline{)0.732}$

Write in standard form. *(pages 78–79)*

**34.** $1.87 \times 10^5$     **35.** $2.98 \times 10^8$     **36.** $7.653 \times 10^7$

**37.** $3.1 \times 10^5$     **38.** $9.082 \times 10^6$     **39.** $8.113 \times 10^7$

Use compatible numbers to estimate the quotient. *(pages 82–83)*

**40.** $82\overline{)635}$     **41.** $63\overline{)1,902}$     **42.** $91\overline{)74.3}$     **43.** $6.3\overline{)52.9}$

If enough information is given, solve the problem. Otherwise, state what information is needed. *(pages 84–85)*

**44.** A television set costing $409 can be bought by making a down payment of $49 and 36 equal monthly payments. How much is each payment?

**45.** In a 100-m race, the winner's time was 10.17 s. The second-place runner was 2 m behind the winner at the finish line. What was the difference in their times?

## ALPHABET SOUP

Don't look too closely or you'll miss this.

| A | EF | HI | KLMN | T | VWXYZ |
|---|----|----|------|---|-------|

---

|  | BCD | G | J | OPQRS | U |
|--|-----|---|---|-------|---|

What rule was used in placing the letters above and below the line?

# International Finance

On one day in 1990, 1 Canadian dollar could be exchanged for 0.8589 American dollars. On the same day, 1 French franc was worth 0.1905 American dollars. A Canadian traveling to France that day would get 4.509 French francs for 1 Canadian dollar (0.8589 ÷ 0.1905).

Find the foreign exchange rates in the business section of a newspaper. Pretend that you are making each trip listed below. The currency used in each country is shown in parentheses. Determine how many units of currency for the country you are visiting you can purchase with 1 unit of currency from the country you are leaving. (*Hint*: Compare the two currencies to the American dollar.)

### Trip

from Australia (dollar) to Belgium (franc)

from Britain (pound) to Canada (Canadian dollar)

from Denmark (krone) to Finland (mark)

from Switzerland (Swiss franc) to Italy (lira)

from Israel (shekel) to Mexico (peso)

# What's My Rule?

Work with a partner. Get a set of tangram pieces and experiment with them for a while to become familiar with the different figures. Compare both their shapes and their sizes.

Then sort the pieces into two groups according to a rule that you make up. Ask your partner to identify the rule you have used. Then reverse roles. Try using more than two groups.

Find the answer.

1. $231 + 986$ is close to
   a. 1,100
   b. 1,200
   c. 1,300
   d. none of these

2. $19.8 + 35.4$ is closest to
   a. 50
   b. 53
   c. 55
   d. none of these

3. 17.259 rounds to
   a. 17.2
   b. 17.25
   c. 17.3
   d. none of these

4. $t \div 21 = 6$
   $t = $ ▒
   a. 126
   b. 27
   c. 15
   d. none of these

5. $41 - w + 3 = 9$
   $w = $ ▒
   a. 12
   b. 44
   c. 35
   d. none of these

6. $m \div 2 = 48 - 14$
   $m = $ ▒
   a. 68
   b. 62
   c. 96
   d. none of these

7. $(90 \times 15) \times 2 = $
   a. 270
   b. 1,352
   c. 210
   d. none of these

8. $42 - 3 \times 2^2 + 8 = $
   a. 164
   b. 14
   c. 38
   d. none of these

9. $5,003 - 749 = $
   a. 4,746
   b. 4,254
   c. 4,364
   d. none of these

10. 
    $$0.403$$
    $$- 0.295$$
    a. 0.292
    b. 0.108
    c. 0.698
    d. none of these

11. $9.007 - 8.5 = $
    a. 0.507
    b. 9.922
    c. 1.57
    d. none of these

12. $3.72 \times 10^4 = $
    a. 3,720
    b. 372,000
    c. 37,200
    d. none of these

13. $56 + 0 + 34 + 44 = $
    a. 144
    b. 134
    c. 154
    d. none of these

14. $7.31 + 12 + 9.2 = $
    a. 28.51
    b. 83.5
    c. 20.23
    d. none of these

15. 
    $$\$98.74$$
    $$+ 36.89$$
    a. \$135.53
    b. \$134.53
    c. \$134.63
    d. none of these

**Problem Solving Check List**

- Too much information
- Too little information
- Multistep problems
- Drawing a picture
- Using a pattern
- Using estimation
- Using guess and check

Remember the strategies you've learned so far. If enough information is given, solve the problem. Otherwise, state what information is needed.

1. The Statue of Liberty in New York occupies about 58 acres. About how many square miles does the Statue of Liberty occupy? (*Hint*: 1 square mile is 640 acres.)

2. In a row of light bulbs, one bulb has 4 bulbs to its left, one bulb has 3 bulbs to its right, and one bulb has 2 bulbs on both sides of it. How many bulbs are in the row?

3. Mrs. Short assigned 3 pages of exercises for homework. She said that the pages were consecutive and that the sum of the page numbers was 996. Which pages did Mrs. Short assign?

4. In the figure below, the vertical, horizontal, and diagonal sums of three numbers are equal. What is $z$?

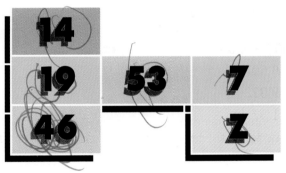

5. Jeff designed a game board in the shape of a rectangle. Its dimensions were 10 in. by 15 in. Jeff realized the board was too small and decided to double both dimensions.

   a. What was the shape of the game board?

   b. What operation would you use to find the areas of the original board and the new board?

   c. How many times larger is the area of the new board than the area of the original one?

6. Harriet drove 50 mi/hr for the first 6 h of a 450-mi trip along the Atlantic Coast. What was her average speed for the remainder of the trip?

7. A stationery store sells pencils at 2 for $.25. If the pencils cost the store owner $.06 each, how much profit is made on a sale of $3 worth of pencils?

8. Lenny had exactly $1 in change. He had exactly 3 times as many nickels as dimes. How many nickels and dimes did he have?

## PAIR-N-THESES

In the computer activity *Calculator Quiz,* you evaluate equations by using the order of operations. Sharpen your skills with this activity. You do not need a computer.

Copy the equation. Then add one or two pairs of parentheses to make the equation true.

1. $8 \div 4 - 2 = 4$
2. $11 - 8 - 5 - 1 = 7$
3. $12 - 6 + 4 - 1 = 3$
4. $12 - 12 \div 4 + 2 = 10$
5. $9 - 4 \times 6 \div 5 \times 3 = 2$

## A-GHAST 🖩

Gas for heating is measured in therms. The Goodheat Gas Company computes each consumer's monthly bill by combining a gas supply charge of $0.3281 per therm with an additional distribution charge of $0.1402 per therm for the first 50 therms and $0.0547 per therm after the first 50 therms. If you use 254.97 therms, what would be the total charge on your bill, rounded to the nearest cent?

## I'M RICH 🖩

About how many years will it take you to earn $1,000,000 if you work 40 hours a week for 52 weeks a year and earn:

- $5 an hour • $10 an hour • $20 an hour • $40 an hour

**DID YOU KNOW . . . ?**
At its present rate of growth, the world's population will double about every 40 yr.

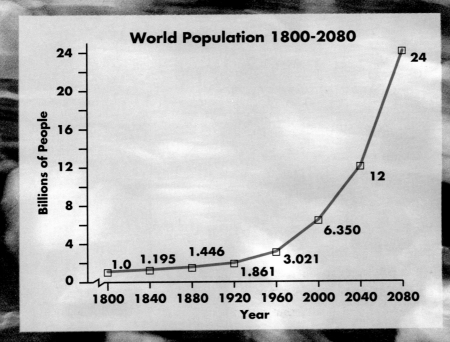

**World Population 1800-2080**

Billions of People

1.0   1.195   1.446   1.861   3.021   6.350   12   24

Year: 1800  1840  1880  1920  1960  2000  2040  2080

**USING DATA**

Collect

Organize

**Describe**

**Predict**

Which population figures in the graph are predictions?

By how much did the world population increase between 1920 and 1960?

Predict the world's population for the year 2020.

## Writing Expressions

The lightning we see takes place between a cloud and the ground. Lightning strikes somewhere on Earth an average of 100 times each second. In 10 seconds (s), lightning would strike about 10 times more.

You can write an **expression** that represents this fact.

- Let $t$ represent the number of seconds.
- Then $100 \times t$, or $100t$, is an expression for the number of times lightning would strike somewhere on Earth in $t$ seconds.

**THINK ALOUD** If you counted 10 s, about how many times, on average, would lightning strike somewhere on Earth?

Other examples:

| Word Phrase | Algebraic Expression |
| --- | --- |
| thirty-seven storms decreased by $m$ storms | $37 - m$ |
| 42 less than $n$ | $n - 42$ |
| eight times $z$ miles | $8 \times z$ or $8z$ |
| $n$ sandwiches divided by twelve campers | $n \div 12$ or $\frac{n}{12}$ |
| $d$ seconds increased by 5 | $d + 5$ |

**GUIDED PRACTICE**

Write as an expression.

1. the sum of 28 and a number $a$

2. eighteen times a number $b$

3. twelve less than a number $c$

4. a number $d$ divided by seven

5. a number $e$ increased by 23

6. twenty decreased by a number $f$

MATH AND SCIENCE

96    LESSON 4–1

Write as an expression. Let $x$ be the unknown value.

**7.** seven more than a number

**8.** ninety-six divided by a number

**9.** five times a number

**10.** twenty-seven more than a number

**11.** a number divided by five

**12.** 128 less than a number

**13.** a number increased by 14

**14.** the product of a number and seven

**15.** twelve decreased by a number

**16.** a number divided by thirteen

**17.** a number increased by 1,000

**18.** a number multiplied by itself

Write as a word phrase.

**19.** $x - 18$

**20.** $4m$

**21.** $29 + q$

**22.** $27 \div z$

**23.** $n + 5$

**24.** $16w$

**25.** $z \div 12$

**26.** $23 - b$

**27.** $\frac{24}{r}$

**28.** $29y$

**29.** $\frac{q}{19}$

**30.** $x - y$

Work with a partner to write the expression.

**31.** Let $t$ represent the temperature before a storm.
Then ▦ represents the temperature after it drops 7°F.

**32.** Let $h$ represent the cost of 1 tent.
Then ▦ represents the cost of 6 tents.

**33.** Let $n$ represent any odd number.
Then ▦ represents the next larger odd number.
Then ▦ represents the next smaller even number.

**34.** Let $w$ represent a whole number.
Then ▦, ▦, and ▦ represent the next
three greater whole numbers.

## Mental Math

Use mental math to match the word phrase
with an expression.

**1.** the number of millimeters in $n$ centimeters

**a.** $n \div 1,000$

**2.** the number of centimeters in $n$ millimeters

**b.** $n \div 10$

**3.** the number of meters in $n$ centimeters

**c.** $n \div 100$

**4.** the number of kilograms in $n$ grams

**d.** $10n$

# Evaluating Expressions

A velodrome is a sports arena with an oval track used for cycling events. One lap around the track at the Marymoor Park velodrome in Redmond, Washington, is 0.4 km.

If a cyclist makes 5 laps of this track, how far has she traveled?

- Let $x$ represent the number of laps a cyclist makes.
- Then $0.4x$ represents the distance in kilometers a cyclist travels around the track.

| | |
|---|---|
| Distance (km) after 1 lap: | $0.4x$ |
| | $0.4 \times 1$ ← Substitute 1 for $x$. |
| | 0.4 km |
| Distance (km) after 3 laps: | $0.4x$ |
| | $0.4 \times 3$ ← Substitute 3 for $x$. |
| | 1.2 km |
| Distance (km) after 5 laps: | $0.4x$ |
| | $0.4 \times 5$ ← Substitute 5 for $x$. |
| | 2.0 km |

If you know the order of operations rules, you can make a 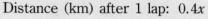 **MATH CONNECTION** to evaluate the expressions below.

Evaluate $\frac{z}{5} + 2$. Use $z = 15$.

$$\frac{z}{5} + 2 = \frac{15}{5} + 2$$
$$= 3 + 2$$
$$= 5$$

Evaluate $a^2 - 3$. Use $a = 6$.

$$a^2 - 3 = 6^2 - 3$$
$$= 36 - 3$$
$$= 33$$

## GUIDED PRACTICE

Evaluate $n + 14$ for the given value of $n$.

**1.** 6 **2.** 12 **3.** 17 **4.** 8.25 **5.** 19.02

Evaluate $\frac{24}{z} + 5$ for the given value of $z$.

**6.** 2 **7.** 6 **8.** 4 **9.** 1.2 **10.** 0.8

Evaluate. Use $x = 2$, $y = 6$, and $z = 8$.

**11.** $7z$    **12.** $10 - y$    **13.** $z \div 4$    **14.** $z^2$

**15.** $x + 5$    **16.** $3x + x - 2$    **17.** $\frac{z}{2}$    **18.** $x + x^2$

**19.** $x + 3x$    **20.** $\frac{28}{x}$    **21.** $\frac{x + 4}{3}$    **22.** $(y - y) + 18$

**23.** $\frac{z}{8} + 7$    **24.** $9 \times (5 + y)$    **25.** $z^2 + z^2$    **26.** $24x - 10x$

**27.** $3.2y - 1.5y$    **28.** $\frac{z}{4} + \frac{z}{2}$    **29.** $6 \times 5(4 - x)$    **30.** $9 + z - x$

Copy and complete.

**31.**

| $a$ | $5a - 2$ |
|-----|----------|
| 2 | $5 \times 2 - 2 = $ ▩ |
| 8 | ▩ |
| 15 | ▩ |

**32.**

| $n$ | $n + 5n$ |
|-----|----------|
| 12 | $12 + 5 \times 12 = $ ▩ |
| 18 | ▩ |
| 45 | ▩ |

**33.**

| $x$ | $x^2 - 7$ |
|-----|-----------|
| 9 | $9^2 - 7 = $ ▩ |
| 14 | ▩ |
| 20 | ▩ |

**CHOOSE** Choose mental math, or pencil and paper to solve.

**34.** A cyclist makes 8 laps around the velodrome in Detroit. How far has the cyclist traveled?

**35.** Who travels farther, a cyclist who makes 6 laps in Los Angeles's velodrome or a cyclist who makes 8 laps in Barcelona's velodrome?

**36.** How many laps must a cyclist make to travel 1 km in Portland's velodrome? in Detroit's velodrome?

| Velodromes | |
|------------|--------------------|
| Location | Distance for 1 Lap |
| Portland, Oregon | 0.250 km |
| Los Angeles, California | 0.333 km |
| Detroit, Michigan | 0.300 km |
| Barcelona, Spain | 0.250 km |

## *Estimate*

You can use clustering to estimate the sum.    $1.461 + 1.54 + 1.4992 \approx 4.5$
Each addend clusters around 1.5.    $1.5 \quad + 1.5 \quad + 1.5 \quad = 4.5$

Use clustering to estimate the sum.

**1.** $4.091 + 3.94 + 3.911$    **2.** $0.542 + 0.478 + 0.4993$

**3.** $10.002 + 9.832 + 10.09 + 0.49 + 0.51$

## Exploring Inverse Operations

We often do something and then we undo it. For example, each activity in the flow chart below is undone by its **inverse** activity.

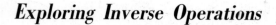

| Input: Tom is sitting. | → | Tom stands up. | → | Tom puts on a hat. | → | Tom takes off a hat. | → | Tom sits down. | → | Output: Tom is sitting. |

**1.** What inverse activity undoes "Tom stands up"?

**2.** If "Tom puts on shoes" were added to the flow chart, what inverse activity would undo it?

**3. IN YOUR WORDS** Is the statement "Tom does not put on a hat" an inverse of the statement "Tom puts on a hat"? Explain.

In mathematics, when two operations undo each other, they are called **inverse operations**.

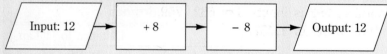

| Input: 12 | → | + 8 | → | – 8 | → | Output: 12 |

**4.** The equation for an input of 12 is $12 + 8 - 8 = 12$.
What equation would describe the input of 6? the input of 36?

**5.** The number 20 is input. If $\boxed{+8}$ is changed to $\boxed{+16}$, what must also change in the flow chart to result in an output of 20?

**6.** What equation describes the input of any number $n$?

Some number tricks use inverse operations.

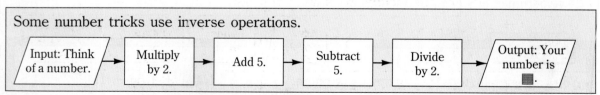

| Input: Think of a number. | → | Multiply by 2. | → | Add 5. | → | Subtract 5. | → | Divide by 2. | → | Output: Your number is ▦. |

**7.** What is the output when we input the number 5?
Try inputting any three other numbers.

**8.** What will the output always be?

**9.** Why does the number trick work?

**10.** Of addition, subtraction, multiplication, and division, which pairs of operations are inverses?

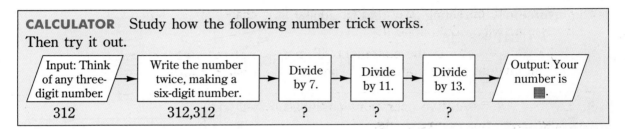

**CALCULATOR** Study how the following number trick works. Then try it out.

| Input: Think of any three-digit number. | → | Write the number twice, making a six-digit number. | → | Divide by 7. | → | Divide by 11. | → | Divide by 13. | → | Output: Your number is ▨. |
|---|---|---|---|---|---|---|---|---|---|---|
| 312 | | 312,312 | | ? | | ? | | ? | | |

**11.** What is the output if the number 392 is input? Try 632, 759, and 104. Does the number trick work for 1,452?

**12.** If output from the flow chart was 761, what was the input?

**13.** In what way can you shorten the number trick?

**14.** For what kinds of numbers does this number trick work? Give some examples.

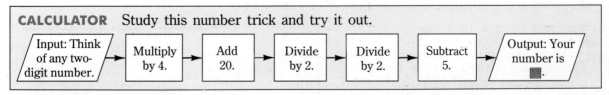

**CALCULATOR** Study this number trick and try it out.

| Input: Think of any two-digit number. | → | Multiply by 4. | → | Add 20. | → | Divide by 2. | → | Divide by 2. | → | Subtract 5. | → | Output: Your number is ▨. |
|---|---|---|---|---|---|---|---|---|---|---|---|---|

**15.** Input the numbers 54, 67, 32, and 99. What is the output of each? Try this number trick on a friend.

**16.** Try 346 and 804. Does the number trick work for three-digit numbers?

**17.** **CREATE YOUR OWN** Make up a number trick of your own.

## Solving Equations
## Using Addition and Subtraction

The Holland and Lincoln tunnels stretch from
New York to New Jersey under the Hudson River.
The Lincoln Tunnel is 8,216 ft long, which is 341 ft
shorter than the length of the Holland Tunnel.
How long is the Holland Tunnel?

Let $h$ represent the length in feet of the
Holland Tunnel.

What length minus 341 equals 8,216?

$$h \quad - \quad 341 \quad = \quad 8{,}216$$

To solve the equation, you can use the operation that
is the inverse of subtracting 341, that is, adding 341.

$$h - 341 = 8{,}216$$
$$h - 341 + 341 = 8{,}216 + 341 \quad \longleftarrow \text{ Add 341 to both sides.}$$
$$h + 0 = 8{,}557$$
$$h = 8{,}557 \quad \longleftarrow \text{ The solution is 8,557.}$$

Check: $h - 341 = 8{,}216$
$8{,}557 - 341 = 8{,}216$ ✔

The Holland Tunnel is 8,557 ft long.

Another example:

$$5.8 + z = 10.2$$
$$5.8 - 5.8 + z = 10.2 - 5.8 \quad \longleftarrow \text{ Subtract 5.8}$$
$$0 + z = 4.4 \qquad\qquad \text{from both sides.}$$
$$z = 4.4 \quad \longleftarrow \text{ The solution is 4.4.}$$

Check: $5.8 + z = 10.2$
$5.8 + 4.4 = 10.2$ ✔

> **The same number can be added or subtracted
> on both sides of an equation.**

### GUIDED PRACTICE

**THINK ALOUD** Which inverse operation would
solve the equation? Then solve and check.

**1.** $x + 9 = 43$      **2.** $t - 12 = 35$

**3.** $15 + n = 56$      **4.** $z - 6.5 = 11.5$

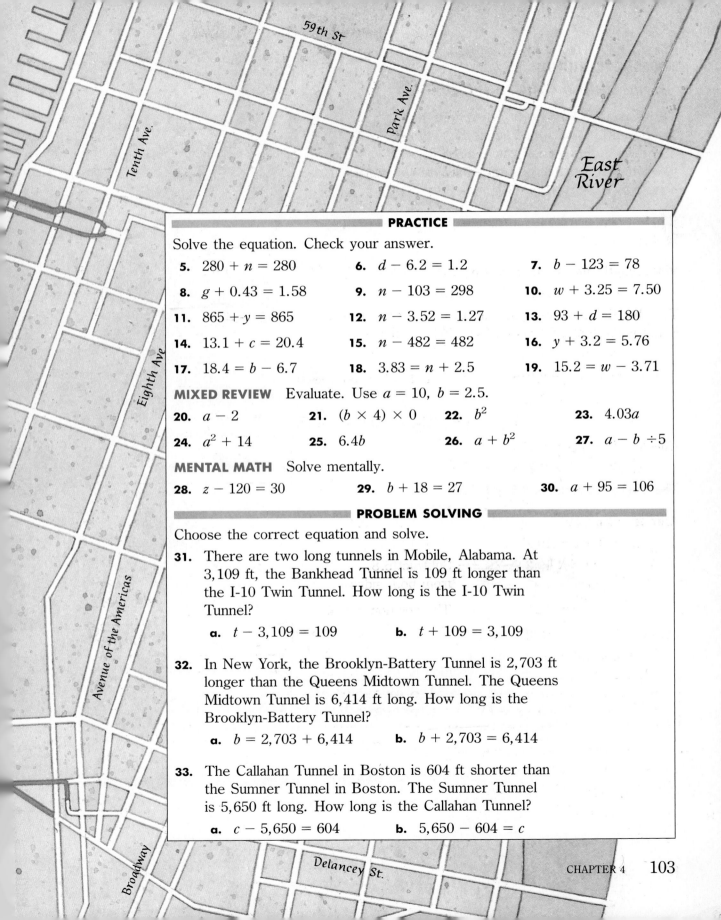

Solve the equation. Check your answer.

**5.** $280 + n = 280$    **6.** $d - 6.2 = 1.2$    **7.** $b - 123 = 78$

**8.** $g + 0.43 = 1.58$    **9.** $n - 103 = 298$    **10.** $w + 3.25 = 7.50$

**11.** $865 + y = 865$    **12.** $n - 3.52 = 1.27$    **13.** $93 + d = 180$

**14.** $13.1 + c = 20.4$    **15.** $n - 482 = 482$    **16.** $y + 3.2 = 5.76$

**17.** $18.4 = b - 6.7$    **18.** $3.83 = n + 2.5$    **19.** $15.2 = w - 3.71$

**MIXED REVIEW**   Evaluate. Use $a = 10$, $b = 2.5$.

**20.** $a - 2$    **21.** $(b \times 4) \times 0$    **22.** $b^2$    **23.** $4.03a$

**24.** $a^2 + 14$    **25.** $6.4b$    **26.** $a + b^2$    **27.** $a - b \div 5$

**MENTAL MATH**   Solve mentally.

**28.** $z - 120 = 30$    **29.** $b + 18 = 27$    **30.** $a + 95 = 106$

**PROBLEM SOLVING**

Choose the correct equation and solve.

**31.** There are two long tunnels in Mobile, Alabama. At 3,109 ft, the Bankhead Tunnel is 109 ft longer than the I-10 Twin Tunnel. How long is the I-10 Twin Tunnel?

    **a.** $t - 3,109 = 109$    **b.** $t + 109 = 3,109$

**32.** In New York, the Brooklyn-Battery Tunnel is 2,703 ft longer than the Queens Midtown Tunnel. The Queens Midtown Tunnel is 6,414 ft long. How long is the Brooklyn-Battery Tunnel?

    **a.** $b = 2,703 + 6,414$    **b.** $b + 2,703 = 6,414$

**33.** The Callahan Tunnel in Boston is 604 ft shorter than the Sumner Tunnel in Boston. The Sumner Tunnel is 5,650 ft long. How long is the Callahan Tunnel?

    **a.** $c - 5,650 = 604$    **b.** $5,650 - 604 = c$

## Solving Equations
## Using Multiplication and Division

If the average length of a triceratops was multiplied by 4, it would equal the average length of a diplodocus, which, at 88 ft, was the longest of the dinosaurs. About how long was a triceratops?

Let $n$ represent the average length of a triceratops in feet.

Four times what number is 88?
$$4n \qquad\qquad = 88$$

Which operation is the inverse of multiplying by 4?

$$4n = 88$$

$$\frac{4n}{4} = \frac{88}{4} \quad \longleftarrow \text{ Divide both sides by 4.}$$

$$n = 22 \quad \longleftarrow \text{ The solution is 22.}$$

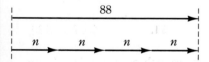

Check: $\quad 4n = 88$
$$4 \times 22 = 88 \ \checkmark$$

A triceratops averaged about 22 ft in length.

Another example:

$$\frac{d}{4} = 1.9 \qquad\qquad\qquad \text{Check: } \frac{d}{4} = 1.9$$

$$\frac{d}{4} \times 4 = 1.9 \times 4 \longleftarrow \text{ Multiply both sides by 4.} \qquad \frac{7.6}{4} = 1.9 \ \checkmark$$

$$d = 7.6 \quad \longleftarrow \text{ The solution is 7.6.}$$

> **You can multiply or divide both sides of an equation by the same number. (Remember, you cannot divide by zero.)**

---

### GUIDED PRACTICE

**THINK ALOUD**  Explain how you would solve and check the equation.

1. $\frac{x}{6} = 9$    2. $6y = 420$    3. $8w = 96$    4. $\frac{k}{12} = 40$

MATH AND SCIENCE

Solve. Check your answer.

**5.** $3a = 48$    **6.** $\frac{p}{6} = 8$    **7.** $\frac{u}{12} = 5$

**8.** $5n = 95$    **9.** $\frac{r}{9} = 5$    **10.** $\frac{n}{11} = 45$

**11.** $8z = 10.4$    **12.** $15z = 150$    **13.** $\frac{n}{11} = 4$

**14.** $\frac{x}{12} = 0$    **15.** $1.1z = 9.9$    **16.** $5k = 65$

**17.** $27e = 216$    **18.** $60x = 240$    **19.** $4c = 6.8$

**20.** $\frac{t}{21} = 14$    **21.** $\frac{m}{0.6} = 12$    **22.** $1.2x = 0.48$

**23.** $3.9c = 1.56$    **24.** $\frac{y}{1.6} = 2.5$    **25.** $6.4 = 4n$

**MIXED REVIEW**    Solve. Check your answer.

**26.** $a + 2.8 = 9.1$    **27.** $\frac{m}{9} = 18$

**28.** $g - 0.75 = 4.26$    **29.** $18b = 576$

**30.** $r - 45 = 12.2$    **31.** $x + 145.7 = 320$

**32.** **CALCULATOR**    Find three values for $a$ in $\frac{a}{7.5}$ so that the expression is equal to a number between 1 and 3.5.

**PROBLEM SOLVING**

Find the underlined fact. The variable represents the unknown. Select the equation that represents the problem and solve.

**33.** The <u>height of a tyrannosaurus in feet</u> times 2.5 equals its length of 45 ft.

**a.** $18 - 12 = w$

**34.** Two times a <u>stegosaurus's length in feet</u> is the 45 ft length of a tyrannosaurus.

**b.** $2.5x = 45$

**35.** A tyrannosaurus's 45-ft length divided by a <u>torosaurus's length in feet</u> is 1.5.

**c.** $\frac{45}{y} = 1.5$

**36.** A tyrannosaurus's height minus 12 is an <u>ornitholestes's length in feet</u>.

**d.** $z \times 2 = 45$

## Problem Solving Strategy:
## Writing and Solving Equations

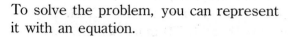

For each show at the Dance Theater
of Harlem, the dancers are on stage for
2 h. After 500 h on stage, how many
shows have been performed?

To solve the problem, you can represent
it with an equation.

- What does the problem ask you to find?
  Decide on a variable to represent this.

  Let $s$ represent the number of shows.

- Make an equation that balances.

| The hours for each show times the number of shows is the total hours. |
|---|
| 2 $\times$ $s$ = 500 |

$2s = 500$     The equation balances. Both $2s$ and 500 represent the number of hours performed.

Solve the equation. Does your answer make sense?

**THINK ALOUD**  Can you write another equation
that represents the problem?

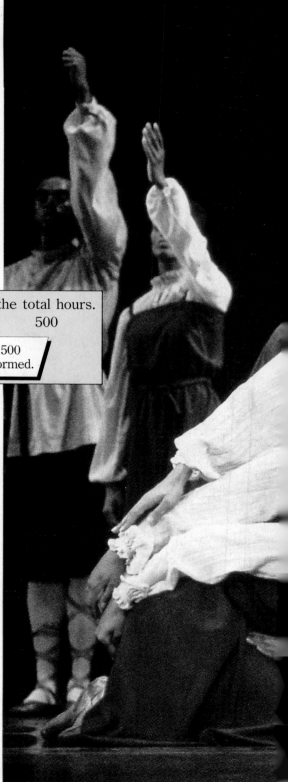

### GUIDED PRACTICE

Decide what the variable represents.
Then choose the equation that represents
the problem and solve.

1. There are 18 dancers in a show. Eleven are
   women. How many male dancers are there?

   a. Let $k$ represent ▦.

   b. Choose: $k + 11 = 18$, $k - 11 = 18$, or $\frac{k}{11} = 18$

2. Each of the 25 performances of a ballet is
   sold out. If the theater seats 224 people,
   how many people will see the ballet?

   a. Let $n$ represent ▦.

   b. Choose: $25n = 224$, $25 \times 224 = n$, or $\frac{25}{n} = 224$

Decide on a variable to represent the unknown quantity. Then write an equation and solve.

3. The first performance of the Dance Theater of Harlem was in 1968. How long ago was that?

4. The Dance Theater of Harlem performs regularly at New York's Aaron Davis Hall, which has 750 seats. Performances are also given at the New York City Center, which has about 1,750 more seats. About how many seats does the City Center have?

5. An amount of money is shared by 18 people to buy ballet tickets. If each ticket costs $22.50, what is the total amount of money that is shared?

6. For 1 wk of performances, the Dance Theater of Harlem charges $175,000. If one performance costs $25,000, how many performances are given in 1 wk?

**CHOOSE** Choose a strategy to solve, if it is possible.

7. A 254-seat theater sells tickets at $12 each. There are eight 3-h shows put on each week, including 2 each on Saturday and Wednesday. At intermission, tea is $1 and fruit juice is $2. In 1 wk, all the shows sell out. How much money was made from ticket sales that week?

8. Tickets for the Dance Theater of Harlem's *Firebird* were $15 each. Props and costumes cost $20,000. What was the profit?

9. A theater sold 214 tickets one day, 194 tickets the second day, and 210 tickets the third day. On the fourth day, the theater sold half the number of tickets sold the second day.

   a. How many tickets were sold on the second day?

   b. On which of the four days were the most tickets sold?

   c. Estimate how many tickets were sold in all.

**Dance Theater of Harlem**

# MIDCHAPTER CHECKUP

Give an expression or equation to show that you understand the situation. Use the variable that is given. Tell whether your answer is an expression or an equation.

**1.** The height $h$ of a tree increases by 15 ft.

**2.** Three classes, each with the same number $s$ of students, have a total of 78 students.

**3.** When a 6-ft-long sandwich was shared equally among a number $f$ of friends, each piece was 2 ft long.

## QUICK QUIZ

Write an expression. Let $m$ be the unknown value. *(pages 96–97)*

**1.** twelve more than a number

**2.** seven less than a number

**3.** fifteen divided by a number

Evaluate. Use $a = 4$, $b = 11$, and $c = 8$. *(pages 98–99)*

**4.** $3a + 9$

**5.** $\dfrac{b - 5}{2}$

**6.** $a + c - 2$

Solve the equation. *(pages 102–105)*

**7.** $r + 12.4 = 23.6$

**8.** $d - 38 = 37$

**9.** $2.5x = 1.5$

Solve. *(pages 106–107)*

**10.** One morning, 88 planes took off from an airport. Each of the airport's 4 runways were used the same number of times.

   **a.** How many runways does the airport have?

   **b.** What equation can be used to find the number of planes that took off from each runway that morning?

   **c.** How many planes took off from each runway that morning?

Write the answers in your learning log.

1. Explain how an equation is different from an expression.

2. Describe how you would evaluate the expression $2a + 3b$.

3. What does the equals sign tell you when solving an equation?

MATH AMERICA

**DID YOU KNOW . . . ?** The Flint Ridge–Mammoth Cave System in Kentucky is the longest cave system in the world. It twists and turns along more than 225 mi. What two cities in your state are about 225 mi apart?

BONUS

Work with a partner. Decide whether the given values for $a$, $b$, and $c$ form a magic square in which all rows, columns, and diagonals have the same sum.

1. $a = 6$, $b = 4$, and $c = 8$

2. $a = 8$, $b = 4$, and $c = 16$

3. $a = 3$, $b = 3$, and $c = 9$

| $2a - b$ | $\dfrac{c - b}{b}$ | $\dfrac{3c}{b}$ |
|---|---|---|
| $\dfrac{ab}{c}$ | $\dfrac{c}{b} + 3$ | $bc - 25$ |
| $2(a - b)$ | $b^2 - 7$ | $4c - 5a$ |

## Graphing Inequalities on a Number Line

Nearly $\frac{1}{8}$ of the world's surface is desert and receives a yearly rainfall of less than 10 in.

The yearly amount of rainfall in deserts can be represented by an inequality.

Let $r$ represent the number of inches of yearly rainfall. The rainfall is less than 10 in.

$$r \quad < \quad 10$$

The $<$ symbol indicates an inequality.

You can illustrate the inequality with a graph.

$r < 10$    The open circle indicates that 10 is not included.

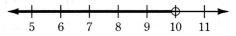

The solid line represents the numbers that are a solution to the given inequality.
(Assume numbers greater than zero in the solution.)

Some solutions are 6, 8, and 9.5.

The rainfall could have been 6 in., 8 in., or 9.5 in.

**THINK ALOUD**   Name three other possible solutions greater than zero. Include some decimal numbers.

Another example:

The amount of rainfall ($r$) is greater than 5 in.

$$r \quad > \quad 5$$

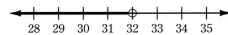

Some solutions are 7, 5.5, and 90.5.

**THINK ALOUD**   Name three other possible solutions.

---

**GUIDED PRACTICE**

Name three possible solutions greater than zero for each inequality.

**1.** $x > 5$

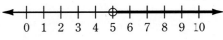

**2.** $w < 32$

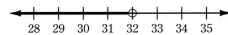

**IN YOUR WORDS**   Explain the reason for your answer.

**3.** Is 5 included on the graph?

**4.** Is 3.5 included on the graph?

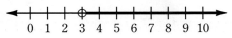

Which of the numbers are solutions to the inequality?
$\frac{1}{3}$, 4, 6.3, 18.2, 48, 957

**5.** $n < 8$

**6.** $n < 17$

**7.** $n > 5$

**8.** $n < 81$

**9.** $n < 6.4$

**10.** $n > 18.6$

Match the inequality with the graph of the solution.

**a.** $x < 25$     **b.** $x > 11$     **c.** $x > 5.5$     **d.** $x > 2.5$

**11.**

**12.**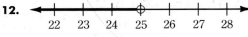

**13.**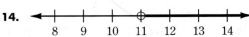

**14.**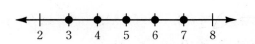

Graph the solution.

**15.** $n > 8$

**16.** $x < 8$

**17.** $x < 7$

**18.** $x > 73.5$

**19.** $n > 42$

**20.** $x > 975$

**21.** $w < 12.5$

**22.** $x > 3 + 2$

Choose the correct inequality that represents
the problem. Then graph the inequality.

**23.** The greatest rainfall in a 12-mo period was 1,044 in.,
in Cherrapunji, Meghalaya, India. What is the rainfall
in a year for any other place in the world compared
with Cherrapunji that year?

**a.** $r < 1,044$     **b.** $r < 12$     **c.** $r > 1,044$

**24.** The least amount of rainfall usually occurs in Arica, Chile.
It receives about 0.03 in. every 12 mo. What is the
rainfall in a year for any other place in the world compared
with Arica?

**a.** $r < 0.03$     **b.** $r > 12$     **c.** $r > 0.03$

**Critical Thinking** 🧩

With a partner, explain the difference between the two
graphs below.

## Mental Math: Solving Inequalities

Mark took 2 h to drive from Colorado Springs to Divide. From Divide he drove to Canon City on a gravel road. The entire trip took less than 7 h. How long could the drive from Divide to Canon City have lasted?

Let $n$ be the driving time from Divide to Canon City.

2 plus what number is less than 7?

$$2 + n < 7$$

To solve the inequality mentally, cover up the variable.

$$2 + \qquad < \qquad 7$$

Try 6:  Is $2 + 6 < 7$?
$\qquad$ $8 > 7$, so 6 is not a solution.

Try 5:  Is $2 + 5 < 7$?
$\qquad$ $7 = 7$, so 5 is not a solution.

**THINK ALOUD**  What can you conclude about numbers greater than or equal to 5?

Try 4:  Is $2 + 4 < 7$?
$\qquad$ $6 < 7$, so 4 is a solution.

**THINK ALOUD**  What can you conclude about numbers less than 5?

Solution: any number less than 5 ($n < 5$). The drive from Divide to Canon City took less than 5 h.

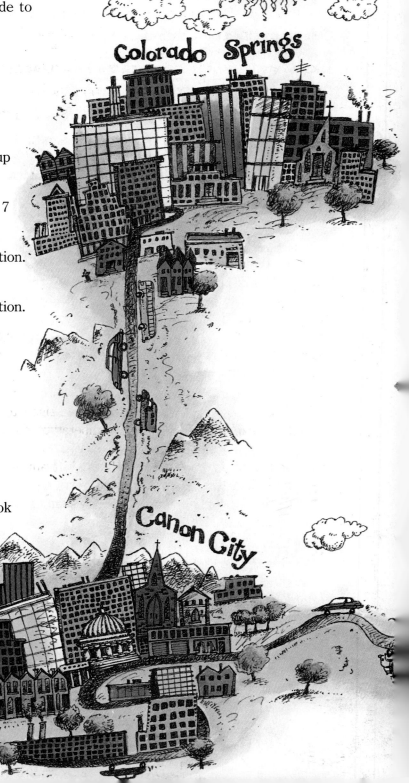

Colorado Springs

Canon City

Write an inequality for the statement.

**1.** 45 minus a number $b$ is greater than 17.

**2.** 1.4 plus a number $p$ is less than 10.

**NUMBER SENSE** Name three possible solutions.

**3.** $y - 5 < 9$

**4.** $x - 3 > 7$

**5.** $8 + n > 10$

Is the given value a solution to the inequality? Write *yes* or *no*.

**6.** $x - 6 > 9$; 25

**7.** $a - 8 < 5$; 15

**8.** $y + 4 < 7$; 1

**9.** $3 + b < 10$; 8

**10.** $a + 8 > 8$; 3

**11.** $m + 0 > 12$; 14

**NUMBER SENSE** Name three possible solutions. SOLVE AND GRAPH

**12.** $y - 2 < 8$

**13.** $n - 5 > 8$

**14.** $a - 7 > 4$

**15.** $x + 8 > 8$

**16.** $m + 5 > 6$

**17.** $a - 12 > 5$

**18.** $7 + a > 11$

**19.** $b - 6 > 3$

**20.** $c - 7 < 14$

**21. CRITICAL THINKING** The equation $x + 3 = 8$ has only one solution. How many solutions does the inequality $x + 3 > 8$ have? Explain.

Match the equality or the inequality with the question. Let $t$ represent the unknown value.

**22.** The temperature in Denver at 9:00 A.M. was 15°C. By noon the temperature had risen to over 23°C. By how much had the temperature risen?

**a.** $15 + t = 23$

**23.** Twenty-three people can take a ski tram at one time. Just before the ski tram starts moving, 15 people decide to take it. How many more people can still go?

**b.** $15 + t > 23$

**24.** One year, the total precipitation in Colorado was 15 in. The next year, the total precipitation was more than 23 in. What was the total precipitation for the 2 yr?

**c.** $15 + 23 < t$

Pueblo

ACME CO

VARIETY

## Exploring Functions

A seventh grade class made a survey to find out what students liked best about their trip to the zoo. The survey had two rules for the question that asked for a favorite animal.

> Rule 1: Select one animal.
> Rule 2: You may not select more than one animal.

The students made these selections.

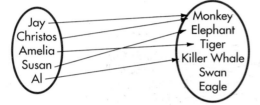

The pairing of students to favorite animals is a **function**, because one and only one animal was chosen by each student.

1. Notice that each student can select only one animal, but two students can select the same animal. Name two students who did.

2. This is *not* a function because rule 1 does not hold. Megan did not choose an animal. How can you make it a function?

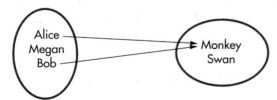

3. This is *not* a function because rule 2 does not hold. Which student did not follow rule 2?

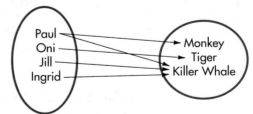

**THINK ALOUD**  Is the statement true for a function? Explain.

4. Each student must pick one animal.

5. Some students can pick two animals.

6. No student can select more than one animal.

7. Two different students can select the same animal.

**8.** The diagrams below show other surveys that asked students to choose a favorite animal. One diagram does *not* show a function. Which one is it? Why?

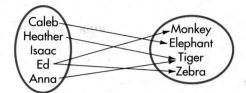
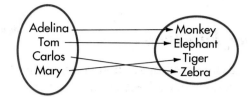

Does the diagram show a function? If not, name the rule that does not hold.

> Rule 1: Each student selects one ride.
> Rule 2: No student may select more than one ride.

**9.**

**10.**

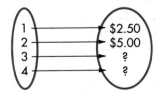
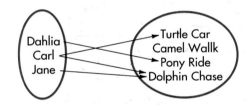

Many functions pair numbers with numbers. As an example, we can pair the number of students (*n*) who go to the zoo with the admission cost (*c*) of $2.50 per student.

**11.** Copy and complete the diagram and the table to show a function for the number of students and the cost.

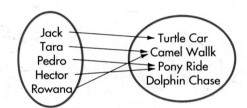

| Number (*n*) | 1 | 2 | 3 | 4 |
|---|---|---|---|---|
| Cost ($) (*c*) | ? | ? | ? | ? |

**12.** Make a table of a function for 1 to 8 students going to the zoo when the admission is $1.75.

Make a function table for *n* from 1 to 6.

**13.** *n* = number of elephants
*e* = number of elephant ears

**14.** *n* = number of zoo train rides
*c* = cost at 75¢ each

**15. CREATE YOUR OWN** Now make up two functions of your own.

## Exploring Function Rules

The Central High School team is in the state
football tournament. Buses are used to take the fans
to games across the state.

The number of buses (b) and the number of fans
that fit (f) in each bus are shown below.

| Buses (b) | 1 | 2 | 3 | 4 | 5 |
|-----------|---|---|-----|-----|-----|
| Fans (f) | 35 | 70 | 105 | 140 | 175 |

1. Explain why the pairing of buses to fans is a function.

2. **IN YOUR WORDS** Explain how the numbers of buses
   and fans are related.

You can write a **function rule** that tells how
the numbers of buses and fans are related.

$$\begin{aligned}\text{number of fans} &= 35 \times \text{number of buses}\\ f &= 35b \qquad \text{function rule}\end{aligned}$$

Use the function rule $f = 35b$ to answer the question.

3. How many people will 10 buses hold?

4. How many buses do you need for 595 people?

Central High School decides to put 32 fans in each bus.
The new function rule is $f = 32b$.

5. Make a table to show the function for 1 to 8 buses.

6. What function rule would indicate that 60 fans fit in each of 10 buses?

Copy and complete the table using the function rule.

7.
| Souvenirs (s) | 1 | 2 | 3 | 4 | 5 | 6 |
|---------------|---|---|---|---|---|---|
| Cost ($) (c) | ? | ? | ? | ? | ? | ? |

Function Rule: $c = 8.95s$

8.
| Players (p) | 11 | 22 | 33 | 44 | 55 | 66 |
|-------------|----|----|----|----|----|----|
| Teams (t) | ? | ? | ? | ? | ? | ? |

Function Rule: $t = \frac{p}{11}$

9. Think of the rows of seats in a football cheering section. Make up a function rule of your own using the number of rows ($r$) and the number of seats in each row ($s$). Let $r$ represent the rows from 1 to 10. Make a table to show your function.

If the pairing has a function rule, write the rule. Otherwise, write *no rule*.

10.
| End of quarter ($q$) | 1 | 2 | 3 | 4 |
|---|---|---|---|---|
| Minutes played ($m$) | 15 | 30 | 45 | 60 |

11.
| Number of fans ($f$) | 1 | 2 | 3 | 4 |
|---|---|---|---|---|
| Cost of tickets in dollars ($t$) | 20 | 40 | 60 | 80 |

12.
| Passes completed ($p$) | 1 | 2 | 3 | 4 |
|---|---|---|---|---|
| Pass length in yards ($l$) | 40 | 5 | 15 | 32 |

13.
| Quarter ($q$) | 1 | 2 | 3 | 4 |
|---|---|---|---|---|
| Points ($p$) | 13 | 7 | 0 | 14 |

14.
| Number of touchdowns ($t$) | 1 | 2 | 3 | 4 |
|---|---|---|---|---|
| Points from touchdowns ($p$) | 6 | 12 | 18 | 24 |

15. Use the function in Exercise 14 to find the number of points scored for 8 touchdowns.

Use the given function rule to complete the table.

16. Minutes ($m$) per Hour ($h$)

| $h$ | 1 | 2 | 3 | 4 | 4.5 |
|---|---|---|---|---|---|
| $m$ | | | | | |

Function Rule: $m = 60h$

17. Feet ($f$) per Yard ($y$)

| $y$ | 0 | 5 | 10 | 15 | 20 |
|---|---|---|---|---|---|
| $f$ | | | | | |

Function Rule: $f = 3y$

Write the rule for the function.

18. Feet ($f$) per Mile ($m$)

| $m$ | 1 | 2 | 3 |
|---|---|---|---|
| $f$ | 5,280 | 10,560 | 15,840 |

Function Rule: $f = $ ▨

19. Ounces ($o$) per Pound ($p$)

| $p$ | 1 | 3 | 5 | 7 |
|---|---|---|---|---|
| $o$ | 16 | 48 | 80 | 112 |

Function Rule: $o = $ ▨

20. **CREATE YOUR OWN** Choose a sport other than football.

a. Make a table showing an aspect of the game that has a function rule.

b. Make a table showing an aspect of the game that does not have a function rule.

# It's ShowTime!

## Problem Solving:
## Representing a Problem

UNDERSTAND
PLAN
REPRESENT
CARRY OUT
LOOK BACK

**READ ABOUT IT**

There are many ways you can represent a problem that will help you solve it.

• You can represent a problem with a picture or diagram.

Using the numerals 3, 4, and 7, how many different three-digit whole numbers can you write? You can use each numeral only once in the three-digit whole number.

| First digit → | 3 | | 4 | | 7 | |
|---|---|---|---|---|---|---|
| Second digit → | 4 | 7 | 3 | 7 | 3 | 4 |
| Third digit → | 7 | 4 | 7 | 3 | 4 | 3 |

• A problem can be represented with an equation.

A freshly baked loaf of bread is about 2 times higher than the unbaked dough. A baked loaf is 4.5 in. high. How high was the dough before baking?

Let $n$ represent the height of the unbaked dough.
$$2n = 4.5$$

• A problem can be represented by a pattern.

Each diagram at the right represents a triangular number. What are the next three triangular numbers?

1    3    6

• You can represent a problem in a table.

What are the first four powers of 4 that when simplified have a 6 in the ones' place?

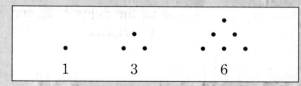

| Power of 4 | Simplified | Ones' Place |
|---|---|---|
| $4^1$ | 4 | 4 |
| $4^2$ | 16 | 6 |
| $4^3$ | 64 | 4 |
| $4^4$ | 256 | 6 |

Work with a partner to show how you would represent the problem in order to solve it. Discuss the following questions.

- *Why did you represent the problem this way?*
- *Is there any other way to represent the problem?*
- *Do all the ways to represent the problem give you the same solution?*

1. Mr. Apple always cuts his homemade pies in straight cuts through the center of the pie. How many pieces would he have after 10 cuts?

2. Four students are waiting in a line to buy muffins. Ann is standing in front of Pete and behind Marie. Carl is standing in front of Marie. Who is first and who is last in line?

3. A baker's worktable has a perimeter of 12 ft. Find three different shapes that the table could be that would have a perimeter of 12 ft.

4. You can go from Denver to Chicago either by plane or by train. After that, there are three ways you might go on to Minneapolis: plane, train, or bus. How many different ways are there that you might choose to go from Denver to Minneapolis?

5. A school uses only two-digit numbers on its baseball uniforms. How many differently numbered uniforms can the team have using the digits 1, 2, and 3? Two of the same number can appear on a uniform.

■ WRITE ABOUT IT

Write a problem that fits the representation.

6.
| Distance | 30 mi | 60 mi | 90 mi |
|----------|-------|-------|-------|
| Time | 0.5 h | 1 h | 1.5 h |

7. $x + 34.5 = 100$

8.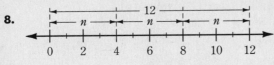

9.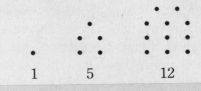

# Investigating Paul Revere's Ride

Listen, my children, and you shall hear
Of the midnight ride of Paul Revere,
On the eighteenth of April, in Seventy-five;
Hardly a man is now alive
Who remembers that famous day and year.

The lines above are the beginning of a famous poem called "Paul Revere's Ride" by Henry Wadsworth Longfellow. The poem tells about an important event in the history of the United States.

Work with a partner.

1. Longfellow published the poem in 1863. How old would someone have had to be at that time to "remember that famous day and year"?

2. One account says that Paul Revere crossed the river from Boston to Charlestown where he began his ride. He traveled first to Medford, then to Arlington, and finally to Lexington. Use the map on page 121 to estimate the total distance he rode.

3. Read the stanza above to yourself. Which lines have the same end rhyme? How would this stanza be different if the ride had been at a time other than midnight? if the year of the ride had been eighty-nine? Rewrite the stanza to include these changes. Be as creative as possible.

MATH AND LITERATURE

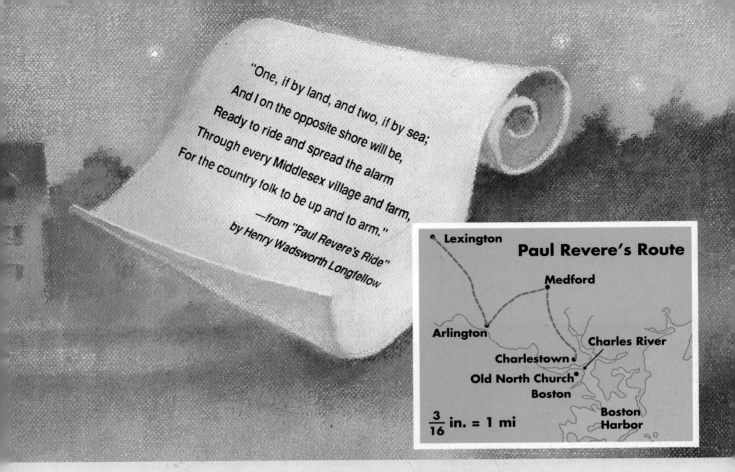

"One, if by land, and two, if by sea;
And I on the opposite shore will be,
Ready to ride and spread the alarm
Through every Middlesex village and farm,
For the country folk to be up and to arm."

—from "Paul Revere's Ride"
by Henry Wadsworth Longfellow

**Paul Revere's Route**

Lexington

Medford

Arlington

Charlestown

Charles River

Old North Church

Boston

Boston Harbor

$\frac{3}{16}$ in. = 1 mi

4. According to other stanzas in the poem, Revere started his ride sometime after "the moon rose over the bay." He and his horse arrived at their destination when "it was two by the village clock." If he averaged about 8 mi/h, about what time did "the moon rise over the bay"?

5. How many lanterns were to be hung in the tower of the Old North Church in Boston if the British troops were coming by a land route? by a water route?

6. What river did Revere have to cross?

7. Find the poem "Paul Revere's Ride" by Longfellow in a book of American poetry. In a short paragraph, explain what the "midnight message of Paul Revere" was.

8. Think of an event that has happened in your lifetime and that involves some type of measurement (for example, distances, time, money, or weight measurements). Then write a short poem about this event. Give your poem to a classmate to read and identify the measurements.

---

**LANGUAGE & VOCABULARY**

Tell whether the price can be represented by an expression, an equation, or an inequality.

1. The price of an item plus 8% sales tax is more than $20.00.

2. the price of an item plus 8% sales tax

3. The price of an item plus 8% sales tax is $10.80.

---

**TEST**

---

**CONCEPTS**

Write as an expression. *(pages 96–97, 100–101)*

1. a number $y$ decreased by 31

2. a number $s$ divided by 5

3. the product of 19 and a number $n$

4. a number $f$ divided by 1.3

Evaluate. Use $a = 4$, $b = 8$, and $c = 2$. *(pages 98–99)*

5. $9a$

6. $13b - 5$

7. $\frac{8c}{2}$

8. $a + 3b - c$

---

**SKILLS**

Solve the equation. *(pages 102–105)*

9. $d - 35 = 64$

10. $203 + r = 391$

11. $0.8m = 1.92$

12. $24.26 = z - 15.1$

13. $\frac{x}{3.1} = 19$

14. $\frac{w}{7} = 3.25$

Is the given value a solution to the inequality?
Write *yes* or *no*. *(pages 110–111)*

15. $f + 11 < 15$; 26

16. $h - 3 > 12$; 17

17. $k - 7 < 3$; 10

Graph the solution. *(pages 112–113)* Solve

18. $p < 9$

$p + 3 < 9$

19. $r > 50$

$r - 5 > 50$

20. $z < 21$

$z - 7 < 21$

Solve. *(pages 102–103, 106–107)*

**21.** A letter carrier emptied two mailboxes on her route. She collected 173 pieces of mail from the first. From both boxes she collected 301 pieces of mail.

    **a.** How many pieces of mail did she collect from the first box?

    **b.** What information is unknown?

    **c.** Choose a variable for the unknown. Then write an equation and solve the problem.

**22.** Gina's backpack seemed too heavy. She removed an item that weighed 3 lb, but the pack still weighed more than 12 lb. How much did the pack weigh before she removed the item?

Choose the correct equation and solve. *(pages 102–103)*

**23.** In New York City, the Lincoln Tunnel is 1,236 ft longer than the Queens Midtown Tunnel. The Queens Midtown Tunnel is 6,414 ft long. How long is the Lincoln Tunnel?

    **a.** $l + 1,236 = 6,414$

    **b.** $1,236 + 6,414 = l$

**LEARNING LOG**

Write the answers in your learning log.

    **1.** Describe two ways an equation and an inequality are different.

    **2.** What does it mean to solve an equation or inequality?

    **3.** What does the open circle on the graph of an inequality mean?

Write as an expression. Let $n$ be the unknown value. *(pages 96–97)*

**1.** a number plus 3

**2.** a number divided by 8

**3.** a number divided by itself

**4.** 2 increased by a number

**5.** the product of 11 and a number

**6.** 75 less than a number

**7.** a number added to itself

**8.** a number multiplied by itself

Evaluate. Use $r = 6$, $s = 8$, and $t = 10$. *(pages 98–99)*

**9.** $3r + 5$

**10.** $\frac{r}{2} - 3$

**11.** $s - 5 + t$

**12.** $2t - 1$

**13.** $(3 \times s) + 2$

**14.** $\frac{(s + 4)}{2}$

**15.** $s^2$

**16.** $t^2 + 9$

Solve. *(pages 102–105)*

**17.** $z + 172 = 300$

**18.** $22 = x - 18$

**19.** $108 = 86 + y$

**20.** $r - 35.4 = 18.7$

**21.** $45.7 = 26.8 + a$

**22.** $31 = c - 13.2$

**23.** $6x = 72$

**24.** $\frac{m}{9} = 12$

**25.** $21f = 105$

**26.** $\frac{h}{3} = 19$

**27.** $\frac{w}{0.9} = 8$

**28.** $4.5n = 90$

**29.** $\frac{x}{23} = 253$

**30.** $3n = 22.95$

Is the given value a solution to the inequality? Write *yes* or *no*.
*(pages 112–113)*

**31.** $r + 7 < 19;\ 7$

**32.** $a - 12 > 8;\ 24$

**33.** $13 + b > 24;\ 15$

**34.** $d - 1 < 32;\ 37$

**35.** $n + 102 > 185;\ 80$

**36.** $m - 15 < 50;\ 27$

Graph the solution. *(pages 110–111)*

**37.** $x > 12$

**38.** $y < 24$

**39.** $m < 8.5$

**40.** $c > 15.5$

Solve. *(pages 106–107, 118–119)*

**41.** A school had $2,070 for special events. If $345 were spent on each event the school sponsored during the year, how many events were held?

**42.** When 3 friends stood on a scale, their total weight was 280 lb. When 2 got off, the scale showed 98 lb. If the 2 friends who got off each weighed the same amount, how much did each weigh?

## Who Uses Functions?

Many real situations exist where you might expect a function rule to apply, but it does not. For example, a bakery might sell one bagel for $.35. If a function rule, such as "cost = $.35 times the number of bagels" were used, you could predict the cost of any number of bagels.

However, stores often charge less when more than one item is purchased. Two bagels might cost $.65. When this happens, you cannot use a function rule to determine the cost of a larger number of bagels.

Visit some stores that post the prices for different numbers of the same item. Try a bookstore, a sporting goods store, or a take-out food shop. Write the prices charged for different numbers of the same item. Then decide whether a function rule exists, and if so, what the rule is.

## Writing Temperature Equations

Newspapers report temperatures in cities throughout the United States. You can use this information to practice writing and reading equations. Work with a partner to choose ten cities from the weather page of today's newspaper. Be sure that each city had a different high temperature yesterday.

Use ten index cards. For each city, write an equation that names yesterday's high temperature on the card. Then write the city's name on the back of the card. When you have completed ten cards, list each city you have used and its temperature on a sheet of paper.

For example, if the high temperature in Philadelphia was 78°F, let 78 be the variable $y$. You could identify Philadelphia by an equation such as $y + 12 = 90$, $y - 19 = 59$, $3y = 234$, or $\frac{y}{26} = 3$.

Exchange the cards and the list with another team. Try to decide what cities are on their list. Look at the back of the card to check.

Find the answer.

**1.**    53
       × 27
   **a.** 457
   **b.** 477
   **c.** 1,411
   **d.** none of these

**2.**    5.94
       × 3.6
   **a.** 2.1384
   **b.** 21.384
   **c.** 213.84
   **d.** none of these

**3.**    0.0072
       × 0.12
   **a.** 0.0864
   **b.** 0.00864
   **c.** 0.000864
   **d.** none of these

**4.** $65\overline{)3,218}$
   **a.** 46 R26
   **b.** 49 R33
   **c.** 44 R58
   **d.** none of these

**5.** $91\overline{)47.32}$
   **a.** 0.52
   **b.** 52
   **c.** 0.052
   **d.** none of these

**6.** $172.04 \div 68 =$
   **a.** 0.253
   **b.** 25.3
   **c.** 2.53
   **d.** none of these

**7.** $m - 5.2 = 14.9$
   $m = $ ▨
   **a.** 9.7
   **b.** 20.1
   **c.** 8.7
   **d.** none of these

**8.** $30x = 165$
   $x = $ ▨
   **a.** 5.5
   **b.** 55
   **c.** 4,950
   **d.** none of these

**9.** $\frac{w}{2.5} = 40$
   $w = $ ▨
   **a.** 16
   **b.** 0.0625
   **c.** 100
   **d.** none of these

What is the best estimate?

**10.** $32 \times 706 =$
   **a.** 2,100
   **b.** 21,000
   **c.** 210,000
   **d.** none of these

**11.** $31\overline{)1,217}$
   **a.** 400
   **b.** 4
   **c.** 40
   **d.** none of these

**12.** $59.8 \div 1.89 =$
   **a.** 30
   **b.** 3
   **c.** 0.03
   **d.** none of these

What is the equivalent value? Use $a = 3$, $b = 4$, and $c = 7$.

**13.** $5a + a + 7$
   **a.** 15
   **b.** 22
   **c.** 18
   **d.** none of these

**14.** $b^2 - 3$
   **a.** 5
   **b.** 15
   **c.** 13
   **d.** none of these

**15.** $3 \times (c + 4)$
   **a.** 33
   **b.** 25
   **c.** 19
   **d.** none of these

# PROBLEM SOLVING REVIEW

- **Too much information**
- **Too little information**
- **Using estimation**
- **Making a list**
- **Making a table**
- **Working backward**

Remember the strategies and types of problems you have had so far. Solve, if possible.

**1.** Sharon has been driving for 3 h. If from now on she averages 50 mi/h, she will complete her 235-mi trip in 2 more hours.

   **a.** How many hours has Sharon already driven?

   **b.** If she can average 50 mi/h, how far will she drive during the next 2 h?

   **c.** How far has she driven during the first 3 h?

**2.** José bought an old baseball card. During the first three years, the card increased $8 in value, then dropped $5, then increased $12. The card is now worth $27. How much did José pay for it?

**3.** Sally bought some books costing $3 each and some magazines costing $2 each. She spent exactly $18. What combinations of books and magazines could she have bought?

**4.** Headrick has decided to wait to buy a new CD player until the bank pays him interest on his savings account. If he has 86 d to wait, about how many weeks must Headrick wait?

**5.** Dinner for 4 friends at Jack O's Tacos cost $23.40. Tax and tip combined added 20% to the bill. To the nearest dollar, what was the total cost of the dinner?

**6.** On the way to school, Mario lent a friend half his money. Then he spent $.50 on orange juice. If he has $.75 left, how much money did Mario have when he left home?

**7.** What is the sum of all the three-digit numbers you can make using the digits 2, 3, and 4 if you do not repeat a digit in a number?

**8.** Dorcas received $4.65 change after paying for two magazines with a $10 bill. One of the magazines cost $1.25 more than the other. What was the total cost of the two magazines?

**9.** Seattle is west of Kansas City. Denver is west of Kansas City but east of Seattle. Cleveland is east of Kansas City but west of New York. What is the correct order of the cities from west to east?

## A SHADY DEAL

Copy the table. Find the hidden number by shading each area in which the value of the expression is 150.

Let $a = 10$, $b = 25$, and $c = 6$.

| | | | |
|---|---|---|---|
| $5a + 10a$ | $3c + a$ | $100 + 5a$ | $4a + 7c$ |
| $8b - 5a$ | $30a$ | $30a - 6b$ | $2a$ |
| $5a + 4b$ | $100 + 2b$ | $bc$ | $20a - 2b$ |
| $10b$ | $b + 5$ | $90 + 10c$ | $10b - 5c$ |
| $7b$ | $40c$ | $25c$ | $8b$ |

## MANY TIMES

Play in pairs. At a signal, make as many true statements as you can by inserting one or more multiplication symbols between two digits. Use a calculator to check. Record your results. The player who finishes first is the winner.

1. $2 \ 2 \ 2 \ 2 \ 2 = 968$

2. $2 \ 2 \ 2 \ 2 \ 2 = 4{,}884$

3. $3 \ 3 \ 3 \ 3 \ 3 = 891$

4. $5 \ 5 \ 5 \ 5 \ 5 \ 5 = 152{,}625$

## WHAT'S YOUR GUESS?

In the computer game *Guess and Test,* you solve word problems by first guessing and then checking. This pencil-and-paper activity will sharpen your problem solving skills. Play with a partner. Each player makes a copy of the chart. Read the clues. Then guess and check. The player who gets the two numbers in the fewest guesses is the winner.

Clues:

a. The sum of the two numbers is 112.

b. Their product is 2,775.

| Guesses | Tests | |
|---|---|---|
| | Sum | Product |
| #1 _____ | | |
| #2 _____ | | |

Discuss how you made your guesses.
Make clues for other numbers for your partner to solve.

# NUMBER THEORY AND FRACTION CONCEPTS 5

**DID YOU KNOW . . . ?**

Tennis was first played in France nearly 900 yr ago. Today, it is the most popular racket sport.

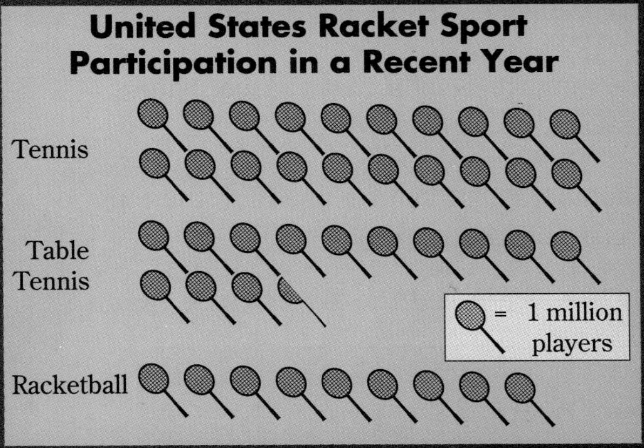
United States Racket Sport Participation in a Recent Year
Tennis
Table Tennis
Racketball
= 1 million players

**USING DATA**

Collect
Organize
Describe
Predict

Which racket sport is played by about 14 million people?

Ask 20 people which racket sports they play. Organize your data into a table. How does your survey compare to the one above?

## Exploring Factors and Divisibility

Grid paper can be used to investigate some interesting numbers.

Shade rectangular regions with the same number of squares as the three at the right on a sheet of grid paper.

1. How many small squares does each rectangle have?

2. There is another rectangular region that can be made with 24 squares. Shade it on your grid paper.

3. List all the whole numbers that can be used for the length and width of a rectangle of 24 squares.

    The numbers you listed are called the **factors** of 24.

> A *factor* is any of two or more numbers that
> are multiplied to obtain a product.

Factors of 24:  1,  2,  3,  4,  6,  8,  12, 24

4. On grid paper, draw all the possible rectangular regions using 36 squares. Then list the factors of 36.

5. Repeat Exercise 4 for rectangles made of 45 and 60 squares. List the factors of 45 and 60.

6. **CRITICAL THINKING**  What number is a factor of any number? Explain.

7. List the factors of the number.
    **a.** 12      **b.** 15      **c.** 18
    **d.** 32      **e.** 50      **f.** 59

The factors of 14 are 1, 2, 7, and 14. Notice how each factor divides into 14 without a remainder. We say 14 is **divisible** by 1, 2, 7, and 14.

$$1\overline{)14} = 14 \qquad 2\overline{)14} = 7 \qquad 7\overline{)14} = 2 \qquad 14\overline{)14} = 1$$

Make a 100 chart on a sheet of grid paper.

| 1 | ② | 3 | ④ | 5̸ | ⑥ | 7 | ⑧ | 9 | ⑩ |
|---|---|---|---|---|---|---|---|---|---|
| 11 | ⑫ | 13 | ⑭ | 1̸5̸ | 16 | 17 | 18 | 19 | 20 |
| 21 | 22 | 23 | 24 | 25 | 26 | 27 | 28 | 29 | 30 |
| 31 | 32 | 33 | 34 | 35 | 36 | 37 | 38 | 39 | 40 |
| 41 | 42 | 43 | 44 | 45 | 46 | 47 | 48 | 49 | 50 |
| 51 | 52 | 53 | 54 | 55 | 56 | 57 | 58 | 59 | 60 |
| 61 | 62 | 63 | 64 | 65 | 66 | 67 | 68 | 69 | 70 |
| 71 | 72 | 73 | 74 | 75 | 76 | 77 | 78 | 79 | 80 |
| 81 | 82 | 83 | 84 | 85 | 86 | 87 | 88 | 89 | 90 |
| 91 | 92 | 93 | 94 | 95 | 96 | 97 | 98 | 99 | 100 |

**8.** Draw a circle around all numbers divisible by 2. Write a rule explaining when a number is divisible by 2.

**9.** Draw a slash (/) through all numbers divisible by 5. Write a rule explaining when a number is divisible by 5.

**10.** Draw a backslash (\\) through all numbers divisible by 10. Write a rule explaining when a number is divisible by 10.

**11.** **a.** **CALCULATOR** Which numbers at the right are divisible by 3?

| 80,004 | 847,395 | 767,534 | 199,989 |
|---|---|---|---|

**b.** Add the digits in each number in Exercise 11a that is divisible by 3. Is the sum of the digits divisible by 3? For example: 987 ⇨ 9 + 8 + 7 = 24 ⇨ 2 + 4 = 6, and 6 is divisible by 3. Now write a divisibility rule for 3.

**12.** **a.** **CALCULATOR** Which numbers in Exercise 11a are divisible by 9?

**b.** Add the digits of each number that is divisible by 9. Is the sum of the digits divisible by 9? Write a divisibility rule for 9.

**13.** **CALCULATOR** Which numbers in Exercise 11a are divisible by 6? Write a divisibility rule for 6.

Your divisibility rules should look something like this.

| A number is divisible by: | |
|---|---|
| 2 if it is even; | 6 if it is divisible by 2 and 3; |
| 3 if the sum of the digits is divisible by 3; | 9 if the sum of the digits is divisible by 9; |
| 5 if the ones' digit is 5 or 0. | 10 if the ones' digit is 0. |

**14.** By which number(s) is the number divisible? 2, 3, 5, 6, 9, 10

    **a.** 102     **b.** 135     **c.** 300     **d.** 5,790     **e.** 7,146     **f.** 13,846

**15.** **CREATE YOUR OWN** Write a divisibility rule for 4.

## Exploring Primes, Composites, and Prime Factorization

You can make a chart of the factors of numbers
to investigate some other interesting numbers.

**1.** Copy and complete the chart below on a sheet of grid paper.

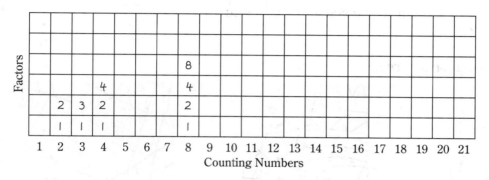

Counting Numbers

**2.** **IN YOUR WORDS** Explain why the number 0 is not
included in the chart.

**3.** Which numbers in your chart have exactly two factors?

> **Numbers that have exactly two factors, namely _1_ and the number itself, are called _prime numbers_.**

**4.** Which numbers in your chart have more than two factors?

> **Numbers that have more than two factors are called _composite numbers_. The numbers _0_ and _1_ are neither prime nor composite.**

List the factors for the number. Is the number _prime_ or _composite_?

**5.** 42    **6.** 60    **7.** 59    **8.** 41    **9.** 39    **10.** 51

**11.** Which numbers less than 80 and greater than 70 are prime?

**12.** Which numbers less than 100 and greater than 89
are composite?

Every composite number can be written as a product of prime factors. This is called the **prime factorization** of a number.

You can use a **factor tree** to find the prime factorization of a number.

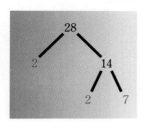

Composite number: 28

Factors: 1, 2, 4, 7, 14, 28

Prime factorization: $2 \times 2 \times 7$

In **exponential form**, $2 \times 2 \times 7$ is $2^2 \times 7$.

**13. IN YOUR WORDS** Explain why 0 and 1 are not used in prime factorizations.

Copy and complete the factor tree.

**14.**
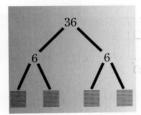

**15.**
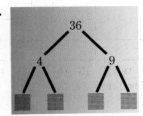

**16.**
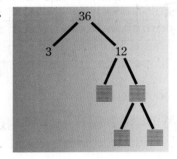

**17.** Did all three factor trees above result in the same prime factorization of 36? Draw another factor tree for 36 that is different from these three.

Use a factor tree to name the prime factorization of the number.

**18.** 48  **19.** 78  **20.** 45  **21.** 54  **22.** 92  **23.** 144

**24.** Copy and complete the chart at the right on grid paper.

**25. IN YOUR WORDS** Describe the prime factors that all multiples of 10 have in common.

**26. CREATE YOUR OWN** Think of another set of numbers like the multiples of 10. Show their prime factors in a chart to discover which ones they have in common.

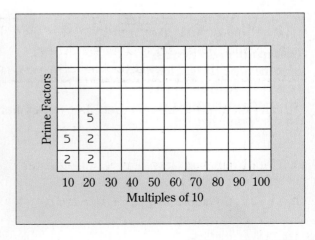

## Greatest Common Factor

People in many cultures have made quilts for important occasions. Many quilts tell interesting stories. You want to make an 8 ft by 10 ft quilt. What is the size of the greatest square you can use?

You can list the factors of 8 and 10 to solve the problem.

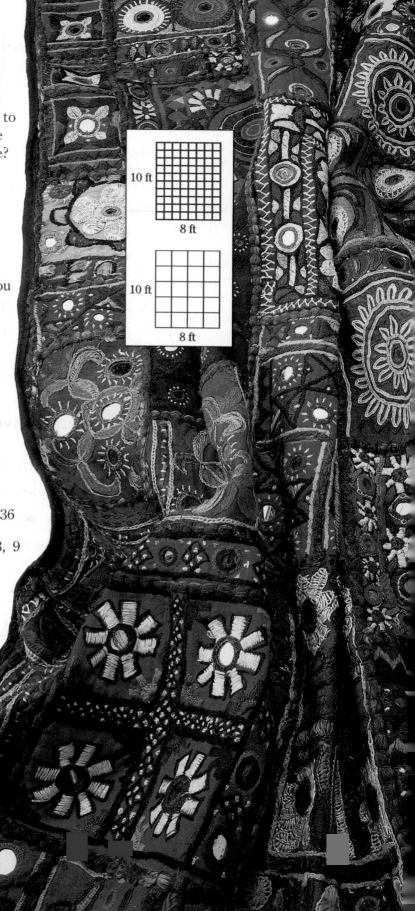

Factors of 8:  1, 2, 4, 8
Factors of 10:  1, 2, 5, 10

The **common factors** 1 and 2 tell you the size of the squares you can use.

The number 2 is called the **greatest common factor (GCF)** of 8 and 10. This is the size of the greatest square that you can use on the quilt.

Another example:

What is the GCF of 18, 27, and 36?

Factors of 18: 1, 2, 3, 6, 9, 18
Factors of 27: 1, 3, 9, 27
Factors of 36: 1, 2, 3, 4, 6, 9, 12, 18, 36

Common factors of 18, 27, and 36: 1, 3, 9

The GCF of 18, 27, and 36 is 9.

**THINK ALOUD** Which whole number is a factor of every number?

**The quilt was made
of old wedding clothes
sewn together in the
Rajasthan region of
north west India.**

List all the factors of the number.

**1.** 36　　　　　**2.** 27　　　　　**3.** 45　　　　　**4.** 72　　　　　**5.** 54

List the common factors. Then name the GCF.

**6.** 6, 9　　　　　**7.** 10, 15　　　　　**8.** 14, 56　　　　　**9.** 21, 84

List the common factors. Name the GCF.

**10.** 4, 6　　　　　**11.** 12, 15　　　　　**12.** 18, 25　　　　　**13.** 14, 42

**14.** 9, 12　　　　　**15.** 18, 45　　　　　**16.** 12, 16　　　　　**17.** 24, 43

**18.** 20, 35　　　　　**19.** 18, 32　　　　　**20.** 12, 20　　　　　**21.** 22, 33

**22.** 21, 63　　　　　**23.** 48, 72　　　　　**24.** 15, 24　　　　　**25.** 40, 27

**26.** 27, 81　　　　　**27.** 45, 65　　　　　**28.** 9, 12, 18　　　　　**29.** 20, 28, 36

**30.** **CRITICAL THINKING** Which is the smallest number that has 2, 3, and 5 as factors?

Find the next three numbers in the pattern.

**31.** 4, 8, 12, 16, ▪, ▪, ▪　　　　　**32.** 90, 180, 270, 360, ▪, ▪, ▪

**33.** 5, 13, 21, 29, ▪, ▪, ▪　　　　　**34.** 34, 79, 124, 169, ▪, ▪, ▪

**35.** 7, 11, 10, 14, 13, ▪, ▪, ▪　　　　　**36.** 2, 10, 3, 11, 4, ▪, ▪, ▪

## Critical Thinking

With a partner, discuss how prime factorization can be used to name the GCF of 28 and 42.

Prime factorization of 28: $2 \times 2 \times 7$

Prime factorization of 42: $2 \times 3 \times 7$

> The GCF contains all the common prime factors of each number.

GCF: $2 \times 7 = 14$, because 2 and 7 are common prime factors.

Use prime factorization to name the GCF.

**1.** 12, 20　　　　**2.** 21, 56　　　　**3.** 39, 52　　　　**4.** 63, 84　　　　**5.** 18, 27, 36

## Least Common Multiple

To increase bicycle sales, a store is giving gifts to its customers. Every 4th customer gets a pair of reflectors and every 6th customer gets a water bottle. Which customer is the first to get both gifts?

The multiples of 4 and 6 help you solve the problem. A **multiple** is the product of a given number and any whole number.

Multiples of 4: 0, 4, 8, 12, 16, 20, 24, 28, 32, 36, . . .
Multiples of 6: 0, 6, 12, 18, 24, 30, 36, . . .

The 12th, 24th, 36th, . . . customers will get both gifts. The 12th customer will be the first to get both.

The number 12 is called the **least common multiple** (**LCM**) of 4 and 6.

What is the LCM of 4, 5, and 10?

Multiples of 4:  4, 8, 12, 16, 20, 24, 28, 32, 36, 40, . . .

Multiples of 5:  5, 10, 15, 20, 25, 30, 35, 40, . . .
Multiples of 10: 10, 20, 30, 40, 50, . . .

Some common multiples of 4, 5, and 10 are 20, 40, 60, . . . The LCM is 20.

When we find the LCM, we disregard the multiple 0 because it is a common multiple of every number.

═══════ **GUIDED PRACTICE** ═══════

List the first six nonzero multiples of the numbers.

**1.** 3, 6           **2.** 7, 9           **3.** 11, 12           **4.** 18, 24

List enough nonzero multiples of the numbers to find the LCM.

**5.** 2, 3           **6.** 6, 8           **7.** 2, 12           **8.** 4, 6, 10

═══════ **PRACTICE** ═══════

Name the LCM.

**9.** 4, 6           **10.** 6, 5           **11.** 2, 6           **12.** 3, 4

**13.** 3, 11         **14.** 8, 12         **15.** 9, 15         **16.** 8, 9

**17.** 10, 15        **18.** 1, 14         **19.** 13, 39        **20.** 16, 1

**21.** 25, 150    **22.** 20, 15    **23.** 9, 21    **24.** 50, 80

**25.** 6, 8, 12    **26.** 4, 5, 6    **27.** 9, 6, 4    **28.** 2, 3, 7

Copy and complete the table.

|  | Numbers | 4, 14 | 20, 25 | 4, 5 | 8, 12 | 30, 10 | 6, 15 |
|---|---|---|---|---|---|---|---|
| **29.** | GCF | 2 | ▤ | ▤ | 4 | ▤ | ▤ |
| **30.** | LCM | 28 | ▤ | 20 | ▤ | ▤ | 30 |
| **31.** | Product | 56 | 500 | ▤ | ▤ | 300 | ▤ |

**32.** **IN YOUR WORDS** Explain how the GCF, LCM, and product are related. Try other pairs of numbers. Does this relationship always work?

**PROBLEM SOLVING**

CHOOSE

Choose mental math or paper and pencil to solve.

**33.** On an assembly line, bicycles are assembled so that every 5th bicycle has reflectors, every 6th has a bell, and every 15th has a basket. What are the first two positions in the assembly line for the bicycles with all three of these features?

**34.** Juan and Maria start cycling on a circular track at the same time but at different speeds. Maria passes Juan every 4 laps. If Maria completes 30 laps of the track, how many times has she passed Juan?

---

## *Critical Thinking*

With a partner, study how prime factorization is used to name the LCM of 24 and 20.

Prime factorization of 24: $2 \times 2 \times 2 \times 3$
Prime factorization of 20: $2 \times 2 \qquad\quad \times 5$
LCM is 120: $\qquad\qquad 2 \times 2 \times 2 \times 3 \times 5$

← The LCM contains all factors of 24 as well as those factors of 20 that are not factors of 24.

Use prime factorization to name the LCM.

**1.** 8, 18    **2.** 28, 40    **3.** 12, 20    **4.** 27, 36    **5.** 9, 12, 15

# Picture This

*Problem Solving:*
*Reading Nonnumerical Graphs*

## ■ READ ABOUT IT

Graphs can be used to show
relationships between two quantities.
One quantity is represented on the
horizontal axis, the other on the
vertical axis.

## ■ TALK ABOUT IT

Work with a partner as you read the
information illustrated in the nonnumerical
graphs at the right.

1. Which two quantities are
   represented on the graph at
   the right?

2. Match the forms of transportation
   to the letters on the graph. Give
   a reason for each matching.

3. In the graph at the right, did both
   runners go the same distance?

4. Which runner went farther in
   the early part of the race?

5. Who ran the distance in the
   shortest amount of time?

6. A cyclist travels the same route
   as the runners. Describe how a line
   representing the cyclist's distance
   and time might look on the graph.

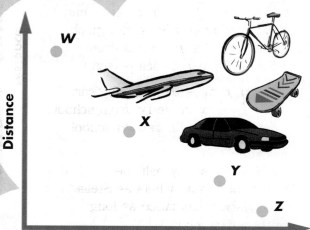

The graph at the right represents Stella's and Fred's trips to school.

7. Stella has a short walk before and after riding a bus. Which line represents Stella's trip to school?

8. How do you think Fred gets to school? Explain.

9. How do the distances Fred and Stella travel to school compare?

10. Discuss how you would represent the following people on the graph. Then copy the graph and draw a line to represent each person.

   • George rides to school by car. He lives twice as far from school as Fred, but he gets to school twice as fast.

   • Alicia lives only half the distance from school as Stella. Yet she takes twice as long to get to school.

## ▪ WRITE ABOUT IT

11. The graph at the right represents a bicycle trip. Write a paragraph describing what is happening. Be sure to include a description of points A, B, C, D, and E in your story.

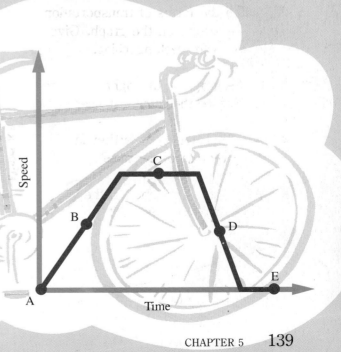

## LANGUAGE & VOCABULARY

Write a sentence for each pair of terms to show that you understand the difference between them.

1. prime number, composite number
2. factor, prime factor
3. factor, multiple
4. common factor, greatest common factor
5. greatest common factor, least common multiple

## QUICK QUIZ

By what is each number divisible? Write *2, 3, 5, 6, 9,* or *10.* *(pages 130–131)*

1. 3,861
2. 7,350
3. 17,045

List the factors. Name the GCF. *(pages 134–135)*

4. 18, 54
5. 12, 64
6. 39, 65

Name the LCM. *(pages 136–137)*

7. 3, 14
8. 9, 12
9. 25, 15

Solve. *(pages 136–137)*

10. The school chorus can perform on stage in rows of either 3, 4, or 5 students with no members left over.
    a. How can the chorus members arrange themselves?
    b. If 5 more students join the chorus, which of the arrangements would no longer be possible?
    c. What is the smallest number of students that can be in the chorus?

Write the answers in your learning log.

1. Most numbers have an even number of factors. Describe numbers that have an odd number of factors.

2. Describe numbers with more than one factor tree.

3. Often students confuse GCF and LCM. Tell how you remember these two ideas.

MATH AMERICA

**DID YOU KNOW . . . ?** The Statue of Liberty is 151 ft tall. It is about 25 times taller than life size. How tall would a statue of you be if it were 25 times your height?

BONUS

A stadium seats 48,060 people for a baseball game. Extra sections are added for a football game, enabling the stadium to seat 56,700. Every section in the stadium contains the same number of seats for both sports. What is the largest number of seats that can be in each section?

## Meaning of Fractions

The flag of Chad is divided into three *equal* parts. The red part is one third of the flag's area. This color can be represented with the fraction $\frac{1}{3}$.

$$\frac{\text{number of red parts}}{\text{total number of parts}} = \frac{1}{3} \begin{array}{l} \longrightarrow \text{ numerator} \\ \longrightarrow \text{ denominator} \end{array}$$

The Nigerian flag also consists of three equal parts. Two of them are green, so two thirds of the flag is green. This color can be represented with the fraction $\frac{2}{3}$.

$$\frac{\text{number of green parts}}{\text{total number of parts}} = \frac{2}{3}$$

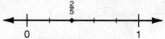

What fraction of the flags at the right have vertical stripes?

$$\frac{\text{number of flags with vertical stripes}}{\text{total number of flags}} = \frac{2}{5}$$

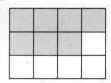

**CRITICAL THINKING** How would you use the flags above to find an example representing the fraction $\frac{5}{5}$?

Chad

Austria

Nigeria

Indonesia

Netherlands

Write the fraction for the shaded parts in the diagram.

**1.**

**2.**

Draw a diagram that represents the fraction.

**3. a.** $\frac{1}{4}$    **b.** $\frac{5}{16}$

**NUMBER SENSE** Write the fraction associated with the letter.

**4.**

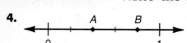

**5.**

**6.**

MATH AND SOCIAL STUDIES

Write the fraction for the shaded parts.

**7.**
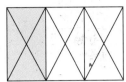

**8.**

**9.**
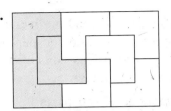

Draw a diagram that represents the fraction.

**10.** $\frac{7}{9}$    **11.** $\frac{2}{3}$    **12.** $\frac{5}{8}$    **13.** $\frac{4}{6}$    **14.** $\frac{3}{11}$    **15.** $\frac{19}{25}$

Write the fraction for the letter.

**16.**

**17.**

**18.**

Czechoslovakia

**19.** Draw a number line from 0 to 1. Illustrate the fractions $\frac{3}{8}$ and $\frac{7}{8}$.

**20.** **ESTIMATE** About how much of Canada's flag is red? About how much of Czechoslovakia's flag is blue?

Canada

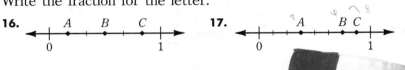

Luxembourg

Ireland

Italy

Colombia

Answer *true* or *false*.

**21.** $\frac{1}{6}$ of the flags have orange.

**22.** $\frac{1}{6}$ of the flags have at least one horizontal red line.

**23.** $\frac{1}{3}$ of the flags have green.

**24.** $\frac{4}{6}$ of the flags are $\frac{1}{3}$ green.

Hungary

Thailand

# Equivalent Fractions

Who is right?

$\frac{3}{12}$ ← blue fish
← fish in all

1 out of every 4
fish is blue. →

**Equivalent fractions** have the same value. To write an
equivalent fraction, multiply the numerator and the denominator
of the given fraction by the same nonzero number.

$$\frac{1}{4} = \frac{1 \times 3}{4 \times 3} = \frac{3}{12}$$

Both are right, because $\frac{1}{4}$ and $\frac{3}{12}$ are equivalent fractions.

Other examples:

$$\frac{2}{5} = \frac{2 \times 2}{5 \times 2} = \frac{4}{10}$$         $$\frac{9}{10} = \frac{9 \times 4}{10 \times 4} = \frac{36}{40}$$

**THINK ALOUD**   Name some other fractions equivalent to $\frac{2}{5}$ and to $\frac{9}{10}$.

―――――――――――――――――― **GUIDED PRACTICE** ――――――――――――――――

**1.** Draw a picture to show that $\frac{4}{8}$ is equivalent to $\frac{1}{2}$.

Name two equivalent fractions for each.       Find the value of *n*.

**2.** $\frac{3}{4}$        **3.** $\frac{5}{9}$        **4.** $\frac{6}{7}$        **5.** $\frac{7}{9} = \frac{n}{18}$        **6.** $\frac{5}{12} = \frac{15}{n}$

Write three fractions equivalent to the given fraction. Use fraction models to help.

**7.** $\frac{1}{3}$     **8.** $\frac{3}{4}$     **9.** $\frac{1}{2}$     **10.** $\frac{5}{9}$     **11.** $\frac{2}{5}$     **12.** $\frac{3}{11}$

**13.** $\frac{3}{5}$     **14.** $\frac{4}{7}$     **15.** $\frac{3}{8}$     **16.** $\frac{5}{16}$     **17.** $\frac{11}{12}$     **18.** $\frac{17}{20}$

Find the value of $n$.

**19.** $\frac{2}{5} = \frac{8}{n}$     **20.** $\frac{3}{7} = \frac{n}{21}$     **21.** $\frac{8}{15} = \frac{n}{60}$     **22.** $\frac{5}{7} = \frac{20}{n}$     **23.** $\frac{6}{13} = \frac{n}{52}$

**24.** $\frac{3}{4} = \frac{n}{72}$     **25.** $\frac{8}{9} = \frac{n}{72}$     **26.** $\frac{12}{25} = \frac{96}{n}$     **27.** $\frac{3}{7} = \frac{48}{n}$     **28.** $\frac{4}{15} = \frac{n}{75}$

**29.** Draw a picture to show that $\frac{2}{3}$ and $\frac{4}{6}$ are equivalent fractions.

**CHOOSE** Choose mental math or paper and pencil to solve.

**30.** Match the fraction with the kind of fish shown in the aquarium.

    **a.** $\frac{1}{3}$     **b.** $\frac{1}{2}$     **c.** $\frac{1}{6}$

**31. CREATE YOUR OWN** Write a fraction problem about the fish in the aquarium.

**32.** Two more of each kind of fish are put in the tank. Write two equivalent fractions that represent what part of the fish in the aquarium are neon tetras.

## Critical Thinking

Suppose you and a partner put 72 fish (guppies, neon tetras, and angelfish) in an aquarium. How many of each kind of fish would you have if the following conditions are met?

- One fourth are neon tetras.
- One half are guppies.
- More than $\frac{1}{6}$ are angelfish.

## Lowest Terms

There are 206 bones in the human body. These bones support the body, protect the internal organs, and aid in movement.

There are 32 bones in the arm and hand. Of these, 8 are found in the wrist.

Can you name the fraction equivalent to $\frac{8}{32}$ that is in **lowest terms**?

If you know how to find the GCF of 8 and 32, you can make a **MATH CONNECTION** to write a fraction in lowest terms equivalent to $\frac{8}{32}$.

Divide the numerator and denominator by the GCF of 8 and 32, 8.

$$\frac{8}{32} = \frac{8 \div 8}{32 \div 8} = \frac{1}{4} \longleftarrow \text{lowest terms}$$

**THINK ALOUD** What is true about a fraction if the GCF of the numerator and denominator is 1?

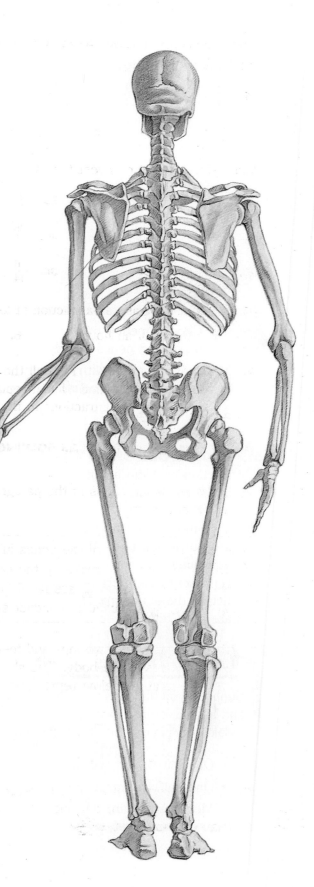

Other examples:

| What is the GCF of 6 and 10? | What is the GCF of 12 and 18? |
|---|---|
| $\frac{6}{10} = \frac{6 \div 2}{10 \div 2} = \frac{3}{5}$ | $\frac{12}{18} = \frac{12 \div 6}{18 \div 6} = \frac{2}{3}$ |

### GUIDED PRACTICE

Is the fraction in lowest terms? Answer *yes* or *no*. If *no*, write the fraction in lowest terms.

1. $\frac{5}{35}$  
2. $\frac{3}{16}$  
3. $\frac{6}{18}$  

4. $\frac{5}{12}$  
5. $\frac{14}{20}$  
6. $\frac{21}{42}$  

7. **THINK ALOUD** If you divide the numerator and denominator of any fraction by the GCF, will the equivalent fraction always be in lowest terms? Explain.

Find the value of $n$.

**8.** $\dfrac{2}{16} = \dfrac{n}{8}$       **9.** $\dfrac{12}{15} = \dfrac{4}{n}$       **10.** $\dfrac{2}{n} = \dfrac{6}{9}$       **11.** $\dfrac{48}{60} = \dfrac{n}{5}$

**12.** $\dfrac{15}{40} = \dfrac{n}{8}$       **13.** $\dfrac{18}{22} = \dfrac{9}{n}$       **14.** $\dfrac{28}{36} = \dfrac{7}{n}$       **15.** $\dfrac{33}{42} = \dfrac{n}{14}$

Write the fraction in lowest terms.

**16.** $\dfrac{8}{16}$    **17.** $\dfrac{10}{15}$    **18.** $\dfrac{7}{13}$    **19.** $\dfrac{16}{20}$    **20.** $\dfrac{15}{45}$    **21.** $\dfrac{8}{20}$

**22.** $\dfrac{9}{21}$    **23.** $\dfrac{6}{27}$    **24.** $\dfrac{35}{50}$    **25.** $\dfrac{28}{32}$    **26.** $\dfrac{13}{28}$    **27.** $\dfrac{45}{81}$

**28.** $\dfrac{23}{46}$    **29.** $\dfrac{18}{81}$    **30.** $\dfrac{16}{44}$    **31.** $\dfrac{16}{96}$    **32.** $\dfrac{84}{140}$    **33.** $\dfrac{150}{210}$

**34.** Write the phrase as a fraction in lowest terms.

     **a.** 20 min of an hour      **b.** 60 d of a 365-d year      **c.** 5 d in June

**35.** **CRITICAL THINKING** Find all the ways in which the numbers 3, 9, 27, and 81 can replace the variables to make equivalent fractions in the equation $\dfrac{a}{b} = \dfrac{c}{d}$.

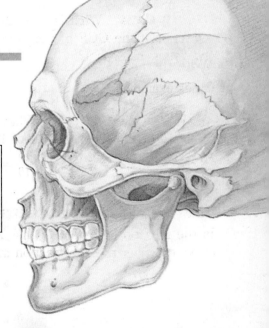

Solve.

**36.** Rewrite the fractions in the paragraph in lowest terms.

> The skull contains $\dfrac{28}{206}$ of the bones in the human body. Of the skull bones, $\dfrac{8}{28}$ make up the cranium, which protects the brain, and $\dfrac{6}{28}$ are facial bones. Of the facial bones, $\dfrac{12}{56}$ are used to conduct sound in the ear.

**37.** The bones in the two legs and feet make up $\dfrac{56}{206}$ of the bones in the body. The shaded region in which rectangle below represents this number of bones?

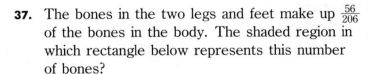

   **a.**          **b.**          **c.**

**38.** Shade a region of a circle to represent the number of bones in the human body that are *not* in the legs and feet.

# Fractions and Mixed Numbers

Jumbo, an elephant in P. T. Barnum's famous circus in the 1880s, weighed $6\frac{1}{2}$ t. The number $6\frac{1}{2}$ is a **mixed number**.

You can write a mixed number as a fraction. This number line shows that $6\frac{1}{2}$ is $\frac{13}{2}$.

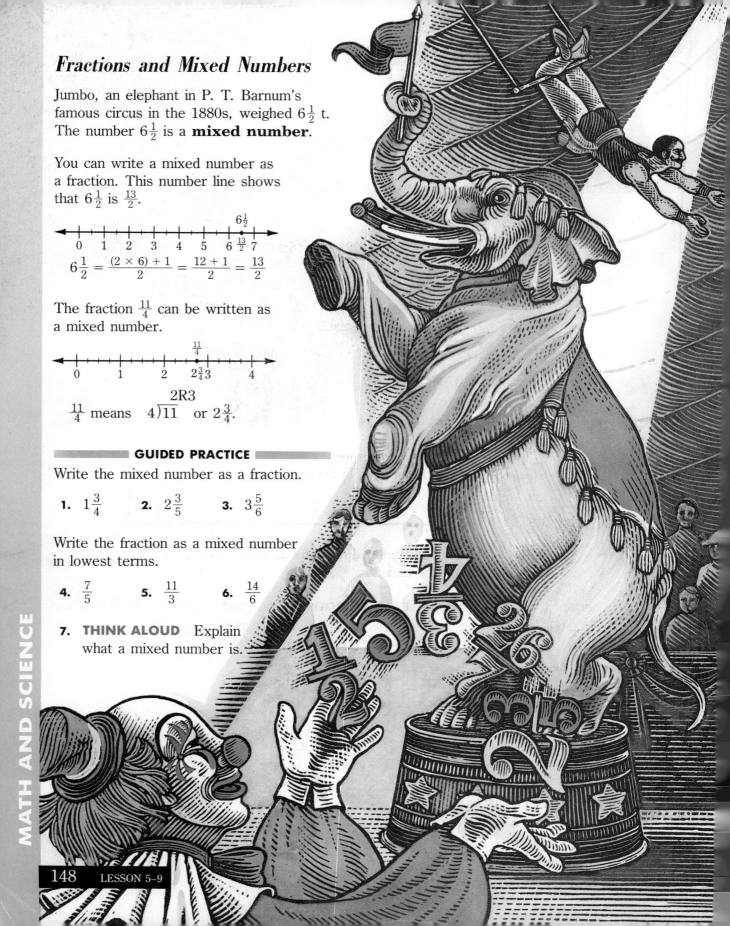

$$6\frac{1}{2} = \frac{(2 \times 6) + 1}{2} = \frac{12 + 1}{2} = \frac{13}{2}$$

The fraction $\frac{11}{4}$ can be written as a mixed number.

$\frac{11}{4}$ means $4\overline{)11}^{\,2R3}$ or $2\frac{3}{4}$.

---
### GUIDED PRACTICE

Write the mixed number as a fraction.

1. $1\frac{3}{4}$    2. $2\frac{3}{5}$    3. $3\frac{5}{6}$

Write the fraction as a mixed number in lowest terms.

4. $\frac{7}{5}$    5. $\frac{11}{3}$    6. $\frac{14}{6}$

7. **THINK ALOUD** Explain what a mixed number is.

Write the mixed number as a fraction.

**8.** $1\frac{3}{8}$    **9.** $2\frac{5}{9}$    **10.** $2\frac{3}{4}$

**11.** $1\frac{7}{9}$    **12.** $3\frac{2}{3}$    **13.** $2\frac{1}{2}$

**14.** $2\frac{9}{10}$    **15.** $3\frac{5}{8}$    **16.** $4\frac{2}{3}$

**17.** $9\frac{4}{5}$    **18.** $9\frac{1}{6}$    **19.** $5\frac{3}{4}$

Write the fraction as a whole or mixed number in lowest terms.

**20.** $\frac{8}{5}$    **21.** $\frac{7}{4}$    **22.** $\frac{13}{8}$

**23.** $\frac{15}{7}$    **24.** $\frac{18}{9}$    **25.** $\frac{14}{8}$

**26.** $\frac{9}{2}$    **27.** $\frac{23}{5}$    **28.** $\frac{26}{7}$

**29.** $\frac{18}{11}$    **30.** $\frac{21}{9}$    **31.** $\frac{29}{7}$

**NUMBER SENSE** Find the measurement in inches represented by the letter. Give the answer in lowest terms.

**32.** *A*    **33.** *B*

**34.** C    **35.** *D*

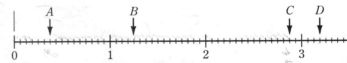

**36. CRITICAL THINKING** Choose from the numbers 1, 2, 3, 5, and 7 to replace the variables in the equation. $\frac{a}{b} = n + \frac{c}{b}$

**PROBLEM SOLVING**

Read carefully. Change each fraction to a mixed number in lowest terms. Use your number sense to select the missing measurements from the fractions listed.

The elephant is the largest living land animal. The largest

**37.** known elephant, an African bull, measured $\frac{79}{6}$ ft tall. One

**38.** record-size elephant tusk is ▦ ft long. The tusk weighs about

**39.** ▦ lb. On average, an elephant's tail measures about

**40.** $\frac{10}{3}$ ft in length. An average elephant's trunk measures about

**41.** 5 ft in length and can hold about ▦ gal of water. An

**42.** elephant also has four back teeth, each weighing about $\frac{17}{2}$ lb.

$\frac{881}{4}$

$\frac{3}{2}$

$\frac{126}{12}$

## Comparing and Ordering Fractions and Mixed Numbers

Did you know that copper is one of the first metals known to human beings? Its use has been traced back to 8000 B.C.

The world's top five copper mining countries produce a total of about 4,656,000 t/yr. The circle graph shows the fraction of the 4,656,000 t of copper each country mines.

Does the USSR mine more copper than Zambia?

If you know how to write an equivalent fraction, you can make a **MATH CONNECTION** to compare two fractions.

Use the **least common denominator (LCD)** to write equivalent fractions so you can compare $\frac{7}{50}$ and $\frac{3}{25}$.

$$\frac{7}{50} = \frac{7}{50} \text{ and } \frac{3}{25} = \frac{6}{50}$$

The LCD, 50, is the least common multiple of the denominators 50 and 25.

Since $\frac{7}{50} > \frac{6}{50}$, $\frac{7}{50} > \frac{3}{25}$.

So the USSR mines more copper than Zambia.

Other examples:

Compare $\frac{7}{8}$ and $\frac{5}{6}$.

$$\frac{7}{8} = \frac{21}{24} \text{ and } \frac{5}{6} = \frac{20}{24}$$

Since $\frac{21}{24} > \frac{20}{24}$, $\frac{7}{8} > \frac{5}{6}$.

Compare $2\frac{3}{5}$ and $2\frac{2}{3}$.

$$2\frac{3}{5} = \frac{13}{5} = \frac{39}{15} \text{ and } 2\frac{2}{3} = \frac{8}{3} = \frac{40}{15}$$

Since $\frac{39}{15} < \frac{40}{15}$, $2\frac{3}{5} < 2\frac{2}{3}$.

### GUIDED PRACTICE

Copy and compare. Choose >, <, or =.

1. $\frac{1}{4}$ ▓ $\frac{1}{3}$

2. $\frac{2}{3}$ ▓ $\frac{5}{8}$

3. $3\frac{1}{6}$ ▓ $3\frac{2}{9}$

4. $1\frac{5}{6}$ ▓ $1\frac{4}{7}$

Order the fractions from the greatest to the least.

5. $\frac{2}{5}, \frac{4}{7}, \frac{2}{3}$

6. $\frac{4}{9}, \frac{6}{11}, \frac{2}{5}$

7. $\frac{1}{3}, \frac{2}{7}, \frac{5}{12}$

8. $\frac{3}{4}, \frac{13}{16}, \frac{19}{24}$

Zambia $\frac{3}{25}$

USSR $\frac{7}{50}$

Chile $\frac{8}{25}$

Canada $\frac{4}{25}$

United States $\frac{13}{50}$

MATH AND SOCIAL STUDIES

Copy and compare. Choose >, <, or =.

**9.** $\dfrac{5}{6} \rule{1cm}{0.5mm} \dfrac{2}{3}$    **10.** $\dfrac{2}{3} \rule{1cm}{0.5mm} \dfrac{5}{9}$    **11.** $\dfrac{3}{8} \rule{1cm}{0.5mm} \dfrac{1}{4}$    **12.** $\dfrac{7}{12} \rule{1cm}{0.5mm} \dfrac{3}{4}$

**13.** $\dfrac{1}{4} \rule{1cm}{0.5mm} \dfrac{2}{8}$    **14.** $\dfrac{3}{4} \rule{1cm}{0.5mm} \dfrac{5}{6}$    **15.** $7\dfrac{1}{2} \rule{1cm}{0.5mm} 2\dfrac{2}{3}$    **16.** $\dfrac{4}{5} \rule{1cm}{0.5mm} \dfrac{3}{4}$

**17.** $2\dfrac{1}{2} \rule{1cm}{0.5mm} \dfrac{15}{6}$    **18.** $\dfrac{5}{6} \rule{1cm}{0.5mm} \dfrac{8}{9}$    **19.** $5\dfrac{4}{5} \rule{1cm}{0.5mm} 5\dfrac{3}{4}$    **20.** $\dfrac{13}{20} \rule{1cm}{0.5mm} \dfrac{3}{4}$

**21.** $2\dfrac{6}{9} \rule{1cm}{0.5mm} 2\dfrac{2}{3}$    **22.** $1\dfrac{7}{9} \rule{1cm}{0.5mm} 1\dfrac{1}{2}$    **23.** $3\dfrac{7}{8} \rule{1cm}{0.5mm} 3\dfrac{11}{12}$    **24.** $\dfrac{18}{5} \rule{1cm}{0.5mm} \dfrac{23}{7}$

**CALCULATOR**  Order from the least to the greatest.

**25.** $2, \dfrac{7}{8}, \dfrac{3}{4}, \dfrac{5}{6}, \dfrac{2}{3}, 1$    **26.** $\dfrac{1}{3}, 1, 2\dfrac{1}{3}, \dfrac{2}{5}, 2\dfrac{1}{2}, 1\dfrac{1}{4}$    **27.** $\dfrac{18}{5}, 3\dfrac{7}{8}, \dfrac{21}{6}, 0.5, \dfrac{4}{1}, 2\dfrac{9}{9}$

**PROBLEM SOLVING**

The circle graph at right shows the top five nickel-producing countries. Use it to solve.

**28.** Match one of the fractions below to each of the countries represented in the circle graph.

  **a.** $\dfrac{1}{4}$    **b.** $\dfrac{1}{10}$    **c.** $\dfrac{7}{40}$

  **d.** $\dfrac{1}{8}$    **e.** $\dfrac{7}{20}$

**29.** One year, Canada produced about 121,800 t of nickel. About how many tons of nickel did the top five countries produce that year in all?

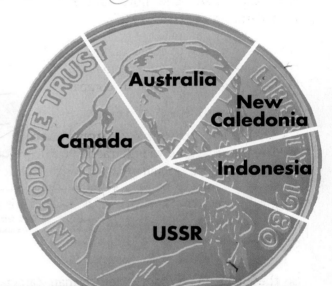

*Australia, New Caledonia, Canada, Indonesia, USSR*

*Mental Math*

To compare each pair of fractions, the product of the pairs of denominators were used as common denominators.

$\dfrac{3}{4} \rule{0.8cm}{0.5mm} \dfrac{2}{3}$    $\dfrac{4}{7} \rule{0.8cm}{0.5mm} \dfrac{5}{8}$    $\dfrac{4}{9} \rule{0.8cm}{0.5mm} \dfrac{3}{7}$    $\dfrac{4}{6} \rule{0.8cm}{0.5mm} \dfrac{6}{9}$

⑨   ⑧      ㉜   ㉟      ㉘   ㉗      ㊱   ㊱

$\dfrac{3 \times 3}{12} \rule{0.8cm}{0.5mm} \dfrac{2 \times 4}{12}$    $\dfrac{4 \times 8}{56} \rule{0.8cm}{0.5mm} \dfrac{5 \times 7}{56}$    $\dfrac{4 \times 7}{63} \rule{0.8cm}{0.5mm} \dfrac{3 \times 9}{63}$    $\dfrac{4 \times 9}{54} \rule{0.8cm}{0.5mm} \dfrac{6 \times 6}{54}$

**1.** In each case, how were the common denominators determined?

**2.** In each case, what will determine if the fractions are equal?

**3.** Look for a pattern to find a short cut for comparing fractions without finding the common denominator.

# Fractions, Mixed Numbers, and Decimals

The weights of the animals shown can be written in decimal form.

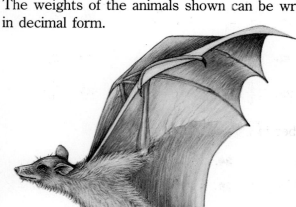

**Bat, $\frac{1}{8}$ lb**

**Grey squirrel, $1\frac{1}{2}$ lb**

Divide. On a calculator:

$$8\overline{)1.000} \quad \overset{0.125}{}$$

1 ÷ 8 = 0.125 (lb)

Change $1\frac{1}{2}$ to $\frac{3}{2}$. Divide.

$$2\overline{)3.0} \quad \overset{1.5}{}$$

3 ÷ 2 = 1.5 (lb)

Use a fraction with a multiple of 10 to help you change the weights of the animals below to fraction form.

**Hummingbird, 0.4 oz**

**Canada Goose, 8.75 lb**

$0.4 = \frac{4}{10} = \frac{2}{5}$ (oz)

$8.75 = 8\frac{75}{100} = 8\frac{3}{4}$ (lb)

---

## GUIDED PRACTICE

Write the fraction as a decimal.

**1.** $\frac{1}{2}$    **2.** $\frac{2}{5}$    **3.** $\frac{4}{10}$    **4.** $\frac{1}{4}$    **5.** $\frac{2}{25}$    **6.** $\frac{3}{50}$

Write the decimal as a fraction or mixed number in lowest terms.

**7.** 0.3    **8.** 0.25    **9.** 6.7    **10.** 0.3    **11.** 0.75    **12.** 4.5

Write the fraction or mixed number in decimal form.

**13.** $\frac{3}{5}$     **14.** $\frac{5}{8}$     **15.** $\frac{9}{20}$     **16.** $\frac{17}{25}$     **17.** $\frac{9}{8}$     **18.** $\frac{7}{10}$

**19.** $\frac{13}{5}$     **20.** $\frac{13}{40}$     **21.** $\frac{85}{100}$     **22.** $\frac{21}{24}$     **23.** $\frac{7}{8}$     **24.** $\frac{3}{16}$

**25.** $\frac{9}{40}$     **26.** $\frac{5}{16}$     **27.** $\frac{17}{32}$     **28.** $4\frac{3}{8}$     **29.** $\frac{125}{500}$     **30.** $\frac{30}{200}$

Write the decimal as a fraction or mixed number in lowest terms.

**31.** 0.6     **32.** 0.9     **33.** 0.45     **34.** 0.125     **35.** 1.3

**36.** 4.23     **37.** 3.6     **38.** 8.75     **39.** 0.08     **40.** 2.32

**41.** 1.125     **42.** 0.625     **43.** 2.375     **44.** 5.004     **45.** 0.0005

**CALCULATOR**   Order from the greatest to the least.

**46.** $1, 0.42, \frac{3}{8}, \frac{2}{5}, \frac{9}{20}, 2, 0.04, \frac{11}{50}$       **47.** $\frac{13}{50}, 0.38, \frac{15}{40}, 3.8, 0.09, 1, \frac{1}{4}, \frac{39}{100}$

**CALCULATOR**   Compute.

**48.** $4.9 + \frac{3}{8}$      **49.** $5.6 + \frac{4}{5}$      **50.** $8.69 + \frac{4}{5}$      **51.** $4.6 - \frac{7}{40}$

Copy and complete the pattern.

**52.** $\frac{1}{8} = 0.125, \frac{2}{8} = 0.250, \frac{3}{8} = 0.375, \frac{4}{8} = \blacksquare, \frac{5}{8} = \blacksquare, \frac{6}{8} = \blacksquare, \frac{7}{8} = \blacksquare, \frac{8}{8} = \blacksquare$

**53.** $\frac{1}{20} = 0.05, \frac{2}{20} = \blacksquare, \frac{3}{20} = 0.15, \frac{4}{20} = 0.20, \frac{5}{20} = \blacksquare, \frac{6}{20} = \blacksquare, \frac{7}{20} = \blacksquare$

**54.** $\frac{1}{50} = \blacksquare, \frac{2}{50} = 0.04, \frac{3}{50} = 0.06, \frac{4}{50} = \blacksquare, \frac{5}{50} = \blacksquare, \frac{6}{50} = 0.12, \frac{7}{50} = \blacksquare$

**55.** $\frac{1}{25} = \blacksquare, \frac{2}{25} = \blacksquare, \frac{3}{25} = 0.12, \frac{4}{25} = 0.16, \frac{5}{25} = 0.20, \frac{6}{25} = \blacksquare, \frac{7}{25} = \blacksquare$

## Mental Math

Use your number sense to find a number in lowest terms that is between the two given numbers in value.

**1.** $\frac{1}{2}, \frac{6}{8}$      **2.** $1\frac{1}{3}, 1\frac{5}{9}$      **3.** $\frac{7}{10}, \frac{1}{2}$      **4.** $2\frac{1}{16}, 2\frac{1}{4}$

**5.** $3\frac{1}{12}, 3\frac{1}{4}$      **6.** $\frac{7}{8}, \frac{15}{16}$      **7.** $9\frac{2}{3}, 10\frac{1}{4}$      **8.** $7\frac{5}{16}, 7\frac{1}{2}$

## Terminating and Repeating Decimals

Did you know that Alaska is the largest state in the United States? California is about $\frac{3}{11}$ as large as Alaska, and Texas is about $\frac{9}{20}$ the size of Alaska.

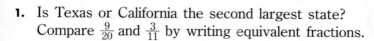

**1.** Is Texas or California the second largest state? Compare $\frac{9}{20}$ and $\frac{3}{11}$ by writing equivalent fractions.

Another way to compare $\frac{9}{20}$ and $\frac{3}{11}$ is to change them to decimal form. You can use a calculator to do this.

**2.** What is the quotient of 9 ÷ 20?

If the remainder is zero when you divide, the decimal is a **terminating decimal.**

**3.** What is the quotient of 3 ÷ 11? Is $\frac{3}{11}$ a terminating decimal? Describe the pattern of the digits in the quotient.

If the remainder in a division never becomes zero, and the digits in the quotient repeat, the decimal is a **repeating decimal.**

**4.** Write a comparison statement using >, <, or = for the decimal equivalents of $\frac{9}{20}$ and $\frac{3}{11}$.

Write the fraction as a terminating decimal.

**5.** $\frac{3}{4}$      **6.** $\frac{16}{25}$      **7.** $\frac{61}{40}$      **8.** $\frac{49}{80}$      **9.** $\frac{27}{32}$      **10.** $\frac{59}{50}$

California is $\frac{3}{11}$ or 0.27272727 . . . the size of Alaska. The three dots mean the digits 2 and 7 repeat forever. We can also write $0.\overline{27}$ to show that this is a repeating decimal. The repeating bar covers only those digits that are continually repeated.

Write the fraction as a repeating decimal. Place a bar over the repeating digits.

**11.** $\frac{5}{9}$      **12.** $\frac{1}{6}$      **13.** $\frac{5}{12}$      **14.** $\frac{11}{27}$      **15.** $\frac{7}{15}$      **16.** $\frac{12}{27}$

**17.** $\frac{12}{41}$      **18.** $\frac{19}{27}$      **19.** $\frac{12}{26}$      **20.** $\frac{14}{11}$      **21.** $\frac{39}{37}$      **22.** $\frac{25}{22}$

**MATH AND GEOGRAPHY**

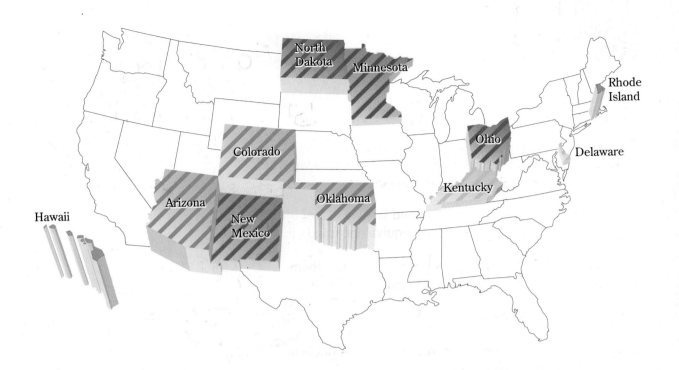

Rewrite each fraction as a decimal. State whether it is a *repeating* or a *terminating* decimal.

**23.** The area of the state of Delaware is about $\frac{1}{20}$ that of the state of Kentucky.

**24.** Ohio has about $\frac{4}{7}$ the area of North Dakota.

**25.** Rhode Island, the smallest state, is about $\frac{3}{16}$ the size of Hawaii.

**26.** Minnesota is about $\frac{2}{3}$ the size of New Mexico.

**27.** Oklahoma is about $\frac{4}{11}$ the size of Arizona, and Colorado is about $\frac{10}{11}$ the area of Arizona.

Write the number as a terminating or a repeating decimal.

**28.** $\frac{2}{5}$    **29.** $\frac{1}{3}$    **30.** $\frac{1}{8}$    **31.** $\frac{4}{15}$    **32.** $\frac{2}{9}$    **33.** $\frac{17}{16}$

**34.** $2\frac{9}{11}$    **35.** $\frac{3}{50}$    **36.** $5\frac{7}{30}$    **37.** $\frac{1}{6}$    **38.** $6\frac{2}{15}$    **39.** $\frac{202}{200}$

**40.** **IN YOUR WORDS** Describe a few fraction denominators that you know will be a terminating decimal. How do you know?

**41.** **IN YOUR WORDS** Describe a few fraction denominators that you know will be a repeating decimal. How do you know?

## Smaller Numbers

Do you recognize what this photograph shows? It is a human hair, magnified 500 times by a scanning electron microscope.

Use a metric ruler for Exercises 1–10.

1. Measure the thickness of the hair in the photograph to the nearest half centimeter.

2. What would be the approximate thickness of a human hair in centimeters? in millimeters?

3. How many human hairs would equal 7 mm? 7 cm?

4. The average thickness of human skin is 19 times greater than the average thickness of human hair. What is the approximate thickness of human skin in centimeters? Use the information from Exercise 2.

An electronic chip is small enough to pass through the eye of a tapestry needle.

5. Measure the length and width of the electronic chip shown. The actual length and width of the chip is about 10 times smaller than the picture. What are the approximate dimensions of the actual chip?

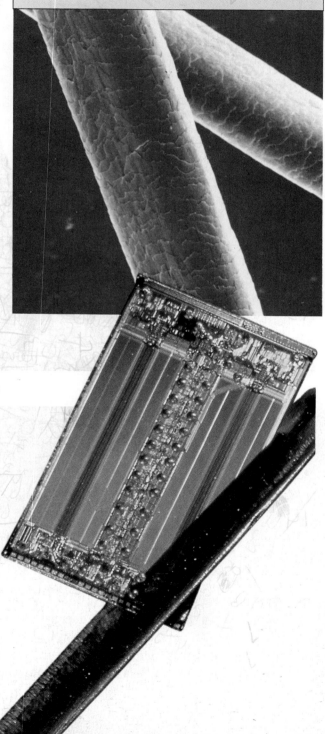

> *To see a World in a Grain of Sand,*
> *And a Heaven in a Wild Flower,*
> *Hold Infinity in the palm of your hand,*
> *And Eternity in an hour.*
>
> — *from "Auguries of Innocence"*
> *by William Blake*

MATH AND SCIENCE

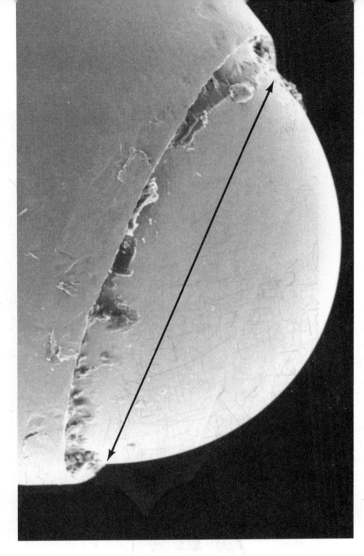

The line across the ball in this picture of the tip of a ball-point pen is about 200 times larger than the actual distance.

6. Measure the line across the ball in centimeters. What is the approximate distance across the ball in a ball-point pen tip in centimeters? in millimeters?

7. About how many ball-point pen tips of this size would equal 1 cm?

8. The ball point on a fine ball-point pen is about 1.6 times smaller than that on a medium ball-point pen. If the distance across the ball tip on a medium pen is about 0.04 cm, about what is the distance across the ball on a fine ball-point pen?

9. The diameter of a nickel is about 2.2 cm. How many times smaller than the diameter of a nickel is the distance across the ball on a medium pen? Use the information in Exercise 8.

10. Only part of a fly's eye is magnified in the photograph at the left. If the entire magnification could be shown, the eye would measure 100 cm across. That is because this photograph has enlarged the fly's eye 400 times. About what would the actual length across the fly's eye be?

## Problem Solving Strategy:
## *Using a Simpler Problem*

Sometimes the numbers in a problem make it appear more difficult than it really is. If you rewrite the problem using simpler numbers, it is easier to solve.

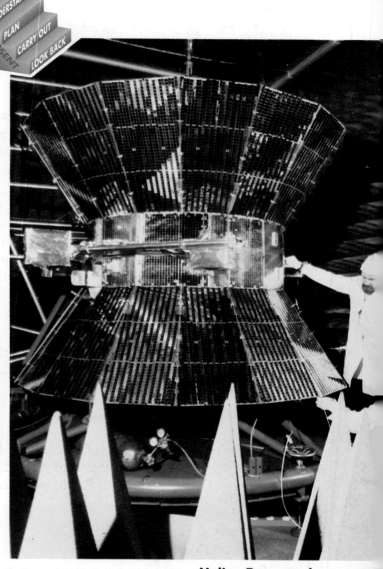

**Problem:**
The research spacecraft *Helios B* came within 27 million miles of the Sun. Traveling at a speed of 124,277.6 mi/h, how many hours did *Helios B* take to get this close to the Sun, which is about 93 million miles from Earth?

- The large numbers in the problem make it appear difficult. Rewrite the problem using simpler numbers.

**Simpler Problem:**
*Helios B* came within about 30,000 mi of the Sun. Traveling at a speed of about 100 mi/h, how many hours did *Helios B* take to get this close to the Sun, which is about 90,000 mi away?

- Which operations would you use to solve the simpler problem?
- Now solve the original problem using the same operations.

Helios B research spacecr

━━━━━━━━━ **GUIDED PRACTICE** ━━━━━━━━━

Solve the simpler problem first, then solve the original problem.

1. **Problem:** What is the quotient of 1 ÷ 500,000,000?

   **Simpler Problem:** What is the quotient of 1 ÷ 5?
   1 ÷ 50? 1 ÷ 500?

2. **Problem:** How many seconds are there in 2 wk?

   **Simpler Problem:** How many seconds are there in 1 min?
   1 h? 1 d?

MATH AND SCIENCE

Solve by using a simpler problem.
Work with a partner.

**3.** The average height of an adult male is $5\frac{3}{4}$ ft. How many men of average height would equal the height of the *Saturn V* rocket, which was 363 ft tall?

**4.** The *Saturn V* rocket launched the first astronauts to go to the Moon. This rocket burned more than 560,000 gal of fuel during the first $2\frac{3}{4}$ min of launch. At that rate, how much did *Saturn V* burn in 1 s?

**5.** *Saturn V* launched *Apollo 11*, which put two men, Armstrong and Aldrin, on the Moon. This historic flight began on July 16, 1969, at 9:32 A.M. and ended on July 24, 1969, at 12:51 A.M. For how many hours and minutes did the flight of *Apollo 11* last?

**6.** The Earth circles the Sun at a speed of 18.5 mi/s (miles per second).

  **a.** What is Earth's speed as it circles the Sun?

  **b.** What is 18.5 mi/s in miles per minute? in miles per hour?

  **c.** How far does Earth travel in 1 d?

**7.** An athlete jogs at a pace of 9.65 km/h. About how many days would it take the athlete to jog a distance equal to the equatorial circumference of Earth, which is 40,064 km?

**CHOOSE** Choose a strategy to solve if possible.

**8.** On average, a guinea pig weighs 1.54 lb. The average 25-yr old woman weighs about 124 lb. A 25-yr old man weighs, on average, about as much as 112 guinea pigs. What is the weight of an average 25-yr old man, to the nearest pound?

**9.** The diameter of the Moon is about 2,100 mi. How many Moon diameters is the Moon away from Earth?

**10.** The distance from Earth to the Sun, 93 million mi, is called 1 astronomical unit (A.U.). The planet Pluto was discovered in 1930, and its average distance from the Sun is 39.53 A.U. About how many miles from the Sun is Pluto?

## Mixed Review

Compute.

1. $963 + 87$
2. $475 + 89$
3. $21,356 + 4,519$
4. $953 + 3,294$
5. $7,246 + 978$
6. $18,000 + 5,628$
7. $53.4 + 19.7$
8. $5.6 + 4.3$
9. $1.51 + 2.7$
10. $1.25 + 5.2$
11. $536.2 + 66.4$
12. $13.19 + 12.20$
13. $567 - 438$
14. $512 - 54$
15. $3,766 - 1,333$
16. $7,442 - 6,999$
17. $12,574 - 10,342$
18. $458,369 - 314,041$
19. $9.5 - 6.3$
20. $16.25 - 10.14$
21. $301.56 - 150.32$
22. $13.45 - 12.54$
23. $34.765 - 17.532$
24. $675.125 - 466.346$
25. $28 \times 28$
26. $37 \times 52$
27. $49 \times 67$
28. $56 \times 980$
29. $631 \times 876$
30. $79 \times 12,458$
31. $587 \times 4,120$
32. $1,234 \times 4,321$
33. $398 \times 19,555$

Compute. Round the answer to the nearest tenth when necessary.

34. $78.2 \times 3.5$
35. $34.6 \times 23.87$
36. $88.88 \times 11.11$
37. $6.75 \times 30.8$
38. $898.5 \times 9.2$
39. $333.33 \times 44.44$
40. $804 \div 12$
41. $2,052 \div 57$
42. $5,590 \div 65$
43. $23,975 \div 685$
44. $18,768 \div 368$
45. $227,574 \div 269$
46. $18 \div 7.5$
47. $3,209.6 \div 47.2$
48. $248.45 \div 25.8$
49. $625.6 \div 122.5$
50. $4,815.2 \div 1.2$
51. $129.73 \div 4.4$

**The French TGV Atlantique is the world's fastest train.**

MATH AND SOCIAL STUDIES

**CHOOSE** Choose mental math, pencil and paper, estimation, or calculator to solve.

**52.** Gustave Eiffel designed both the 300-m-high Eiffel Tower in Paris and the 46.05-m-high Statue of Liberty in New York City. How much higher is the Eiffel Tower?

**53.** The Arc de Triomphe was built between 1806 and 1836 to commemorate Napoleon's victories. For how long has the Arc de Triomphe been completed?

**54.** The world's fastest electric train runs between Paris and Lyon at an average speed of 169.9 mi/h. Its top speed is about 1.9 times faster than its average. About what is the top speed of this train?

**55.** Chicago's O'Hare Airport handled about 56.3 million people in a recent year, about 2.8 times more than Orly Airport in Paris. About how many people went through Orly?

Use the bar graph to answer the question.

**56.** About what is the total population of the five cities?

**57.** Which city has about $\frac{1}{5}$ the population of Paris?

**58.** Which two cities together have about the same population as Marseille?

**59.** **CREATE YOUR OWN** Use the information in the bar graph to write a word problem. Give it to a partner to solve.

**Eiffel Tower, Paris, France**

**Population of Five French Cities**

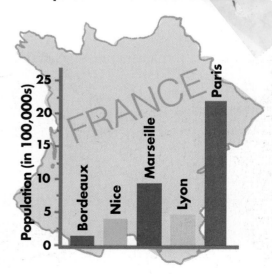

# CHAPTER CHECKUP

---

## LANGUAGE & VOCABULARY

Explain why each statement is true.

1. $\frac{4}{8} = \frac{1}{2}$    2. $\frac{13}{3} = 4\frac{1}{3}$

3. $\frac{7}{9} > \frac{5}{10}$    4. $\frac{3}{6} < 0.65$

5. $0.\overline{18} > 0.18$

---

## TEST ✓

Name the GCF and LCM for the pair of numbers. *(pages 134–137)*

1. 3, 12    2. 5, 20    3. 6, 16    4. 20, 12    5. 14, 21

6. Write the mixed number as a fraction. *(pages 148–149)*

a. $1\frac{8}{9}$    b. $7\frac{3}{5}$    c. $9\frac{5}{8}$

Write the prime factorization.

7. 72    8. 136

Write the fraction as a whole or mixed number in lowest terms. *(pages 146–149)*

9. $\frac{16}{4}$    10. $\frac{14}{8}$    11. $\frac{27}{6}$

Write the fraction as a decimal or the decimal as a fraction. *(pages 152–153)*

12. $\frac{5}{8}$    13. $\frac{34}{50}$    14. $\frac{18}{24}$    15. 0.0625    16. 0.4

Write as a terminating or repeating decimal. *(pages 154–155)*

17. $\frac{5}{6}$    18. $\frac{7}{11}$    19. $\frac{17}{40}$    20. $3\frac{1}{9}$    21. $\frac{15}{16}$

---

## SKILLS

Write the value of $n$. *(pages 142–147)*

22. $\frac{4}{9} = \frac{16}{n}$    23. $\frac{7}{12} = \frac{n}{36}$    24. $\frac{15}{35} = \frac{3}{n}$    25. $\frac{n}{45} = \frac{2}{5}$

Compare. Choose >, <, or =. *(pages 150–151)*

26. $\frac{5}{6}$ ▓ $\frac{3}{4}$    27. $\frac{3}{5}$ ▓ $\frac{9}{15}$    28. $1\frac{1}{2}$ ▓ $1\frac{7}{9}$    29. $3\frac{1}{2}$ ▓ $\frac{14}{4}$

Solve by using a simpler problem. *(pages 158–159)*

**30.** The planet Pluto is usually described as being farthest from the Sun, but at one point in its orbit Pluto is 4 million miles closer to the Sun than Neptune is at its closest distance to the Sun, 2 billion, 766 million miles. Even at its closest point to the Sun, Pluto is 2 billion, 670 million, 600 thousand miles farther from the Sun than Earth is at its closest point.

   **a.** What is the closest Neptune comes to the Sun?

   **b.** What is the closest Pluto comes to the Sun?

   **c.** What is the closest Earth comes to the Sun?

Choose mental math or pencil and paper to solve. *(pages 136–137)*

**31.** On Bernie's used car lot, every 4th car has power windows, every 5th car has power locks, and every 10th car has power seat adjusters. If there are 75 cars lined up in the lot, which cars would have all three features?

**32.** Larry is building a model car using a scale of $\frac{2}{5}$. If a part of the real car is 45 in. long, how long will that part be on Larry's scale model?

**LEARNING LOG**

Write the answers in your learning log.

   **1.** How do you think cross products got their name?

   **2.** Tell where you find mixed numbers on the number line.

   **3.** Describe three ways you can decide whether two fractions are equal.

# EXTRA PRACTICE

List the factors. Name the GCF. *(pages 134–135)*

**1.** 6, 15      **2.** 9, 21      **3.** 15, 25      **4.** 16, 40      **5.** 63, 35

Name the LCM. *(pages 136–137)*

**6.** 9, 7      **7.** 6, 9      **8.** 5, 11      **9.** 4, 14      **10.** 24, 30

Write a fraction for each letter. *(pages 142–143)*

**11.**    **12.**    **13.**

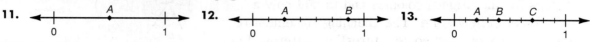

Find the value of *n*. *(pages 144–147)*

**14.** $\frac{1}{7} = 4n$      **15.** $\frac{3}{n} = \frac{36}{48}$      **16.** $\frac{n}{24} = \frac{5}{6}$      **17.** $\frac{3}{8} = \frac{12}{n}$

Write the mixed number as a fraction. *(pages 148–149)*

**18.** $1\frac{2}{3}$      **19.** $2\frac{3}{4}$      **20.** $8\frac{1}{6}$

Write as a whole or mixed number in lowest terms.
*(pages 148–149)*

**21.** $\frac{7}{5}$      **22.** $\frac{21}{7}$      **23.** $8\frac{22}{6}$

Compare. Choose >, <, or =. *(pages 150–151)*

**24.** $\frac{3}{7} \ \blacksquare\ \frac{5}{8}$      **25.** $\frac{2}{9} \ \blacksquare\ \frac{5}{18}$      **26.** $4\frac{7}{9} \ \blacksquare\ 4\frac{9}{12}$      **27.** $3\frac{12}{18} \ \blacksquare\ 3\frac{2}{3}$

Write the fraction as a decimal. *(pages 152–153)*

**28.** $\frac{8}{20}$      **29.** $\frac{35}{40}$      **30.** $\frac{12}{5}$

Write the decimal as a fraction or mixed number in lowest terms.
*(pages 152–153)*

**31.** 0.09      **32.** 0.875      **33.** 2.375

Write as a terminating or repeating decimal. *(pages 154–155)*

**34.** $\frac{3}{5}$      **35.** $\frac{2}{3}$      **36.** $\frac{4}{9}$      **37.** $2\frac{5}{6}$      **38.** $\frac{8}{11}$

Solve. *(pages 158–159)*

**39.** Mount McKinley is 20,320 ft high. Mount Whitney is 14,491 ft.
high. Mount Alverstone is 9 ft higher than Mount Whitney.
What is the difference in height between Mount McKinley and
Mount Alverstone?

# The American Flag

The American flag has changed as new states have been admitted to the Union. At first, both a new star and stripe were added for each new state. In 1818, Congress decided to return to the original 13 stripes for the original colonies and to add only a star for each new state. The changing placement of the stars has created some interesting patterns. For example, from 1912 through 1959, the flag had 48 stars arranged in six rows of eight stars.

Find pictures of the American flag in different years. Draw a picture of one of the flags. Then write a short explanation of why the stars in that flag are arranged in the pattern you see.

At some point in the future, a 51st state may join the United States. How do you think the flag might look then? Try to design a flag with 51 stars so that the arrangement of the stars has an appealing look. Compare your ideas with others in the class.

## RELATIVELY PRIME NUMBERS

Whole numbers greater than 1 are either prime or composite. However, two or more composite numbers can be relatively prime. Numbers are relatively prime if the only factor they have in common is 1. For example, 25 and 36 form a pair of relatively prime numbers. No factor of 25 (1, 5, 25) is also a factor of 36 (1, 2, 3, 4, 6, 9, 12, 18, 36) except for 1. Are 49 and 54 relatively prime?

Work with a partner. Make up some pairs of numbers, some of which are relatively prime. Exchange your list with another team. Try to find the pairs that are relatively prime.

Find the answer.

**1.** 66 is divisible by
  **a.** 3, 5
  **b.** 2, 3, 6
  **c.** 2, 3, 6, 9
  **d.** none of these

**2.** Which of these is a prime number?
  **a.** 57
  **b.** 77
  **c.** 71
  **d.** none of these

**3.** A prime factorization of 54 is
  **a.** $3 \times 3 \times 6$
  **b.** $3 \times 3 \times 2 \times 2$
  **c.** $3 \times 3 \times 3 \times 2$
  **d.** none of these

**4.** A solution to $x - 9 < 4$ is
  **a.** 15
  **b.** 14
  **c.** 13
  **d.** none of these

**5.** A solution to $m + 3 > 12$ is
  **a.** 8
  **b.** 9
  **c.** 10
  **d.** none of these

**6.**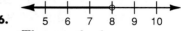
The graph shows
  **a.** $x < 8$
  **b.** $x = 8$
  **c.** $x > 8$
  **d.** none of these

**7.** The GCF of 10 and 36 is
  **a.** 2
  **b.** 6
  **c.** 10
  **d.** none of these

**8.** The LCM of 8 and 12 is
  **a.** 16
  **b.** 24
  **c.** 36
  **d.** none of these

**9.** The LCM of 2, 3, and 9 is
  **a.** 9
  **b.** 12
  **c.** 18
  **d.** none of these

**10.** $4 \times 4 \times 4 \times 4 \times 4 =$
  **a.** $4^5$
  **b.** $5^4$
  **c.** 20
  **d.** none of these

**11.** 5.2 million =
  **a.** 5,000,002
  **b.** 52,000,000
  **c.** 5,002,000
  **d.** none of these

**12.** $(9 \times 10^2) + (7 \times 10^1) =$
  **a.** 97
  **b.** 907
  **c.** 970
  **d.** none of these

**13.** Which number is between 6.904 and 6.980?
  **a.** 6.019
  **b.** 6.915
  **c.** 6.991
  **d.** none of these

**14.** Which number is less than 378.42?
  **a.** 378.39
  **b.** 378.50
  **c.** 379.02
  **d.** none of these

**15.** 0.085 is between which two numbers?
  **a.** 0.081 and 0.084
  **b.** 0.008 and 0.0089
  **c.** 0.80 and 0.90
  **d.** none of these

Remember the strategies and types of problems you've had so far. Solve, if possible.

1. For an auto race around a $2\frac{1}{2}$-mi oval, the cars line up side by side. When the race begins, the fastest car completes 7 laps in the time the slowest car completes 6 laps.

   a. How far is it around the track?

   b. How far has the fastest car traveled when it completes the first 7 laps?

   c. How far will each car have traveled the next time the fastest car and the slowest car meet at the starting line?

2. A mashed potato recipe makes 2 servings for each potato used. If Marietta follows the recipe how many servings can she prepare?

3. If the pattern continues, how many dots will be in the tenth term of this sequence?

4. How many line segments of any length are in the figure?

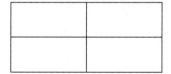

5. A baseball diamond is a square 30 yd on a side. For a football game, the diamond becomes part of the football field, a 100-yd by 53-yd rectangle. In square yards, how much of the football field is not part of the baseball diamond?

6. Randall paid for a $.45 drink with exact change. If he did not have any pennies, how many different combinations of coins could he have used?

7. Twenty-five riders started a 20 mi bicycle race. At 15 mi, 7 riders had dropped out. Everyone else completed the race. How many riders finished?

8. Cornell checked in for a 12:15 P.M. flight that took off 20 minutes late. If he checked in $1\frac{1}{2}$ h before takeoff, what time did he check in?

9. How many times does the digit 2 appear in the page numbers of a 128-page book?

## PRIME TIME RIDDLES

Divide me by 3 and you get a 2-digit prime. Multiply me by 3 and you get a 2-digit composite number. Who am I?

We are 3-digit numbers less than 150. We are products of two 2-digit prime numbers. Who are we?

## QUICK FACTOR

Work with a partner. See who can completely write the prime factorization for each number the fastest. To get you started, one factor is given.

1. 24,840 {factor: 23}

2. 5,814 {factor: 19}

3. 108,108 {factor: 7}

## NUMBER DETECTIVE

In the computer activity *Remainder Clues,* players use clues about divisors and remainders to try to guess a mystery number. This activity for partners will help you decide whether a certain remainder is appropriate for a given divisor and dividend. You do not need a computer.

Players A and B secretly choose numbers from the table. Player A then gives Player B a clue about his or her number. For instance, a clue for 62 could be: "My number divided by 4 has a remainder of 2." Player B would then eliminate any number in the table that doesn't have a remainder of 2 when it is divided by 4.

Player B then gives a clue about his or her number and Player A checks the table. Play continues until either player guesses the other's number. Only one guess is permitted on each turn.

| 56 | 57 | 58 | 59 | 60 | 61 | 62 |
|----|----|----|----|----|----|----|
| 63 | 64 | 65 | 66 | 67 | 68 | 69 |
| 70 | 71 | 72 | 73 | 74 | 75 | 76 |

# FRACTIONS: ADDITION AND SUBTRACTION 6

**DID YOU KNOW . . . ?**
On an average day, Americans watch about 1.5 billion hours of television!

The bar graph shows that America's teen-agers watch a lot of television for relaxation. Yet, watching television is not the most popular relaxation activity.

**How Teen-agers Spend Their Relaxation Time Each Day**

- Talking on the telephone
- Watching television
- Listening to records/tapes
- Reading for pleasure

Activities

0   $\frac{1}{2}$   1   $1\frac{1}{2}$   2   $2\frac{1}{2}$   3   $3\frac{1}{2}$   4

Time in Hours

**USING DATA**
Collect
Organize
Describe
Predict

Ask 20 friends to tell you how much time they spend per day on each of their favorite leisure time activities. Organize the information you collect in a table and make a bar graph similar to the one above.

How does your bar graph compare with the one above?

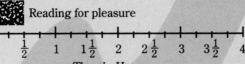

## Exploring Estimating Perimeters

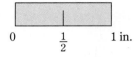

1. The diagram at the right shows the inch (in.) divided into halves, fourths, eighths, and sixteenths. Draw line segments that are $\frac{1}{2}$ in., $\frac{2}{4}$ in., $\frac{4}{8}$ in., and $\frac{8}{16}$ in. in length. What do you notice?

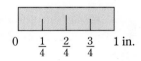

Is the measurement *greater than* or *less than* $\frac{1}{2}$ in.?

**2.** $\frac{1}{4}$ in.    **3.** $\frac{3}{4}$ in.    **4.** $\frac{1}{8}$ in.    **5.** $\frac{7}{8}$ in.

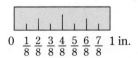

Use the diagram to help you estimate the length.
Is the length closer to *0 in.* or to *1 in.*?

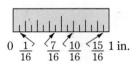

**6.** $\frac{5}{8}$ in.    **7.** $\frac{3}{8}$ in.    **8.** $\frac{2}{16}$ in.    **9.** $\frac{3}{16}$ in.

**10.** $\frac{5}{16}$ in.    **11.** $\frac{7}{16}$ in.    **12.** $\frac{9}{16}$ in.    **13.** $\frac{13}{16}$ in.

14. **IN YOUR WORDS** Is there a way to tell whether a fractional measurement is closer to 0 in. or to 1 in. without using the diagram? If so, describe it.

Use what you discovered in Exercise 14 to tell whether the fraction is closer to *0* or to *1*.

**15.** $\frac{9}{10}$    **16.** $\frac{6}{42}$    **17.** $\frac{8}{11}$    **18.** $\frac{3}{5}$    **19.** $\frac{4}{7}$

20. The perimeter of a plane figure is the distance around the figure. By adding the lengths of the sides, a student found the perimeter of this triangle to be $5\frac{9}{16}$ in. Estimate to see whether the answer is reasonable. Round to the nearest inch.

$1\frac{5}{16}$ in. ⇨ 1 in.

$1\frac{3}{4}$ in. ⇨ 2 in.

$2\frac{1}{2}$ in. ⇨ 3 in. ◁ We round $\frac{1}{2}$ in. to 1 in.

What is an estimate for the perimeter?
Is a perimeter of $5\frac{9}{16}$ in. *reasonable* or *unreasonable*?

$2\frac{1}{2}$ in.    $1\frac{3}{4}$ in.

$1\frac{5}{16}$ in.

Is the given perimeter reasonable? Use estimation to decide.

**21.**

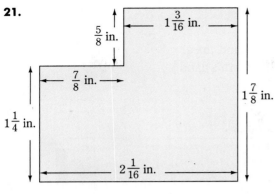

$\frac{5}{8}$ in.

$1\frac{3}{16}$ in.

$\frac{7}{8}$ in.

$1\frac{7}{8}$ in.

$1\frac{1}{4}$ in.

$2\frac{1}{16}$ in.

Perimeter: $7\frac{7}{8}$ in.

**22.**

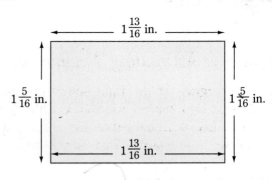

$1\frac{13}{16}$ in.

$1\frac{5}{16}$ in.

$1\frac{5}{16}$ in.

$1\frac{13}{16}$ in.

Perimeter: $9\frac{1}{4}$ in.

Use a ruler to measure. Does the perimeter fall between
the measurements?

**23.**

Between: 5 in. and 7 in.

**24.**

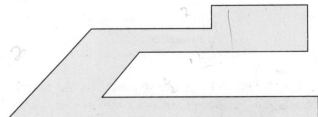

Between: 9 in. and 10 in.

**25.** Does Figure A or Figure B have the greater perimeter?
Use measurements and estimation to decide.

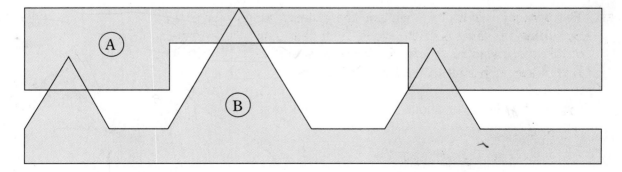

Draw the given figure so that it has a perimeter of between 8 in.
and 10 in. Label the dimensions.

**26.** any triangle      **27.** a square      **28.** any other figure

# Adding and Subtracting Fractions: Same Denominators

The continent of Asia covers about $\frac{3}{10}$ of the world's land area, while Africa covers about $\frac{2}{10}$. What total fraction of Earth's land area do these two continents cover?

Add to find the total area. Why is it easy to add $\frac{3}{10}$ and $\frac{2}{10}$?

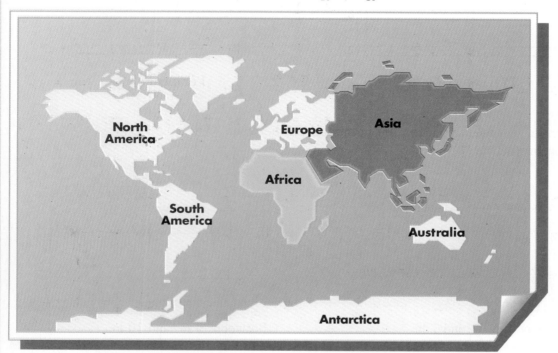

| Add the numerators. Why? | | Give the sum in lowest terms. |
|---|---|---|
| $\frac{3}{10}$ | 3 tenths | |
| $+\ \frac{2}{10}$ | 2 tenths | |
| $\frac{5}{10}$ | 5 tenths | $\frac{5}{10} = \frac{1}{2}$ |

The two continents cover about $\frac{1}{2}$ of Earth's land area.

Other examples:

$$4\frac{6}{12}$$
$$+\ \frac{7}{12}$$
$$4\frac{13}{12} = 5\frac{1}{12}$$

$$\frac{7}{9}$$
$$-\ \frac{1}{9}$$
$$\frac{6}{9} = \frac{2}{3}$$

$$8\frac{4}{5}$$
$$-\ 1\frac{2}{5}$$
$$7\frac{2}{5}$$

Add or subtract. Give the answer in lowest terms.

**1.** $\frac{3}{5} + \frac{1}{5}$   **2.** $\frac{5}{6} - \frac{1}{6}$   **3.** $5\frac{2}{8} + 4\frac{5}{8}$   **4.** $8\frac{7}{9} - 4\frac{4}{9}$   **5.** $4\frac{3}{8} + 9\frac{7}{8}$

**PRACTICE**

Add or subtract. Give the answer in lowest terms.

**6.** $\frac{1}{5} + \frac{1}{5}$   **7.** $\frac{3}{8} + \frac{2}{8}$   **8.** $\frac{4}{6} - \frac{1}{6}$   **9.** $\frac{3}{4} + \frac{3}{4}$   **10.** $\frac{7}{8} - \frac{5}{8}$

**11.** $\frac{4}{5} - \frac{2}{5}$   **12.** $\frac{2}{3} + \frac{2}{3}$   **13.** $\frac{3}{5} + \frac{3}{5}$   **14.** $\frac{7}{8} + \frac{1}{8}$   **15.** $\frac{5}{12} - \frac{1}{12}$

**16.** $2\frac{2}{6} + 1\frac{5}{6}$   **17.** $2\frac{3}{7} - 1\frac{1}{7}$   **18.** $4\frac{2}{3} + 1\frac{2}{3}$   **19.** $14\frac{2}{5} - 9\frac{1}{5}$   **20.** $16\frac{2}{8} + 4\frac{7}{8}$

**21.** $5\frac{8}{9} - 3\frac{4}{9}$   **22.** $4\frac{6}{13} + 2\frac{5}{13}$   **23.** $3\frac{7}{11} - \frac{5}{11}$   **24.** $3\frac{1}{4} + 3\frac{1}{4}$   **25.** $11\frac{6}{10} - 9\frac{4}{10}$

**MIXED REVIEW**   Compute.

**26.** $3.4 \times 2$   **27.** $5.47 \times 10$   **28.** $1\frac{3}{4} - \frac{1}{4}$   **29.** $29 + 2^2$

**30.** $3.64 \div 1.4$   **31.** $\frac{5}{6} + 1\frac{1}{6}$   **32.** $18 \div 0.09$   **33.** $57 - 4^2$

**MENTAL MATH**   Solve for $n$ mentally.

**34.** $\frac{7}{8} - n = \frac{5}{8}$   **35.** $\frac{5}{9} + n = \frac{8}{9}$   **36.** $4\frac{2}{3} - n = 1\frac{1}{3}$   **37.** $\frac{2}{7} + \frac{4}{7} + n = 1\frac{2}{7}$

**PROBLEM SOLVING**

 Choose paper and pencil or calculator to solve.

**38.** Match the continent to the region in the circle graph.

**39.** Which is the largest continent?

**40.** What is the sum of all the fractions for the continents? What should it be? Give a possible reason for the difference.

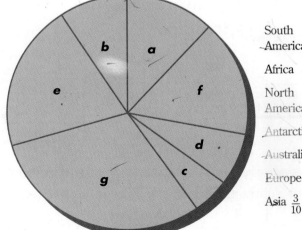

**The Seven Continents as Fractions of the World's Land Area**

South America $\frac{3}{25}$

Africa $\frac{1}{5}$

North America $\frac{4}{25}$

Antarctica $\frac{9}{100}$

Australia $\frac{1}{20}$

Europe $\frac{7}{100}$

Asia $\frac{3}{10}$

1 Measure    $\frac{1}{4}$ ⇑ note    $\frac{1}{8}$ ⇑ note    $\frac{1}{2}$ ⇑ note    1 whole note ⇑

## Adding and Subtracting Fractions: Denominators That Are Multiples

From *Old Folks at Home*, by Stephen Foster. Also known as *Swanee River*.

The different types of notes tell you how long to hold a note as you play the music. Find one note in the music above that is held for the same time as two $\frac{1}{8}$ notes (♪) and one $\frac{1}{4}$ (♩) note.

Add $\frac{1}{8} + \frac{1}{8} + \frac{1}{4}$ to solve this problem.

To add fractions with different denominators, you can make a MATH CONNECTION.

- You know how to find equivalent fractions.
- You know how to add fractions with the same denominator.

What is the lowest common denominator (LCD) of 8 and 4?

$$\frac{1}{8} = \frac{1}{8}$$
$$\frac{1}{8} = \frac{1}{8}$$
$$+ \frac{1}{4} = + \frac{2}{8}$$
$$\frac{4}{8} = \frac{1}{2} \quad \longleftarrow \boxed{\text{lowest terms}}$$

One half note (♩) is held for the same time.

Stephen Foster, great American songwriter, wrote many songs about the beauty of the South.

Other examples:

$$\boxed{\text{What is the LCD of 8 and 24?}} \longrightarrow$$

$$\frac{15}{24} = \frac{15}{24}$$
$$- \frac{3}{8} = - \frac{9}{24}$$
$$\frac{6}{24} = \frac{1}{4} \quad \longleftarrow \boxed{\text{lowest terms}}$$

$$\frac{3}{4} = \frac{15}{20}$$
$$+ \frac{17}{20} = + \frac{17}{20}$$
$$\frac{32}{20} = 1\frac{3}{5}$$

$$\longleftarrow \boxed{\text{What is the LCD of 4 and 20?}}$$

---

## GUIDED PRACTICE

Add or subtract. Give the answer in lowest terms.

1. $\frac{3}{4} - \frac{1}{2}$     2. $\frac{7}{10} + \frac{2}{5}$     3. $\frac{1}{4} + \frac{3}{8}$     4. $\frac{5}{12} - \frac{1}{6}$     5. $\frac{8}{9} + \frac{5}{18}$

MATH AND MUSIC

**PRACTICE**

Add or subtract. Give the answer in lowest terms.

**6.** $\dfrac{1}{6} + \dfrac{1}{2}$  **7.** $\dfrac{1}{4} + \dfrac{7}{12}$  **8.** $\dfrac{5}{6} - \dfrac{1}{2}$  **9.** $\dfrac{2}{3} + \dfrac{13}{15}$  **10.** $\dfrac{1}{2} - \dfrac{2}{4}$

**11.** $\dfrac{3}{5} - \dfrac{11}{30}$  **12.** $\dfrac{11}{27} + \dfrac{4}{9}$  **13.** $\dfrac{4}{5} - \dfrac{3}{25}$  **14.** $\dfrac{5}{6} - \dfrac{7}{36}$  **15.** $\dfrac{15}{16} + \dfrac{1}{32}$

**16.** $\dfrac{4}{9} + \dfrac{1}{3}$  **17.** $\dfrac{4}{5} + \dfrac{3}{25}$  **18.** $\dfrac{5}{6} - \dfrac{7}{24}$  **19.** $\dfrac{13}{27} + \dfrac{5}{9}$  **20.** $\dfrac{3}{4} - \dfrac{5}{12}$

**21.** $\dfrac{19}{25} - \dfrac{9}{50}$  **22.** $\dfrac{3}{4} + \dfrac{3}{8}$  **23.** $\dfrac{6}{9} - \dfrac{6}{18}$  **24.** $\dfrac{11}{12} + \dfrac{20}{24}$  **25.** $\dfrac{6}{7} - \dfrac{3}{14}$

**26.** $\dfrac{1}{2} + \dfrac{3}{4} + \dfrac{1}{2}$  **27.** $\dfrac{4}{5} - \dfrac{4}{10} + \dfrac{2}{5}$  **28.** $\dfrac{3}{4} + \dfrac{1}{2} - \dfrac{3}{8}$  **29.** $\dfrac{5}{6} + \dfrac{1}{2} - \dfrac{1}{3}$

**MIXED REVIEW**  Compute. Give the answer in lowest terms if necessary.

**30.** $5.7 + 0.45$  **31.** $4\dfrac{5}{6} - \dfrac{1}{6}$  **32.** $\dfrac{3}{8} + \dfrac{3}{4}$  **33.** $8.51 - 7$

**34.** $\dfrac{11}{12} - \dfrac{1}{2}$  **35.** $6 - 2.3$  **36.** $\dfrac{5}{9} + 8\dfrac{4}{9}$  **37.** $0.6 + 0.042$

Complete the function table. Give the answer in lowest terms.

**38.**

| $a$ | $\dfrac{1}{8}$ | $\dfrac{2}{8}$ | $\dfrac{3}{8}$ | $\dfrac{4}{8}$ | $\dfrac{5}{8}$ |
|---|---|---|---|---|---|
| $a + \dfrac{1}{8}$ | ? | ? | ? | ? | ? |

**39.**

| $b$ | $\dfrac{9}{10}$ | $\dfrac{8}{10}$ | $\dfrac{7}{10}$ | $\dfrac{6}{10}$ | $\dfrac{5}{10}$ |
|---|---|---|---|---|---|
| $b - \dfrac{1}{10}$ | ? | ? | ? | ? | ? |

**MENTAL MATH**  Solve for $n$ mentally.

**40.** $\dfrac{2}{7} + n = 1$  **41.** $n - \dfrac{2}{3} = \dfrac{2}{3}$  **42.** $\dfrac{19}{25} - n = 0$

**PROBLEM SOLVING**

**CHOOSE**  Use the music for *Swanee River* on page 174.
Choose mental math or paper and pencil to solve.

**43.** For each measure of the music for *Swanee River* shown, add the fractions that represent each kind of note in the measure. What is the sum in each case?

**44.** The *Swanee River* music requires that a whole note ( $\circ$ ) gets four beats.
 **a.** How many beats does a $\dfrac{1}{2}$ note get? a $\dfrac{1}{4}$ note? an $\dfrac{1}{8}$ note?
 **b.** How many beats are there in each measure of *Swanee River*?

CHAPTER 6  **175**

## Adding and Subtracting Fractions: Any Denominators

A student surveying colleges in the United States used this circle graph to get information on degrees earned at historically African American institutions of higher learning in a past year. What fraction of the enrolled students earned either a bachelor's or a master's degree?

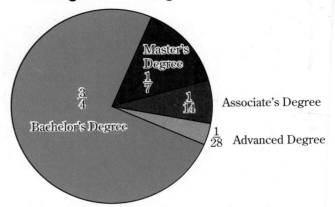

**Degrees Earned at Historically African American Institutions of Higher Learning**

Master's Degree $\frac{1}{7}$

$\frac{3}{4}$ Bachelor's Degree

$\frac{1}{14}$ Associate's Degree

$\frac{1}{28}$ Advanced Degree

Since you know how to write equivalent fractions and how to add fractions with the same denominator, you can make a MATH CONNECTION to add $\frac{3}{4} + \frac{1}{7}$.

What is the LCD of 4 and 7?

$$
\begin{array}{rcl}
\frac{3}{4} & = & \frac{21}{28} \\
+\frac{1}{7} & = & +\frac{4}{28} \\
\hline
& & \frac{25}{28}
\end{array}
$$

Almost all of the students, or $\frac{25}{28}$, received these two degrees.

**CRITICAL THINKING**  Which degree did twice as many students receive as the associate degree?

Another example:

What is the LCD of 8 and 9?

$$
\begin{array}{rcl}
\frac{6}{8} & = & \frac{54}{72} \\
-\frac{5}{9} & = & -\frac{40}{72} \\
\hline
& & \frac{14}{72} = \frac{7}{36}
\end{array}
$$

lowest terms

COLLIS P. HUNTINGTON MEMORIAL BUILDING

**Tuskegee Institute, Tuskegee, Alabama**

---

## GUIDED PRACTICE

Add or subtract. Give the answer in lowest terms.

**1.** $\frac{3}{8} - \frac{1}{4}$

**2.** $\frac{2}{5} + \frac{2}{6}$

**3.** $\frac{7}{8} - \frac{2}{3}$

**4.** $\frac{1}{6} + \frac{5}{8}$

**5.** $\frac{4}{6} - \frac{1}{8}$

Find the sum or the difference in lowest terms.

**6.** $\dfrac{5}{9} + \dfrac{1}{4}$      **7.** $\dfrac{7}{8} - \dfrac{3}{5}$      **8.** $\dfrac{2}{6} + \dfrac{1}{3}$      **9.** $\dfrac{4}{8} + \dfrac{4}{6}$      **10.** $\dfrac{6}{9} + \dfrac{1}{3}$

**11.** $\dfrac{2}{3} - \dfrac{2}{6}$      **12.** $\dfrac{8}{10} - \dfrac{3}{4}$      **13.** $\dfrac{5}{6} - \dfrac{7}{9}$      **14.** $\dfrac{10}{12} + \dfrac{3}{18}$      **15.** $\dfrac{1}{8} + \dfrac{1}{5}$

**16.** $\dfrac{3}{10} + \dfrac{4}{15}$      **17.** $\dfrac{6}{9} - \dfrac{3}{15}$      **18.** $\dfrac{6}{11} - \dfrac{2}{5}$      **19.** $\dfrac{4}{5} - \dfrac{17}{24}$      **20.** $\dfrac{7}{12} + \dfrac{4}{9}$

**21.** $\dfrac{7}{8} - \dfrac{3}{4}$      **22.** $\dfrac{6}{7} - \dfrac{5}{9}$      **23.** $\dfrac{15}{20} + \dfrac{1}{5}$      **24.** $\dfrac{6}{8} + \dfrac{2}{7}$      **25.** $\dfrac{7}{16} - \dfrac{2}{12}$

**MIXED REVIEW**    Compute.

**26.** $5\dfrac{2}{6} + 8\dfrac{3}{6}$      **27.** $3.524 \times 1.8$      **28.** $\dfrac{4}{5} + \dfrac{5}{6}$      **29.** $6.5 \div 0.0013$

**30.** $0.08 + 0.4$      **31.** $1\dfrac{10}{12} - \dfrac{3}{12}$      **32.** $0.2 - 0.06$      **33.** $\dfrac{4}{5} - \dfrac{4}{15}$

**MENTAL MATH**    Compute mentally.

**34.** $\dfrac{2}{3} + \dfrac{1}{6} + \dfrac{1}{3}$      **35.** $\dfrac{5}{8} + \dfrac{1}{2} + \dfrac{3}{8}$      **36.** $\dfrac{7}{8} + \dfrac{1}{8} - \dfrac{1}{4}$

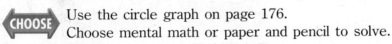 Use the circle graph on page 176.
Choose mental math or paper and pencil to solve.

**37.** What fraction of the students received a degree other than the associate degree?

**38.** What fraction of the students earned a master's or an advanced degree?

**39.** Ask 12 classmates which academic degree they might choose to work toward in college. Write a fraction to show how many of the 12 classmates made each choice.

## Critical Thinking

Work with a partner.
What is the total number of different ways possible to combine one class with one after school activity?

| Class | After School Activity |
|---|---|
| Mathematics | Basketball Team |
| English | Glee Club |
| Home Economics | Debating Team |
| Social Studies | Drama Club |

## Adding and Subtracting Mixed Numbers

American Al Oerter won the gold medal in the discus throw in four straight Olympic games, an amazing feat.

Use the bar graph to find out how much farther Oerter threw the discus in the 1968 Olympics than in the 1964 Olympics.

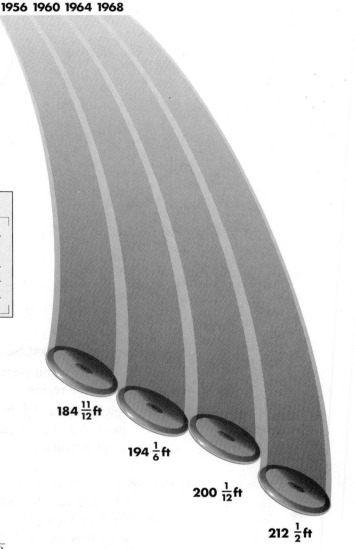

1956  1960  1964  1968

$184\frac{11}{12}$ ft

$194\frac{1}{6}$ ft

$200\frac{1}{12}$ ft

$212\frac{1}{2}$ ft

| Write equivalent fractions. | Subtract. |
|---|---|
| $212\frac{1}{2} = \quad 212\frac{6}{12}$ | $212\frac{6}{12}$ |
| $-\ 200\frac{1}{12} = -\ 200\frac{1}{12}$ | $-\ 200\frac{1}{12}$ |
| | $12\frac{5}{12}$ |

Al Oerter threw the discus $12\frac{5}{12}$ ft farther in 1968 than in 1964.

**THINK ALOUD** What $12\frac{5}{12}$ ft is in feet and inches?

Another example:

$$2\frac{1}{3} = \quad 2\frac{4}{12}$$

What is the LCD of 3 and 4?

$$+\ 4\frac{3}{4} = +\ 4\frac{9}{12}$$

$$6\frac{13}{12} = 7\frac{1}{12}$$

═══ **GUIDED PRACTICE** ═══

Give the sum or difference in lowest terms.

**1.** $3\frac{1}{2} + 5\frac{1}{3}$     **2.** $4\frac{2}{3} + 5\frac{1}{6}$     **3.** $5\frac{3}{8} - 2\frac{1}{4}$     **4.** $8\frac{5}{6} - 2\frac{1}{4}$

═══ **PRACTICE** ═══

Give the sum or difference in lowest terms.

**5.** $1\frac{1}{2} + 1\frac{1}{4}$     **6.** $5\frac{2}{3} + 4\frac{1}{9}$     **7.** $7\frac{3}{4} - 7\frac{1}{2}$     **8.** $6\frac{1}{5} - 1\frac{1}{10}$

**9.** $3\frac{2}{5} + 4\frac{5}{6}$     **10.** $5\frac{3}{8} + 1\frac{1}{4}$     **11.** $12\frac{1}{3} - 3\frac{1}{4}$     **12.** $4\frac{7}{8} - 1\frac{1}{2}$

**13.** $7\frac{1}{3} + 3\frac{1}{6}$      **14.** $8\frac{3}{4} - 1\frac{1}{2}$      **15.** $4\frac{1}{5} + 3\frac{1}{3}$      **16.** $4\frac{1}{3} - 4\frac{1}{8}$

**17.** $5\frac{1}{4} - 1\frac{1}{6}$      **18.** $4\frac{5}{6} - \frac{1}{8}$      **19.** $7\frac{5}{8} + 2\frac{1}{10}$      **20.** $2\frac{3}{5} + 4\frac{4}{10}$

**21.** $6\frac{3}{4} + 3\frac{5}{6}$      **22.** $5\frac{5}{12} - 4\frac{1}{3}$      **23.** $6\frac{5}{12} + \frac{7}{18}$      **24.** $12\frac{5}{9} - 6\frac{3}{8}$

**25.** $3\frac{1}{4} + 4\frac{1}{4} + 6\frac{1}{8}$      **26.** $5\frac{3}{8} + \frac{1}{16} + 3\frac{3}{4}$      **27.** $7\frac{2}{3} + \left(3\frac{3}{5} - 1\frac{1}{3}\right)$

**MIXED REVIEW**   Compute.

**28.** $4\frac{2}{9} + 3\frac{2}{6}$      **29.** $14.8 - 6.5$      **30.** $6\frac{4}{5} - 2\frac{6}{10}$      **31.** $2.7 \div 0.3$

**32.** $5\frac{8}{21} - 4\frac{2}{7}$      **33.** $22.1 + 16.3$      **34.** $50.4 \div 6.3$      **35.** $4.2 \times 3.1$

Evaluate. Use $a = 2\frac{1}{2}$, $b = 3\frac{7}{8}$, $c = \frac{1}{5}$.

**36.** $3\frac{2}{3} + a + 6\frac{1}{8}$      **37.** $6\frac{7}{8} + a - c$      **38.** $(b - a) - c$

---

**PROBLEM SOLVING**

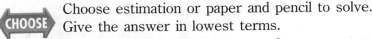

Choose estimation or paper and pencil to solve.
Give the answer in lowest terms.

**39.** The women's discus weighs about $2\frac{3}{16}$ lb. The men's discus weighs twice this amount. About what is the weight of a men's discus?

**40.** In the 1988 Olympics, the winning throw in the men's discus was $225\frac{3}{4}$ ft. The best women's discus throw in that Olympics was $11\frac{5}{12}$ ft farther. What was that distance?

---

**Mental Math** 🧩

You can count on to subtract mentally.

$1 - \frac{3}{5}$

Start with $\frac{3}{5}$. Count on by $\frac{1}{5}$'s to 1.

$1 - \frac{3}{5} = \frac{2}{5}$

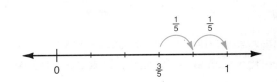

Count on to subtract mentally.

**1.** $1 - \frac{4}{5}$      **2.** $2 - \frac{2}{3}$      **3.** $3 - \frac{1}{2}$      **4.** $7 - \frac{7}{9}$      **5.** $2 - \frac{5}{8}$

# Renaming Before Subtracting

The osprey uses its large wings to dive from great heights to catch fish. The wingspan of the osprey averages $4\frac{1}{2}$ ft. The osprey's body length averages only $1\frac{5}{6}$ ft.

How much longer is the osprey's average wingspan than its average body length?

The diagram represents the problem.

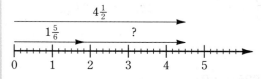

| Write equivalent fractions. What is the LCD of 2 and 6? | Rename. | Subtract. |
|---|---|---|
| $4\frac{1}{2} = \quad 4\frac{3}{6}$  $-1\frac{5}{6} = -1\frac{5}{6}$ | $4\frac{3}{6} = 3\frac{6}{6} + \frac{3}{6}$  $= 3\frac{9}{6}$ | $3\frac{9}{6}$  $-1\frac{5}{6}$  $2\frac{4}{6} = 2\frac{2}{3}$ |

*Why can't we subtract?*

**THINK ALOUD** How would you estimate the difference between $4\frac{1}{2}$ and $1\frac{5}{6}$?

Another example:

| Rename 6 as $5\frac{4}{4}$. | Subtract. |
|---|---|
| $6$  $-2\frac{1}{4}$ | $5\frac{4}{4}$  $-2\frac{1}{4}$  $3\frac{3}{4}$ |

GUIDED PRACTICE

Find the value of $n$.

**1.** $5\frac{1}{3} = 4\frac{n}{3}$  **2.** $7\frac{2}{5} = 6\frac{n}{5}$  **3.** $15\frac{3}{8} = 14\frac{11}{n}$  **4.** $7\frac{1}{4} = 6\frac{n}{4}$  **5.** $8\frac{5}{8} = 7\frac{13}{n}$

Give the answer in lowest terms.

**6.** $5\frac{1}{3} - 1\frac{2}{3}$  **7.** $7\frac{2}{5} - 2\frac{4}{5}$  **8.** $15\frac{3}{8} - 5\frac{3}{4}$  **9.** $9\frac{1}{4} - 1\frac{2}{3}$

Subtract. Give your answer in lowest terms.

**10.** $9\frac{2}{5} - 2\frac{4}{5}$      **11.** $6\frac{3}{8} - 2\frac{7}{8}$      **12.** $9\frac{5}{12} - 8\frac{9}{12}$      **13.** $15\frac{5}{9} - 12\frac{7}{9}$

**14.** $45\frac{7}{12} - 9\frac{11}{12}$      **15.** $40 - 7\frac{5}{12}$      **16.** $15 - 8\frac{7}{9}$      **17.** $10\frac{4}{6} - 4\frac{5}{6}$

**18.** $34\frac{5}{8} - \frac{7}{8}$      **19.** $30\frac{3}{9} - 19\frac{7}{9}$      **20.** $7\frac{1}{6} - 2\frac{5}{12}$      **21.** $5\frac{1}{8} - 1\frac{3}{4}$

**22.** $50\frac{7}{12} - 18\frac{15}{24}$      **23.** $12 - 10\frac{6}{9}$      **24.** $7\frac{4}{5} - 2\frac{9}{10}$      **25.** $5\frac{1}{4} - 2\frac{4}{6}$

**26.** $17 - 6\frac{5}{9}$      **27.** $9\frac{2}{9} - 8\frac{5}{8}$      **28.** $6\frac{2}{4} - 1\frac{4}{5}$      **29.** $40 - 21\frac{9}{10}$

**MIXED REVIEW** Compute.

**30.** $391 \times 4.57$      **31.** $2\frac{5}{8} + \frac{3}{4}$      **32.** $9,825 + 697$      **33.** $3\frac{1}{6} - 2\frac{1}{2}$

**34.** $\frac{2}{9} + \frac{5}{9} + \frac{1}{2}$      **35.** $3,528 \div 28$      **36.** $48 - 6\frac{1}{2}$      **37.** $0.179 - 0.099$

**MENTAL MATH** Solve for *n* mentally.

**38.** $8\frac{4}{5} - n = 3\frac{2}{5}$      **39.** $13\frac{2}{3} - n = 4\frac{1}{3}$      **40.** $24\frac{3}{4} - n = 14\frac{1}{2}$

 Choose estimation or paper and pencil to solve. Use the graph below.

**41.** California condors are the largest flying bird in the United States. What is the difference between the condor's average body length and wingspan?

**42.** What is the difference between the average wingspan of the condor and the peregrine falcon?

**43.** Estimate the number of times longer the bald eagle's average wingspan is than its body length.

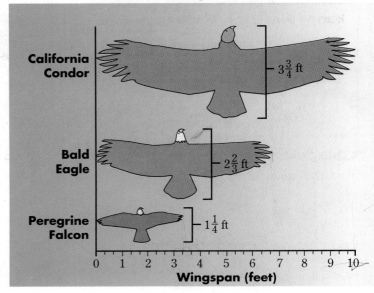

**Average Body Length and Wingspan of Some Endangered Birds**

California Condor — $3\frac{3}{4}$ ft

Bald Eagle — $2\frac{2}{3}$ ft

Peregrine Falcon — $1\frac{1}{4}$ ft

Wingspan (feet)

## LANGUAGE & VOCABULARY

Explain in your own words how each pair of activities is similar and how each pair is different.

1. Adding fractions with the same denominators and adding fractions with different denominators.

2. Finding the LCM of two numbers and finding the LCD of two fractions.

3. Subtracting fractions and subtracting mixed numbers.

4. Subtracting mixed numbers without renaming and subtracting mixed numbers with renaming.

## QUICK QUIZ

Find the sum or difference in lowest terms. *(pages 172–181)*

1. $\frac{3}{5} + \frac{4}{5}$   2. $12\frac{5}{6} - 7\frac{3}{6}$   3. $\frac{7}{10} - \frac{1}{2}$

4. $\frac{3}{9} + \frac{7}{18}$   5. $\frac{2}{3} + \frac{3}{5}$   6. $\frac{11}{12} - \frac{3}{10}$

7. $4\frac{2}{7} + 5\frac{1}{3}$   8. $12\frac{1}{5} - 3\frac{2}{4}$   9. $18 - 9\frac{3}{8}$

Solve. *(pages 178–179)*

10. A 5-mi race consists of 20 laps around a $\frac{1}{4}$-mi track.

   a. How far will a runner have gone when she completes 20 laps?

   b. Jackie has run $3\frac{1}{4}$ mi. How can you find out how many miles she must run to complete the race?

   c. How far must Jackie run to complete the race?

Write the answers in your learning log.

1. When will the common denominator for an addition or a subtraction problem be different than the original denominators?

2. Your friend has trouble finding the LCD when adding fractions. You want to help him. What would you tell him to check first?

MATH AMERICA

**DID YOU KNOW . . . ?** Old Faithful, a geyser in Yellowstone National Park, erupts every 73 min. If it erupted at 8:00 A.M., during what classes would it erupt for the rest of your school day?

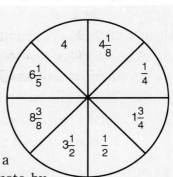

BONUS

a. $\blacksquare \frac{\blacksquare}{\blacksquare} + \blacksquare \frac{\blacksquare}{\blacksquare} = 7\frac{5}{8}$

b. $\blacksquare - \blacksquare \frac{\blacksquare}{\blacksquare} = 2\frac{1}{4}$

c. $\blacksquare \frac{\blacksquare}{\blacksquare} + \frac{\blacksquare}{\blacksquare} - \frac{\blacksquare}{\blacksquare} = 6\frac{9}{20}$

d. $\blacksquare \frac{\blacksquare}{\blacksquare} - \frac{\blacksquare}{\blacksquare} = 7\frac{7}{8}$

Use the fractions or mixed numbers in the circle. Work with a partner. Use estimation to fill in the boxes. Check your estimate by using a calculator.

Circle values: $4$, $4\frac{1}{8}$, $\frac{1}{4}$, $1\frac{3}{4}$, $\frac{1}{2}$, $3\frac{1}{2}$, $8\frac{3}{8}$, $6\frac{1}{5}$

# *Problem Solving Strategy: Guess and Check*

At the amusement park, there are 94 cups (c) of water in four jars. You are told each jar contains $2\frac{1}{3}$ more cups than the jar to its left. You can win a prize by guessing the correct number of cups in jar 1.

Ask yourself questions to be sure you understand the problem.

- How many jars in all are there?
- How does the number of cups in each jar compare to the number of cups in the jar to its right?

Often the best way to solve a problem is to guess and check. List your guesses in a table.

| | Jar 1 | Jar 2 | Jar 3 | Jar 4 | Total |
|---|---|---|---|---|---|
| 1st Guess: $8\frac{1}{3}$ | $8\frac{1}{3}$ | $10\frac{2}{3}$ | 13 | $15\frac{1}{3}$ | $47\frac{1}{3}$ |
| 2nd Guess: 25 | 25 | ? | ? | ? | ? |

← Should the next guess be a higher number or a lower number? Should it be a mixed number?

← How many cups would be in jars 2, 3, and 4? Why was 25 a good guess? Why was it bad? How can you make the next guess better?

Now make a new guess and solve the problem.
Be sure your answer is reasonable.

- Do the numbers add up to 94?
- Does each jar contain $2\frac{1}{3}$ more cups than the one to its left?

========= **GUIDED PRACTICE** =========

Make a table. Use the guess and check strategy to solve.

1.  Suppose there are 100 c of water in five jars. Each jar contains $2\frac{1}{2}$ more cups of water than the jar to its left.

    a.  How many jars are there?

    b.  Which jar contains the most water?

    c.  How many cups of water are there in jar 1?

2.  Now suppose there are 108 c of water in four jars. Each jar contains $2\frac{2}{3}$ fewer cups of water than the jar to its left. How many cups of water are there in jar 4?

### Four Aces Amusement Park

Admission:
Adults .................... $8.00
Children (under 12) ...... $6.50
Children (under 5) ....... $4.75

All rides are free once you get in.

Use the guess and check strategy to solve.

3. The 4 members of the Lee family pay a total of $24 for admission to the park. How many adults, children under 12, and children under 5 are in the Lee family?

4. Enrique, Mario, Juana, Rita, and Rosa Sanchez paid a total of $32.50 to enter the park. How many tickets were purchased at each price?

5. Anders, Dag, Hilde, Inga, and Berta Olsen pay a total of $34 for admission to the park. How many of the five members of the Olsen family are adults? are children under 12? are children under 5?

6. Jay bought 2 of one type of souvenir and 3 of another for a total of $19. If one type of souvenir cost a half dollar more than the other, what was the price of each?

**PROBLEM SOLVING**

**CHOOSE** Choose a strategy to solve.

7. Brigid counted 24 out-of-state license plates in the amusement-park parking lot. There were 10 from Alabama, 5 from Florida, and 3 from Tennessee. What fractional part of the out-of-state plates were not from Alabama, Florida, or Tennessee?

8. **CRITICAL THINKING** In which state do you think the park was located? Defend your choice.

9. Andrea bought 2 cats. She exchanged each cat for 2 dogs. Each dog was exchanged for 2 horses. Each horse was exchanged for 2 fish. If this pattern continued, how many pets would Andrea have after six exchanges?

10. When Greg got home from the park, he had five coins of four different types totaling $1. What coins and how many of each did he have?

## Exploring Measurement

Measuring is comparing. The earliest humans did not need to make accurate comparisons. They could tell by looking whether a cave was large enough for a family to live in.

**1.** Describe a situation in which you measure this way today.

Later on, people began to use different units of measure.

- The inch we use today came from the width of a thumb.
- A foot was the length of a foot.
- A yard was the distance from the nose to the tip of the middle finger of the outstretched arm.

**2.** Measure the length and the width of your math book using thumb widths.

**3.** About how many of your feet equal 1 yd? Measure by using the nonstandard foot and yard above.

**4.** Measure the length of your classroom in your foot lengths.

**5.** Measure the length of your classroom blackboard in the nonstandard yard.

**6. IN YOUR WORDS** Compare your measurements with those of your classmates. What problems are caused by these nonstandard units of measure?

Our system of measuring length has **standard units** that are always the same. The smallest unit is the inch. Any measurement requiring more precision must be done using fractional parts of an inch.

Use a ruler to measure the following to the nearest eighth of an inch.

**7.** the length of your shoe

**8.** the length of a desk top

**9.** the width of a pencil

**10.** the length of this phrase

11. **CRITICAL THINKING** How would you change our measurement system to make it easier to use?

The earliest known standard unit was the **cubit.** It was the distance from the tip of the middle finger to the elbow, and it varied in length in different parts of the ancient world. The **royal cubit,** used by the Egyptians in building the pyramids, was $20\frac{1}{2}$ in.

12. Use a ruler to measure the cubit of your arm and a partner's arm to the nearest eighth of an inch.

13. How do the lengths of each of your cubits compare to the $20\frac{1}{2}$ in.?

Some ancient units were smaller than the cubit.

the **span**          the **palm**          the **digit**

14. Measure the span, the palm, and the digit of your hand and a partner's hand to the nearest eighth of an inch.

**ESTIMATE** Use the span, palm, and digit measurements from Exercise 14 to estimate each length in inches. Do not use paper and pencil.

15. the length of a calculator

16. the length of a notebook

17. the length of the word "length"

18. the height of your chair

19. the width of a quarter

20. the height of the classroom door

21. **IN YOUR WORDS** Describe how you can use your span to estimate the height of the classroom ceiling.

22. **CREATE YOUR OWN** Write a paragraph describing your bedroom. Use only cubits, spans, palms, and digits when you describe your bedroom and the size of the objects in it.

# Customary Units: Length

Several customary units of length are shown in the illustration. The chart below shows how they are related.

> 12 inches (in.) = 1 foot (ft)
> 36 in. = 1 yard (yd)
> 3 ft = 1 yd
> 5,280 ft = 1 mile (mi)

Why do we multiply by 12 to change from feet to inches?

4 ft = ▓ in.

> Is the number of inches *more* or *less* than 4?
> 4 ft = 48 in.

Why do we divide by 3 to change from feet to yards?

15 ft = ▓ yd

> Is the number of yards *more* or *less* than 15?
> 15 ft = 5 yd

About one ft

About one in.

About one yd

Notice how you rename as you add and subtract measures.

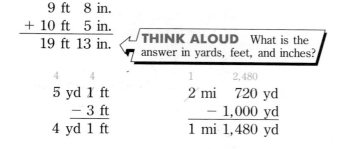

```
    9 ft   8 in.
+ 10 ft   5 in.
  19 ft  13 in.
```

> **THINK ALOUD** What is the answer in yards, feet, and inches?

```
   4     4              1      2,480
  5 yd 1 ft          2 mi   720 yd
    − 3 ft             − 1,000 yd
  4 yd 1 ft          1 mi 1,480 yd
```

---

## GUIDED PRACTICE

Copy and complete.

**1.** 9 yd = ▓ in.

**2.** 4 yd = ▓ ft

**3.** 360 in. = ▓ yd

**4.** 2 mi = ▓ ft

**5.** 33 ft = ▓ yd

**6.** 33 ft = ▓ in.

**7. NUMBER SENSE** What is an object whose height you would measure in inches? in feet? in yards?

**8. THINK ALOUD** Explain how you would find the difference between 1 mi and 100 yd.

Copy and complete.

**9.** 12 ft = ▦ in.          **10.** 54 ft = ▦ yd          **11.** 18 ft = ▦ in.

**12.** 3 mi = ▦ ft          **13.** 3 yd = ▦ in.          **14.** 10 yd = ▦ in.

**15.** 4 yd = ▦ ft 12 in.          **16.** 5 ft = 2 ft ▦ in.          **17.** 4 yd = ▦ yd 9 ft

**18.** 6 yd = ▦ ft          **19.** 9 ft = ▦ in.          **20.** 2 yd 15 in. = ▦ in.

**NUMBER SENSE**  Choose the best estimate.

**21.** the depth of a fish pond
   **a.** 48 yd   **b.** 48 ft   **c.** 48 in.

**22.** the distance around a garage
   **a.** 3 ft   **b.** 30 ft   **c.** 3 mi

**23.** the height of a stop sign
   **a.** 8 ft   **b.** 48 ft   **c.** $\frac{1}{4}$ mi

**24.** the length of a toothbrush
   **a.** $\frac{1}{2}$ in.   **b.** 20 in.   **c.** $\frac{1}{2}$ ft

**MIXED REVIEW**  Compare. Choose >, <, or =.

**25.** 9 ft ▦ 3 yd          **26.** 2 mi ▦ 10,400 ft          **27.** 33 yd ▦ 100 ft

Compute.

**28.**    5 ft 8 in.
        + 8 ft 9 in.

**29.**   10 ft  4 in.
        −  6 ft 11 in.

**30.**    2 mi 960 yd
        + 8 mi 900 yd

**31.**    3 yd 2 ft 8 in.
        − 1 yd 2 ft 9 in.

**CHOOSE** ⟩  Use the diagram. Choose paper and pencil or calculator to solve.

**32.** The perimeter of Boston Common is about 2,182 yd. About how long, in yards, is the side for which no dimension is given?

**33.** If you walked the perimeter of Boston Common, how many miles would you walk?

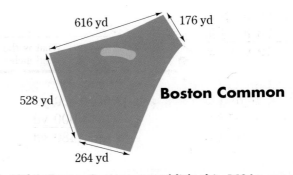

Boston Common

616 yd
176 yd
528 yd
264 yd

The Boston Common, established in 1634, was the first public park in the colonies.

## Critical Thinking 🧩

Discuss how you would change each measurement to inches.

**1.** $\frac{1}{4}$ yd     **2.** $\frac{1}{3}$ ft     **3.** $6\frac{1}{2}$ ft     **4.** $1\frac{2}{3}$ yd     **5.** $8\frac{1}{6}$ ft     **6.** $2\frac{3}{4}$ yd

# Customary Units: Capacity

The chart shows how the customary units of capacity are related.

| |
|---|
| 8 fluid ounces (fl oz) = 1 cup (c) |
| 2 c = 1 pint (pt) |
| 2 pt = 1 quart (qt) |
| 4 qt = 1 gallon (gal) |

Why do we multiply by 2 to change from pints to cups?

14 pt = ▓ c    $\leftarrow$ Is the number of cups *more* or *less* than 14?
14 pt = 28 c

Why do we divide by 4 to change from quarts to gallons?

48 qt = ▓ gal    $\leftarrow$ Is the number of gallons *more* or *less* than 48?
48 qt = 12 gal

**THINK ALOUD** How would you find the number of fluid ounces in 1 pt? in 1 qt?

Notice how you add and subtract units of capacity.

$$\begin{array}{r} 5 \text{ qt } 7 \text{ pt} \\ + 3 \text{ qt } 2 \text{ pt} \\ \hline 8 \text{ qt } 9 \text{ pt} \end{array} = 12 \text{ qt } 1 \text{ pt} = 3 \text{ gal } 1 \text{ pt}$$

simplest form

$$\begin{array}{r} \overset{0\quad 8}{2} \text{ gal } \cancel{0} \text{ qt} \\ - 5 \text{ qt} \\ \hline 3 \text{ qt} \end{array}$$

$$\begin{array}{r} \overset{0\quad 16}{2} \text{ c } \cancel{0} \text{ fl oz} \\ - \quad\quad 10 \text{ fl oz} \\ \hline 1 \text{ c } 6 \text{ fl oz} \end{array}$$

---

**GUIDED PRACTICE**

Which unit of capacity is appropriate? Choose *fl oz*, *c*, *pt*, *qt*, or *gal*.

**1.** a bathtub          **2.** a tube of toothpaste          **3.** a car's gasoline tank

Copy and complete.

**4.** 3 gal = ▓ qt     **5.** 4 pt = ▓ c     **6.** 12 qt = ▓ pt     **7.** 36 c = ▓ pt

**8. THINK ALOUD** How much of a gallon is 1 qt? 2 qt?

Copy and complete.

**9.** 72 fl oz = ▤ c

**10.** 16 qt = ▤ gal

**11.** 160 pt = ▤ c

**12.** 22 pt = ▤ c

**13.** 9 gal = ▤ qt

**14.** 64 fl oz = ▤ pt

**15.** 12 c = ▤ fl oz

**16.** 100 gal = ▤ pt

**17.** $13\frac{1}{2}$ qt = ▤ c

**MIXED REVIEW**  Compare. Choose >, <, or =.

**18.** 5 yd ▤ 14 ft

**19.** 15,840 ft ▤ 3 mi

**20.** 200 fl oz ▤ 30 c

**NUMBER SENSE**  Choose the best estimate.

**21.** a small fishbowl
   **a.** 3 qt   **b.** 3 c   **c.** 3 fl oz

**22.** a bathtub
   **a.** 200 fl oz   **b.** 20 qt   **c.** 20 gal

**23.** a can of soup
   **a.** 10 c   **b.** 10 fl oz   **c.** 10 qt

**24.** a bottle of dish detergent
   **a.** 20 pt   **b.** $\frac{1}{2}$ c   **c.** 20 fl oz

Copy and complete. Use the appropriate unit of capacity.

**25.** 240 fl oz = 15 ▤

**26.** 14 gal = 112 ▤

**27.** $4\frac{1}{2}$ qt = 18 ▤

Compute. Give the answer in simplest form.

**28.**   3 gal 2 qt
       + 1 gal 6 qt

**29.**   8 pt 0 c
       − 5 pt 3 c

**30.**   1 c  9 fl oz
       + 0 c 16 fl oz

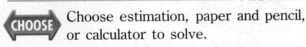 Choose estimation, paper and pencil, or calculator to solve.

**31.** Nutritionists recommend we drink 8 c of water every day. How many quarts is that in 1 wk? How many gallons is that in 4 wk?

**32.** It takes about 150 gal of water to make the paper for just 1 Sunday newspaper. The circulation of the Sunday *New York Times* is 1,663,000. About how many gallons of water does it take to produce this many copies?

**33.** **CREATE YOUR OWN**  Each person in the United States uses an average of 70 gal of water per day. Create a math problem about this fact. Give it to a friend to solve.

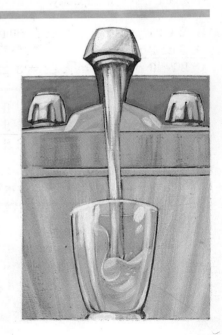

# Customary Units: Weight

One of the largest rainbow trout ever caught weighed 42 lb 2 oz.

Rainbow trout usually weigh about 1 lb.

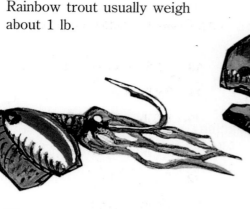

The weight tied to the fishing line is 1 oz.

> 16 ounces (oz) = 1 pound (lb)
> 2,000 lb = 1 ton (t)

Why do we multiply by 16 to change from pounds to ounces?

4 lb = ▓ oz

Is the number of ounces *more* or *less* than 4?
4 lb = 64 oz

Why do we divide by 2,000 to change from pounds to tons?

10,000 lb = ▓ t

Is the number of tons *more* or *less* than 10,000?
10,000 lb = 5 t

Notice how you add and subtract units of weight.

$$
\begin{array}{r}
4 \text{ lb} \quad 9 \text{ oz} \\
+ \ 3 \text{ lb} \quad 5 \text{ oz} \\
\hline
7 \text{ lb} \ 14 \text{ oz}
\end{array}
$$

⟨ simplest form ⟩

$$
\begin{array}{r}
^{3} \quad ^{2,000} \\
4 \text{ t} \quad \emptyset \text{ lb} \\
- \qquad 650 \text{ lb} \\
\hline
3 \text{ t} \ 1,350 \text{ lb}
\end{array}
$$

---

## GUIDED PRACTICE

Find the missing number.

**1.** 9 lb = ▓ oz

**2.** 24,000 lb = ▓ t

**3.** 160 oz = ▓ lb

**4.** 7 t = ▓ lb

**5.** 5 lb = ▓ oz

**6.** 10 t = ▓ lb

**NUMBER SENSE**   Name an object with the given weight.

**7.** about 2 lb          **8.** about 2 oz          **9.** about 2 t

**10. THINK ALOUD**   What is $7\frac{1}{2}$ lb in pounds and ounces?

**PRACTICE**

Copy and complete.

**11.** 4 t = ▨ lb

**12.** 24 oz = ▨ lb

**13.** 19 lb 8 oz = ▨ lb

**14.** 16 lb = ▨ oz

**15.** 12 lb 15 oz = ▨ oz

**16.** 28 lb = ▨ oz

**17.** 18,000 lb = ▨ t

**18.** 15,000 lb = ▨ t

**19.** $5\frac{1}{2}$ lb = ▨ lb ▨ oz

**MIXED REVIEW**   Compute.

**20.** 14 yd = ▨ ft

**21.** 12 qt = ▨ gal

**22.** 5 t = ▨ lb

**23.** 2 lb = ▨ oz

**24.** 10 pt = ▨ qt

**25.** 72 in. = ▨ ft

**NUMBER SENSE**   Choose the best estimate.

**26.** a hamburger

    **a.** 4 oz   **b.** 2 lb   **c.** $\frac{1}{2}$ oz

**27.** a dictionary

    **a.** 12 oz   **b.** 2 lb   **c.** 42 lb

**28.** a loaded truck

    **a.** 400 lb   **b.** 2 t   **c.** 40,000 oz

**29.** an apple

    **a.** $\frac{1}{2}$ lb   **b.** 1 lb   **c.** 64 oz

Compute. Give the answer in simplest form.

**30.**    12 lb 15 oz
    + 18 lb 10 oz

**31.**    30 lb 2 oz
    − 14 lb 9 oz

**32.**    6 t 1,400 lb
    +     1,800 lb

**PROBLEM SOLVING**

**CHOOSE**   Choose mental math, paper and pencil, or calculator to solve.

**33.** A record-size catch for a walleye was 25 lb. How many 25-lb walleyes would weigh a total of 1 t?

**34.** Which two record-size fish in the table differ in weight by 2 lb 7 oz?

**35.** Represent the information in the table with a bar graph.

| Record Fish Catches | |
| --- | --- |
| Smallmouth bass | 11 lb 15 oz |
| Lake whitefish | 14 lb 6 oz |
| Yellow perch | 4 lb 3 oz |
| White catfish | 17 lb 7 oz |
| Bluegill | 4 lb 12 oz |
| Pickerel | 9 lb 6 oz |

# Problem Solving: Multistep Problems

A jogger takes 30 min to complete 13 laps around a 0.25-mi track. If this speed is maintained, how long will it take the jogger to complete a 26-mi marathon?

This problem requires several steps to solve.

**STEP 1:** How many miles did the jogger run in 30 min?

THINK ALOUD  Why does $13 \times 0.25$ answer the question?

$13 \times 0.25 = 3.25$ (mi)

**STEP 2:** What is the jogger's speed in miles per hour?

THINK ALOUD  Why does multiplying 3.25 by 2 answer this question?

$3.25 \times 2 = 6.5$ (mi/h)

**STEP 3:** At a speed of 6.5 mi/h, how long will it take to run 26 mi?

THINK ALOUD  Why does dividing 26 by 6.5 answer this question? Solve this last step yourself.

**CRITICAL THINKING**  Is it reasonable to assume that a jogger can run at the same speed for 26 mi? Why or why not?

---

## GUIDED PRACTICE

Use several steps to solve.

1. A jogger runs 8 laps on a 0.25-mi track in 15 min. How many hours would it take to run a 26-mi marathon if the jogger could maintain her speed?

2. In the 1988 Olympics, Florence Griffith-Joyner set a world record for running 200 m with the time of 21.34 s.
   a. What was the distance of this race?
   b. Was the distance run in *more than* or *less than* than 1 min?
   c. If this pace were maintained, about how far would Griffith-Joyner run in 1 min?

**Fastest Swimming Speeds**

| Stroke | Speed over 100m |
|---|---|
| Backstroke | 1.83 m/s |
| Breaststroke | 1.62 m/s |
| Freestyle | 2.07 m/s |
| Butterfly | 1.89 m/s |

---
**PRACTICE**
---

Use the information shown above to solve, if necessary.

**3. IN YOUR WORDS** A record holder swims 0.5 km in 308 s. What stroke do you think was used?

**4.** How far would the fastest butterfly swimmer travel in 1.5 min?

**5.** About how much longer would it take the fastest breaststroke swimmer than the fastest backstroker to swim 200 m?

**6.** A dolphin can swim 16.6 m/s. By about how many seconds would a dolphin defeat a human swimming freestyle over a distance of 200 m?

**7.** A downhill skier has been recorded as traveling at a speed of 2 mi/min. At this speed, how many minutes would it take to complete a 2.5-mi ski run?

**8.** The record speed for roller skaters is a little more than 24 mi/h. What is this speed in miles per minute? At this speed, what distance can be skated in 40 s?

**CHOOSE** Choose a strategy to solve, if possible.

**9.** In the 1988 Olympics, Carl Lewis ran 100 m in a record 9.92 s. At that speed, how long would it take him to complete one lap around the Olympic track?

**10.** One way to arrange the letters at the right is shown. How many different ways are possible?

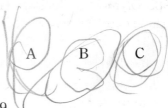

**11.** If you multiplied 3 by itself once, the result is 9. What would be the digit in the ones' place if 3 were multiplied by itself 10 times?

## LANGUAGE & VOCABULARY

Decide whether the unit is appropriate for the measurement.
Explain your decision.

1. using yards to measure a student's height

2. using feet to measure the distance between cities

3. using gallons to measure the water in a swimming pool

4. using fluid ounces to measure the fuel in a car's gas tank

5. using tons to measure a horse's weight

## TEST ✓

### CONCEPTS

Copy and complete. *(pages 188–193)*

1. 48 ft = ▨ yd

2. 6 ft = ▨ in.

3. 2 yd 1 ft = ▨ in.

4. 3 pt = ▨ c

5. 96 fl oz = ▨ pt

6. 3 gal = ▨ qt

7. $2\frac{1}{4}$ lb = ▨ lb ▨ oz

8. 3 lb 7 oz = ▨ oz

9. 212,000 lb = ▨ t

### SKILLS

Find the sum or difference in lowest terms. *(pages 172–181)*

10. $\frac{4}{9} - \frac{1}{9}$

11. $\frac{4}{7} + \frac{5}{7}$

12. $8\frac{3}{12} - 2\frac{1}{12}$

13. $5\frac{2}{3} + 9\frac{2}{3}$

14. $\frac{3}{4} + \frac{2}{12}$

15. $\frac{5}{9} - \frac{3}{18}$

16. $\frac{7}{10} + \frac{12}{30}$

17. $\frac{5}{7} - \frac{5}{14}$

18. $\frac{8}{9} - \frac{3}{5}$

19. $\frac{5}{6} + \frac{7}{9}$

20. $\frac{6}{11} - \frac{1}{4}$

21. $4\frac{3}{8} + 1\frac{1}{16}$

22. $12\frac{1}{2} + 9\frac{2}{3}$

23. $7\frac{1}{4} - 2\frac{5}{6}$

24. $15 - 6\frac{1}{7}$

## PROBLEM SOLVING

Use the guess-and-check strategy to solve. *(pages 184–185)*

**25.** Two friends paid a total of $8.05 for their lunches of pizza and milk. Ben paid $.85 more than Cal. Pizza is $1.25 per slice and milk is $.70 per glass or $1.10 per container.

  **a.** How much in all did Ben and Cal spend on lunch?

  **b.** If they each ordered milk, what do you suppose is the largest number of pizza slices they could have ordered?

  **c.** What did each boy have for lunch?

Use several steps to solve. *(pages 194–195)*

**26.** A restaurant uses an average of 3 lb 8 oz of butter per hour during the time it is open. If the restaurant is open 6 h/d every day, how much butter will be used in 2 wk?

Solve.

**27.** In a gym class competition, Jaime's two jumps were $12\frac{1}{2}$ ft and $9\frac{2}{3}$ ft. What was the combined distance of his jumps?

**LEARNING LOG**

Write the answers in your learning log.

**1.** Do you think a carrot would be a good standard unit of measure? Why or why not?

**2.** Study examples where you change from a smaller unit of measure to a larger unit of measure. Describe what happens and why.

Write the answer in lowest terms. *(pages 172–181)*

**1.** $\frac{1}{8} + \frac{3}{8}$   **2.** $\frac{7}{10} - \frac{4}{10}$   **3.** $9\frac{3}{5} - 6\frac{1}{5}$

**4.** $3\frac{5}{12} + 8\frac{4}{12}$   **5.** $\frac{3}{7} - \frac{2}{14}$   **6.** $\frac{8}{9} + \frac{1}{18}$

**7.** $\frac{11}{20} + \frac{9}{40}$   **8.** $\frac{4}{16} + \frac{3}{8}$   **9.** $\frac{5}{12} + \frac{3}{6}$

**10.** $\frac{1}{8} + \frac{2}{4}$   **11.** $\frac{8}{10} - \frac{3}{5}$   **12.** $\frac{6}{12} + \frac{3}{4}$

**13.** $\frac{4}{18} - \frac{1}{6}$   **14.** $\frac{5}{6} - \frac{2}{5}$   **15.** $\frac{1}{7} + \frac{1}{8}$

**16.** $\frac{4}{6} - \frac{1}{2}$   **17.** $\frac{6}{7} + \frac{2}{3}$   **18.** $2\frac{1}{2} + 1\frac{3}{6}$

**19.** $5\frac{2}{7} + 6\frac{1}{14}$   **20.** $6\frac{3}{5} - \frac{2}{4}$   **21.** $1\frac{8}{10} + 3\frac{1}{5}$

**22.** $16 + 4\frac{1}{8}$   **23.** $4\frac{4}{9} - 3\frac{1}{7}$   **24.** $8\frac{1}{7} + 9\frac{1}{8}$

**25.** $12 - 6\frac{1}{2}$   **26.** $3 - 2\frac{5}{7}$   **27.** $3\frac{1}{6} - 2\frac{5}{6}$

**28.** $7\frac{3}{5} - 2\frac{3}{4}$

Copy and complete. *(pages 188–193)*

**29.** 2 mi = ▨ ft   **30.** 17 ft = ▨ in.

**31.** 1 yd 11 in. = ▨ in.   **32.** 9 yd = ▨ in.

**33.** 20 pt = ▨ gal   **34.** 48 fl oz = ▨ pt

**35.** 32 gal = ▨ pt   **36.** 80 fl oz = ▨ c

**37.** 3 t = ▨ lb   **38.** 5 lb 3 oz = ▨ oz

**39.** 48 oz = ▨ lb   **40.** 16 lb = ▨ oz

Solve. *(pages 184–185, 194–195)*

**41.** Two friends compare their ages. The difference between their ages is 3 yr and the product of their ages is 238 yr. How old is the older friend?

**42.** A fish tank is filled at the rate of $\frac{1}{2}$ gal/min. At that rate, how long will it take to put 14 gal into the tank?

## A Stock Market Investment

Many people invest in the stock market to try to earn money. Buying shares in a company shows confidence in a company and its ability to be profitable. Because so many people have these investments, you can find daily reports on the stock market in newspapers and on radio and television.

Find the stock market news in the financial section of a newspaper. Choose five public companies to "invest" in. The stock market report will show the number of shares sold the day before, the final (closing) price of a share, and the daily change in price.

Pretend that you have bought 10 shares of stock in each company you chose at the closing price in the report. Notice that the price and change are given as fractions or mixed numbers, not decimals. Change the fraction to a decimal, rounded to the nearest hundredth.

Keep a daily record of the price of your shares for at least two weeks. Also, record the amount your stocks have gained or lost from the previous day. At the end of the two weeks, compare the price of each stock with the price when you "bought" it. Then multiply each final value by 10 for the 10 shares you "own." Did you make or lose money?

### NO CONNECTIONS

Copy the drawing. Use each number from 1 to 8 once. Fill the boxes so that no boxes that touch, even at corners, have consecutive numbers.

### MENUS OF MEALS

Plan menus for a weekend. Use cookbooks to decide what foods you need to include for balanced meals and how much of each food to buy. Make a grocery list and estimate how much the food will cost.

# CUMULATIVE REVIEW

Find the answer.

**1.** $\frac{16}{24} =$

 **a.** $\frac{2}{4}$

 **b.** $\frac{2}{3}$

 **c.** $\frac{3}{4}$

 **d.** none of these

**2.** $\frac{3}{5}$ is less than

 **a.** $\frac{5}{6}$

 **b.** $\frac{3}{10}$

 **c.** $\frac{1}{3}$

 **d.** none of these

**3.** $\frac{5}{8} =$

 **a.** 0.625

 **b.** 1.6

 **c.** 0.58

 **d.** none of these

**4.** 3.125 =

 **a.** $3\frac{1}{4}$

 **b.** $3\frac{1}{6}$

 **c.** $3\frac{1}{12}$

 **d.** none of these

**5.** $\frac{7}{10} - \frac{6}{12} =$

 **a.** $\frac{1}{2}$

 **b.** $\frac{1}{5}$

 **c.** $\frac{1}{3}$

 **d.** none of these

**6.** $\frac{3}{7} + \frac{5}{14} =$

 **a.** $\frac{8}{14}$

 **b.** $\frac{8}{21}$

 **c.** $\frac{11}{14}$

 **d.** none of these

**7.** 7 km =

 **a.** 700 m

 **b.** 7,000 m

 **c.** 0.007 m

 **d.** none of these

**8.** 0.085 L =

 **a.** 85 mL

 **b.** 850 mL

 **c.** 8.5 mL

 **d.** none of these

**9.** 1,400 g =

 **a.** 14 kg

 **b.** 140 kg

 **c.** 1.4 kg

 **d.** none of these

Round to the given place.

**10.** 3,749 (tens)

 **a.** 3,700

 **b.** 3,740

 **c.** 4,000

 **d.** none of these

**11.** 16,421 (hundreds)

 **a.** 16,000

 **b.** 16,300

 **c.** 16,400

 **d.** none of these

**12.** 2.458 (tenths)

 **a.** 2.4

 **b.** 2.46

 **c.** 2.5

 **d.** none of these

# PROBLEM SOLVING REVIEW

**Problem Solving Check List**

- **Using guess and check**
- **Multistep problems**
- **Using estimation**
- **Working backward**

Remember the strategies and types of problems you've had so far. Solve.

1. Three friends combine their money to buy a gift. Theresa has $2.50, Paula has $1.50, and Ann has $1\frac{1}{2}$ times as much as the other two together.

   **a.** How much does Paula have?

   **b.** How much does Ann have?

   **c.** How much more do they need to buy a $12.00 gift?

2. When John stands on the scale holding his cat, the scale shows 125 lb. John weighs 95 lb more than his cat. How much do John and his cat each weigh?

3. Three classes with 34 students each come to the auditorium. Four classes with 27 students each follow them. If the room has 600 seats, how many seats will still be empty?

4. During a basketball game, 2 players drank 1.5 c of water each. The other 3 players drank 2.5 c each. How much water altogether did the players drink?

5. Mr. Jaskowiak uses the formula $C = \$3.00 + \$.12m$ to determine the cost ($C$) of traveling to work, where $m$ is the distance in miles. What is the cost of a 15-mi round trip?

6. The Pizza Palace allows the use of up to three $.55 coupons per pizza. To find the cost of a pizza, the owner uses the formula $C = \$9.00 - \$.55n$ where $n$ is the number of coupons. What is the lowest cost for 1 pizza?

7. Caesar can join the math club if he has a 90 average in math. His four test scores are 93, 83, 86, and 90. How much less than 90 is Caesar's average?

Is the answer *reasonable* or *unreasonable*? If unreasonable, explain why and find a reasonable answer.

8. Several friends had $2\frac{1}{3}$ mi to hike to reach their destination. They hiked $\frac{1}{3}$ of the way and rested. How far did they hike before resting?

   *Answer:* They hiked $1\frac{1}{6}$ mi.

9. A dressmaker has 26 yd of fabric. If each dress requires 2.75 yd, how many dresses can be made from the fabric?

   *Answer:* 9 dresses

## DID YOU KNOW ...?

Admission to a movie was 25¢ in the late 1930s. How much more money would a theater that holds 125 people take in now than in the late 1930s?

## STACK THEM UP

The dimensions of three boxes are shown below. How can you arrange them in a stack so that the total height is $9\frac{7}{16}$ in.?

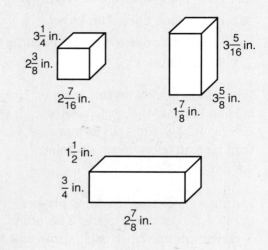

$3\frac{1}{4}$ in.

$2\frac{3}{8}$ in.

$2\frac{7}{16}$ in.

$3\frac{5}{16}$ in.

$3\frac{5}{8}$ in.

$1\frac{7}{8}$ in.

$1\frac{1}{2}$ in.

$\frac{3}{4}$ in.

$2\frac{7}{8}$ in.

## DIGIT DILEMMA

In the computer activity *Fraction Challenge I,* you place the digits from 1 to 9 into the fraction equations to form true statements. For this pencil-and-paper activity, you supply missing digits to form fraction equations.

Use each digit only once for the set of equations. You won't need all the digits for Set 1, but you will use all of them for Set 2. All fractions must be in lowest terms.

Digits:

$$1\ 2\ 3\ 4\ 5\ 6\ 7\ 8\ 9$$

**1.** $\dfrac{\blacksquare}{2} + \dfrac{\blacksquare}{3} = \dfrac{7}{\blacksquare}$    $\dfrac{\blacksquare}{5} + \dfrac{2}{\blacksquare} = \dfrac{31}{35}$    $\dfrac{\blacksquare}{9} + \dfrac{5}{\blacksquare} = \dfrac{77}{72}$

**2.** $\dfrac{\blacksquare}{\blacksquare} + \dfrac{\blacksquare}{4} = \dfrac{5}{4}$    $\dfrac{\blacksquare}{\blacksquare} + \dfrac{\blacksquare}{3} = \dfrac{19}{6}$    $\dfrac{\blacksquare}{8} + \dfrac{1}{\blacksquare} = \dfrac{11}{\blacksquare}$

**DID YOU KNOW . . . ?**

There are about 240 species of trees growing in the United States that are valuable sources of wood and lumber.

$\frac{1}{4}$ of the deciduous trees in the United States are oaks or hickories.

$\frac{2}{3}$ of the trees in the United States are deciduous. That is they have leaves that fall.

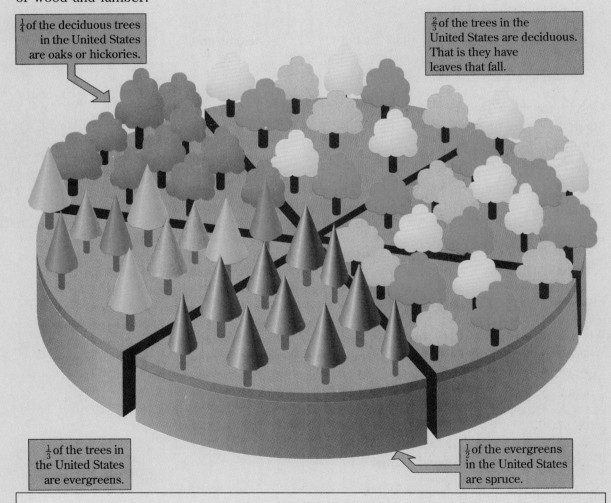

$\frac{1}{3}$ of the trees in the United States are evergreens.

$\frac{1}{2}$ of the evergreens in the United States are spruce.

**USING DATA**

Collect
Organize
**Describe**
Predict

What fraction of all the trees in the United States are spruce?

What fraction of the deciduous trees in the United States are not oak or hickory?

What fraction of all the trees in the United States are not oak or hickory?

## Multiplying Fractions

About three fifths of the population of South America live in Brazil and Argentina. About $\frac{1}{6}$ of the people in these two countries live in the cities of São Paulo and Buenos Aires. What fraction of the population of South America is that?

You must find $\frac{1}{6}$ of $\frac{3}{5}$, or multiply $\frac{1}{6} \times \frac{3}{5}$.

Find the product by:

- representing the total population with a square grid divided into sixths and fifths
- shading a part that is $\frac{1}{6}$ by $\frac{3}{5}$

First think about the denominators.
Shade by going up sixths and over fifths.

$$\frac{1}{6} \times \frac{3}{5} = \frac{?}{?}$$

Since the square has 30 parts, the denominator of the answer is 30.

Now think about the numerators.
Shade by going up $\frac{1}{6}$ and over $\frac{3}{5}$.

$$\frac{1}{6} \times \frac{3}{5} = \frac{?}{30}$$

What part of the square is shaded?
What is the numerator of the product?

$$\frac{1}{6} \times \frac{3}{5} = \frac{1 \times 3}{6 \times 5} = \frac{3}{30} = \frac{1}{10}$$

About $\frac{1}{10}$ of all South Americans live in São Paulo and Buenos Aires.

> **To multiply fractions, multiply the numerators.
> Then multiply the denominators. Write the resulting
> fraction in lowest terms.**

To save time, you can divide out common factors before multiplying. This process is called **canceling**.

$$\frac{1}{6} \times \frac{3}{5} = \frac{1}{\overset{}{6}} \times \frac{\overset{1}{3}}{5} = \frac{1}{10}$$
$$\phantom{\frac{1}{6} \times \frac{3}{5} = \frac{1}{6}}{}_{2}$$

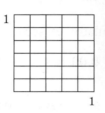

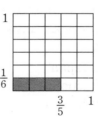

---

**GUIDED PRACTICE**

Draw a square diagram for each.

**1.** $\frac{1}{3}$ of $\frac{1}{2}$    **2.** $\frac{2}{3} \times \frac{3}{5}$

Multiply. Write the product in lowest terms.

**3.** $\frac{4}{5}$ of $\frac{5}{8}$    **4.** $\frac{2}{3} \times \frac{3}{7}$    **5.** $\frac{4}{7} \times \frac{4}{5}$

Write the product in lowest terms.

**6.** $\frac{3}{7}$ of $\frac{4}{5}$  **7.** $\frac{3}{5}$ of $\frac{2}{9}$  **8.** $\frac{5}{8} \times \frac{0}{7}$  **9.** $\frac{1}{6} \times \frac{3}{5}$  **10.** $\frac{5}{10} \times \frac{7}{10}$

**11.** $\frac{3}{4} \times \frac{5}{6}$  **12.** $\frac{7}{8} \times \frac{5}{7}$  **13.** $\frac{5}{4} \times \frac{4}{5}$  **14.** $\frac{9}{8} \times \frac{8}{9}$  **15.** $\frac{7}{8} \times \frac{1}{6}$

**16.** $\frac{2}{5} \times \frac{3}{5}$  **17.** $\frac{7}{9} \times \frac{3}{7}$  **18.** $\frac{1}{8} \times \frac{6}{7}$  **19.** $\frac{5}{2} \times \frac{2}{5}$  **20.** $\frac{4}{5} \times \frac{1}{10}$

**21.** $\frac{0}{4} \times \frac{5}{6}$  **22.** $\frac{1}{5} \times \frac{12}{20}$  **23.** $\frac{7}{8} \times \frac{2}{14}$  **24.** $\frac{1}{10} \times \frac{50}{100}$  **25.** $\frac{0}{12} \times \frac{0}{8}$

**26.** $\frac{1}{5} \times \frac{5}{6} \times \frac{1}{6}$  **27.** $\frac{2}{3} \times \frac{1}{2} \times \frac{1}{4}$  **28.** $\frac{7}{8} \times \frac{4}{5} \times \frac{1}{3}$

**MIXED REVIEW** Compute.

**29.** $95 \times 76$  **30.** $\frac{1}{3} + 6\frac{1}{2}$  **31.** $216 \div 6$  **32.** $15 - 1\frac{7}{8}$

**33.** $0.4 \times 0.11$  **34.** $19 - 1.63$  **35.** $2.4 \div 0.2$  **36.** $0.24 + 0.9$

**CALCULATOR** Use a calculator to solve.

**37.** $\frac{3}{5} \times 0.42$  **38.** $0.09 \times \frac{7}{8}$  **39.** $\frac{3}{4} \times 1.36$  **40.** $\frac{5}{8} \times 4.9$

**CHOOSE** Use the circle graph. Choose mental math or paper and pencil to solve. Write your answers in lowest terms.

**41.** About $\frac{1}{7}$ of the population of Venezuela live in the capital city of Caracas. What fraction of the population of South America is in Caracas?

**42.** About $\frac{7}{20}$ of Chile's population live in the capital city of Santiago. What fraction of South Americans live in Santiago?

**43.** What fraction of South America's population live in Peru, Brazil, or Venezuela?

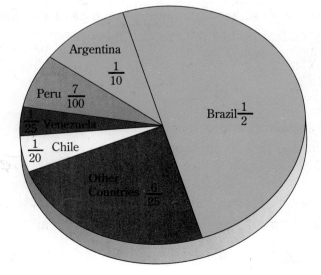

**Approximate Population of South America**

Argentina $\frac{1}{10}$; Peru $\frac{7}{100}$; $\frac{1}{25}$ Venezuela; $\frac{1}{20}$ Chile; Brazil $\frac{1}{2}$; Other Countries $\frac{6}{25}$

## Multiplying Fractions and Whole Numbers

Pure gold is 24 k (karats). Gold that is 18 k is $\frac{18}{24}$, or $\frac{3}{4}$, pure gold and $\frac{1}{4}$ other metals. How many ounces of pure gold are there in an 18-k chain that weighs 2 oz?

The diagram shows $\frac{3}{4}$ of 2 squares, or $\frac{3}{4} \times 2$.

Go up $\frac{3}{4}$ and across 2.

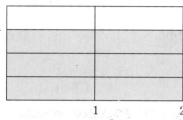

Can you see that $\frac{3}{4} \times 2$ is $1\frac{1}{2}$?

If you know that $2 = \frac{2}{1}$, you can make a MATH CONNECTION to multiply $\frac{3}{4} \times 2$.

$$\frac{3}{4} \times 2 \quad = \frac{3}{\underset{2}{\cancel{4}}} \times \frac{\overset{1}{\cancel{2}}}{1} = \frac{3}{2} = 1\frac{1}{2}$$

The chain contains $1\frac{1}{2}$ oz of pure gold.

> **To multiply a fraction by a whole number, write the whole number as a fraction and multiply.**

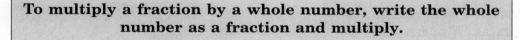

### GUIDED PRACTICE

Explain how to find the product in lowest terms.

1. $\frac{4}{5} \times 3$
2. $\frac{7}{8} \times 4$
3. $\frac{3}{4} \times 20$
4. $12 \times \frac{1}{3}$
5. $\frac{5}{6} \times 0$

### PRACTICE

Write the product in lowest terms.

6. $3 \times \frac{5}{6}$
7. $\frac{5}{8} \times 16$
8. $\frac{7}{8} \times 4$
9. $\frac{3}{4} \times 9$
10. $7 \times \frac{1}{3}$

11. $\frac{2}{5} \times \frac{3}{5}$
12. $\frac{7}{8} \times 1$
13. $\frac{7}{8} \times \frac{5}{7}$
14. $5 \times \frac{2}{5}$
15. $\frac{4}{5} \times \frac{5}{4}$

16. $0 \times \frac{7}{8}$
17. $\frac{5}{16} \times 0$
18. $\frac{3}{4} \times \frac{4}{3}$
19. $\frac{2}{3} \times 12$
20. $16 \times \frac{1}{8}$

**21.** $\frac{0}{12} \times 6$  **22.** $\frac{7}{16} \times 8$  **23.** $25 \times \frac{3}{20}$  **24.** $0 \times \frac{0}{50}$  **25.** $\frac{3}{32} \times 16$

**26.** $\frac{3}{5} \times \frac{2}{9}$  **27.** $7 \times \frac{5}{14}$  **28.** $\frac{7}{10} \times 30 \times \frac{1}{3}$  **29.** $\left(\frac{1}{6} + \frac{3}{4}\right) \times \frac{2}{3}$

**MIXED REVIEW** Compute.

**30.** $14.67 \times 53.11$  **31.** $\frac{7}{12} + \frac{3}{8}$  **32.** $687.09 + 54.23$  **33.** $\frac{12}{14} - \frac{5}{7}$

**34.** $6\frac{2}{7} + 5\frac{5}{6}$  **35.** $231.76 - 230.81$  **36.** $12\frac{1}{6} - 5\frac{10}{12}$  **37.** $945.73 + 34.6$

Use **MENTAL MATH** to solve the equation.

**38.** $\frac{2}{5}n = \frac{6}{35}$  **39.** $\frac{5}{6}n = \frac{15}{42}$  **40.** $\frac{3}{4}n = 1$  **41.** $\frac{11}{16}n = 0$

═══════════════════ **PROBLEM SOLVING** ═══════════════════

**CHOOSE** Use the information on page 206.
Choose paper and pencil or calculator to solve.

**42.** The largest known coin was 14 k, weighed 365 lb, and was worth \$1 million. How many pounds of pure gold did it contain?

**43.** At \$420/oz, what is the value of the gold in a 12-k medallion that weighs $\frac{15}{16}$ oz?

**44.** How long is a line of 1,000,000 pennies that are side by side? Each penny is $\frac{3}{4}$ in. wide.

## Mental Math

You can use mental math to multiply a whole number by a fraction with a numerator of 1.

- How many coins are there in all?
- What part of the coins are gold?
- How many of the coins are gold?

$\frac{1}{3}$ of 15 = 5 ⟹ 15 ÷ 3 = 5

Multiply mentally.

**1.** $\frac{1}{5}$ of 40  **2.** $\frac{1}{7} \times 42$  **3.** $\frac{1}{3}$ of 18  **4.** $\frac{1}{10} \times 360$  **5.** $\frac{1}{6}$ of 24

**6.** $\frac{3}{8}$ of 24 (*Hint:* Find $\frac{1}{8}$ of 24 first.)  **7.** $\frac{2}{5} \times 20$  **8.** $24 \times \frac{5}{6}$

## Multiplying With Mixed Numbers

Devin worked $2\frac{3}{4}$ h of overtime on Monday making a patio. How many hours of regular pay did this earn him?

You need to multiply $1\frac{1}{2}$ by $2\frac{3}{4}$.

**ESTIMATE** You can estimate the product of $1\frac{1}{2}$ and $2\frac{3}{4}$ by rounding to whole numbers. What do you estimate the product to be?

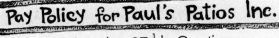

Pay Policy for Paul's Patios Inc.

- A full workweek is $37\frac{1}{2}$ h. Overtime is over $37\frac{1}{2}$ h.

- Overtime during the week or on Saturdays earns $1\frac{1}{2}$ h of regular pay per hour worked.

- Overtime on Sundays or holidays earns $1\frac{3}{4}$ h of regular pay per hour worked.

If you know how to multiply fractions and how to change mixed numbers to fractions, you can make a **MATH CONNECTION** to multiply mixed numbers.

$$1\frac{1}{2} \times 2\frac{3}{4} = \frac{3}{2} \times \frac{11}{4} = \frac{33}{8} = 4\frac{1}{8}$$

Is this answer close to your estimate?

Devin earned $4\frac{1}{8}$ h of regular pay.

Other examples:

$$\frac{3}{4} \times \frac{4}{3} = \frac{\overset{1}{\cancel{3}}}{\cancel{4}} \times \frac{\overset{1}{\cancel{4}}}{\cancel{3}} = 1$$

$$\frac{1}{2} \times 2 = 1$$

$$\frac{2}{3} \times 1\frac{1}{2} = \frac{\overset{1}{\cancel{2}}}{\cancel{3}} \times \frac{\overset{1}{\cancel{3}}}{\cancel{2}} = 1$$

**CRITICAL THINKING** In each of the examples above, can you multiply the first factor by a different factor and still get 1?

> **Two numbers whose product is 1 are called reciprocals.**

$\frac{3}{4}$ and $\frac{4}{3}$ are called reciprocals. Name some other pairs of numbers that are reciprocals.

=== GUIDED PRACTICE ===

Find the reciprocal of the number.        Write the product in lowest terms.

**1.** 7        **2.** $\frac{3}{8}$        **3.** $5\frac{1}{2}$        **4.** $1\frac{3}{5} \times 10$   **5.** $1\frac{2}{7} \times 7$

=== PRACTICE ===

Write the reciprocal of the number.

**6.** $\frac{3}{4}$        **7.** $4\frac{5}{6}$        **8.** $1\frac{1}{7}$        **9.** $\frac{1}{8}$        **10.** 6        **11.** 1

Write the product in lowest terms. Estimate to see if your answer is reasonable.

**12.** $\frac{1}{4} \times 2\frac{1}{3}$  **13.** $2\frac{4}{5} \times 15$  **14.** $49 \times 1\frac{2}{7}$  **15.** $4\frac{4}{7} \times 3\frac{1}{2}$

**16.** $4\frac{3}{5} \times 3$  **17.** $6 \times 6\frac{7}{8}$  **18.** $\frac{5}{31} \times 6\frac{1}{5}$  **19.** $7\frac{1}{5} \times 0$

**20.** $2\frac{1}{4} \times 1\frac{2}{3}$  **21.** $\frac{3}{4} \times 1\frac{1}{3}$  **22.** $10\frac{3}{4} \times \frac{2}{3}$  **23.** $2\frac{3}{7} \times 2\frac{1}{4}$

**24.** $5\frac{1}{3} \times 2\frac{5}{8}$  **25.** $6\frac{3}{5} \times 1\frac{3}{4}$  **26.** $3\frac{4}{9} \times 8\frac{1}{10}$  **27.** $5\frac{9}{10} \times 8$

**28.** $\frac{1}{4} \times 1\frac{1}{4}$  **29.** $\frac{9}{10} \times 1\frac{1}{9}$  **30.** $8\frac{7}{8} \times 40$  **31.** $5\frac{1}{3} \times \frac{3}{16}$

**MIXED REVIEW**    Compute.

**32.** $\frac{3}{8} + \frac{3}{4}$  **33.** $5 - 4\frac{2}{3}$  **34.** $1\frac{1}{4} \times 1\frac{1}{4}$  **35.** $5\frac{1}{5} + 6\frac{4}{9}$

**36.** $7 - 6\frac{3}{5}$  **37.** $\frac{4}{5} + 1\frac{1}{3}$  **38.** $5\frac{3}{5} \times \frac{3}{7}$  **39.** $\frac{1}{4} \times \frac{3}{5} \times \frac{8}{9}$

**40. CRITICAL THINKING**    What number has no reciprocal? Why not?

**PROBLEM SOLVING**

**CHOOSE**    Use the chart on page 208.
Choose paper and pencil or calculator to solve.

**41.** Susan worked $5\frac{1}{2}$ h of overtime on Thanksgiving Day. How many hours of regular pay did she earn?

**42.** In the first week of July, Mandy worked a full workweek. Also, she worked $3\frac{1}{2}$ h on July 4th. At \$8/h, what was her salary that week?

**43.** Ashley worked a full workweek plus 6 h and 20 min overtime on Saturday. What was ~~his~~ Her salary that week if he earns \$8/h?

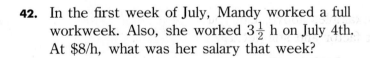

**Critical Thinking**

Work with a partner.

**1.** What are the products of:
$\frac{3}{4} \times 1$, $\frac{3}{4} \times 0$, $\frac{3}{4} \times \frac{1}{2}$, $\frac{3}{4} \times \frac{1}{4}$?

**2. IN YOUR WORDS**    Explain the value of the product you get when you multiply by a fraction less than 1.

# Problem Solving Strategy:
## *Using Estimation*

A museum was given discounted prices on the cost of several Native American crafts to aid the museum in setting up its exhibit of Native American arts and crafts.

Suppose the museum had $170 to buy 2 large baskets. Would that amount of money be enough?

An estimated answer is all that is needed to solve the problem.

- Round the cost of 1 large basket to make the calculation easier.
- Estimate the total cost at the regular price.
- What would you do to find the amount of the discount?
- Estimate the discounted price of 2 large baskets.

**THINK ALOUD** Can you estimate the discounted price in fewer steps?

$\frac{1}{3}$ off regular prices shown

large basket — $119.95
bear mask — $74.95
totem pole — $49.99
bookmark — $4.95
small planter — $62.95

$\frac{1}{4}$ off regular prices shown

drum — $265.95
Cherokee "e tsi" mother doll — $25.00

---

## GUIDED PRACTICE

Estimate. Do not calculate.

1. The museum wants to buy a totem pole.
   a. What is the regular price?
   b. What amount close to the regular price is easy to multiply by $\frac{1}{3}$?
   c. Estimate the discounted price.

2. **IN YOUR WORDS** The discounted price for 2 bear masks is about $90. Is that about right? Explain.

3. Would $12 be enough to buy three bookmarks?

4. About how much less would the large basket and the small planter cost at the discounted price?

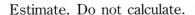
Estimate. Do not calculate.

5. How much money does the museum save by buying the drum at a discount?

6. About what is the discounted price of the drum?

7. Is $50 enough to buy the Cherokee "e tsi" mother doll and a totem pole at the discounted prices?

8. **CREATE YOUR OWN** Write two problems using the information on these two pages. Give them to a friend to solve.

9. **IN YOUR WORDS** With a budget of $400, which discounted items from both pages would you buy for the museum? Explain and defend your choices in a paragraph.

CHOOSE Choose a strategy to solve, if possible.

10. A hiking trail near the museum starts at one marker and goes 2 mi north, then 3 mi east, 5 mi south, 4 mi east, and 3 mi north to another marker. How far apart are the two markers?

11. Miguel bought a bear mask at the discounted price. What was his change?

12. How much change did Lara receive when she bought a Cherokee "e tsi" mother doll at the discounted price? She gave the clerk $20 and paid $.94 sales tax.

Decide whether the product *must be*, *can be*, or *cannot be* greater than at least one factor. Support your answer with at least one example.

1. multiplying a fraction by a fraction

2. multiplying a fraction by a whole number

3. multiplying a fraction by a mixed number

4. multiplying a whole number by a mixed number

## QUICK QUIZ ✔

Write the product in lowest terms. *(pages 204–209)*

1. $\frac{5}{6}$ of $\frac{7}{8}$

2. $\frac{4}{5}$ of $\frac{3}{10}$

3. $\frac{0}{8} \times 7$

4. $16 \times \frac{3}{8}$

5. $\frac{5}{9} \times 30$

6. $\frac{2}{3} \times 8\frac{1}{2}$

7. $13 \times 2\frac{1}{5}$

8. $7\frac{3}{4} \times 3\frac{2}{5}$

9. $2\frac{1}{8} \times 5\frac{2}{3}$

Solve. *(pages 210–211)*

10. A 247-mi car trip can be shortened by about $\frac{1}{4}$ using a short cut. Mr. and Mrs. Spence have 6 gal of gas in their tank. Their car averages 30 mi/gal.

   a. If they do not use the short cut, how far must Mr. and Mrs. Spence drive?

   b. How can you find out the distance they must drive using the short cut?

   c. Do they have enough gas to complete the trip either way?

Write the answers in your learning log.

1. Describe the size of the answer when you multiply two mixed numbers.

2. Explain how dollars and cents are like mixed numbers.

MATH AMERICA

BONUS

**DID YOU KNOW . . . ?** In 1689, one of the colonies had 23 public schools— more than any other colony. How many public schools are there in your state? Compare the two numbers with a fractional statement.

Work with a partner. Use a calculator.

A recipe for an apple dessert uses the following ingredients:

3 c bread crumbs

$1\frac{1}{4}$ c sugar

$\frac{1}{2}$ c butter

$\frac{1}{2}$ tsp cinnamon

3 large apples

$\frac{1}{4}$ tsp nutmeg

Directions:   Bake in a 3-qt baking dish for 30 min at 375°F.

To make $1\frac{1}{2}$ times the recipe, which ingredients and directions must be changed? Write the new recipe.

# Dividing Fractions and Whole Numbers

A recipe for 1 batch of pancakes calls for $\frac{2}{3}$ c of milk. How many batches of pancakes can you make with 4 c of milk?

There are at least two ways to find out.

Use division:

- How many $\frac{2}{3}$ c are in 4 c?
  $$4 \div \frac{2}{3} = ?$$
- The diagram at the right shows that 6 batches can be made with 4 c of milk.
  $$4 \div \frac{2}{3} = 6$$

Use multiplication:

- First find out how many batches can be made from 1 c of milk.
  You can get $1\frac{1}{2}$, or $\frac{3}{2}$, batches from 1 c of milk.
- Then multiply to find out the number of batches in 4 c.
  $$4 \times \frac{3}{2} = 6$$
  You can make 6 batches of pancakes with 4 c of milk.

Notice that dividing 4 by $\frac{2}{3}$ has the same result as multiplying 4 by $\frac{3}{2}$. This is because $\frac{3}{2}$ is the reciprocal of $\frac{2}{3}$.

$$4 \div \frac{2}{3} = 4 \times \frac{3}{2} = 6$$

**To divide by a fraction, multiply by its reciprocal.**

## GUIDED PRACTICE

Find the value of $n$.

**1.** $15 \div \frac{3}{5} = 15 \times n$ 

**2.** $28 \div \frac{4}{9} = 28 \times n$

Write the quotient in lowest terms.

**3.** $5 \div \frac{1}{4}$

**4.** $12 \div \frac{3}{4}$

Write the quotient in lowest terms.

**5.** $3 \div \frac{1}{2}$    **6.** $5 \div \frac{1}{3}$    **7.** $4 \div \frac{1}{5}$    **8.** $7 \div \frac{1}{8}$    **9.** $4 \div \frac{1}{20}$

**10.** $6 \div \frac{2}{3}$    **11.** $1 \div \frac{3}{4}$    **12.** $1 \div \frac{7}{8}$    **13.** $3 \div \frac{3}{10}$    **14.** $4 \div \frac{2}{5}$

**15.** $9 \div \frac{9}{11}$    **16.** $5 \div \frac{3}{4}$    **17.** $7 \div \frac{3}{4}$    **18.** $10 \div \frac{5}{6}$    **19.** $3 \div \frac{11}{20}$

**20.** $7 \div \frac{2}{3}$    **21.** $15 \div \frac{1}{3}$    **22.** $32 \div \frac{4}{5}$    **23.** $5 \div \frac{4}{4}$    **24.** $20 \div \frac{2}{5}$

**25.** $19 \div \frac{12}{12}$    **26.** $21 \div \frac{7}{8}$    **27.** $32 \div \frac{16}{25}$    **28.** $6 \div \frac{34}{34}$    **29.** $100 \div \frac{3}{5}$

**MIXED REVIEW**    Compute.

**30.** $18 - \frac{3}{4}$    **31.** $18 \div \frac{3}{4}$    **32.** $9\frac{1}{3} \times \frac{5}{6}$    **33.** $9\frac{1}{3} + \frac{5}{6}$

**34.** $48 \div \frac{3}{8}$    **35.** $\frac{3}{8} \times 48$    **36.** $4\frac{1}{3} + 1\frac{1}{2}$    **37.** $4\frac{1}{3} - 1\frac{1}{2}$

**MENTAL MATH**    Use the pattern to solve mentally.

**38.** If $10 \div \frac{1}{2} = 20$, what is $10 \div \frac{1}{4}$?    $10 \div \frac{1}{8}$?    $10 \div \frac{1}{16}$?

Solve using the Sculptor's Dough recipe.

**39.** Phil made an eagle using the Sculptor's Dough recipe for 6 c. If an eagle takes $\frac{3}{4}$ c of dough, how many eagles can he make from 1 batch of dough?

**40.** Cathy's model of a snowflake used about $\frac{2}{5}$ c of dough. How many snowflakes can she make from $\frac{1}{2}$ batch of dough?

**41.** How much water and salt would you use to make the dough with only 3 c of flour?

Sculptor's Dough (makes 6 cups)
1$\frac{3}{4}$ c water
4 c flour
2 c salt
Mix all 3 ingredients together.
Add more water as needed. Shape the dough into several flat designs. Bake in oven at 200 °F for about 3 h.

## Dividing Fractions

How many $\frac{1}{4}$-lb hamburgers can be made from $\frac{3}{4}$ lb of meat?

- How many $\frac{1}{4}$ lb are in $\frac{3}{4}$ lb?

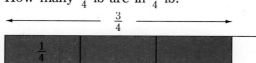

Do you see that three $\frac{1}{4}$-lb hamburgers can be made from $\frac{3}{4}$ lb of meat?

To divide, multiply by the reciprocal of $\frac{1}{4}$.

$$\frac{3}{4} \div \frac{1}{4} = \frac{3}{4} \times \frac{\overset{1}{\cancel{4}}}{1} = 3$$

How many $\frac{1}{8}$-lb hamburgers can be made with the same amount of meat?

- How many $\frac{1}{8}$ lb are in $\frac{3}{4}$ lb?

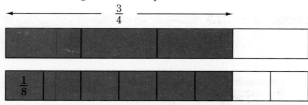

Can you count six $\frac{1}{8}$-lb hamburgers in $\frac{3}{4}$ lb?

Multiply by the reciprocal of $\frac{1}{8}$.

$$\frac{3}{4} \div \frac{1}{8} = \frac{3}{\underset{1}{\cancel{4}}} \times \frac{\overset{2}{\cancel{8}}}{1} = 6$$

How can $\frac{5}{6}$ lb of meat be shared equally between Pat and Lou?

- What is $\frac{5}{6}$ divided by 2?

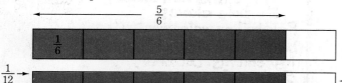

Pat's
Lou's

Multiply by the reciprocal of 2.

$$\frac{5}{6} \div 2 = \frac{5}{6} \times \frac{1}{2} = \frac{5}{12}$$

Do you see that Pat and Lou would get $\frac{5}{12}$ lb of meat each?

═══════════ **GUIDED PRACTICE** ═══════════

Write the quotient in lowest terms.

**1.** $\frac{7}{8} \div \frac{3}{4}$   **2.** $\frac{3}{4} \div \frac{7}{8}$   **3.** $\frac{4}{5} \div 4$   **4.** $\frac{5}{6} \div \frac{5}{6}$   **5.** $\frac{1}{6} \div 6$

═══════════ **PRACTICE** ═══════════

Write the quotient in lowest terms.

**6.** $\frac{3}{4} \div \frac{2}{3}$   **7.** $\frac{3}{4} \div \frac{3}{4}$   **8.** $\frac{4}{5} \div \frac{3}{4}$   **9.** $\frac{3}{4} \div 1$   **10.** $\frac{3}{4} \div 3$

**11.** $\frac{6}{11} \div 4$   **12.** $\frac{5}{8} \div 10$   **13.** $\frac{7}{9} \div 14$   **14.** $\frac{2}{3} \div 36$   **15.** $\frac{4}{9} \div \frac{4}{5}$

**16.** $\dfrac{6}{1} \div \dfrac{1}{6}$    **17.** $\dfrac{5}{9} \div \dfrac{1}{3}$    **18.** $\dfrac{1}{16} \div 4$    **19.** $\dfrac{4}{5} \div \dfrac{14}{5}$    **20.** $\dfrac{18}{19} \div 12$

**21.** $\dfrac{8}{9} \div \dfrac{2}{3}$    **22.** $\dfrac{9}{10} \div 45$    **23.** $\dfrac{8}{15} \div \dfrac{16}{25}$    **24.** $\dfrac{8}{11} \div \dfrac{8}{11}$    **25.** $\dfrac{3}{8} \div \dfrac{7}{12}$

**26.** $\dfrac{4}{7} \div \dfrac{10}{14}$    **27.** $\dfrac{7}{9} \div 13$    **28.** $\dfrac{9}{12} \div \dfrac{7}{6}$    **29.** $\dfrac{8}{7} \div \dfrac{4}{9}$    **30.** $\dfrac{14}{9} \div \dfrac{6}{4}$

**31.** $\left(\dfrac{2}{3} + \dfrac{1}{8}\right) \div \dfrac{1}{2}$    **32.** $\left(\dfrac{7}{8} - \dfrac{1}{4}\right) \div 4$    **33.** $\left(\dfrac{4}{5} \times \dfrac{10}{20}\right) \div \dfrac{8}{9}$

**MIXED REVIEW**    Compute.

**34.** $4\dfrac{1}{2} + \dfrac{5}{6}$    **35.** $3\dfrac{1}{3} - \dfrac{7}{8}$    **36.** $\dfrac{5}{6} \times 1\dfrac{1}{2}$    **37.** $\dfrac{4}{5} \div \dfrac{3}{8}$

**38.** $9\dfrac{1}{3} + 6\dfrac{1}{2}$    **39.** $5\dfrac{3}{4} - 2\dfrac{9}{10}$    **40.** $3\dfrac{1}{4} \times 3\dfrac{1}{4}$    **41.** $\dfrac{1}{2} \div \dfrac{4}{5}$

---

**PROBLEM SOLVING**

**CHOOSE** Choose paper and pencil or mental math to solve.

**42.** You want to make spicy orange herbal tea but have only 1 tea bag. How much of each other ingredient would you need?

**43.** How many tablespoons of honey are used per cup of orange juice in this recipe?

**44.** Suppose this is a recipe for 4 c of tea. In that case, how could you modify it to make 10 c?

"Spicy Orange Herbal Tea"
4 c boiling water
2 herbal lemon tea bags
½ c orange juice
3 T honey
1 in. cinnamon stick
5 whole cloves
Pour boiling water over the tea bags. Add the remaining ingredients. Let brew 5 min before serving.

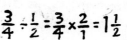

$\dfrac{3}{4} \div \dfrac{1}{2} = \dfrac{3}{4} \times \dfrac{2}{1} = 1\dfrac{1}{2}$
This answer is weird!
When you divide the answer should get smaller!

---

*Critical Thinking*

• With a partner, continue the pattern for the next three divisions.

$8 \div 8,\ 8 \div 4,\ 8 \div 2,\ 8 \div 1,$
$8 \div \dfrac{1}{2},\ 8 \div \dfrac{1}{4},\ \blacksquare\ \blacksquare\ \blacksquare$

• Explain the value of the quotient you get when you divide by a fraction less than 1.

# Dividing With Mixed Numbers

Two square pieces of wood measuring $5\frac{1}{8}$ in. on a side are needed for the ends of the CD (compact disk) holder at the right. Could you use a board that is 11 in. long and $5\frac{1}{8}$ in. wide for the 2 end pieces?

If you know how to divide fractions and how to change mixed numbers to fractions, you can make a **MATH·CONNECTION** to divide 11 by $5\frac{1}{8}$.

---

Change $5\frac{1}{8}$ to $\frac{41}{8}$.

$$11 \div 5\frac{1}{8} \implies 11 \div \frac{41}{8}$$

Multiply by the reciprocal of $5\frac{1}{8}$, or $\frac{8}{41}$.

$$11 \times \frac{8}{41} = \frac{88}{41} = 2\frac{6}{41}$$

---

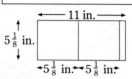

The 11-in. board could be used.

Another example:

$$2\frac{1}{4} \div 1\frac{1}{2} = \frac{9}{4} \div \frac{3}{2} = \frac{\overset{3}{9}}{\underset{2}{4}} \times \frac{\overset{1}{2}}{\underset{1}{3}} = \frac{3}{2} = 1\frac{1}{2}$$

---

### GUIDED PRACTICE

Write the quotient in lowest terms.

1. $3\frac{3}{7} \div \frac{6}{7}$
2. $3\frac{1}{2} \div 1\frac{1}{2}$
3. $9\frac{3}{4} \div 1\frac{7}{8}$
4. $6\frac{2}{3} \div 1\frac{1}{9}$

### PRACTICE

Write the quotient in lowest terms.

5. $8\frac{2}{3} \div 4\frac{1}{3}$
6. $8\frac{2}{3} \div 8\frac{2}{3}$
7. $4 \div 2\frac{1}{2}$
8. $6\frac{3}{4} \div 40\frac{1}{2}$

9. $5\frac{3}{5} \div \frac{4}{7}$
10. $\frac{16}{15} \div 3\frac{1}{5}$
11. $15\frac{3}{4} \div 15\frac{3}{4}$
12. $8\frac{7}{8} \div \frac{7}{8}$

13. $8\frac{2}{3} \div 1\frac{5}{8}$
14. $0 \div 3\frac{4}{5}$
15. $4\frac{4}{5} \div 1$
16. $2\frac{1}{10} \div 5\frac{1}{5}$

17. $\frac{5}{6} \div 2\frac{1}{2}$
18. $6\frac{3}{4} \div 7\frac{1}{4}$
19. $13\frac{1}{2} \div 3\frac{3}{8}$
20. $25\frac{1}{3} \div 3\frac{1}{6}$

**21.** $5\frac{1}{2} \div \frac{3}{8}$  **22.** $\left(4\frac{1}{2} \times \frac{2}{4}\right) \div \frac{1}{2}$  **23.** $\left(\frac{4}{5} - \frac{6}{10}\right) \div 1\frac{1}{2}$

**MIXED REVIEW**  Compute.

**24.** $6\frac{1}{7} - \frac{5}{7}$  **25.** $\frac{3}{8} \times \frac{4}{5}$  **26.** $2\frac{1}{2} + \frac{3}{4}$  **27.** $2\frac{1}{4} \div 1\frac{1}{2}$

**28.** $9\frac{1}{3} \times \frac{3}{4}$  **29.** $\frac{5}{16} + 1\frac{1}{8}$  **30.** $\frac{5}{6} \div \frac{5}{6}$  **31.** $3 - 1\frac{2}{3}$

**NUMBER SENSE**  Is the quotient *greater than* or *less than* 1?

**32.** $6 \div 2\frac{1}{2}$  **33.** $2\frac{3}{4} \div 11$  **34.** $5 \div \frac{3}{4}$  **35.** $2\frac{1}{3} \div 9\frac{1}{2}$

---

**PROBLEM SOLVING**

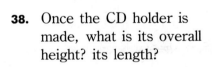 Choose mental math, estimation, or paper and pencil to solve.

**36.** **IN YOUR WORDS**  Explain why you would not want to cut all 5 pieces for the CD holder at the right from the same board.

**37.** You have a $10\frac{1}{2}$ in. by $9\frac{3}{4}$ in. piece of wood that is $\frac{1}{4}$ in. thick. Is that enough to cut the 3 long rectangular pieces? Prove your answer with a sketch on grid paper. Let each square on the grid represent 1 in.$^2$.

**38.** Once the CD holder is made, what is its overall height? its length?

**39.** A single CD is about $\frac{7}{16}$ in. thick. About how many CDs could you store in this holder?

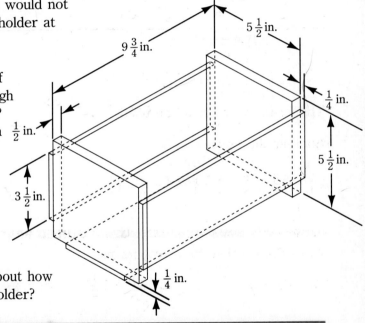

---

*Estimate*

Compatible numbers can help you estimate the quotient of mixed fractions.

$43\frac{1}{2} \div 6\frac{1}{8} = ?$  ⇨  $42 \div 6 = 7$  ⇨  So, $43\frac{1}{2} \div 6\frac{1}{8}$ is about 7.

Use compatible numbers to estimate.

**1.** $58 \div 5\frac{3}{5}$  **2.** $25\frac{3}{8} \div 3\frac{1}{9}$  **3.** $34\frac{5}{16} \div 8\frac{2}{13}$  **4.** $105\frac{1}{3} \div 8\frac{2}{3}$

# Problem Solving Strategy: Making A Table

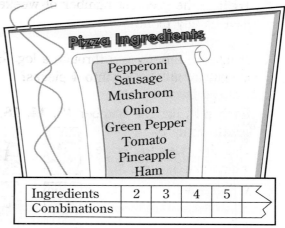

Some problems can be solved when you put the information in a table and look for a pattern.

At a party, every person shook hands with every other person once. If there were 16 people at the party, how many handshakes took place?

Think of fewer people at the party. How many handshakes would there be if there were 2 people at the party? 3 people? 4 people?

Record what you learned from the diagrams into the table.

| People | 1 | 2 | 3 | 4 | 5 | 6 | 7 |
|--------|---|---|---|---|----|----|---|
| Handshakes | 0 | 1 | 3 | 6 | 10 | 15 | ? |

Look at the number of handshakes. Can you see a pattern? How many handshakes would there be for 7 people?

Now, continue the pattern to find out how many handshakes took place among the 16 people at the party.

---

**GUIDED PRACTICE**

Make a table to help you find a pattern that solves the problem.

1. You must choose exactly 2 ingredients on a pizza from the list shown.

   a. How many ingredients are there in all to select from?

   b. How many different combination pizzas could you choose if there were only 2 ingredients on the list? 3 ingredients? 4 ingredients?

   c. How many different combination pizzas could you choose from the list of all 8 ingredients?

**Pizza Ingredients**

Pepperoni
Sausage
Mushroom
Onion
Green Pepper
Tomato
Pineapple
Ham

| Ingredients | 2 | 3 | 4 | 5 | |
|-------------|---|---|---|---|--|
| Combinations | | | | | |

Make a table to help you find the pattern that solves the problem.

**2.** If the pattern were continued, how many toothpicks would it take to make 25 squares?

**3. a.** How many small triangles, , are on triangular grids $A$, $B$, and $C$?

    **b.** How many small triangles would a triangular grid with 10 rows have?

**4.** How many triangles, of the sizes shown below, are in the triangular grid $A$? $B$? $C$?

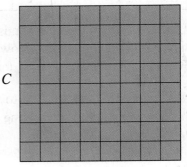

**5.** How many squares of the sizes shown below are on checkerboards $A$, $B$, and $C$?

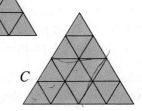

**6.** Find all of the different sized squares on checkerboard $C$. How many squares, of all different sizes are there?

CHOOSE  Choose a strategy to solve.

**7.** What is the greatest number of weekend days you can have in any month?

**8.** It takes 5 min to saw through a log. How long will it take to cut the log into 4 pieces?

**9.** Each card has the number **12**, **15**, **18**, or **20** on its back. Use the clues to decide which number is on each card.

• The numbers on **C** and **B** are multiples of 5.

• The number on **D** is greater than that on **B**.

• The number on **A** is less than that on **C**.

# Planning a Tree Planting Project

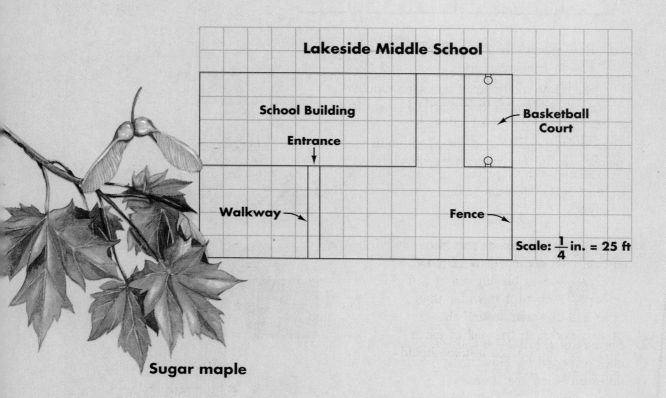

**Sugar maple**

The Lakeside Nursery is donating as many sugar maple, white ash, and red maple trees as needed for landscaping to the new Lakeside Middle School.

Pretend that you have been appointed to a task force to plan the tree-planting project. The job of your task force is to determine the number of trees needed and the number of volunteers needed to get the job done and to oversee the project.

Work in a small group.

1. Copy the scale drawing of the Lakeside School grounds. Use the scale to decide where there is room to plant the trees.

2. Agree on the number and kind of trees that will be planted. Use the chart on page 223 to help you decide. On the scale drawing show the location of the new trees.

222  LESSON 7–9

MATH AND ECOLOGY

**3.** Write the Lakeside Nursery a letter stating the number of trees of each type you will need. Be sure to thank them for donating the trees. Tell them when and where the trees are to be delivered. What else might be included in your letter?

| Type of Tree | Dimensions of Full-grown Tree | Suggested Spacing Between Trees |
|---|---|---|
| sugar maple | 60–80 ft high 40–60 ft wide | 20 ft |
| white ash | 60–80 ft high 40–60 ft wide | 20 ft |
| red maple | 50–70 ft high 30–50 ft wide | 15 ft |

Continue the planning by answering the questions.

**4.** Estimate that it will take 2 workers about 1 h to plant each tree. How many volunteers will you need to get the trees planted? Would you include only students on your project or also members of the community? Why?

Red maple

**5.** Each tree delivered from the nursery is about 10 to 12 ft tall. Holes need to be dug about 2 ft deep and about 1 ft wider than the ball of earth around the tree's roots. If the ball of earth is 30 in., how wide a hole should be dug for each tree?

**6.** What types of equipment will you need to plant the trees? How will you lift the trees? How will you dig the holes? Decide on a plan to get the equipment.

White ash

**7.** Can the tree planting be completed in one weekend? What factors might influence the completion of the job?

Congratulations! You and the tree-planting task force have done a great job.

## LANGUAGE & VOCABULARY

1. Explain how to find the reciprocal of a mixed number.

2. Explain how to divide $\frac{1}{8}$ by $\frac{6}{7}$.

Make up one problem to fit each situation.

3. dividing a whole number by a fraction so that the quotient is greater than the whole number

4. dividing a whole number by a fraction so that the quotient is equal to the whole number

## TEST ✓

### CONCEPTS

Write the reciprocal of the number. *(pages 208–209)*

1. 3
2. $\frac{1}{7}$
3. $2\frac{1}{4}$
4. $\frac{5}{9}$
5. $4\frac{2}{3}$

### SKILLS

Write the product in lowest terms. *(pages 204–209)*

6. $\frac{1}{4}$ of $\frac{1}{3}$
7. $\frac{2}{5}$ of $\frac{5}{6}$
8. $\frac{3}{8} \times \frac{2}{3}$
9. $\frac{6}{9} \times \frac{1}{2}$

10. $\frac{2}{1} \times \frac{3}{8}$
11. $\frac{3}{11} \times 4$
12. $\frac{2}{9} \times 8$
13. $28 \times \frac{3}{7}$

14. $2\frac{1}{2} \times \frac{3}{4}$
15. $\frac{1}{4} \times 4\frac{1}{5}$
16. $1\frac{1}{3} \times 7\frac{2}{5}$
17. $3\frac{5}{9} \times 2\frac{1}{5}$

Write the quotient in lowest terms. *(pages 214–219)*

18. $7 \div \frac{2}{5}$
19. $25 \div \frac{2}{3}$
20. $9 \div \frac{3}{7}$
21. $\frac{7}{9} \div 12$

22. $\frac{9}{11} \div \frac{3}{5}$
23. $\frac{4}{8} \div \frac{1}{5}$
24. $8\frac{3}{5} \div \frac{1}{5}$
25. $6\frac{2}{9} \div 2\frac{1}{3}$

Estimate. Do not calculate. *(pages 210–211)*

**26.** Two bookcases, each with 7 shelves, are empty. Each shelf holds about 20 books. The library receives a shipment of 6 cartons, each containing 50 books.

    **a.** How many empty shelves are there?

    **b.** About how many books can fit on the 2 bookcases?

    **c.** About how many books in the shipment will not fit on the shelves?

Solve. *(pages 220–221)*

**27.** Make a table to help you find the pattern that solves the problem. Square banquet tables seat 4 people, 1 on each side. If the tables are lined up as shown in the picture, what is the fewest number of tables needed to seat 25 dinner guests?

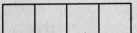

**28.** A 25-ft piece of timber is to be cut into pieces, each $\frac{2}{3}$ ft long. How many $\frac{2}{3}$-ft pieces can be cut? How much timber will be left?

**LEARNING LOG**

Write the answers in your learning log.

  **1.** Your friend says $4\frac{3}{5}$ and $\frac{5}{23}$ are reciprocals. Explain this thinking.

  **2.** A multiplication problem with whole numbers can be checked by dividing. Explain how this method would work with fractions. Include an example.

# EXTRA PRACTICE

Write the reciprocal of the number. *(pages 208–209)*

**1.** $6$ **2.** $\frac{1}{5}$ **3.** $\frac{7}{9}$ **4.** $2$ **5.** $9\frac{3}{8}$

**6.** $1\frac{1}{2}$ **7.** $14$ **8.** $\frac{3}{11}$ **9.** $10$ **10.** $7\frac{2}{5}$

Write the answer in lowest terms. *(pages 204–209, 214–219)*

**11.** $\frac{1}{3} \times \frac{0}{8}$ **12.** $\frac{2}{5} \times \frac{3}{2}$ **13.** $\frac{6}{7} \times \frac{1}{2}$ **14.** $\frac{0}{9} \times \frac{0}{5}$

**15.** $\frac{3}{7} \times 15$ **16.** $8 \times \frac{1}{5}$ **17.** $2 \times \frac{13}{12}$ **18.** $\frac{1}{9} \times 11$

**19.** $\frac{1}{3} \times 2\frac{1}{5}$ **20.** $2\frac{1}{2} \times \frac{4}{9}$ **21.** $3 \times 8\frac{1}{7}$ **22.** $4\frac{1}{3} \times 2\frac{3}{8}$

**23.** $56 \times \frac{1}{7}$ **24.** $3\frac{7}{9} \times 2\frac{1}{5}$ **25.** $\frac{2}{5} \times 3\frac{1}{4}$ **26.** $27 \times 1\frac{5}{6}$

**27.** $8 \div \frac{1}{5}$ **28.** $12 \div \frac{1}{5}$ **29.** $7 \div \frac{3}{4}$ **30.** $15 \div \frac{2}{3}$

**31.** $\frac{5}{9} \div 3$ **32.** $\frac{1}{4} \div 11$ **33.** $\frac{3}{10} \div 14$ **34.** $\frac{3}{7} \div 8$

**35.** $\frac{1}{2} \div \frac{2}{9}$ **36.** $\frac{2}{3} \div \frac{1}{6}$ **37.** $\frac{7}{15} \div \frac{8}{9}$ **38.** $\frac{2}{5} \div \frac{4}{3}$

**39.** $2\frac{5}{6} \div \frac{3}{5}$ **40.** $3\frac{5}{8} \div 1\frac{1}{4}$ **41.** $\frac{7}{16} \div 1\frac{5}{9}$ **42.** $4\frac{11}{12} \div 5\frac{1}{3}$

Solve. *(pages 210–211, 220–221)*

**43.** A roller coaster has 6 cars. Each car can hold 4 people. A ride takes 3 min and there are 150 people in line. The ride is closing in 30 min. Will all the people be able to ride?

**44.** During a sale, you pay \$10 for the first shirt you buy. If you buy 2 shirts, you pay \$10 plus $\frac{1}{2}$ of \$10 for the second. If you buy 3 shirts, you pay \$20 plus $\frac{1}{3}$ of \$10 for the third, and so on. How much would you pay for 10 shirts?

## Multiplying with Unit Fractions

The ancient Egyptians did almost all computations using unit fractions, or fractions with a numerator of 1. Although this was difficult, much of what was known several thousand years ago can still be applied today. Here are some examples.

- To double the size of any fraction whose denominator is an even number, divide the denominator by 2. Using this method for $2 \times \frac{1}{8}$ leads to thinking $8 \div 2 = 4$, so $2 \times \frac{1}{8} = \frac{1}{4}$.

- To double any fraction whose denominator is divisible by 3, divide the denominator by 3 to get a quotient $q$. Then write the double as $\frac{1}{2q} + \frac{1}{6q}$. To double $\frac{1}{27}$, divide 27 by 3 to get the quotient 9. Then the double of $\frac{1}{27}$ is $\frac{1}{2 \times 9} + \frac{1}{6 \times 9}$, or $\frac{1}{18} + \frac{1}{54}$.

Work with a partner. Write ten unit fractions and discuss which ones can be doubled by either method above. Work together to write the double for each of those that you can. Find out about other methods the ancient Egyptians used to perform computations.

## A Shopping Spree

Choose a mail-order catalog. Pretend that you have just been given $500 and that your goal is to spend as much of it as possible on items from the catalog. In addition to deciding what you want to purchase, think about whether you have to pay sales tax and shipping charges.

You can find answers to these questions in your catalog. Remember that both sales tax and shipping charges must be deducted from the $500. How close can you come to spending exactly $500?

## One Line Design

Try to draw the design at the bottom without lifting your pencil from the paper and without retracing any lines. After you do this, make up other designs that can be drawn without lifting the pencil or retracing. Give them to a friend to try to draw.

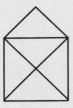

Find the answer.

**1.** $3\frac{1}{8} + 2\frac{5}{6} =$

   **a.** $5\frac{3}{7}$

   **b.** $5\frac{23}{24}$

   **c.** $5\frac{1}{6}$

   **d.** none of these

**2.** $12 - 5\frac{3}{7} =$

   **a.** $6\frac{4}{7}$

   **b.** $7\frac{4}{7}$

   **c.** $6\frac{3}{7}$

   **d.** none of these

**3.** $\frac{3}{7} \times \frac{4}{9} =$

   **a.** $\frac{3}{4}$

   **b.** $\frac{7}{16}$

   **c.** $\frac{4}{21}$

   **d.** none of these

**4.** $2\frac{1}{7} \times 3\frac{5}{8} =$

   **a.** $7\frac{43}{56}$

   **b.** $6\frac{5}{56}$

   **c.** $6$

   **d.** none of these

**5.** $2 \div \frac{4}{7} =$

   **a.** $\frac{2}{7}$

   **b.** $3\frac{1}{2}$

   **c.** $1\frac{1}{7}$

   **d.** none of these

**6.** $3\frac{5}{9} \div 1\frac{1}{5} =$

   **a.** $2\frac{26}{27}$

   **b.** $4\frac{4}{15}$

   **c.** $1\frac{13}{32}$

   **d.** none of these

Find the matching value.

**7.** $\frac{2}{9}$

   **a.** $0.\overline{2}$

   **b.** $0.29$

   **c.** $0.11$

   **d.** none of these

**8.** $\frac{3}{8}$

   **a.** $0.378$

   **b.** $0.37$

   **c.** $0.375$

   **d.** none of these

**9.** $4\frac{9}{11}$

   **a.** $4.9$

   **b.** $4.\overline{81}$

   **c.** $4.81$

   **d.** none of these

**10.** 6 yd

   **a.** 216 in.

   **b.** 12 ft

   **c.** 24 ft

   **d.** none of these

**11.** 9 qt, 1 pt

   **a.** 2 gal, 1 qt

   **b.** 37 qt

   **c.** 19 c

   **d.** none of these

**12.** 4 lb, 5 oz

   **a.** 133 oz

   **b.** 69 oz

   **c.** 20 oz

   **d.** none of these

# PROBLEM SOLVING REVIEW

Remember the strategies and types of problems you've had so far. Solve.

**Problem Solving Check List**

- Too much information
- Too little information
- Working backward
- Using guess and check

1. Ally built a number tetrahedron (figure with 4 faces). The smallest number on a face is 12; the largest is 30. The numbers are all consecutive multiples of the same number.

   a. How many faces are on the tetrahedron?

   b. How can you find the other numbers on the faces?

   c. What is the sum of the numbers on the faces?

2. The winning team scored 5 points less than 3 times the number of points the losing team scored. The winning team scored 40 points. How many points did the losing team score?

3. Mark enlarged a 5-in. by 7-in. photo so that the short edge of the enlargement was $12\frac{1}{2}$ in. If the ratio of the sides stayed the same, how long was the long edge of the enlargement?

4. Between 8 A.M. and noon, the temperature rose 5°F, fell 4°F, fell 3°F, and rose 2°F. If the temperature at noon was 2°F, what was the temperature at 8 A.M.?

5. A truck carrying cargo weighs 32,365 lb when fully loaded. At two stops, the driver unloads 7 yd$^3$ and 12 yd$^3$ of cargo. What is the weight of the truck then?

6. Bart's school has 6 doors. Each day he enters through 1 door and leaves through a different door. How many days can he do this before he must repeat a combination?

7. A driver travels east for 25 mi, turns north and goes another 15 mi. To return home over the same roads, in what directions will she have to travel?

8. On Monday the highest temperature was 80°F. On Tuesday the highest temperature was 15% lower than on Monday. On Wednesday the highest temperature reached 90% of Tuesday's temperature. To the nearest degree, what was Wednesday's highest temperature?

## THE WEIRD SERIES

Estimate the values of $A$ and $B$.

$$\frac{9}{8} \times \frac{7}{6} \times \frac{5}{4} \times \frac{3}{2} = A$$

$$\frac{2}{3} \times \frac{4}{5} \times \frac{6}{7} \times \frac{8}{9} = B$$

What special relationship do the values of $A$ and $B$ have?

Find the values of $A$ and $B$, and write them in simplest form. Compare your estimates with the actual values of $A$ and $B$.

## FRACTION MADNESS

Work with a partner or in a small group to answer the problems.

1. Study the equation. Write two sets of keystrokes that will give you the answer.

$$\frac{33}{12} \times \frac{15}{27} \times \frac{36}{30} \times \frac{24}{44} = 1$$

2. Study the equation. Write a set of keystrokes that will give you the answer.
(*Hint:* Remember reciprocals.)

$$\frac{9}{24} \div \frac{6}{16} \times \frac{40}{72} \div \frac{35}{63} = 1$$

## CHANGING AND REARRANGING

In the computer game *Fraction Challenge II*, players find missing digits to complete fraction multiplication and division problems. This activity, which you can do with a pencil and paper, helps you develop skills at writing multiplication and division problems with fractions.

Use each group of six numbers to create fraction equations. Work with a partner to try and create as many true equations as possible. Use the models with the missing digits to help.

1 3 5 6 9 10 [multiplication]          2 4 4 4 6 12 [division]

**DID YOU KNOW . . . ?**

One reason that the Golden Gate Bridge survived the California earthquake of October 17, 1989, is its design.

The roadway of this suspension bridge hangs from steel cables that are supported by two high towers. This design lets the bridge flex during high winds and earthquakes.

The part of the San Francisco-Oakland Bay Bridge that collapsed has a less flexible, cantilever design. Its roadway is supported by towers that can be affected by earth tremors.

Alcatraz Island

Treasure Island

**San Francisco - Oakland Bay Bridge**

OAKLAND

*San Francisco Bay*

**Golden Gate Bridge**

Yerba Buena Island

SAN FRANCISCO

**USING DATA**

Collect

Organize

Describe

Predict

Bridges and buildings should be designed to help them survive earthquakes, fires, floods, and windstorms. Ask 15 people if they have experienced an earthquake, tornado, hurricane, flood, or fire. Find out whether good design helped to protect them.

Work with your classmates to combine data and make a bar graph.

## Exploring Basic Figures

A **plane** is like a flat surface that goes on and on without end. It contains an infinite number of **points**, or exact locations.

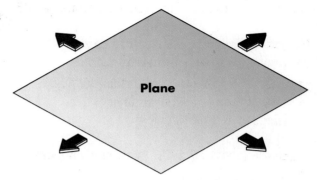

Plane

1. Name some objects that look like parts of planes.

Use plane 1 at right for Exercises 2–9.

2. How many points can you see?

**3. THINK ALOUD** How many points can you not see? Explain.

A **line** is a set of points that extends without end in opposite directions.

> You say, "line *MP*" or "line *PM*."
> You write $\overleftrightarrow{MP}$ or $\overleftrightarrow{PM}$.

M     N     O     P

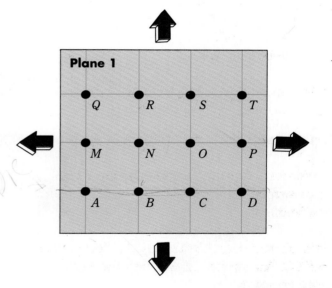

**Plane 1**

Q   R   S   T

M   N   O   P

A   B   C   D

4. What are three other names for $\overleftrightarrow{MP}$?

5. How many lines can be drawn through *B* and *D*? any two points?

6. How many lines can be drawn that connect *S* with any point shown?

7. **THINK ALOUD** How many lines in the plane contain point *S*?

A **line segment** is a part of a line with two endpoints.

> You write $\overline{MN}$ or $\overline{NM}$.
>
> M         N    You say "line segment *MN*" or "line segment *NM*."

8. If $\overline{ST}$ is 1 cm long, name all segments you can draw that measure 3 cm.

Line segments of the same length are **congruent**.

9. Name four line segments that can be drawn congruent to $\overline{MO}$. Repeat for $\overline{SC}$.

**10.** In plane 2, do $\overleftrightarrow{HJ}$ and $\overleftrightarrow{FK}$ intersect at point $J$, point $K$, or point $F$?

Remember that lines extend without end.

**11.** Do $\overleftrightarrow{KF}$ and $\overleftrightarrow{GM}$ intersect at some point?

**12.** Do $\overleftrightarrow{HK}$ and $\overleftrightarrow{GM}$ intersect at some point?

**Parallel lines** are lines that never intersect and are in the same plane.

**13.** Are $\overleftrightarrow{HK}$ and $\overleftrightarrow{GM}$ parallel lines? Name two other pairs of parallel lines you could draw.

A **ray** is a part of a line with one endpoint.

The endpoint is $A$.

$A$      $B$

You write $\overrightarrow{AB}$.
You say, "ray $AB$."

**14.** In plane 3, what is another name for $\overrightarrow{AE}$?

**15.** Name all the rays shown in plane 3.

Two rays with the same endpoint form an **angle**. The common endpoint is a **vertex**.

In plane 3, ray $AB$ and ray $AC$ form angle $BAC$. You write $\angle BAC$ with the vertex in the middle.

**16.** Name the rays that form $\angle DAF$.

**17.** Are $\angle BAC$ and $\angle CAE$ the same angle?

**18.** Name all angles shown in plane 3.

**19.** **CREATE YOUR OWN** Use two pieces of paper to construct a model of two planes like planes 4 and 5. Where do the two planes intersect?

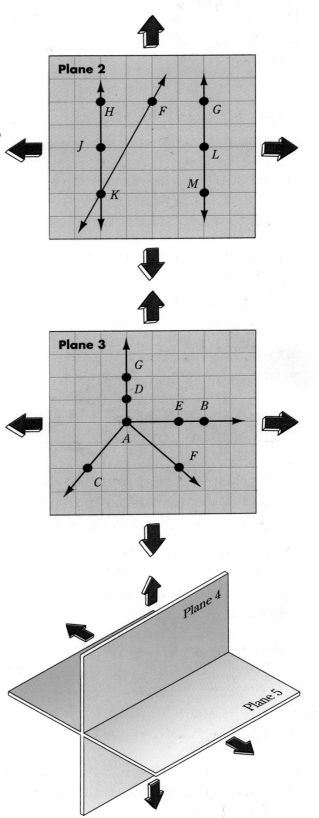

## Measuring Angles

A ship's navigator uses angles to stay on course at sea. The ship in the diagram is on a course 60° from north. Navigation angles have three digits and are measured clockwise from north with a compass.

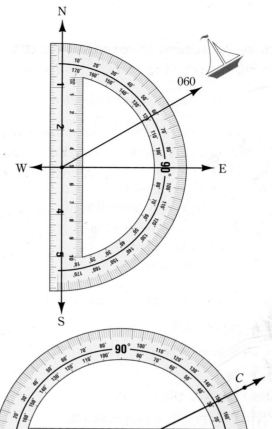

To measure the navigation angle above, use the outer scale of a protractor. Why?

**STEPS** Place the center of the protractor at the vertex of the angle.

Line up one side of the angle with 0°.

To draw an angle with a measure of 30°, use the inner scale of a protractor. Why?

**STEPS** Draw ray *AB*.

Place the protractor's center mark at the vertex, *A*. Line up 0° with ray *AB*.

Mark point *C* at 30° and draw ray *AC*.

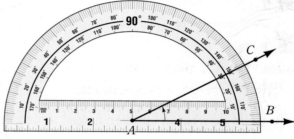

A ship sailing an easterly course forms a **right angle** with north measuring 90°. A right angle has **perpendicular** sides.

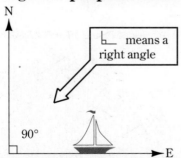

⌐ means a right angle

90°

An **acute angle** measures less than 90°.

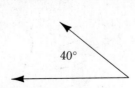

40°

A ship on a southerly course forms a **straight angle** with North.

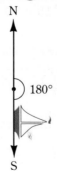

180°

An **obtuse angle** measures greater than 90° and less than 180°.

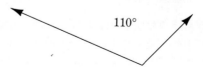

110°

Is the angle *acute*, *right*, *obtuse*, or *straight*?

**1.** 90°          **2.** 137°          **3.** 40°          **4.** 120°          **5.** 5°          **6.** 180°

Use a protractor to complete. (m∠FED means "the measure of ∠FED is")

**7.** m∠*FED* = ▓ °          **8.** m∠*JKL* = ▓ °          **9.** m∠*WXY* = ▓ °

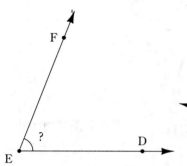

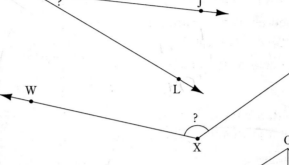

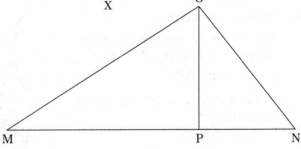

Use the figure at right to answer.

**10.** Which segment is perpendicular to segment *MN*? Identify the two right angles.

**11.** **ESTIMATE** Name one obtuse, one straight, and one acute angle.

Use a protractor to draw an angle with the given measure.

**12.** 20°          **13.** 150°          **14.** 75°          **15.** 90°          **16.** 128°          **17.** 9°

Estimate the position of each buoy in relation to north. Use the compass readings.

**18.** *B*          **19.** *C*          **20.** *D*

**21.** E          **22.** *F*          **23.** G

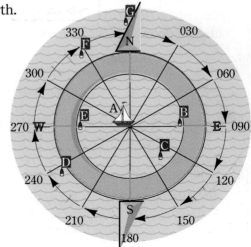

## Exploring Angle Relations

Many designs for stained glass are based on relations between angles. Use a protractor to explore some angle relations in the design on page 237.

**Congruent angles** are angles with the same measure. Angles *HIC* and *NOG* are congruent angles. Both measure 135°.

1. Find an angle congruent to ∠*AIB*.

2. What are the measures of ∠*FOG*, ∠*CLE*, and ∠*UOV*? Which two of these angles are congruent?

**Vertical angles** have rays going in opposite directions from the same point. All pairs of vertical angles are congruent. Angles *AIB* and *RIS* are vertical angles.

3. Measure ∠*CLD* and ∠*TLU*. What kind of angles are they? Are they congruent?

4. Find two other pairs of vertical angles in the design.

**Adjacent angles** have a common vertex and a common side, but no interior points in common. ∠*QIR* and ∠*RIS* are adjacent angles.

5. Do ∠*TLU* and ∠*ULM* have a common vertex? a common side? What can you conclude?

6. Find two other pairs of adjacent angles in the design.

7. **CRITICAL THINKING** Are pairs of adjacent angles always congruent?

---

**Two angles are complementary angles if the sum of their measures is 90°.**

**Two angles are supplementary angles if the sum of their measures is 180°.**

---

8. Find two angles in the design that are:
   **a.** complementary   **b.** supplementary

9. Use a protractor and ruler to draw:
   a. any angle supplementary to a 45° angle
   b. any angle complementary to a 25° angle

10. **CREATE YOUR OWN** Design a stained glass window that has an example of each kind of angle relation studied in this lesson.

# Problem Solving:
## Venn Diagrams

You can use **Venn diagrams**
to represent a collection of objects or events.

Days beginning with the letter *S*        Saturday
                                            Sunday

When two collections have nothing in common,
the figures in a Venn diagram do not overlap.

**Collection 1:**                                    Monday          **Collection 2:**
                                                     Tuesday
Days beginning        Saturday                       Wednesday       Days you
with the letter *S*   Sunday                         Thursday        usually go
                                                     Friday          to school

**THINK ALOUD**   How would you draw a Venn diagram
representing two collections with some items in common?

Try drawing a Venn diagram for collections 1 and 3.

> Collection 1: days beginning with the letter *S*
> Collection 3: days with six letters

> (*Hint*:   How many figures will you draw? What days
>            will you use? Can figures overlap?)

How would you draw a Venn diagram when one collection
is contained entirely within another collection? Draw a Venn
diagram for collections 2 and 4.

> Collection 2: days you usually go to school
> Collection 4: days beginning with the letter *T*

> (*Hint*:   Can one figure be inside the other?)

Do your Venn diagrams look like these?

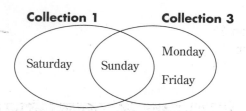

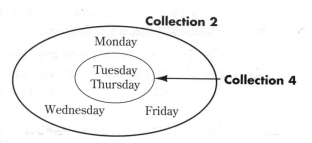

**1.** Look at the Venn diagram and answer the question.

   **a.** What kind of objects are represented in this Venn diagram?

   **b.** What are the two collections represented in this Venn diagram?

   **c.** Which school day has 8 letters?

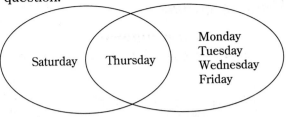

Draw a Venn diagram.
Use the collections at right.

   **2.** 𝔸 and 𝔹       **3.** 𝔹 and ℂ

   **4.** 𝔸 and 𝔾       **5.** ℂ and 𝔻

   **6.** ℂ and 𝔼       **7.** 𝔸 and ℂ

   **8.** 𝔾 and ℂ       **9.** 𝔻 and 𝔽

**10.** ℂ and 𝔽

Months of the Year:

𝔸: months with exactly 30 days
𝔹: months with 31 days
ℂ: months beginning with the letter *J*
𝔻: months that have the letters *ber*
𝔼: months that have four letters
𝔽: months with some summer vacation days
𝔾: all months

Describe the collection of numbers the Venn diagram shows.

**11.**

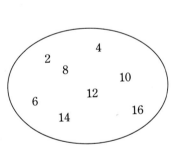

**12.**

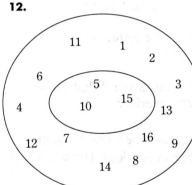

**13.**

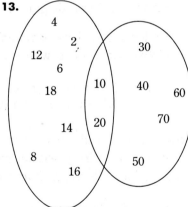

## Critical Thinking

How would you draw a Venn diagram to represent three collections? Think about these collections.

   Collection 1: multiples of 3 that are less than 35
   Collection 2: multiples of 5 that are less than 35
   Collection 3: multiples of 2 that are less than 35

Draw the diagram.

## Exploring Polygons

Use the workmasters with geometric
figures and polygon properties.

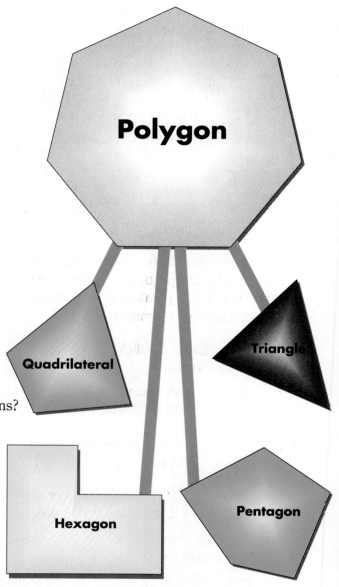

1. A **polygon** is a closed, plane figure
   made from three or more line segments.
   Two of your **geometric figures** are
   *not* polygons. Write their letters.

| Polygons | Number of Sides |
|----------|-----------------|
| Triangle | 3 |
| Quadrilateral | 4 |
| Pentagon | 5 |
| Hexagon | 6 |
| Octagon | 8 |

2. Sort the rest of the geometric figures
   by the number of sides they have.
   Which are triangles? quadrilaterals? pentagons?
   Is *E* or *F* a hexagon?

3. Figures *C*, *D*, and *F* are **regular
   polygons**. Regular polygons have
   all sides and angles congruent.
   Name two other figures that
   are regular polygons.

4. Quadrilaterals with exactly one
   pair of parallel sides are called
   **trapezoids**. They cannot have two
   sets of parallel sides. Name the figures
   that are trapezoids.

5. Place these quadrilaterals in two rows.

   Row 1:    *M*    *K*    *L*    *N*      ⇨ These are **parallelograms**.
   Row 2:    *R*    *S*    *P*    *Q*      ⇨ These are not parallelograms.

   a. Find the **polygon properties** that apply
      to a parallelogram.

   b. **IN YOUR WORDS** Now write your own definition
      of a parallelogram.

**6.** Place these figures in two rows.

Row 1:    *N*     *O*     *C*         ⇨ rectangles

Row 2:    *I*    *J*    *K*    *L*    *M*    ⇨ all other parallelograms

**CRITICAL THINKING**   Do rectangles have all the properties of parallelograms? Are rectangles parallelograms? What other property do rectangles have?

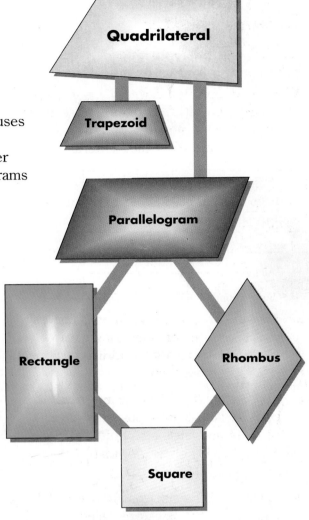

**7.** Place these figures in two rows.

Row 1:   *C*   *J*   *L*      ⇨ rhombuses

Row 2:   *N*   *O*   *I*   *K*   *M*   ⇨ all other parallelograms

**CRITICAL THINKING**   Do rhombuses have all the properties of parallelograms? Are rhombuses parallelograms? What other property do rhombuses have?

**8.** Place these parallelograms in two rows.

Row 1:    all rectangles
Row 2:    all rhombuses

**THINK ALOUD**   Which figure belongs in both rows? Why?

**9.** **IN YOUR WORDS**   Tell why a square is both a rectangle and a rhombus.

**10.** Use the descriptions below to check your answers to Exercises 5–9.

---

**A parallelogram is a quadrilateral with opposite sides parallel. Notice that opposite sides are also congruent.**

**A rhombus is a parallelogram with all sides congruent.**

**A rectangle is a parallelogram with only right angles.**

**A square can be described as a rectangle with all sides congruent, or as a rhombus with only right angles.**

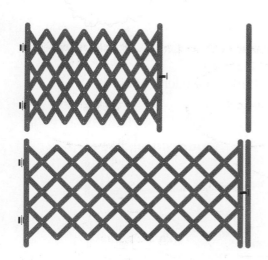

## Problem Solving: Making Generalizations

When the safety gate is partially open, many figures on it look like rhombuses. When closed, the figures look like squares.

**THINK ALOUD** What properties do squares and rhombuses have in common? What property does a square have that other rhombuses do not have?

When we generalize, we tell how ideas or things are related. The generalization, "A square is a rhombus," says that rhombuses make up a larger class of figures than squares. A Venn diagram can be used to show generalizations.

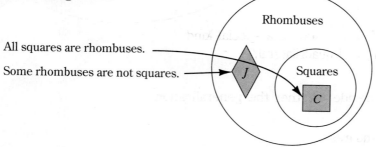

All squares are rhombuses.

Some rhombuses are not squares.

Are all properties of parallelograms also true for rhombuses?

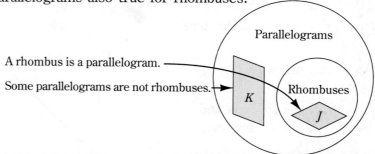

A rhombus is a parallelogram.

Some parallelograms are not rhombuses.

## GUIDED PRACTICE

1. Use the Venn diagram to answer the question.

   **a.** What three figures are in the Venn diagram?

   **b.** With what figures does a square share properties?

   **c.** Where would you place a trapezoid?

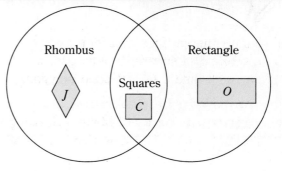

Is the generalization true? Write *yes* or *no*.

**2.** No trapezoid is a parallelogram.

**3.** Some trapezoids are parallelograms.

**4.** All trapezoids are parallelograms.

Complete each generalization with *All, Some,* or *No.*

**5.** _____ parallelograms are quadrilaterals.

**6.** _____ rectangles are parallelograms.

**7.** _____ quadrilaterals are rectangles.

**8.** _____ rectangles are quadrilaterals.

**9.** _____ trapezoids are parallelograms.

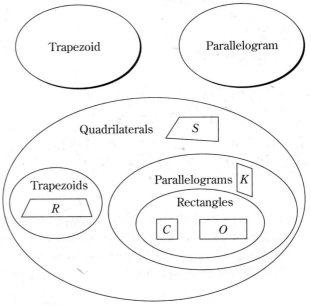

**10. CRITICAL THINKING** Why is a square a special kind of rectangle, parallelogram, and quadrilateral?

Draw a Venn diagram. Then decide whether the generalization is *true* or *false.*

**11.** Some rectangles are not squares.

**12.** Some parallelograms are not rectangles.

**13.** Some trapezoids are not quadrilaterals.

**CHOOSE** Choose any strategy to solve.

**14.** How many triangles can you find altogether? Explain your answer.

**15.** Why can't you make a two-sided polygon?

**16.** Name the vertices that identify a triangle, a square, a pentagon, a hexagon, and a seven-sided polygon.

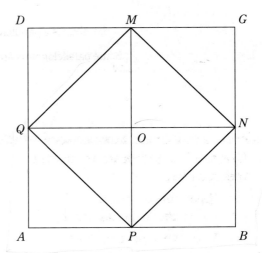

**17. CREATE YOUR OWN** Make a drawing that contains different kinds of polygons. Ask a friend to list all the polygons.

# Classifying Triangles

With seven sticks of the lengths shown, you could make several different kinds of triangles.

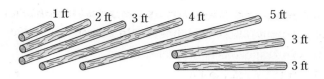

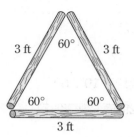

An **equilateral triangle** has all sides and angles congruent.

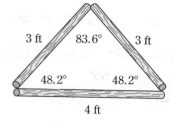

An **isosceles triangle** has two congruent sides and two congruent angles.

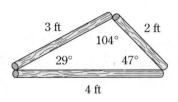

A **scalene triangle** has no congruent sides or congruent angles.

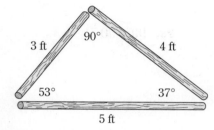

A **right triangle** has a right angle.

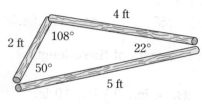

An **obtuse triangle** has one obtuse angle.

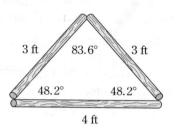

An **acute triangle** has all acute angles.

Add the three angle measures for each triangle above. What is the sum in each case?

> **The sum of the measures of the angles of a triangle is 180°.**

**THINK ALOUD**   If you use any three of the seven sticks, will you always be able to make a triangle? Why or why not?

---
### GUIDED PRACTICE

Name the triangle with the given property.

**1.** all acute angles

**2.** two congruent angles

**3.** no congruent angles

**4.** one obtuse angle

**NUMBER SENSE**   The measures of two angles of a triangle are given. What is the measure of the third angle? Explain your answer.

**5.** 110°, 35°

**6.** 60°, 60°

Is a triangle that has these side lengths or angle measures *equilateral*, *isosceles*, or *scalene*?

**7.** 5 in., 7 in., 5 in.

**8.** $8\frac{1}{2}$ in., $8\frac{1}{2}$ in., $8\frac{1}{2}$ in.

**9.** 2 in., 3 in., 4 in.

**10.** 20°, 90°, 70°

**11.** 60°, 60°, 60°

**12.** 99.6°, 40.2°, 40.2°

Is a triangle with these angle measures *right*, *obtuse*, or *acute*?

**13.** 40°, 40°, 100°

**14.** 60°, 60°, 60°

**15.** 110°, 10°, 60°

**16.** 90°, 45°, 45°

**17.** 80.2°, 90°, 9.8°

**18.** 29.5°, 79.1°, 71.4°

**19.** **CRITICAL THINKING**  Can a triangle have two obtuse angles? Explain.

The measures of two angles of a triangle are given.
What is the measure of the third angle?

**20.** 60°, 80°

**21.** 125°, 45°

**22.** 55°, 64.2°

**23.** 90°, 30.5°

Can you make a triangle with segments of these lengths?
Write *yes* or *no*.

**24.** 1 in., 3 in., 5 in.

**25.** 4 in., $3\frac{1}{2}$ in., 10 in.

**26.** 10 in., $6\frac{1}{4}$ in., 4 in.

Is the generalization *true* or *false*?

**27.** Some right triangles can be scalene.

**28.** No equilateral triangles are right.

**29.** All scalene triangles are obtuse.

**30.** No isosceles triangles are obtuse.

## Critical Thinking

A **diagonal** of a polygon is a line segment that joins two nonadjacent vertices. Draw the polygon and its diagonals. Complete the table.

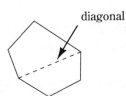

diagonal

Look for a pattern in the numbers. Then predict the number of diagonals in an octagon. Check your answer by drawing an octagon with its diagonals.

| Polygon | △ | □ | ⬠ | ⬡ | ⬠ |
|---|---|---|---|---|---|
| Number of sides | 3 | 4 | | | |
| Number of diagonals | | | | | |

---

**LANGUAGE & VOCABULARY**

---

For the pair of terms, write one sentence describing how the terms are the same and one sentence describing how they are different.

1. line—line segment

2. line segment—ray

3. intersecting line segments—parallel line segments

4. scalene triangle—equilateral triangle

5. isosceles right triangle—isosceles obtuse triangle

---

**QUICK QUIZ**

---

Is the angle *acute, right, obtuse,* or *straight*? *(pages 234–237)*

1. 92°    2. 159°    3. 17°    4. 180°

Is a triangle with these angle measures *right, obtuse,* or *acute*?
*(pages 232–233, 240–241, 244–245)*

5. 60°, 71°, 49°    6. 108°, 35°, 37°    7. 13°, 90°, 77°

The measures of two angles of a triangle are given. What is the measure of the third angle? *(pages 244–245)*

8. 123°, 31°    9. 68°, 72°

Solve. *(pages 238–239)*

10. All the students in class 7-152 study at least one of two languages. Sixteen study only Spanish, 9 study only French, and 3 study both languages.

   a. How many different languages are studied?

   b. Does the Venn diagram at right represent the situation?

   c. How many students are in the class?

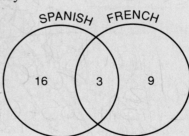

Write the answers in your learning log.

1. How are pictures of lines, segments, and rays different from symbols of lines, segments, and rays?

2. Explain how a right angle can help identify acute and obtuse angles.

3. Your friend thinks vertical angles are adjacent. What is wrong with this thinking?

**MATH AMERICA**

**BONUS**

**DID YOU KNOW . . . ?** The game of basketball was invented and developed in the United States. A high school basketball court is 84 ft long and 50 ft wide. How many times could your classroom fit into an area that size?

The drawing shows all the exterior angles of two polygons. Trace the polygons. Measure each exterior angle with a protractor. Add the measures of the exterior angles of each polygon.

Draw some other polygons. Measure each exterior angle, and add those measures. What generalization do you think you can make about the sum of the measures of the exterior angles of any polygon?

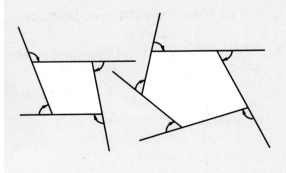

## Exploring Reflections, Rotations, and Translations

Reflections, rotations, and translations are motions that change the positions of figures. These motions are often used in tiling designs.

Many designs are based on a **reflection** (flip) of an object in a line.

1. Notice how the figures are reflected along the vertical and horizontal lines. What are the images of $\overline{AB}$? Are the images congruent to $\overline{AB}$?

2. $\overline{AC}$ and $\overline{CE}$ are congruent. What other segments are congruent to them?

3. **CREATE YOUR OWN** On dot paper make a design of your own with vertical and horizontal reflections.

Designs can also be created by the **rotation** (turn) of an object about a point.

4. Cut out a trapezoid as shown. Rotate it to the four positions. How many degrees did it rotate between the original position and each new position?

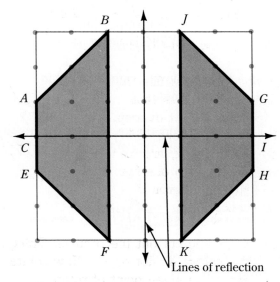

Lines of reflection

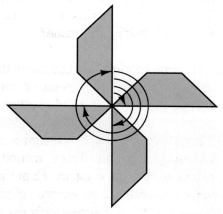

5. **THINK ALOUD** The rotation images at right result from 60° rotations about the given point. Can you think of another kind of motion that would result in images in the same positions?

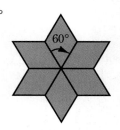

60°

6. Is point $A$, point $B$, or point $C$ the center of the rotation? To test a point, trace the shaded figure and the point. Rotate your paper about that point.

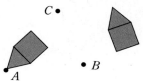

$C \bullet$

$\bullet B$

$A$

A **translation** (slide) is another way to create a tiling design. During translation, the figure should not flip or turn.

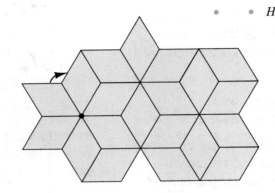

**7.** What is the translation image of $\overline{DC}$?

**8.** $\overline{DC}$ and $\overline{HG}$ are congruent. Are $\overline{AB}$ and $\overline{EF}$ congruent? Are $\overline{DH}$ and $\overline{CG}$ congruent?

**9.** Are $\overline{DH}$ and $\overline{CG}$ parallel?

A **tessellation** fills the plane with figures that touch but do not overlap. Some tessellations, like the one at right, are made by starting with one figure and rotating it around different points.

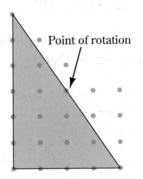

**10.** Copy and cut out the triangle. Trace around the cutout on dot paper. Now rotate it 180° about the given point of rotation.
Trace around the shape in its new position. What new polygon is made?

**11.** Use your triangle to tessellate the plane using rotations. Your point of rotation can change to the midpoint of another side.

**12.** **CREATE YOUR OWN** Design a tiling pattern using these ideas. Cut out a polygon. Trace around it. Then translate, reflect, or rotate it and trace again. Experiment with altering the polygon before moving it, as shown. If your polygon does not tessellate the plane, try a different polygon or use more than one figure.

Original

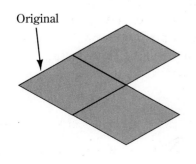

Original

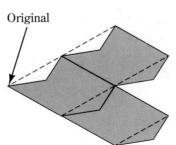

Original

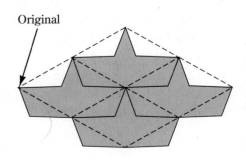

# Congruent Figures

This quilt block pattern is made up of a tessellation of congruent triangles and diamonds.

**Congruent figures** have the same size and shape.

Translations, rotations, and reflections can be used to form congruent figures.

**THINK ALOUD** One pair of congruent triangles in the quilt can be formed by starting with the purple triangle and rotating it about the point shown. What other congruent figures in the quilt are formed by reflection? by translation?

For congruent figures, corresponding sides and angles are congruent. Marks (|, ||, |||) are placed on corresponding sides of $\triangle ABC$ and $\triangle DEF$ to show that the sides are congruent. We write $\triangle ABC \cong \triangle DEF$, where $\cong$ means "is congruent to."

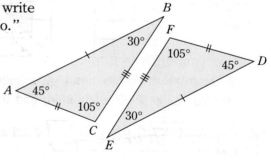

Corresponding Sides
$\overline{AB} \cong \overline{DE}$
$\overline{BC} \cong \overline{EF}$
$\overline{AC} \cong \overline{DF}$

Corresponding Angles
$\angle BAC \cong \angle EDF$
$\angle ACB \cong \angle DFE$
$\angle ABC \cong \angle DEF$

Where do corresponding sides appear in the quilt?

The triangles are congruent. Name all sets of corresponding sides and angles.

**1.**

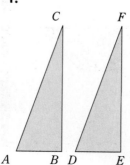

**2.**

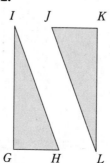

**3.**

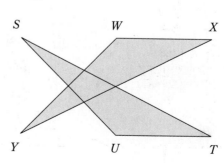

Are the figures congruent? Did you use a translation, rotation, or reflection to decide?

**4.**
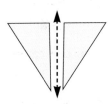

**5.**
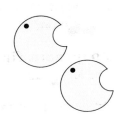

**6.**
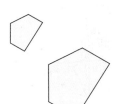

**7.**

P.

$\triangle MNO$ and $\triangle PQR$ are congruent. Find the missing measure.

**8.** $\overline{PR}$    **9.** $\overline{MN}$    **10.** $\overline{NO}$

**11.** $\angle MNO$    **12.** $\angle PRQ$    **13.** $\angle RPQ$

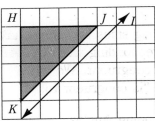

Line $I$ is a reflection line. Draw the figure and the reflection image on grid paper. Identify all sets of congruent sides and angles.

**14.**
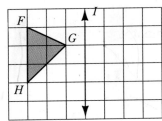

**15.**
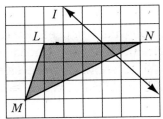

**16.**

**17. CREATE YOUR OWN** Design a quilt block pattern. Try to use reflection, rotation, and translation images.

**Critical Thinking**

Image $B$ is congruent to original $A$ after two motions, reflection followed by translation. Use dot paper to find two motions to prove that image $D$ is congruent to original $C$.

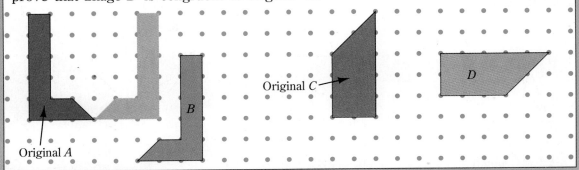

Original $A$

Original $C$

$D$

$B$

## Symmetry

A design that has symmetry has a harmonious balance and is pleasing to the eye. One type of symmetry is **line symmetry**.

A figure with line symmetry can be folded so that the two parts of the figure are congruent. The fold is called the **line of symmetry**.

You can use some clear plastic to check for symmetry (or to draw parts of symmetric figures).

**STEPS** Hold the plastic upright on the line of symmetry.

Look through the plastic to see the image.

Decide whether the parts coincide (or draw the image).

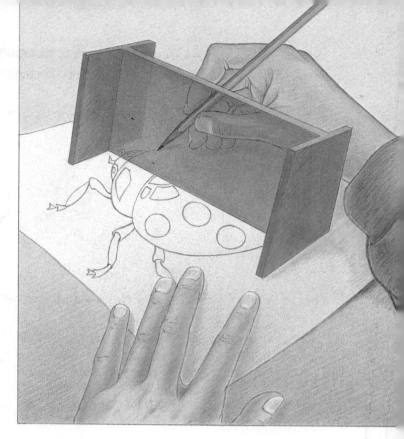

An equilateral triangle has three lines of symmetry. Trace the triangle three times, drawing a different line of symmetry on each tracing. Use clear plastic or folding to show each line is a line of symmetry.

**CRITICAL THINKING**  What types of triangles are formed by the three lines of symmetry?

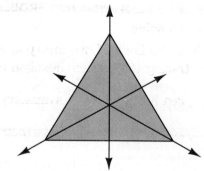

======== **GUIDED PRACTICE** ========

How many lines of symmetry does the figure have? To decide, draw, cut out, and fold the figure. Draw all lines of symmetry.

**1.**    **2.**    **3.**    **4.**

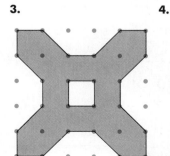 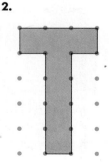 

Draw the figure. Then cut out and fold the figure to find the lines of symmetry. Draw them.

**5.**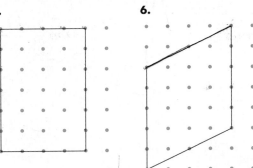

**6.**

**7.**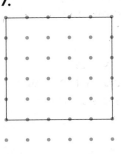

**8.**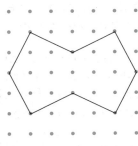

The hexagon at right shows two lines of symmetry. Name all figures congruent to the figure.

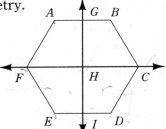

**9.** the pentagon with vertices *A, G, I, E, F*

**10.** the trapezoid with vertices *A, B, C, F*

**11.** the trapezoid with vertices *E, F, H, I*

Draw a figure to solve.

**12.** Show all of the lines of symmetry in a regular hexagon. Start by tracing the regular hexagon above.

**13.** What polygon has no lines of symmetry?

**14.** What polygon has five lines of symmetry?

**15.** How many lines of symmetry does a circle have?

A design was made by folding paper as shown. Draw the completed design.

**16.**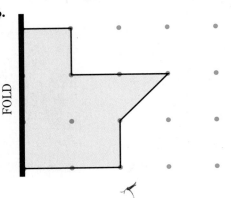

**17.**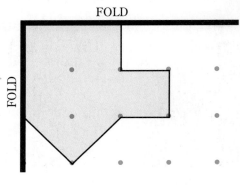

# Circles and Circumference

Meteor Crater in Arizona has a diameter of about 1 mi. How does its radius compare to its diameter?

About how many times longer is the circumference than the diameter?

Use a piece of yarn or a narrow strip of paper to find out. Measure the circumference and the diameter in the photograph of the crater.

The straight-line distance from the two points on the rim of the crater through the center is the **diameter** (d).

Diameter ≈ 1 mi

Radius

The **radius** (r) is the distance from the center of the crater to any point on the rim.

The exact ratio of the circumference to the diameter of a circle is called **pi** ($\pi$). It is about 3.14 or $\frac{22}{7}$. You write:

$$\frac{C}{d} = \pi, \text{ or } \frac{C}{d} \approx 3.14$$
$$C = \pi d, \text{ or } C \approx 3.14 \times d$$

The distance around the rim of the crater is the **circumference** (C).

**CRITICAL THINKING** How would you write an expression for the circumference of a circle if you know its radius?

Mt. Vesuvius, in Italy, is the only active volcano on the mainland of Europe. The radius of its crater rim is 1,000 ft. About what is the circumference of its crater rim?

$$C = \pi \times d$$
$$\approx 3.14 \times 2,000 \approx 6,280$$

$$C = \pi \times 2 \times r$$
$$\approx 3.14 \times 2 \times 1,000 \approx 6,280$$

$D = 2 \times r$, so
$C = \pi \times 2 \times r$

The circumference of the crater is about 6,280 ft.

---

## GUIDED PRACTICE

Find the circumference. Use $\pi \approx 3.14$. Round to tenths.

**1.**

4 ft

**2.**

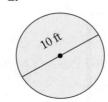

10 ft

**3.**

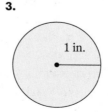

1 in.

**4.**

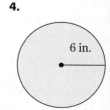

6 in.

Find the circumference. Use $\pi \approx 3.14$. Round to tenths.

**5.** $d = 8$ in.          **6.** $d = 2$ yd          **7.** $r = 2$ yd          **8.** $r = 1.2$ ft

**9.** d = 15 in.          **10.** $d = 2.5$ ft          **11.** $r = 0.5$ in.          **12.** $r = 3.4$ in.

Find the circumference. Use $\pi \approx \frac{22}{7}$.

**13.** $d = \frac{7}{8}$ yd          **14.** $r = 1\frac{1}{6}$ mi          **15.** $d = 1{,}449$ mi          **16.** $r = 4{,}200$ ft

**ESTIMATE**   About what is the perimeter of the figure?

**17.**

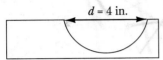
$d = 4$ in.

**18.**
$d = 40$ ft **19.**

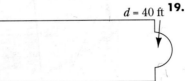

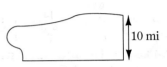
10 mi

Find the length of each figure. Use $\pi \approx 3.14$. *Hint:* Notice how the three figures are alike and how they are different.

**20.**

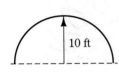
10 ft

**21.**

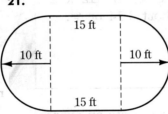
15 ft
10 ft     10 ft
15 ft

**22.**

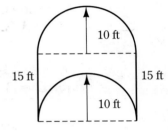
10 ft
15 ft     15 ft
10 ft

Solve. Use $\pi \approx 3.14$. Round your answer to tenths.

**23.** The world's largest crater on an inactive volcano is Haleakala, located in Hawaii. The circumference of the crater is about 20 mi. About what is the diameter of the crater?

**24.** Mauna Loa, in Hawaii, is the world's largest volcano. It rises 30,000 ft from the ocean floor and has a diameter at its base of 60 mi. About what is the circumference at the base of Mauna Loa?

**25.** On March 27, 1980, the crater of the Mount Saint Helens volcano measured 250 ft in diameter. The volcano erupted that day. Twelve days later, the crater measured 1,700 ft across. By how much did the circumference increase?

**26. CREATE YOUR OWN**   Use a compass and straightedge. Draw a figure with line segments and parts of circles. Ask a friend to find the length of the figure.

# Area: Rectangles and Triangles

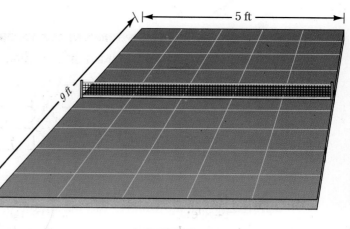

An official table for table tennis measures 9 ft by 5 ft. What is its area in square feet (ft²)?

The **area** of a plane figure measures the surface it covers. By counting squares, you can see that the area of the table is 45 ft².

You can also calculate the area using a formula.

| **Area (A) of a rectangle = base × height** |
| :---: |
| **= bh** |

$A = bh$
$= 9 \times 5$
$= 45 \text{ ft}^2$

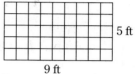

**THINK ALOUD** What is the formula for the area of a square?

A triangular race course for sailboats is shown by $\triangle ABC$ in the diagram. What is the area of the race course in square miles (mi²)?

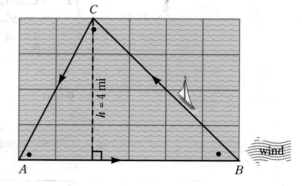

Count squares to find the area of the triangle and of the rectangle. Is the area of the triangle *half* the area of the rectangle?

The **height**(h) of a triangle is the length of a segment that is perpendicular to the base (b). This formula gives the area of a triangle.

| **Area (A) of a triangle = ½ area of rectangle** |
| :---: |
| **= ½ (base × height)** |
| **= ½ bh** |

$A = \frac{1}{2} bh$
$= \frac{1}{2} \times 6 \times 4$
$= \frac{1}{2} \times 24$
$= 12 \text{ mi}^2$

---

## GUIDED PRACTICE

Find the area.

1.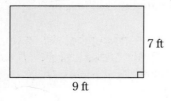
   7 ft
   9 ft

2.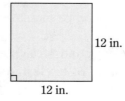
   12 in.
   12 in.

3.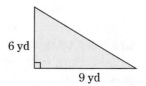
   6 yd
   9 yd

**4.** Each square represents 1 in$^2$. Estimate the area of each figure.

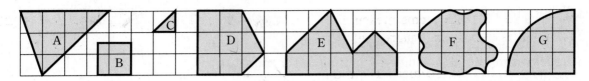

Find the area.

**5.** rectangle:
$b = 9$ in.; $h = 3$ in.

**6.** triangle
$b = 20$ in.; $h = 8$ in.

**7.** triangle:
$b = 6.5$ yd; $h = 9.2$ yd

**8.** rectangle:
$b = 10$ in.; $h = 8\frac{1}{4}$ in.

**9.** triangle:
$b = 30$ in.; $h = 14$ in.

**10.** rectangle:
$b = 6.5$ yd; $h = 9.2$ yd

Find the unknown dimension.

**11.** rectangle:
$A = 21$ ft$^2$; $b = 2$ ft
What is the height?

**12.** rectangle:
$A = 34.1$ in.$^2$; $h = 5.5$ in.
What is the base?

**13.** Triangle:
$A = 36$ yd$^2$; $b = 8$ yd
What is the height?

Find the area of a square with side $s$.

Find the length of the square.

**14.** $s = 12$ in.

**15.** $s = 9\frac{1}{4}$ ft

**16.** $A = 81$ yd$^2$

**17.** $A = 10,000$ mi$^2$

Find the area of the rectangle and all triangles in the figure.

**18.**

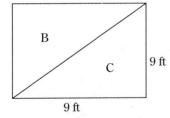

**19.**

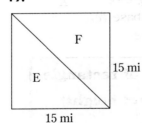

**20.**

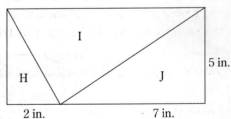

**21.** A football field is 360 ft by 160 ft. The playing area for field hockey is 300 ft by 180 ft. Which field is larger?

**22.** At the half-time show for a football game, the band made a triangular formation. What area was covered by the band if the base of the triangle was 15 yd and the height was 32 yd?

**23.** A rectangular ice-skating rink has a floor with an area of 2,112 yd$^2$. The length of the floor is 66 yd. What is the width?

**24.** A sailboat has a triangular sail with an area of 77 ft$^2$. If the height of the triangle is 14 ft, how many feet long is the base?

# Area: Parallelograms and Trapezoids

If you know how to find the area of a rectangle, you can use a **MATH CONNECTION** to find the area of a parallelogram.

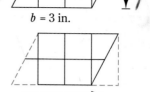

Cut out a parallelogram from grid paper, as shown. Transform the parallelogram into a rectangle by cutting out a triangular piece from one end and moving it to the other end.

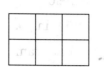

Are the areas of the rectangle and of the parallelogram the same?

---

**Area ($A$) of a parallelogram = base × height**
$$= bh$$

---

$$A = bh$$
$$= 3 \times 2$$
$$= 6 \text{ in.}^2$$

You can use a similar **MATH CONNECTION** to find the area of a trapezoid.

Cut out a trapezoid from grid paper, as shown.

Trace around it. Then rotate it and trace again to form a parallelogram.

How does the area of the trapezoid compare to the area of the parallelogram?

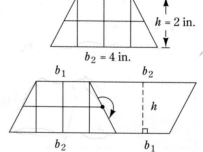

---

**Area ($A$) of a trapezoid = $\frac{1}{2}$ area of parallelogram**
$$= \frac{1}{2} \text{ (sum of bases)} \times \text{height}$$
$$= \frac{1}{2} (b_1 + b_2) \times h$$

---

$$A = \frac{1}{2} (b_1 + b_2) \times h$$
$$= \frac{1}{2} (2 + 4) \times 2 = 6 \text{ in.}^2$$

---

## GUIDED PRACTICE

**1.** Find the area of the parallelogram.

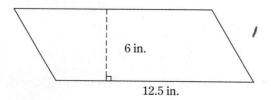

**2.** Find the area of the trapezoid.

Find the area.

**3.**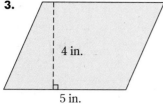

4 in.

5 in.

**4.**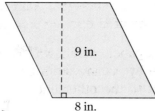

9 in.

8 in.

**5.**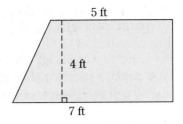

5 ft

4 ft

7 ft

**6.** parallelogram:
$b = 6\frac{1}{2}$ in., $h = 3\frac{1}{2}$ in.

**7.** trapezoid:
$b_1 = 5$ ft, $b_2 = 8$ ft, $h = 3.2$ ft

**8.** parallelogram:
$b = 10\frac{1}{4}$ in., $h = 12\frac{1}{2}$ in.

**9.** trapezoid:
$b_1 = 2.5$ ft, $b_2 = 1.3$ ft, $h = 1.8$ ft

**10.** What is the height?
parallelogram:
$A = 16$ mi$^2$; $b = 4$ mi

**11.** What is the base?
parallelogram:
$A = 11$ ft$^2$; $h = 5\frac{1}{2}$ ft

**12.** What is the height?
trapezoid:
$A = 7$ ft$^2$;  $b_1 = 10$ ft;
$b_2 = 4$ ft

Find the area.

**13.**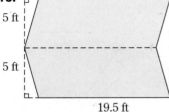

5 ft

5 ft

19.5 ft

**14.**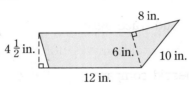

8 in.

$4\frac{1}{2}$ in.

6 in.

10 in.

12 in.

**15.**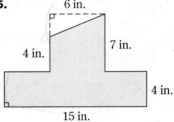

6 in.

4 in.

7 in.

4 in.

15 in.

Make drawings on inch grid paper to solve.

**16.** Draw two different parallelograms each with an area of 9 in.$^2$.

**17.** Sketch three different trapezoids each with an area of 12 in.$^2$.

*Critical Thinking*

**1.** What is the area of the given polygon shown in the figure?

    **a.** rectangle *BDFG*
    **b.** parallelogram *ABFG*
    **c.** parallelogram *CEFG*

**2.** How are these three polygon areas related? Why?

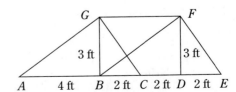

G      F

3 ft      3 ft

A    4 ft    B   2 ft   C   2 ft   D   2 ft   E

## Area: Circles

A sprinkler is rotating in a full circle
to water part of a lawn. The watered circle
has a radius of 2 yd. What is the area of the circle?

You need a formula that gives the area of a circle
for which the radius is known. First, estimate the
area of this circle by drawing one square outside the
circle and another one inside the circle. What are the
areas of these two squares?

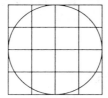    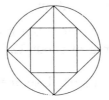

The area of the outer square is 16 yd$^2$.     The area of the inner square is 8 yd$^2$.
  Write that as $4 \times (2^2)$ yd$^2$, or $4r^2$.       Write that as $2 \times (2^2)$ yd$^2$, or $2r^2$.

A good estimate for the area of the circle would be between 8 yd$^2$
and 16 yd$^2$, or about 12 yd$^2$. You can write that as $3 \times 2^2$ yd$^2$, or $3r^2$.

The actual formula for the area of a circle uses the number $\pi$.
In the work you just did, $3r^2$ is an approximation for $\pi r^2$.

**Area ($A$) of a circle = $\pi r^2$**

The ancient Egyptians worked out a value of $4\left(\frac{8}{9}\right)^2$, or
about 3.16, for $\pi$. By putting a square around a circle
and marking off the corners, they formed an octagon
that had almost the same area as the circle.

You can use 3.14 in the formula as an estimate for $\pi$.
Using this formula for the sprinkler problem, you will
find that the area of the circle is 12.6 yd$^2$.

**NUMBER SENSE**   What is a good estimate of the area
of a circle that has a radius of 1 yd?

=== **GUIDED PRACTICE** ===

1. How do you find the area of a circle that has a radius
   of 3 yd? What is the area rounded to tenths?

2. How do you find the area of a circle that has a diameter of 9 in.?
   What is the area rounded to tenths?

Find the area. Use $\pi \approx 3.14$. Round the answer to tenths.

**3.**
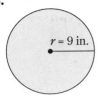
$r = 9$ in.

**4.**

$r = 20$ yd

**5.**

$r = 7$ ft

**6.**
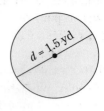
$d = 1.5$ yd

**7.** $r = 2.5$ ft

**8.** $r = 1.4$ in.

**9.** $d = 18$ in.

**10.** $d = 10$ ft

**11.** $r = 16$ in.

**12.** $r = 40$ in.

**13.** $d = 50$ yd

**14.** $d = 22.2$ ft

**15. CRITICAL THINKING** What is the radius of a circle that has an area of about $12.56$ in.$^2$?

Find the area of the shaded part. Use $\pi \approx 3.14$. Round to tenths.

**16.**
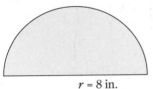
$r = 8$ in.

**17.**
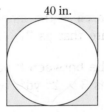
40 in.

40 in.

**18.**
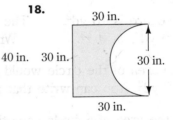
30 in.

30 in.    30 in.

30 in.

30 in.

**19.**
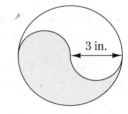
3 in.

**20.** Six sprinklers, with a radius of 10 yd each, are used to water a large lawn. About what is the area of the watered part of the lawn?

**21.** A rotating sprinkler swings through a 90° angle in a quarter turn. How many degrees does it swing through in a half turn? in a full turn? in three full turns?

## Critical Thinking

Use these figures and draw any others you need to answer the question.

1. What happens to the perimeter and the area of a rectangle when the length and the width double? Explain.

2. What happens to the circumference and the area of a circle when the radius doubles? Explain.

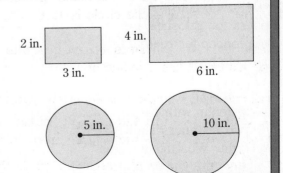

2 in.

3 in.

4 in.

6 in.

5 in.

10 in.

# Investigating Fasteners 🖩 🧩

Many of the machines and tools that you use every day did not exist 100 yr ago. One of these inventions is the zipper.

The drawings at right are similar to ones you might find in a sewing book published around 1900. They show two different kinds of fasteners used at the time.

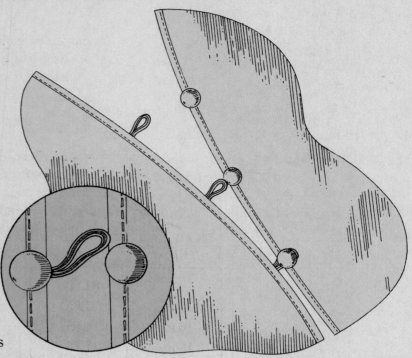

Work with a partner.

1. Write a description of each drawing. How are the fasteners similar? How are they different?

The zipper, or zip fastener, was invented in 1891 by Whitcomb L. Judson and made practical in 1913 by Gideon Sundback. At least ten more years went by before manufacturers would even consider using zippers for galoshes and even longer for ready-made clothes.

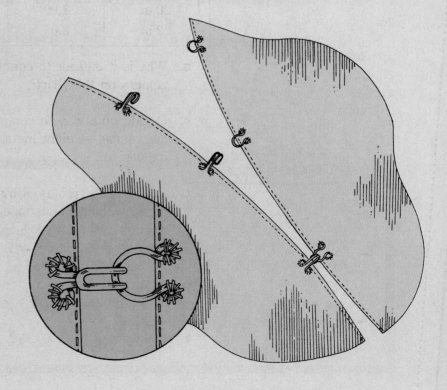

2. Compare a zipper fastener with the two fasteners shown at right. What advantages does the zipper have? disadvantages?

MATH AND HISTORY

A zipper is made of three parts.
- dozens of identical metal or plastic hooks
- two strips of fabric
- a Y-shaped slider

Use the chart and a calculator to answer these questions.

| Plastic Zippers | | | Metal Zippers Medium-Weight | | | Metal Zippers Heavy-Weight | |
| --- | --- | --- | --- | --- | --- | --- | --- |
| Size | Price | | Size | Price | | Size | Price |
| 7 in. | $1.20 | | 12 in. | $1.80 | | 6 in. | $1.25 |
| 9 in. | 1.25 | | 14 in. | 1.85 | | 7 in. | 1.40 |
| 12 in. | 1.35 | | 16 in. | 1.85 | | 9 in. | 1.40 |
| 16 in. | 1.50 | | 18 in. | 1.85 | | 11 in. | 1.45 |
| 20 in. | 1.60 | | 20 in. | 1.90 | | | |
| 22 in. | 1.65 | | 22 in. | 2.05 | | | |

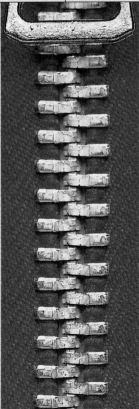

**3.** Why is it difficult to compare the prices of the different zippers on the chart?

**4.** Decide on a way to compare the prices of plastic and medium-weight metal zippers. Which are more expensive?

**5.** Compare the prices of medium-weight and heavy-weight metal zippers by computing the average price per inch for each type. Round amounts to the nearest cent and organize your work in a chart.

**6.** What factors besides price would you consider before deciding what kind of zipper to buy?

**7.** What other fasteners have you used? How do they compare to zippers in performance? Do they cost *more than* or *less than* zippers?

## Mixed Review

Write as fractions or as mixed numbers in lowest terms.

**1.** $\frac{9}{12}$     **2.** $\frac{36}{24}$     **3.** $0.45$     **4.** $6.75$     **5.** $5\frac{11}{7}$     **6.** $7\frac{16}{6}$

Find the missing numerator.

**7.** $8\frac{3}{4} = 8\frac{?}{8}$     **8.** $8\frac{3}{5} = 7\frac{?}{5}$     **9.** $13\frac{1}{6} = \frac{?}{6}$     **10.** $5\frac{7}{8} = \frac{?}{8}$

Write the reciprocal of the number.

**11.** $5$     **12.** $\frac{5}{2}$     **13.** $9$     **14.** $\frac{4}{7}$     **15.** $1$     **16.** $2\frac{7}{8}$

**17.** Explain what it means for one number to be the reciprocal of another.

**18.** Explain how two fractions can be simplified before multiplying.

Give the answer in lowest terms.

**19.** $\frac{3}{5} \times \frac{2}{5}$     **20.** $\frac{3}{5} - \frac{2}{5}$     **21.** $\frac{3}{5} \div \frac{2}{5}$     **22.** $\frac{3}{5} + \frac{2}{5}$

**23.** $9 \times \frac{2}{3}$     **24.** $\frac{5}{9} \div 25$     **25.** $\frac{11}{12} \times 18$     **26.** $56 \div \frac{7}{8}$

**27.** $3\frac{2}{3} - 2\frac{1}{4}$     **28.** $3\frac{2}{3} \div 2\frac{1}{4}$     **29.** $3\frac{2}{3} + 2\frac{1}{4}$     **30.** $\frac{2}{3} \times 2\frac{1}{4}$

**31.** $2\frac{1}{6} - \frac{5}{9}$     **32.** $3\frac{1}{5} \times 3\frac{1}{5}$     **33.** $5\frac{1}{2} \div 8.25$     **34.** $6\frac{1}{3} \times 0.8$

**35.** $15 - 3\frac{3}{4}$     **36.** $2\frac{1}{3} + 9$     **37.** $84 \div \frac{1}{12}$     **38.** $95 \times \frac{3}{5}$

**39.** $300 \div \frac{1}{2}$     **40.** $\frac{5}{8} \times 400$     **41.** $250 - 48\frac{5}{9}$     **42.** $\frac{1}{26} \div \frac{5}{13}$

Use mental math to solve.

**43.** $a + 2\frac{1}{3} = 6\frac{2}{3}$     **44.** $\frac{6}{7}b = 0$     **45.** $c \div \frac{4}{5} = 1$     **46.** $3\frac{1}{4} \div d = 3\frac{1}{4}$

**47.** $e - 3\frac{3}{4} = \frac{1}{4}$     **48.** $1\frac{2}{9}f = 2\frac{4}{9}$     **49.** $g + \frac{5}{6} = 6\frac{5}{6}$     **50.** $h \div 3\frac{1}{2} = 2$

Write as a variable expression. Use $n$ as the variable.

**51.** two-thirds less than a number

**52.** a number increased by $4\frac{1}{2}$

**53.** $3\frac{4}{5}$ divided by some number

**54.** $\frac{4}{5}$ of some number

**55.** a number divided by $\frac{7}{8}$

**56.** the product of $6\frac{7}{8}$ and some number

Write the variable expression in words.

**57.** $z - \frac{2}{9}$  **58.** $n \div \frac{3}{8}$  **59.** $\frac{4}{5} + a$  **60.** $6\frac{7}{8} - c$  **61.** $32\frac{3}{4} \div a$

**PROBLEM SOLVING**

CHOOSE Solve. Choose mental math, estimation, pencil and paper, or calculator.

**62.** In 1985, Mexico's exports equaled $1\frac{4}{7}$ times its imports. If its imports in 1985 were worth \$14 million, what was the value of Mexico's exports that year?

**63.** It has been predicted that in the year 2100 the population of Mexico will be 196 million, or about $2\frac{3}{8}$ times what it was in 1987. About what was Mexico's population in 1987?

**64.** In 1987, the world's most populous country, China, had about $12\frac{4}{5}$ times as many residents as had Mexico. If Mexico's population was 82 million in 1987, what is a good estimate for China's population in 1987?

**65.** Juarez, Mexico, would need $30\frac{4}{5}$ additional inches of rain each year to equal the average yearly rainfall in Seattle, Washington. If Seattle's average rainfall is $38\frac{3}{5}$ in., what is the average rainfall in Juarez?

**66.** Approximately 15 out of every 100 Mexicans live in Mexico City. Use your answer from Exercise 63 to find the population of Mexico City in 1987.

**67.** The state of Texas occupies 262,000 mi² of land. Mexico takes up 761,000 mi². Is Texas about $\frac{2}{5}$, $\frac{3}{8}$, $\frac{1}{3}$, or $\frac{1}{4}$ the size of Mexico?

**Mexico City, Mexico**

# CHAPTER CHECKUP

---

## LANGUAGE & VOCABULARY

---

Write a sentence to answer the question.

1. How do you know whether two figures are congruent?

2. How do you know whether a figure has a line of symmetry?

3. How do you decide whether a figure is a parallelogram or a trapezoid?

---

## TEST ✓

---

### CONCEPTS

Is the angle *acute, right, obtuse,* or *straight*? *(pages 234–237)*

1. 109°    2. 45°    3. 90°    4. 175°    5. 180°

Is a triangle that has these side lengths *equilateral, isosceles,* or *scalene*? *(pages 244–245)*

6. 4 cm, 5 cm, 6 cm    7. 8 in., 8 in., 8 in.

8. Use a protractor. m∠ABC = ▦°

Are the figures congruent? Name the polygons in Exercises 9 and 11.

9.     10.     11.

Copy the figure. Draw the lines of symmetry. *(pages 252–253)*

12.    13.    14.

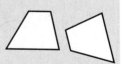

---

### SKILLS

---

Find the circumference and area of the circle. Use $\pi \approx 3.14$. Round the answer to tenths. *(pages 254–255, 260–261)*

15. $d = 10$ yd    16. $d = 3.5$ in.    17. $r = 6$ ft    18. $r = 5.5$ cm

Find the area of the figure. *(pages 256–259)*

**19.** rectangle
$h = 8$ cm
$b = 12$ cm

**20.** triangle
$b = 2.5$ yd
$h = 3.4$ yd

**21.** parallelogram
$b = 7.5$ in.
$h = 4$ in.

**22.** trapezoid
$b_1 = 2$ ft; $b_2 = 3$ ft
$h = 1.5$ ft

## PROBLEM SOLVING

Use a Venn diagram to solve. *(pages 238–239, 242–243)*

**23.** A survey showed that of 50 people asked, 22 say they read newspapers daily and 35 say they watch TV news daily.

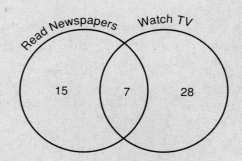

**a.** How many people were questioned?

**b.** Does the Venn diagram at right represent this situation?

**c.** Do *some, all,* or *none* of the 50 people read newspapers and watch TV news daily?

**24.** A roof brace for a new house is shaped like a right triangle with a base of 2.5 yd and a height of 3.4 yd. How many square yards of insulation will be needed to fill the interior of the brace?

**LEARNING LOG**

Write the answers in your learning log.

**1.** You know the diameter of a circle. Explain how to find the radius.

**2.** The woman working in the cafeteria tells you the two pieces of bread used to make a sandwich are congruent. What does she mean?

**3.** Explain to your friend why we use the label *square units* when finding the area of a circle.

Use a protractor to complete. *(pages 234–235)*

**1.** $m\angle ABC = $ ▦

**2.** $m\angle FGH = $ ▦

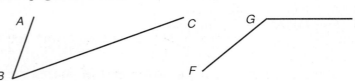

Is a triangle that has these side lengths or angle measures equilateral, isosceles, or scalene? *(pages 244–245)*

**3.** 7 cm, 8 cm, 10 cm

**4.** $9\frac{1}{2}$ in., $12\frac{1}{2}$ in., $15\frac{1}{2}$

**5.** 35°, 35°, 110°

**6.** 103°, 39°, 38°

**7.** 65°, 60°, 55°

**8.** 7 yd, 7 yd, 7 yd

Are the figures congruent? *(pages 250–251)*

**9.**

**10.**
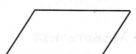

**11.**

How many lines of symmetry does the figure have? Copy the figure and draw the lines of symmetry. *(pages 252–253)*

**12.**

**13.**

**14.**

Find the circumference. Use $\pi \approx 3.14$. Round the answer to tenths. *(pages 254–255)*

**15.** $d = 32$ in.

**16.** $r = 17.5$ ft

**17.** $r = 9.2$ m

**18.** $d = 2.9$ cm

Find the area. *(pages 256–259)*

**19.** rectangle
$l = 7$ m
$w = 18$ m

**20.** parallelogram
$b = 7.5$ in.
$h = 15.8$ in.

**21.** trapezoid
$b_1 = 2$ m
$b_2 = 3.8$ m
$h = 1.7$ m

Find the area of the circle. Use $\pi \approx 3.14$. Round to tenths. *(pages 260–261)*

**22.** $r = 5.4$ ft

**23.** $d = 25.8$ in.

**24.** $r = 49.7$ yd

Solve. *(pages 238–239, 242–243)*

**25.** Decide whether the generalization "Some line segments are rays" is *true* or *false*.

# Circles of Cities

How many cities are within 10 mi of your city or town? You can find out this way.

1. Find a road map of your state or the part of your state that your city or town is in.

2. Locate your city or town on the map. Tape one end of a piece of string to the mark for your town.

3. Determine the number of miles represented by 1 in. on the map.

4. Calculate the number of inches of string that represents 10 mi. For example, if 1 in. on the map represents 2 mi, mark off a length of 5 in. on the string.

5. Tie a pencil to the string at the length you calculated and draw a circle with your city or town at the center.

6. Make a list of all the cities and towns inside the circle. They are all within 10 mi. of your city or town.

## A *Different Angle* on Angle Measurement

A different way to think of angle measurement is to think of holding one ray of the angle stationary while rotating the other ray around the vertex. If the two rays begin as a single ray, like ———→, then a 90° angle can be thought of as a $\frac{1}{4}$ turn, as shown at right.

$\frac{1}{4}$ turn = 90°

Thinking of angle measurement this way relates an angle to a fractional part of 360°. Work with a partner. One person models a turn using two pencils as rays. The other writes the turn and the angle equivalent. Some turns to try are $\frac{1}{3}$, $\frac{1}{2}$, $\frac{3}{4}$, $\frac{1}{8}$, $\frac{3}{8}$, $\frac{5}{8}$, $\frac{7}{8}$, and 1 whole turn. What other fractional turns can you use that will result in an angle with a whole number of degrees?

### DID YOU KNOW . . . ?
There are 435 seats in the United States House of Representatives. Each of our states is allowed a certain number of representatives based on the state's population. What fraction of the total number of seats do your state representatives occupy?

Find the answer.

**1.** circle, $d = 5$ ft
circumference = ▨
Use $\pi \approx 3.14$.
- **a.** 15.70 ft
- **b.** 7.90 ft
- **c.** 19.63
- **d.** none of these

**2.** triangle, $b = 12$ ft
$h = 15$ ft,
area = ▨
- **a.** 180 ft$^2$
- **b.** 90 ft$^2$
- **c.** 27 ft$^2$
- **d.** none of these

**3.** trapezoid, $b_1 = 10$ cm
$b_2 = 14$ cm, $h = 8$ cm
area = ▨
- **a.** 152 cm$^2$
- **b.** 96 cm$^2$
- **c.** 192 cm$^2$
- **d.** none of these

**4.** $138.7 + 96.09 =$
- **a.** 234.16
- **b.** 325.69
- **c.** 235.79
- **d.** none of these

**5.** $\$37.95 + \$.76 =$
- **a.** \$38.61
- **b.** \$38.71
- **c.** \$37.71
- **d.** none of these

**6.** $0.6 + 24.9 + 0.184 =$
- **a.** 246.84
- **b.** 27.34
- **c.** 25.684
- **d.** none of these

**7.** $3,000 - 1,823 =$
- **a.** 1,177
- **b.** 1,077
- **c.** 1,223
- **d.** none of these

**8.** $12.9 - 7.12 =$
- **a.** 20.02
- **b.** 4.97
- **c.** 5.78
- **d.** none of these

**9.** $0.0316 - 0.007 =$
- **a.** 0.0386
- **b.** 0.0246
- **c.** 0.0309
- **d.** none of these

Find the matching value.

**10.** 37.51 million
- **a.** 37,000,051
- **b.** 37,051,000
- **c.** 37,510,000
- **d.** none of these

**11.** 97 hundredths
- **a.** 0.97
- **b.** 0.097
- **c.** 0.0097
- **d.** none of these

**12.** $(4 \times 10^2) + (3 \times 10^0)$
- **a.** 403
- **b.** 430
- **c.** 4,030
- **d.** none of these

**13.** $29 \times (7 \times 6) =$
- **a.** 377
- **b.** 1,218
- **c.** 908
- **d.** none of these

**14.** $32 - (4 + 3^2) =$
- **a.** 37
- **b.** 25
- **c.** 19
- **d.** none of these

**15.** $8 \times (15 - 5) \div 8 =$
- **a.** 3
- **b.** 8
- **c.** 10
- **d.** none of these

Remember the strategies and types of problems you've had so far. Solve.

1. Barry's lunch of an omelet and milk cost $3.75. Bob had only a glass of milk and spent $2.95 less than Barry. What was their total bill?

2. A car averages 20 mi/gal of gas. If gas costs $1.60/gal, how much does it cost to drive the car 400 mi?

3. Sue bought a dress for $60 and wants a coat that costs 2.5 times as much as the dress. If she originally had $200, how much more money does she need to buy the coat?

4. Training for a marathon, Tony ran 50 mi/wk for exactly one half year. Altogether, how far did he run by the end of this period?

5. Steve wrote his three-number combination in code. The first number is a multiple of 7 whose digits add to 8. The second is a prime number between 55 and 60. The third has 9 factors and the sum of its 2 digits is 9. What is Steve's combination?
   (*Hint:* All 3 numbers have 2 digits.)

6. A lumber mill cuts planks $\frac{7}{8}$ in. thick. The log that is being cut is exactly 9 in. thick.

   a. How thick is each plank?

   b. How many planks can be cut from the log?

   c. How thick will the remaining piece be?

7. A three-speed electric fan turns 900 revolutions per minute on low. It turns $1\frac{1}{2}$ times faster on medium than on low. It turns $1\frac{1}{2}$ times faster on high than on medium. How fast does the fan turn on high?

8. Roberto studied $\frac{1}{2}$ h Monday, $\frac{3}{4}$ h Tuesday, and 1 h Wednesday. If he continues this pattern on Thursday and Friday, how many hours will he have studied for the 5 d?

9. A machine pays $.05 for each bottle returned. The machine took 72 bottles one week and 85 bottles the next week. How much more did the machine pay out the second week than the first week?

10. A ladder is leaning against the side of a 35-ft building. If the ladder is 26 ft long and the base of the ladder is 10 ft from the building, does the ladder reach the top of the building?

## COVER IT UP

Keiko wants to carpet her room, shown below. The carpeting comes in a roll that is 1.9 m wide. What is the least amount of uncarpeted floor space Keiko will have left if she does not want to pay extra for cutting carpet to a different width?

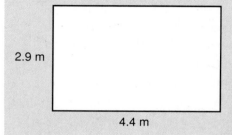

2.9 m

4.4 m

## WASTE NOT

Work in a group of three or four people. Use a metric ruler and make these rectangles.

|   | length | width |
|---|--------|-------|
| A→ | 15.2 cm | 1.6 cm |
| B→ | 3.3 cm | 4 cm |
| C→ | 12.5 cm | 2.1 cm |

Cutting from only one side, find the least amount of paper you could cut from each rectangle so that the area of each rectangle will be a whole number. Draw where you would cut. Compare your answers with other groups.

## CAUSING A PROBLEM

In the computer activity *Guess and Test*, you use clues about perimeter and area to guess the width and length of rectangles. This activity, which does not require a computer, will help you develop the skills you need for *Guess and Test*.

One way to write word problems is to work backward, beginning with your answers, and then creating clues.

Example:

Answer                  Problem

*Jorge is 13. Jan is 9.*  The sum of Jorge's and Jan's ages is 22 and the product is 117. How old are Jorge and Jan?

Use this method to create two word problems. Trade papers with a classmate and try to solve each other's word problems.

**DID YOU KNOW . . . ?**
The ratio of body weight to brain weight of the brachiosaurus is 80,000 lb to 1 lb!

A 12,000-lb elephant has a 1,000 to 1 ratio of body weight to brain weight.

For every 50 lb of a 150-lb human, there is 1 lb of brain weight - a 50 to 1 ratio.

A 220-lb dolphin has a 110 to 1 ratio of body weight to brain weight.

**USING DATA**

Collect
Organize
Describe
Predict

Describe how the brain sizes of these animals compare with one another.

Research the body and brain weights of other mammals. Organize all of the data into a table.

# Comparatively Speaking

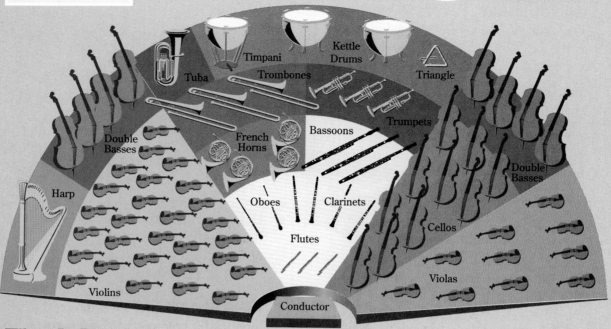

## What Is Ratio?

The Boston Pops Symphony Orchestra normally has the instruments shown above.

Several ratios can be written about this orchestra. A **ratio** is a special way of comparing two numbers. Some ratios are shown at right.

Of the 84 musicians, 28 are violinists.

all musicians to violinists ⇨ 84 to 28
violinists to all musicians ⇨ 28 to 84

There are 3 trumpet players and 1 tuba player.

trumpet players to tuba players ⇨ 3 to 1
tuba players to trumpet players ⇨ 1 to 3

The cello is about twice as long as the viola.

cello length to viola length ⇨ 2 to 1
viola length to cello length ⇨ 1 to 2

### TALK ABOUT IT

Work with a partner. Use the picture above to help you answer the question.

1. What is the ratio of all the strings to all of the instruments in the orchestra?

2. What is the ratio of violas to all of the strings other than violas?

MATH AND MUSIC

**3.** What is the ratio of double basses to all string instruments of any type?

**4.** What is the ratio of French horns to clarinets?

**5.** **IN YOUR WORDS** Describe a situation involving only the woodwinds that has a ratio of 2 to 3.

**6.** What is the ratio of violas to cellos?

**7.** **ESTIMATE** What is the ratio of the length of a flute to the length of a bassoon?

To make them easier to interpret, ratios are usually stated using the smallest possible numbers. An example is shown below.

Of 84 musicians, 4 play percussion instruments.

all instruments to percussion instruments ⇨ 84 to 4
in smallest possible numbers ⇨ 21 to 1

Solve using the smallest possible numbers.

**8.** There are 2 kettle drums and 4 percussion instruments in all. What is the ratio of kettle drums to all percussion instruments?

**9.** Describe a situation involving the brass instruments that has a ratio of 1 to 1.

**10.** What is the ratio of percussion instruments to woodwinds?

**11.** **ESTIMATE** What is the ratio of the length of a trumpet to the length of a trombone?

**WRITE ABOUT IT**

Write a paragraph about a musical group you know. Use as many ratios as you can to describe the musicians and their instruments.

## *Exploring Ratios*

Refer to the colored pattern block polygons at the right.

The ratio of red to green is 5 to 4. You can also write the ratio using the ratio sign, 5:4, or as a quotient (fraction), $\frac{5}{4}$.

Write the ratio for the polygons at the right as a quotient and using the ratio sign.

**1.** red to yellow    **2.** green to all polygons

Solve.

**3.** Which polygons at the right have a ratio of 4:5? 12:5? 3:4? $\frac{3}{12}$?

**4.** Is 12 to 5 the ratio of red polygons to all polygons? Why or why not?

Use the polygons at the left to write the ratio.

**5.** triangles to squares

**6.** squares to all polygons

**7.** Which polygons have a ratio of 1:8? $\frac{3}{3}$? 6:2? $\frac{8}{2}$?

The triangles and the remaining polygons above have been grouped in sets of 2 at the right.

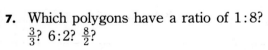

**8.** Write the ratio of sets of 2 triangles to all sets of 2.

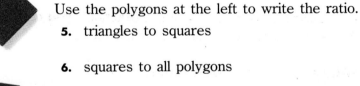

Two equally good ways of showing the ratio of triangles to all polygons are 2:8 and 1:4. Such ratios are called **equal ratios**.

Use the 12 rhombuses and the 6 triangles at the right to answer.

9. What is the ratio of triangles to rhombuses?

10. Can both the triangles and the rhombuses be put into sets of 2?

11. What is the ratio of sets of 2 triangles to sets of 2 rhombuses?

Since $\frac{6}{12}$ and $\frac{3}{6}$ are equally good ways of stating the ratio of triangles to rhombuses, they are equal ratios.

12. Arrange the polygons to show that $\frac{2}{4}$ and $\frac{1}{2}$ can also be used to describe the ratio of triangles to rhombuses.

13. The ratio of triangles to all polygons in the set is $\frac{6}{18}$. Use the polygons to find three other equal ratios comparing the triangles to all polygons.

If you write a ratio as a quotient (fraction), you can divide to find an equal ratio in lowest terms.

$$\frac{12}{6} = \frac{12 \div 6}{6 \div 6} = \frac{2}{1}$$

Write as a ratio in lowest terms.

14. $\frac{12}{4}$     15. 8 to 12     16. 9 : 12     17. 24 to 36     18. 10 : 100     19. 8.5 to 17

---

**A *proportion* is a statement that two ratios are equal.**

---

Since you know how to multiply or divide to write an equivalent fraction, you can make a **MATH CONNECTION** to work with a proportion.

Do the two ratios make a proportion? Choose = or ≠.

20. $\frac{4}{8}$ ▦ $\frac{1}{3}$     21. $\frac{12}{36}$ ▦ $\frac{1}{3}$     22. $\frac{17}{51}$ ▦ $\frac{1}{3}$     23. $\frac{4}{8}$ ▦ $\frac{6}{12}$

Copy and complete the proportion.

24. $\frac{1}{3} = \frac{▦}{12}$     25. $\frac{12}{48} = \frac{1}{▦}$     26. $\frac{10}{50} = \frac{1}{▦}$     27. $\frac{14}{42} = \frac{▦}{6}$

## *Exploring Proportional Thinking*

Commuters in China make good use of bicycles. In fact, for every 10 cars in China, there are 2,500 bicycles. That means that for every 1 car there are 250 bicycles.

You are using proportional thinking when you say, "10 cars is to 2,500 bicycles as 1 car is to 250 bicycles."

**1.** Write the proportion above using two ratio signs. Repeat writing the ratios as quotients.

You use proportional thinking to read and to make graphs. The pictograph shows how students get to school.

**2.** What ratio of faces to students was used to make the pictograph?

| How Students Get to School | |
|---|---|
| Walk | ☺ ☺ ☺ ☺ |
| Bicycle | ☺ ☺ ☺ ☺ ☺ ☺ |

1 ☺ = 25 students

**3.** If there were 1 face for every student, how many faces would there be in the Bicycle row?

**4.** How many faces are there in the Walk row? How many students does that represent?

**Commuters in Beijing, China**

You use proportional thinking to compare pairs of ratios. Can the two ratios form a proportion? Write *yes* or *no*.

**5.** 3 bicycles is to 6 pedals, 1 bicycle is to 2 pedals

**6.** 3 is to 6, 6 is to 9     **7.** 4:5, 28:33     **8.** $\frac{4}{5}$, $\frac{28}{35}$

**9.** **IN YOUR WORDS** Explain how you compared the ratios in Exercises 7 and 8.

Use proportional thinking to rearrange the four numbers
into a proportion.

**10.** 1, 4, 20, 5    **11.** 1, 2, 12, 6    **12.** 6, 7, 28, 24    **13.** 2, 12, 18, 3

You use proportional thinking to write a proportion equation
and make a table.

In rural China, there are about 4 bicycles to every 5 households,
or 8 bicycles to every ▓ households. Think: 4 is to 5 as 8 is to ▓?

$\frac{4}{5} = \frac{8}{▓}$ ➭ Double 4 to get 8, so double the 5. ➭ $\frac{4}{5} = \frac{8}{10}$

Copy and complete the table.

**14.**

| Households | 5 | 10 | 20 | 40 |
|---|---|---|---|---|
| Bicycles | 4 | 8 | ▓ | ▓ |

**15.**

| Bicycles | 1 | 10 | ▓ | 40 |
|---|---|---|---|---|
| Wheels | 2 | ▓ | 60 | ▓ |

In China's cities there are about 8 bicycles to every 5 households.
That's a ratio of 8:5.

**16. IN YOUR WORDS** Are the ratios 8:5 and 40:30 proportional? Explain.

**17.** Use the 8:5 ratio to make a table for 8, 16, 24, 32, 40, and 48 bicycles.

Yai Yee rode her bicycle for 18 mi in 3 h.

$\frac{18 \text{ mi}}{3 \text{ h}}$    The ratio, $\frac{18 \text{ mi}}{3 \text{ h}}$, is called a rate because miles are compared to hours.

**A rate compares two quantities of different kinds.**

You use proportional thinking when you change the ratio to lowest
terms and say, "18 mi is to 3 h as 6 mi is to 1 h."

$\frac{18 \text{ mi}}{3 \text{ h}} = \frac{6 \text{ mi}}{1 \text{ h}}$    The ratio, $\frac{6 \text{ mi}}{1 \text{ h}}$, is called a unit rate. In short form, we write 6 mi/h.

**A ratio of a quantity to 1 is called a *unit rate*.**

**MENTAL MATH** Use proportional thinking to solve mentally.

**18.** A motorbike travels at the rate of 36 mi/gal of gas. At this rate,
how many miles would the motorbike travel on 10 gal of gas?

**19.** In a 20-mi bicycle race, Kim traveled at a speed of 5 mi/h.
At that rate, how long did she take to complete the race?

## Solving Proportions 🔲

In the proportion at the right, the arrows show the **cross products** $4 \times 9$ and $6 \times 6$.

$$\frac{4}{6} \times \frac{6}{9}$$

**THINK ALOUD** Multiply the cross products. What do you notice?

> **The *cross products* of a proportion are equal.**

**CRITICAL THINKING** Can a proportion be written for the two ratios? If so, write it.

$\frac{2}{16}$ and $\frac{3}{24}$ $\qquad\qquad$ $\frac{3}{4}$ and $\frac{2}{3}$ $\qquad\qquad$ $\frac{21}{9}$ and $\frac{14}{6}$

You use proportional thinking to write a proportion and you use cross products to solve for an unknown.

The purple at the right is a mixture of 8 parts red and 6 parts blue. How many parts red are needed to make this purple if 12 parts blue are used?

Use proportional thinking to set up the proportion. Let $n$ represent the number of red parts.

8 red is to 6 blue as $n$ red is to 12 blue.

$\qquad\qquad$ 8:6 as $n$:12

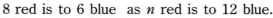

$$\frac{\text{red}}{\text{blue}} \longrightarrow \frac{8}{6} = \frac{n}{12} \longleftarrow \frac{\text{red}}{\text{blue}}$$

$6n = 8 \times 12$ ◁ Use the cross products to solve.

$6n = 96$

$\dfrac{6n}{6} = \dfrac{96}{6}$

$n = 16$

$\dfrac{8}{6} = \dfrac{16}{12}$ ◁ Check by substituting 16 for $n$.

$8 \times 12 = 6 \times 16$

$96 = 96$ ✔ $\qquad$ 8 ⊠ 12 ⊡ 6 ▣ 16

Sixteen parts red are needed to make the purple.

═══════════ **GUIDED PRACTICE** ═══════════

Use cross products to choose = or ≠.

**1.** $\frac{4}{7} \equiv \frac{5}{8}$ $\qquad$ **2.** $\frac{15}{12} \equiv \frac{20}{16}$ $\qquad$ **3.** $\frac{7}{9} \equiv \frac{5}{7}$ $\qquad$ **4.** $\frac{5}{16} \equiv \frac{2}{5}$

MATH AND ART

Solve. Check your answer.

**5.** $\dfrac{3}{4} = \dfrac{x}{20}$

**6.** $\dfrac{4}{x} = \dfrac{8}{5}$

**7.** $\dfrac{\text{cost}}{\text{pounds}} \longrightarrow \dfrac{\$5.99}{7} = \dfrac{x}{12} \longleftarrow \dfrac{\text{cost}}{\text{pounds}}$

---

## PRACTICE

Use cross products. Choose = or ≠.

**8.** $\dfrac{11}{20} \blacksquare \dfrac{1}{2}$

**9.** $\dfrac{18}{10} \blacksquare \dfrac{27}{15}$

**10.** $\dfrac{4}{18} \blacksquare \dfrac{10}{45}$

**11.** $\dfrac{7}{8} \blacksquare \dfrac{4}{5}$

Solve the proportion. Use pencil and paper or a calculator.

**12.** $\dfrac{3}{8} = \dfrac{15}{x}$

**13.** $\dfrac{3}{4} = \dfrac{r}{16}$

**14.** $\dfrac{12}{15} = \dfrac{x}{45}$

**15.** $\dfrac{7}{15} = \dfrac{14}{a}$

**16.** $\dfrac{m}{10} = \dfrac{1}{2}$

**17.** $\dfrac{15}{2} = \dfrac{x}{8}$

**18.** $\dfrac{24}{8} = \dfrac{12}{n}$

**19.** $\dfrac{6}{12} = \dfrac{9}{d}$

**20.** $\dfrac{14}{16} = \dfrac{35}{x}$

**21.** $\dfrac{5}{12} = \dfrac{c}{30}$

**22.** $\dfrac{4}{6} = \dfrac{5}{p}$

**23.** $\dfrac{1}{4} = \dfrac{5}{f}$

**24.** $\dfrac{5}{b} = \dfrac{2}{7}$

**25.** $\dfrac{16}{x} = \dfrac{2}{3}$

**26.** $\dfrac{5}{8} = \dfrac{2}{t}$

**27.** $\dfrac{1}{5} = \dfrac{q}{16}$

**CALCULATOR** Solve.

**28.** $\dfrac{3.7}{x} = \dfrac{11.1}{9}$

**29.** $\dfrac{5.6}{7.2} = \dfrac{2.8}{t}$

**30.** $\dfrac{4.2}{x} = \dfrac{9}{10.5}$

**31.** $\dfrac{u}{0.99} = \dfrac{1.35}{2.43}$

---

## PROBLEM SOLVING

Choose the proportion. Solve the problem.

**32.** The orange color at the right uses 13 parts yellow and 3 parts warm red. How many parts yellow are needed if 24 parts warm red are used?

    **a.** $\dfrac{13}{3} = \dfrac{24}{x}$     **b.** $\dfrac{13}{3} = \dfrac{x}{24}$

**33.** Paint costs \$3.96/fl oz. At that rate, what does $1\frac{1}{4}$ fl oz cost?

    **a.** $\dfrac{\$3.96}{1} = \dfrac{1.25}{x}$     **b.** $\dfrac{\$3.96}{1} = \dfrac{x}{1.25}$

---

## Estimate

You can use compatible numbers to estimate the unknown in a proportion.

$$\dfrac{9}{34} = \dfrac{n}{12} \quad \Rightarrow \quad \dfrac{1}{4} = \dfrac{n}{12} \quad \Rightarrow \quad \text{1 is to 4 as } n \text{ is to 12.} \quad n \approx 3$$

Use compatible numbers to estimate the value of the variable.

**1.** $\dfrac{7}{15} = \dfrac{x}{2}$

**2.** $\dfrac{8}{13} = \dfrac{2}{x}$

**3.** $\dfrac{n}{11} = \dfrac{5}{21}$

**4.** $\dfrac{4}{9} = \dfrac{n}{44}$

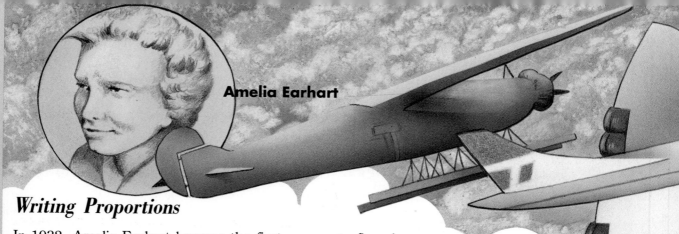

Amelia Earhart

# Writing Proportions

In 1932, Amelia Earhart became the first woman to fly solo across the Atlantic Ocean. She flew 2,026 mi, from Newfoundland to Ireland, at a speed of 135 mi/h. At that speed, how many hours did her transatlantic flight take?

Let $x$ represent the flight time in hours.

Think: 2,026 mi is to $x$ as 135 mi is to 1 h.

$$2{,}026 : x = 135 : 1$$

$$\frac{\text{miles}}{\text{hours}} \longrightarrow \frac{2{,}026}{x} = \frac{135}{1} \longleftarrow \frac{\text{miles}}{\text{hours}}$$

Keep the order in each ratio the same.

$$135x = 2{,}026 \times 1$$

$$\frac{135x}{135} = \frac{2{,}026}{135}$$

Use cross products to solve.

$$x = 15.007$$

Amelia Earhart's transatlantic flight took about 15 h.

**THINK ALOUD**  How would you check your answer?

**CRITICAL THINKING**  Explain why the speed, 135 mi/h, is also called a unit rate.

═══════════════ GUIDED PRACTICE ═══════════════

Copy and complete the proportion.

1. The fastest time in which a glider has flown 625 mi is about 7 h. How many miles is that per hour?

$$\frac{\text{miles}}{\text{hours}} \longrightarrow \frac{625}{7} = \frac{\blacksquare}{1} \longleftarrow \frac{\text{miles}}{\text{hour}}$$

2. **CRITICAL THINKING**  Which proportion does *not* represent the problem at the right? Why? Now solve the problem.

a. $\dfrac{5{,}090}{1} = \dfrac{\blacksquare}{50}$    b. $\dfrac{5{,}090}{\blacksquare} = \dfrac{50}{1}$

> In 1908, Glen Curtis flew an airplane 5,090 ft at a speed of 50 ft/s. How many seconds did the flight last?

**The Concorde**

**CHOOSE** Write a proportion. Choose mental math, paper and pencil, or calculator to solve.

3. Orville Wright made the first airplane flight, near Kitty Hawk, North Carolina, in 1903. He flew 120 ft in 12 s. At that rate, how far did he fly in 6 s? in 1 s?

4. Two British flyers, Alcock and Brown, made the first nonstop transatlantic flight in 1919. They flew a distance of 1,960 mi in 16 h. What was their speed in miles per hour?

Joseph Kittinger's balloon

5. In 1984, Joseph Kittinger became the first person to fly solo across the Atlantic in a balloon. His average speed was 42 mi/h. If Kittinger's flight took 84 h, how many miles did he fly?

6. Charles Lindbergh was the first man to fly solo 3,600 mi across the Atlantic from New York to Paris in 1927. If Lindbergh's speed was about 107 mi/h, how long did his flight last?

7. In 1986, Americans Richard Rutan and Jeana Yeager made the first nonstop flight around the world without refueling. They flew a total of 25,012 mi at an average speed of 115 mi/h. To the nearest hour, how many hours did Rutan and Yeager fly?

8. In 1978, the Concorde flew 3,600 mi from Paris to New York in 3.5 h. What was the Concorde's speed in whole miles per hour?

**CREATE YOUR OWN** Write a word problem to fit the proportion.

9. $\frac{2}{3} = \frac{?}{27}$

10. $\frac{2}{\$5} = \frac{?}{\$7.50}$

11. $\frac{4}{5} = \frac{?}{1,000}$

## Rates and Comparison Shopping

When shopping, you often find different quantities of the same item sold at different prices. In such cases, you can use proportional thinking to find the better buy.

Which is the better buy of Italian plum tomatoes?

**75¢/6 oz**

**$1.85/lb**

To decide, find the unit rates, or the cost of 1 oz, for each.

Let $x$ represent the cost per ounce (cost/oz).

75¢ is to 6 oz as $x$ is to 1 oz.

$$\frac{\text{cost}}{\text{ounces}} \longrightarrow \frac{\$.75}{6} = \frac{x}{1} \longleftarrow \frac{\text{cost}}{\text{ounces}}$$

$$\frac{6x}{6} = \frac{\$.75}{6}$$

$$x = \$.125, \text{ or } 13\text{¢}$$

The unit rate is 13¢ for 1 oz, or 13¢/oz.

$1.85 is to 16 oz as $x$ is to 1 oz.

$$\frac{\text{cost}}{\text{ounces}} \longrightarrow \frac{\$1.85}{16} = \frac{x}{1} \longleftarrow \frac{\text{cost}}{\text{ounces}}$$

$$\frac{16x}{16} = \frac{\$1.85}{16}$$

$$x = \$.115625, \text{ or } 12\text{¢}$$

The unit rate is 12¢ for 1 oz, or 12¢/oz.

Which is the better buy?

You can also find the cost per ounce using a calculator.

$$0.75 \boxed{\div} 6 \boxed{=} 0.125 \qquad\qquad 1.85 \boxed{\div} 16 \boxed{=} 0.115625$$

━━━━━━━━━━━━━━ **GUIDED PRACTICE** ━━━━━━━━━━━━━━

Find the unit rate.

1. 70¢ for 2 oz parsley flakes

2. $1.89 for 3 lb onions

3. 96¢ for 8 tomatoes

4. $7.50 for $1\frac{1}{2}$ lb Gorgonzola cheese

Find the unit rate to determine the better buy.

5. Which is the better buy for the Parmesan cheese at the right?

$1\frac{1}{2}$ lb

**$ 11.98**

**$ 3.99**

9 oz

MATH AND HOME ECONOMICS

Find the better buy. Use a calculator, mental math, or pencil and paper.

**6.** jar of olives, $1.89/12 oz    can of olives, $2.29/lb

**7.** pasta salad, $2.20/8 oz    pasta salad, $9.38/2 lb

**8.** lasagna noodles, $3.98/2 lb    lasagna noodles, $2.29/lb

**9.** 1 can olive oil, $13.32/gal    two bottles olive oil, $9.38/2 qt

**10.** ricotta cheese, $3.05/12 oz    ricotta cheese, $3.29/lb

**11.** fresh garlic, $.50/4 oz    garlic powder, $.60/3 oz

**12.** mozzarella cheese, $3.29/12 oz    mozzarella cheese, $2.49/8 oz

**13.** tomato sauce, $1.29/14 fl oz    tomato sauce, $.85/7½ fl oz

**14. CRITICAL THINKING** Suppose you will be serving 3 people 16 fl oz of soup each. Which is the more economical buy, if you do not wish to buy too much more soup than you will need?

**4 cans for $ 5.16**

**5 cans for $ 5.79**

---

## Mental Math

You can use proportional thinking and equivalent fractions to find the better buy mentally.

Which is the better buy for apples, 6 for 74¢ or a dozen for $1.59?

Think: $\frac{6}{0.74} = \frac{12}{?}$.

Double 6 to get 12, so also double 0.74.
$\frac{6}{0.74} = \frac{12}{1.48}$, so it is better to buy 12/$1.48 than 12/$1.59.

Is one a better buy than the other? If so, which one?

**1.** 4 for 79¢ or 12 for 99¢

**2.** 15 for $70 or 3 for $16

**3.** 8 for $1.09 or 4 for $0.49

**4.** 10 for $13 or 40 for $50

---

## LANGUAGE & VOCABULARY

Use the term in a sentence to show that you know its meaning.

1. ratio
2. cross products
3. rate
4. unit rate
5. proportion

---

## QUICK QUIZ

Solve the proportion. Check your answer. *(pages 280–281)*

1. $\dfrac{8}{24} = \dfrac{x}{36}$
2. $\dfrac{a}{17} = \dfrac{6}{51}$
3. $\dfrac{8}{12} = \dfrac{20}{x}$
4. $\dfrac{15}{m} = \dfrac{3}{8}$

Find the better buy. *(pages 284–285)*

5. cereal: 10 oz for $1.79 or 13 oz for $2.09
6. paper towels: 50 sheets for $1.09 or 65 sheets for $1.35
7. light bulbs: 4 for $3.28 or $.85 each
8. oranges: 12 for $1.00 or 15 for $1.50
9. olives: 8 oz for $1.45 or 10 oz for $1.69

Solve. *(pages 276–279, 282–283)*

10. Bamboo, a very fast growing plant, has been known to grow as much as 35 in. in 1 d. Some seaweeds can grow as much as 1 yd in 1 d.

    a. Has a bamboo plant ever been known to grow as much as 1 yd in 1 d?

    b. How could you find the maximum growth for either plant in 1 wk?

    c. If a bamboo plant could continue growing at the rate of 35 in./d, how much would it grow in 1 wk?

Write the answers in your learning log.

1. Describe two ways you can test to see whether two ratios form a proportion.

2. Your friend thinks the four numbers in a proportion can be arranged any way. Explain why you agree or disagree with this thinking.

MATH AMERICA

**DID YOU KNOW . . . ?** About 3 out of every 10 workers in the United States work in an agricultural career. Poll your classmates. Ask whether anyone in their families works in an agriculture-related job. Compare your reduced ratio to the national ratio. Are the two proportional? What could explain the differences?

## BONUS

The menu of the Bet You Can't Buy Just One restaurant includes these items and prices:

Orange juice: 3 for $1.95          Milk: 2 for $.99

Apples: 3 for $.79          Baked potato: 2 for $2.45

Tuna sandwich: 2 for $2.15          Egg salad sandwich: 2 for $1.99

Yogurt: 3 for $2.39          Tea: 2 for $1.27

How much does each order cost? Round to the nearest cent.

1. 5 orange juices
2. 1 tuna sandwich
3. 3 milks
4. 3 egg sandwiches
5. 7 apples
6. 2 yogurts
7. 1 baked potato
8. 1 tea

# Jot it Down

## Problem Solving:
### Writing Problems

UNDERSTAND
PLAN
REPRESENT
CARRY OUT
LOOK BACK

**READ ABOUT IT**

When the *Titanic* began its first voyage, at noon on April 10, 1912, from Southampton, England, to New York City, it was the largest ship in the world. It was 882 ft long, weighed 46,328 t, and carried about 2,227 people. Its 3 anchors alone weighed a total of 31 t.

The *Titanic* was nicknamed "The Unsinkable Ship." But at 11:40 P.M. on the night of April 14, it struck an iceberg about 400 mi off the coast of North America and began to sink.

The *Carpathia*, a ship about 60 mi from the *Titanic* at the time, raced to the scene in answer to the *Titanic*'s distress signals. When it arrived on the scene $4\frac{1}{2}$ h later, it found only 705 of the *Titanic*'s passengers and crew in lifeboats.

As the *Titanic* sank 12,460 ft to the ocean floor, it broke into two pieces, which now rest 1,970 ft apart.

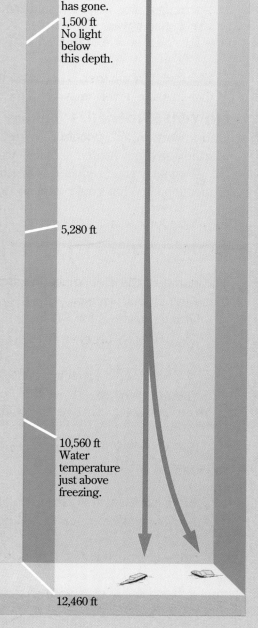

437 ft
Deepest point a scuba diver has gone.

1,500 ft
No light below this depth.

5,280 ft

10,560 ft
Water temperature just above freezing.

Washington Monument 555 ft

Sears Tower 1,454 ft

Statue of Liberty 305 ft

12,460 ft

The *Titanic* was thought to be lost forever, but it was located in 1985 by a French and American team. Two years later, Congress moved to make the *Titanic* an international memorial.

## ■ TALK ABOUT IT

Use the information about the *Titanic* on pages 288 and 289.

1. This proportion was used to solve a problem.

$$\frac{\text{miles}}{\text{hours}} \longrightarrow \frac{60}{4\frac{1}{2}} = \frac{x}{1}$$

The answer was, *The* Carpathia *traveled at a speed of 13* $\frac{1}{3}$ *mi in 1 h.* What was the question?

2. Work with a partner. Discuss what problem you can write that has the given answer. Tell what information is needed to write the problem.

   a. about 1,522 people

   b. about 2.4 mi

   c. 62,000 lb

   d. 73 yr

   e. about 0.4 mi

## ■ WRITE ABOUT IT

Work with a partner. Use the information on pages 288 and 289.

3. Devise a math problem that involves ratio.

4. Devise a math problem involving time.

5. Write a problem involving depth.

6. Write a problem that requires division to find its solution.

7. Write a problem in which a unit of measurement is changed to another unit.

8. Write a problem for which the answer cannot be found because not enough information is given.

9. Write a problem that contains too much information.

Now exchange problems with another pair of partners and solve.

## Exploring Similar Polygons

Polygons having the same shape, but
not necessarily the same size, are called
**similar** polygons.

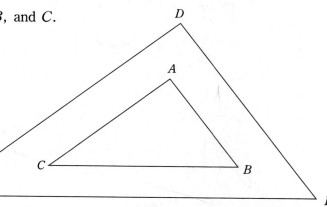

1. Follow the steps to make a triangle similar
   to △ABC, but larger.

   • Trace △ABC. Label the vertices A, B, and C.

   • Place a ruler along $\overline{AB}$. Draw line
     $\overline{DE}$ parallel to $\overline{AB}$ along the other
     edge of the ruler.

   • Repeat for the other two sides
     of △ABC. Use a ruler to
     extend the lines until they
     intersect and form △DEF.

   • Label the vertices of the
     larger triangle D, E,
     and F.

If you worked carefully, △DEF should be similar to △ABC.

2. $\overline{DE}$ and $\overline{AB}$ are called corresponding
   sides of the similar triangles. Why?

3. Which side of △ABC corresponds to
   $\overline{FD}$ of △DEF? Which side corresponds
   to $\overline{FE}$?

Use a centimeter ruler to compare the lengths in the diagram above.
Write the ratio in lowest terms.

4. length of $\overline{CB}$ : length of $\overline{FE}$

5. length of $\overline{AB}$ : length of $\overline{DE}$

6. length of $\overline{AC}$ : length of $\overline{DF}$

7. What do you notice about the ratios
   you wrote in Exercises 4–6?

8. What do you think is true about
   the corresponding sides of similar
   figures?

9. Why are ∠ABC and ∠DEF called
   corresponding angles?

10. Which angle of △DEF corresponds
    to ∠ACB of △ABC? Which angle
    corresponds to ∠FDE?

11. Use a protractor to measure ∠DFE and ∠ACB. How do they compare in size?

12. Use a protractor to compare ∠CAB and ∠ABC with their corresponding angles. How do they compare in size?

13. **CRITICAL THINKING** Use a protractor and a ruler to draw ~~five~~ *three* different pairs of similar triangles. Can you draw a pair of triangles with congruent angles that are not similar?

---

**Two figures are *similar* when their corresponding angles are congruent and their corresponding sides are in proportion.**

---

The two triangles at the right are similar. The ratio of $\overline{LM}$ to $\overline{RS}$ is 3:2.

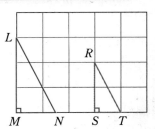

14. Without measuring, what is the ratio of $\overline{MN}$ to $\overline{ST}$? the ratio of $\overline{LN}$ to $\overline{RT}$?

15. **IN YOUR WORDS** It is easy to find the corresponding sides and angles for the triangles in Exercise 14. For the polygons below it is not so easy. Trace and turn the polygons to find the corresponding sides and angles.

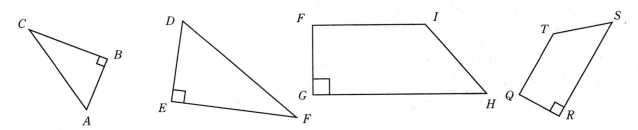

Trace the pairs of similar polygons. Mark the corresponding angles and sides.

16.

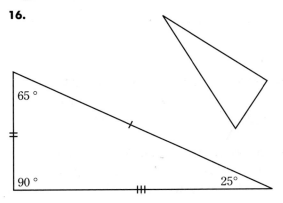

17.

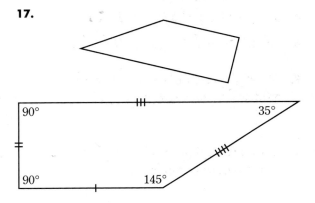

## *Similar Polygon Applications*

Marla is sewing a pillow with an African design. The instructions show a reduced version of the design. If the length of the finished pillow will be 14 in., what will be its width?

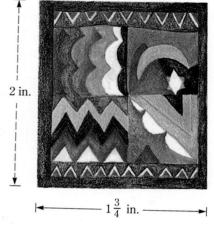

Set up a proportion to solve the problem. Let $w$ be the width of the pillow in inches.

$1\frac{3}{4}$ in. is to 2 in. as 14 in. is to $w$.

Reduced size:    Actual size:

$\frac{\text{length} \longrightarrow}{\text{width} \longrightarrow} \frac{1.75}{2} = \frac{14}{w} \frac{\longleftarrow \text{length}}{\longleftarrow \text{width}}$

$1.75w = 2 \times 14$    ⟵ Use cross products.

$\frac{1.75w}{1.75} = \frac{28}{1.75}$

$w = 16$

$\frac{1.75}{2} = \frac{14}{16}$    ⟵ Check by substituting 16 for $w$.

$1.75 \times 16 = 2 \times 14$

$28 = 28$ ✔

**Traditional African designs**

The width of the finished pillow will be 16 in.

The figures in the design are similar. What is the length of side $x$ of the large triangle?

Use corresponding sides to set up the proportion.

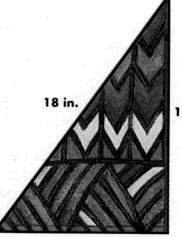

$\frac{\text{large} \longrightarrow}{\text{small} \longrightarrow} \frac{16}{4} = \frac{x}{3} \frac{\longleftarrow \text{large}}{\longleftarrow \text{small}}$

18 in.    16 in.

$4x = 16 \times 3$

$\frac{4x}{4} = \frac{48}{4}$

$x = 12$    ⟵ How would you check this answer?

4 in.

3 in.    x in.

The length of the side $x$ of the large triangle is 12 in.

━━━━━━━━━━━━━━━━━━━━━━━━ **GUIDED PRACTICE** ━━━━━━━━━━━━━━━━━━━━━━━━

The figures are similar. Copy and complete the proportion. Solve for the value of the unknown.

12 in.

**1.** $\frac{10}{15} = \frac{x}{▥}$    **2.** $\frac{▥}{4} = \frac{12}{y}$

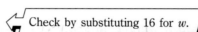

9 in.    6 in.

15 in.

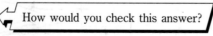

y

x    4 in.

10 in.

The figures are similar. Write a proportion to solve for the unknown.

**3.**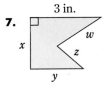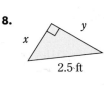
2 ft   x ft   4 ft   8 ft   8 ft

**4.**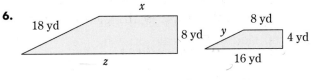
9 in.   x   3 in.   2 in.

**5.**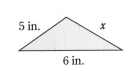
y   6 in.   9 in.   5 in.   x   6 in.

**6.**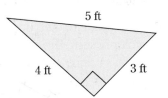
x   18 yd   8 yd   z   8 yd   y   8 yd   16 yd   4 yd

**7.**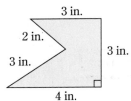
3 in.   x   w   z   y   2 in.   3 in.   3 in.   3 in.   4 in.

**8.**
x   y   2.5 ft   4 ft   5 ft   3 ft

Write a proportion to solve.

**9.** A slide image is $1\frac{3}{8}$ in. wide and $\frac{7}{8}$ in. high. When the image is projected onto a screen, it is 88 in. wide. How high is the projected image?

**10.** You want to enlarge the pillow design on page 292 so that the pillow becomes 3 ft wide. How long will it be?

**11.** A photograph that is 8 in. wide and 10 in. long is reduced on a photocopy machine to 3 in. long. How wide is the reduced photograph?

**12.** In some parts of Africa, houses are painted colorfully. A pattern for these painted African houses is shown at the right, on $\frac{1}{4}$ in. grid paper. Measure the height of the front/back piece of the house. To what size square would the grid have to be enlarged to make the actual height of this piece 12 in. tall?

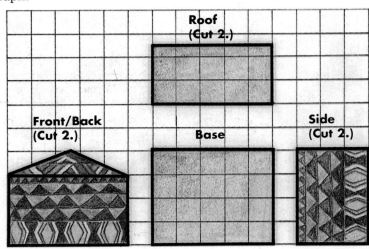

Roof (Cut 2.)

Front/Back (Cut 2.)   Base   Side (Cut 2.)

## Scale Drawings and Similarity

Some Kickapoo people live in traditional compounds in parts of Texas, Oklahoma, Kansas, and northern Mexico. Some live in cities and towns.

What is the length along the top side of the scale drawing of the compound? What is its actual length?

Use the scale to set up a proportion. Let $x$ represent the actual length in feet.

0.5 in. is to 10 ft as 2.75 in. is to $x$ ft.

$$\frac{\text{inches}}{\text{feet}} \longrightarrow \frac{0.5}{10} = \frac{2.75}{x} \longleftarrow \frac{\text{inches}}{\text{feet}}$$

$$0.5x = 10 \times 2.75 \quad \boxed{\text{Use cross products.}}$$

$$\frac{0.5x}{0.5} = \frac{27.5}{0.5}$$

$$x = 55$$

$$\frac{0.5}{10} = \frac{2.75}{55} \quad \boxed{\text{Check by substituting 55 for } x.}$$

$$0.5 \times 55 = 10 \times 2.75$$

$$27.5 = 27.5 \checkmark$$

0 inches   1   2   3

**Scale: 0.5 in. = 10 ft**
**Mexican Kickapoo Compound**
**Scale: 0.5 in. = 10 ft**

ramada

summer house

winter house

cookhouse

The **scale** is the ratio of a length in the drawing to the actual length.

The actual length across the top of the compound is 55 ft.

---

**GUIDED PRACTICE**

Use a ruler and the scale to find the length in miles.   **Scale: $\frac{1}{4}$ in. = 150 mi**

1.

2.

3.

4. Use a ruler and the scale to find the actual length of a cookhouse in the compound.

Use a ruler and the scale to find the length in yards.    **Scale: 0.5 in. = 5 yd**

**5.** |————————|    **6.** |————————————|    **7.** |————————|    **8.** |——————|

Use a ruler and the scale to find the length in miles.    **Scale: $\frac{1}{8}$ in. = 2 mi**

**9.** |——————————|    **10.** |————|    **11.** |————————————|    **12.** |——————|

■ **PROBLEM SOLVING** ■

 Use a ruler and the scale. Choose estimation, paper and pencil, or a calculator to solve.

Refer to the Kickapoo winter house at the right.

**13.** What is the actual length (*a*) of the Kickapoo winter house at the right?

**14.** What is the actual size of the opening to the winter house (*b*)?

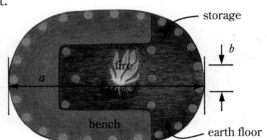

**Scale: $\frac{1}{4}$ in. = $2\frac{1}{2}$ ft**

Refer to the map.

**15.** What is the actual distance from Oklahoma City to Tulsa?

**16.** What is the actual distance between McLoud, Oklahoma, and San Antonio, Texas?

**17.** Find two cities that are about 600 mi apart.

**18.** Estimate the length of the Oklahoma/Texas border.

**Scale: 0.5 in. = 100 Mi**

## Problem Solving Strategy: Using Proportions

UNDERSTAND
PLAN
REPRESENT
CARRY OUT
LOOK BACK

For centuries, artists have worked with proportions. For example, Greek sculptors worked with a body height to head height ratio of 8 to 1.

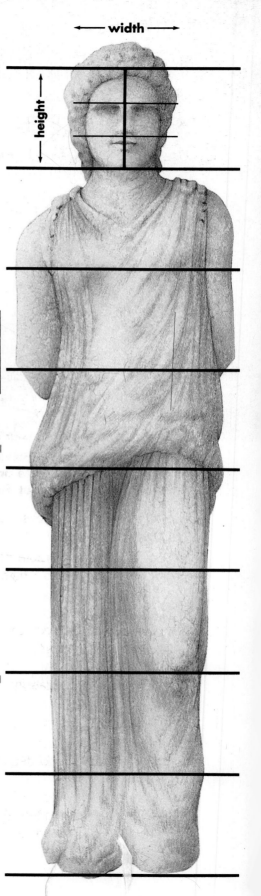

width

height

Suppose you want to make a clay sculpture of a human with a head 2 in. high. Using the Greek sculptors' 8 to 1 ratio, what would be the total height of the sculpture?

**THINK ALOUD**  Does each proportion represent the problem? Explain.

| | | |
|---|---|---|
| human body height → | $\dfrac{8}{1} = \dfrac{x}{2}$ | ← sculpture body height |
| human head height → | | ← sculpture head height |
| human body height → | $\dfrac{8}{x} = \dfrac{1}{2}$ | ← human head height |
| sculpture body height → | | ← sculpture head height |

Now solve the problem.

════════ **GUIDED PRACTICE** ════════

Write a proportion to solve.

**1.** A sculpture of a human with a head height of 3 in. is made using the 8 to 1 ratio.

   **a.** What is the head height of the sculpture?

   **b.** Explain what the 8 to 1 ratio means.

   **c.** What is the total body height of the sculpture?

**2.** For the sculpture described in Exercise 1, what is the height of the figure to the waist?

════════ **PRACTICE** ════════

Write a proportion to solve.

**3.** The most common head shape is oval. In an oval head, the ratio of width to height is about 2:3. For the sculpture described in Exercise 1, about how wide should the head be?

**4.** The head usually is "five eyes" wide. For the sculpture described in Exercise 1, how wide should each eye be?

MATH AND ART

**The images of George Washington, Thomas Jefferson, Theodore Roosevelt, and Abraham Lincoln are on Mount Rushmore, in South Dakota. Each head is about 60 ft high, about the height of a five-story building!**

Use the 8:1 or the 2:3 sculptor's ratio to write a proportion and solve.

5. If Washington's whole body had been sculpted, how high would it have been?

6. If Lincoln had been sculpted from the waist to the head, how many stories high would he have been?

7. Together, approximately how wide are all four heads?

8. About what would be the combined width of Jefferson's two eyes?

CHOOSE   Choose a strategy to solve.

9. **IN YOUR WORDS**   Measure your total height and the height of your head. Explain how your body and head height compares to the 8 to 1 ratio described on page 296.

10. The heads on Mount Rushmore were sculpted from models $\frac{1}{12}$ their size. About how high were the models?

11. How many times higher are the heads on Mount Rushmore than your head?

# Planning a Window-Washing Business

Imagine that you and some friends want to start a summer business. You decide that washing windows might be a good way to earn money. What kind of planning must you do?

Work in a small group. Use a calculator when necessary.

1. Decide how much money you will need to start your business. Your start-up costs for this business will be the cost of your cleaning supplies. Make a chart like the one below and fill it in.

MATH AND ECONOMICS

298    LESSON 9–12

**2.** Total your start-up costs.

**3.** If the start-up costs are shared equally among all members of your group, how much must each member contribute?

**4.** Sometimes partners do not share the start-up costs or the profits equally. For example, they might share the start-up costs and the profits in the ratio 1:2:3. If your start-up costs were $18, how much would each person contribute if three people shared the costs in the ratio 1:2:3? Explain.

| Equipment Needed | cost |
| --- | --- |
| | |
| | |
| | |
| Total | |

**5.** What are some advantages and disadvantages to business partners of sharing start-up costs equally? of not sharing start-up costs equally? Decide how your group will share the start-up costs for your window-washing business. Write a ratio to show this.

**6.** Suppose you decide to work 8 h/wk. Your group can wash 6 windows in 1 h. You will charge $4.00 per window. How many windows can you wash each week? How much would your group make each week if each of you works 8 h/wk?

**7.** Use the start-up costs from Exercise 4 and your answer from Exercise 6. If three people shared the start-up costs and the profits in a 1:2:3 ratio, how much would each receive for the first week's work? Remember to subtract your start-up costs from the week's profits. Explain your answer.

**8.** Suppose that business slows down. To stay in business, how can you vary the services your business provides without adding to your start-up costs? Now suppose business grows so much that there is too much work for you and your partners to handle. What are some things you can do to adjust to this possibility?

**9.** Exercises 1–9 are based on a window-washing business. List ten other jobs that you could do in the summer to earn money. Be creative. Discuss the advantages and disadvantages of each job.

**10.** Select one job from Exercise 9. Apply the types of questions asked about the window-washing business to this job. Could you earn money in this business? Explain.

## Mixed Review

Find the LCM.

**1.** 5, 10
**2.** 4, 5
**3.** 4, 6
**4.** 10, 18
**5.** 12, 14

Find the GCF.

**6.** 20, 30
**7.** 10, 15
**8.** 36, 40
**9.** 36, 42
**10.** 36, 45

Write the fraction in lowest terms.

**11.** $\frac{10}{30}$
**12.** $\frac{5}{30}$
**13.** $\frac{4}{16}$
**14.** $\frac{16}{72}$
**15.** $\frac{14}{16}$

Compute.

**16.** $578 + 324$
**17.** $23 \times 754$
**18.** $972 - 631$
**19.** $5,074 \div 86$

**20.** $359,988 \div 524$
**21.** $6,627 - 4,738$
**22.** $11,931 + 12,001$
**23.** $491 \times 5,561$

**24.** $3.4 + 16.2$
**25.** $71.6 \times 71.6$
**26.** $225.6 \div 56.4$
**27.** $89.6 - 9.7$

**28.** $57.125 + 41.92$
**29.** $57.125 - 41.92$
**30.** $14.57 \times 16.2$
**31.** $22.75 + 18.31$

**32.** $10.73 - 10.67$
**33.** $378.41 \times 27.8$
**34.** $464.16 \div 77.36$
**35.** $663.6 \div 55.3$

Compute. Write the answer in lowest terms.

**36.** $\frac{3}{4} + \frac{1}{2}$
**37.** $\frac{3}{8} + \frac{5}{16}$
**38.** $\frac{11}{12} - \frac{2}{3}$
**39.** $\frac{7}{11} \times \frac{1}{4}$

**40.** $\frac{3}{4} \times \frac{4}{5}$
**41.** $\frac{6}{8} \div \frac{1}{2}$
**42.** $12\frac{5}{16} - 10\frac{1}{2}$
**43.** $\frac{8}{9} \div \frac{4}{5}$

**44.** $20\frac{5}{16} - 17\frac{1}{2}$
**45.** $2\frac{3}{5} + 8\frac{1}{10}$
**46.** $1\frac{1}{4} \times 2\frac{1}{5}$
**47.** $12\frac{2}{3} \div 2\frac{2}{3}$

**Luzon,
Philippines**

Choose estimation, mental math, pencil and paper, or calculator to solve.

**48.** Estimate the part of the Philippine flag that is red.

**49.** Spanish explorers colonized the Philippines in the 1500s. In 1898, Spain gave the Philippines to the United States. On July 4, 1946, the Philippines became independent. For how many years has the Philippines been independent?

**50.** There are about 66,156,000 people living in the Philippines, on about 116,000 mi² of land. About how many persons is that per square mile?

**51.** Nearly half the population of the Philippines live on Luzon, the largest island. About how many people is that? Use the information in Exercise 50.

**52.** Luzon has an area of about 40,000 mi². What is the ratio in lowest terms of the area of Luzon to the total area of the country? Use the information in Exercise 50.

**53.** Use an inch ruler to measure along the black line on the map at right. About how many miles is the distance along the length of the country?

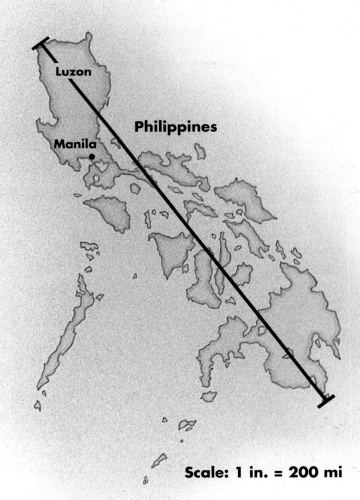

**Scale: 1 in. = 200 mi**

---

**LANGUAGE & VOCABULARY**

Is the statement *true* or *false*?

**1.** The only figures that can be similar are polygons.

**2.** All rectangles are similar.

**3.** A scale drawing can be smaller than the original.

---

**TEST** ✓

---

**CONCEPTS**

Use cross products to choose = or ≠. *(pages 280–281)*

**1.** $\dfrac{2}{9} \rule{1cm}{0.5mm} \dfrac{4}{15}$

**2.** $\dfrac{10}{15} \rule{1cm}{0.5mm} \dfrac{30}{45}$

**3.** $\dfrac{8}{7} \rule{1cm}{0.5mm} \dfrac{12}{9}$

**4.** $\dfrac{14}{20} \rule{1cm}{0.5mm} \dfrac{21}{30}$

**SKILLS**

Solve for the unknown value. Check your answer.
*(pages 280–281)*

**5.** $\dfrac{3}{9} = \dfrac{5}{x}$

**6.** $\dfrac{7}{12} = \dfrac{x}{36}$

**7.** $\dfrac{1}{8} = \dfrac{6}{x}$

**8.** $\dfrac{r}{12} = \dfrac{12}{16}$

Find the better buy. *(pages 284–285)*

**9.** peanut butter: 12 oz for $1.75 or 18 oz for $2.35

**10.** bread: 24-oz loaf for $1.67 or 32-oz loaf for $2.49

The figures are similar. Write a proportion to solve for the
unknown value. *(pages 290–293)*

**11.**
8 in.
2 in.
9 in.
x

**12.**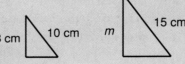
8 cm   10 cm   m   15 cm

**13.**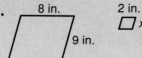
27 m
y
x
60 m   12 m
45 m

**14.**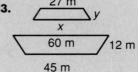
a   18 ft
20 ft   24 ft

Use a ruler and the scale to find the length in feet. *(pages 294–295)*

Scale: $\frac{1}{4}$in. = 3 ft          **15.**                                    **16.**

**PROBLEM SOLVING**

Write a proportion to solve. *(pages 296–297)*

**17.** A building is being constructed from a scale model that is 4 ft high. The scale used to construct the building is 1 in. = 10 ft.

  **a.** What is the height of the scale model?
  **b.** What does a scale of 1 in. = 10 ft mean?
  **c.** What will the height of the actual building be?

Write a proportion. Solve. *(pages 276–279, 282–283)*

**18.** David paid $4.83 for 3 gal of gasoline. At that rate, how much will Rosella pay for 8 gal of gasoline?

**19.** A photograph with dimensions 14 in. by 20 in. is to be enlarged. Will the enlargement have the same shape as the original if its dimensions are 21 in. by 30 in?

**LEARNING LOG**

Write the answers in your learning log.
  **1.** Your friend thinks all pieces of paper are similar. Explain what is wrong with this thinking.

  **2.** What is important to remember when using proportions to solve problems?

Use cross products to choose = or ≠. *(pages 280–281)*

**1.** $\dfrac{3}{12} \blacksquare \dfrac{9}{48}$

**2.** $\dfrac{7}{15} \blacksquare \dfrac{21}{45}$

**3.** $\dfrac{20}{12} \blacksquare \dfrac{16}{10}$

**4.** $\dfrac{9}{25} \blacksquare \dfrac{3}{8}$

Solve the proportion. Check your answer. *(pages 280–281)*

**5.** $\dfrac{1}{5} = \dfrac{6}{x}$

**6.** $\dfrac{2}{3} = \dfrac{x}{21}$

**7.** $\dfrac{2}{5} = \dfrac{8}{x}$

**8.** $\dfrac{12}{32} = \dfrac{18}{m}$

**9.** $\dfrac{y}{4} = \dfrac{42}{56}$

**10.** $\dfrac{6}{x} = \dfrac{8}{12}$

**11.** $\dfrac{5}{9} = \dfrac{n}{45}$

**12.** $\dfrac{14}{2} = \dfrac{42}{a}$

Find the better buy. *(pages 284–285)*

**13.** salt: 16 oz for $.59 or 18 oz for $.75

**14.** vinegar: 20 oz for $.45 or 32 oz for $.60

**15.** rice: 32 oz for $1.39 or 48 oz for $1.89

**16.** frankfurters: 8 for $2.49 or 12 for $2.70

The figures are similar. Write a proportion to solve for the unknown value. *(pages 292–293)*

**17.**

**18.**

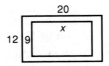

**19.**

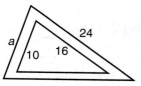

**20.**

Use a ruler and the scale to find the length. *(pages 294–295)*

**21.** |————————————————|    Scale: 0.5 in. = 3 yd

**22.** |——————————————————————|    Scale: 0.25 in. = 6 ft

**23.** |————————————————————|    Scale: $\frac{1}{8}$ in. = 4 mi

Solve. *(pages 282–283, 296–297)*

**24.** A model of an airplane that is 150 ft long is built to a scale of $\frac{1}{8}$ in. = 1 ft. How long will the model be?

**25.** For the airplane described above, the ratio of the wingspan to the length is 3 to 4. How long is the wingspan of the actual plane? of the model?

# MAKING A SCALE MODEL DRAWING

Some examples of scale models are blueprints, photographs, maps, dolls, and television pictures. You can make scale model drawings this way.

- Tape several sheets of centimeter graph paper together to use for an enlargement.
- Draw a simple design on another sheet of graph paper.
- Enlarge the design using a 1:2 ratio. For example, make every segment that is 1 cm long in the original 2 cm long in the enlargement.

Try several designs. By doubling the length of each segment, by what ratio does the area of the figure increase?

# Fast Times

Choose a race. It could be the Boston Marathon, the Indianapolis 500, an Olympic swim meet, or any race you are interested in. Use an almanac to find the winning times for the race over a period of years. Make a graph of the data. See if you can predict from your graph what the winning time may be 10 yr from now.

# Scales of Squares

Play with a partner. On a piece of paper, make a game board like the one below. Take turns putting your first initial in a circle. The winner is the player whose initials are in 4 circles that, when connected, would make a square.

$$\begin{matrix} \bigcirc & \bigcirc & \bigcirc & \bigcirc \\ \bigcirc & \bigcirc & \bigcirc & \bigcirc \\ \bigcirc & \bigcirc & \bigcirc & \bigcirc \\ \bigcirc & \bigcirc & \bigcirc & \bigcirc \end{matrix}$$

Find the answer.

**1.** $3{,}459 \times 28 =$
    **a.** 92,282
    **b.** 34,590
    **c.** 96,852
    **d.** none of these

**2.** $27.09 \times 0.6 =$
    **a.** 162.54
    **b.** 1.6254
    **c.** 0.16254
    **d.** none of these

**3.** $0.039 \times 0.003 =$
    **a.** 0.000117
    **b.** 0.00117
    **c.** 0.0117
    **d.** none of these

**4.** $3{,}843 \div 25 =$
    **a.** 112 R 13
    **b.** 153 R 18
    **c.** 152 R 18
    **d.** none of these

**5.** $\$16.28 \div 22 =$
    **a.** $7.40
    **b.** $358.16
    **c.** $.74
    **d.** none of these

**6.** $83.41 \div 0.19 =$
    **a.** 43.9
    **b.** 4.39
    **c.** 439
    **d.** none of these

Solve for $x$.

**7.** $\dfrac{x}{24} = \dfrac{35}{60}$
    **a.** 14
    **b.** 16
    **c.** 20
    **d.** none of these

**8.** $\dfrac{10}{16} = \dfrac{x}{24}$
    **a.** 12
    **b.** 15
    **c.** 18
    **d.** none of these

**9.** $\dfrac{25}{40} = \dfrac{20}{x}$
    **a.** 30
    **b.** 32
    **c.** 36
    **d.** none of these

Find the best estimate.

**10.** $418 \div 83 =$
    **a.** 5
    **b.** 6
    **c.** 50
    **d.** none of these

**11.** $2{,}421 \div 59 =$
    **a.** 30
    **b.** 50
    **c.** 40
    **d.** none of these

**12.** $26.8 \div 0.31 =$
    **a.** 90
    **b.** 9
    **c.** 900
    **d.** none of these

Evaluate the expression. Use the value of the given variable.

**13.** $x^2 - x$
Use $x = 9$.
    **a.** 0
    **b.** 72
    **c.** 90
    **d.** none of these

**14.** $3(9 - y)$
Use $y = 2$.
    **a.** 27
    **b.** 25
    **c.** 21
    **d.** none of these

**15.** $7 - (m \div 3)$
Use $m = 6$.
    **a.** $\dfrac{1}{3}$
    **b.** 5
    **c.** 4
    **d.** none of these

# PROBLEM SOLVING REVIEW

Remember the strategies and types of problems you have done so far. Solve.

1. Lee measured his room and drew a scale model of it. The drawing was a rectangle 6 in. by 9 in. The scale was $\frac{1}{2}$ in. = 1 ft.

   a. What scale did Lee use?

   b. How can you find the actual dimensions of the room?

   c. What are the dimensions of the room?

2. Kim has $2.35 in coins. Her friend has exactly $1.00 more in coins. They combine their money and exchange it for bills. What is the fewest number of bills they can receive?

3. Carla delivers balloon bouquets that come in three sizes: small, for $7.95; medium, for $12.95; and large, for $22.95. She earns $2.00 per delivery. How much does she earn for delivering 3 small, 3 medium, and 4 large bouquets?

4. Stan ran the first lap of a race in 2 min 48 s. He ran each of the remaining laps in 3 min 19 s. What was his time for the entire race?

5. Mercedes had $10. She bought 1 pen for $2.95, labels for $.59, and envelopes for $2.19. How much more did she spend for the pen than the envelopes?

6. Grover Cleveland served as President of the United States from 1885 to 1889 and from 1893 to 1897. How many years elapsed between the beginning of his first term and the end of his second term?

7. Jan traveled from Buffalo to Memphis, from Memphis to New Orleans, and from New Orleans to Mobile. She could choose from 3 flights, 4 trains, and 2 buses. How many choices did Jan have?

8. Sun drew a coordinate grid. He plotted the points represented by the ordered pairs: (1, 3), (2, 5), and (3, 7). If he continued the pattern, what are the coordinates of the next ordered pair?

9. A baby weighed 7 lb 4 oz at birth. During the next two months, the baby gained 13 oz, lost 3 oz, and then gained 6 oz. How much did the baby weigh after two months?

## EASY AS PI

On a calculator with eight digits, $\pi$ equals 3.1415927. Some people use 3.14 to estimate $\pi$, while some use $\frac{22}{7}$. Write $\frac{22}{7}$ as a decimal.

Find three nonequivalent fractions that give 3.141 as a quotient when all the decimal places to the right of the thousandths' place are dropped.

## WHAT'S THE RATIO?

In the computer activity *Ratio Maze*, you find your way out of a maze by finding equivalent ratios. This pencil-and-paper activity will build your skills at writing equivalent ratios.

Write three equivalent ratios using the numbers in each box.

1. $\boxed{2\ 3\ 4\ 5\ 6\ 10}$

2. $\boxed{6\ 9\ 10\ 12\ 15\ 18}$

3. $\boxed{10\ 12\ 15\ 18\ 25\ 30}$

4. $\boxed{6\ 12\ 16\ 18\ 32\ 48}$

## SMART SHOPPING

Which price gives you the most for your money?

Salty Sam's salt: 1 lb $0.60

XYZ Salt: 1 lb, 12 oz $0.89

Salt-o'-the-Earth: 26 oz $0.99

How much would 64 oz of the best buy cost, using the same unit price?

**DID YOU KNOW . . . ?**

Every day each American throws out an average of 4 lb of trash. If you loaded all of this trash into garbage trucks, it would fill 63,000 of them.

The diagram shows the percent of materials typically found in American trash.

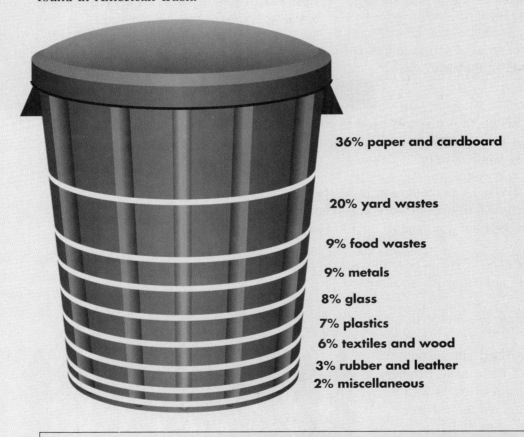

36% paper and cardboard

20% yard wastes

9% food wastes

9% metals

8% glass

7% plastics

6% textiles and wood

3% rubber and leather

2% miscellaneous

**USING DATA**
Collect
Organize
Describe
Predict

Ask 20 people who bring their lunches to school the following:

• Is your food wrapped in paper, foil, or plastic?
• Are the wrappings recycled when you are finished eating?
• Do you use a reusable container for your lunch?
• Do you care about the environment?

Organize your data with that of your classmates into a table.

## EXPLORE

### Exploring the Meaning of Percent

In about the last 50 yr, 40% of the world's original rain forest cover has been destroyed.

The tropical rain forests support about 50% of the world's species of plants and animals.

It is estimated that about 12% of the 40,000 mi² of tropical forest left in 1980 may be gone by the year 2000.

In each example above, a percent is used to describe a fact about tropical rain forests. **Percent** is a special ratio that compares a number to 100.

1. **IN YOUR WORDS**  A percent sign is written at the right. Explain how the sign itself helps you remember the meaning of percent as the ratio of a number to 100, or per hundred.

2. **IN YOUR WORDS**  Explain how the word *percent* can help you remember its meaning.

3. Name and define two words that have *cent* as a prefix.

The illustration at the right contains 100 trees. If 20 of them have needles, you can say the ratio of trees with needles to the total number of trees is 20:100, or 20%.

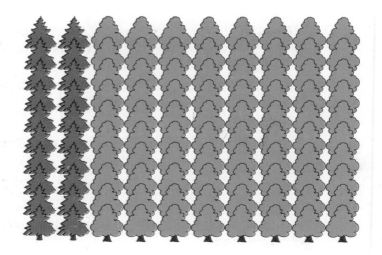

4. The remaining trees are broad-leaved. What percent of the trees are broad-leaved?

5. Suppose 50 of the trees at the right are tropical. What percent of the trees are tropical?

MATH AND ECOLOGY

The diagram shows 100. What percent of the diagram is shaded?

**6.**

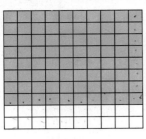

**7.**

**8.**

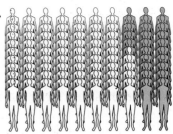

**ESTIMATE** Estimate the percent that is shaded.

**9.**

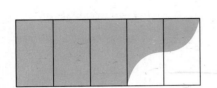

**10.**

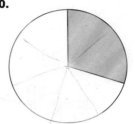

**11.**

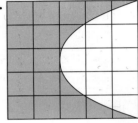

**12.** In 1950, 30 acres out of every 100 acres of land on Earth was forest. The ratio of forest to land was 30:100. What percent is this?

**13.** By the year 2000, about 7 acres out of every 100 acres of land on Earth will be forest. This is a ratio of $\frac{7}{100}$. What percent is this?

**14.** In some areas, all of the trees are protected. What is the ratio of trees to protected trees in these areas? What percent is this?

Write the ratio as a percent.

**15.** 35 out of 100    **16.** 9 out of 100    **17.** $\frac{1}{100}$    **18.** 5:100

Write the percent as a ratio.

**19.** 30%    **20.** 1%    **21.** 100%    **22.** 67%    **23.** 4.5%

Draw and shade a 10-by-10 grid to represent the percent.

**24.** 95%    **25.** 15%    **26.** 37%    **27.** 80%    **28.** 41%

**IN YOUR WORDS** Explain the meaning of the estimate.

**29.** It is estimated that over 20% of the rain forest in Brazil has already been destroyed to clear land for settlers.

**30.** **IN YOUR WORDS** Work with a partner. Use a newspaper to find three uses of percent. Explain the meaning of each percent you find.

# Fractions and Percent

In a basketball game, Patrena scored on 1 of the 4 free throws she attempted. On what percent of her free throws did Patrena score?

You can make a **MATH CONNECTION** to change a fraction to a percent.

- You know a percent is a ratio per 100.
- You know how to write equivalent fractions.

What fraction with a denominator of 100 is equivalent to $\frac{1}{4}$?

$$\frac{1}{4} = \frac{25}{100} = 25\%$$    1 $\boxed{\div}$ 4 $\boxed{=}$ 0.25

Patrena scored on 25% of her free throws.

Another example:

Gino's team won 2 of 3 games. What percent is this?

$$\begin{array}{r} 0.66\frac{2}{3} \\ \overline{3)2.00} \end{array} = 66\frac{2}{3}\%$$    2 $\boxed{\div}$ 3 $\boxed{=}$ 0.6666666

Basketball statistics often record this as 0.667. Why is it misleading to call this a percent?

**THINK ALOUD**  Does $\frac{2}{3}$ exactly equal 0.6666666, on a calculator? Explain.

If you know that *percent* means "per hundred," you can make a **MATH CONNECTION** to change a percent to a fraction.

$$20\% = \frac{20}{100} = \frac{1}{5} \qquad 5\% = \frac{5}{100} = \frac{1}{20} \qquad 12\frac{1}{2}\% = \frac{12.5}{100} = \frac{125}{1,000} = \frac{1}{8}$$

## GUIDED PRACTICE

Write in percent form.

**1.** $\frac{1}{10}$    **2.** $\frac{1}{2}$    **3.** $\frac{3}{8}$    **4.** $\frac{7}{25}$    **5.** $\frac{4}{4}$    **6.** $\frac{1}{3}$

Write as a fraction in lowest terms or as a whole number.

**7.** 80%    **8.** 35%    **9.** 100%    **10.** 72%    **11.** 6%    **12.** $87\frac{1}{2}\%$

Write in percent form. Use a calculator, mental math, or pencil and paper.

**13.** $\frac{3}{4}$       **14.** $\frac{27}{50}$       **15.** $\frac{3}{5}$       **16.** $\frac{6}{6}$       **17.** $\frac{5}{8}$       **18.** $\frac{16}{64}$

**19.** $\frac{12}{18}$       **20.** $\frac{7}{20}$       **21.** $1$       **22.** $\frac{0}{45}$       **23.** $\frac{24}{25}$       **24.** $\frac{15}{60}$

**25.** $\frac{32}{40}$       **26.** $\frac{12}{36}$       **27.** $\frac{21}{24}$       **28.** $\frac{3}{8}$       **29.** $\frac{45}{135}$       **30.** $\frac{125}{500}$

Write as a fraction in lowest terms or as a whole number.

**31.** 56%       **32.** 43%       **33.** 2%       **34.** 18%       **35.** 70%       **36.** 17%

**37.** 45%       **38.** 68%       **39.** 24%       **40.** 100%       **41.** 80%       **42.** 32%

**43.** 1%       **44.** 72%       **45.** 31%       **46.** 95%       **47.** 5%       **48.** 8%

**MIXED REVIEW**  Compute.

**49.** $\frac{1}{2} + \frac{3}{8}$       **50.** $\frac{3}{5} \times \frac{1}{6}$       **51.** $6.2 - 1.004$       **52.** $180 \div \frac{2}{3}$

**53.** $15\frac{1}{3} - \frac{5}{9}$       **54.** $0.25 + 0.087$       **55.** $\frac{5}{6} \div 1\frac{1}{5}$       **56.** $0.7 \times 950$

**MENTAL MATH**  Write as a percent. Compute mentally.

**57.** $\frac{1}{2}$       **58.** $\frac{1}{10}$       **59.** $\frac{1}{4}$       **60.** $\frac{1}{3}$       **61.** $\frac{1}{5}$       **62.** $\frac{2}{3}$

CHOOSE  Use the table to answer to the nearest percent.
Choose mental math, paper and pencil or calculator.

**63.** What percent of the team's total points were scored by player 1?

**64.** Which player scored 25% of the team's total points?

**65.** What percent of the total field goals attempted were made?

**66.** Which player scored on 100% of the free throws she attempted?

**67.** **CREATE YOUR OWN**  Write two math problems using the facts in the table.

### Basketball Scores

| Player | Field Goals Made | Field Goals Attempted | Free Throws Made | Free Throws Attempted | Total Points |
|---|---|---|---|---|---|
| **1** | 11 | 21 | 5 | 6 | 27 |
| **2** | 1 | 3 | 1 | 2 | 3 |
| **3** | 2 | 8 | 2 | 3 | 6 |
| **4** | 6 | 12 | 7 | 9 | 19 |
| **5** | 2 | 10 | 2 | 2 | 6 |
| **6** | 5 | 7 | 3 | 4 | 13 |
| **7** | 1 | 4 | 0 | 0 | 2 |
| **8** | 0 | 0 | 0 | 0 | 0 |
| **9** | 0 | 0 | 0 | 0 | 0 |
| **10** | 0 | 1 | 0 | 0 | 0 |
| **Totals** | **28** | **66** | **20** | **26** | **76** |

# Decimals and Percent

About 0.8 of all the animals on Earth are insects. About 0.01 of all the animals on Earth are mammals.

These numbers are easier to compare if they are written as percents.

If you know that percent means per hundred, you can make a **MATH CONNECTION** to change decimals to percents.

Start by changing to a fraction with a denominator of 100. Why?

$$0.8 = \frac{8 \times 10}{10 \times 10} = \frac{80}{100} = 80\% \qquad 0.01 = \frac{1}{100} = 1\%$$

About 80% of all the animals on Earth are insects. About 1% are mammals.

> Why are 80% and 1% easier to compare?

**Animals on Earth**

Mammals

Insects

Other examples:

$$0.75 = \frac{75}{100} = 75\% \qquad 0.453 = \frac{453 \div 10}{1,000 \div 10} = \frac{45.3}{100} = 45.3\%$$

$$20\% = \frac{20}{100} = 0.20 \qquad 37.5\% = \frac{37.5}{100} = 0.375$$

**THINK ALOUD** Why does the decimal point move when you change a decimal to a percent? a percent to a decimal?

## GUIDED PRACTICE

Write the decimal as a percent.　　　　Write the percent as a decimal.

**1.** 0.25　　　**2.** 0.02　　　**3.** 0.8　　　**4.** 70%　　　**5.** 7%　　　**6.** 12.5%

## PRACTICE

Write the percent as a decimal.

**7.** 10%　　　**8.** 19%　　　**9.** 42%　　　**10.** 36%　　　**11.** 27%　　　**12.** 99%

**13.** 66.7%　　**14.** 100%　　**15.** 7.6%　　**16.** 11.9%　　**17.** 6.5%　　**18.** 50%

**19.** 3.25%　　**20.** 0.9%　　**21.** 1.9%　　**22.** 11.75%　　**23.** 0.5%　　**24.** 3.8%

Write the decimal as a percent.

**25.** 0.25      **26.** 0.35      **27.** 0.1      **28.** 0.11      **29.** 0.8      **30.** 0.06

**31.** 0.001      **32.** 0.31      **33.** 0.031      **34.** 0.1667      **35.** 0.991      **36.** 0.121

**37.** 0.083      **38.** 0.705      **39.** 0.4567      **40.** 1      **41.** 0.005      **42.** 0.0002

**MIXED REVIEW**   Write as a decimal.

**43.** $\frac{1}{2}$      **44.** $\frac{3}{5}$      **45.** $\frac{35}{100}$      **46.** $\frac{7}{8}$      **47.** $\frac{9}{9}$      **48.** $\frac{1}{20}$

**MENTAL MATH**   Name the fraction and the decimal.

**49.** 25%      **50.** 75%      **51.** 50%      **52.** 10%      **53.** 60%      **54.** 80%

---

**PROBLEM SOLVING**

**CHOOSE**   Choose mental math, paper and pencil, or calculator to solve.

**55.** About 0.2 of all insects on Earth are butterflies and moths. What percent of all insects are not butterflies or moths?

**A mammal is a backboned animal that feeds its young on mother's milk.**

**56.** There are about 1,000,000 known insect species on Earth today. Of these, about 112,000 are ants or bees. In lowest terms, what is the ratio of ants or bees to total insects known today?

**57.** Of the known living species on Earth, 71% are insects, 11% are other animals, and 18% are plants. Model these facts with a 10-by-10 square grid.

## *Critical Thinking*

Work with a partner. Use the diagram to solve.

1. What percent of the insects shown are ants? flies?

2. What percent of the insects are either ants or flies?

3. What percent of the insects are bees?

# Writing Percents
# Greater Than 100%

In the year 2000, the population of Alaska is expected to be 119% of what it was in 1990. This means that for every 100 people in Alaska in 1990, there will be 119 in the year 2000. This is a ratio of $\frac{119}{100}$.

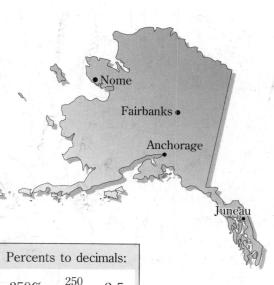

You can write this ratio as a percent.   $\frac{119}{100} = 119\%$

You can work with percents greater than 100% just like you work with those less than 100%.

| Fractions to percents: | Decimals to percents: | Percents to decimals: |
|---|---|---|
| $\frac{5}{4} = 5 \div 4 = 1.25$ or 125% | $3.45 = 345\%$ | $250\% = \frac{250}{100} = 2.5$ |

## GUIDED PRACTICE

Write as a percent.

1. $\frac{120}{100}$     2. 1.75     3. 4     4. $\frac{3}{2}$     5. $\frac{5}{3}$

Write as a decimal.

6. 112%     7. 350%     8. 700%     9. 175%     10. 250%

## PRACTICE

Write as a percent.

11. 1.09     12. 11     13. $\frac{104}{100}$     14. 8     15. $\frac{450}{100}$

Write as a decimal.

16. 120%     17. 225%     18. 500%     19. 125%     20. 700%

Express the percent as a ratio per 100.

21. Alaska's area is about 219% that of Texas.

22. Juneau's population is about 110% of Fairbanks's population.

23. **NUMBER SENSE**   In some cases, percents greater than 100 do not make sense. For example, *150% of the cars in the parking lot are black*, does not make sense. Name two other situations where it is not sensible to have a percent greater than 100.

## Writing Percents Less Than 1%

**City Hall, Nome, Alaska**

In Alaska, about 0.6% of the population lives in Nome. Percents even less than 1% are important. About 0.6% of the 588,000 people in Alaska is 3,500 people!

To work with percents less than 1%, you use the same procedures as working with other percents. For example, we can change from one form to another.

Percents to decimals:

$$0.75\% = \frac{0.75 \times 100}{100 \times 100} = \frac{75}{10,000} = 0.0075$$

$$\frac{1}{2}\% = \frac{0.5 \times 10}{100 \times 10} = \frac{5}{1,000} = 0.005$$

Decimals to percents:

$$0.006 = \frac{6}{1,000} = \frac{6 \div 10}{1,000 \div 10} = \frac{0.6}{100} = 0.6\%$$

Fractions to percents:

$$\frac{1}{500} = \frac{1 \div 5}{500 \div 5} = \frac{0.2}{100} = 0.2\%$$

---
**GUIDED PRACTICE**
---

Write as a decimal.

**1.** 0.2%　　**2.** 0.8%　　**3.** 0.25%　　**4.** 0.7%　　**5.** $\frac{1}{4}\%$

Write as a percent.

**6.** 0.005　　**7.** 0.002　　**8.** 0.0055　　**9.** $\frac{0.7}{100}$　　**10.** $\frac{1}{400}$

---
**PRACTICE**
---

Write as a decimal.

**11.** 2%　　**12.** 0.2%　　**13.** 0.02%　　**14.** 0.6%　　**15.** $\frac{3}{4}\%$

Write as a percent.

**16.** 0.0075　　**17.** 0.001　　**18.** 0.0006　　**19.** 0.008　　**20.** 0.0014

**21.** $\frac{0.75}{100}$　　**22.** $\frac{0.1}{100}$　　**23.** $\frac{0.04}{100}$　　**24.** $\frac{2}{1,000}$　　**25.** $\frac{1}{800}$

**26. IN YOUR WORDS** Think about a quick way of changing 0.6% to a decimal. Write a sentence describing this short cut.

# Percent Sense

## When Do We Use Percent?

### 🖾 READ ABOUT IT

Percents help us to make comparisons. Because *percent* means "per hundred", we can compare very large and small things in terms of 100.

For example, percents make it easy to realize how large the Pacific Ocean is compared to 100% of the ocean water on Earth.

**Our Earth's Oceans**

Pacific Ocean 47%

### 🖾 TALK ABOUT IT

Working with a partner, discuss what the percent means. Talk about how percent is making a comparison in terms of 100.

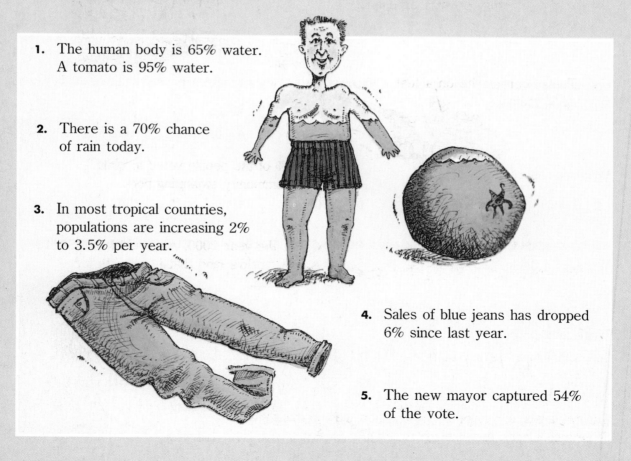

1. The human body is 65% water. A tomato is 95% water.

2. There is a 70% chance of rain today.

3. In most tropical countries, populations are increasing 2% to 3.5% per year.

4. Sales of blue jeans has dropped 6% since last year.

5. The new mayor captured 54% of the vote.

**6.**

## Pitchers with at least 270 wins

|  | Wins | Losses | Wins/Total | Percent |
|---|---|---|---|---|
| Tom Seaver | 311 | 205 | 0.603 | 60.3% |
| Phil Niekro | 318 | 274 | 0.537 | 53.7% |
| Steve Carlton | 329 | 244 | 0.574 | 57.4% |
| Tommy John | 288 | 231 | 0.555 | 55.5% |
| Cy Young | 511 | 313 | 0.620 | 62.0% |

**7.** Only 25% of the world's paper is recycled.

**8.** 50% of the teenagers polled said they study 2 h every evening except on weekends.

**9.** Paula scored 90% on a test of 50 items.

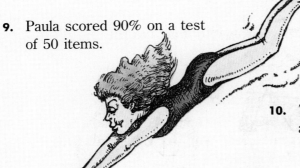

**10.** 72% of the people voted to build a community swimming pool.

**11.** By the year 2000, we could lose 18% of the world's land that is suitable for farming.

## ⬛ WRITE ABOUT IT

Work with a partner.

Cut out a percent example from a newspaper or magazine.
Write a paragraph explaining how the percent is used.

EXPLORE

**The baseball team has won 30 of the 60 games they have played. That is 50% of the games played.**

## *Exploring Percent Models*

A percent bar diagram can be used to represent situations involving percent.

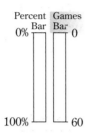

To make percent bar diagrams, you work from the top down. In this situation, each bar represents the games played. One represents the *percent* of games played and the other the *number* of games played.

**1.** Why is there a 0 on the games bar across from the 0% point on the percent bar? Why are the bottoms of the bars marked 100% and 60?

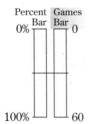

A line has been drawn across the diagram to show the part of the games the team has won.

**2.** How far down the bar was the line drawn?

**3.** How did you know to draw the line at that point?

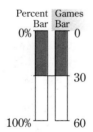

The games bar has been labeled.

**4.** Why was the 30 placed at the middle of the games bar? Why were the top halves of the bars shaded?

**5.** What should be placed on the percent bar across from the 30?

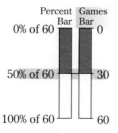

The completed bar diagram is shown. The math sentence that represents the situation is shaded.

**6.** What part of the bars would have been shaded if the team had won all 60 games? no games?

**7.** How would the diagram change if the team had played 80 games?

The percent bar diagram shows the baseball games in which Melinda got at least one hit.

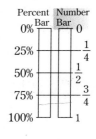

**8. a.** In how many games did she play?

**b.** In how many games did she get at least one hit? What percent is this?

When making a percent bar diagram to fit a situation, it is helpful to be able to draw the line across the bars in *about* the right place. Knowing these fraction/percent relationships can help: $\frac{1}{4} = 25\%$, $\frac{1}{2} = 50\%$, $\frac{3}{4} = 75\%$.

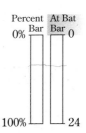

**9.** Describe where the line would cross the bars for the given percent.

    **a.** 80%      **b.** 15%      **c.** 40%

Sometimes in a percent problem the percent will not be given. In such cases, the other numbers in the problem will help you draw the line across the bars.

Todd got a hit 15 of the 24 times he came to bat.

**10.** What is half of 24? Did Todd get a hit *more than* or *less than* half of his times at bat? Where would you draw the line?

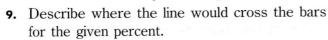

Describe where you would draw the line across a percent bar diagram for the situation.

**11.** 75 stolen bases in 80 attempts

**12.** 2 of 50 games rained out

Julio got a hit 80% of the times he came to bat. If he batted a total of 25 times, how many hits did he get? Use the percent bars at the right to answer.

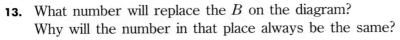

**13.** What number will replace the *B* on the diagram? Why will the number in that place always be the same?

**14.** Would you say that 25 is *100%* of Julio's times at bat or *80%* of the times Julio got a hit?

**15.** Which letter should be replaced by 80%? Which letter cannot be replaced with a number from the problem?

Draw and label a percent bar diagram for the example.

**16.** 75% of 80 is 60.      **17.** 40% of 25 is 10.      **18.** 2 out of 20 is 10%.

# *Finding the Percent of a Number*

From 1889 to 1989, 12% of North Carolina's 25 governors were Republicans. All the others were Democrats. How many governors were Republicans?

Percent bars can model this problem.

Let $x$ be the number of Republican governors.

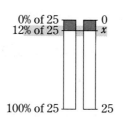

12% of the 25 governors were Republican.

12% of 25 is what number?
$$0.12 \times 25 = x$$
$$3 = x$$

If you know how to change a percent to a decimal and how to multiply decimals, you can make a **MATH CONNECTION** to find the percent of a number.

There were three Republican governors.

Another example:

What is 12% of 400?
$$12\% \times 400 = x$$
$$0.12 \times 400 = x$$
$$48 = x$$

Let $x$ be the unknown number.

**State Capitol Building, Raleigh, North Carolina.**

Use the percent bars to check.

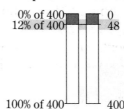

---

**GUIDED PRACTICE**

Write an equation and solve.

**1.**
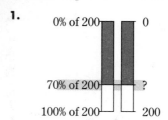

**2.**
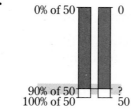

**3.**
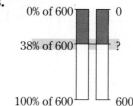

**4.** What is 60% of 900?

**5.** What is 5% of 120?

**6.** What is $\frac{1}{2}$% of 600?

MATH AND SOCIAL STUDIES

Find the percent of the number. Use percent bars to help.

**7.** 50% of 480     **8.** 7% of 84     **9.** 50% of 9     **10.** 10% of 450

**11.** 1% of 350     **12.** 75% of 40     **13.** 5% of 80     **14.** 0.5% of 80

**15.** 0.1% of 80     **16.** 0.6% of 456     **17.** 2% of 96     **18.** 0.05% of 350

**19.** 0.5% of 800     **20.** $\frac{1}{2}$% of 1,000     **21.** $37\frac{1}{2}$% of 40

**MIXED REVIEW**  Compute.

**22.** $0.2 \times 86$     **23.** $\frac{3}{4} \times 96$     **24.** $25\% \times 28$     **25.** $\frac{1}{2} \times 52$

**26.** $40\% \times 40$     **27.** $0.1 \times 75$     **28.** $\frac{4}{5} \times 55$     **29.** $50\% \times 120$

**CALCULATOR**  Compute.

**30.** $62\frac{1}{2}$% of 8,440     **31.** 98% of 3,662     **32.** 17% of 5.66     **33.** $\frac{1}{4}$% of 228.4

**PROBLEM SOLVING**

**CHOOSE** Choose mental math, paper and pencil, or calculator to solve.

**34.** About 40% of North Carolina's 53,669 mi$^2$ is farmland. How many square miles is that?

**35.** There are about 6 million people in North Carolina. About 21% of them are under age 15, and about 11% are 65 or older. About how many people are between the ages of 15 and 65?

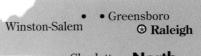

Winston-Salem • • Greensboro  ⊕ **Raleigh**  • Charlotte  **North Carolina**

**36.** Of about $2\frac{3}{4}$ million workers in North Carolina, about 30% are in manufacturing. How many workers are in manufacturing?

**Estimate**

Compatible numbers help you estimate the percent of a number.

9% of 105  is close to  ⇨10% × 105 = 10.5  So 9% of 105 is about 10.

Estimate.

**1.** 11% of 256     **2.** 47% of 600     **3.** 9% of 185     **4.** 24% of 320

# Finding the Percent

In the northern hemisphere, June 21 has more daylight than
any other day. On this day Barrow, Alaska, has daylight
for 24 h, while Philadelphia has 15 h of daylight. What percent
of the day is daylight in Philadelphia on June 21?

Set up percent bar models for the problem.
Are the labels correct?

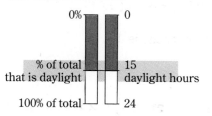

Let *n* represent the percent of daylight in
Philadelphia on June 21.

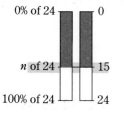

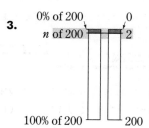

15 h out of 24 h
are sunlight.

What percent is 15 out of 24?

$$n \times 24 = 15$$
$$\frac{n \times 24}{24} = \frac{15}{24}$$
$$n = 0.625 \text{ or } 62.5\%$$

On June 21, 62.5% of the day in Philadelphia is daylight.

Another example:

24 is what percent of 96?

$$n \times 96 = 24$$
$$\frac{n \times 96}{96} = \frac{24}{96}$$
$$n = 0.25, \text{ or } 25\%$$

Use a percent bar diagram to check.

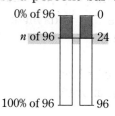

---

## GUIDED PRACTICE

Write an equation and solve.

**1.**

0% of 80 — 0
*n* of 80 — 12
100% of 80 — 80

**2.**

0% of 600 — 0
*n* of 600 — 240
100% of 600 — 600

**3.**

0% of 200 — 0
*n* of 200 — 2
100% of 200 — 200

**4.** What percent of 12 is 3?

**5.** 45 is what percent of 360?

**6.** What percent is $\frac{18}{54}$?

MATH AND GEOGRAPHY

Write an equation and solve. Use percent bars to help.

**7.** 12 is what percent of 15?

**8.** What percent of 40 is 13?

**9.** What percent is 15 out of 80?

**10.** 96 is what percent of 120?

**11.** What percent of 6 is 2?

**12.** 15 is what percent of 15?

**13.** What percent is 19 out of 76?

**14.** 32 is what percent of 128?

**15.** What percent is 250 out of 2,000?

**16.** 1 is what percent of 6?

**17.** What percent is $\frac{14}{112}$?

**18.** What percent is $\frac{64}{16}$?

**MIXED REVIEW** Compute.

**19.** $45\% \times 150 = $ ▨

**20.** 13 out of 65 = ▨ %

**21.** $9\frac{1}{2}\% \times 800 = $ ▨

**22.** ▨ $\% = \frac{72}{360}$

**23.** ▨ $= 28\%$ of 1,000

**24.** $\frac{54}{162} = $ ▨ %

**NUMBER SENSE**  Is the percent *greater than* or *less than* 10%?

**25.** 2 of 60

**26.** 10 of 30

**27.** 2 of 25

**28.** 4 of 43

**29.** 6 of 58

**30.** 8 of 81

CHOOSE   Use the percent bars to solve.
Choose mental math, paper and pencil, or calculator.

**31.** What percent of the day is daylight in Houston on June 21?

**32.** On June 21, which city has daylight for more than 75% of the day?

**33.** **IN YOUR WORDS**  Which city has more daylight in the summer? Why?

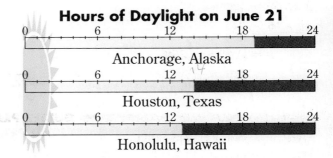

**Hours of Daylight on June 21**

Anchorage, Alaska

Houston, Texas

Honolulu, Hawaii

---

**Mental Math**

Think of a fraction in lowest terms to help you find the percent.

15 of 60 ➪ $\frac{15}{60}$ ➪ $\frac{1}{4}$ ➪ 25%

Compute the percent mentally.

**1.** 25 of 50

**2.** $50 of $500

**3.** 12 of 48

# *Finding the Original Number*

In the 1984 Presidential election, Ronald Reagan received close to 60% of the popular vote. If he received more than 54 million votes, about how many people voted in the election?

Percent bars can represent this problem.

Why are the labels correct?

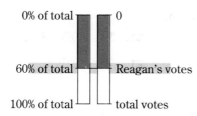

0% of total — 0

60% of total — Reagan's votes

100% of total — total votes

Let *n* represent the total number of votes.

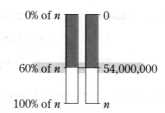

0% of *n* — 0

60% of *n* — 54,000,000

100% of *n* — *n*

60% of what is 54?

$$0.60 \times n = 54$$

$$\frac{0.60 \times n}{0.60} = \frac{54}{0.60}$$

$$n = 90$$

About 90 million (90,000,000) people voted in the election.

Another example:

42 is 20% of what number?

$$0.2 \times n = 42$$

$$\frac{0.2 \times n}{0.2} = \frac{42}{0.2}$$

$$n = 210$$

Use a percent bar diagram to check.

Use percent bars to check.

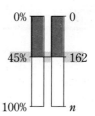

0% of 210 — 0

20% of 210 — 42

100% of 210 — 210

---

**GUIDED PRACTICE**

Write an equation and solve.

**1.**

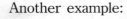

0% — 0

50% — 26

100% — *n*

**2.**

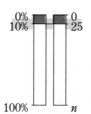

0% — 0

10% — 25

100% — *n*

**3.**

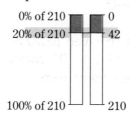

0% — 0

45% — 162

100% — *n*

**4.** 37 is 20% of what number?

**5.** 80% of what number is 72?

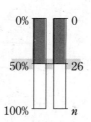

Write an equation and solve. Use percent bars to check.

**6.** 25% of what number is 8?

**7.** 35 is 20% of what number?

**8.** 12 is 75% of what number?

**9.** 40% of what number is 12?

**10.** 35% of what number is 7?

**11.** 720 is 18% of what number?

**12.** 75 is 50% of what number?

**13.** 25% of what number is 14?

**14.** $37\frac{1}{2}$% of what number is 40?

**15.** 7.2 is 80% of what number?

**MIXED REVIEW** Write an equation, and then solve for $n$.

**16.** $n$ % of 40 is 20?

**17.** 50% of 80 is $n$.

**18.** 9 is 30% of $n$.

**19.** 52% of $n$ is 13.

**20.** $n$ % of 60 is 12.

**21.** 75% of 300 is $n$.

**MENTAL MATH** Find the unknown value mentally.

**22.** 50% of what number is 60?

**23.** 25% of what number is 10?

■■■■■■■■■■■■■■■ **PROBLEM SOLVING** ■■■■■■■■■■■■■■■

 Choose paper and pencil or calculator to solve.

**24.** In the 1984 Presidential election, Ronald Reagan captured 97% of the 538 electoral college votes. How many electoral votes did he get?

**25.** Officially, George Bush received 53.37% of the popular vote, or 48,886,097 votes, in 1988. About how many votes were cast in total that year?

**26.** In the 1960 Presidential election, John Kennedy received about 50.08% and Richard Nixon received about 49.92% of the 68,335,642 votes cast. About how many votes did each candidate receive?

**27.** **CRITICAL THINKING** In 1984, Ronald Reagan received 97% of the electoral college votes but only about 60% of the popular vote. How do you account for such a big difference?

## Exploring Mental Math and Percent

If you know how to write a percent as a fraction, you can make a **MATH CONNECTION** to find a percent mentally.

Write the fraction and percent that tell what part of the bar is shaded.

**1.** 　　**2.** 　　**3.** 　　**4.**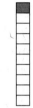

Since $25\% = \frac{1}{4}$, finding 25% of a number is like taking $\frac{1}{4}$ of that number. 25% of $80 = \frac{1}{4}$ of $80 = 4\overline{)80} = 20$.

**5.** Since $20\% = \frac{1}{5}$, what is 20% of 50?

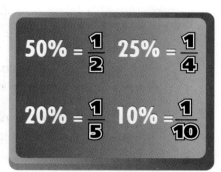

Use the fraction equivalent to find the percent of the number mentally.

**6.** 50% of 60　　**7.** 25% of 60　　**8.** 20% of 60

**9.** 10% of 60　　**10.** 20% of 40　　**11.** 10% of 50

**12.** 25% of 120　**13.** 50% of 360　**14.** 25% of 360

50% of what number is 4? You know that half of the number you want is 4.

> 50% are showing. How many in all?

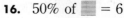

If half of a number is 4, you can multiply $4 \times 2$ to find the number.

**15.** Since $20\% = \frac{1}{5}$, 20% of ▤ = 8?

Find the original number mentally.

**16.** 50% of ▤ = 6　　　**17.** 25% of ▤ = 6　　　**18.** 20% of ▤ = 6

**19.** 10% of ▤ = 6　　　**20.** 25% of ▤ = 3　　　**21.** 20% of ▤ = 10

**22.** 10% of ▤ = 15　　**23.** 50% of ▤ = 100　　**24.** 50% of ▤ = 1,000

If you can find 25% of a number in your head, you can make a MATH CONNECTION to find 75% of a number.

**25.** How many times larger is 75% than 25%? If 25% of 28 is 7, and 75% is three times larger than 25%, what is 75% of 28?

**26.** How many times larger is 40% than 10%? If 10% of 30 is 3, what is 40% of 30?

Compute mentally.

**27.** 25% of 12

**28.** 75% of 12

**29.** 20% of 15

**30.** 40% of 15

**31.** 60% of 20

**32.** 75% of 20

**33.** 20% of 25

**34.** 40% of 10

The members of a school band needed to sell 80 boxes of greeting cards to raise money for a trip. The percent bar diagram shows how they did. By the end of week 4, they had sold 120 boxes. This was more than 100% of their goal.

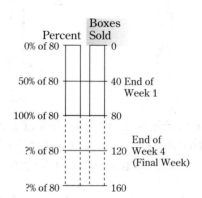

**35.** How many boxes had to be sold to double their goal? Was the goal doubled?

**36.** If the goal had been doubled, what percent of their goal would have been reached?

**37.** What percent of their goal was reached by selling 120 boxes of cards?

**38.** To find 150% of 60, think
  **a.** What is 100% of 60?
  **b.** What is 50% of 60?
  **c.** If 100% is 60, and 50% is 30, what is 150% of 60?

**39.** To find 125% of 40, think:
  **a.** What is 100% of 40?
  **b.** What is 25% of 40?
  **c.** What is 125% of 40?

**40.** To find 120% of 50, think:
  **a.** What is 100% of 50?
  **b.** What is 20% of 50?
  **c.** What is 120% of 50?

**41.** To find 110% of 80, think:
  **a.** What is 100% of 80?
  **b.** What is 10% of 80?
  **c.** What is 110% of 80?

Compute mentally.

**42.** 150% of 10

**43.** 125% of 12

**44.** 110% of 40

**45.** 200% of 10

**46.** 125% of 20

**47.** 100% of 20

**48.** 175% of 20

**49.** 160% of 20

**50.** **IN YOUR WORDS** Describe how you can think about 1% of 320 to help you find 3% of 320.

---
**LANGUAGE & VOCABULARY**
---

Write a sentence to explain how you would:

1. change a fraction to a percent
2. change a percent to a fraction
3. change a decimal to a percent
4. change a percent to a decimal
5. find a percent of a number

---
**QUICK QUIZ**
---

Write as a percent. *(pages 312–317)*

1. $\frac{13}{20}$     2. $\frac{12}{16}$          3. 0.43          4. 0.195

5. 1.32          6. 0.0028

Find the percent of the number. *(pages 322–323)*

7. 3% of 82

Write an equation and solve. *(pages 324–327)*

8. What percent is 24 out of 80?

9. 40% of what number is 50?

Solve. *(pages 326–327)*

10. Leslie counted birds on a walk in the park. She saw 23 pigeons
    and 7 robins.

    a. How many robins did Leslie see?

    b. How can you find the percent of the birds that were robins?

    c. What percent were robins?

Write the answers in your learning log.

1. Write one or more sentences telling what is important to remember when dealing with percents.

2. Describe a way to find 25% of a number mentally.

MATH AMERICA

**DID YOU KNOW . . . ?** In the 1920's, people in the United States could buy a dozen large eggs for 68¢, a quart of whole milk for 17¢, and a pound of butter for 70¢. By what percentage has the price of each item changed in more than 70 years?

BONUS

In the state in which Marilyn lives, sales tax on restaurant meals is 7%. When a tip is appropriate, Marilyn always leaves exactly 15% of the bill. The past two nights, she has eaten at a self-service restaurant where the bill before tax was $11.55 and at a cafe with waitress service where the bill before tax was $10.15. Which dinner cost more? How much more? Round to the nearest cent. Make up some other restaurant problems.

## Problem Solving:
## Estimating Tips and Sales Tax

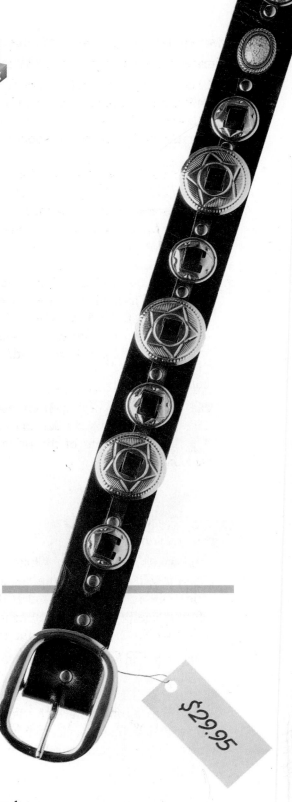

UNDERSTAND
PLAN
REPRESENT
CARRY OUT
LOOK BACK

Jacek has $50 to spend at an international student fair. He is about to buy a hand-embroidered tablecloth for $44.95. If the sales tax is 6%, does he have enough money to buy the tablecloth?

Compatible numbers can help you estimate the sales tax.

- Think: $44.95 is close to $50. The sales tax is about 6% of $50.

- Think: 6% is 6 × 1%. What is 1% of $50? What is 6% of $50?

- Now estimate the cost including the sales tax on your own. Does Jacek have enough money?

The food bill at the Polish pavilion is $29.45. The usual amount for a tip is about 15% of the bill. About how much should you leave for a tip?

- Think: $29.45 is close to $30. The tip is about 15% of $30.

- Think: 15% is 10% + 5%. What is 10% of $30? What is 5% of $30? What is 15% of $30?

- Now estimate a fair tip on your own.

━━━━━━━━━━━━━━━ **GUIDED PRACTICE** ━━━━━━━━━━━━━━━

Estimate the solution to the problem.

1. Dahlia wants to buy a hand-crafted belt for $29.95 and a leather handbag for $34.59. The sales tax is 5%.

   a. What is the sales tax?

   b. Would the cost of the two items be *more than* or *less than* $62?

   c. Is the total cost, with sales tax, *more than* or *less than* $70?

2. Luigi bought a $5.75 lunch at the German food stand. He would like to leave a 15% tip. About how much should the tip be?

Estimate the solution to the problem.

**3.** Ernest bought a windbreaker for $45 and two Chinese silk scarfs for $15 each. The sales tax was 7.8%. About how much did he spend?

**4.** The tax paid on three Italian take-out dinners costing $42 was $4.90. About what percent of the price was tax?

**5.** Morana and Tony had two Japanese meals for a total of $11.50. The sales tax was 6%. About how much change would Morana and Tony get from a $20 bill if they left a 15% tip?

**6.** Rhonda bought a $64.99 painting, a $14.49 cookbook, and an Egyptian scarf for $19.29. About what was the total cost if the sales tax was 7%?

**7.** Mrs. Thomas wants to buy 4 yd of silk from Thailand to make a dress. The silk costs $9.95/yd plus a 5% sales tax. About how much should Mrs. Thomas expect to spend?

**8.** José buys a $29.50 meal at the East Indian pavilion. The sales tax on the food is 5% and José wants to include a 15% tip. About how much money will José pay for the meal?

**9.** At the Dutch pavilion, $3.50 is charged for 1 lb of Gouda cheese. This price *includes* a sales tax of 21¢. About what percent of the price is the tax?

**10.** In some places, people can use the amount of sales tax they pay to estimate the tip. If you pay $3.42 sales tax, at 8.25%, about how much money would you leave for a 15% tip?

**CHOOSE** Choose a strategy to solve.

**11.** Jana wants to buy a $40 Chinese kite on sale at 25% off the regular price. There is an additional 10% off the sale price if you pay cash. What would the cash price for the kite be if the sales tax is 5.2%?

**12.** Art left a $1.20 tip for his meal. If the tip was about 15% of the cost of the meal, what was the cost of the meal?

**13.** **CRITICAL THINKING** Marina estimated the solution to Exercise 8 by multiplying $30 by 1.2. Explain why her method works.

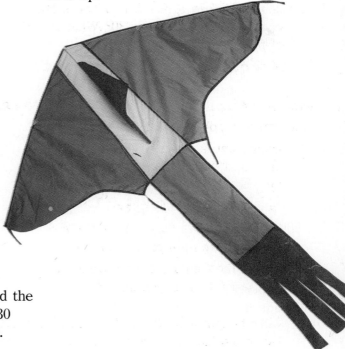

## *Using Percents Greater Than 100%*

Lori wants to buy a pair of jeans for $34. Sales tax is 8%. What is the total amount of money Lori must pay for the jeans?

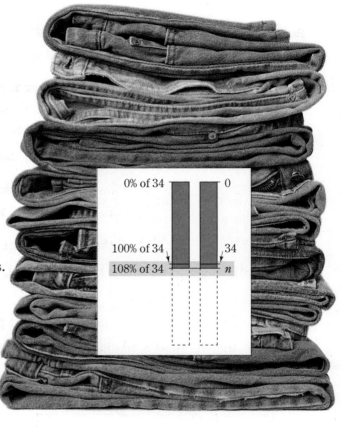

Lori has to pay:

$$
\begin{array}{rl}
100\% & \text{of the cost of the jeans} \\
+\ \ 8\% & \text{sales tax} \\
\hline
108\% &
\end{array}
$$

The percent bars represent this situation. Let $n$ represent the total amount Lori pays.

108% of $34 is what number?

$$1.08 \times 34 = n$$
$$36.72 = n$$

On a calculator:  1.08 $\boxed{\times}$ 34 $\boxed{=}$ 36.72

In all, Lori must pay $36.72 for the jeans.

Julio paid $14, including tip, for his dinner at Sparto's restaurant. That was 112% of the price of the dinner on the menu. What was the price of the dinner on the menu?

The percent bars represent this situation. Let $x$ represent the menu price of the dinner.

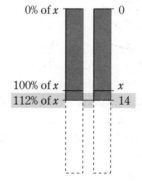

112% of what number is $14?

$$1.12 \times x = 14$$
$$\frac{1.12 \times x}{1.12} = \frac{14}{1.12}$$
$$x = 12.5$$

On a calculator:  14 $\boxed{\div}$ 1.12 $\boxed{=}$ 12.5
The price of Julio's dinner on the menu was $12.50.

**GUIDED PRACTICE**

What percent of the cost is the total amount paid?
Include the percent of tax or tip.

**1.** $75 with a 6% sales tax    **2.** $22.50 with a 15% tip    **3.** $3.95 with a 7% sales tax

Write an equation and solve.

**4.** What is 105% of $30?    **5.** What percent is $\frac{\$10.35}{\$9}$?    **6.** 180% of what is 360?

━━━━━━━━━━━━━━━━━━━━━━━━━ PRACTICE ━━━━━━━━━━━━━━━━━━━━━━━━━

Write an equation and solve. Use percent bars to help.

**7.** What is 120% of 48?    **8.** 150% of 8 is what?    **9.** What percent is $\frac{285}{95}$?

**10.** 200% of what is 124?    **11.** What is 105% of 90¢?    **12.** 150% of what is 36?

Add a 15% tip to find the amount to be paid for the meal.

**13.** $9.95    **14.** $25.17    **15.** $5.29    **16.** $8.44

Add a 5.5% sales tax to find the amount to be paid for the item.

**17.** sweater: $24    **18.** jacket: $49    **19.** boots: $81

**MIXED REVIEW** Compute.

**20.** 20% of what is 15?    **21.** 45 is what percent of 90? **22.** What is 72% of 300?

**23.** What percent of 50 is 5?    **24.** What is 115% of 85?    **25.** 180% of what is 360?

**CALCULATOR** Copy and complete the function table.

**26.**

| $n$ | 30% | 60% | 90% | 120% | 150% |
|-----|-----|-----|-----|------|------|
| 280$n$ | ? | ? | ? | ? | ? |

**27.**

| $n$ | 40% | 80% | 120% | 160% | 200% |
|-----|-----|-----|------|------|------|
| 320$n$ | ? | ? | ? | ? | ? |

━━━━━━━━━━━━━━━━━━━━━━━━━ PROBLEM SOLVING ━━━━━━━━━━━━━━━━━━━━━━━━━

**CHOOSE** Choose paper and pencil or calculator to solve.

**28.** The sales tax in Willis, Texas, is 7% and in New Waverly, Texas, it is 9%. Drew lives in New Waverly. If it takes $1.50 worth of gas to drive to Willis and back, how much would Drew save by driving to Willis to buy a $200 weed eater?

**29.** Ruth and Carl ordered 2 Mexican dinners at $8.80 each. A tax of 5% and a 15% tip was paid on the cost of the 2 meals. How much did Ruth and Carl pay in all?

**30.** **CREATE YOUR OWN** Make up a math problem involving sales tax or tips. Give it to a friend to solve.

## EXPLORE

### *Exploring the Percent of Increase and Decrease*

Aaron wants to buy a new racing bicycle. Last year the price of the bicycle was $240. Now the price is $360. By what percent did the price of the bicycle increase?

1. By what amount did the price of the bicycle increase?

2. The **percent of increase** is the ratio of the increase to the original amount. Copy and complete the percent of increase ratio for this problem.

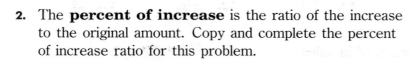

$$\frac{\text{amount of increase}}{\text{original amount}} \rightarrow \frac{?}{\$240} = \blacksquare\% \leftarrow \text{percent of increase}$$

The ratio of the amount of increase to the original amount is given. Find the percent of increase.

3. $\dfrac{\$100}{\$125}$     4. $\dfrac{\$20}{\$25}$     5. $\dfrac{\$350}{\$700}$     6. $\dfrac{\$120}{\$150}$     7. $\dfrac{\$15}{\$20}$

Suppose you know that the price of a three-speed bicycle increased by 12%. Last year the bicycle sold for $150. The percent bar model at the right can help you find this year's price. Let $p$ represent this year's price.

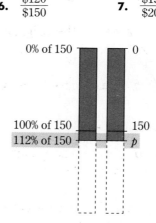

8. Would this year's price be *more than* or *less than* 100% of $150?

9. What percent of 150 is this year's price?

10. What is this year's price?

Find this year's price.

11. A TV set that cost $750 last year has a price this year that is 8% higher.

12. A baseball trading card that cost $24 last year increased in value by 25%.

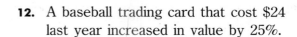

The present value of Bettina's car is $7,200. Last year the value was $9,600. By what percent did the value of her car decrease?

**13.** By what amount did Bettina's car decrease in value?

**14.** The **percent of decrease** is the ratio of the decrease to the original amount. Copy and complete the percent of decrease ratio for this problem.

$$\underset{\text{original amount}}{\overset{\text{amount of decrease}}{\phantom{x}}} \begin{array}{c} \rightarrow \\ \rightarrow \end{array} \frac{?}{\$9,600} = \blacksquare\% \leftarrow \text{percent of decrease}$$

The ratio of the amount of decrease to the original amount is given. Find the percent of decrease.

**15.** $\dfrac{\$1.50}{\$6}$  **16.** $\dfrac{\$2.40}{\$20}$  **17.** $\dfrac{\$.45}{\$3}$  **18.** $\dfrac{\$.72}{\$1.80}$  **19.** $\dfrac{\$4}{\$6}$

Bruce knows his jeep has decreased in value by 25% from its original value. If the present value is $8,400, what was the original price of the jeep?

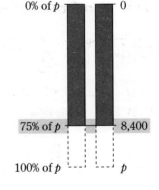

Let $p$ represent the original price.

**20.** Is the *original price* or the *present value* of the jeep equal to 100% of $8,400?

**21.** What percent of the original price of Bruce's jeep is $8,400?

**22.** What was the original price of the jeep?

Find the original price.

**23.** A sailboat decreased in value by 20%. It is now worth $3,200.

**24.** A van is now valued at $18,000 after a 40% decrease.

In business, the percent of increase is called the **percent of profit**. The percent of decrease is the **percent of loss**.

Does the situation have a *profit* or a *loss*? Find the percent of profit or loss.

**25.** A storekeeper pays $4.50 for a book and sells it for $9.

**26.** One month, a business has $50,000 in sales and $70,000 in expenses.

# Problem Solving:
## Using an Interest Formula

| The amount of money borrowed is called the **principal.** | The interest **rate** is usually given as a percent of the principal you pay for a certain period of time, usually 1 yr. | How long you keep the money is called the **time.** |

There is a formula that tells how interest, $I$, principal, $p$, rate, $r$, and time, $t$, are related.

$I = p \times r \times t$

The **interest**, $I$, is what the bank charges you for the loan.

The table shows how the values in the formula depend on each other. As one value changes, so do the others.

| $I = p \times r \times t$ | Interest ($I$) | Principal ($p$) | Rate ($r$) | Time ($t$) |
|---|---|---|---|---|
| $8 = 100 \times 0.08 \times 1$ | $8 | $100 | 8% | 1 yr |
| $4 = 100 \times 0.08 \times 0.5$ | $4 | $100 | 8% | $\frac{1}{2}$ yr |
| $17 = 100 \times 0.085 \times 2$ | $17 | $100 | 8.5% | 2 yr |
| $6 = 100 \times 0.08 \times 0.75$ | $6 | $100 | 8% | 9 mo |

Change 9 mo to $\frac{3}{4}$ yr.

Juan borrows $800 from the bank at $8\frac{1}{2}$ % for 2 yr. How much money must Juan pay back to the bank after 2 yr?

- Would the $8\frac{1}{2}$% be substituted for the $I$, $p$, $r$, or $t$ in the formula?
- Remember that Juan must pay back the $800 plus the interest charged.
- Now solve the problem.

Use the interest formula to solve.

1. Tanya borrowed $1,000 for 4 yr at $10\frac{1}{2}\%$.

   a. What was the interest rate?

   b. What would the $1,000 be substituted for in the interest formula?

   c. How much will Tanya owe the bank after 4 yr?

Use the interest formula to solve.

2. Riva took out a 5-yr, $8,000 loan to buy a car. If the interest rate is 16%, how much interest will she pay on the loan after 5 yr?

3. Angela borrows $1,000 from the bank at 11% for 6 mo. How much will Angela owe the bank after 6 mo?

4. Sharon paid $95 interest on a 2-yr loan. The interest rate was $12\frac{1}{2}\%$. How much money did she borrow?

5. Paul paid $135 interest on a 3-yr loan with a principal of $300. What was the interest rate?

6. How much more interest is paid on a $1,000,000 loan for 1 yr at 12% than at 11.5%?

7. **IN YOUR WORDS** How can you work Exercise 6 without figuring the interest on both loans and subtracting?

8. Antonio borrows $3,200 at a yearly interest rate of 12%. How much will he owe the bank if he keeps the money for only 6 mo? for only 3 mo?

9. The Ching family borrows $18,000 at 11.5% to renovate their house. How much money will the Ching family owe the bank after $1\frac{1}{2}$ yr?

10. Suppose you put $1,024 into a savings account that earns 9.5% simple interest per year. How much money will you have in your savings account after 1 yr?

**CHOOSE** Use the circle graph. Choose any strategy to solve.

11. Pat earns $1,500/mo. How much of that pays her rent?

12. If Pat does not buy any clothing one month, how much of her $1,500 salary could she save?

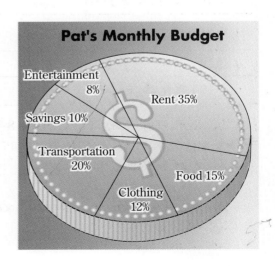

Pat's Monthly Budget

Entertainment 8%
Rent 35%
Savings 10%
Transportation 20%
Food 15%
Clothing 12%

# Making Decisions About Credit Cards

Credit cards are convenient because they are easy to carry. People who have credit cards do not need to carry around a lot of money.

Credit cards can also be used to borrow money. For example, if you make a $400 purchase, you do not have to pay the entire amount when the bill comes due. The credit card company adds a finance charge to the unpaid balance. You have "borrowed" from the credit card company the amount of the bill you did not pay. The finance charge is **interest** you must pay for borrowing this money.

Work in a small group. Use the information given for three imaginary credit cards. A calculator or computer will be useful.

| Card Name | *Credi*Card | BUYER'S plus | *SavCred* |
|---|---|---|---|
| **Annual Fee** | $20 | $25 | $0 |
| **Minimum Monthly Payment** | 15% of balance | 10% of balance | 25% of balance |
| **Interest Rate for Monthly Finance Charge** | 1.3% | 1.4% | 1.7% |

1. Discuss which credit card seems to offer the best terms. What factors might affect your decision to choose one credit card over the others?

2. Annie Anderson charges about $300/mo on her credit card. She pays the bill in full every month. Which credit card offers the best terms for Annie? Explain.

3. Bill Bateman plans to use his credit card to buy a $2,000 furnace for his home. He will not use the card for any other purchases. He plans to buy the furnace in September and pay $500 per month. Copy and complete the chart to determine how much Bill will pay per month in finance charges on each of the three cards.

| Month | | CrediCard | BUYER'S plus | SavCred |
|---|---|---|---|---|
| Sept | Amount of Bill | $2,000.00 | $2,000.00 | $2,000.00 |
| | Amount paid | 500.00 | 500.00 | 500.00 |
| Oct | Unpaid Balance | $1,500.00 | $1,500.00 | $1,500.00 |
| | Interest | 19.50 | 21.00 | 25.50 |
| | Amount paid | 500.00 | 500.00 | 500.00 |
| Nov | Unpaid Balance | $1,019.50 | | |
| | Interest | 13.25 | | |
| | Amount paid | 500.00 | | |
| Dec | Unpaid Balance | | | |
| | Interest | | | |
| | Amount paid | | | |
| Jan | Unpaid Balance | | | |
| | Interest | | | |
| | Amount paid | | | |

4. Use the chart from Exercise 3. Find the total finance charges Bill will pay for the five months for each of the cards. Then add the annual fee to the finance charge total for each card. Which credit card offers the best terms for Bill?

5. Clyde Carlyle plans a $4,800 credit card purchase and will not use the card again for any other purpose. He will pay the minimum monthly payment or $400.00 per month, whichever is greater. Create a chart similar to Bill's and decide which card is best. Give reasons for your choice. Do not forget the annual fees.

6. **IN YOUR WORDS** Write a paragraph explaining how to decide which of the three credit cards to choose.

---

## LANGUAGE & VOCABULARY

Tell whether the result will be >, <, or = 100%.

1. the total cost of a purchase, including sales tax, compared to the price of the item

2. the value of a share of stock that drops by 50% and then increases by 100%

3. the height of Mount St. Helens after its eruption compared to its height before the eruption

4. the depth of a lake following a heavy rain compared to its depth before the rain

---

## TEST ✓

### CONCEPTS

Write as a percent. *(pages 312–317)*

1. $\frac{9}{36}$
2. $\frac{35}{105}$
3. 0.07
4. 0.467
5. $\frac{325}{100}$
6. 9
7. 0.008
8. $\frac{1}{400}$

### SKILLS

Find the percent of the number. *(pages 322–323)*

9. 10% of 380
10. 3% of 82
11. 0.07% of 640

Write an equation and solve. *(pages 324–327, 334–335)*

12. 9 is what percent of 30?
13. 21 is what percent of 50?
14. 114 is what percent of 500?
15. 63 is 45% of what number?
16. 80% of what number is 52?
17. 256 is 25% of what number?
18. What number is 130% of 27?
19. 108% of what number is 108?

Write the percent as a decimal and as a fraction in lowest terms. *(pages 312–314)*

20. 6%
21. 42%
22. 75%
23. 98%

## PROBLEM SOLVING

Estimate the solution to the problem. *(pages 332–333)*

**24.** The food bill for Patricia's dinner was $12.05. Sales tax was 5% and she left a 15% tip.

   **a.** What percent was the sales tax? What percent was the tip?

   **b.** About how many times greater was the tip than the tax?

   **c.** Estimate the total of the tax and tip on the dinner.

Use the interest formula to solve. *(pages 338–339)*

**25.** Which will cost Alberto more in interest payments: $2,000 borrowed for 1 yr at 6%, or $3,000 borrowed for 2 yr at 3%? How much more?

**26.** On her last science test, Chartia scored 80% by answering 52 questions correctly. How many questions were on the test?

**LEARNING LOG**

Write the answers in your learning log.

  **1.** What does "percent sense" mean to you?

  **2.** A bank advertises that it will pay 8% interest on deposits. What does that mean?

Write as a percent. *(pages 312–317)*

**1.** $\frac{18}{36}$    **2.** $\frac{8}{40}$    **3.** $\frac{7}{8}$    **4.** $\frac{12}{12}$    **5.** $\frac{16}{24}$

**6.** 0.75    **7.** 0.1    **8.** 0.375    **9.** 0.87    **10.** 0.08

**11.** 0.075    **12.** 0.603    **13.** 0.210    **14.** 0.012    **15.** 0.15

**16.** 2    **17.** $\frac{147}{100}$    **18.** $\frac{9}{5}$    **19.** 2.65    **20.** 1.03

**21.** 0.009    **22.** 0.0078    **23.** 0.0081    **24.** $\frac{1}{200}$    **25.** $\frac{1}{250}$

Find the percent of the number. *(pages 322-323)*

**26.** 2% of 28    **27.** 85% of 190    **28.** 0.25% of 80

**29.** 0.8% of 150    **30.** $\frac{1}{2}$% of 200    **31.** 0.03% of 96

Write an equation and solve. *(pages 324–327, 334–335)*

**32.** 18 is what percent of 45?    **33.** 48 is what percent of 200?

**34.** 9 is what percent of 54?    **35.** 16 is 40% of what number?

**36.** 54 is 75% of what number?    **37.** 70% of what number is 63?

**38.** 20% of what number is 2.2?    **39.** What number is 150% of 18?

**40.** What number is 115% of 32?    **41.** 175% of what number is 42?

Solve. *(pages 332–333, 338–339)*

**42.** Jackson bought a sandwich for $3.50 and a fruit drink for $1.25. If the tax was 7%, how much did he pay, to the nearest cent?

**43.** Roberto borrowed $1,600 for $1\frac{1}{2}$ yr from a bank charging 14% yearly interest. How much did he have to repay the bank at the end of the time of the loan?

MORTGAGE RATES

A mortgage is a loan, usually made by a bank, that is used to buy a home. Talk with an adult in your home or visit a bank to talk with a loan officer to answer these questions.

1. Why is the interest rate lower if the time of the loan is shorter?

2. Why is the "annual" rate sometimes different from the "annual percentage rate"?

3. Why would a home buyer choose an adjustable interest rate mortgage (one whose rate changes) rather than one with an interest rate that remains the same for the time of the loan?

## NONSENSE PERCENTS

Percents are used often in everyday conversation. However, some of the uses do not reflect an understanding of what percent really means. Read the statement and think about why, although it may sound good, it really does not make sense.

1. "He always tries his best. He makes a 110% effort."

2. "I agree with you 1,000%."

3. "There is a 100% chance of rain tomorrow."

4. "Prices reduced almost 100%!"

## Comparison Shopping

Different states throughout the United States charge different sales tax rates. Some states charge no sales tax. As a result, the same item can cost a consumer different prices, depending on where the item is bought.

Work with a partner. Find sales tax rates in an almanac. Then use a calculator to determine the difference in cost of the item bought in each location.

- a $219 bicycle bought in Alabama or Florida
- a $500 television set bought in Nebraska or Ohio
- a $12,000 car bought in Montana or Wyoming

Make up some comparisons. Some cities or counties also charge a sales tax. Find the sales tax where you live. To what items does it apply?

# CUMULATIVE REVIEW

Find the answer.

1. Which number is less than 82,097?
   a. 82,107
   b. 82,709
   c. 81,970
   d. none of these

2. Which number is greater than 7.060?
   a. 7.6
   b. 7.059
   c. 7.010
   d. none of these

3. 17.04 is between which two numbers?
   a. 17.00 and 17.05
   b. 17.05 and 17.10
   c. 16.95 and 17.00
   d. none of these

4. $38 - r = 19$
   a. 38
   b. 19
   c. 57
   d. none of these

5. $g - 8 = 26$
   a. 16
   b. 18
   c. 34
   d. none of these

6. $107 - d = 68$
   a. 41
   b. 175
   c. 49
   d. none of these

7. $47m = 282$
   a. 6
   b. 60
   c. 13,254
   d. none of these

8. $11.3 - x = 6.5$
   a. 5.2
   b. 4.8
   c. 17.8
   d. none of these

9. $\frac{y}{7} = 58$
   a. 8.3
   b. 406
   c. 0.12
   d. none of these

10. A solution to $b - 8 < 17$ is ?
    a. 25
    b. 26
    c. 27
    d. none of these

11. A solution to $x + 9 > 13$ is ?
    a. 4
    b. 3
    c. 22
    d. none of these

12. 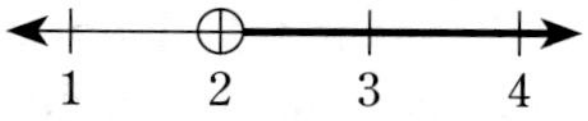
    The graph shows ?
    a. $x > 2$
    b. $x = 2$
    c. $x < 2$
    d. none of these

13. What are the prime factors of 72?
    a. 3, 3, 2, 2, 2
    b. 2, 2, 3, 3, 3
    c. 3, 3, 8
    d. none of these

14. 54 is divisible by what numbers?
    a. 2, 3, 5, 6, 9
    b. 2, 3, 6, 9
    c. 2, 3, 5, 9
    d. none of these

15. Which number is a prime number?
    a. 49
    b. 57
    c. 59
    d. none of these

# PROBLEM SOLVING REVIEW

**Problem Solving Check List**

- Multistep problems
- Using guess and check
- Using a formula
- Using a pattern
- Using an equation
- Using proportion

Remember the strategies and types of problems you've had so far. Solve.

1. Jen was trying to make a train. She left her home at 3:30 P.M. for the 45-min trip to the station. This should have left her 15 min to find and board the train.

   a. At what time did Jen leave her home?

   b. What time was her train scheduled to leave?

   c. The trip to the station took 1h 10 min. By how much did she miss her train?

2. During a baseball game, one team had 12 hits. The opponents had $1\frac{1}{2}$ times as many hits. How many hits did the teams have altogether?

3. Alex bought two pieces of electronic equipment advertised for $200 and $300. The store took 8% off because he paid cash. How much did he pay?

4. The greatest depth of the Pacific Ocean is 36,198 ft. Mount Everest is 29,028 ft tall. How much greater are the combined heights of Mount Everest and 7,965-ft Mount Olympus than the depth of the deepest part of the Pacific?

5. A recipe for 4 people uses 1 lb spaghetti, $1\frac{1}{2}$ lb tomatoes, 1 tsp garlic powder, and other ingredients. If the recipe were increased to serve 6, how many pounds of tomatoes would be needed?

6. To make her purchases, Adrienne borrowed $400 at 14% interest for 1 yr. How much must she repay the bank?

7. A bicycle is on sale for $232. If this is 80% of its original price, what was its price before the sale?

8. Paolo bought 1 lb peppers, twice as much asparagus, and $\frac{1}{4}$ lb less beans than asparagus. How many pounds of beans did he buy?

9. Use each digit from 2 through 9 once to form two 4-digit numbers that have the greatest possible difference.

10. An airline ticket that usually sells for $220 can be purchased in advance for $187. What percent of the usual price is saved with advance purchase?

11. Niabi has $3.75 in dimes and nickels. She has twice as many dimes as nickels. How many nickels does she have?

## OOPS! ▦

Find the mistakes that the waiter made when he wrote up the bill. Figure the correct bill.

| | |
|---|---|
| dinner for 3 | $30.85 |
| 3 milks | + 2.25 |
| | 33.10 |
| 6% tax | + 1.99 |
| | 35.09 |
| 1 ice cream | + 1.20 |
| | 37.29 |
| 6% tax | + 2.24 |
| total | $39.53 |

## TAXI TIPPERS ▦

Reggie, Maria, Jack, and Eli took a taxi to the airport. Each fare was $8.

The first rider left the lowest tip. Only two riders left the customary tip of 15%. Reggie, the last rider, paid a total of $9.50. Jack gave the cab driver a 10% tip. Maria took the cab immediately after Eli.

Tell the order of the riders and how much each paid for the ride.

## QUICK WAY 💻

In the computer activity *Making Sense of Percents,* you use estimation to guess the percent of a number. This pencil-and-paper activity will help you become familiar with one of the estimation techniques used in that game.

You can use the 10% method when a percent is close to a multiple of 10%. For example, 61% of 2,986 is about 60% of 3,000.

$$10\% \text{ of } 3,000 = 300$$
$$6 \times 300 = 1,800 \quad \text{so, } 61\% \text{ of } 2,986 \approx 1,800.$$

Compete with a friend. See how many seconds it takes each of you to estimate all the problems using the 10% method.

1. 41% of 2,977
2. 69% of 8,012
3. 71% of 48,904
4. 19% of 20,086
5. 38% of 41,101
6. 89% of 98,900

**DID YOU KNOW . . . ?**

Two winners of the Olympic 400-m freestyle swimming race became Hollywood stars. Johnny Weissmuller, the 1924 winner, played Tarzan. The 1932 winner, Buster Crabbe, played Flash Gordon.

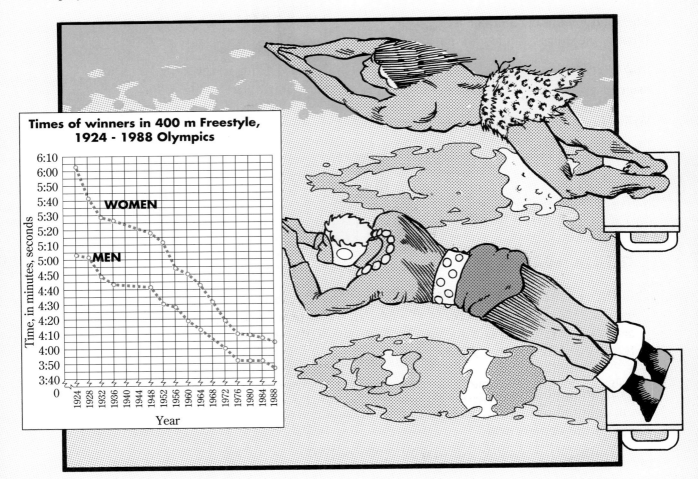

**Times of winners in 400 m Freestyle, 1924 - 1988 Olympics**

**USING DATA**

Collect
Organize
**Describe**
Predict

By about how many seconds did the men's winning time improve from 1960 to 1988? the women's winning time?

Did men or did women improve more from 1948 to 1988? Why do you think this is so?

## Exploring Proportional Thinking and Percent

The percent bar diagram can be used to set up proportions to solve percent problems. Here is a completed diagram for 75% of 68.

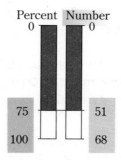

The ratio for the percent bar is $\frac{75}{100}$. What is the equal ratio for the number bar?

The ratios on the left and on the right of the diagram give us the proportion $\frac{75}{100} = \frac{51}{68}$.

Write the proportion that fits the diagram.

**1.**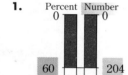

**2.**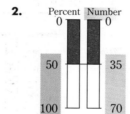

**3.**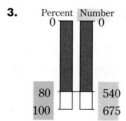

**4.** What number is found in each of the proportions in Exercises 1–3? Why will this be true for all percent problems?

> A survey of 360 seventh graders revealed that 80% made their own breakfasts. How many students is that?

You can complete the percent bar because the 80% is given. Use the answers to Exercises 5–8 to copy and complete the number bar.

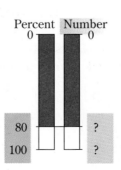

**5.** Does 100% represent the *total number* of students in the survey or the *number who make their own breakfasts*?

**6.** Does 80% represent the *total number* of students in the survey or the *number who make their own breakfasts*?

**7.** Is 360 the *total number* of students in the survey or the *number who make their own breakfasts*?

**8.** Why does the proportion below fit this problem?
$$\frac{80}{100} = \frac{n}{360}$$

Copy the percent bar diagram. Set up a $\frac{a}{100} = \frac{c}{d}$ proportion for the problem. Do not solve.

**9.** Of 60 students who play baseball after school, 25% ride the bus. How many students ride the bus?

**10.** Of 90 students who take Spanish, 30% also study music. How many Spanish language students study music?

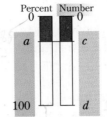

A student survey showed that 17 out of the 25 students who have gym during last period of the day have math during first period. What percent is that?

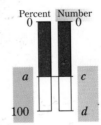

**11.** Is the 17 represented by the *c* or by the *d* on the percent bar diagram? Which letter represents the 25?

**12.** What represents the unknown percent?

**13.** Write a proportion for the percent problem.

Draw a percent bar diagram. Then write a proportion and solve.

**14.** 14% of 150 = ▇.

**15.** ▇% of 48 is 18.

**16.** 27 out of ▇ is $37\frac{1}{2}$%.

**17.** Of 52 girls asked, 39 preferred track and field to volleyball. What percent of the girls preferred track and field?

**18.** In a survey, 65%, or 78 students, asked to have science class in the morning. How many students were surveyed?

**CREATE YOUR OWN**  Write a problem to fit the percent bar diagram.

**19.**

**20.**

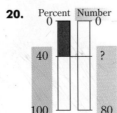

**21.**

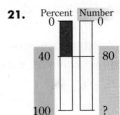

## Using Proportion and Percent

It has been projected that by the year 2000 the population of Florida will be 120% of what it was in 1990. If the 1990 population was about 12.8 million, about what will it be by the year 2000?

**NUMBER SENSE**  Will the answer be *greater than* or *less than* 12.8 million? Why?

Write and solve the proportion. Let $n$ represent the population in the year 2000.

When the percent is greater than 100%, you may want to read the diagram upward and write the ratios so that 100 is a denominator.

$$\frac{120}{100} = \frac{n}{12.8}$$
$$100n = 12.8 \times 120$$
$$\frac{100n}{100} = \frac{1{,}536}{100}$$
$$n = 15.36$$

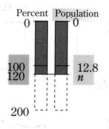

$$\frac{100}{120} = \frac{12.8}{n}$$
$$100n = 12.8 \times 120$$
$$\frac{100n}{100} = \frac{1{,}536}{100}$$
$$n = 15.36$$

**THINK ALOUD**  Why was the 12.8 million placed opposite the 100?

By the year 2000, Florida's population will be about 15.36 million.

Other examples:

24 is 8% of what number?

$$\frac{8}{100} = \frac{24}{n}$$
$$8n = 100 \times 24$$
$$\frac{8n}{8} = \frac{2{,}400}{8}$$
$$n = 300$$

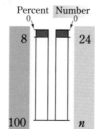

What percent of 192 is 48?

$$\frac{n}{100} = \frac{48}{192}$$
$$192n = 100 \times 48$$
$$\frac{192n}{192} = \frac{4{,}800}{192}$$
$$n = 25 \ (\%)$$

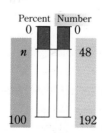

======== GUIDED PRACTICE ========

Use a proportion to solve. Use percent bars to help.

**1.** 40% of 60 is what number?

**2.** What percent of 30 is 24?

**3.** What percent of 24 is 30?

Use a proportion to solve.

**4.** 30% of what number is 7.5?

**5.** 5% of what number is 10?

**6.** What percent of 75 is 15?

**7.** What percent of 18 is 6?

**8.** 18 is what percent of 6?

**9.** What percent of 60 is 6?

**10.** 23% of what number is 20.7?

**11.** What percent of 300 is 9?

**12.** 6% of what number is 15?

**13.** What percent of 8 is 3?

**14.** 52% of $n$ is 33.8.

**15.** 40% of $n$ is 36.

Write a problem to fit the question.

**16.** 12 is 30% of what number?

**17.** 9 is what percent of 45?

**18.** 0.6% of what number is 2.4?

**19.** What percent of 5.2 is 3.9?

**20.** **IN YOUR WORDS** Why is the word *percent* a good name for fractions with a denominator of 100?

 Choose paper and pencil or calculator to solve.

**21.** The Everglades are about 2,746 mi$^2$ and Lake Okeechobee covers about 25.5% of the Everglades. About how many square miles is Lake Okeechobee?

**22.** About 580 mi of Florida's 1,350-mi coastline is on the Atlantic Ocean and the rest is on the Gulf of Mexico. About what percent of Florida's coastline is on the Gulf of Mexico?

**23.** **WRITE YOUR OWN** In 1513, Juan Ponce de León landed on Florida's east coast and claimed the region for Spain. In 1565, Pedro Menéndez de Avilés of Spain founded St. Augustine, now the oldest city in the United States. Use these facts to write a problem.

# Problem Solving:
## Using Percent of Commission

A salesperson is often paid a **commission**, which is a percent of the total sales the person makes.

Juanita sells computers and earns 8% commission on her sales. One day she sold a computer for $1,947. How much commission did she earn that day?

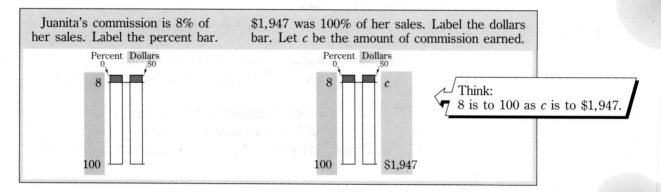

Juanita's commission is 8% of her sales. Label the percent bar.

$1,947 was 100% of her sales. Label the dollars bar. Let $c$ be the amount of commission earned.

Think:
8 is to 100 as $c$ is to $1,947.

What proportion represents this problem? Now solve the problem.

**CRITICAL THINKING** Why do you think a person who sells expensive items is often paid a commission?

━━━━━━━━━━━━━━━ **GUIDED PRACTICE** ━━━━━━━━━━━━━━━

Write a proportion to solve.

1. Lap-Cheung sells computers and earns $12\frac{1}{2}$% commission on his sales. He would like to earn $5,000 in commission in the next month.
   a. What percent of his sales is Lap-Cheung's commission?
   b. To get $5,000 in commission, would Lap-Cheung have to sell *less than* or *more than* $5,000 worth of computers?
   c. How much in total computer sales must Lap-Cheung have in order to make $5,000 in commission?

2. Alicia received a commission of $120 for selling a printer worth $2,000. What percent of total sales is her commission?

3. Jason earns a 15% commission selling jewelry. One week he sold 2 necklaces at $450 each, 5 rings at $799 each, and 15 bracelets at $150 each. How much commission did he earn that week?

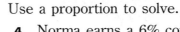

Use a proportion to solve.

**4.** Norma earns a 6% commission on sales, plus a base salary of $400/mo. Last month, she earned a total of $1,300. What were her total sales?

**5.** Angie earned $78 in commission for selling a $600 pair of gold earrings. What percent is her commission?

**6.** What would Hiroshi earn for selling 3 Egyptian paintings for $12,500 each, if his commission is 5.2% of his total sales?

**7.** Rosa is paid a base salary of $1,800/mo plus commission. One month she made $10,000 in sales and her total income was $3,000. What percent is her commission?

**8.** Errol earns a 15% commission for selling African art. For the sale of 1 wood carving, he earned $120 in commission. What was the value of the carving he sold?

**CHOOSE** Choose a strategy to solve.

**9.** Last year, Renete earned $36,000 in commission. Owing to more sales this year, she will earn 125% of that amount. What will she earn this year?

**10.** The Art and Jewelry Shoppe requires a down payment of 20% of the price of any item purchased on credit. What is the price of a wall hanging that requires a down payment of $120?

**11.** Enzo bought a $230 suit on credit, paying $24.50/mo for 12 mo. How much would Enzo have saved had he paid for the suit all at once?

**CREATE YOUR OWN** Create your own commission problem to fit the percent bar diagram.

**12.**

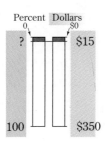

**13.**

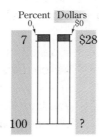

**14.**

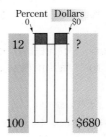

## LEARNING LOG

Match the situation with the appropriate expression.

**1.** 15% of the 40 students joined the club.  **a.** 40% of 150

**2.** Of 150 books on a reading list, 40% were fiction.  **b.** 15% of 40

**3.** The length of the photo is 150% of its 15 cm width.  **c.** 150% of 40

**4.** 40% of the 15-mi trip is complete.  **d.** 150% of 15

**5.** 150% more than last year's 40 voters are expected to vote this year.  **e.** 40% of 15

## QUICK QUIZ

Solve using a proportion. *(pages 352–353)*

**1.** 40% of what number is 56?  **2.** 75% of what number is 48?

**3.** What percent of 50 is 45?  **4.** What percent of 35 is 28?

**5.** 24 is what percent of 8?  **6.** What percent of 125 is 55?

**7.** 27 is what percent of 18?  **8.** 48 percent of $x$ is 18.

**9.** 165% of what number is 42.9?

Use a proportion to solve. *(pages 354–355)*

**10.** Last month, Arthur earned a commission of 7% on sales of $15,000 in addition to his base salary of $500.

  **a.** What was Arthur's rate of commission?

  **b.** Were Arthur's total earnings for the month less than or greater than $15,000?

  **c.** What were Arthur's total earnings for the month?

Write the answers in your learning log.

1. When using a proportion to find a percent, what is an important thing to remember?

2. You have learned two ways to solve percent problems. Describe the two ways and tell which way you prefer and why.

**DID YOU KNOW . . . ?** The United States Capitol stands on Capitol Hill in Washington, D.C. The building has 540 rooms and 658 windows. How many rooms and windows does your state capitol have? See whether you can write proportions to compare the two sets of numbers.

The Mark Down Clothing Store deducts 15% from the selling price of a garment at the end of each week it remains unsold. If a $249 coat goes on sale and remains unsold, how many weeks will it take for the price to drop below $150?

## Discount

A **discount** is a *decrease* in the regular price of an item. A discount of 20% tells you that you save 20¢ on every dollar of the regular price.

The discount on a pair of roller skates is 20%. How much would you save on a pair of roller skates that regularly sells for $49? What is the sale price?

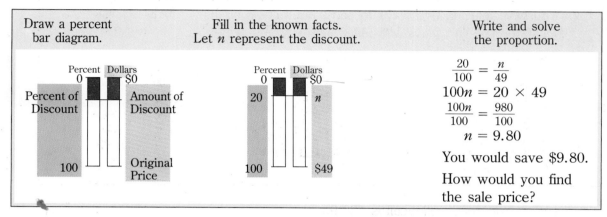

| Draw a percent bar diagram. | Fill in the known facts. Let $n$ represent the discount. | Write and solve the proportion. |
|---|---|---|

$$\frac{20}{100} = \frac{n}{49}$$
$$100n = 20 \times 49$$
$$\frac{100n}{100} = \frac{980}{100}$$
$$n = 9.80$$

You would save $9.80.

How would you find the sale price?

**CRITICAL THINKING**  The shaded part of the dollars bar is the amount of the discount. What does the unshaded part represent? How can you use this information to find the sale price?

=========================== **GUIDED PRACTICE** ===========================

Find the amount of discount and the sale price.

1. original price: $125
   discount: 15%

2. original price: $23
   discount: 5%

3. original price: $65
   discount: 50%

=============================== **PRACTICE** ===============================

Find the amount of discount and the sale price.

4. original price: $43.50
   discount: 30%

5. original price: $49.88
   discount: 50%

6. original price: $1,230
   discount: 20%

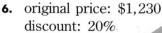

7. A $59.99 skateboard now costs $54. What is the percent of discount?

8. Which is cheaper, a $49.99 skateboard with a 20% discount, or a $54.99 skateboard with a 25% discount?

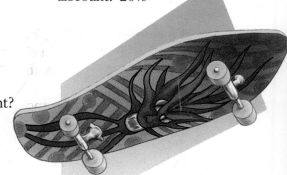

9. If a skateboard is on sale for $49 which is a 30% discount, what was the original price?

## Markup

Stores buy goods and then sell them at increased prices. The amount of the price increase is called the **markup**.

Dino's Sports buys volleyballs for $14.99 each. If a volleyball is marked up by 40%, what is its selling price?

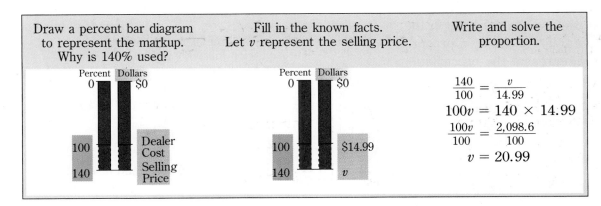

| Draw a percent bar diagram to represent the markup. Why is 140% used? | Fill in the known facts. Let $v$ represent the selling price. | Write and solve the proportion. |
|---|---|---|
| Percent Dollars — 0 $0, 100 Dealer Cost, 140 Selling Price | Percent Dollars — 0 $0, 100 $14.99, 140 $v$ | $\dfrac{140}{100} = \dfrac{v}{14.99}$  $100v = 140 \times 14.99$  $\dfrac{100v}{100} = \dfrac{2{,}098.6}{100}$  $v = 20.99$ |

Dino's selling price of a volleyball is $20.99.

### GUIDED PRACTICE

Find the missing value.

1. cost to store: $52.50
   markup: 50%
   selling price: ▒

2. cost to store: $25
   markup: ▒%
   selling price: $45

3. cost to store: ▒
   markup: 40%
   selling price: $32.55

### PRACTICE

The cost to Dino's Sports is given. Find the selling price.

4. baseball bat: $12.00
   markup: 45%

5. baseball: $9.50
   markup: 100%

6. soccer ball: $3.25
   markup: 80%

7. swim goggles: $5.30
   markup: 120%

8. sport bag: $7.99
   markup: 60%

9. fishing pole: $15.99
   markup: 65%

10. Dino's buys a shirt for $15.99, marks it up 50%, and sells it at a 25% discount. What is the profit?

11. Dino's sells a bicycle for $280. The markup was 40%. What did Dino's pay for the bike?

12. A dozen junior tennis rackets are bought for a total of $96. Dino's marks them up by 40%. What is the selling price of *each* racket?

13. **IN YOUR WORDS** If Dino's marks up an item by 50% and then sells it at a 50% discount, do they make a profit? Explain.

## Proportions and Circle Graphs

The circle graph shows what happens to the precipitation that falls each year on the land over Earth. About how much precipitation evaporates back into the air each year?

What Happens to Precipitation on Earth's Land Area

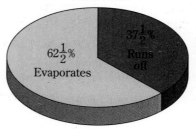

$62\frac{1}{2}\%$ Evaporates

$37\frac{1}{2}\%$ Runs off

You can use the percents in the circle graph to set up a proportion. Let $e$ represent the precipitation that evaporates, in cubic kilometers.

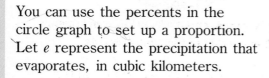

On average, about 96,000 km³ of precipitation fall every year.

$62\frac{1}{2}$ is to 100 as $e$ is to 96,000.

$$\frac{62.5}{100} = \frac{e}{96,000}$$

$$100e = 62.5 \times 96,000$$

$$\frac{100e}{100} = \frac{6,000,000}{100}$$

$$e = 60,000$$

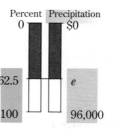

Percent   Precipitation

About 60,000 km³ of precipitation evaporates each year.

**CRITICAL THINKING**   What are two ways of finding out how much precipitation runs off the land on Earth in a year?

## GUIDED PRACTICE

Use the information in the circle graph below to set up a proportion and solve for $n$.

1. The circle represents 4,200 people.
   a. How many is 25% of the people?
   b. How many people are represented by $n$?

2. The circle represents 180 mi.
   a. How many is 60% of the miles?
   b. How many miles are represented by $n$?

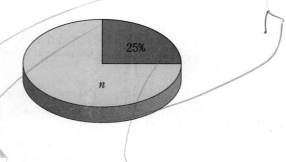

25%

$n$

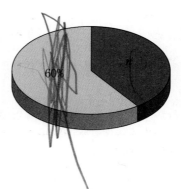

60%

$n$

MATH AND SCIENCE

Use the information in the circle graph to set up a proportion and solve.

**3.** On average, about how much precipitation in the United States returns unused to the sea each day?

**4.** About how much precipitation in the United States evaporates each day?

**5.** About how much precipitation in the United States is used by people each day?

**What Happens to Precipitation in the United States**

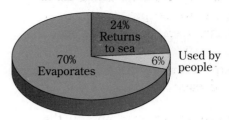

On average, about 16 km³ of precipitation fall every day in the United States.

**How Water is Used in the United States**

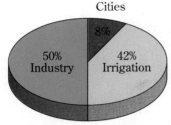

On average, about 280 billion gallons of water are used each day.

**6.** About how many gallons of water are used daily for irrigation?

**7.** About how many gallons of water do United States industries use each day?

**8. IN YOUR WORDS** How can you find the amount of water used by cities without using percents?

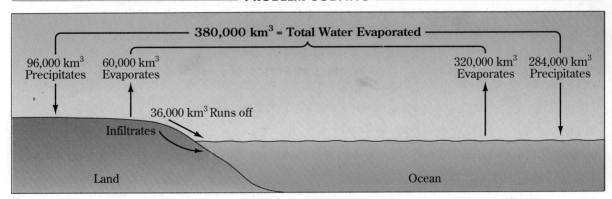

**CHOOSE** Use the diagram above.
Choose paper and pencil or calculator to solve.

**9.** What percent of the water that evaporates comes from the oceans?

**10.** What percent of the total precipitation falls on land?

**11. IN YOUR WORDS** With nearly 320,000 km³ of water evaporating each year from our oceans, why are the water levels not dropping?

## Problem Solving:
## Estimating with Percents

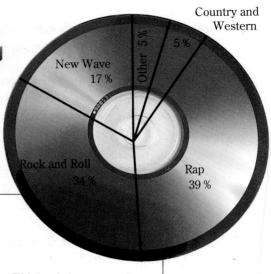

A survey was made recently in Houston, Texas, of the music preferences of 990 teen-agers. The circle graph shows the results.

About how many teen-agers preferred rock and roll?

| Draw a percent bar diagram. | Is 990 *all teen-agers surveyed* or *those who liked rock and roll?* | |
|---|---|---|
| 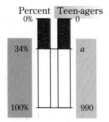 | Percent / Teen-agers bar diagram with 0%, 34%, 100% and 0, a, 990 | Think of the proportion representing the problem. $$\frac{34}{100} = \frac{a}{990}$$ |

There are two ways to estimate the solution.

**Method 1:** Since 34% is close to $33\frac{1}{3}\%$, or $\frac{1}{3}$, think:

$$\frac{1}{3} = \frac{\equiv}{990}.$$

**Method 2:** Since 990 is close to 1,000, think:

$$\frac{34}{100} = \frac{\equiv}{1,000}.$$

Now use both methods to estimate the solution. Which method was easier? Why?

====== GUIDED PRACTICE ======

Use the circle graph above to answer.

1.  **a.** What percent of the teen-agers preferred country-and-western music?

    **b.** What is 1% of 990? 5% of 990?

    **c.** Estimate the number of teen-agers who preferred country-and-western music.

    **d.** If you can estimate 5% of 990 how can you use it to estimate the number of teen-agers who preferred new-wave music (17%)?

Use the circle graph to estimate the solution.

**Age Preference of 990 Seventh Grade Students**

**2.** About what percent of students prefer to be the same age as they are? About how many students is that?

**3.** About what percent of students would prefer to be older? About how many students is that?

**4.** About what percent of students would prefer to be younger? About how many students is that?

To be older 63%

To be younger 10%

To be same age 27%

 **CHOOSE** Choose any strategy to estimate the solution.

**5.** The Longhorn Music Shop made $17,946 during a recent sale. If their profit was 15% of their total sales, about how much profit was made during the sale?

**6.** A local radio station plays country-and-western music for 21 min of every hour. About what percent of each hour is country-and-western music played?

**7.** A rock-and-roll CD is on sale for $3.05 less than its regular price. If the discount is 25%, about what is the regular price of the CD?

**8.** To buy a $595 CD player, Jake makes an 18% down payment. About how much is the down payment?

**9.** Lucia saves 50% of her weekly paycheck and spends 50% of what is left on audio tapes. About how much did Lucia earn one week if she bought $14.98 worth of audio tapes?

## Critical Thinking

Work with a partner.

**1.** How many quarters are there in $2.75?

**2.** $2.75 \div 0.25$

**3.** $275 \div 25$

**4.** $2\frac{3}{4} \div \frac{1}{4}$

• How did you solve Exercise 1? Did you use a different method to solve Exercises 2–4?

• Which method is easier? Defend your choice.

# Investigating Batting Averages

Next time you watch or listen to a baseball game, notice what different statistics are mentioned. A player's batting average is the ratio of the number of hits the player gets to the number of times the player is at bat. It can be computed using this formula:

$$B = \frac{h}{a} \text{ (written as a decimal rounded to thousandths)}$$

where $h$ = number of hits
$a$ = number of times at bat

The table has batting data for a baseball team that plays 20 games a season.

| Player | First half of season | | Second half of season | | Entire season | |
|---|---|---|---|---|---|---|
| | At–bats | Hits | At–bats | Hits | At–bats | Hits |
| Mario | 60 | 20 | 70 | 12 | 130 | 32 |
| Jack | 75 | 24 | 50 | 8 | 125 | 32 |
| Rita | 58 | 12 | 68 | 7 | 126 | 19 |
| Ana | 73 | 15 | 48 | 5 | 121 | 20 |
| Yoko | 62 | 13 | 72 | 8 | 134 | 21 |
| Omar | 72 | 16 | 52 | 6 | 124 | 22 |
| Julia | 60 | 10 | 60 | 10 | 120 | 20 |
| Jason | 58 | 11 | 58 | 11 | 116 | 22 |
| Takashi | 55 | 9 | 55 | 8 | 110 | 17 |
| Lani | 72 | 10 | 74 | 10 | 146 | 20 |
| Kate | 30 | 6 | 35 | 4 | 65 | 10 |
| David | 37 | 8 | 25 | 3 | 62 | 11 |

Work with a partner. Use the table on page 364 and a calculator.

1. Find each player's batting average for the first half of the season, the second half of the season, and the entire season.

2. Who had the highest batting average for the entire season?

3. Did that person have the highest batting average in the first half of the season? in the second half?

4. Compare Mario's and Jack's batting averages for the first half of the season, the second half of the season, and the entire season. Try to explain why such a situation can happen.

5. Compare the first half, second half, and season batting averages for Mario, Ana, and David. Does it seem as if you can find the seasonal batting average by averaging the batting averages for the two halves of the season?

6. Compare the first half, second half, and season batting averages for Julia, Takashi, and Lani. Does it seem as if you can find the seasonal batting average by averaging the batting averages for the two halves of the season?

7. Do your answers to Exercises 5 and 6 agree? Look for differences between the two groups of batting averages that might explain the reason.

## *Mixed Review*

Compute.

**1.** $17{,}340 \div 68$ **2.** $922 + 211$ **3.** $6{,}741 - 5{,}630$ **4.** $412 \times 42$

**5.** $895.43 - 312.44$ **6.** $73.01 + 147.77$ **7.** $431.6 - 1.27$ **8.** $2{,}344.8 \div 586.2$

**9.** $\frac{7}{8} \div \frac{1}{2}$ **10.** $5\frac{1}{4} \times 5\frac{1}{4}$ **11.** $9\frac{5}{6} + 2\frac{3}{4}$ **12.** $2\frac{1}{3} - 1\frac{1}{2}$

**13.** $\frac{7}{8} \times 1\frac{1}{3}$ **14.** $1\frac{5}{8} \div \frac{1}{2}$ **15.** $6\frac{8}{12} + \frac{5}{6}$ **16.** $4\frac{1}{2} - 3\frac{7}{8}$

Write as a percent.

**17.** $\frac{3}{4}$ **18.** $\frac{2}{3}$ **19.** 0.35 **20.** 0.7 **21.** 0.005 **22.** $\frac{9}{4}$

Write as a fraction in lowest terms.

**23.** 0.4 **24.** 0.04 **25.** 45% **26.** 6% **27.** 120% **28.** 0.5%

Write as a decimal.

**29.** $\frac{3}{8}$ **30.** $\frac{4}{5}$ **31.** 16% **32.** 4% **33.** 0.25% **34.** 105%

Find the missing number.

**35.** 30% of ▒ is 54. **36.** ▒% of 35 is 14. **37.** 180% of 320 is ▒.

**38.** 30% of 423 is ▒. **39.** 1% of ▒ is 80. **40.** ▒% of 20 is 40.

**41.** 16% of ▒ is 36. **42.** ▒% of 56 is 28. **43.** 150% of 400 is ▒.

**44.** $33\frac{1}{3}$% of 423 is ▒. **45.** 0.5% of ▒ is 80. **46.** ▒% of 30 is 45.

Create a true proportion by solving for $n$.

**47.** $\frac{3}{4} = \frac{15}{n}$ **48.** $\frac{2}{3} = \frac{n}{108}$ **49.** $\frac{35}{20} = \frac{5}{n}$ **50.** $\frac{9}{5} = \frac{n}{100}$

**51.** $\frac{3}{4} = \frac{n}{15}$ **52.** $\frac{24}{36} = \frac{n}{108}$ **53.** $\frac{3.5}{20} = \frac{5}{n}$ **54.** $\frac{9}{4} = \frac{n}{100}$

CHOOSE
Choose estimation, mental math,
paper and pencil, or calculator to solve.

**55.** Of China's working population
of over 520 million people, 70% are
farmers. How many people is that?

**56.** About 78 million of China's
520 million workers are in
manufacturing or mining. What
percent of China's workers is that?

**57.** The Qin dynasty, which completed
the Great Wall of China, ruled from
221 B.C. to 206 B.C. For how many
years was the Qin dynasty in power?

**58.** The Great Wall covers 4,000 mi of the
northern border of China. In 1794,
the Great Wall celebrated its 2,000th
birthday. How old is it today?

**59.** Eastern China contains 50%
of the land area but only 10% of the
population of the country. If about
110 million people live in eastern
China, about what is the country's
total population?

**60.** About $\frac{1}{5}$ of the world's population
live in China. If China recently had
a population of about 1,098,000,000,
about what was the population
of the world at that time?

**61.** In 1990, China produced goods
valued at $225 billion.

   **a.** About how much money came
from agricultural goods?

   **b.** About how much money came
from nonagricultural sources?

**62** **CREATE YOUR OWN** Write a math
problem about China. Give it to
a friend to solve.

**Production in China**

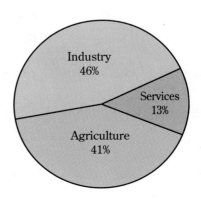

---

### LANGUAGE & VOCABULARY

Write *true* or *false*. If false, give a counterexample.

1. If one store discounts an item 20% and another store discounts the same item 30%, you will save money by shopping at the second store.

2. A store offering no discount can have a lower price than a store selling the same item at a 15% discount.

3. A store marks up prices in order to make a profit.

4. A large markup followed by a large discount can result in the same selling price as a small markup followed by a small discount.

5. A 30% discount on an original price of $150 is a smaller discount than a 15% discount on an original price of $150.

---

### TEST

---

#### CONCEPTS

Solve using a proportion. *(pages 352–353)*

1. 40% of what number is 8.6?

2. 80% of what number is 27?

3. 16 is what percent of 50?

4. 4.2 is what percent of 12?

5. What percent of 30 is 72?

6. 2% of what number is 55?

#### SKILLS

Find the amount of the discount and the sale price. *(page 358)*

7. Original price: $29.95

   Discount: 20%

8. Original price: $38.50

   Discount: 25%

9. Original price: $175.40

   Discount: 15%

10. Original price: $1,860

    Discount: 35%

The cost to the store and the markup are given. Find the selling price. *(page 359)*

**11.** Coat: $45

Markup: 75%

**12.** Computer: $525

Markup: 80%

**13.** Game: $15

Markup: 110%

**14.** Book: $9

Markup: 65%

**15.** Shoes: $35

Markup: 75%

**16.** Glasses: $38.50

Markup: 100%

Use the information in the circle graph to set up a proportion and solve. *(pages 360–361)*

**17.** How many students chose spring vacation as their favorite?

**18.** How many students chose summer?

**19.** How many students chose winter?

Favorite School Vacations
600 Responses

Winter 32%
Summer 45%
Spring 23%

## PROBLEM SOLVING

Use a proportion to solve. *(pages 354–355)*

**20.** Sally earned $3,000 in salary and commission one month. Of this, $1,800 was commission on $22,500 in sales.

  **a.** How much did Sally earn in commission?

  **b.** What proportion will give Sally's percent of commission?

  **c.** What percent of sales is Sally's commission?

Estimate. *(pages 362–363)*

**21.** During one January, it rained 9 d. About what percent of the days did it rain?

**22.** At a sale, a discount of 35% was offered on all computers. How much would you save on a computer that regularly sells for $1,860? What is the sale price?

## LEARNING LOG

Write the answers in your learning log.

  **1.** A newspaper advertisement says "Up to 50% off." Explain what this means to you.

  **2.** A toy store is having a 20% off everything sale. How would you estimate the sale price of items in the store?

# EXTRA PRACTICE

Solve using a proportion. *(pages 352–355)*

**1.** What percent of 38 is 9.5?

**2.** 68 is 34% of what number?

**3.** What percent of 126 is 44.1?

**4.** What percent of 14 is 42?

**5.** 4% of what number is 25?

**6.** 32% of what number is 22?

**7.** What percent of 17 is 22.1?

**8.** 456 is 120% of what number?

**9.** What percent of 8 is 27.2?

**10.** What percent of 16 is 52?

Find the amount of the discount and the sale price. *(page 358)*

**11.** Original price: $75

Discount: 15%

**12.** Original price: $36

Discount: 20%

**13.** Original price: $120

Discount: 35%

**14.** Original price: $79

Discount: 50%

**15.** Original price: $5,600

Discount: 25%

**16.** Original price: $885

Discount: 45%

Find the selling price for the given cost and markup. *(page 359)*

**17.** TV: $300

Markup: 90%

**18.** Phone: $20

Markup: 115%

**19.** Radio: $17.50

Markup: 80%

**20.** Shirt: $15.75

Markup: 100%

**21.** Lamp: $23.10

Markup: 110%

**22.** Rug: $55

Markup: 85%

Use the information in the circle graph to set up a proportion and solve. *(pages 360–361)*

**23.** The graph represents 3,400 students.

   **a.** How many students is 40% of the students?

   **b.** How many students are represented by $x$?

**24.** The graph shows how one student spends her time.

   **a.** How much time does she spend studying?

   **b.** How much time does she spend reading?

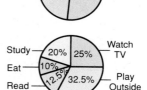

The graph represents 8 h of a day.

Solve. *(pages 354–355, 362–363)*

**25.** Roberto earned $3,920 in commission on sales of $24,500. What percent is his commission?

**26.** Angela was absent from school 11 out of 180 school days last year. About what percent of the school year was she absent?

# International Percents

Choose a country other than the United States. Do research to learn about its money.

- What is the monetary unit called?
- What denominations are used?
- What is the current value of one unit of the country's currency in United States money?

You can set up and solve a proportion to determine the value in United States money of each unit of the country's money. For example, in France, the monetary unit is the French franc. One denomination of the French franc is the 50-franc note. If 1 French franc has a value equal to $.23, you can use the following proportion to determine the value in United States money of a 50-franc note:

$$\frac{1}{.23} = \frac{50}{x}$$

Use proportions to determine the value in United States money of each denomination used in the country you have chosen.

# Comparison Shopping

Supermarkets compete for business in many ways. One goal of supermarkets is to convince consumers that they have the lowest prices. But is one supermarket really less expensive than another?

Work with a group. Make a list of about 15 or 20 common items and their most common size. Have members of your group visit at least two supermarkets to record the prices of the items.

- List the items and prices in both stores in a table.
- Can you see a pattern?
- Are prices in one store consistently lower than those in another? If the answer is *yes*, what might explain the fact that people continue to shop in the more expensive store? Is price the only concern of consumers?

## Math Scavenger Hunt

Look through a newspaper for these examples of percents.

- a percent greater than 100%
- a percent that refers to a population
- a percent that refers to time
- a percent less than 100%
- a percent that refers to money
- a percent used in a graph

# CUMULATIVE REVIEW

Find the answer.

1. What is the LCM of 9 and 15?
   a. 3
   b. 30
   c. 135
   d. none of these

2. What is the LCM of 3, 5, and 6?
   a. 15
   b. 30
   c. 90
   d. none of these

3. What is the GCF of 18 and 27?
   a. 9
   b. 18
   c. 36
   d. none of these

4. $\frac{15}{35} = $ ▦
   a. $\frac{3}{5}$
   b. $\frac{3}{7}$
   c. $\frac{5}{7}$
   d. none of these

5. $\frac{7}{12} = $ ▦
   a. $\frac{14}{21}$
   b. $\frac{14}{36}$
   c. $\frac{21}{36}$
   d. none of these

6. $\frac{7}{8}$ is greater than ▦.
   a. $\frac{5}{6}$
   b. $\frac{9}{10}$
   c. $\frac{11}{12}$
   d. none of these

7. $\frac{5}{8} + \frac{7}{10} = $ ▦
   a. $\frac{12}{18}$
   b. $1\frac{13}{40}$
   c. $1\frac{1}{4}$
   d. none of these

8. $\frac{12}{16} - \frac{1}{4} = $ ▦
   a. $\frac{11}{12}$
   b. $\frac{1}{2}$
   c. $\frac{1}{4}$
   d. none of these

9. $2\frac{1}{3} + 5\frac{2}{5} = $ ▦
   a. $7\frac{1}{5}$
   b. $7\frac{3}{8}$
   c. $7\frac{11}{15}$
   d. none of these

10. All squares are ▦.
    a. trapezoids
    b. kites
    c. rectangles
    d. none of these

11. All parallelograms are ▦.
    a. quadrilaterals
    b. rectangles
    c. squares
    d. none of these

12. All trapezoids are ▦.
    a. parallelograms
    b. rhombuses
    c. rectangles
    d. none of these

13. $\frac{14}{27} = \frac{x}{81}$
    a. 28
    b. 42
    c. 56
    d. none of these

14. $\frac{15}{8} = \frac{75}{x}$
    a. 45
    b. 32
    c. 40
    d. none of these

15. 7 oranges: $1.33
    1 orange: $x$
    a. $9.31
    b. $.13
    c. $.19
    d. none of these

# PROBLEM SOLVING REVIEW

Remember the strategies and types of problems you've had so far. Solve.

1. A school district owns a 40-seat bus, a 15-seat minibus, and two station wagons, one with 9 seats and one with 7 seats.

    a. How many seats does the bus have?

    b. How can you find out the total number of ways students can be transported using 1, 2, 3, or 4 vehicles?

    c. How many different ways can students be transported using 1, 2, 3, or 4 vehicles?

2. A parade begins at 10:45 A.M. Each band takes 2 min to pass the reviewing stand. If the parade lasts 2 h 25 min, at what time does it end?

3. A juice machine dispenses 10 oz bottles. There is a total of 1 gal 12 oz of juice in the machine. How many bottles are in the machine?

4. Of 20 students asked, 12 said they liked the school lunch. At that rate, how many of 200 students would probably say they liked the lunch?

5. Ruth bought a pair of jeans that were priced at $39.95. She received a 10% employee's discount. How much did the jeans cost her?

6. If Corey lived 4 blocks closer to school, he would live twice as far from school as Jorge. If Jorge lives 3 blocks from school, how far from school does Corey live?

7. Five friends shared a dinner check evenly. The check was $65.50 and they decided to give the waiter a 15% tip. To the nearest dollar, how much did each friend pay?

8. A $2\frac{1}{2}$ h film has 2 reels: one $1\frac{1}{3}$h long and one $1\frac{1}{6}$h long. An intermission comes between the reels. If the reels are played in reverse order, how much earlier would the intermission be?

9. Apples are 5 for $1.00 and oranges are 3 for $1.00. Arthur spent $7.00 and came home with 29 pieces of fruit. What did he buy?

10. A school lunchroom offered a choice of chicken, tuna, or pizza. Seventy-five more students had pizza than chicken, and 60 more students had chicken than tuna. If 165 tunas were served, how many lunches were served in all?

## THINKING IN CIRCLES

The circle graph gives the budget breakdown for the drama club this year. How would the graph change if someone donated rehearsal space to the club for free? Give the new percentages.

## ZEROING IN

Use a calculator to find a percent of 893 that is within the given range.

Range
1. 50–100
2. 70–95
3. 71.5–72.5
4. 71.9–72.2
5. 71.93–71.97

## GETTING INTERESTED

In *EduCalc*, you learn to use a computer spreadsheet to compute compound interest—that is, interest earned on interest. This pencil-and-paper activity will help you become familiar with how compound interest works.

This spreadsheet shows how much interest a deposit of $500 will earn after 4 yr in an account that pays 5% interest compounded annually.

| End of Year | Principal | x Interest Rate | = Interest | Total |
|---|---|---|---|---|
| 1 | 500.00 | 0.05 | 25.00 | 525.00 |
| 2 | 525.00 | 0.05 | 26.25 | 551.25 |
| 3 | 551.25 | 0.05 | 27.56 | 578.81 |
| 4 | 578.81 | 0.05 | 28.94 | 607.75 |

Set up a similar table, and use a calculator to compute the compound interest and the new totals. Use the annual compound interest shown.

1. $1,200; 5%; 6 yr
2. $800; 6%; 10 yr
3. $985; 6%; 6 yr
4. $1,420; $6\frac{1}{4}$%; 4 yr
5. $1,340; $5\frac{1}{2}$%; 5 yr
6. $800; $9\frac{3}{4}$%; 5 yr

**DID YOU KNOW . . . ?**

For every bird that becomes extinct, the world also may lose 90 insects, 35 plants, and 2 fish. For every 2 birds that become extinct, 1 mammal also may be lost.

**Number of Species That May
Become Extinct Along with One Bird**

1 Square represents 1 species

Insects

Plants

Bird

Fish

Mammal

**USING DATA**
- Collect
- Organize
- Describe
- **Predict**

Find out about 5 birds that are in danger of becoming extinct.

By the year 2000, it is predicted that 1 in 20 of today's bird species may become extinct. This equals about 400 to 500 different species of birds. Predict how the bird extinctions may affect insects, plants, fish, and mammals by the year 2000.

# EXPLORE

## Exploring Surveys

A seventh grade class was writing a story about
the graduating eighth grade class for the school newspaper.
They decided to use a questionnaire to make a survey of the eighth graders.

Erick and Lara were partners for this project. Follow along on
their part of the project. It will give you ideas on how to write
questions and to collect and organize data.

To get started on the survey each student had to develop a
question that would help to gather clear data about an interesting topic.

**Lara's Question:**

*How much time do you spend studying?*

**Erick's Question:**

*What was the last important item you bought?*

Lara and Erick exchanged questions so that they could comment
on each other's questions. They could ask about the meaning of an
unclear question, point out data that would be hard to organize, or
mention anything to help the other person write a better question.

Erick and Lara exchanged questions and received these comments.

**Comments on Lara's Question:**

- *Do you include studying during school hours?*

- *Will students really know in general how much time they spend studying?*

**Comments on Erick's Question:**

- *What does "important" mean? New socks? A radio?*

- *Will you want to put the responses into categories?*

- *Or have choices in categories?*

1. **THINK ALOUD**   What other comments might be made about
   their questions?

Then they rewrote their own questions to make the questions better.

**Lara's New Question:**

*How much time did you spend studying after school yesterday?*

(a) 0–15 min
(b) 16–60 min
(c) more than 60 min

**Erick's New Question:**

*What was the last item you bought for $10 or more with your own money?*

MATH AND LANGUAGE ARTS

2. **THINK ALOUD**   How did Erick and Lara respond to the comments on their questions?

3. **CREATE YOUR OWN**   Choose an interesting topic and write a question. Exchange questions with a partner. Give helpful comments. Then rewrite your own question.

The students put all the questions together into one questionnaire. Then they discussed how they would collect the data.

4. Lara didn't want her question to be asked on a Monday. Can you tell why?

Once the questionnaires had been filled out by the eighth graders, each seventh grade student tallied and organized the raw data for his or her question.

| Lara's Tallied Data: | | Lara's Organized Data: | |
|---|---|---|---|
| | | *Minutes* | *Number of Responses* |
| 0–15 min ~~HHT HHT HHT HHT HHT HHT~~ IIII | | *0–15* | 34 |
| 16–60 min ~~HHT HHT HHT HHT HHT~~ III | | *16–60* | 28 |
| more than 60 min ~~HHT HHT HHT~~ III | | *more than 60* | 18 |

| Erick's Tallied Data | | | |
|---|---|---|---|
| CD ~~HHT HHT~~ II | record album ~~HHT~~ III | shorts II | video movie ~~HHT~~ |
| blouse IIII | audio tape ~~HHT HHT HHT~~ | software IIII | soccer ball I |
| T-shirt ~~HHT~~ I | clock I | radio I | CD player I |
| book ~~HHT~~ I | cassette player II | purse III | pizza I |
| jeans IIII | video game II | football I | guitar strings I |

5. Work with a partner to sort Erick's data by putting similar objects into a category. For instance, you could put the football and the soccer ball into a category called Sports Equipment. Then make a table of organized data like Lara's.

Your class may want to make a survey and write a story about the results for the school newspaper. You can collect and organize data for the questions you wrote in Exercise 3.

# Sampling and Predicting

The sales manager of Smart Sporting Goods wants to predict the number of students at Carver High School who might purchase school jackets. The manager can use a sample to predict the percent of students who are likely jacket buyers.

A **population** is an entire group about whom information is wanted. The population in this example is students at Carver High School.

A **sample** is a part, or subset, of the population. You collect information about the sample in order to make a prediction about the population. To do this you use proportional thinking to draw conclusions about the population from the sample.

All students at Carver High School

Some students at Carver High School

When a sample has characteristics that are very similar to the population, it is called a **representative sample.** The best chance to ensure representativeness is to use a **random sample.**

Random selections are made when every member of the population has an equally likely chance of being selected. One way to get a random sample of students at the high school is to put separate slips with each student's name into a box, mix the name slips, and draw some name slips.

**THINK ALOUD**   Suppose the sales manager asks students at the junior after-school volleyball game whether they would buy the jacket. Would the results of this sample group give a good prediction for the entire student body? Would this be a representative sample?

━━━━━━━━━━━━━━━━━━━━ **GUIDED PRACTICE** ━━━━━━━━━━━━━━━━━━━━

Use the diagram.

1. Name the population and the sample.

2. Explain why this sample is neither representative nor random.

Students at Carver High School

Carver High School Music Club

Name the population and the sample in Exercises 3–8.

**3.**

Students in
Homeroom 303

10 Students whose names
were drawn from a hat

**4.**

People in Indiana

Girls at a high
school in Indiana

**5.** A magazine subscription company wants information about all the people in the United States.
They survey the people in a nursing home in California.

**6.** The manager of a restaurant leaves customer surveys at the entrance to the restaurant one evening. He wants to know how all his customers feel about the service at the restaurant.

**7.** You want to select 10 members of the band to complete a survey about uniforms. You pick names of band members from a hat.

**8.** A research company wants information about high school students across the country.
They interview students at one high school in Florida.

**9.** Which samples in Exercises 3–8 are random samples of the population? Explain.

**10. CRITICAL THINKING** Sometimes it's very difficult to obtain random samples. Use the examples in Exercises 4, 5, 6, and 8 to discuss why.

**11.** A principal wants to know how many students in her school are interested in attending a field trip to the modern art museum. How might she get a representative sample of 80 students from the population of 1,200 students?

**12.** The seventh grade class at Washington School wants to have a committee of eight typical students represent them at an all-school meeting. How might the students be selected?

**13.** A town wants to build a swimming pool. How could you sample 100 out of 2,500 townspeople to find out how many would buy season swimming passes?

# Double Bar Graphs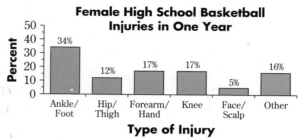

The single bar graphs below show the types of injuries received by students playing high school basketball during one year.

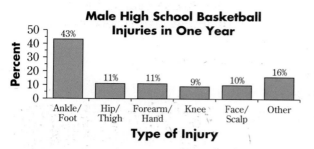

**Male High School Basketball Injuries in One Year**

43% 11% 11% 9% 10% 16%

Ankle/Foot | Hip/Thigh | Forearm/Hand | Knee | Face/Scalp | Other

**Type of Injury**

**Female High School Basketball Injuries in One Year**

34% 12% 17% 17% 5% 16%

Ankle/Foot | Hip/Thigh | Forearm/Hand | Knee | Face/Scalp | Other

**Type of Injury**

**THINK ALOUD** How do the injuries for males and for females compare? The **mode** is the event that occurs most frequently. What injury is the mode for males? for females?

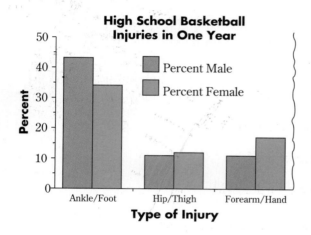

**High School Basketball Injuries in One Year**

Percent Male
Percent Female

Ankle/Foot | Hip/Thigh | Forearm/Hand

**Type of Injury**

You can compare injuries for males and for females more easily on a double bar graph.

**STEPS** Label the horizontal axis as Injury.

Label the vertical axis as Percent.

Since the greatest percent on either single bar graph is 43%, the vertical axis can stop at 50%. Each division can represent 5%.

Use separate and distinct bars for males and for females.

## GUIDED PRACTICE

Copy and complete the double bar graph by using facts from the single bar graphs. Use the graph to answer the question.

**1.** Which injuries occurred more often for males than for females?

**2.** Which injury occurred most often overall?

**3.** **ESTIMATE** Which injury occurred about twice as often for females as for males? How can you tell?

**4.** **CRITICAL THINKING** Which type of injury will probably be the mode for females in the year after the one graphed?

**5.** **THINK ALOUD** How do you think this data was obtained? Discuss the sample, the population, and the survey question(s).

| Players in High School Sports | | |
|---|---|---|
| Sport | Players | Players Injured |
| Football | 1,021,685 | 374,678 |
| Wrestling | 273,334 | 82,987 |
| Basketball | 697,907 | 162,981 |

This table shows the number of players injured at least once during one year in three different high school sports.

Graph the information. Write the names of the sports in alphabetical order on the horizontal axis. Make 11 divisions on the vertical axis, each representing 100,000 players.

**6.** Draw a single bar graph showing the total number of players in each sport.

**7.** Draw a single bar graph showing the number of players injured playing each sport.

**8.** Use your two single bar graphs. Draw a double bar graph comparing the total number of players to the number of players injured for each sport.

Is the statement *true* or *false*? Explain.

**9.** Based on the number of players, football was the mode.

**10.** There were fewer players than injured players in each sport.

**11.** For each sport, over half the players were injured.

**12.** Wrestling had fewer injured players than did basketball.

**ESTIMATE** About what was the percent of players injured that year?

**13.** football     **14.** basketball     **15.** wrestling

**PROBLEM SOLVING**

Solve. Use the data in the table.

**16. CALCULATOR** Find the percent of players who were injured in each sport.

**17.** Which sport had the greatest risk of injury? Explain.

**18.** Make a single bar graph showing the percent of injury in each of the three sports in the table above.

**19. IN YOUR WORDS** Compare your single bar graph of the percent of injury to your single bar graph of the number of injuries. Discuss how the two graphs are alike. Tell how and why they are different.

## Mean and Median 🔲

Over the last 200 years the population of the New England states has grown dramatically, as you can see in the chart below. (The populations are rounded to the nearest thousand.)

|  | 1790 | 1890 | 1990 |
|---|---|---|---|
| Maine | 97,000 | 661,000 | 1,212,000 |
| New Hampshire | 142,000 | 377,000 | 1,412,000 |
| Vermont | 85,000 | 332,000 | 562,000 |
| Massachusetts | 379,000 | 2,239,000 | 5,880,000 |
| Rhode Island | 69,000 | 346,000 | 1,002,000 |
| Connecticut | 238,000 | 746,000 | 3,279,000 |
| **Total** | 1,010,000 | 4,701,000 | 13,347,000 |

You can represent the "average" population for the New England states in 1790 by the mean or the median.

The **mean** is the sum of the data items divided by the number of data items.

$$\frac{\text{total population}}{\text{number of states}} \quad \Longrightarrow \quad \frac{1,010,000}{6} \quad \Longrightarrow \quad 168,333.33$$

The mean population of the six states in 1790 was about 168,000.

The **median** is the middle number in a set of data arranged in order.

After putting the state populations in order, you will find *two* middle numbers, 97,000 and 142,000. When you have an even number of data items, the median is the mean of the two middle numbers.

$$\frac{97,000 + 142,000}{2} = 119,500$$

The median population in 1790 was 119,500.

**THINK ALOUD**   Since the 1790 population of Massachusetts was so much greater than the other states, the median may be a better representation of the average population than the mean. Explain.

Maine

Vermont

New Hampshire

Massachusetts

Connecticut

Rhode Island

**Newfane, Vermont**

Use the chart on page 382 for Exercises 1–9.
Suppose the population of Massachusetts in 1790
had been 250,000.

1. Find the new mean population for the
   New England states for that year.

2. Find the new median population for the
   New England states for that year. (*Hint:*
   Remember to put the state populations in order.)

3. Did both the mean and the median change
   with the changed population? Why or why not?

4. **CRITICAL THINKING**  Why did the mean get
   closer to the median? Which would you use to best
   show the "average"?

**PRACTICE**

Find the mean of the population.

5. the New England states in 1890

6. the New England states in 1990

Find the median of the population.

7. the New England states in 1890

8. the New England states in 1990

**PROBLEM SOLVING**

Solve. Use pencil and paper or a calculator.

9. Change the 1890 population of Massachusetts to 750,000.

   a. Find the mean (to the nearest thousand). Did it change
      with the changed population? Why or why not?

   b. Find the median (to the nearest thousand). Did it change
      with the changed population? Why or why not?

10. **IN YOUR WORDS**  When do you think the average should
    be reported as the median? as either the mean or the median?

11. Chris calculated the median population of the New England
    states in 1990 this way: $\frac{562,000 + 5,880,000}{2}$. What was his error?

CHAPTER 12   383

# Double Line Graphs

The table shows two heart rates for a 12 year-old girl.

| Minutes | 1 | 2 | 3 | 4 | 5 | 6 | 7 | 8 | 9 | 10 |
|---|---|---|---|---|---|---|---|---|---|---|
| Heart Rate at Rest | 86 | 88 | 87 | 89 | 90 | 87 | 87 | 90 | 88 | 87 |
| Heart Rate After Exercise | 190 | 185 | 147 | 117 | 103 | 105 | 98 | 90 | 92 | 89 |

You can show the after-exercise heart rate with a line graph.

**STEPS**   Draw the horizontal and the vertical axes on grid paper.

Label the horizontal axis as minutes.

Label the vertical axis as heart rate. Use multiples of 20 from 0 to 200, since the highest rate is 190.

Plot the after-exercise heart rates and join with segments to make a line graph.

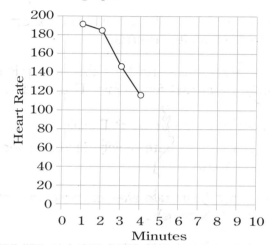

## GUIDED PRACTICE

1. Copy the graph started above.

2. What is the next point you should show?

3. Complete the graph using the after-exercise heart rates shown.

4. What points would you plot to show at-rest heart rates?

5. On the same grid, make a line graph of the at-rest heart rates. Use a different colored pencil.

6. What would you title this graph?

7. **CRITICAL THINKING**   About how long does it take heart rate after exercise to return to heart rate at rest? What factors could influence this recovery time?

Use this table, showing heart-rate data for an adult man, for Exercises 8–13.

| Minutes | 1 | 2 | 3 | 4 | 5 | 6 | 7 | 8 | 9 | 10 |
|---|---|---|---|---|---|---|---|---|---|---|
| Heart Rate at Rest | 50 | 48 | 60 | 51 | 54 | 52 | 55 | 53 | 56 | 58 |
| Heart Rate After Exercise | 111 | 104 | 80 | 81 | 72 | 64 | 65 | 57 | 53 | 57 |

**8.** Make a line graph for the man's heart rate after exercise.

**9. NUMBER SENSE** What would you expect the man's heart rate to be 15 min after exercise?

**10.** Make another line graph on the same grid showing the man's heart rate at rest for 10 min. Use a different colored pencil.

Is the statement *true* or *false*? Explain.

**11.** The man's heart rate rapidly decreases for the first 5 min after exercise.

**12.** The man's heart rate after exercise will probably gradually slow down to 0 beats/min.

**13.** The man's heart rate after exercise will probably level off to about 55 beats/min if he continues to rest.

Solve. Use your line graphs of the heart rates of the girl and of the man.

**14.** About how long does it take for the man's heart rate to return to "normal" after exercising?

**15. IN YOUR WORDS** Compare the after-exercise and at-rest heart rates of the 12-year-old girl and the adult man. What similarities and differences do you see?

**16.** A doctor looked at the line graphs for the girl and the man and remarked that they both appeared to be in good physical condition. The graph of another person's after-exercise and at-rest rates is shown at right. What physical condition do you think the person is in? Why?

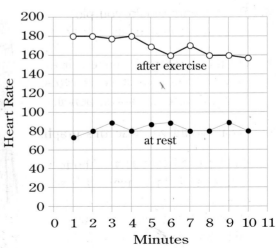

CHAPTER 12   **385**

# Problem Solving:
## Choosing an Appropriate Graph

A science class grew bean seedlings under three different
conditions. Students watered some of the seedlings with tap water,
some with bleach water, and some with salt water. Each day the
students measured the heights of the seedlings and calculated an
average height for each type of watering.

**THINK ALOUD**   How would an average height for several seedlings
be calculated?

The table below has the data for the average heights of the
seedlings for the first five days of the experiment.

| Average Height of Seedlings | | | | | |
|---|---|---|---|---|---|
| | **Day 1** | **Day 2** | **Day 3** | **Day 4** | **Day 5** |
| Tap water | 0.2 cm | 1.3 cm | 2.5 cm | 3.8 cm | 5.2 cm |
| Bleach water | 0.2 cm | 0.5 cm | 0.5 cm | 0.5 cm | 0.5 cm |
| Salt water | 0.2 cm | 1.0 cm | 1.9 cm | 2.3 cm | 2.8 cm |

The two graphs below are from students' reports about their experiment.

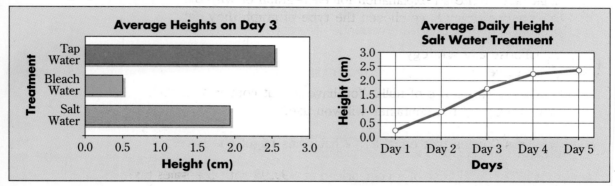

**THINK ALOUD**   Which of the graphs above is a bar graph?
a line graph? Use the line graph to estimate the heights at $2\frac{1}{2}$ d
of the seedlings treated with salt water.

> **When data are organized by nonnumerical categories,
> you can use bar graphs or pictographs.**
>
> **When data are organized numerically, you can use
> bar graphs, pictographs, or line graphs.**

**THINK ALOUD**   The data in the first graph should not be shown
as a line graph. Discuss why.

MATH AND SCIENCE

1. Use the information in the box at the bottom of page 386.

   a. What kind of graphs can you use for data that is organized by numerical categories?

   b. Are types of watering treatments numerical or nonnumerical data?

   c. Ruth has a record of her height on each of her birthdays. What kind of graph would you use to show the data?

Use the table on page 386. What types of graph can be used to represent the data set?

2. the average heights for five days of the seedlings treated with salt water

3. the average height on day 5 for seedlings treated all three ways

4. **CREATE YOUR OWN** Use the data in the table to make a line graph for the average daily growth of seedlings under bleach water treatment for five days.

5. **IN YOUR WORDS** Find several graphs in newspapers or magazines. Write an explanation for each graph of why the graph makers may have chosen the type of graph they did.

**CHOOSE** Choose any strategy to solve.

6. A recipe calls for 3 c of milk. You have a 1-qt container of milk. What fraction of the container will you use?

7. Laura has 9 coins that equal $1. What coins might she have?

8. What is the total cost of a coat priced at $99.98 with 5% sales tax?

## *Estimate*

When several data items are close to the same number, you can round them to that number to make a mental estimate of the mean.

Example: 57, 58, 60, 62, 64, 90, 100
Round 57, 58, 60, 62, and 64 to 60; multiply 60 by 5 (300), add the other numbers to 300 (490), and divide 490 by 7 to get a mean of 70.

Estimate the mean mentally.

1. 31, 30, 29, 30, 36    2. 60, 76, 77, 81, 83, 100    3. 39, 49, 47, 52, 51, 61

# Relative Frequency

Middle schools are organized in different ways. The bar graph allows you to compare different types of middle schools that existed in 1970–71. For example, you can see there were over twice as many schools for grades 6–8 as for grades 5–8.

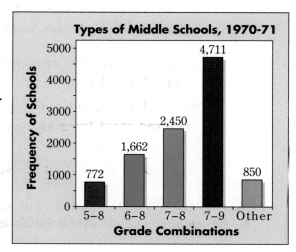

**THINK ALOUD** Why can't you see how many schools for grades 5–8 there were compared to all the middle schools?

To make such a comparison, you can find a relative frequency. A **relative frequency** is a ratio that compares a part to the whole.

**THINK ALOUD** How can you find the whole, or the *total*, number of middle schools?

You can construct a **relative frequency table** from the information in the bar graph.

**STEPS** Make a chart with three columns. Put the grade combinations in the first column.

Show each grade combination's frequency (the part) in the second column. Find the total number of schools (the whole).

Find the relative frequency by using a calculator to divide the part by the whole. Round the quotient to the nearest hundredth.

| Types of Middle Schools, 1970-71 | | |
|---|---|---|
| Grade Combination | Frequency (Part) | Relative Frequency (Part ÷ Whole) |
| 5–8 | 772 | 0.07 or 7% |
| 6–8 | 1,662 | ☐ or ☐ |
| 7–8 | 2,450 | ☐ or ☐ |
| 7–9 | ☐ | ☐ or ☐ |
| Other | ☐ | ☐ or ☐ |
| Total (whole) | 10,445 | |

The relative frequency of middle schools for grades 5–8 is about 0.07. In 1970–71, about 7% of all middle schools were for grades 5–8.

**THINK ALOUD** What grade combination does your school have? In 1970–71 what percent of middle schools had that combination?

---

### GUIDED PRACTICE

1. **CALCULATOR** Copy and complete the relative frequency table above. Round the relative frequencies to hundredths. Then write them as percents.

2. **THINK ALOUD** How do you think the data on page 388 about middle schools was obtained? Discuss the sample, the population, and the question(s) that may have been asked.

---
**PRACTICE**
---

Refer to your relative frequency table.

3. **ESTIMATE** Find a grade combination that
   a. occurred about twice as often as did grades 7–8.
   b. occurred almost half as often as did grades 6–8.
   c. occurred in about 1 out of every 4 middle schools.

4. **IN YOUR WORDS** Explain why the sum of the relative frequencies should always be close to 1.00, or 100%.

5. What is the sum of the relative frequencies in percents? Is it close to 1.00, or 100%?

---
**PROBLEM SOLVING**
---

Refer to the bar graph at right.

6. **CALCULATOR** Make a relative frequency table for types of middle schools in 1986–87. Round the relative frequencies to hundredths. Then write each relative frequency as a percent.

7. **ESTIMATE** Find a grade combination for 1986–1987 that fits the description.
   a. occurred about twice as often as did grades 7–9?
   b. occurred in about 1 out of every 10 middle schools?
   c. occurred in about $\frac{1}{4}$ of all middle schools?

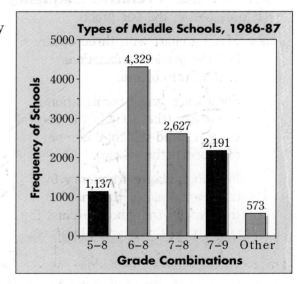

8. What is the mode for the grade combinations?

9. **IN YOUR WORDS** Explain how to find the mode by using either the bar graph or your relative frequency table.

10. **CREATE YOUR OWN** Make a double bar graph of the relative frequencies for 1970–1971 and 1986–87. Use it to predict which grade combination will be most common in 1997–98.

Write a sentence describing the relationship between the two terms.

**1.** sample, population

**2.** data items, mean

**3.** middle number, median

**4.** time, line graph

**QUICK QUIZ** ✓

Name the population and the sample. *(pages 378–379)*

**1.** A national mail order clothing company wants to know how customers feel about the quality of their products. They send questionnaires to customers in 5 states.

**2.** A TV game show hostess asks each viewer to send in a post card. The producer wants to determine the age range of the audience. Those who send in cards may win a prize. On a later show, the hostess draws 100 post cards from a drum.

Use the data from the table. *(pages 380–385, 388–389)*

The table shows Parent-Teacher Association membership in two schools for 4 years.

**3.** Make a double bar graph of this data.

**4.** Find the mean and the median of the Coolidge membership.

**5.** In what year was the Fillmore membership about $\frac{3}{4}$ of the 1991 Fillmore membership?

|      | Fillmore | Coolidge |
|------|----------|----------|
| 1988 | 85       | 112      |
| 1989 | 96       | 115      |
| 1990 | 108      | 130      |
| 1991 | 110      | 135      |

Solve. *(pages 386–387)*

**6.** The table shows the average price of gasoline during a 4-wk period.

  **a.** What was the average price of regular gasoline during week 3?

  **b.** How can you compare the average prices of the gasoline?

  **c.** What type of graph can be used to represent the average prices of both gasolines?

| Week | Regular | Premium |
|------|---------|---------|
| 1    | $1.09   | $1.28   |
| 2    | $1.15   | $1.25   |
| 3    | $1.17   | $1.39   |
| 4    | $1.21   | $1.43   |

**LEARNING LOG**

Write the answers in your learning log.

1. Explain the advantage of having a large sample when attempting to make predictions.

2. Your math test grades are 42, 100, 85, 82, and 88. Would you rather have your teacher use the mean or the median to represent your final grade? Explain.

**MATH AMERICA**

**DID YOU KNOW . . . ?** In 1976, the United States celebrated its bicentennial, or 200th, birthday. What birthday will your city or town celebrate this year? Express your city or town's age in centuries. Use fractions if necessary.

**BONUS**

Conduct a survey. Choose a representative sample of students from your grade. Ask them to name their favorite news broadcaster.

Consider these questions in conducting your survey:

- How will you get a representative sample?
- How many students will you need to ask?
- How can you best display your data?

Predict the results of your survey. How do the results compare with your prediction? Are they what you expected? How can you explain the results?

## Measuring Chance

What do you think is the chance that one of your classmates will become President of the United States tomorrow?

If you answered *no chance*, you are right. Mathematically, the probability of this happening is 0.

**Probability (*P*)** is a measure of chance.

- Events that are impossible have a probability of 0. The probability that a car traveling under its own power down the highway has no wheels is 0.

- Events that are certain to happen have a probability of 1. For example, the probability that the day after next Tuesday will be a Wednesday is 1.

- Events that are uncertain have a probability between 0 and 1. The probability of getting a head when tossing a penny is $\frac{1}{2}$, or 0.5.

=== GUIDED PRACTICE ===

1. **THINK ALOUD**   Give one example of the event.
   a. an event that has a probability of 0
   b. an event that has a probability of 1
   c. an event that has a probability between 0 and 1

2. Could the number represent a probability? Write *yes* or *no*.
   a. 5     b. $\frac{6}{10}$     c. 0.04     d. $1\frac{1}{5}$     e. 45%     f. 95     g. 150%

=== PRACTICE ===

Is the probability *0, 1,* or *between 0 and 1*?

3. You toss a nickel and it will land heads up.

4. You will drive a car to school tomorrow.

5. It will rain tomorrow.

6. It will snow somewhere in the Rocky Mountains next year.

Write the probability of the event. Then rewrite the sentence so that the probability is 0.

**7.** There will be at least one full moon in the spring.

**8.** March will follow February.

Write the probability of the event. Then rewrite the sentence so that the probability is between 0 and 1.

**9.** A cat will fly to the top of a tree to escape a dog.

**10.** Someone will be born in the United States today.

Is the probability statement close to the truth? Write *yes* or *no*. Explain your answer.

**11.** The probability that the next person you see will be a twin is 0.9.

**12.** The probability a new teacher will be left handed is $\frac{1}{6}$.

---

**PROBLEM SOLVING**

Use your number sense and the graph to solve.

**13.** In which city is the chance of rain closest to 0 for any random day?

**14.** In which city is the chance of rain greater than 50% on any random day?

**15.** List the cities in order from the least to the greatest according to the chance of rain on any random day.

**16.** **IN YOUR WORDS** Tell why probabilities range from 0 to 1.

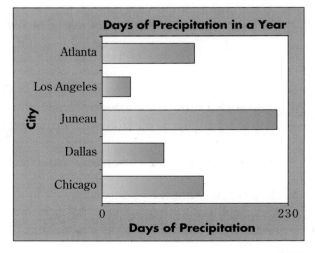

**Days of Precipitation in a Year**

City: Atlanta, Los Angeles, Juneau, Dallas, Chicago

0 — Days of Precipitation — 230

# *Equally Likely Outcomes*

Do you think the chances of spinning a 1, 2, 3, or 4 are the same, or equal, on each of these spinners?

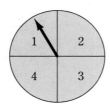

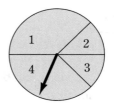

Yes, the chances are the same, because the regions are the same size. This spinner has equally likely outcomes.

No, the chances are not equal because the regions are not the same size.

Suppose you closed your eyes and drew one card from the hat. Does each card have an equally likely chance of being drawn?

No, each card does not have an equally likely chance because the folded card would feel different. The difference probably would be noticed by the person who is drawing.

A situation has **equally likely outcomes** when each result has the same chance of occurring.

## GUIDED PRACTICE

Write *yes or no*. Explain.

1. Are heads and tails equally likely outcomes in a penny toss?

2. You reach into your lunch bag with your eyes closed. Is the selection of the sandwich or of the orange equally likely?

3. Are even numbers and odd numbers equally likely outcomes on the toss of a 1–6 number cube?

4. Three different sandwiches, peanut butter, jelly, and peanut butter and jelly, are made with bread from the same loaf, wrapped in wax paper, and put in a bag. Is the selection of any one by reaching into the bag without looking equally likely?

5. Without looking, are you equally likely to draw a blue marble as a red marble from a bag that contains 6 red marbles and 3 blue marbles that are all the same size?

Write *equally likely* or *not equally likely* for the outcomes.

**6.** an even number or an odd number

**7.** red, blue, or green

**8.** green or yellow

**9.** rolling a 1, 2, 3, 4, 5, or 6 on a 1–6 number cube

**10.** rolling a composite number or a prime number on a 1–6 number cube

**11.** having 3, 4, 5, 6, or 7 letters in a person's first name

**12.** Either a male or a female will be the next new student to join your class.

**13.** The next person you meet will be left-handed or right-handed.

Blue and red are equally likely outcomes on the spinner at right. Is it likely that the data set comes from this spinner? Explain.

**14.** blue: 492
red: 508

**15.** blue: 249
red: 751

**16.** blue: 36
red: 41

**17.** blue: 912
red: 948

## Critical Thinking

**1.** You ask a person to select one of the numbers, 1, 2, 3, or 4. Do you think that all four outcomes are equally likely?

**2.** Work in a group of four. Each of you should ask 25 people to select one of the numbers *1, 2, 3,* or *4.* Compile your data on one tally sheet. Does it appear that each of the choices was equally likely? Why or why not?

**3.** If you asked another 100 people the same question, do you think your results would change greatly? Explain.

## *Exploring the Meaning of Probability*

Mrs. Foy ran an experiment with her class. She put 12 cubes of the same size and shape in a bag. Some cubes were green. Some were blue.

**THINK ALOUD**  Is the probability of drawing a blue cube *0, 1,* or *between 0 and 1*?

Each of her 25 students took 2 turns drawing a cube from the bag without looking. After each draw, the cube was returned to the bag and the bag was shaken. Each cube in the bag had an equally likely chance of being drawn.

The results of the 50 draws in this experiment were tallied as shown.

| Blue | ‖‖ ‖‖ ‖‖ ‖‖ ‖‖ ‖‖ ‖‖ | 32 |
|---|---|---|
| Green | ‖‖ ‖‖ ‖‖ ‖‖ | 18 |

The relative frequency of an outcome is its **experimental probability.** For blue, it was 32 out of 50, or $\frac{32}{50}$. For green, it was 18 out of 50, or $\frac{18}{50}$.

With a large number of trials, the experimental probability gives a good estimate of the **actual probability**. Sometimes you can tell the actual probability by looking at the possible outcomes. Then you would use the following ratio.

Probability ($P$) of an event $= \dfrac{\text{number of favorable outcomes}}{\text{total number of possible outcomes}}$

Mrs. Foy emptied the bag so that the students could look at the cubes and find the actual probabilities.

$$P \text{ (blue)} = \frac{\text{number of blue cubes}}{\text{total number of cubes}} = \frac{8}{12}, \text{ or } \frac{2}{3}$$

$$P \text{ (green)} = \frac{\text{number of green cubes}}{\text{total number of cubes}} = \frac{4}{12}, \text{ or } \frac{1}{3}$$

You write $P$ (blue). You say, "the probability of blue."
You write $P$ (green). You say, "the probability of green."

1. **THINK ALOUD**  How close was the experimental probability to the actual probability for drawing a blue cube? a green cube?

Some students experimented with tossing a 1–6 number cube 60 times. The table shows the tally for the frequency of each number tossed.

| | |
|---|---|
| 1: 𝍸 \|\|\| | 4: 𝍸 𝍸 |
| 2: 𝍸 𝍸 \|\| | 5: 𝍸 𝍸 |
| 3: 𝍸 𝍸 \| | 6: 𝍸 \|\|\|\| |

**2.** Use the data table. Write the experimental probability as a fraction and as a decimal.

**a.** tossing a 4  **b.** tossing a 3

**3.** Look at the 1–6 cube. Find the actual probability as a fraction and as a decimal.

**a.** tossing a 4  **b.** tossing a 3

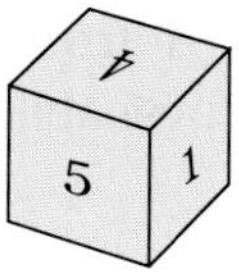


**4.** Use a number cube to do a probability experiment. Work with a partner. Toss the cube 80 times. Tally your results. What experimental probabilities do you find for each outcome in Exercise 3?

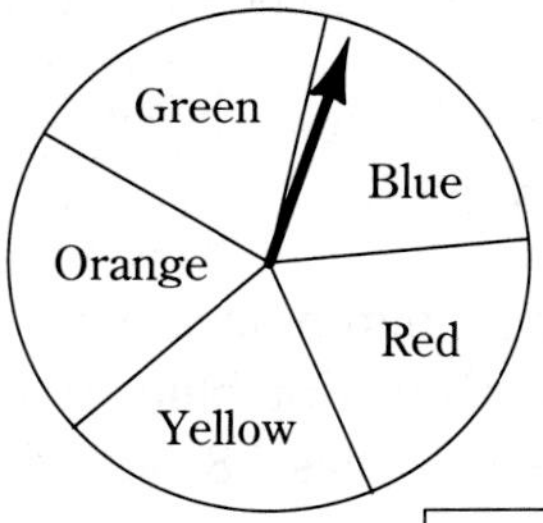


Some students spun a spinner like the one at right 100 times and recorded the results below.

**5.** Find the experimental probability and the actual probability for the event. Write each as a fraction, as a decimal, and as a percent.

**a.** spinning red  **b.** spinning green

**c.** spinning yellow  **d.** spinning red or yellow

| | |
|---|---|
| Red | 17 |
| Yellow | 21 |
| Orange | 18 |
| Green | 19 |
| Blue | 25 |

**6. THINK ALOUD** How do you think the experimental probability and the actual probability for each of the events in Exercise 5 will compare after 20 spins? after 500 spins?

**7.** Work with a partner. Use a five-section spinner like the one above. Complete 100 trials. How do your experimental probabilities compare to those in Exercise 5?

**8. CREATE YOUR OWN** Work in a small group. Design a probability experiment using different-colored objects of the same size, such as marbles or pencils. Find the experimental probability and the actual probability for the event(s) in your experiment.

## Exploring Good Estimates of Probability

Playing the Guess $P(X)$ game with a partner will help you explore some ideas about probability. Player 1 will know the actual probability of selecting an $X$ from looking at the squares. Player 2 will try to determine the probability by using experimental data.

### GUESS P(X)

Materials:   6 small squares (3 labeled with $X$, 3 labeled with $O$).

a calculator

a record sheet like this one for each player:

| | | | | | | |
|---|---|---|---|---|---|---|
| Is it $X$ or $O$? | | | | | | |
| How many $X$'s so far? | | | | | | |
| How many looks so far? | | | | | | |
| Relative frequency $\left(\frac{X\text{'s}}{\text{Looks}}\right)$ | | | | | | |

Rules:

1. Player 1 turns all the squares face down and mixes them. Player 2 points to three squares.

2. Player 1 looks at the three squares, places them face down in a row, and puts the others aside.

3. Player 2 chooses one of the squares, looks at it, answers the three questions on the record sheet, calculates and writes the relative frequency, and puts back the square face down.

4. Player 1 mixes the three squares again.

5. Player 2 repeats the steps in rule 3.

6. Play continues until Player 2 wants to guess the probability of turning over an $X$. (Choices are $0$, $\frac{1}{3}$, $\frac{2}{3}$, or $1$.)

7. Both players look at the three squares and calculate the actual probability. If the guess is correct, Player 2 receives 1 point for each look. If not, Player 2 receives 25 points.

8. Players change roles for the next round. After four rounds, the player with the lower score wins.

1. **THINK ALOUD** What happens to the relative frequency as you take more looks?

2. **CRITICAL THINKING** What is the highest relative frequency possible? What would it indicate? What is the lowest relative frequency possible? What would it indicate?

3. **THINK ALOUD** How is the relative frequency used to estimate the probability of choosing a square with an $X$?

4. Use your record sheet from a game. Change the relative frequencies to decimals. Write the decimals for each round in a row in the order of play. Look for patterns that describe how the relative frequency changes in the earlier part of a round as compared with how it changes in the later part of a round.

5. **CRITICAL THINKING** When you play a round of this game, the first relative frequencies usually vary greatly. Later in a round, they tend to stabilize. Why do you think this happens?

> **The Law of Large Numbers says that if you run a large number of experiments, the experimental probability you find will be close to the actual probability.**

6. During a round of the Guess $P(X)$ game, a player turned over these squares in 16 looks: $O, O, X, X, X, O, X, X, O, X, O, X, X, X, O, O$. Make a relative frequency table for the data. Change the relative frequencies to decimals and write them in order of play. What pattern do you see?

7. **CRITICAL THINKING** How would you change the rules to play this game with ten squares?

8. **NUMBER SENSE** Suppose you are playing this game with 100 squares, 50 with $X$'s and 50 with $O$'s. Fifty squares have been turned over and you are Player 2. About how many looks would you want to take before you would guess the probability using the Law of Large Numbers? Explain.

T = Boys          H = Girls

| Coin 1 | Coin 2 | Coin 3 |
|--------|--------|--------|
| H | T | T |
| H | H | H |
| T | T | H |
| H | T | H |
| T | T | T |
| T | H | T |
| H | T | H |
| T | H | T |
| H | H | T |
| H | H | T |
| H | H | H |
| H | H | T |
| T | H | T |
| H | T | H |
| H | T | H |
| H | H | T |
| T | H | T |
| H | H | T |
| T | H | T |
| T | H | T |
| T | H | T |
| T | T | T |
| T | H | H |
| H | H | T |
| T | T | T |
| H | T | H |
| T | H | H |
| T | T | T |
| T | T | T |
| H | H | H |
| T | T | T |
| T | H | H |
| H | T | T |
| T | H | H |
| H | T | H |
| H | T | T |
| H | H | H |
| H | H | T |
| T | T | T |
| T | H | T |
| T | H | T |
| H | T | T |
| H | H | H |
| T | H | T |
| H | H | T |
| T | T | H |
| H | H | T |
| H | H | T |
| H | H | T |

# Problem Solving:
## Simulation

Some probability problems are solved using an experiment that imitates the problem. This kind of experiment is called a **simulation**. A simulation gives a good estimate of the actual probability of an event.

Mr. and Mrs. Otero have no children yet. What is the probability that the three children they want to have will all be boys?

You can simulate this problem with a random device.

**STEPS** Select a random device. The toss of a coin could represent a child's position in a family. Tails (T) could represent a boy. Heads (H) could represent a girl.

Design the event. A family of three children could be simulated by tossing three coins.

Find the desired event. Having three coins land tails up (T, T, T) could represent a three-boy family.

Use the Law of Large Numbers. Run 500 events. The relative frequency of three tails will be a good estimate of the probability of a three-boy family.

These were the results after 500 tosses of three coins.

| Event | Frequency | Event | Frequency |
|-------|-----------|-------|-----------|
| (T, T, T) | 65 | (H, H, T) | 65 |
| (T, T, H) | 59 | (H, T, H) | 62 |
| (T, H, T) | 62 | (T, H, H) | 61 |
| (H, T, T) | 66 | (H, H, H) | 60 |

**NUMBER SENSE** Why do these events all represent different types of families?

**THINK ALOUD** Use the data to find the relative frequency of three-boy families. What is the experimental probability that a couple's three children will all be boys?

================ GUIDED PRACTICE ================

1. Look at the frequency table to answer.
   **a.** How many different types of families are possible?
   **b.** How many of these family types are all boys?
   **c.** What is the actual probability of a three-boy family?

2. **THINK ALOUD**   Discuss how the experimental probability and the actual probability compare for a family in which all three children are boys.

3. Consider a family with a girl born first and then two boys born later.
   a. Which event represents this kind of family?
   b. How many times did this event occur in the simulation?
   c. What is the relative frequency of this event as a percent?
   d. What is the experimental probability of this event as a percent?

Use the frequency table on page 400 to answer.

4. Which event represents a three-girl family? What is the frequency of this event?

5. What is the relative frequency of a three-girl family as a percent?

6. What is the experimental probability of a three-girl family?

7. What is the actual probability of a three-girl family? How does this compare with the experimental probability?

8. Which event represents a family with two girls born first and then a boy? What are the experimental probability and the actual probability for this event?

**CHOOSE**  Choose any strategy to solve.

9. The number of different ways that three coins can be tossed is eight. How many different ways can four coins be tossed?

10. Jorge told his brother to walk 4 blocks north of their house, to turn left and walk 2 blocks, to turn left again and walk 3 more blocks, and to turn left one more time and walk 3 blocks to find their meeting place. After his brother left, Jorge cut across one block to get to the meeting place. In what direction did he go?

11. Marta gave her sister Juana 60¢. She gave her at least one quarter, one dime, one nickel, and one penny. How many different ways could Marta have given Juana 60¢?

## Mixed Review

**Carnival** in Rio de Janiero, Brazil

Compute.

**1.** $694 \times 36$   **2.** $674 - 433.76$   **3.** $87.89 + 268.54$   **4.** $1,627.5 \div 2.5$

**5.** $\frac{6}{8} \div \frac{3}{4}$   **6.** $6\frac{2}{3} \times 5\frac{1}{2}$   **7.** $2\frac{1}{6} + 2\frac{1}{4}$   **8.** $5\frac{1}{4} - 2\frac{1}{2}$

Make a true proportion by solving for $n$.

**9.** $\frac{6}{8} = \frac{9}{n}$   **10.** $\frac{n}{21} = \frac{1}{3}$   **11.** $\frac{8}{n} = \frac{14}{56}$   **12.** $\frac{12}{16} = \frac{n}{36}$

Write as a percent.

**13.** $0.16$   **14.** $0.95$   **15.** $1$   **16.** $\frac{3}{4}$   **17.** $0.04$

Write as a decimal.

**18.** $\frac{1}{2}$   **19.** $100\%$   **20.** $37\frac{1}{2}\%$   **21.** $50\%$   **22.** $19.1\%$

Find the unknown.

**23.** What percent is 15 out of 60?   **24.** What is 80% of 60?

**25.** 75% of what number is 48?   **26.** What percent is 17 out of 68?

**27.** What is 40% of 75?   **28.** 65% of what number is 156?

**29.** What percent is 72 out of 300?   **30.** What is 25% of 496?

**31.** 20% of what number is 105?   **32.** What percent is 232 out of 400?

**33.** What is 12.5% of 2?   **34.** 35% of what number is 210?

Use the graph and the map. Choose pencil and paper, calculator, or estimation to solve.

**35.** Every spring, in Rio de Janeiro's famous *Carnival*, neighborhoods compete to have the showiest costumes and parades. *Carnival* lasts for 4 days and 4 nights. For about what percent of 1 wk does it last?

**36.** About how many times greater was Brazil's population in 1900 than in 1800?

**37.** About how many times greater will Brazil's population be in the year 2000 than it was in 1900?

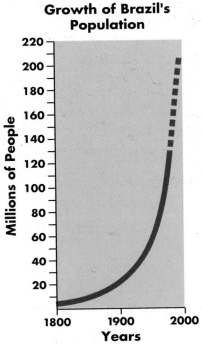

**38.** In 1960, Brazil's capital was moved from Rio de Janeiro to Brasilia. Use the scale and a ruler to find the approximate distance between Rio de Janeiro and Brasilia.

**39.** When swollen by rain, the Amazon River flows at about 3 mi/h, which is about 200% of its average speed. About what is its average speed?

**40.** From 1930, when the competition was first held, to 1990, soccer's World Cup has been played 14 times and Brazil has won it 3 times. About what percent of the time has Brazil won the World Cup?

# Making Decisions About After-School Activities ✎

How do you go about making decisions? You can use a chart in the decision-making process.

In the chart below, Alice analyzed three after-school activities according to four factors. A score of *1, 2,* or *3* shows the rank, or importance, of each factor, with 3 being the *most important* for a factor and 1 being the *least important*.

| FACTOR | SCHOOL NEWSPAPER | SWIM TEAM | GUITAR LESSONS |
|---|---|---|---|
| COST | 3 | 2 | 1 |
| TIME | 2 | 1 | 3 |
| STATUS | 2 | 3 | 1 |
| FUN | 2 | 1 | 3 |

For example, Alice ranked the cost factor because she wants to spend as little money as possible. Taking guitar lessons gets a score of 1 because it is the most expensive choice. Joining the swim team gets a score of 2 because it is less expensive than guitar lessons. Working on the school newspaper gets a score of 3 because it is free.

Work with a partner. Use the data on page 404 to solve.

1. Alice did not want to spend a lot of time on after-school activities. According to the ranking, which activity is the least time consuming? the most time consuming?

2. Which activity does Alice consider the most fun? the least fun?

3. Total the scores for each activity. Which activity received the highest score? Would you rank these activities in the same way? Explain.

The factors themselves in a decision-making chart may be weighted to show the value assigned to them by the chart maker. In this expanded chart, Alice has weighted the factors according to her personal preferences. Her weighted scores range from 10 (*most important*) to 1 (*least important*).

| FACTOR | WEIGHT | SCHOOL NEWSPAPER | | SWIM TEAM | | GUITAR LESSONS | |
|---|---|---|---|---|---|---|---|
| | | SCORE | WEIGHTED SCORE | SCORE | WEIGHTED SCORE | SCORE | WEIGHTED SCORE |
| COST | 6 | 3 | 18 | 2 | | 1 | |
| TIME | 5 | 2 | | 1 | | 3 | |
| STATUS | 1 | 2 | | 3 | | 1 | |
| FUN | 10 | 2 | | 1 | | 3 | |

4. According to the chart, which factor, the time involved or the amount of fun, is more important to Alice? Explain.

5. Copy and complete the chart. Find the total of the weighted scores for each activity. Which activity is now valued most?

6. When you create a decision-making chart, you can include any factors. For example, in the chart above you might include *Friends involved* and assign a score of 3 if there are many friends participating in the activity. What other factors might you add to the chart?

7. You must also decide upon the scoring and weighting system you will use. What are some advantages of scoring an activity from 10 to 1 instead of from 3 to 1? What are some disadvantages?

8. Working alone, create your own decision-making chart for out-of-school activities. Share your chart with the class.

════════════════ LANGUAGE & VOCABULARY ════════════════

Write *true* or *false*. If *false*, tell why.

1. Every event has a probability of at least 0 and at most 1.

2. If a situation has 2 equally likely outcomes and 20 trials are done, the results will always be 10 of each outcome.

3. A simulation with a large number of trials will always give the actual probability of the event.

─────────────────── TEST  ───────────────────

════════════════ CONCEPTS ════════════════

Name the population and the sample. *(pages 378–379)*

1. A guidance counselor wants to know how many seventh graders want to start a class newspaper. She asks the seventh grade students with whom she meets on Monday.

2. A radio station wants to know how its audience feels about an issue. Listeners are asked to call and express their opinions.

Use the data in the table. *(pages 394–397)*

3. If you randomly choose 1 student from class 7-315, what is the probability that the student was absent in September?

4. Each month, one student with perfect attendance is honored by selecting a name at random. During which month was there an equally likely chance that the student chosen was from either class?

Students with Perfect Attendance

|  | Class 7-305 (20 students) | Class 7-315 (18 students) |
|---|---|---|
| September | 15 | 18 |
| October | 13 | 13 |
| November | 8 | 11 |
| December | 12 | 13 |

════════════════ SKILLS ════════════════

Use the data from the table above. *(pages 382–383, 388–389)*

5. Find the mean number of students in class 7-305 with perfect attendance from September through December.

**6.** In class 7-305, during which month was the relative frequency of students with perfect attendance 65%?

Is the probability *0, 1,* or *between 0 and 1*? *(pages 392–393)*

**7.** May 1998, will follow July 1998.

**8.** Monday, May 17, will follow Sunday, May 16.

━━━━━━━━━━━ **PROBLEM SOLVING** ━━━━━━━━━━━

**9.** Use the data from the table on page 406. *(pages 386–387)*

   **a.** During which month was the total number of students with perfect attendance the lowest?

   **b.** What type of graphs can be used to compare the number of students with perfect attendance during the 4 mo?

   **c.** Why would a line graph not be appropriate to compare the number of students absent in September?

Use a simulation. *(pages 400–401)*

**10.** One of 8 different posters is packed inside a music magazine. Stanley wants to predict the number of magazines he would have to buy in order to collect all 8 posters. He ran a simulation using the spinner and tallied his results.

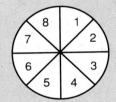

Poster 1: |||      Poster 2: |      Poster 3: ||||      Poster 4: ┼┼┼┼

Poster 5: |||      Poster 6: |||      Poster 7: ||||      Poster 8: ||

How many magazines did Stanley's simulation tell him he would need to buy?

**11.** During 4 consecutive weeks a ski resort had the following amounts of snow: 15 in., 13 in., 8 in., and 12 in. What was the mean weekly amount of snow?

**LEARNING LOG**

Write the answers in your learning log.

  **1.** Describe what is meant by "chance."

  **2.** When you roll two number cubes, how would you determine what sums are equally likely to occur?

# EXTRA PRACTICE

Name the population and the sample. *(pages 378–379)*

1. A college wants to know about the interests of its freshman students. A questionnaire is sent to all students whose last name begins with the letter *S*.

2. To learn about their customers' tastes, a music store questions every tenth person who enters the store.

Use the data from the table. *(pages 380–385, 388–389)*

3. Make a double bar graph of the data.

4. Find the mean weekly sales for each store.

5. During which week did Sounds sell about 40% of its monthly total of CD players?

CD Players Sold in Two Stores

| Week of | Tunetown | Sounds |
|---------|----------|--------|
| June 3  | 38       | 29     |
| June 10 | 52       | 72     |
| June 17 | 102      | 128    |
| June 24 | 85       | 96     |

6. Find the relative frequency of Tunetown's June 3 weekly sales compared to its monthly total.

Is the probability *0, 1,* or *between 0 and 1*? *(pages 392–393)*

7. Humans will walk on Mars this year.

8. Humans will walk on Mars during the 21st century.

Write *equally likely* or *not equally likely* for the outcomes in the situation. *(pages 394–395)*

9. Rolling an even or odd number on a cube numbered 1 through 6.

10. Tossing 1 coin and the results being 1 head.

Solve. *(pages 386–387, 400–401)*

11. What type of graph can be used to represent the data set? The average daily temperature in Seattle, Washington during July.

12. Sandy has 6 sweaters she wants to wear, but she wants to vary the order in which she wears them. She ran a simulation using a number cube and got these results:

    3    1    4    3    6    5    1    3    2

    If each number represents a different sweater, how many days would it take for her to wear all 6 sweaters?

## GRAPHS IN ADS

Companies often use graphs in their advertisements. When used properly, a graph can make information clear to the reader. However, sometimes graphs are included only because they look official and the information in the graph may have little to do with the claim being made for the product.

Work with a group. Find several advertisements in newspapers or magazines that use graphs. Write a short paragraph summarizing your feelings about the effectiveness of the graphs you have found.

## WHAT'S NORMAL

Words like *normal*, *typical*, and *average* are used in conversation, in the written media (newspapers, magazines), and on radio and television every day. Some examples are references to *normal* rainfall for a day, the height of the *typical* person, or the *average* price of shares of stock. These words may refer to the mean, median, or mode of a set of data.

Find references using the words *normal*, *typical*, or *average*. For each one decide whether it refers to the mean, median, or mode of the data being considered. You may not be able to determine which was intended. If you cannot tell, make a note of that also. Decide which of the three, mean, median, or mode, is used most commonly.

# Pizza Pieces

You can slice a pizza into 2 pieces with 1 cut. You can slice a pizza into 4 pieces with 2 cuts. Show how you can slice a pizza into 7 pieces with 3 cuts. What is the greatest number of pieces you can slice with 4 cuts?

Find the answer.

**1.** $3\frac{1}{5} \times 1\frac{7}{8}$

   **a.** $3\frac{7}{40}$

   **b.** $4\frac{7}{40}$

   **c.** 6

   **d.** none of these

**2.** $\frac{3}{8} \div 4$

   **a.** $\frac{3}{32}$

   **b.** $1\frac{1}{2}$

   **c.** $\frac{3}{8}$

   **d.** none of these

**3.** $12\frac{1}{2} \div \frac{2}{3}$

   **a.** $8\frac{1}{3}$

   **b.** $25\frac{2}{3}$

   **c.** $18\frac{3}{4}$

   **d.** none of these

**4.** An angle less than 90° is
   **a.** obtuse
   **b.** acute
   **c.** straight
   **d.** none of these

**5.** An angle of exactly 180° is
   **a.** acute
   **b.** right
   **c.** obtuse
   **d.** none of these

**6.** Circumference of circle: $d = 9$m, $\pi \approx 3.14$
   **a.** 28.26 m
   **b.** 14.1 m
   **c.** 63.6 m
   **d.** none of these

**7.** $\frac{3}{20} = \underline{\ ?\ }$
   **a.** 30%
   **b.** 20%
   **c.** 15%
   **d.** none of these

**8.** $0.062 = \underline{\ ?\ }$
   **a.** 0.62%
   **b.** 6.2%
   **c.** 62%
   **d.** none of these

**9.** $18.5\% = \underline{\ ?\ }$
   **a.** 0.0185
   **b.** $\frac{185}{1000}$
   **c.** 18.5
   **d.** none of these

**10.** $3.72 = \underline{\ ?\ }$
   **a.** 372%
   **b.** 37.2%
   **c.** 0.372%
   **d.** none of these

**11.** $\frac{207}{100} = \underline{\ ?\ }$
   **a.** 20.7%
   **b.** 0.207%
   **c.** 2.07%
   **d.** none of these

**12.** $0.8\% = \underline{\ ?\ }$
   **a.** 0.8
   **b.** 0.08
   **c.** 0.008
   **d.** none of these

Find the matching value.

**13.** 2 yd 3 in.
   **a.** 27 in.
   **b.** 75 in.
   **c.** 39 in.
   **d.** none of these

**14.** 1 gal 2 pt
   **a.** 20 c
   **b.** 16 c
   **c.** 12 c
   **d.** none of these

**15.** 3 lb 1 oz
   **a.** 17 oz
   **b.** 49 oz
   **c.** 97 oz
   **d.** none of these

# PROBLEM SOLVING REVIEW

**Problem Solving Check List**

- Too much information
- Too little information
- Multistep problems
- Using guess and check
- Using percents
- Using estimation
- Drawing a picture

Remember the strategies and types of problems you've had so far. Solve.

1. One hundred students were asked to name their favorite pet. Twenty eight percent chose a cat, 23% a parrot, and 7% a lizard. The rest chose a dog.

   a. What percent of the students chose a cat as their favorite?

   b. Which pet was preferred by the most students?

   c. How many more students chose a dog than a lizard?

2. After filling her car's gas tank, Shirley went on a 300-mi trip. The gas tank holds 12 gal and the car averages 42 mi/gal. To the nearest gallon, how much gas was left after the trip?

3. Oak Street is 16 blocks long. A traffic signal is to be placed at every other intersection along Oak Street and at both ends. How many traffic signals are needed?

4. A phone call costs $.25 for the first 3 min and $.10 for each additional minute, but on weekends, the first 3 min are $.20 and each extra minute is $.07. How much cheaper is a 15-min call on the weekend?

5. After math class, $\frac{1}{3}$ of the students went to gym. Of those that were left, $\frac{1}{2}$ went to lunch and the rest of the students stayed to talk with their teacher. How many went to the gym?

6. Vivian and Richard were running for class president. A total of 347 votes were cast. Vivian received 79 votes more than Richard. How many votes did each candidate receive?

7. A spinner has 8 equal sections. Six sections are green and two are red. In 500 spins, about how many times would you expect the spinner to stop on green?

8. Four boys determine that the mean of their heights is 60 in. If a 5th boy joins them, how tall must he be if the mean height of the 5 boys is 61 in.?

9. A rectangular picture measuring 5 in. by 8 in. is in a rectangular frame that measures 9 in. by 12 in. What is the area of the border?

10. Last week, Jason's after-school job paid him $24.00 plus a 15% bonus. What were his total earnings for the week?

## I'LL TAKE $7\frac{1}{2}$ ▦

A large insurance company employs 40,580 people. A sample was taken of 1,250 of those employees. Of those sampled, 500 were in favor of an 8-h workday, instead of the $7\frac{1}{2}$-h workday they currently have.

How many of the 40,580 would you expect to be in favor of the longer work day? How many more hours will be worked for the company in one day if the company goes to an 8-h work day?

## STARTING SALARIES ▦

The annual salaries of the 20 employees of a company are:

$14,280; $15,490; $15,575; $16,280;

$16,575; $17,200; $17,485; $20,450;

$26,475; $32,571; $32,890; $32,927;

$33,100; $33,250; $34,800; $34,956;

$35,103; $36,428; $36,792; $50,211

Sam joined the company, and will earn $\frac{1}{2}$ the sum of the median plus the mean. What is Sam's salary?

## SIMPLY CIRCULAR 💻

In the computer activity *Animal Farm*, you must shift two types of animals in and out of a pen until you reach a target ratio of one type of animal to the total number of animals. This activity will help you work with ratios in this way.

Look at the initial ratio in each problem below. Try to change this to the target ratio in exactly the number of steps indicated by the spaces. At each step you add or subtract just one black or white circle.

| | | Initial Ratio | Steps | Target |
|---|---|---|---|---|
| 1. | white circles / circles in all | $\frac{3}{4}$ | | $\frac{1}{4}$ |
| 2. | black circles / circles in all | $\frac{5}{6}$ | | $\frac{3}{8}$ |

**DID YOU KNOW . . . ?**

The baseball card for rookie Mickey Mantle, issued in 1952, recently sold for $6,000!

The bar graph shows how the values of some collectors' items have changed over the last 10 yr.

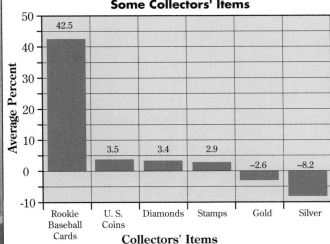

**Average Percent of Increase or Decrease Some Collectors' Items**

| Collectors' Items | Average Percent |
|---|---|
| Rookie Baseball Cards | 42.5 |
| U.S. Coins | 3.5 |
| Diamonds | 3.4 |
| Stamps | 2.9 |
| Gold | −2.6 |
| Silver | −8.2 |

**USING DATA**

Collect
Organize
**Describe**
Predict

Describe what happened to the value of silver in the last 10 yr.

About how many times greater is the percent of increase in the value of rookie baseball cards than the value of stamps in the last 10 yr?

## Integers

Pensacola, Florida, is about 5 m above sea level, and New Orleans, Louisiana, is about 1 m below sea level.

Distances above and below sea level can be recorded using positive and negative numbers. To record Pensacola's altitude you can write $^+5$ or 5. For the altitude of New Orleans, you can write $^-1$.

The numbers $^+5$ and $^-1$ are called **integers**. The set of integers is made up of the counting numbers (1, 2, 3, . . .), their opposites ($^-1$, $^-2$, $^-3$, . . .), and 0.

**THINK ALOUD**  Why is 5 the same as $^+5$?

Integers can be graphed on a number line. Numbers to the left of 0 are negative and those to the right of 0 are positive.

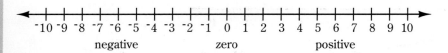

The numbers 7 and $^-7$ are opposites. **Opposite numbers** are on opposite sides of 0 but are the same distance from 0. The distance an integer is from 0 is called its **absolute value**.

The absolute value of 7 is 7. We write: $|7| = 7$.
The absolute value of $^-7$ is 7. We write: $|^-7| = 7$.

Other examples:

| Number | Opposite |
|---|---|
| 15° below zero ($^-15°$) | 15° above zero (15°) |
| 8 s before liftoff ($^-8$ s) | 8 s after liftoff (8 s) |

**THINK ALOUD**  What is the absolute value of $^-15$? of 15? Do opposites have the same absolute value?

===== GUIDED PRACTICE =====

Use the number line. Write the integer, its opposite, and its absolute value.

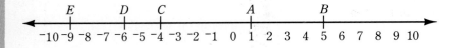

**1.** $A$      **2.** $B$      **3.** $C$      **4.** $D$      **5.** $E$

MATH AND GEOGRAPHY

Name the opposite in words. Write the original number and its opposite as integers.

**6.** You owe $6.  **7.** 5 mi north  **8.** The temperature is 5° below 0.

Name the opposite of the integer.

**9.** 1  **10.** 6  **11.** ⁻6  **12.** ⁻9  **13.** 5

Write the absolute value of the integer.

**14.** ⁻3  **15.** ⁻12  **16.** 45  **17.** ⁻62  **18.** ⁻100

**19. NUMBER SENSE** What number is its own opposite?

**20. NUMBER SENSE** Name the opposite of the opposite of ⁻2.

Copy the number line. Graph the integer and name its opposite.

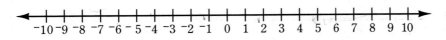

**21.** 6  **22.** ⁻6  **23.** 8  **24.** ⁻4  **25.** ⁻2

**26.** Name two integers that are 7 units from 0.

**27.** Name two integers that have an absolute value of 7.

**28. CRITICAL THINKING** Tell the value(s) of $n$.

 **a.** $n = |23|$  **b.** $|n| = 23$  **c.** $|-n| = 23$

**MENTAL MATH** Name the next three integers in the pattern.

**29.** ⁻8, ⁻5, ⁻2, ▦, ▦, ▦  **30.** 18, 10, 2, ▦, ▦, ▦

Use the graph.

**31.** How far (in meters) is Death Valley below sea level?

**32.** How far (in meters) above sea level is Shreveport, Louisiana?

**33.** Name the listed city that is the least above sea level.

**34.** Denver, Colorado, is called the mile-high city. Write its altitude as an integer.

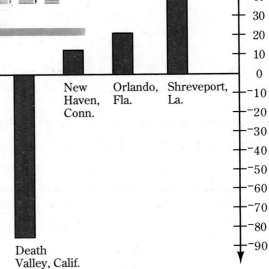

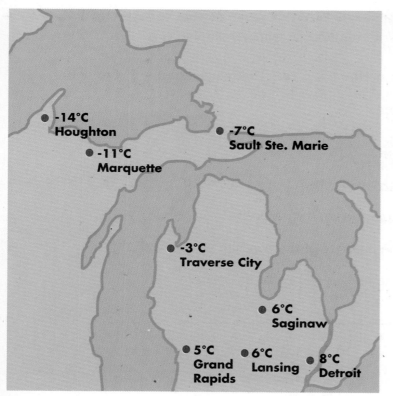

## Comparing and Ordering Integers

Temperature is measured in degrees Celsius (°C) in the metric system. The weather map shows some expected high temperatures for some Michigan cities on a day in February.

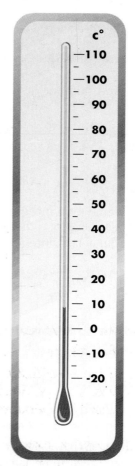

Since numbers above 0 are greater than numbers below 0, they represent a warmer temperature than those below 0.

5°C is warmer than ⁻14°C
5°C > ⁻14°C

A number line is often used to compare integers.

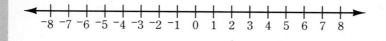

5 is to the right of ⁻3. → 5 > ⁻3 *or* ⁻3 < 5
⁻8 is to the left of 6. → ⁻8 < 6 *or* 6 > ⁻8

**THINK ALOUD**  Locate any two integers on the number line. Is the integer to the left always less than the integer to the right?

══════════════ **GUIDED PRACTICE** ══════════════

Use the number line to compare. Write *left* or *right* for the first blank, and choose < or > for the second blank.

1. 4 is to the ▦ of 3. 4 ▦ 3

2. ⁻1 is to the ▦ of 0. ⁻1 ▦ 0

3. ⁻5 is to the ▦ of ⁻4. ⁻5 ▦ ⁻4

4. ⁻3 is to the ▦ of ⁻6. ⁻3 ▦ ⁻6

MATH AND GEOGRAPHY

Name the integer.

**5.** two to the left of 0

**6.** five to the right of 0

**7.** three to the left of ⁻1

**8.** six to the right of ⁻3

Compare. Choose >, <, or =.

**9.** 2 ▧ 4

**10.** ⁻2 ▧ ⁻4

**11.** 4 ▧ ⁻2

**12.** ⁻4 ▧ 2

**13.** ⁻6 ▧ ⁻8

**14.** ⁻14 ▧ ⁻6

**15.** ⁻7 ▧ 0

**16.** ⁻3 ▧ 5

**17.** |⁻5| ▧ |3|

**18.** |⁻6| ▧ |⁻4|

**19.** |⁻12| ▧ |8|

**20.** |⁻3| ▧ |3|

**MENTAL MATH** Write in order from the least to the greatest.

**21.** ⁻8, 4, ⁻7, 2

**22.** 5, ⁻7, ⁻10, 3

**23.** ⁻12, 4, ⁻9, 6

**24.** 0, ⁻2, 4, ⁻3, 2

**25.** ⁻8, 6, |⁻2|, ⁻4

**26.** 0, |⁻1|, 6, |2|, ⁻4

**NUMBER SENSE** Write the next three integers in the pattern.

**27.** 5, 3, 1, ⁻1, ___, ___, ___

**28.** ⁻8, ⁻6, ⁻4, ___, ___, ___

**29.** 10, 5, 0, ⁻5, ___, ___, ___

**30.** 10, ⁻10, 20, ⁻20, 30, ___, ___, ___

Use the table to solve.

**31.** Which state had the highest record temperature? the lowest record temperature?

**32.** Record the low temperatures in order from least to greatest.

**33.** What is the difference between the least and greatest record low temperatures?

**34.** For which state does the absolute value of the record high and the record low differ by 1°C?

### Record Lowest and Highest Temperature to Nearest °C

| State | Lowest | Highest |
|-------|--------|---------|
| Alaska | ⁻62 | 38 |
| Florida | ⁻19 | 43 |
| Indiana | ⁻37 | 47 |
| Michigan | ⁻46 | 45 |
| North Dakota | ⁻51 | 49 |
| Virginia | ⁻34 | 43 |

## *Exploring a Model for Integers*

Benjamin Franklin discovered many properties of electricity. He suggested calling opposite electrical charges positive and negative. The idea of charged particles can be used to help you understand operations with integers.

You can use cubes or models to represent charged particles. Choose one color to represent positively charged particles, or positive integers, and a different color to represent negatively charged particles, or negative integers. Use a sheet of paper as a workmat.

Let ▆ represent the integer 1. Let ▢ represent the integer ⁻1.

The workmat at right contains 3 ▆ charges. The integer represented is 3.

**1.** Place 4 ▢ on your workmat. What integer is represented?

**2.** Clear your workmat. Put 5 ▆ on it. What integer is represented?

**3.** Represent the integer with charged particles.

   **a.** ⁻2        **b.** ⁻5        **c.** ⁻8        **d.** ⁺6

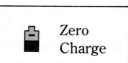
Zero Charge

The ▆ and the ▢ are opposite charges. When you combine a ▆ and a ▢, a zero charge results.

Show 7 ▆ on your workmat. Then place 3 ▢ on it.

**4.** How many ▢ charges can you make?

**5.** Make the zero charges. What integer is represented? Remove the zero charges. What integer is represented now?

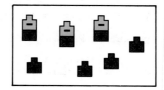

**6.** **IN YOUR WORDS** Explain why removing the 3 zero charges doesn't change the integer represented.

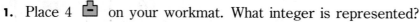

7. Show 5 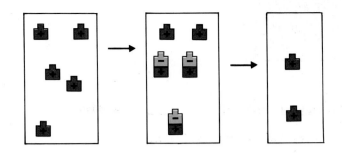 on your workmat. Put on 3 ☐. Make as many zero charges as you can and then remove them. What integer is represented by the remaining charges?

Follow the directions. Tell what integer is represented.

8. Show 4 ☐ . Put on 3 ☐ .

9. Show 3 ☐ . Put on 8 ☐ .

10. Show 7 ☐ . Put on 5 ☐ .

11. Show 2 ☐ . Put on 6 ☐ .

12. **THINK ALOUD** Show 3 ☐ . on your workmat. What could you do to take out 2 ☐ ?

   a. Put 2 zero charges on the workmat. Does this change the integer represented on the workmat?

   b. Can you take out 2 ☐ now?

   c. What integer is represented after you take out 2 ☐ ?

Zero Charges

13. Show 2 ☐ on your workmat. Can you take out 5 ☐ ?

   a. How many zero charges must be placed on the workmat?

   b. What integer is represented after you take out 5 ☐ ?

How many zero charges do you need to place on the workmat to take out the given charge? What is the integer represented?

14. Show 6 ☐ . Take out 4 ☐ .

15. Show 3 ☐ . Take out 5 ☐ .

16. Show 4 ☐ . Take out 1 ☐ .

17. Show 2 ☐ . Take out 8 ☐ .

18. **CREATE YOUR OWN** Write a charged particle problem using positive charges and negative charges. Challenge a friend to name the integer you represented.

# Adding Integers

In the Game of Twelve, players take turns spinning positive and negative integers. They keep track of their spins and totals on a sheet like this one. The first player to reach 12 points wins.

Dana's first spin is ⁻2. Her second spin is +5. How many points does she have?

You can use charged particles to represent her spins of ⁻2 and 5 on your workmat.

DANA
SPIN 1   -2
SPIN 2    5
TOTAL
SPIN 3
TOTAL

| Start with 2 ⊟. | Put on 5 ⊞. | Make zero charges, if possible. | What is on the workmat? |
|---|---|---|---|
| 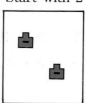 | 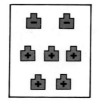 | 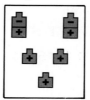 |  |

Dana has 3 points after two spins.

**THINK ALOUD**  Look at the examples at right.

What can you say about the sum if all the charges are positive? if all are negative?

What can you say about the sum if there are more negative charges than positive? if there are more positive charges than negative?

a.  5 + 8 = 13
b.  6 + ⁻9 = ⁻3
c.  12 + ⁻5 = 7
d.  8 + ⁻2 = 6
e.  ⁻15 + 9 = ⁻6
f.  ⁻2 + ⁻6 = ⁻8

Notice that in b, c, d, and e the sign of the sum is the same as the sign of the integer with the greater absolute value.

> **The sum of two positive integers is positive.**
> **The sum of two negative integers is negative.**
> **The sum of a positive integer and a negative integer will have the same sign as the integer with the greater absolute value.**

**CALCULATOR**  Use the ± to change an integer to its opposite. To enter a negative integer, first enter its absolute value and then press ±.

For ⁻6 + 2, press 6 ± + 2 =.  ⁻6 + 2 = ⁻4

For ⁻5 + ⁻3, press 5 ± + 3 ± =.  ⁻5 + ⁻3 = ⁻8

For 14 + ⁻32, press 14 + 32 ± =.  14 + ⁻32 = ⁻18

Add. Think of charged particles.

**1.** $^-8 + 14$     **2.** $16 + ^-9$     **3.** $19 + ^-7$     **4.** $^-15 + 15$     **5.** $^-9 + ^-21$

**6. CRITICAL THINKING** What is the sum of any integer and its opposite?

**PRACTICE**

Decide whether the sum will be positive or negative. Then add.

**7.** $^-9 + 4$     **8.** $^-7 + 6$     **9.** $^-6 + ^-9$     **10.** $3 + ^- 7$

**11.** $10 + ^-8$     **12.** $^-9 + ^-5$     **13.** $6 + ^-12$     **14.** $^-7 + ^-4$

**15.** $6 + ^-15$     **16.** $^-8 + ^-17$     **17.** $^-9 + 9$     **18.** $5 + ^-6$

**19.** $^-10 + ^-3$     **20.** $28 + ^-25$     **21.** $15 + ^-35$     **22.** $^-50 + 25$

Add. Use charges if necessary.

**23.** $^-4 + ^-2 + ^-3$     **24.** $5 + ^-2 + ^-1$     **25.** $^-6 + ^-2 + 4$     **26.** $^-7 + ^-9 + ^-3$

**27.** $9 + 2 + ^-9$     **28.** $^-1 + ^-6 + 4$     **29.** $6 + ^-12 + 6$     **30.** $^-5 + ^-3 + 2$

**MIXED REVIEW** Compute.

**31.** $6.2 \times 0.3$     **32.** $\frac{3}{4} \times \frac{4}{5}$     **33.** $15 \div 0.5$     **34.** $\frac{1}{5} + \frac{3}{4}$

**35.** $3.8 - 2.02$     **36.** $\frac{4}{7} + \frac{2}{3}$     **37.** $0.3 + 4.9$     **38.** $7 \div \frac{2}{3}$

**CALCULATOR** Name the sum.

**39.** $^-38 + 78$     **40.** $^-83 + 138$     **41.** $197 + ^-139$     **42.** $^-182 + 423$

**MENTAL MATH** Make the sum with a positive and a negative integer.

**43.** $8$     **44.** $^-7$     **45.** $15$     **46.** $^-12$     **47.** $0$

**PROBLEM SOLVING**

Dick Chamberlain uses his own method of keeping score in golf. Par is zero. One over par is 1, one under par is $^-1$, two over par is 2, two under par is $^-2$, and so on. Remember, the *low* score in golf wins.

**48.** Which player had the lowest score? the highest?

**49.** Arrange the players by name from the lowest score to the highest score.

**50.** If Rob and Ruth were partners and played Ron and Roya, which team won?

| Hole | Rob | Ruth | Ron | Roya |
|------|-----|------|-----|------|
| 1 | $^-2$ | 1 | $^-1$ | 2 |
| 2 | $^-1$ | 2 | 0 | 1 |
| 3 | 0 | $^-1$ | 1 | 1 |
| 4 | 2 | 3 | $^-2$ | 2 |
| 5 | 3 | 0 | 1 | $^-1$ |
| 6 | $^-1$ | 1 | $^-1$ | 2 |
| 7 | 0 | $^-1$ | 1 | $^-1$ |
| 8 | 1 | 2 | 2 | 2 |
| 9 | 2 | 1 | $^-1$ | 3 |

## Subtracting Integers

A hot-air balloonist
noticed that the air
temperature at an
altitude of 1,050 m was ⁻2°C
while the air temperature
at ground level was 5°C.
What was the difference
between the air temperatures?

You can use
charged particles
to represent
the subtraction
5 − ⁻2.

Show 5 ⊞ .  To take out 2 ⊟ , put in 2 zero charges.  What do you have left?

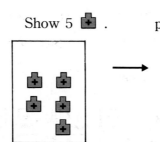

The difference between the air temperatures was 7°C.

**THINK ALOUD**  The pairs of equations below show examples of
subtracting an integer and adding its opposite. Instead of
subtracting an integer, what can you do?

| | | | |
|---|---|---|---|
| ⁻4 − 7 = ⁻11 | 3 − ⁻2 = 5 | 6 − 9 = ⁻3 | ⁻6 − ⁻14 = 8 |
| ⁻4 + ⁻7 = ⁻11 | 3 + 2 = 5 | 6 + ⁻9 = ⁻3 | ⁻6 + 14 = 8 |

### To subtract an integer, add its opposite.

**CALCULATOR**  You can use the $\pm$ key when you want to find
the difference between two integers.

For 32 − ⁻59, press 32 $-$ 59 $\pm$ $=$ .
For ⁻67 − ⁻95, press 67 $\pm$ $-$ 95 $\pm$ $=$ .
For ⁻59 − 23, press 59 $\pm$ $-$ 23 $=$ .

━━━━━━━━━━━━━━━━ **GUIDED PRACTICE** ━━━━━━━━━━━━━━━━

Use charged particles on your workmat to find the difference.

**1.** 5 − ⁻3    **2.** ⁻8 − ⁻2    **3.** ⁻2 − 8    **4.** ⁻11 − ⁻5

Subtract the integer by adding its opposite.

**5.** 7 − ⁻3    **6.** ⁻9 − ⁻12    **7.** 5 − 11    **8.** ⁻2 − 10

Solve. Use a calculator, mental math, or pencil and paper.

**9.** $^-5 - 2$     **10.** $3 - {}^-8$     **11.** $4 - {}^-6$     **12.** $2 - 11$

**13.** $^-2 - 9$     **14.** $^-4 - {}^-7$     **15.** $^-6 - 13$     **16.** $10 - {}^-4$

**17.** $0 - 6$     **18.** $0 - {}^-6$     **19.** $3 - {}^-11$     **20.** $^-7 - {}^-12$

**21.** $^-5 - 6$     **22.** $^-3 - 8$     **23.** $14 - {}^-5$     **24.** $2 - 9$

**25.** $^-3 + {}^-4 - 2$     **26.** $7 - {}^-3 + 2$     **27.** $^-5 - 1 + {}^-4$     **28.** $5 - 6 - {}^-9$

**MIXED REVIEW** Compare. Choose $>$, $<$, or $=$.

**29.** $6 + {}^-2$  $3 - {}^-5$     **30.** $^-6 + {}^-4$ ▧ $^-2 - 8$     **31.** $^-5 - {}^-1$ ▧ $0 - 6$

**32.** $2 - {}^-6$ ▧ $^-7 + 3$     **33.** $5 - {}^-2$ ▧ $^-4 + 1$     **34.** $^-7 + {}^-1$ ▧ $^-3 - {}^-5$

**CALCULATOR** Name the missing integer that makes the equation true.

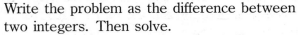

**35.** $2 \;\boxed{\pm}\; \boxed{+}\; ▧ \; \boxed{=} \; 7$

**36.** $4 \;\boxed{\pm}\; \boxed{+}\; ▧ \;\boxed{\pm}\; \boxed{=} \; {}^-12$

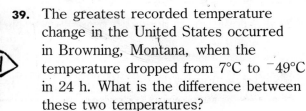

**37.** ▧ $\boxed{-}\; 5 \;\boxed{\pm}\; +6 \;\boxed{=}\; 13$

**38.** $7 \;\boxed{\pm}\; \boxed{+}\; ▧ \;\boxed{-}\; 5 \;\boxed{=}\; {}^-4$

Write the problem as the difference between two integers. Then solve.

**39.** The greatest recorded temperature change in the United States occurred in Browning, Montana, when the temperature dropped from 7°C to ⁻49°C in 24 h. What is the difference between these two temperatures?

**40.** The greatest recorded temperature change in the world occurred in Verkhoyansk, USSR. Temperatures changed from −70°C to 37°C. What is the difference between these two temperatures?

**41.** Garopan, Saipan, located in the Mariana Islands in the Pacific Ocean, during a nine-year period recorded the least change in temperature on record. The temperature ranged from a high of 31°C to a low of 20°C. What is the difference between these two temperatures?

# Problem Solving:
## Using Logic

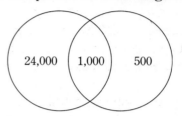

The city health department wants to send a pamphlet about
free vaccines to all families with children and to all teachers.
There are 25,000 families with children in the city. Of the city's
1,500 teachers, 1,000 have children. How many pamphlets
does the health department need to print?

The solution to problems often requires organizing and examining
data. A Venn diagram is one way to organize the data.

Start by entering the
available information.

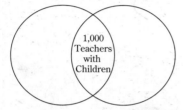

25,000 families          1,500 teachers
with children

Now you can see how
to complete the Venn diagram.

Families with          Teachers without
children;               children:
no one is a teacher:    1,500 − 1,000
25,000 − 1,000

The health department needs to print 25,500 pamphlets.

─────────────────────────── **GUIDED PRACTICE** ───────────────────────────

1. Use the Venn diagram at right to tell whether the statements
   are *true* or *false*.

   **a.** There are more car owners than home owners.

   **b.** All car owners are home owners.

   **c.** If there are 25,000 car owners and 1,000 home
   owners, then there are 24,000 car owners who
   do not own homes.

Use the Venn diagram. Fill in the blanks with *All, Some,* or *No*.

2.

   **a.** ____ home owners are students.

   **b.** ____ students are home owners.

3.

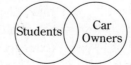

   **a.** ____ students are car owners.

   **b.** ____ car owners are students.

Solve. Make a Venn diagram to help.

**4.** In a class, 13 students went to a doctor last year, 18 went to a dentist, and 5 went to both. If all the students saw either a doctor or dentist, how many students are in the class?

**5.** Amy is taller than Beth but shorter than Tom. Who is the tallest?

**6.** A politician claims that all home owners and all skilled workers will vote for him since he has supported them in the past. How many votes will he get if there are 15,000 home owners, 3,000 skilled workers, and 1,800 skilled workers who own homes?

**7.** A salesperson made calls to 20 homes with dogs, 28 homes with cats, and 18 homes with birds. Five of the homes with dogs also had birds, 11 homes with cats also had birds, and 3 homes with dogs also had cats. One home had all three kinds of animals. How many homes were called?

 Choose any strategy to solve.

**8.** On a recent math test, Sally scored higher than Dennis and Kelleen but lower than Vincent. Kelleen had a lower score than Dennis. Name the students in order from the highest score to the lowest.

**9.** In a class, 11 students have one or more sisters, 16 have one or more brothers, 4 have one or more brothers and sisters, and 5 have neither a brother nor a sister. How many students are in the class?

**10.** Earl spent $4.20 for 1 milk, 2 hamburgers, and an apple. Enid bought 2 milks, one hamburger, and 2 apples for $3.30. If Eric bought 1 milk, 1 hamburger, and 1 apple, how much did his meal cost?

**11.** If a lawn-mowing service can mow a lawn 100 m by 100 m in 1 h, how long should it take to mow a lawn 50 m by 50 m?

## *Multiplying Integers*

In chemistry, an electrically charged atom or group of atoms is called an ion. The charge on an ion may be either positive or negative. The table at right gives the names and charges of some common ions.

| Name | Charge |
|---|---|
| Tin (Stannic) | +4 |
| Carbonate | ⁻2 |
| Mercury | +2 |
| Phosphate | ⁻3 |
| Fluoride | ⁻1 |
| Sodium | +1 |

If there are 5 carbonate ions, what is the total charge?

You can write the expression $5 \times {}^-2$ to represent the situation.

You multiply positive integers as you do whole numbers. You can use patterns to name the product of $5 \times {}^-2$.

$$5 \times 2 = 10$$
$$5 \times 1 = 5$$
$$5 \times 0 = 0$$
$$5 \times {}^-1 = {}^-5$$
$$5 \times {}^-2 = {}^-10$$

To continue the pattern, these products must be negative.

The charge on 5 carbonate ions is ⁻10.

**NUMBER SENSE**   Since $5 \times {}^-2$ means ${}^-2 + {}^-2 + {}^-2 + {}^-2 + {}^-2$, tell how you could use charged particles to show that $5 \times {}^-2 = {}^-10$.

To multiply two negative integers, look at the pattern.

$$^-5 \times 2 = {}^-10$$
$$^-5 \times 1 = {}^-5$$
$$^-5 \times 0 = 0$$
$$^-5 \times {}^-1 = 5$$
$$^-5 \times {}^-2 = 10$$

To continue the pattern, these products must be positive.

> **The product of two positive integers or two negative integers is a positive integer.**
> **The product of a positive integer and a negative integer is a negative integer.**

**THINK ALOUD**   What is the product of any integer and 0?

Other examples:

$$^-3 \times {}^-5 = 15 \qquad\qquad {}^-3 \times 5 = {}^-15$$

$$3 \times 5 = 15 \qquad\qquad 3\ \boxed{\times}\ 5\ \boxed{\pm}\ \boxed{=}\ {}^-15$$

**Atomium Sculpture, Brussels, Belgium**

**MATH AND SCIENCE**

State whether the product is *positive*, *zero*, or *negative*.

**1.** $8 \times ^-2$      **2.** $^-3 \times ^-6$      **3.** $^-6 \times 4$      **4.** $^-12 \times 0$

**5. THINK ALOUD**   Explain why the product of $^-1 \times ^-2 \times ^-3$ is $^-6$.

Simplify. Use a calculator, mental math, or pencil and paper.

**6.** $3 \times ^-2$      **7.** $^-5 \times 8$      **8.** $^-4 \times ^-3$      **9.** $^-6 \times 0$

**10.** $^-2 \times 7$      **11.** $6 \times 9$      **12.** $^-6 \times ^-7$      **13.** $4 \times ^-9$

**14.** $^-7 \times ^-4$      **15.** $^-2 \times 5$      **16.** $5 \times 0$      **17.** $^-9 \times ^-8$

**18.** $5 \times ^-7$      **19.** $^-6 \times 8$      **20.** $^-7 \times ^-7$      **21.** $^-12 \times 2$

**22.** $^-3 \times 5 \times ^-4$      **23.** $^-5 \times ^-2 \times ^-1$      **24.** $3 \times ^-2 \times 2$      **25.** $^-6 \times 2 \times 4$

**26.** $^-3 \times |^-8|$      **27.** $|^-3| \times ^-8$      **28.** $|^-3| \times |^-8|$      **29.** $^-3 \times ^-8$

**MIXED REVIEW**   Compute.

**30.** $^-5 + 1$      **31.** $^-3 + ^-6$      **32.** $5 + ^-8$      **33.** $8 + ^+3$

**34.** $^-6 - ^-6$      **35.** $3 + ^-9$      **36.** $^-17 - 3$      **37.** $^-14 + ^-8$

**ESTIMATE**   Estimate. Be sure the sign is correct.

**38.** $2 \times ^-396$      **39.** $^-247 \times ^-4$      **40.** $^-117 \times 5$      **41.** $^-8 \times 412$

**42.** $^-104 \times ^-81$      **43.** $^-212 \times 197$      **44.** $^-48 \times 402$      **45.** $^-203 \times ^-23$

**46. CALCULATOR**   Name four pairs of integers that have a product of $^-558$.

Use the chart on page 426 to find the total charge.

**47.** 3 tin ions and 6 carbonate ions

**48.** 7 sodium ions and 4 phosphate ions

**49.** 10 mercury ions and 8 fluoride ions

**50. CRITICAL THINKING**   A molecule is formed by 2 or more ions whose total charge is 0. Could 3 mercury ions and 2 phosphate ions form a molecule?

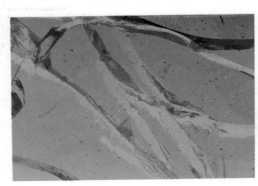

## Dividing Integers

During a 5-d period, the stock market index decreased 20 points. What was the average daily change in the stock market index?

You can use a related multiplication fact to divide.

$$^-20 \div 5 = \blacksquare \quad \overleftarrow{\text{What number multiplied by 5 gives } ^-20?}$$

$$\blacksquare \times 5 = {}^-20 \longrightarrow {}^-4 \times 5 = {}^-20$$

So, $^-20 \div 5 = {}^-4$.

The average daily change was a loss of 4 points.

Other examples:

| Divide. | Related Multiplication Fact | Conclude. |
|---|---|---|
| $^-20 \div {}^-5 = \blacksquare$ | $4 \times {}^-5 = {}^-20$ | $^-20 \div {}^-5 = 4$ |
| $20 \div {}^-5 = \blacksquare$ | $^-4 \times {}^-5 = 20$ | $20 \div {}^-5 = {}^-4$ |
| $20 \div 5 = \blacksquare$ | $4 \times 5 = 20$ | $20 \div 5 = 4$ |

> **The quotient of two positive integers or two negative integers is a positive integer.**
> **The quotient of a positive integer and a negative integer is a negative integer.**

**CALCULATOR** $35 \div {}^-5$; $35$  $5$   $^-7$ $\qquad$ $^-48 \div {}^-6$; $48$  $\div$ $6$ $\pm$ $=$ $8$

The quotient of 0 divided by any other integer is 0.

$$0 \div {}^-8 = 0 \qquad 0 \div 5 = 0$$

**CRITICAL THINKING** Use the relationship between multiplication and division to explain why you cannot divide an integer by 0.

═══════════════ **GUIDED PRACTICE** ═══════════════

Is the quotient *positive*, *negative*, or *zero*?

**1.** $^-24 \div {}^-3$ $\qquad$ **2.** $^-36 \div 9$ $\qquad$ **3.** $^-27 \div {}^-3$ $\qquad$ **4.** $0 \div 4$

Find the quotient by writing a related multiplication fact.

**5.** $^-10 \div 5$ $\qquad$ **6.** $14 \div {}^-7$ $\qquad$ **7.** $^-15 \div {}^-3$ $\qquad$ **8.** $18 \div 6$

Divide. Use a calculator, mental math, or pencil and paper.

**9.** $^-64 \div 8$      **10.** $^-48 \div 6$      **11.** $54 \div ^-9$      **12.** $20 \div ^-2$

**13.** $^-72 \div ^-8$      **14.** $^-35 \div 7$      **15.** $^-18 \div ^-9$      **16.** $^-50 \div 5$

**17.** $0 \div ^-9$      **18.** $16 \div ^-2$      **19.** $^-66 \div ^-11$      **20.** $^-30 \div ^-5$

**21.** $^-70 \div 10$      **22.** $^-7 \div 1$      **23.** $^-28 \div 7$      **24.** $^-24 \div ^-2$

**25.** $51 \div 17$      **26.** $84 \div |^-4|$      **27.** $|^-46| \div ^-2$      **28.** $|^-45| \div |^-3|$

**MIXED REVIEW**   Compute.

**29.** $^-8 + 3$      **30.** $^-5 \times ^-8$      **31.** $12 - ^-9$      **32.** $15 + ^-7$

**33.** $^-3 \times 7$      **34.** $^-6 - ^-4$      **35.** $^-4 - ^-6$      **36.** $^-12 + ^-8$

**CALCULATOR**   Multiply or divide.

**37.** $756 \div ^-21$      **38.** $^-1,316 \div ^-47$      **39.** $^-153 \times ^-209$      **40.** $^-82,804 \div ^-254$

**41.** $4,293 \div 81$      **42.** $198 \times ^-278$      **43.** $115,116 \div ^-318$      **44.** $^-125,697 \div ^-429$

**45.** Over 7 business days a stock dropped 14 points. What was its average drop per day?

**46.** Five days ago the ABC Corporation's stock was 30 points lower. Did the stock rise or fall in the last 5 days? By how much did it rise or fall on average each day?

## Critical Thinking

You can use four $^-2$'s to write an equation equal to 1.

$$(^-2 + ^-2) \div (^-2 + ^-2) = 1$$

Use only the integer $^-2$ exactly four times and the operations of addition, subtraction, multiplication, and division to write an equation that equals the number.

**1.** 0      **2.** 2      **3.** 3      **4.** 4      **5.** 5      **6.** 6

**7. CREATE YOUR OWN**   Use four $^-2$'s to write equations that equal other integers.

━━━━ **LANGUAGE** & **VOCABULARY** ━━━━

Tell whether the situation can most clearly be represented by *addition, subtraction, multiplication,* or *division* of integers.

1. determining your location after driving 9 mi west, then driving 12 mi east

2. finding your depth in a cave after descending 25 m/h for 5 h.

3. determining the number of minutes needed for a plane to climb to 2,400 ft if it climbs at the rate of 600 ft/min

4. finding the difference in temperature between two cities, one whose temperature is 15°C and the other whose temperature is ⁻4°C

5. finding the total loss in value for a share of stock whose value has dropped $4/wk for each of the past 3 wk

━━━━ **QUICK QUIZ**  ━━━━

Name the opposite. *(pages 414–415)*

1. You walk up 3 flights of stairs.          2. ⁻14

Compare. Write >, <, or =. *(pages 416–417)*

3. 2 ▦ ⁻18          4. ⁻11 ▦ 11

Solve. *(pages 418–423, 426–429)*

5. ⁻12 + 7          6. 0 − ⁻9          7. ⁻8 × 6

8. ⁻56 ÷ 7          9. ⁻81 ÷ ⁻9

Solve. *(pages 424–425)*

10. In one apartment building, all apartments have at least 1 telephone. There are regular telephones in 32 apartments, cordless telephones in 10 apartments, and both kinds in 8 apartments.

    a. How many apartments have both kinds of telephones?

    b. Are there more regular or more cordless telephones?

    c. What is the fewest number of apartments that can be in the building? Draw a Venn diagram to verify your answer.

Write the answers in your learning log.

1. Your friend was absent yesterday. Explain how to draw a number line that includes positive and negative numbers. Describe how to tell where the smallest and largest numbers are located.

2. Explain how adding positive charges and negative charges represents adding integers.

**MATH AMERICA**

**BONUS**

**DID YOU KNOW . . . ?** The Pony Express delivered letters from St. Joseph, Missouri, to Sacramento, California, covering 1,966 miles in about 10 days. Estimate how long it would have taken to send a letter from your school to Sacramento by Pony Express. How long does it take today to send a letter from your school to Sacramento?

This magic square uses only the first 9 counting numbers. What is the sum of each row, column, and diagonal?

| 8 | 1 | 6 |
|---|---|---|
| 3 | 5 | 7 |
| 4 | 9 | 2 |

You can create other magic squares this size using other numbers as long as you keep the relative positions of the numbers constant. In this magic square, 2 has been added to the number in each cell above. What is the sum?

| 10 | 3 | 8 |
|----|---|---|
| 5 | 7 | 9 |
| 6 | 11 | 4 |

Make another magic square. Use the integers: ⁻5, ⁻4, ⁻3, ⁻2, ⁻1, 0, 1, 2, 3.

Does the "magic" still work? Does every row, column, and diagonal have the same sum?

## Solving Addition and Subtraction  Equations with Integers

One of the most freakish changes in temperature occurred in Spearfish, South Dakota, in 1943. In just two minutes, the temperature increased 27°C to reach a high of 7°C.

To find the original temperature, let $t$ represent the original temperature. Then write and solve the equation, $t + 27 = 7$.

**THINK ALOUD**  What operation can you use to get $t$ by itself on one side of the equation? Explain.

$$t + 27 = 7$$

> Subtraction is the inverse of addition.

$$t + 27 - 27 = 7 - 27$$

> Subtract 27 from both sides.

$$t + 0 = {}^-20$$

$$t = {}^-20$$

> The solution is $^-20$.

Check:  $t + 27 = 7$
$^-20 + 27 = 7$ ✔

The original temperature was $^-20$°C.

Another example:

$$n - 4 = 15$$

$$n - 4 + 4 = 15 + 4$$

> Add 4 to both sides.

$$n + 0 = 19$$

$$n = 19$$

> The solution is 19.

Check:  $n - 4 = 15$
$19 - 4 = 15$ ✔

> **You can add or subtract the same integer on both sides of an equation.**

MATH AND SCIENCE

Solve and check the equation. Explain how you did it.

**1.** $x + 8 = 27$  **2.** $y - 14 = 32$  **3.** $t - 8 = {}^-12$  **4.** $z + 12 = {}^-16$

■■■■■■■■■■■■■■■■■■■■■■■■■■■■ **PRACTICE** ■■■■■■■■■■■■■■■■■■■■■■■■■■■■

Solve and check. Use a calculator, mental math, or pencil and paper.

**5.** $n + 6 = 2$  **6.** $x + 8 = {}^-7$  **7.** $y + 15 = 5$

**8.** $n - 6 = {}^-3$  **9.** $t - 8 = {}^-11$  **10.** $t - 14 = {}^-16$

**11.** $8 = 2 + m$  **12.** $n + {}^-5 = {}^-6$  **13.** ${}^-7 + k = {}^-7$

**14.** $r - 5 = {}^-6$  **15.** $y + 3 = {}^-10$  **16.** $t - 5 = {}^-8$

**17.** $p + {}^-7 = {}^-12$  **18.** $m - {}^-5 = {}^-5$  **19.** $h - 9 = {}^-4$

**MIXED REVIEW**  Evaluate. Use $a = {}^-2$, $b = 6$, and $c = {}^-5$.

**20.** $a + 8$  **21.** $7 + a$  **22.** $b + {}^-8$  **23.** $c - {}^-4$

**24.** $a + {}^-b$  **25.** $c - b$  **26.** $b - a$  **27.** $a - b - c$

**NUMBER SENSE**  Name the integer if it exists.

**28.** the least positive integer  **29.** the least integer

**30.** the greatest positive integer  **31.** the greatest negative integer

■■■■■■■■■■■■■■■■■■■■■■■■■■■■ **PROBLEM SOLVING** ■■■■■■■■■■■■■■■■■■■■■■■■■■■■

In the troposphere, the lowest part of the earth's atmosphere, temperatures drop about 5.6°C for every kilometer of altitude.

The formula below gives the temperature ($t$) at a point in the troposphere if you know the ground temperature ($g$) and the altitude of the point in kilometers ($k$).

$$t = g - 5.6k$$

Use the formula to complete the table.

| | Ground level temperature | Temperature at 5 km | Temperature at 20 km | Temperature at 50 km | Temperature at 75 km |
|---|---|---|---|---|---|
| **32.** | 18°C | | | | |
| **33.** | 6°C | | | | |
| **34.** | ${}^-5$°C | | | | |

## Solving Multiplication and Division Equations with Integers

During a recent 7-d drought in the Southwest, the water level in a reservoir decreased 14 cm. About how much did the water level change 'each day during this period?

Let $n$ represent the average daily change in centimeters.

$7n$ represents the change in 7 d.

$7n = {}^-14$

Since you know how to solve addition and subtraction equations with integers, you can use a MATH-CONNECTION to solve this equation.

**Cracked earth near Beatty, Nevada**

**THINK ALOUD**   What operation can you use to get $n$ by itself on one side of the equation? Explain.

$7n = {}^-14$  ⟵ Division is the inverse of multiplication.

$\dfrac{7n}{7} = \dfrac{{}^-14}{7}$  ⟵ Divide both sides by 7.

$n = {}^-2$  ⟵ The solution is $^-2$.

Check:

$7n = {}^-14$

$7(^-2) = {}^-14$ ✔

The water level changed about $^-2$ cm each day.

Another example:

$\dfrac{x}{{}^-3} = 2$

$\dfrac{x}{{}^-3} \times {}^-3 = 2 \times {}^-3$  ⟵ Multiply both sides by $^-3$.

$x = {}^-6$  ⟵ The solution is $^-6$.

Check:

$\dfrac{x}{{}^-3} = 2$

$\dfrac{{}^-6}{{}^-3} = 2$ ✔

> **You can multiply or divide both sides of an equation by the same nonzero integer.**

434    LESSON 13–10

Explain how you would solve and check the equation.
First name the operation you would use.

**1.** $3n = {}^-12$   **2.** $\frac{x}{4} = {}^-2$   **3.** ${}^-3t = 24$   **4.** $\frac{n}{{}^-5} = {}^-4$

Solve.

**5.** $\frac{x}{5} = {}^-7$   **6.** ${}^-3k = 27$   **7.** $9b = {}^-54$   **8.** $\frac{n}{{}^-9} = 8$

**9.** ${}^-12x = 60$   **10.** $\frac{t}{{}^-4} = {}^-8$   **11.** $\frac{y}{4} = 10$   **12.** ${}^-6y = {}^-30$

**13.** $\frac{m}{12} = {}^-4$   **14.** $6z = {}^-48$   **15.** $\frac{x}{8} = {}^-15$   **16.** ${}^-7n = {}^-56$

**17.** ${}^-8x = 80$   **18.** $\frac{p}{13} = {}^-11$   **19.** ${}^-4b = 52$   **20.** $\frac{x}{{}^-7} = 23$

**21.** ${}^-8z = 96$   **22.** $\frac{r}{{}^-21} = {}^-6$   **23.** ${}^-14a = {}^-168$   **24.** ${}^-15n = {}^-180$

**MIXED REVIEW**   Give the answer in lowest terms.

**25.** $\frac{2}{3} + \frac{3}{5}$   **26.** $\frac{4}{5} - \frac{2}{3}$   **27.** $\frac{21}{30} \times \frac{4}{7}$   **28.** $\frac{3}{7} \div \frac{7}{12}$

**29.** $5\frac{2}{3} + 2\frac{1}{6}$   **30.** $7\frac{1}{3} \div 3\frac{2}{3}$   **31.** $2\frac{3}{4} \times 1\frac{5}{7}$   **32.** $6\frac{1}{2} - 2\frac{3}{8}$

**NUMBER SENSE**   Solve the equation. Look for a pattern.

**33.** $2a = 2$   **34.** $3a = {}^-9$

**35.** $4a = 36$   **36.** $5a = {}^-135$

**37.** Write the next two equations that continue the pattern
begun in Exercises 33–36.

Write the equation and solve.

**38.** If an irrigation pond is being
filled at the rate of 10 L/s, how
long will it take to increase the
amount of water in the pond
by 500 L?

**39.** If water is pumped from an
irrigation pond at the rate of
8 L/s, how long will it take
to decrease the amount of water
in the pond by 512 L?

**40.** An irrigation pond was being filled at the rate of 11 L/s.
Water was being drained out simultaneously at the rate of
9 L/s. How many minutes did it take to increase the water
in the pond by 600 L ?

# Coordinate Plane

The map of Washington, D.C., at right is on a number grid called a **coordinate plane.**

In the coordinate plane, the horizontal number line is called the **x-axis**. The vertical number line is called the **y-axis**. The two lines meet at a point called the **origin** (0, 0).

- On the map, what is located at (0, 0)?

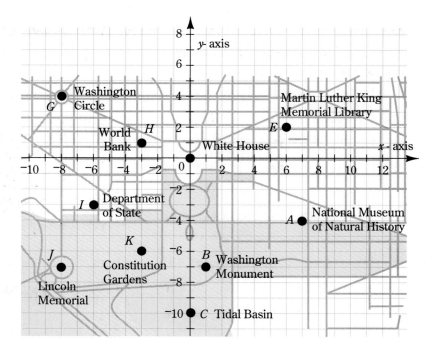

Point *A* is called the **graph** of the ordered pair (7, ⁻4). You can locate point *A* by starting at origin (0, 0) and moving 7 units to the right and 4 units down. The numbers 7 and ⁻4 are called the **coordinates** of *A*.

- What is located at (7, ⁻4)?

- What are the coordinates of *I*, the Department of State?

**THINK ALOUD**  Do (7, ⁻4) and (⁻4, 7) name the same point? Why is the order of naming the coordinates important?

---

**GUIDED PRACTICE**

Use the grid above. Name the ordered pair.

**1.**  $E(\blacksquare, 2)$

**2.**  $I(^-6, \blacksquare)$

**3.**  $C(\blacksquare, \blacksquare)$

Name the landmark located at the given coordinates. Use the grid above.

**4.**  (⁻3, 1)

**5.**  (⁻8, ⁻7)

**6.**  (1, ⁻7)

MATH AND GEOGRAPHY

Write the letter of the point named
by the ordered pair.

**7.** ($^-$3, 4)    **8.** (3, 5)

**9.** (5, $^-$2)    **10.** ($^-$7, $^-$2)

**11.** (2, 7)    **12.** ($^-$1, 1)

**13.** ($^-$3, 1)    **14.** (1, $^-$2)

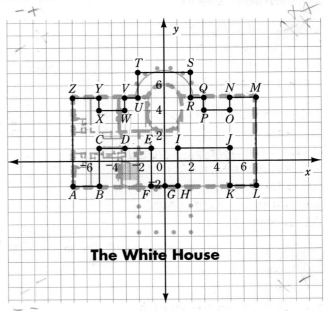

**The White House**

Name the ordered pair for each point.

**15.** $Z$    **16.** $B$    **17.** $N$

**18.** $G$    **19.** $X$    **20.** $T$

**21.** $L$    **22.** $I$    **23.** $R$

**24.** $V$    **25.** $C$    **26.** $M$

Find the distance between the pair of points.

**27.** $M$ and L    **28.** $J$ and $K$    **29.** $C$ and $E$    **30.** $S$ and $T$

**31.** $X$ and P    **32.** $M$ and $Z$    **33.** $C$ and $I$    **34.** $F$ and $L$

**35.** Draw and label an $x$-axis and a $y$-axis on graph paper.
Graph and label each ordered pair:

$A($$^-$2, 6$)$, $B(0, 10)$, $C(2, 6)$, $D(3, $$^-$9$)$, $E(0, $$^-$10$)$, $F($$^-$3, $$^-$9$)$, and $G(0, 5)$.

Connect the points:

$A$ to $B$, $B$ to $C$, $C$ to $D$, $D$ to $E$, $E$ to $F$, $F$ to $A$, $A$ to $G$, $C$ to $G$,
and $B$ to $E$.

**36.** **CREATE YOUR OWN**  Plot and connect ordered pairs to create
a figure. See whether a classmate can draw your figure.
Give her or him the ordered pairs for the points and tell her
or him which points to connect.

**37.** **CRITICAL THINKING**  Graph any three ordered pairs such
that each $x$-coordinate is 2 more than each $y$-coordinate.

**a.** Draw a line through these points.

**b.** Name the coordinates of any other two points on this line.

**c.** What do you notice about the coordinates of these points?

## Exploring Coordinate Transformations

A translation (slide) of a figure in the coordinate plane does not change its size or shape, only its location. The result of a translation is called the translation image.

Trace and cut out △*ABC*. Copy the table.

1. Record the coordinates for points *A*, *B*, and *C*.

Start with your triangle on △*ABC*. Perform the translation. Record the coordinates of the translation image.

2. 5 units to the right, 0 units up or down

3. 2 units to the right, 3 units up

4. 1 unit left, 2 units down

5. **CREATE YOUR OWN**  Start with △*ABC*. Make any translation you wish. Record the coordinates of the translation image.

| Triangle | Coordinates | | |
|---|---|---|---|
| | *A* | *B* | *C* |
| *ABC* | | | |
| Image after 5*R*,0 | | | |
| Image after 2*R*,3*U* | | | |
| Image after 1*L*,2*D* | | | |
| Your Image | | | |

6. How do the translation images compare to the original triangle?

7. **IN YOUR WORDS**  Explain how you would find the *x*- or *y*-coordinates for the translation image resulting from the translation.

a. 3 units to the right

b. 4 units up

c. 6 units down

d. 1 unit down

e. 1 unit to the left, 2 units up

f. 2 units to the right, down 3 units

A reflection (flip) of a figure in the coordinate plane also does not change the shape or size of the figure. The line over which a figure is reflected is called the **line of reflection** and the result of a reflection is called the **reflection image**.

Trace $\triangle DEF$. Cut it out. Copy the table.

**8.** Record the coordinates for points $D$, $E$, and $F$.

Start with your triangle on $\triangle DEF$. Perform the reflection. Record the coordinates of the reflection image.

**9.** reflection over the $y$-axis

**10.** reflection over the $x$-axis

| Triangle | Coordinates | | |
|---|---|---|---|
| | D | E | F |
| *DEF* | | | |
| Reflection Image over *y*-axis | | | |
| Reflection Image over *x*-axis | | | |

**11. CRITICAL THINKING** How do the coordinates of the reflection image compare to the original coordinates?

**12.** Copy the coordinate system and $\triangle TUV$ on a sheet of grid paper.

   **a.** Reflect $\triangle TUV$ over the $y$-axis

   **b.** Translate the reflection image of $\triangle TUV$ 6 units to the left. What are the coordinates of the vertexes of the image?

**13.** Copy the coordinate system and the original $\triangle TUV$ on a sheet of grid paper.

   **a.** Translate $\triangle TUV$ 6 units to the left.

   **b.** Reflect the translation image of $\triangle TUV$ over the $y$-axis. What are the coordinates of the vertexes of the image?

   **c.** Compare your results with Exercise 12.

**14. CRITICAL THINKING** Are translation and reflection commutative operations?

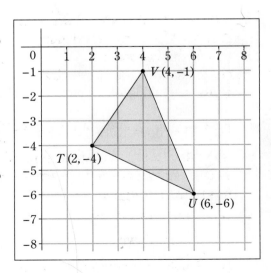

# Problem Solving:
# Working Backward

Most problem solving situations present you with information and ask you to determine a solution. Sometimes, however, you know the solution and how it was found, but you need to find the beginning condition. A strategy used to solve this kind of problem is working backward.

Marcia is flying from Detroit to Los Angeles. Her plane leaves at 9:45 A.M. and she wants to be at the airport $\frac{3}{4}$ h before departure. She can drive to the airport in 50 min and she needs $1\frac{1}{2}$ h to dress and have breakfast. For what time should she set her alarm clock?

**THINK ALOUD**   What do you want to know? What facts do you know? How can you work backward to answer the question?

| Marcia's plane leaves at 9:45 A.M. She wants to arrive $\frac{3}{4}$ h before this. | She will take about 50 min to drive to the airport. | She needs $1\frac{1}{2}$ h to dress and eat before she leaves. |
| --- | --- | --- |

9:45 A.M. $- 0:45 = 9:00$ A.M.  9:00 A.M. $- 0:50 = 8:10$ A.M.  8:10 A.M. $- 1:30 = 6:40$ A.M.

Marcia should set the alarm clock for 6:40 A.M.

<hr>

## GUIDED PRACTICE

1. Read the story to answer the questions.

   Ruth is thinking of a number. If she multiplies the number by 3 and divides by 2, she gets 6.

   **a.** What does Ruth get after multiplying her number by 3 and dividing by 2?

   **b.** To work backward, what is the first step to take?

   **c.** What is the number Ruth is thinking of?

2. Dick is thinking of a number. If he divides the number by 2, then multiples it by 3, and finally divides by 0.9, the result is ⁻5. What is the number?

Solve.

3. Annie's plane leaves at 10:35 A.M. It takes $1\frac{1}{2}$ h to get to the airport from her house. If she allows 30 min to check in and get to the gate, what time should she leave the house?

4. Willie was thinking of a number. If he adds 8 to it, subtracts $\frac{1}{2}$ and then subtracts 5, he gets 1. What number was Willie's number?

5. Mary bought a cassette player with half of her money. Then she spent $15 more. After that, she spent half of her remaining money on tapes. Then she spent $18 on head phones. If she had $12 left, how much did she have before she bought the cassette player?

6. Sandy paid $14.90 for taxi fare from the airport to the hotel, including a $2.00 tip. Sky Cab charges $1.90 for the first mile plus $.20 for each additional $\frac{1}{5}$ mi. How many miles did Sandy travel from the airport to the hotel?

7. Carlos deposited his paycheck in a new savings account on Monday. On Tuesday, he withdrew $25.00 to buy a concert ticket. He deposited $37.50 on Wednesday and then withdrew $20.00 on Thursday to spend at the concert. On Friday, he withdrew $18.75 to buy a shirt. If his savings account then contained $56.25, what amount did Carlos deposit on Monday?

 Choose any strategy to solve.

8. Name the simplest value of the continuous fraction.

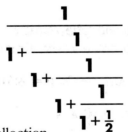

$$1 + \cfrac{1}{1 + \cfrac{1}{1 + \cfrac{1}{1 + \cfrac{1}{1 + \frac{1}{2}}}}}$$

9. Mr. Ryan divided his stamp collection among his children. Roger got $\frac{1}{2}$ of the stamps, Rose got $\frac{1}{4}$ of the stamps, Ray got $\frac{1}{5}$ of the stamps, and Ruth got 1,000 stamps. How many stamps did Mr. Ryan have in his collection?

10. Think of a number. Add 4, multiply by 3, subtract 4, and multiply by 3. Add together the digits of the result. If the answer has more than 1 digit, keep adding digits until it is a single-digit number. Is it 6? Try other numbers.

---

### LANGUAGE & VOCABULARY

---

Each situation can be represented by an equation. Without solving the equation, tell whether the solution will be *positive* or *negative*.

1. If a number $y$ is increased by 5, the result is $^-9$.

2. A number $b$ multiplied by $^-3$ equals $^-21$.

3. Dividing a number $x$ by 8 gives a quotient of $^-7$.

4. If 24 is subtracted from a number $q$, the difference is 8.

5. When a number $m$ is subtracted from 10 the result is $^-3$.

---

### TEST ✓

---

#### CONCEPTS

Name the opposite of the integer. *(pages 414–415)*

1. $^-2$      2. $18$      3. $1$      4. $0$      5. $^-25$

Write the absolute value of the integer. *(pages 414–415)*

6. $^-6$      7. $^-47$      8. $36$

Compare. Write $>$, $<$, or $=$. *(pages 416–417)*

9. $0 \, \blacksquare \, ^-3$      10. $^-15 \, \blacksquare \, 8$      11. $|^-9| \, \blacksquare \, |9|$

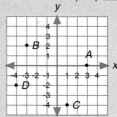

Name the ordered pair for the point. *(pages 436–439)*

12. $A$      13. $B$

14. $C$      15. $D$

#### SKILLS

Solve. *(pages 418–423, 426–429, 432–435)*

16. $^-4 + 17$      17. $31 - {}^-14$      18. $^-16 \times 4$      19. $48 \div {}^-6$

20. $x + 14 = 5$      21. $y - 8 = {}^-3$      22. $^-4k = 36$      23. $\dfrac{m}{7} = {}^-9$

---

Use a Venn diagram. *(pages 424–425)*

**24.** In a survey, 21 students liked gym class, 44 liked library period, and 9 liked both.

  **a.** How many students liked library period?

  **b.** Did more students like gym than library?

  **c.** What is the smallest number of students that could have been surveyed? Draw a Venn diagram to verify your answers.

Solve. *(pages 440–441)*

**25.** If you subtract 6 from a number, then divide by 3, and finally add 2, the result is 16. What is the number?

**26.** Overnight a temperature of $y°C$ dropped 8°C to ⁻3°C. What was the temperature before the drop?

LEARNING LOG

Write the answers in your learning log.

  **1.** Describe two inverse operations used in mathematics and two inverse operations that are not mathematical.

  **2.** You just graphed the point (4, 5). Now explain to your friend how to graph the point (⁻4, ⁻5).

Name the opposite of the integer. *(pages 414–415)*

**1.** ⁻3   **2.** 8   **3.** 0   **4.** ⁻100   **5.** 15

Write the absolute value of the integer. *(pages 414–415)*

**6.** 21   **7.** ⁻2   **8.** 150   **9.** ⁻81   **10.** ⁻14

Compare. Write >, <, or =. *(pages 416–417)*

**11.** ⁻3 ▦ 4   **12.** 12 ▦ ⁻15   **13.** 0 ▦ 9   **14.** ⁻8 ▦ ⁻4

**15.** ⁻23 ▦ 0   **16.** ⁻5 ▦ ⁻10   **17.** |⁻6| ▦ |6|   **18.** 6 ▦ ⁻16

Solve. *(pages 418–423, 426–429, 432–435)*

**19.** ⁻2 + ⁻8   **20.** ⁻9 − 3   **21.** 0 − ⁻8   **22.** 13 + ⁻13

**23.** ⁻9 ÷ ⁻3   **24.** ⁻15 × 2   **25.** 14 × ⁻5   **26.** ⁻40 ÷ 10

**27.** 25 + ⁻27   **28.** 18 − ⁻12   **29.** 0 × 7   **30.** ⁻81 ÷ 9

**31.** $a + 16 = 4$   **32.** $c - 4 = {}^{-}9$   **33.** $e - {}^{-}2 = 15$   **34.** $\frac{g}{6} = {}^{-}6$

**35.** $m + {}^{-}8 = {}^{-}21$   **36.** ${}^{-}7p = {}^{-}35$   **37.** $\frac{r}{8} = 2$   **38.** $\frac{t}{-3} = 21$

**39.** $\frac{x}{5} = {}^{-}35$   **40.** $n - {}^{-}3 = {}^{-}8$   **41.** $x + {}^{-}9 = 13$   **42.** $x - 3 = 9$

Name the ordered pair for the point. *(pages 436–439)*

**43.** $A$   **44.** $B$

**45.** $C$   **46.** $D$

**47.** $E$   **48.** $F$

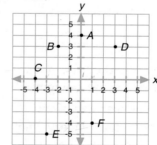

Solve. *(pages 424–425, 440–441)*

**49.** In one farming community, soybeans are grown on 7 farms, corn is grown on 7 farms, and both crops are grown on 3 farms. What is the smallest number of farms that can be in the community?

**50.** Arnold left home with some money in his pocket. He spent half of what he had on lunch, then he spent $1.20 on a magazine, and still had $1.50. How much did Arnold have when he left home?

## GUESS MY POLYGON

Play this game with a group. You will need a geoboard, rubber band, and centimeter graph paper. One player is the Polygon Placer and the others are the guessers.

1. Using the geoboard as a coordinate grid, the Polygon Placer makes a polygon with a rubber band. The polygon must fit in the first quadrant and no coordinate can exceed 4. The polygon shown has vertexes with coordinates $A$ (1, 0), $B$ (2, 1), $C$ (3, 1), $D$ (3, 3), and $E$ (1, 3).

2. The guessers draw a coordinate grid on their sheets of graph paper. The $x$ and $y$ axes need only go 4 units each in the positive direction.

3. The Guessers take turns naming the coordinates of a point. The Placer must tell whether the point named is a vertex of the polygon.

4. On any turn a Guesser can show his or her figure to the Placer. The first player who correctly copies the Placer's polygon wins the round.

5. Play until each player has been the Polygon Placer.

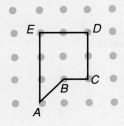

## Large Number Estimates

We often hear statements about the size of populations that seem too large to count. For example, you might read that 250,000 people watched a parade. Do you think that is an exact number or an estimate? How is a number like that obtained? One way to estimate crowds is to count the number of people within a small area and multiply by the number of similar areas.

You can use this principle to make a large number estimate in your school. Look around your classroom. Is either the floor or the ceiling covered with tiles? If either is, work with a partner to estimate the number of tiles that are in the entire building. If your building doesn't have this, estimate the number of pencils in the school.

## Six in a Row

Find six consecutive integers that add up to 369. After you find the answer, think about how you would make up a question like this one. Then make up two or three "In a Row" questions and share them with a friend.

Find the answer.

**1.** 30% of 86
- **a.** 2.58
- **b.** 258
- **c.** 25.8
- **d.** none of these

**2.** 18 is what percent of 96?
- **a.** 187.5%
- **b.** 18.75%
- **c.** 1.875%
- **d.** none of these

**3.** 40% of what number is 24?
- **a.** 9.6
- **b.** 60
- **c.** 96
- **d.** none of these

**4.** $\frac{23}{100} = \frac{x}{56}$
- **a.** 12.88
- **b.** 1.288
- **c.** 128.8
- **d.** none of these

**5.** $\frac{0.3}{100} = \frac{n}{42}$
- **a.** 1.26
- **b.** 12.6
- **c.** 126
- **d.** none of these

**6.** $\frac{160}{100} = \frac{y}{89}$
- **a.** 1.424
- **b.** 14.24
- **c.** 142.4
- **d.** none of these

**7.** original price: $95
discount: 15%
selling price:
- **a.** $14.25
- **b.** $80
- **c.** $80.75
- **d.** none of these

**8.** original price: $23
discount: 7%
selling price:
- **a.** $21.39
- **b.** $16
- **c.** $1.61
- **d.** none of these

**9.** cost: $38
markup: 70%
selling price:
- **a.** $108
- **b.** $54.29
- **c.** $64.60
- **d.** none of these

**10.** 81, 76, 82, 94
mean =
- **a.** 333
- **b.** 83.25
- **c.** 82.5
- **d.** none of these

**11.** 1, 8, 3, 7, 8
median =
- **a.** 7
- **b.** 8
- **c.** 5.4
- **d.** none of these

**12.** 6, 9, 7, 8, 9, 11
median =
- **a.** 8.5
- **b.** 8
- **c.** 9
- **d.** none of these

**13.** $^-7$ is between
- **a.** $^-6$ and 0
- **b.** $^-10$ and $^-6$
- **c.** $^-4$ and 0
- **d.** none of these

**14.** $^-23$ is greater than
- **a.** 0
- **b.** 15
- **c.** $^-36$
- **d.** none of these

**15.** $^-8$ is less than
- **a.** $^-35$
- **b.** $^-2$
- **c.** $^-15$
- **d.** none of these

# PROBLEM SOLVING REVIEW

**Problem Solving Check List**

- Too much information
- Too little information
- Multistep problems
- Making a graph
- Using a pattern
- Using an equation
- Using percents

Remember the strategies and types of problems you've had so far. Solve.

1. A staircase is made with 5 bricks in the bottom row, 4 in the next, then 3, 2, and 1. Another staircase follows the same pattern, but has 2 additional rows of bricks.

   a. How many bricks are in the bottom row of the smaller staircase?

   b. How many bricks are needed to build the smaller staircase?

   c. How many more bricks does the larger staircase need than the smaller one?

2. An elevator runs between ⁻2s (subbasement) to + 7 (7th floor). Edgar rode from the main floor (0), up to the 5th floor, then to the subbasement. How many floors did he pass by?

3. A racing bicycle has 2 gear positions in front and 6 in the rear. If a rider must select a combination of a front gear and a back gear, how many choices does the rider have?

4. Arizona became the 48th state in 1912. Delaware became the first state 125 yr earlier. In what year did Delaware become a state?

5. An airline ticket that normally sells for $362 can be bought at discount for $248. Estimate the total savings for a family buying 5 tickets.

6. A car maker guarantees its cars for 7 yr or 70,000 mi, whichever comes first. If an owner has had her car 5 yr and has driven 57,328 mi, which is likely to come first, 7 yr of ownership or 70,000 mi?

7. A driver is making a trip of 250 mi in desert and 150 mi in mountains. His car averages 25 mi/gal in the desert, but only 18 in mountains. What is the fewest whole number of gallons of gas the driver should expect to use?

8. Scientists estimate that 6,500 objects are orbiting the Earth. About 21% are dead satellites and about 6% are live satellites. About how many more satellites are dead than are live?

9. In 1986, Brook Junior High School raised $120 from a plant sale. By 1988, the amount increased to $165. In 1990, it was $210. If the pattern continues, predict how much the school will earn in 1994. Make a graph.

## TECHNOLOGY

## GIVE ME A SIGN 🔢

Change one operational sign in each problem so that a true statement is formed.

$(98 + 121) \div 11 + {}^-78 = 1{,}000$

$({}^-40 + {}^-6) - (8 \div {}^-2) = {}^-50$

${}^-120 \div (36 + {}^-30) + ({}^-420 \div 21) = 0$

Make up two more problems like these for a classmate to solve.

## GIVE ME THE TRUTH 🔢

Insert one or two pairs of parentheses so that a true statement is formed.

$98 + {}^-27 - 34 - {}^-85 = {}^-48$

${}^-79 \times 56 \div {}^-8 \times {}^-34 - {}^-17 = {}^-9{,}401$

${}^-91 + 43 \div {}^-117 + 125 = {}^-6$

$246 \div {}^-41 - {}^-846 - {}^-126 = 714$

## OFF THE BOARD 💻

In the computer activity *Operation Integer*, you move spaceships on a coordinate plane by adding or subtracting integer values for $x$ or $y$ coordinates. This pencil-and-paper activity will help you become familiar with moving a point on the coordinate plane.

Work with a partner. You will need a graph labeled from ${}^-15$ to $15$ on both the $x$- and $y$-axes. You will also need a number cube and a coin. Each player places a marker at $(0, 0)$. Move the marker according to these rules. Take turns.

1. Flip the coin. Heads means "add to $x$-coordinate." Tails means "add to $y$-coordinate."

2. Roll the number cube. This is the absolute value of the number to be added to the appropriate coordinate. Add a positive integer on the first turn, then alternate between positive and negative on the other turns.

Play until one player's marker has moved off the graph.

448    TECHNOLOGY

**DID YOU KNOW . . . ?**

Icebergs are made up of fresh water. If an iceberg 1 mi long, $\frac{1}{3}$ mi wide, and 500 ft thick melted, it would provide enough water for 8 million people to each have 1,000 qt per day for a month!

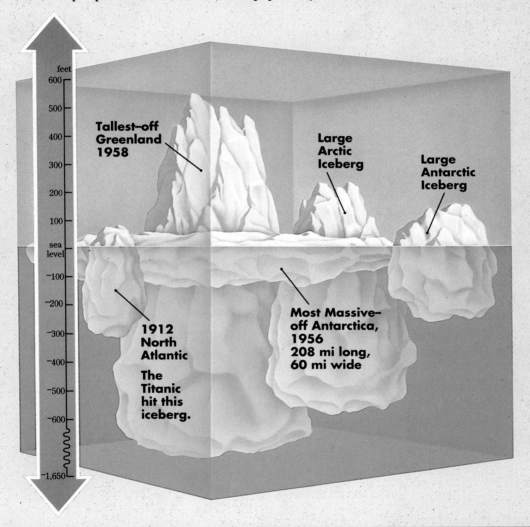

feet
600
500
400
300
200
100
sea level
-100
-200
-300
-400
-500
-600
-1,650

**Tallest–off Greenland 1958**

**Large Arctic Iceberg**

**Large Antarctic Iceberg**

**1912 North Atlantic**

**The Titanic hit this iceberg.**

**Most Massive– off Antarctica, 1956 208 mi long, 60 mi wide**

**USING DATA**

**Collect**

**Organize**

Describe

Predict

Measure several ice cubes to find the volume of each. Then melt the ice cubes. Measure the amount of water you get. Record your measurements in a table.

# Shaping Our World

## Geometry Around Us

**READ ABOUT IT**

The influence of the Chinese and the Japanese on the art of Europe and other parts of the world came about in part through the trade of cobalt blue and white pottery.

**Japanese dish, Late 17th century**

**Chinese vase, Early 15th century**

Pottery can be built up by hand, made from molds, or thrown (formed) on a pottery wheel. Master craftspeople throw clay into cylinders or other round pots on a rotating pottery wheel. The artist begins with a piece of clay, exerts the right amount of pressure, and forms the shape.

**Chinese vase, Middle 14th century**

1. Designs on many early works of art did not follow the shape, or contour, of the potteries. Which piece of art on these pages shows this kind of design?

2. Repeated designs can be created by rotations. The dish at right has five equally spaced designs made from rotations. What is the measure of the angle of rotation?

3. Discuss the rotations and angles of rotation on the Japanese dish on page 450.

4. Are there repeated designs or rotations on the vases? Discuss them.

5. Do you see any line symmetry on the dishes? Explain.

**Chelsea plate
Middle 18ᵗʰ century**

■ **WRITE ABOUT IT**

Use the three vases on pages 450 and 451 as examples.

6. Which vases were thrown on a wheel?

7. Which vase was probably made by combining different parts, each thrown on a wheel? Explain.

8. Which vase was made from several flat slabs like prisms? Explain.

9. Do you see any Asian influences in the Dutch tulip vase? Explain.

**Dutch Tulip vase,
Late 17ᵗʰ century**

# Squares and Square Roots

In ancient times, people used geometry to understand numbers. You can, too, by making a **MATH CONNECTION**

What is the area of the square at right?

What is $3^2$?

How does $3^2$ relate to the length of a side and the area of the square?

The **square** of any number is that number multiplied by itself. $3^2 = 3 \times 3 = 9$
You read: *The square of 3, or 3 squared, is 3 times 3, or 9.*

If you know that the area of a square is 9 cm$^2$, then each side is 3 cm. Similarly, if you know that 9 is the square of a number, then 3 is the number because $3^2 = 9$.

The symbol for a positive square root is $\sqrt{\phantom{x}}$. You write $\sqrt{9} = 3$. You read: *The positive square root of 9 is 3.*

**THINK ALOUD** Remember what you learned about multiplying integers. What is $^-3 \times {}^-3$, or $(^-3)^2$? Is $^-3$ also a square root of 9?

**CALCULATOR** Other examples:

$29^2 = 841$                     $\sqrt{55,696} = 236$

$30^2 = 900$                     $\sqrt{56,169} = 237$

Estimate, then find $29.2^2$.     Estimate, then find $\sqrt{56,000}$.

━━━━━━━━━━━━━ **GUIDED PRACTICE** ━━━━━━━━━━━━━

Read the exercise aloud. Then explain how to find the square or square root, and tell what it is.

**1.** $6^2$  **2.** $4.1^2$  **3.** $\sqrt{16}$  **4.** $\sqrt{\dfrac{4}{9}}$  **5.** $\sqrt{\dfrac{36}{9}}$  **6.** $\left(\dfrac{1}{3}\right)^2$

**7.** What solutions does $x^2 = 25$ have? What is the positive value of $x$?

Find the square of the number.

**8.** $9^2$  **9.** $1^2$  **10.** $10^2$  **11.** $0^2$  **12.** $12^2$

**13.** $(^-2)^2$  **14.** $\left(\frac{1}{2}\right)^2$  **15.** $\left(\frac{1}{10}\right)^2$  **16.** $(^-5)^2$  **17.** $25^2$

Find the positive square root of each number.

**18.** $\sqrt{25}$  **19.** $\sqrt{36}$  **20.** $\sqrt{0}$  **21.** $\sqrt{100}$  **22.** $\sqrt{121}$

**23.** $\sqrt{225}$  **24.** $\sqrt{81}$  **25.** $\sqrt{1}$  **26.** $\sqrt{900}$  **27.** $\sqrt{49}$

**28.** $\sqrt{\frac{4}{16}}$  **29.** $\sqrt{\frac{1}{4}}$  **30.** $\sqrt{\frac{1}{25}}$  **31.** $\sqrt{\frac{49}{81}}$  **32.** $\sqrt{\frac{64}{9}}$

**33. a.** Write the squares of each whole number from 1 to 10.

**b.** Write the numbers whose square roots are the whole numbers from 1 to 10. What do you observe?

**CALCULATOR** Find a number with a square between the given numbers.

**34.** 6 and 7  **35.** 9,000 and 10,000  **36.** 0.1 and 0.2

**37.** 600 and 700  **38.** 90 and 100  **39.** 0.7 and 0.8

Use $=$ or $\neq$ to make *true* sentences.

**40.** $5^2 \times 7^2$ ▓ $(5 \times 7)^2$  **41.** $5^2 + 7^2$ ▓ $(5 + 7)^2$

**42.** $8^2 \times 9^2$ ▓ $(8 \times 9)^2$  **43.** $8^2 + 9^2$ ▓ $(8 + 9)^2$

**44. CREATE YOUR OWN** Create and solve other examples like those in Exercises 40–43. What conclusions can you reach?

## Critical Thinking

Work with a partner. The figures below show that 1, 4, and 9 are square numbers. Find the next three square numbers.

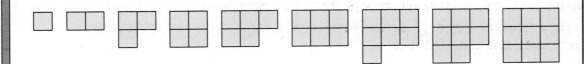

## EXPLORE

## *Exploring the Pythagorean Theorem*

Early Egyptian surveyors were called *harpedonaptai,* or "rope stretchers." They used ropes with 12 equally spaced knots to make right angles when they were laying out the boundaries of pieces of land.

**THINK ALOUD**  Why are right angles important in surveying land?

Use centimeter graph paper, scissors, and a centimeter ruler.

1.  Cut strips of paper of four different lengths: 3 cm, 4 cm, 5 cm, and 6 cm. Which three can be put together to form a right triangle?

The tomb of Ramses IX of Egypt, built about 1140 B.C. near Thebes. It shows a 3-4-5 right triangle.

2.  In a right triangle, the side opposite the right angle is called the **hypotenuse**. The other sides are called **legs**.

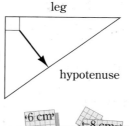

   **a.**  How long is the hypotenuse of your right triangle?

   **b.**  How long are the legs?

3.  Cut out eight squares with sides of the following lengths: 3 cm, 4 cm, 5 cm, 6 cm, 8 cm, 10 cm, 12 cm, and 13 cm. On each square, mark the length of one side and mark the area of the square.

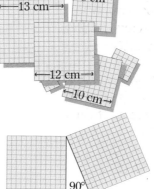

4.  Experiment to see how many ways you can arrange three of your squares to make a right triangle as shown.

List the lengths of sides and areas of squares that can be arranged to form right triangles.

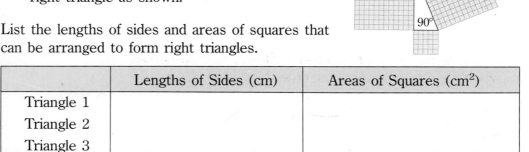

| | Lengths of Sides (cm) | Areas of Squares (cm²) |
|---|---|---|
| Triangle 1 | | |
| Triangle 2 | | |
| Triangle 3 | | |

MATH HISTORY

**5.** Make a list of some squares that form triangles that are not right triangles.

|  | Lengths of Sides (cm) | Areas of Squares (cm²) |
|---|---|---|
| Triangle 1 |  |  |
| Triangle 2 |  |  |
| Triangle 3 |  |  |

**6.** Look at your lists from Exercises 4 and 5. Can you discover any relationships between the areas? (*Hint*: Think about adding squares on the legs and comparing the sums of their areas with the area of a square added on the hypotenuse.)

**7.** If you did not discover a relationship in Exercise 6, work through this example.

| area of square on hypotenuse | $(5 \text{ cm})^2 \longrightarrow 25 \text{ cm}^2$ |
| area of square on one leg | $(3 \text{ cm})^2 \longrightarrow 9 \text{ cm}^2$ |
| area of square on other leg | $(4 \text{ cm})^2 \longrightarrow 16 \text{ cm}^2$ |

Notice that $25 \text{ cm}^2 = 9 \text{ cm}^2 + 16 \text{ cm}^2$.

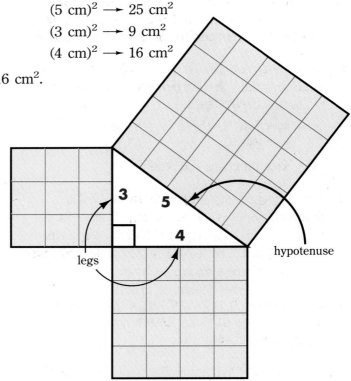

The relationship in Exercises 6 and 7 is known as the **Pythagorean Theorem.** It was named for Pythagoras, a Greek mathematician who studied in Babylonia, Egypt, and Italy about 2,500 y ago.

The Pythagorean Theorem states that for a right triangle, the square of the length of the hypotenuse equals the sum of the squares of the lengths of the legs.

**8.** Look at your lists from Exercises 4 and 5. Does the Pythagorean Theorem work for right triangles? for other triangles?

**9. CALCULATOR** Is a triangle with sides of these lengths a right triangle?

**a.** 7 cm, 24 cm, 25 cm    **b.** 8 cm, 11 cm, 14 cm

## Construction: Designs

Many designs can be made using only a compass and a straightedge. A straightedge is a ruler without numbers or units.

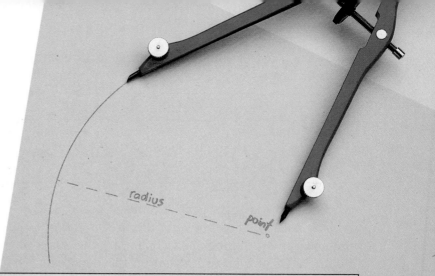

radius
point

1. Practice the construction. Then use it for Exercises 2–7.

---

### Construction: Arcs of a circle

| Use a compass to draw a circle with center $C$ and radius $\overline{CQ}$. | Do not change the compass opening. Place the compass point at $Q$. Strike a mark on the circle. | Place the compass point on the mark. Strike again. Repeat around the circle. |
| --- | --- | --- |

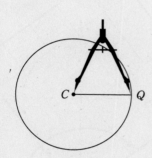

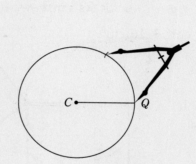

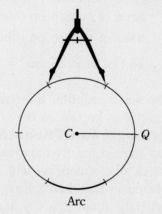

Arc

---

Use the construction above to make the figure.
Then, construct the design or create a new one of your own.

**2.** a regular hexagon    **3.** an equilateral triangle    **4.** a trapezoid

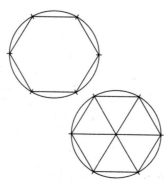

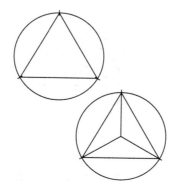

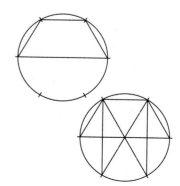

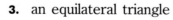

MATH AND ART

Construct the design.

**5.**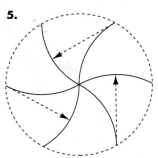

**6.**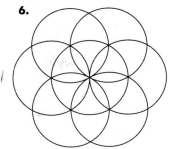

**7.**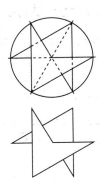

**8.** Practice the construction. Then use it for Exercises 9–12.

| Construction: Perpendicular lines | | |
|---|---|---|
| Draw a circle with center $P$. Draw diameter $\overline{AB}$. | Set the compass opening to about the length of the diameter. Place the compass point at $A$. Strike two marks as shown. | Repeat at $B$ so that the marks intersect. Draw $\overleftrightarrow{CD}$. It is perpendicular to $\overline{AB}$. |

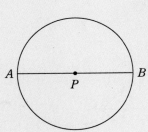

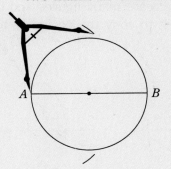

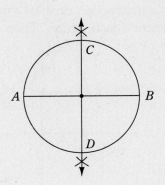

Construct the design.

**9.**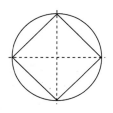

**10.**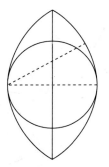

**11.**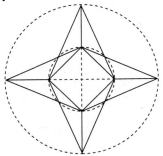

**12. CREATE YOUR OWN** Use the constructions to make a design of your own.

## Construction: Bisecting Segments and Angles

When you construct a perpendicular line by placing the compass point at the ends of a line segment, you also bisect the segment, or divide it into two congruent parts. In the construction at right, $\overleftrightarrow{DE} \perp \overline{AB}$ and $\overleftrightarrow{DE}$ bisects $\overline{AB}$.

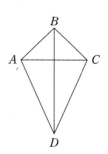

1. What are the two congruent segments on $\overline{AB}$?

2. What line is perpendicular to $\overline{AB}$?

3. At what point does $\overleftrightarrow{DE}$ bisect $\overline{AB}$?

4. How many right angles are formed? Name them.

This construction enables you to create many figures and designs. Construct each figure. Then use it to copy the design or to make your own.

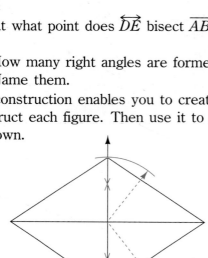
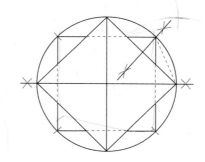

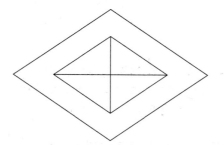
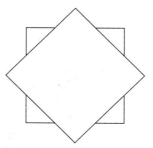

5. **THINK ALOUD**   In the kite at right there are two pairs of congruent sides. Name them. What property do you think the diagonals of a kite have? Construct a kite.

To bisect an angle, you divide it into two congruent angles.

| Construction: Bisecting of an angle | | |
|---|---|---|
| Draw an angle. Label the vertex $M$. Place the compass point at $M$ and strike equal lengths along the rays. Label the points $N$ and $P$. | With the compass point at $N$, strike an arc as shown. | Repeat with the point at $P$ without changing the compass radius. Label $Q$. Draw $\overrightarrow{MQ}$. |

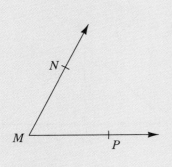 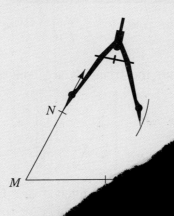

6. Use the construction above.

 a. What angle was bisect

 b. What ray bisected

 c. Name the two

 d. Copy the c

7. Trace the tri

 a. Bisect t
    What d

 b. Draw
    Bisect

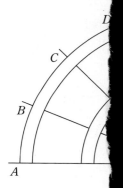

# Construction: Triangles

Triangles are rigid figures. The three sides alone determine a triangle's shape. Once the three sides are known, the angles are determined.

> **Two triangles are congruent when the three sides of one triangle are congruent to the three sides of the other triangle.**

This rule is called the side-side-side rule.
You can shorten it to the SSS rule.

SSS rule to decide whether the triangles are congruent.

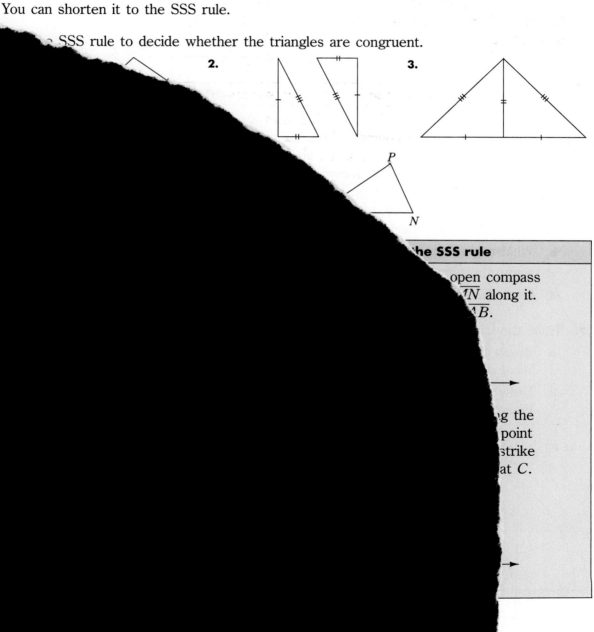

**2.**

**3.**

*P*

*N*

he SSS rule

open compass
*N* along it.
*B*.

g the
point
strike
at *C*.

Use the SSS rule to construct a congruent figure.

**5.**

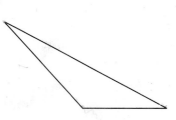

**6.**

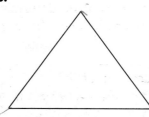

**7.**

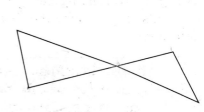

**8.** You can construct a right triangle if you know the lengths of the two legs. Copy this construction of a right triangle.

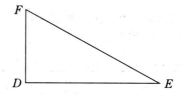

---

### Construction: Right △GHI congruent to △DEF

| Construct perpendicular lines. Label point $G$. | Measure $DE$ with the compass. With the compass point at $G$, strike an arc as shown. Extend the segment if necessary. Label point $H$. | Measure $DF$ with the compass. With the compass point at $G$, mark $I$. Draw right △GHI. How do you know that △GHI is a right triangle? |
|---|---|---|
| 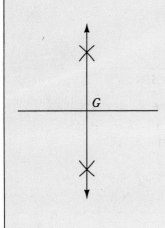 | 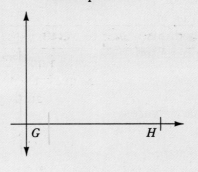 | 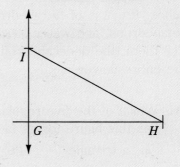 |

---

Construct the figures.

**9.**

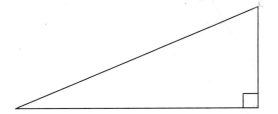

**10.**

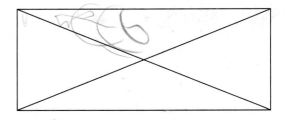

## Construction: Space Figures

Many beautiful crystals have faces that are regular polygons. A salt crystal is shaped like a **cube**. A diamond crystal is shaped like an **octahedron**. Cubes and octahedrons are called **space figures**. A space figure has three dimensions—length, width, and height.

There are exactly five regular space figures. They have faces that are congruent regular polygons. See the drawings at right.

A space figure with its interior is a **solid**. The solids of the five regular space figures are called **Platonic solids** and were named for the Greek philosopher Plato.

The ancient Greeks believed that the universe was made of these five solids. They thought the earth was made of cubes, fire was of tetrahedrons, air of octahedrons, and water of icosahedrons. For them, the dodecahedron represented the entire universe.

1. Which of the five regular space figures has this figure for its faces?
   **a.** a triangle      **b.** a square
   **c.** a pentagon

2. Two faces meet at a line segment called an **edge**. Tell how many edges the figure has.
   **a.** a cube          **b.** a tetrahedron

3. Edges meet in points called **vertexes**. Tell how many edges meet at each vertex.
   **a.** a tetrahedron   **b.** an octahedron
   **c.** an icosahedron  **d.** a dodecahedron

Salt crystals (sodium chloride)

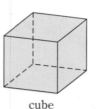

cube            tetrahedron

octahedron

icosahedron          dodecahedron

MATH HISTORY

**4.** Copy this construction to make a model of a tetrahedron.

---

**Construction: Tetrahedron**

Draw a large circle. Strike six arcs around the circle. Draw equilateral triangle △*ABC*.

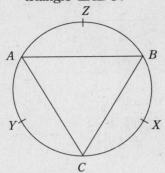

Draw segments $\overline{AX}$, $\overline{BY}$, and $\overline{CZ}$.

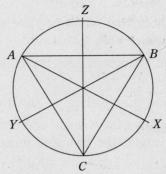

Draw △*MNP* as shown.

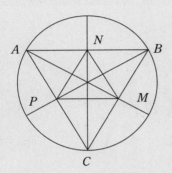

Cut out △*ABC*. Fold along $\overline{MN}$, $\overline{NP}$, and $\overline{MP}$ to make the tetrahedron.

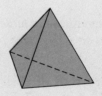

---

**5.** A tetrahedron can be used to construct an octahedron.

  **a.** Make a copy of the construction for the tetrahedron.

  **b.** Trace it twice so that the parts match at $\overline{ST}$ as shown.

  **c.** Cut along the outside edges. Fold along other segments. Construct the octahedron.

**6. CREATE YOUR OWN** Describe a plan you could follow to construct a cube. Try your plan.

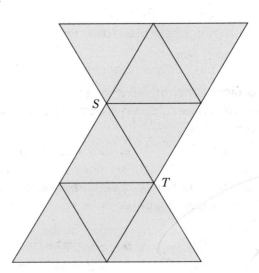

---

**LANGUAGE & VOCABULARY**

---

Write *true* or *false*.

1. Every number that has a positive square root also has a negative square root.

2. Every right triangle meets the conditions of the Pythagorean theorem.

3. Constructing the bisector of any angle requires a protractor.

4. If three angles of a triangle are congruent to three angles of another triangle, the triangles must be congruent.

---

**QUICK QUIZ** ✓

---

Find the square of the number. *(pages 452–455)*

1. $7^2$       2. $(^-4)^2$       3. $\left(\frac{1}{3}\right)^2$

Find the positive square root of each number. *(pages 452–455)*

4. $\sqrt{64}$       5. $\sqrt{625}$       6. $\sqrt{\frac{1}{16}}$

Use the construction for exercises 7–9. *(pages 456–463)*

7. Name the bisected angle.

8. Name the angle bisector.

9. Name the congruent angles created by the angle bisector.

10. Mr. Salazar wants to enclose a plot of land to use as a vegetable garden. He has 52 ft of fencing to use.

     **a.** How much fencing does Mr. Salazar have available?

     **b.** If he builds his garden in the shape of a square, how long can each side be?

     **c.** If he builds his garden in the shape of a square, what will be the area of the garden?

Write the answers in your learning log.
1. Your friend thinks that the Pythagorean Theorem will work for all triangles. What is wrong with this thinking?

2. Explain what will be true if you correctly bisect a line segment or angle.

**DID YOU KNOW . . . ?** In 1960 Americans generated an average of 2.5 lb/d of garbage per person. Twenty-five years later, we were generating about 3.5 lb/d. How much garbage is collected in your city or town in a week? About how many pounds is that per person per day?

In the drawing at right, *r* is the radius of the large circle that fits in the corner. The corner is a right angle. Tell how you could find the radius of the smaller circle in the corner.

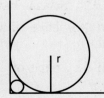

# Problem Solving Strategy:
# Creating and Using Formulas

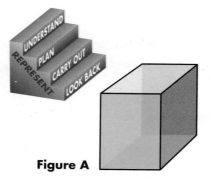

A formula uses symbols to show relationships. Creating a formula for a relationship lets you work with the relationship more easily.

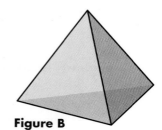

**Figure A**

**Figure B**

Study the space figures A–F. Can you find a formula to relate the number of faces (*F*), edges (*E*), and vertexes (*V*) in each figure?

You can count faces, edges, and vertexes and collect information in a chart like this one.

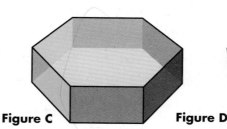

**Figure C**　　　**Figure D**

| Space Figure | F | E | V |
|:---:|:---:|:---:|:---:|
| A | 6 | 12 | |
| B | | | |
| C | | | |

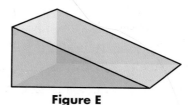

**Figure E**

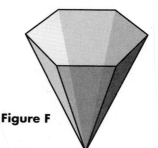

**Figure F**

Which formula is correct for all of the space figures?

**a.** $F + V = E$　　　**b.** $F + V = E + 2$　　**c.** $F + E = V - 1$

Check the formula you chose using this space figure. If the relationship you chose is not correct, you may need to count again.

**THINK ALOUD** Explain the formula in your own words.

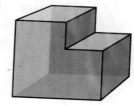

Figure X

═══════════════ **GUIDED PRACTICE** ═══════════════

**1.** Use the formula $F + V = E + 2$ and Figures G and H to answer.

　**a.** What three variables are related by the formula?

　**b.** Do the space figures at right satisfy the formula?

　**c.** If $F = 5$ when $V = 5$, what is $E$?

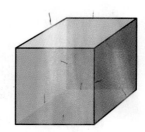

**Figure G**　　　**Figure H**

466　　LESSON 14–8

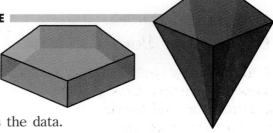

Use the formula to find the missing variable.

**2.** $F = 7$       $V = 10$       $E = ?$

**3.** $F = 6$       $V = ?$       $E = 10$

**4.** Use the chart to write a formula that relates the data.

| C | D |
|---|---|
| 12.56 cm | 4 cm |
| 21.98 cm | 7 cm |
| 35.17 cm | 11.2 cm |

$C$ = circumference of a circle
$d$ = diameter
$\pi \approx 3.14$

**5.** Use the formula from Exercise 4 to show that when the diameter of a circle is 6.8 cm, the circumference is about 21.35 cm.

**6.** Use the chart to write a formula that relates the data.

| A | r |
|---|---|
| 3.14 cm$^2$ | 1 cm |
| 12.56 cm$^2$ | 2 cm |
| 78.5 cm$^2$ | 5 cm |

$A$ = area of circle
$r$ = radius
$\pi \approx 3.14$

**7.** Use the formula from Exercise 6 to show that when the radius of a lid is 8 cm, the area is about 200.96 cm$^2$.

Solve. Tell what formula you used.

**8.** The first Ferris wheel was built in 1893 in Chicago. Its diameter was about 75 m. After the Ferris wheel revolved 20 times, about how far did the passengers travel?

**9.** Four years later, a Ferris wheel was built in London with an area of about 6,400 m$^2$. Did this Ferris wheel have a greater diameter than the one built in Chicago?

Choose any strategy to solve.

**10.** What is the next number in the pattern: 1, 5, 3, 7, 5, 9, 7, . . . ?

**11.** A 1-L bottle of orange juice costs $1.25. A 2-L bottle of the same juice costs $2.39. Only three 2-L bottles are left. How much will 10-L of orange juice cost?

**12.** Rosa gave half of her baseball card collection to Sam. He gave half of what Rosa gave him to Harold. Harold gave half of the cards he got from Sam to Herman. Herman already had 8 baseball cards. The cards he got from Harold doubled his collection. How many baseball cards does Rosa now have?

## Exploring Surface Area of Prisms and Pyramids

A cube is a special example of a prism. All **prisms** have two bases that are congruent polygons on parallel planes.

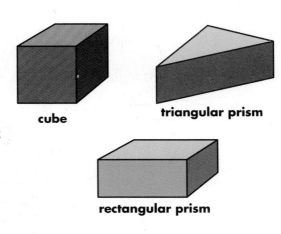

cube          triangular prism

rectangular prism

1. For any prism, what are the shapes of the faces that are not bases?

2. What is the name of a rectangular prism with square bases and square faces?

The **surface area** of a space figure is the sum of the areas of the faces. To find the surface area, you can use a pattern.

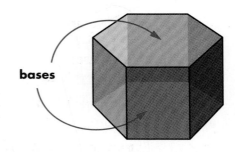

bases

hexagonal prism

3. What is the surface area of this rectangular prism? Answer these questions to help you find out.

   a. How do you find the area of face E?

   b. What other face has the same area?

   c. Is there a face with the same area as face B? face A?

4. Draw the pattern on centimeter graph paper. Cut it out to make the rectangular prism. What pairs of faces have the same areas?

5. **IN YOUR WORDS** Write a paragraph explaining how to find the surface area of any rectangular prism.

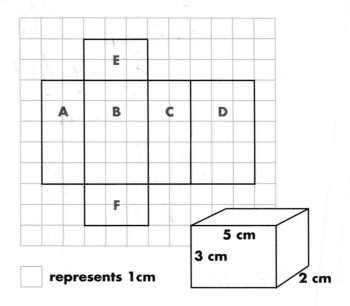

represents 1cm

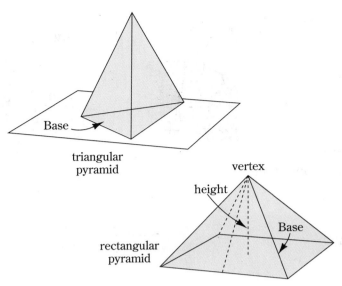

triangular
pyramid

vertex

height

Base

rectangular
pyramid

A **pyramid** has only one base and is named according to the shape of the base. A segment from a vertex perpendicular to the base is called the height of the pyramid. The height is not related to surface area, but to the volume of the pyramid.

**6.** For a pyramid, what are the shapes of the faces that are not the base?

**7.** What is the name of a triangular pyramid with all faces congruent?

**8.** **a.** What is the surface area of the pyramid at right? Count squares or use formulas. Remember: The area of a triangle $= \frac{1}{2}(b \times h)$.

**b.** Draw the pattern on centimeter graph paper. Cut it out to make the pyramid. Describe the positions of the faces with the same areas.

**c.** **IN YOUR WORDS** Write a paragraph explaining how you found the surface area.

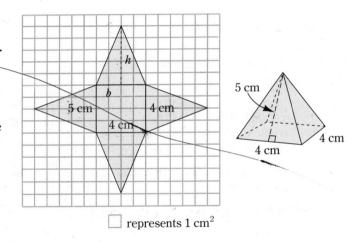

$h$

$b$

5 cm

4 cm

4 cm

5 cm

4 cm

4 cm

☐ represents 1 cm$^2$

Find the surface area.

**9.**

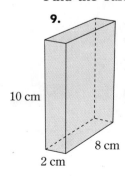

10 cm

8 cm

2 cm

**10.**

square base

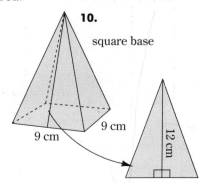

9 cm

9 cm

12 cm

**11.**

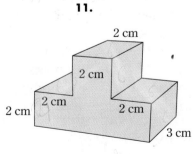

2 cm

2 cm

2 cm

2 cm

2 cm

2 cm

3 cm

**12.** a triangular pyramid with the area of each face equal to 24 cm$^2$

**13.** a cube with the lengths of each side equal to $m$

## *Exploring Surface Area of Curved Surfaces*

All faces of prisms and pyramids are polygons. However, some space figures have faces that cannot be contained in a plane. These faces are called curved surfaces. Many of these surfaces are found in nature.

| **Spheres** | | |
|---|---|---|
| The Sun, the Moon, and the planets resemble **spheres**. All points on the surface of a sphere are the same distance from the center. | 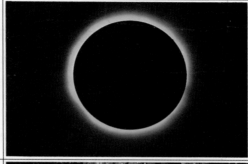 |  |
| **Cylinders** | | |
| A tree trunk resembles a cylinder. The two bases of the cylinder are congruent and on parallel planes. |  |  |
| **Cones** | | |
| An erupting volcano looks like a cone. A cone has one base. |  |  |

**1.** Which figure above has these qualities?

    **a.** one circular base and one curved surface

    **b.** all points equidistant from one point

    **c.** two flat faces and one curved surface

    **d.** exactly one curved surface

MATH AND SCIENCE

To find the surface area of a cylinder, you can use a pattern.

2. Estimate the surface area of the cylinder by counting and piecing together squares.

3. Draw the pattern. How long is the rectangle? Cut out the pattern and make the cylinder.

   (*Hint:* How does the length of the rectangle relate to the circumference of the circle? If you know the radius or diameter, how can you find the circumference?)

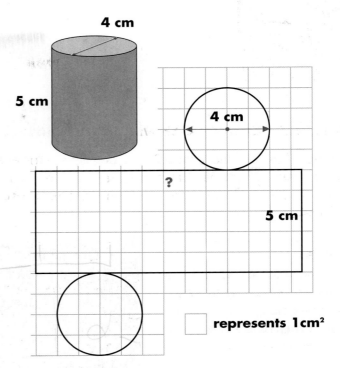

□ represents 1 cm²

4. What other method could you use to find the surface area? Choose a method and use it.

   (*Hint 1:* Use the formula for the area of a circle to find the area of each base. $A = \pi \times r^2$ .)

   (*Hint 2:* The length of the rectangle is the same as the circumference of the circular base. $C = \pi \times d$. What is the area of the rectangle?)

5. Compare your estimates for the surface area obtained in Exercises 2 and 4.

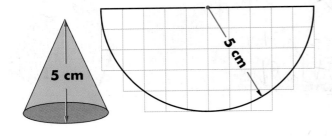

This is a pattern for the curved surface of a cone.

6. Estimate the surface area of this part of the cone.

7. Draw the pattern on centimeter graph paper. Cut it out and bend it to make the curved surface.

8. Draw the flat face.

9. Estimate the surface area of the cone.

## Problem Solving: Visual Perception

A drafter draws designs or plans to construct tools, utensils, cars, and other objects. For some objects, it is necessary to draw a **cross section** of the object so you can see a hidden part.

To make a cross section of this faucet handle, you would cut through the handle along a plane. The shape of the figure the plane cuts is called the **cross section**.

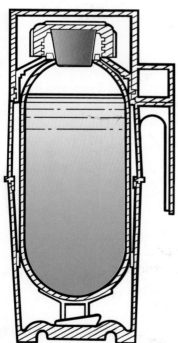

The picture at the left shows a cross section of an object you often use. What is the object? Answer these questions to help you decide.

What could a cross section look like from a different direction?

Is the object's shape more like a prism, cylinder, or sphere?

What is contained within the object?

---

### GUIDED PRACTICE

1. Use the diagram at right to answer.
   a. What does the diagram show?
   b. What is the shape of the cross section?
   c. What is the shape of the cross section of a sphere when the plane does not pass through the center of the sphere?

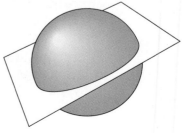

MATH AND INDUSTRIAL ARTS

Which shapes can be cross sections of the figure on the left?

**2.**
   **a.**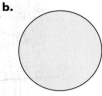
   **b.**
   **c.**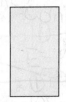
   **d.**

**3.**
   **a.**
   **b.**
   **c.**
   **d.**

Draw the shape of the cross section. Use a compass if necessary.

**4.**
   **5.**
   **6.**

**7.**
   **8.**
   **9.**

**CHOOSE** Choose any strategy to solve.

**10.** Judith bought a pair of jeans at an outlet sale. The original price was $50.00. She received the regular 20% outlet discount and, in addition, a 25% discount on the first discounted price because of the sale. How much did she pay for the jeans?

**11.** Roger made 5 model cars and wants to put them on a shelf. He is trying to decide how to arrange them and wants to try every possible way. How many different ways can he arrange the cars on a shelf?

**12.** About how many days in all will there be in the 21st century? (*Hint:* It begins January 1, 2001 and ends December 31, 2100.)

# Volume: Prism and Pyramid

This refrigerator holds 18 cubic feet (18 ft³) of food. Estimate the size of a cubic foot and show it using your hands.

The **volume** of a space figure measures the amount of space inside it. The volume of a rectangular prism with dimensions 3 ft by 3 ft by 2 ft, is 18 ft³.

---

| **The volume (V) of any prism is the product of the area of the base (B) and the height (h).** | **The volume (V) of a pyramid is one third of the volume of a prism with the same base (B) and height (h).** |
|---|---|
| $V = Bh$ | $V = \frac{1}{3}(Bh)$ |

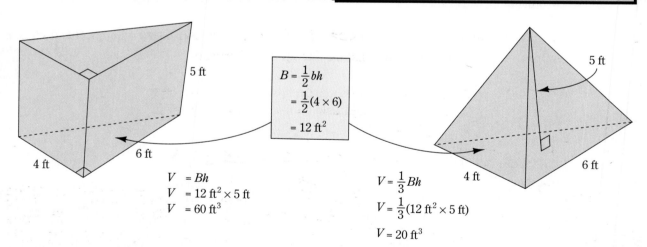

$$B = \frac{1}{2}bh$$
$$= \frac{1}{2}(4 \times 6)$$
$$= 12 \text{ ft}^2$$

5 ft
6 ft
4 ft

$V = Bh$
$V = 12 \text{ ft}^2 \times 5 \text{ ft}$
$V = 60 \text{ ft}^3$

5 ft
4 ft
6 ft

$V = \frac{1}{3}Bh$
$V = \frac{1}{3}(12 \text{ ft}^2 \times 5 \text{ ft})$
$V = 20 \text{ ft}^3$

Find the volume. Write the formula you used.

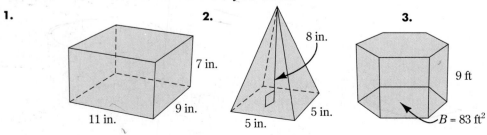

**1.**
7 in.
9 in.
11 in.

**2.**
8 in.
5 in.
5 in.

**3.**
9 ft
$B = 83 \text{ ft}^2$

Find the volume.

**4.**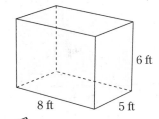
6 ft
8 ft     5 ft

**5.**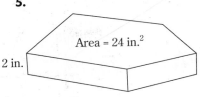
Area = 24 in.²
2 in.

**6.**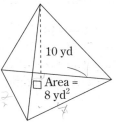
10 yd
Area = 8 yd²

**7.**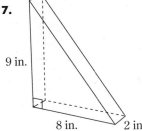
9 in.
8 in.     2 in.

**8.**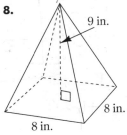
9 in.
8 in.     8 in.

**9.**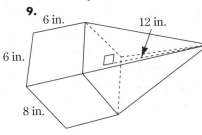
6 in.          12 in.
6 in.
8 in.

**10.** a cube with length of side:   **a.** 10 in.   **b.** 11 ft   **c.** s feet

Find the height.

**11.** a prism with a volume of 308 in.³ and a base area of 28 in.²

**12.** a pyramid with a volume of 255 in.³ and a base area of 45 in.²

**13.** Name one possible set of dimensions for an 18 ft³ freezer.

**14.** **IN YOUR WORDS**  You want to buy a freezer. Use the ad below to write two questions you should ask yourself before buying it.

## *Volume: Cylinder*

A springform pan used for baking has a removable rim fastened with a spring. When the rim is removed, the sides of the cake look perfect. One standard size for a springform pan is 10 in. in diameter and $2\frac{1}{2}$ in. in height. What is its volume?

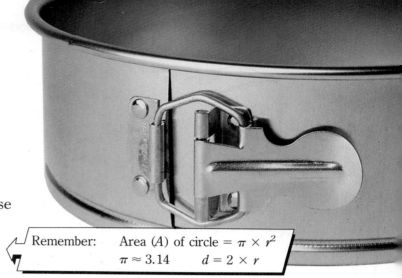

First, you find the area of the circular base and multiply by a height of 1 in.

For the volume of one layer:
$V = (\pi \times r^2) \times 1$
$V \approx (3.14 \times 5^2) \times 1$, or
78.50 in.$^3$

Remember:     Area ($A$) of circle = $\pi \times r^2$
$\pi \approx 3.14$     $d = 2 \times r$

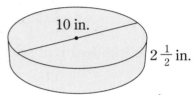

Then for the entire cylinder, multiply by a height of $2\frac{1}{2}$ in.

$V \approx 78.5$ in.$^3$ $\times 2.5$, or 196.25 in.$^3$

The pan holds about 200 in.$^3$.

---

**The volume of a cylinder is found by multiplying the area of its base ($B$) times its height ($h$).**
**Volume ($V$) = Area of Base ($B$) × height ($h$)**
$$V = B \times h$$

---

**THINK ALOUD**   For what other space figure is the same formula used to find its volume?

**CALCULATOR**   Could you multiply this way—$3.14 \times 2.75 \times 16$—to find the volume of the cylinder? Explain your answer.

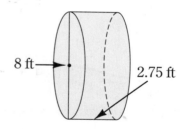

8 ft ⟶    2.75 ft

---

**GUIDED PRACTICE**

Find the volume. Explain how you used the formula.

**1.**

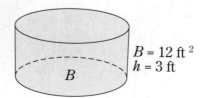

$B = 12$ ft$^2$
$h = 3$ ft

$B$

**2.**

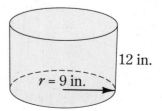

12 in.

$r = 9$ in.

MATH AND HOME ECONOMICS

Find the volume of the cylinder. Use 3.14 for $\pi$.

**3.** $r = 3$ ft

  $h = 7$ ft

**4.** $r = 9$ ft

  $h = 3$ ft

**5.** $r = 17$ yd

  $h = 11$ yd

**6.** $d = 19$ in.

  $h = 17$ in.

**7.** $d = 82$ ft

  $h = 25$ ft

**8.** $d = 3\frac{1}{2}$ yd

  $h = 2\frac{1}{4}$ yd

Find the volume.

**9.**

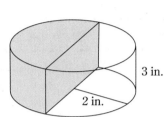

3 in.

2 in.

**10.**

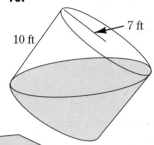

10 ft

7 ft

**11.**

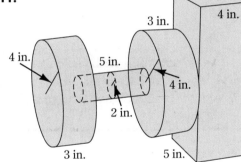

4 in.   5 in.   3 in.   4 in.

3 in.   2 in.   5 in.

4 in.   12 in.

**12. CALCULATOR** Find the radius and the height of two different cylinders, each with a volume between 50 in.$^3$ and 60 in.$^3$

**13.** Springform pans come in two standard sizes with diameters of 7 in. and 10 in. Both pans have the same height. Compare their volumes.

**14. CRITICAL THINKING** Why do you think the two sizes of pans in Exercise 13 are the standard sizes?

**15.** Some springform pans look like the one at right. What is its volume?

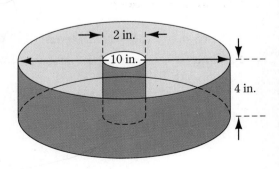

2 in.   10 in.   4 in.

## Mixed Review

Compute.

**1.** $28,182 \div 77$     **2.** $913 + 302$     **3.** $7,650 - 4,721$     **4.** $613.4 - 1.58$

**5.** $\frac{5}{8} \times 2\frac{1}{6}$     **6.** $4\frac{5}{8} \div \frac{1}{4}$     **7.** $10\frac{11}{12} + \frac{10}{24}$     **8.** $9\frac{3}{8} - 3\frac{7}{8}$

Solve for $n$ in the proportion.

**9.** $\frac{n}{35} = \frac{12}{60}$     **10.** $\frac{8}{20} = \frac{n}{45}$     **11.** $\frac{9}{15} = \frac{33}{n}$     **12.** $\frac{14}{n} = \frac{8}{24}$

Find the unknown.

**13.** 75% of what number is 90?     **14.** What is 80% of 385?

**15.** What is 60% of 610?     **16.** 25% of what number is 111?

**17.** What percent is 258 out of 516?     **18.** What is 50% of 270?

**19.** 90% of what number is 198?     **20.** What percent is 161 out of 460?

Compute.

**21.** $9 + {}^-3$     **22.** $1 - 5$     **23.** $2 \times {}^-4$     **24.** ${}^-4 \div 2$

**25.** ${}^-1 - 6$     **26.** $7 + {}^-4$     **27.** $4 \div {}^-2$     **28.** ${}^-7 \times {}^-3$

**29.** ${}^-5 \times 2$     **30.** ${}^-4 \div {}^-2$     **31.** ${}^-12 + {}^-8$     **32.** $5 - {}^-3$

**33.** ${}^-16 \div 4$     **34.** $4 \times {}^-6$     **35.** ${}^-2 - {}^-12$     **36.** ${}^-15 + 15$

**37.** ${}^-20 + {}^-10$     **38.** ${}^-12 - 21$     **39.** ${}^-4 \times {}^-4$     **40.** $20 \div {}^-10$

**Niamey, Niger**

Use the map and the table. Choose estimation, mental math, pencil and paper, or calculator to solve.

**41.** About 6,894,000 people live in Niger.

   **a.** About 1 person out of every 23 people in Niger owns a radio. About how many people own radios?

   **b.** Less than 1% of the population owns a television. About how many people, at most, own televisions?

   **c.** About 4 out of every 5 people live in rural areas. About how many people live in urban areas?

**42.** The Niger River is the third largest river in Africa. It is about 252 mi longer than the 2,348-mi Mississippi River. About how long is the Niger River?

**43.** Niger's capital, Niamey, is located at about 13° N latitude and 2° E longitude. What is the latitude and longitude of Mount Gréboun, Niger's highest point?

**44.** *Sahara* comes from an Arabic word meaning "desert." The United States, which has an area of about 3,619,000 mi², is only about 119,000 mi² larger than the Sahara. About how large is the Sahara?

**45.** Estimate the distance from Mount Gréboun to Niamey.

**46.** Draw a double bar graph of the average monthly high and low temperatures for Niamey.

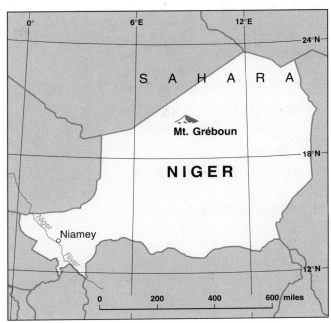

| Niamey's Average High and Low Temperatures | | |
|---|---|---|
| January | 93°F | 61°F |
| February | 91°F | 64°F |
| March | 102°F | 72°F |
| April | 106°F | 79°F |
| May | 106°F | 81°F |
| June | 100°F | 77°F |
| July | 93°F | 75°F |
| August | 90°F | 72°F |
| September | 93°F | 73°F |
| October | 97°F | 73°F |
| November | 99°F | 66°F |
| December | 93°F | 59°F |

# Investigating Water and Ice

Ice is water that has frozen solid. Raindrops are water, but snow, sleet, frost, and hail are ice. Ice has many uses because it is cold. It helps to keep foods fresh, to chill beverages, and to treat injuries.

Pure water changes to ice, or freezes, when it is cooled to 32°F. This temperature is the freezing point of water.

Almost all substances contract, or grow smaller, as they cool. Water contracts as it cools to 39°F. Then it begins to expand, or grow larger. When water freezes, it increases in volume by about $\frac{1}{11}$.

When the temperature around ice becomes warmer than 32°F, ice begins to melt into water. The temperature of the ice and the melted water will stay at 32°F until all the ice has melted.

Work with a partner. You will need nonglass containers, some water, a ruler, packaging materials, and a freezer. A thermometer may be helpful.

MATH AND SCIENCE

1. Use a tall container. Pour water in it to a depth of at least $5\frac{1}{2}$ in., but don't fill the container. Freeze the water in the container. Measure the height of the ice.

2. Did the ice increase in volume? If so, by what fraction did it increase? Do your results agree with the information given on page 480?

3. Use your results from Exercises 1 and 2 to explain the situations.

   a. Water pipes may burst in very cold weather.

   b. Ice floats in water.

4. Imagine that you have the blocks of ice shown below. If all three are placed on a sidewalk on a warm day, which do you think will completely melt first? Explain.

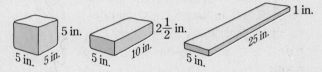

5. For most uses of ice, it is important to keep it so cold that it doesn't melt or that it melts very slowly. List some ways to keep ice cold.

6. Can you think of a better way to keep ice from melting? List your ideas.

7. Have a contest. Make several blocks of ice using the same amount of water and the same kind of container. Use whatever materials you like (but nothing involving electricity) to "package" the ice. See whose packaging best keeps the ice from melting.

8. In Exercise 7, how can you determine when the ice has completely melted without opening the "packages" of ice? (*Hint*: Read the fourth paragraph on page 480.)

---
### LANGUAGE & VOCABULARY
---

Match the figure with its description.

1. a figure with two congruent triangular bases     **a.** cone
2. a figure with six congruent faces     **b.** triangular prism
3. a figure with one square base and four congruent triangular faces     **c.** cylinder
4. a figure with one base and no polygon faces     **d.** cube
5. a figure with two circular bases     **e.** square pyramid

---
### TEST ✓
---

==== **CONCEPTS** ====

Find the square of the number. *(pages 452–455)*

1. $11^2$     2. $23^2$     3. $1^2$     4. $4^2$     5. $(^-6)^2$

Find the positive square root of each number. *(pages 452–455)*

6. $\sqrt{169}$     7. $\sqrt{400}$     8. $\sqrt{1}$     9. $\sqrt{\frac{25}{64}}$     10. $\sqrt{\frac{1}{36}}$

Use the construction. Points $Q$ and $X$ were found by striking arcs from points $M$ and $N$. Line $QX$ is to be drawn. Complete each statement. *(pages 458–461)*

11. $\overleftrightarrow{QX}$ and $\overline{MN}$ will be _____.

12. Segments $MO$ and $ON$ are _____.

==== **SKILLS** ====

Find the volume. Use 3.14 for $\pi$. *(pages 468–471, 474–477)*

13.
$h = 10$ in.
$A = 81$ in.$^2$

14.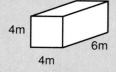
4m
6m
4m

15.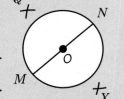
$r = 3$ ft    $h = 12$ ft

16. A cube with length of side 15 in.

17. A pyramid with base area 100 m$^2$ and height 12 m.

18. A cylinder with diameter 12 yd and height 12 yd.

For Exercises 14 and 15 find the surface area also.

Find the height. *(pages 474–475)*

**19.** A prism with volume of 539 in.$^3$ and base area of 77 in.$^2$

**20.** A pyramid with volume of 405 in.$^3$ and base area of 135 in.$^2$

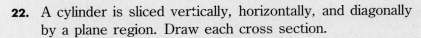 **PROBLEM SOLVING**

Solve. *(pages 472–473, 466–467, 476–477)*

**21.** Use the space figure.

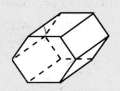

   **a.** What is the shape of the figure?

   **b.** How many faces ($F$), vertexes ($V$), and edges ($E$) does the figure have?

   **c.** Does the figure satisfy the formula $F + V = E + 2$?

**22.** A cylinder is sliced vertically, horizontally, and diagonally by a plane region. Draw each cross section.

**23.** A cylindrical oil tank has a radius of 3 ft for its base and a height of 12 ft. What is the volume of the tank? Use 3.14 for $\pi$.

 **LEARNING LOG**

Write the answers in your learning log.

   **1.** Describe in your own words what is meant by surface area.

   **2.** Explain how you would make a cylinder using a flat piece of paper.

Find the square of the number. *(pages 452–455)*

**1.** $3^2$  **2.** $9^2$  **3.** $16^2$  **4.** $13^2$  **5.** $24^2$

**6.** $(^-16)^2$  **7.** $(^-2)^2$  **8.** $\left(\frac{3}{8}\right)^2$  **9.** $0^2$  **10.** $\left(\frac{2}{3}\right)^2$

Find the positive square root of each number. *(pages 452–455)*

**11.** $\sqrt{16}$  **12.** $\sqrt{144}$  **13.** $\sqrt{256}$  **14.** $\sqrt{961}$  **15.** $\sqrt{289}$

**16.** $\sqrt{0}$  **17.** $\sqrt{100}$  **18.** $\sqrt{\frac{4}{9}}$  **19.** $\sqrt{\frac{16}{9}}$  **20.** $\sqrt{\frac{81}{36}}$

Constructions. *(pages 456–463)*

**21.** Draw line segment $PQ$. Construct the perpendicular bisector of $\overline{PQ}$. Label the point of intersection $O$. How many right angles are formed? What can you say about segments $PO$ and $OQ$?

**22.** Draw $\angle ABC$. Construct the bisector of $\angle ABC$ with ray $BD$. What can you say about $\angle ABD$ and $\angle CBD$?

**23.** Draw obtuse triangle $FGH$. Construct triangle $JKL$ congruent to triangle $FGH$. What can you say about the corresponding sides and angles of the two triangles?

Find the volume. Use 3.14 for $\pi$. *(pages 468–471, 474–477)*

**24.**

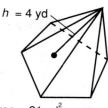

$h = 4$ yd

Area = 21 yd$^2$

**25.**

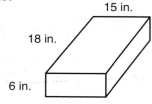

15 in.

18 in.

6 in.

**26.**

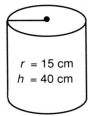

$r = 15$ cm
$h = 40$ cm

Solve. *(pages 466–467)*

**27.** Use the table to write a formula that relates the data.

| C | M |
|---|---|
| $1.15 | 1 |
| $1.30 | 2 |
| $1.45 | 3 |
| $1.60 | 4 |

$C$ = cost of a train ride

$M$ = number of miles ridden

**28.** Can the intersection of a plane region and a cube be a point? a line segment? Explain.

## What is the Volume of a **Rock** 🧩

Can you find the volume of an irregularly shaped object, such as a rock? One way is to measure the amount of water it displaces. You will need a liter container with markings and several rocks that will fit into the container.

Work with a partner. First estimate the volume of each rock. Remember a liter container has a volume of 1,000 mL or 1,000 cm³ Then measure the volume of each rock,

- Put water in the container to the 300 mL line.

- Place a rock in the container, making sure it is completely submerged. If it is not completely under water, remove it and add 100 ml of water. Replace the rock and check whether the water covers it. Continue if necessary.

- Read the level of the water in the container. Subtract the amount that was in the container before the rock was submerged. The difference is the volume of the rock.

- Repeat with the other rocks.

How do your estimates compare with your findings?

### Are Volume and Surface Area Related?

What happens to the ratio of surface area to volume as the size of a figure increases? You will need at least 64 small cubes.

Build or draw cubes with different edge lengths—1 unit, 2 units, 3 units, 4 units, and so on. Make a table showing the length of the edge, the surface area, the volume, and the surface area to volume ratio.

What do you notice about the ratio as the size of the figure increases?

### NUMBERS FROM NUMBERS

Try to make every number from 1 through 25 this way. Use each of the last 4 digits of a telephone number just once with any operation (addition, subtraction, multiplication or division) and with parentheses.

Example: 1237

$$7 - (3 + 2 + 1) = 1$$
$$(7 - 3) \div (2 \times 1) = 2$$
$$7 - ((3 - 1) \times 2) = 3$$

A green cube numbered 1–6 is tossed once. Find the probability.

**1.** $P(3) =$
- **a.** $\frac{1}{3}$
- **b.** $\frac{1}{2}$
- **c.** $\frac{3}{6}$
- **d.** none of these

**2.** $P(\text{odd}) =$
- **a.** $\frac{1}{2}$
- **b.** $\frac{1}{4}$
- **c.** $\frac{1}{8}$
- **d.** none of these

**3.** $P(\text{green}) =$
- **a.** $\frac{1}{3}$
- **b.** $\frac{3}{4}$
- **c.** 1
- **d.** none of these

Find the answer.

**4.** $(^-3) - (^-8) =$
- **a.** 5
- **b.** $^-11$
- **c.** $^-5$
- **d.** none of these

**5.** $12 \times (^-4) =$
- **a.** 48
- **b.** $^-48$
- **c.** $^-16$
- **d.** none of these

**6.** $(^-56) \div (^-7) =$
- **a.** 9
- **b.** 8
- **c.** $^-8$
- **d.** none of these

**7.** $m - 9 = ^-4$
- **a.** $^-5$
- **b.** $^-13$
- **c.** 5
- **d.** none of these

**8.** $x + ^-3 = 14$
- **a.** 11
- **b.** 17
- **c.** $^-11$
- **d.** none of these

**9.** $\frac{t}{15} = ^-5$
- **a.** $^-3$
- **b.** 75
- **c.** $^-75$
- **d.** none of these

**10.** $\sqrt{324} =$
- **a.** 32
- **b.** 18
- **c.** 24
- **d.** none of these

**11.** $\sqrt{9} =$
- **a.** 6
- **b.** 9
- **c.** 3
- **d.** none of these

**12.** $36^2 =$
- **a.** 1,296
- **b.** 906
- **c.** 1,196
- **d.** none of these

**13.** Volume =
- **a.** 26 in.$^3$
- **b.** 78 in.$^3$
- **c.** 446 in.$^3$
- **d.** none of these

**14.** Volume =
- **a.** 225 m$^3$
- **b.** 90 m$^3$
- **c.** 75 m$^3$
- **d.** none of these

**15.** Volume =
- **a.** 188.4 ft$^3$
- **b.** 754 ft$^3$
- **c.** 94.2 ft$^3$
- **d.** none of these

Remember the strategies and types of problems you've had so far. Solve.

**Problem Solving Check List**

- Drawing a picture
- Using a formula
- Multistep problems
- Using guess and check
- Making a generalization
- Using patterns

1. A copying machine is used 8 h/d. During the first hour, 50 copies were made; 75 copies during the second; 105 during the third; and 140 during the fourth hour.

   a. How many copies are made during the first hour?

   b. If the pattern continues, how many copies will be made during the fifth hour?

   c. If the pattern continues, how many copies will be made during the day?

2. The letters of the word EASTERNER are each written on a tile and placed in a bag. What is the probability that a tile drawn randomly will contain either an $E$ or an $A$?

3. Each row in the design on an Acoma Indian bowl contains a rectangle alternating with 4 triangles. There are 6 rows and each row has 8 rectangles. What is the total number of triangles?

4. The formula for the total cost $(C)$ of a visit to an amusement park is $C = 3N + 1.25R$ where $N$ is the number of people and $R$ is the number of rides. What would it cost a family of 3 to go on 11 rides?

5. Five friends visit the park in Exercise 4. When they left they noticed that the total cost of the rides was exactly twice what they paid for admission. How many rides had they gone on?

6. To determine the monthly service charge of a checking account, a bank uses the formula $C = 5 + 0.25N$. If $N$ is the number of checks above 10, what is the service charge for 20 checks?

7. A board game spinner is 50% red and 25% blue. The rest of the spinner is green. Of 160 spins, how many would you expect to be green?

8. The desks in room 325 are arranged in 5 rows of 6 desks. One day, a different number of students were absent in each row, but no row was empty. What is the largest number that could have been present?

9. A carpenter cuts boards from planks using the formula $B = \frac{P}{2} - 1$, where $B$ is the length of a board and $P$ is the length of the plank. If the carpenter has a 12-ft board, how long was the plank?

## TWO BY TWO BY TWO 🖩

A large box measures 126 cm by 144 cm by 286 cm. How many cubes can you place in the box, if each cube measures:

**1.** 2 cm × 2 cm × 2 cm?

**2.** 4 cm × 4 cm × 4 cm?

**3.** 8 cm × 8 cm × 8 cm?

## BUY THE C-SIDE 🖩

In the grid below, each square represents 35 $mi^2$. Each square mile costs $10. How much does each region cost?

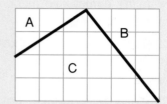

## MAKING IT FIT 💻

In the computer activity *Congruent Triangles*, you must be able to create a triangle congruent to another triangle, placing it on a coordinate grid so that the vertices are at points on the grid. This activity, which does not require a computer, will help you develop skills at placing a triangle on a coordinate grid.

Using a metric ruler, measure the sides of each triangle. Then measure the coordinate grid. How can you draw the triangles on the grid so that each vertex is at a point on the grid? You may flip or turn the triangles.

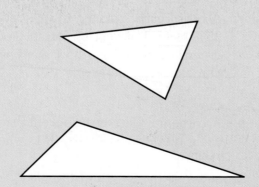

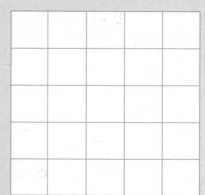

**DID YOU KNOW . . . ?**

Two of the 40 people who were President of the United States before 1992 had the same birthday. James K. Polk and Warren G. Harding were both born on November 2.

The Probability of Two People in a Group Sharing the Same Birthday

**USING DATA**
- Collect
- Organize
- Describe
- Predict

If 20 people are together in one place, what is the probability of two people sharing the same birthday?

Ask 23 people for their birth dates. Now ask 60 people for their birth dates. How many duplicate birth dates did you find? Do your findings agree with the graph?

# More Than Meets the Eye

## Problem Solving:
## *Misleading Graphs*

### 📖 READ ABOUT IT

Graphs are sometimes used to give misleading impressions.

The data in the table at right have been used to make the two different graphs below.

| Year | Persons per Household |
|------|------------------------|
| 1930 | 4.11 |
| 1960 | 3.33 |
| 1990 | 2.60 |

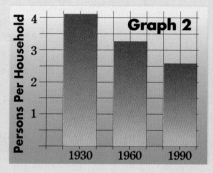

The table and graph show the number of skiers during some recent ski seasons as reported by the United States ski industry.

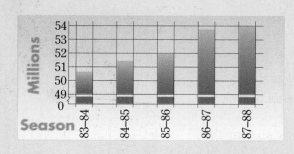

| Season | Skiers (in millions) |
|--------|----------------------|
| '83–'84 | 50.6 |
| '84–'85 | 51.4 |
| '85–'86 | 51.9 |
| '86–'87 | 53.7 |
| '87–'88 | 53.9 |

The graph at right was used to show how the percent of adults who have high school diplomas has increased over time.

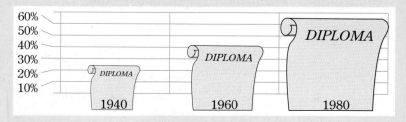

Use the graphs and the data table for the number of persons per household to answer Exercises 1 and 2.

1. In the data table, how do the number of persons per household in 1930 and in 1990 compare? How does the area covered by the 1930 bar compare with the area covered by the 1990 bar in the two graphs?

2. Why might someone incorrectly use Graph 1 in an article titled, "The Shrinking American Family"?

Use the graph and the data table for the number of skiers per season to answer Exercises 3 and 4.

3. How many skiers were there in the 1983–84 season? in the 1987–88 season? By how much did the number of skiers increase from the 1983–84 season to the 1987–88 season?

4. Does the graph or the table give a stronger impression that the popularity of skiing is rising rapidly? Explain.

Use the graph for the number of adults with high school diplomas to answer Exercises 5 and 6.

5. Look at the heights of the diplomas. About how many times more people completed high school in 1980 as in 1940?

6. Compare the areas of the diplomas for 1940 and 1980 on the graph. About how many times larger is the area of the 1980 diploma than the area of the 1940 diploma?

■ WRITE ABOUT IT

7. Write a paragraph explaining why Graph 1 showing the change in size of households gives a false impression.

8. Redraw the graph of the ski industry statistics so that the horizontal scale starts at zero. Use divisions of 10 (for millions). Explain why this graph gives a more accurate impression.

9. Explain why the areas of the diplomas make the graph for adults with diplomas misleading. Is it the width or the height of the diplomas that accurately reflects the increase in the number of people completing high school?

# Line Plots

Some facts, or statistics, about the players on a recent United States soccer team are listed in the table below.

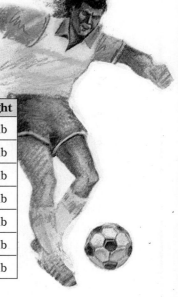

| Player | Age | Height | Weight | Player | Age | Height | Weight |
|---|---|---|---|---|---|---|---|
| Sonny Askew | 25 | 6'1" | 175 lb | Paul Hammond | 29 | 6'1" | 195 lb |
| Chico Borja | 23 | 5'11" | 155 lb | Hayden Knight | 25 | 6'1" | 175 lb |
| Dan Canter | 22 | 6'1" | 175 lb | Arnold Mausser | 28 | 6'2" | 185 lb |
| Tony Crescitelli | 25 | 5'11" | 180 lb | Alan Merrick | 32 | 5'10" | 170 lb |
| Pedro Debrito | 23 | 6'1" | 170 lb | Rob Olson | 23 | 6'1" | 175 lb |
| Jeff Durgan | 21 | 6'1" | 175 lb | Bruce Savage | 21 | 5'9" | 155 lb |
| Rudy Glenn | 24 | 6'2" | 185 lb | Perry VanDerBeck | 23 | 5'10" | 155 lb |

You can graph the ages of the players on a **line plot**. Line plots are usually used only when you are plotting fewer than 25 data items.

You can make a line plot by following these steps.

**STEPS** Identify the range by subtracting the smallest number from the largest. The smallest number is 21 and the largest is 32.

Range = 32 − 21 = 11

Make a horizontal line and label it with numbers. Because the range is 11, there should be at least 12 numbers on the line. The lowest number should be 21 or less and the highest number should be 32 or more to cover the whole age range.

Mark an $x$ above the line for each player's age.

**Ages of Soccer Players**

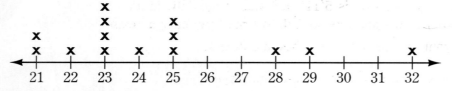

**THINK ALOUD** What does the line plot tell you about the data?

================================ GUIDED PRACTICE ================================

Use the data in the table above.

**1.** What is the oldest player's age? What is the youngest player's age?

Use the data in the table on page 492.

2. Where do the players' ages seem to cluster? What is the range of heights in inches?

3. **IN YOUR WORDS**  What ages would you expect most soccer players to be?

4. Where are the gaps in the ages? Why do you think this is so?

5. Make a line plot of the players' heights. Convert each height to inches.

6. Are there clusters? Are there gaps? What conclusions can you make by looking at the line plot of the players' heights?

7. **THINK ALOUD**  By using the line plots, how could you find the mode? the median? In each case, explain.

8. **CRITICAL THINKING**  Why do you think that a line plot is usually used only for sets of data with fewer than 25 entries?

9. Make a line plot of the players' weights. Use multiples of 5 lb on the scale.

10. Can the conclusion be drawn just by looking at your line plot of the players' weights? Write *yes* or *no*. If *no*, tell why.
    a. Most of the players are between 170 lb and 185 lb.
    b. The total weight of the players is more than 1 t.
    c. Some of the players are a little too heavy for their height.
    d. Three of the players are quite a bit lighter than the others.
    e. The light players tend to be the short players.
    f. The mode for the weights of the players is 175 lb.

Suppose that a 23-year-old player who is 5'11'' tall and weighs 165 lb and a 26-year-old player who is 6' tall and weighs 170 lb joined the soccer team.

11. Add these data to your line plots for weights and heights.

12. What conclusions would you now make about the players' heights? the players' weights?

13. **CREATE YOUR OWN**  Choose data from a newspaper or magazine. Make a line plot. Use fewer than 25 entries. Be sure some of the statistics are repeated so that a line plot is a sensible way to organize the data.

# Stem-and-Leaf Plots

All states are trying to increase the graduation rate for high school students. The table below shows the high school graduation rates for each state and the District of Columbia. Each rate is rounded to the nearest percent.

| | | | | | |
|---|---|---|---|---|---|
| Ala........ 67% | Fla.........62% | La.......... 63% | Nebr....... 88% | Ohio....... 80% | Tex.........64% |
| Alaska.....68% | Ga......... 63% | Maine......77% | Nev.........65% | Okla........72% | Utah .......80% |
| Ariz........63% | Hawaii .....71% | Md.........77% | N.H.........73% | Oreg....... 74% | Vt......... 78% |
| Ark........ 78% | Idaho...... 79% | Mass....... 77% | N. J.........78% | Pa......... 79% | Va.........74% |
| Calif....... 67% | Ill..........76% | Mich....... 68% | N. Mex.....72% | R. I......... 67% | Wash.......75% |
| Colo........73% | Ind......... 72% | Minn.......91% | N. Y........64% | S. C........ 64% | W. Va.......75% |
| Conn...... 90% | Iowa....... 89% | Miss........63% | N. C. ......70% | S. Dak......82% | Wis.........86% |
| Del........ 71% | Kans....... 82% | Mo......... 76% | N. Dak..... 90% | Tenn....... 67% | Wyo........81% |
| D.C........57% | Ky......... 69% | Mt.........87% | | | |

You can make a **stem-and-leaf plot** to organize this data. Think of each data item as a *stem* and a *leaf*. For these numbers, the stems will be the tens' digits and the leaves will be the ones' digits.

**STEPS**  Find the stems. They are all the tens' digits between the smallest and largest values.

| Stem | Leaf |
|---|---|
| 9 | |
| 8 | |
| 7 | |
| 6 | |
| 5 | |

List the stems vertically with a line to their right.

Now go through the list, separating each value into its stem and its leaf. The first value is 67% for Alabama.

| Stem | Leaf |
|---|---|
| 9 | |
| 8 | |
| 7 | |
| 6 | 7 |
| 5 | |

Put the leaf for each item to the right of the stem. The leaf for Alabama, 7, goes to the right of the stem 6.

Continue plotting this way until all the data have been listed.

| Stem | Leaf |
|---|---|
| 9 | 010 |
| 8 | 927802061 |
| 7 | 8311962777638202498455 |
| 6 | 7837239383547474 |
| 5 | 7 |

**THINK ALOUD**  What can be done now to organize the data better?

1. Make a new stem-and-leaf plot of the data by arranging the leaves for each stem from smallest to largest.

2. Are there any clusters or gaps in this data?

3. In which stem would you expect to find the median value?

4. **THINK ALOUD** How are a bar graph and a stem-and-leaf plot alike? How are they different?

5. Make a stem-and-leaf plot for the high school dropout rate for each state and the District of Columbia.

   (*Hint:* Each high school dropout rate can be found by subtracting the graduation rate from 100%.)

6. **CRITICAL THINKING** How does the stem-and-leaf plot for the dropout rate compare with that for the graduation rate?

Imagine you are writing a story for your school newspaper about the dropout rates in the United States based on the information from Exercise 5. Use the stem-and-leaf plot to complete the news story.

7. Many educators are concerned about the high school dropout rate in the United States. More than half the states have a dropout rate of __a.__ or higher. The highest dropout rate is __b.__ . The place with the lowest dropout rate is Minnesota, with a rate of __c.__ .

8. **IN YOUR WORDS** Add to the news story by writing one more sentence that contains a factual statement.

9. **CREATE YOUR OWN** Find data in a magazine or newspaper appropriate for a stem-and-leaf plot. Then plot the data.

# Box Plots

Recently, an estimated 2.5 million camcorders were sold in a year. That year a buyers' guide reported the prices of more than 100 models. The **box plot** shows a summary of the prices of VHS camcorders.

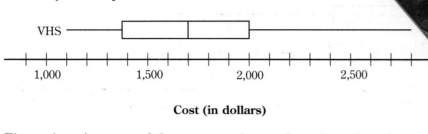

Cost (in dollars)

Five values in a set of data are used to make a box plot: the median, the upper and lower quartiles, and the upper and lower extremes.

The median is the middle number of the data set and separates it into an upper and a lower half.

The quartiles are the middle numbers of the upper half and the lower half; they separate the data into quarters, or fourths.

The extremes are the largest and the smallest values.

You can see these values clearly in a box plot

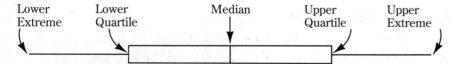

**THINK ALOUD**  A box plot is sometimes called a "box-and-whiskers" plot. Which parts make up the box? Which parts are the whiskers?

**CRITICAL THINKING**  The data are separated into fourths in a box plot. What part of the data is in the box? What part of the data is in the whiskers? Why is the right whisker longer than the left one?

═══════════════════ **GUIDED PRACTICE** ═══════════════════

Estimate the range of prices.

1. the middle 50% of the VHS camcorders

2. the lower half of the VHS camcorders

3. the lower quarter of the VHS camcorders

The buyers' guide described three types of camcorders: high quality super VHS and Hi8, compact, and standard VHS. The prices for these types are shown in the box plots.

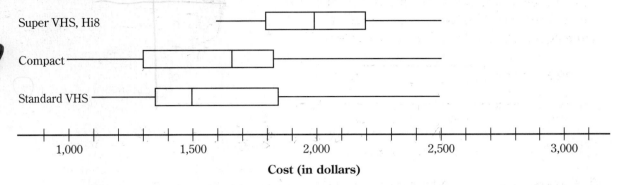

Cost (in dollars)

Use the box plots to answer the question for each kind of camcorder.

**4.** Estimate the value of the lower extreme.

**5.** Describe the range of the lower quarter.

**6.** Describe the range of the lower half.

**7.** Estimate the median price.

**8.** Estimate the range of the middle 50%.

**9.** Estimate the range of the upper quarter.

**PROBLEM SOLVING**

Refer to the box plots for the three kinds of camcorders.

**10. IN YOUR WORDS** Compare the prices of the compact, the standard VHS, and the super VHS camcorders.

**11.** The middle 50% of the prices for the compact and the standard VHS camcorders are about the same, but the medians are different. Explain.

*Critical Thinking*

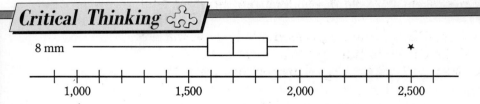

This box plot shows the prices of 8-mm camcorders. The star represents an extreme value compared to the rest of the prices, called an **outlier.** Outliers are shown separately to represent the data set accurately.

Why is it misleading to draw the whisker all the way to the star?

# Construction: Circle Graph

In the 1988 Olympics, the USSR won the most medals. Its athletes received 132 medals. Of these, 55 were gold, 46 were silver, and 31 were bronze.

You can show these data in a circle graph that represents the proportions of gold, silver, and bronze medals.

1. Start by using a proportion to find the number of degrees for each section of the circle. Round to the nearest degree. Remember, there are 360° around the center of a circle.

| Medals | Gold | Silver | Bronze |
|---|---|---|---|
| **Part** / **Whole** | $\dfrac{55}{132}$ | $\dfrac{46}{132}$ | $\dfrac{31}{132}$ |
| **Proportion** | $\dfrac{55}{132} = \dfrac{n}{360}$ | $\dfrac{46}{132} = \dfrac{p}{360}$ | $\dfrac{31}{132} = \dfrac{q}{360}$ |
| | $55 \times 360 = 132 \times n$ | $46 \times 360 = 132 \times p$ | $31 \times 360 = 132 \times q$ |
| | $n = \dfrac{55 \times 360}{132}$ | $p = \dfrac{46 \times 360}{132}$ | $q = \dfrac{31 \times 360}{132}$ |
| | $n = 150°$ | $p = 125°$ | $q = 85°$ |

2. You can use a compass, a protractor, and a straightedge to construct the circle graph.

**STEPS** Draw a circle with a radius.

Use the protractor to measure the degrees needed to represent the gold medals (150°).

Draw the second side of the central angle. Write "gold" as a label for the section.

Use the protractor to measure the degrees needed to represent the silver medals (125°). Draw the angle. Label the section "silver."

The remaining section will be for the bronze medals. Check the angle measure with your protractor. It should be 85°. Label the section.

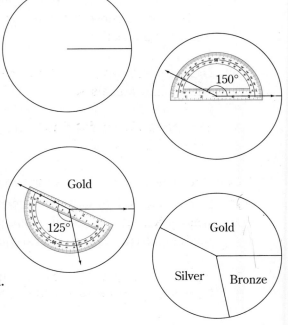

**3.** Look at your circle graph. Estimate the fractional part of the circle graph represented by each section.

**4.** About what fraction of the medals were gold? bronze? silver?

**5.** **ESTIMATE** About what percent of the medals were gold? bronze? silver?

The chart shows the number of gold, silver, and bronze medals won by East Germany and the United States in the 1988 Olympics.

| | Gold | Silver | Bronze |
|---|---|---|---|
| **East Germany** | 37 | 30 | 35 |
| **United States** | 36 | 27 | 31 |

**6.** For East Germany, how many degrees of a circle would be needed to represent the gold medals? the silver medals? the bronze medals?

**7.** Draw a circle graph to show the proportions of gold, silver, and bronze medals won by East Germany.

**8.** **ESTIMATE** What fractional part of the East Germany circle graph is each section?

**9.** For the United States, how many degrees of a circle would be needed to represent the gold medals? the silver medals? the bronze medals?

**10.** Draw a circle graph to show the proportions of gold, silver, and bronze medals won by the United States.

**11.** **ESTIMATE** What fractional part of the United States circle graph is each section?

**CRITICAL THINKING** Use your three circle graphs to answer.

**12.** If you referred to nothing other than the graphs, would you be able to tell which country—the USSR, East Germany, or the United States—won the most medals in 1988? Explain.

**13.** By looking at just the graphs, what comparisons can you make between the countries' athletes?

## LANGUAGE & VOCABULARY

Write *true* or *false*.

1. A line plot makes the mode of a set of data easily visible?

2. The middle stem in a stem-and-leaf plot will always have the largest number of leaves.

3. In a box plot, the upper and lower extremes must be equidistant from the median.

QUICK QUIZ ✓

The table shows the number of tickets to the school play sold by students in room 212. Use the data. *(pages 492–499)*

| | | |
|---|---|---|
| Bill 34 | Sally 29 | Eddie 28 |
| Donna 24 | Arnold 24 | Paul 22 |
| Winnie 24 | Sue 29 | Wanda 22 |
| Johnny 24 | Mike 27 | Julio 40 |
| Michael 35 | Michelle 20 | Charlene 28 |

1. What is the range of the data?

2. Make a line plot of the data.

3. Name the stems you would use to make a stem-and-leaf plot.

4. Name the median and upper and lower quartiles you would use to make a box plot.

5. Tell how to make a circle graph.

Solve. *(pages 490–491)*

6. The graph shows the number of books in one class library.

    a. About how many novels are in the library?

    b. What impression does the graph give about the number of novels compared to the number of biographies?

    c. About how many more novels are there than biographies?

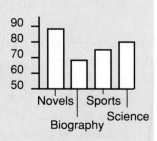

Write the answers in your learning log.

1. In what ways can a graph not tell the real truth.

2. Explain what is meant by the range of ages of the members of your family.

3. When you look at a circle graph, what does the whole circle represent?

MATH AMERICA

**DID YOU KNOW . . . ?** Refined sugar is the only known food that provides only calories and no nutrients. The average American consumes nearly 100 lb of sugar/yr. 36% is eaten directly and the rest is eaten as an ingredient in prepared foods. If each member of your class consumes the average amount, how many pounds of sugar would the class eat in a year? Of that, how many pounds would come from prepared foods?

BONUS

"In what year is your birthday?" In China people can answer this question with the name of an animal. Find out what animals the Chinese years are named for. Then answer the question.

## Sample Space

Leah works at the Salty Seafood Shop. Her uniform includes 3 skirts (blue, white, and striped) and 2 blouses (blue and striped). How many different outfits can she make?

Each outfit can be thought of as an **outcome**. There are several ways to figure out the number of all possible outcomes.

### • Use an organized list.

| Blue blouse with each skirt | | Striped blouse with each skirt | |
|---|---|---|---|
| blue blouse, blue skirt | (b,b) | striped blouse, blue skirt | (s,b) |
| blue blouse, white skirt | (b,w) | striped blouse, white skirt | (s,w) |
| blue blouse, striped skirt | (b,s) | striped blouse, striped skirt | (s,s) |

This list of all possible outcomes is called the **sample space**. There are 6 possible outcomes in the sample space.

### • Use a tree diagram.

List the blouses.   Connect to the skirts.   Sample Space

blue
— blue ——————— (blue, blue)      (b, b)
— white —————— (blue, white)     (b, w)
— striped ————— (blue, striped)   (b, s)

striped
— blue ——————— (striped, blue)    (s, b)
— white —————— (striped, white)   (s, w)
— striped ————— (striped, striped) (s, s)

There are 6 possible outcomes in the sample space.

### • Use a lattice.

List the skirts across the top and the blouses down the side. Write the outfits in the cells.

| **Blouses** | **Skirts** | | |
|---|---|---|---|
| | blue | white | striped |
| blue | b, b | b, w | b, s |
| striped | s, b | s, w | s, s |

There are 6 possible outcomes in the sample space.

### • Use the basic counting principle.

2 blouses, 3 skirts ⟶ 2 × 3 = 6 outcomes

**When you know the number of outcomes for each event, you can multiply those numbers to find the number of outcomes in the sample space for the multiple event.**

Eric can choose from 4 types of shirts and 3 types of slacks for his park district uniform. Find the number of different outfits he can wear.

1. Use an organized list.

2. Use a tree diagram.

3. Use a lattice.

4. Use the basic counting principle.

5. What is the sample space for the above problem?

6. How many outcomes are there in the sample space?

Jason bought 2 pairs of shorts (yellow and blue) and 4 T-shirts (yellow, blue, green, and red). Find the total number of possible outfits.

7. Use an organized list.

8. Use a tree diagram.

9. Use a lattice.

10. Use the basic counting principle.

11. If Jason also bought a pair of green shorts, how many combinations of clothing could he then make? Use the method of your choice.

12. **CRITICAL THINKING** Jason's mother said he could buy 6 pieces of clothing. How many T-shirts and shorts are needed to get the greatest number of outfits?

Identify a situation for the sample space.

13.

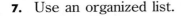

| | | heads | (H, H) |
| heads | | | |
| | | tails | (H, T) |
| | | heads | T, H |
| tails | | | |
| | | tails | (T, T) |

14.

| | 1 | 2 | 3 | 4 | 5 | 6 |
|---|---|---|---|---|---|---|
| 1 | 1, 1 | 2, 1 | 3, 1 | 4, 1 | 5, 1 | 6, 1 |
| 2 | 1, 2 | 2, 2 | 3, 2 | 4, 2 | 5, 2 | 6, 2 |
| 3 | 1, 3 | 2, 3 | 3, 3 | 4, 3 | 5, 3 | 6, 3 |
| 4 | 1, 4 | 2, 4 | 3, 4 | 4, 4 | 5, 4 | 6, 4 |
| 5 | 1, 5 | 2, 5 | 3, 5 | 4, 5 | 5, 5 | 6, 5 |
| 6 | 1, 6 | 2, 6 | 3, 6 | 4, 6 | 5, 6 | 6, 6 |

15. **CREATE YOUR OWN** Describe a situation that has a sample space of 24 outcomes.

## Probability of Multiple Events

The swim team members couldn't decide among three choices—the Dolphins, the Porpoises, and the Pisces—for a new name. They also had a tie in the vote for swim suit colors between purple and blue.

So the coach put cards with the names in one box and cards with the colors in another. A card from each box would be picked without looking.

Vicki wanted the team name to be the Porpoises and the suit color to be purple. She listed the sample space.

| | |
|---|---|
| Porpoises, blue | Porpoises, purple |
| Dolphins, blue | Dolphins, purple |
| Pisces, blue | Pisces, purple |

Since the outcomes are equally likely, the probability of her choice was 1 out of 6, or $\frac{1}{6}$.

Eric's choice was the Dolphins with blue suits. He used the basic counting principle to match each name with each color. There were $2 \times 3$, or 6, possibilities. The probability of his choice was 1 out of 6, or $\frac{1}{6}$.

**THINK ALOUD** Explain how you could use a tree diagram or a lattice to find the probability of a name and color choice.

========== GUIDED PRACTICE ==========

1. Find the probability of the choice *Dolphins, purple* from the names Dolphins, Porpoises, Pisces, and Waves and the colors purple, blue, and green. Use an organized list, a tree diagram, a lattice, or the basic counting principle to list the sample space.

2. **IN YOUR WORDS** Why did you choose the method you used to list the sample space?

At the swim meet, the swimmers picked sweat pants and sweat shirts from two team boxes. By the time Benjy got to the box, there were only 2 sweat shirts (1 small and 1 medium) and 3 sweat pants (1 small, 1 medium, and 1 large) left.

**3.** List the sample space for all the possible combinations of sweat shirts and sweat pants.

**4.** Use your favorite method to find the probability that Benjy selected a medium sweat shirt and medium sweat pants by reaching into the boxes without looking.

**5.** What is the probability that Benjy picked out both a small sweat shirt and small sweat pants?

**PROBLEM SOLVING**

The coach can assign swimmers to lane 1, lane 2, lane 3, or lane 4. The coach always has the swimmers pick lane numbers out of a hat.

**6.** Jenny is going to swim in two races. Find the probability that Jenny will get lane 4 for both races if she gets to pick first from the hat for each race. Solve by listing the sample space.

**7.** Alissa is going to swim in only two races. She likes lane 3 and lane 4 equally well. Find the probability that she will get in a lane she likes for both races if she gets to pick first for each race.

**8.** Alex likes even numbers. Find the probability that he will draw even-numbered lanes for both of his two races if he gets to pick first.

**9.** Hamid is going to swim in three races. What is the probability that he will swim in lane 4 for all three races if he gets to pick first for each?

**10.** Maria is the star of the team. She will swim in four races. What is the probability that she will swim in lane 4 for all four races if she picks first for each race?

## Independent Events

The Oakton Middle School Volunteer Club has 5 members, 2 boys and 3 girls. Whenever there is a request for help, the club members draw 1 of their 5 names out of a hat to see who will give the help. All 5 names go back into the hat at the end of the day.

Mr. Buono is recovering from an illness and has asked to have his lawn mowed on two Fridays.

On the first Friday, 1 of the 5 names is drawn.
On the second Friday, 1 of the 5 names is drawn.

The two drawings are called **independent events** because the name drawn on the first Friday has no effect on the name drawn on the second Friday.

What is the probability that a girl's name will be chosen both times?

You could use a lattice to find the sample space. You would find that the probability that a girl's name will be chosen both times is 9 out of 25, or $\frac{9}{25}$.

You also could reason that the probability of a girl being chosen is 3 out of 5, or $\frac{3}{5}$, on the first Friday and 3 out of 5, or $\frac{3}{5}$, on the second Friday. When you find the probability this way, you are using the **multiplication principle**.

You could use a lattice to find the sample space.

|   | g  | g  | g  | b  | b  |
|---|----|----|----|----|----|
| g | gg | gg | gg | gb | gb |
| g | gg | gg | gg | gb | gb |
| g | gg | gg | gg | gb | gb |
| b | bg | bg | bg | bb | bb |
| b | bg | bg | bg | bb | bb |

The probability of a girl's name being chosen both times is 9 out of 25, or $\frac{9}{25}$.

---

**Multiplication Principle: To find the probability of two independent events occurring at the same time, find the product of the individual probabilities.**

$$P(A \text{ and } B) = P(A) \times P(B)$$

---

First Friday: $P(g)$      Second Friday: $P(g)$      Both Fridays: $P(g \text{ and } g)$

$$\frac{3}{5} \qquad \times \qquad \frac{3}{5} \qquad = \qquad \frac{9}{25}$$

---

### GUIDED PRACTICE

The club had a request from Mrs. Wells at its last meeting. She needed someone to pick up her mail on Monday and Friday of this week.

1. Will the drawings for the names of the helpers on the two days be independent events? Explain.

2. What is the probability that a boy will be chosen on both days?

Remember, there are 2 boys and 3 girls in the Volunteer Club.
What is the probability of the event?

3. A girl will be selected on both days to pick up mail
   for Mrs. Wells.

4. A girl will pick up Mrs. Wells's mail on the first day and a boy
   will pick it up on the second day.

## PROBLEM SOLVING

The homeless shelter needs someone to help serve dinner on each
of two Saturday nights. The Volunteer Club consists of 1 eighth grader,
2 seventh graders, and 2 sixth graders.

5. What is the probability that the two volunteers selected
   will be seventh graders?

6. What is the probability that an eighth grader will be selected
   the first week and a seventh grader will be selected the next?

7. What is the probability that a boy will be selected the first
   week and a girl will be selected the second week?

8. What is the probability that the eighth grader will be picked
   twice? Explain your answer.

## Critical Thinking

Use this pet fact: 57 out of 100 households have pets.

How many households out of 100 do not have pets?

The two events, households with pets and households without
pets, cover all the possibilities. They are **complementary events**.

Name the complementary event.

1. In the United States, 4 out of 5 dog
   owners give their dogs table scraps.

2. Table scraps are not given to their cats
   by 69 out of 100 cat owners.

3. Snakes are disliked by 3 out of 11 people.

## Dependent Events

Sometimes the Oakton Middle School Volunteer Club has more than one request for help on a given day, as shown in the notice at right.

Remember, there are 2 boys and 3 girls in the club and they draw names to select the helper.

To select the first helper, 1 of the 5 names is drawn. To select the second helper, 1 of the 4 names *remaining* is drawn.

The two drawings are called **dependent** events because the second selection is influenced by the first selection.

What is the probability that two boys' names will be selected? The probability of selecting a boy's name on the first draw is $\frac{2}{5}$.

**THINK ALOUD**  Suppose that a boy's name was drawn on the first draw. What is the probability that a boy's name will be selected on the second draw?

You can use the multiplication principle to find the probability of selecting a boy's name on both draws.

$$P(\text{boy, 1st draw}) \times P(\text{boy, 2nd draw}) = P(\text{boy, both draws})$$
$$\frac{2}{5} \qquad \times \qquad \frac{1}{4} \qquad = \qquad \frac{2}{20}$$

> **When two events are dependent, the outcome of one event influences the outcome of the other event. To use the multiplication principle for dependent events, you must think about how the first event affects the second event.**

### GUIDED PRACTICE

Jenny Johnson asked for volunteers to deliver breakfast and lunch to her handicapped mother on Thursday.

1. Are these selections dependent or independent events?

2. What is the probability that a boy will be selected to deliver breakfast and a girl will be selected to deliver lunch?

Refer to the situation in Guided Practice. Find the probability.

**3.** Two girls will be selected to deliver the meals.

**4.** A girl will be selected to deliver breakfast and a boy will be selected to deliver lunch.

Remember, the Volunteer Club consists of 1 eighth grader, 2 seventh graders, and 2 sixth graders. There are 2 boys and 3 girls in the club.

The nursing home needs two helpers to serve dinner on Saturday night this week.

**5.** Are the selections of the two helpers independent or dependent events? Explain.

**6.** What is the probability that the two helpers are both sixth graders?

**7.** What is the probability that the two helpers are both girls?

The homeless shelter needs one person to pick up donation packages at the park on each of the next two Sundays.

**8.** The club selects a volunteer each week by drawing a name from the hat containing the five names. Are the selections independent or dependent events? Explain.

**9.** What is the probability that the two volunteers are both seventh graders?

**10.** What is the probability that a boy is selected the first week and a girl is selected the second week?

## Critical Thinking

**Odds** are ratios that compare favorable outcomes to unfavorable outcomes. If the probability that it will snow today is 4 out of 10, the odds in favor of it snowing are 4 to 6 and the odds against it are 6 to 4.

What are the odds in favor of and against the event?

**1.** thunderstorm when the probability of a storm is 3 out of 5

**2.** sunny day when the probability of a cloudy day is 74%

**3.** fog when the forecast for clear air is 50%

## Problem Solving Strategy:
## Draw a Picture

Students in Mr. Sosa's math class use calculators often. Sometimes calculators get broken. Alicia needs a calculator. There are 3 calculators in the left drawer and 2 calculators in the right drawer.

One of the calculators in the right drawer is not working, but the students don't know that. What is the probability that Alicia will select the broken calculator?

A good strategy for solving this problem is to draw and use fractional areas of a unit square, like the one at right. Into how many sections is this square cut up? The area of each section is what fraction of the area of the square?

First, you can show the probability of selecting each of the drawers. Since the probability for selecting each drawer is $\frac{1}{2}$, draw a vertical line dividing the unit square into two equal parts.

Second, show the probability of selecting each calculator within each drawer. Label each section "working" or "broken."

| Left | Right |
|---|---|
| | |

The probability of selecting each calculator in the left drawer is $\frac{1}{3}$. Draw two horizontal lines to divide the left half of the square into thirds.

| Left | Right |
|---|---|
| working | |
| working | |
| working | |

The probability of selecting each calculator in the right drawer is $\frac{1}{2}$. Draw a horizontal line to divide the right half of the square in half.

| Left | Right |
|---|---|
| working | working |
| working | |
| | broken |
| working | |

Next, identify what portion of the whole square is labeled as broken. Three of the 12 small sections represent the probability of selecting a broken calculator. The probability that Alicia will select a broken calculator is $\frac{3}{12}$, or $\frac{1}{4}$.

1. Use the unit square and the story to answer.

   Huong needs a calculator. There are 2 calculators in one box and 4 calculators in another box. Each box contains one calculator that is not working properly.

   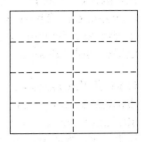

   a. Into how many parts is the square divided? What fraction of the area of the square is each part?

   b. Divide the unit square into parts that represent the probability of selecting each box. Then divide each part into sections that represent the probability of selecting each calculator. Label each section as "working" or "broken." What portion of the square represents working calculators?

   c. What is the probability that Huong will select a working calculator?

**PRACTICE**

Show your work by sketching a copy of the unit square and its fractional parts. Use it to solve the problem.

2. Ian needs a timer. There are 2 timers in the left drawer and 5 timers in the right drawer. In the right drawer 3 of the timers are not working.

   a. What is the probability that Ian will select a working timer?

   b. What is the probability that he will select a timer that is not working?

3. Ina needs a stopwatch. There are 3 stopwatches in the left drawer and only 1 in the right drawer. The one in the right drawer is broken, but the three in the left drawer are working.

   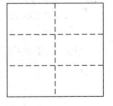

   a. What is the probability that Ina will select a working stopwatch?

   b. What is the probability that she will select a broken stopwatch?

 Choose any strategy to solve.

4. A sweater with an original price of $50 has been marked down 10% 3 times. What is its price now?

5. How many times are the hour hand and the minute hand of a clock lined up together in one day?

6. How many ways can the 5 letters, *l*, *e*, *a*, *r*, and *n*, be arranged?

## Exploring Combinations and Permutations

Jenny, Amir, and some friends were playing a word game with tiles that had letters on one side.

Four tiles remained. They were placed face down.

On Amir's turn he was to pick three tiles. He could get these different sets of letters:

These four sets of possibilities are called **combinations**. There were four combinations of three letters that Amir could get.

It turned out that Amir picked the first combination: t n a .
He then listed all the possible arrangements using the three letters:

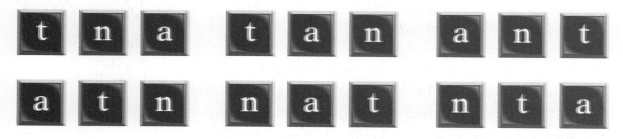

1. **THINK ALOUD** How many arrangements made real words? How many arrangements made nonsense words?

These different arrangements of the three letters are called **permutations**. In a permutation, the order, or arrangement, is important. Amir found 6 permutations using all three letters.

2. What combinations could Jenny pick if she were to select two of the four letters without looking?

3. If Jenny had picked b and a for her two letters, what would be all the permutations using both letters?

When listing all possible outcomes, it is important to know whether you are looking for all combinations or all permutations. In combinations, the arrangement, or order does not matter. In permutations, the order of every outcome is important.

Some friends were playing a word game. Tell whether you would look for a *combination* or a *permutation* to answer the question.

**4.** Pierre was to select three of the letters at random. What possible sets might he have picked if he picked without looking?

**5.** Pierre was to make real and nonsense words with his three letters. What words could he make?

**6.** Alexis already had picked four letters. What arrangements of these letters could she make?

**7.** Sue was to pick two letters on her turn. Three letters were left. What sets of letters might she have picked without looking?

During another game, the last five tiles had these letters: *b, a, u, k, c.*

**8.** Pierre was to select three of the letters without looking. List all the combinations he might have picked.

**9.** Pierre picked *b, a,* and *c.* List all the possible permutations.

**10.** Alexis picked *b, a, k,* and *c.* List all the possible permutations.

**11.** Sue was to pick two letters on her turn. List all the combinations she might have picked.

Carmen and Adelita were playing the same word game. The last four tiles had these letters: *a, e, n, t.*

**12.** What are all the possible combinations for two letters?

**13.** What are all the possible combinations for three letters?

**14.** Adelita picked *a* and *n.* What are the permutations of these two letters?

**15.** Carmen picked *e, n,* and *t.* What are the permutations of these three letters?

**16.** How many of the permutations in Exercise 15 are real words?

**17.** **CREATE YOUR OWN** Make cards for six different letters. Choose different numbers of letters and find all possible combinations and permutations.

## Mixed Review

Compute.

**1.** $240.72 \div 68$

**2.** $0.677 + 87.4$

**3.** $65.39 - 454.6$

**4.** $8.2 \times 0.52$

**5.** $\frac{5}{6} \times 3\frac{1}{8}$

**6.** $8\frac{3}{8} \div \frac{1}{4}$

**7.** $7\frac{5}{6} + \frac{5}{12}$

**8.** $19\frac{1}{6} - 3\frac{5}{12}$

Solve for $n$ in the proportion.

**9.** $\frac{n}{90} = \frac{14}{20}$

**10.** $\frac{8}{24} = \frac{n}{15}$

**11.** $\frac{8}{17} = \frac{24}{n}$

**12.** $\frac{6}{n} = \frac{9}{12}$

Find the unknown.

**13.** 85% of what number is 595?

**14.** What is 55% of 165?

**15.** What is 25% of 360?

**16.** 20% of what number is 30?

**17.** What percent of 80 is 12?

**18.** What is 10% of 600?

**19.** 35% of what number is 217?

**20.** What percent of 400 is 260?

Compute.

**21.** $4 + {}^-1$

**22.** $3 - 8$

**23.** ${}^-3 \times 4$

**24.** ${}^-6 \div 3$

**25.** $1 - {}^-5$

**26.** ${}^-6 + {}^-4$

**27.** ${}^-14 \div 7$

**28.** ${}^-3 \times {}^-3$

**29.** ${}^-1 \times {}^-1$

**30.** ${}^-10 \div 5$

**31.** $6 + {}^-5$

**32.** ${}^-4 - {}^-10$

**33.** ${}^-8 \div {}^-2$

**34.** $3 \times {}^-5$

**35.** ${}^-7 - {}^-12$

**36.** ${}^-12 + {}^-7$

**37.** ${}^-5 + {}^-1$

**38.** $9 - 14$

**39.** $12 \times {}^-20$

**40.** ${}^-24 \div {}^-6$

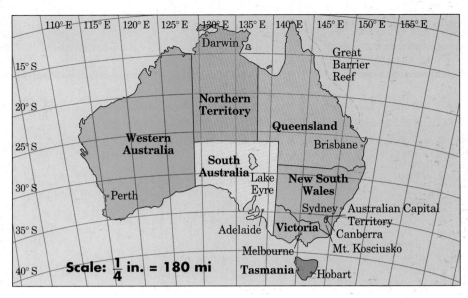

Scale: $\frac{1}{4}$ in. = 180 mi

CHOOSE Choose estimation, mental math, pencil and paper, or calculator to solve.

Use the map to match each state or territory to its area.

| | | | |
|---|---|---|---|
| **a.** 920 mi$^2$ | **b.** 26,200 mi$^2$ | **c.** 87,900 mi$^2$ | **d.** 309,500 mi$^2$ |
| **e.** 380,070 mi$^2$ | **f.** 519,770 mi$^2$ | **g.** 666,900 mi$^2$ | **h.** 975,100 mi$^2$ |

**41.** Northern Territory    **42.** South Australia    **43.** Queensland

**44.** New South Wales    **45.** Victoria    **46.** Tasmania

**47.** Western Australia    **48.** Australian Capital Territory

**49.** In 1851, gold was discovered in Australia. As a result, the population rose from about 400,000 in 1850 to about 1,100,000 in 1860. By about what percent did the population rise during this time period?

**50.** Use the map scale to estimate the flying distance in miles between the cities.

   **a.** Brisbane and Adelaide    **b.** Sydney and Perth    **c.** Darwin and Hobart

**51.** Lake Eyre in South Australia is completely dry most of the year. The lake, 52 ft below sea level, is Australia's lowest point. Mt. Kosciusko in New South Wales, 7,310 ft high, is Australia's highest point. What is the difference between these two points?

**52.** What is the approximate latitude and longitude of Perth? of Australia's capital city, Canberra?

## LANGUAGE & VOCABULARY

Complete each sentence with the appropriate expression from this list: *sample space, basic counting principle, independent events, dependent events.*

1. Two events whose probabilities do not influence one another are

   _____.

2. Multiplying outcomes to find total possible outcomes is one use of the _____.

3. The list of all possible outcomes of an event is the

   _____.

4. Two events, the second of which is influenced by the first, are

   _____.

## TEST

### CONCEPTS

The line plot shows the number of officially sanctioned 300 games bowled by the top 17 bowlers. *(pages 492–497)*

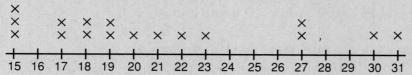

1. What is the range of the data?

2. Make a stem-and-leaf plot of the data.

3. What is the median?

4. What is the upper extreme of the data?

Construct a circle graph of the data. *(pages 498–499)*

5. A marketing research company needs to make a graph of the number of visitors, in millions, to 3 cities in a recent year. The data from these cities is: Los Angeles, 45, San Diego, 30, and New York City, 15.

Solve. *(pages 502–509, 512–513)*

Bill has 4 books (3 novels and 1 play) and 5 magazines (2 sports and 3 news). He wants to take a book and a magazine on a trip.

**6.** Find the number of different combinations he can take.

**7.** What is the probability that if Bill picks without looking, he will select a novel and a sports magazine?

**8.** If Lawrence decides to take only 2 books, what is the probability that if he picks without looking, he will choose a novel followed by a play?

**PROBLEM SOLVING**

**9.** Use the graph to answer. *(pages 490–491)*

   **a.** What was the average family size in 1960?

   **b.** Does the graph make it seem that the average family size in 1988 is half that in 1960?

   **c.** By how much did the average family size decrease from 1960 to 1988?

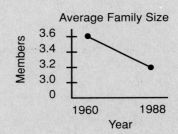
Average Family Size

Solve. *(pages 510–511)*

**10.** Maria has 2 boxes of eggs, one with 3 eggs and one with 4 eggs. One egg in each box is bad, but she doesn't know it. She needs 1 egg. What is the probability that she will pick a bad one?

**11.** Four girls and 5 boys are on a baseball team. A captain and a co-captain are to be chosen. If one must be a girl and one a boy, how many different combinations are possible?

LEARNING LOG

Write the answers in your learning log.

**1.** Dan says the letters of his name have more permutations than the letters of Ann's name. Do you agree with him? Explain.

**2.** The odds are 4 to 3 you have English, math, social studies, or science at any given period during the day. Explain.

Use the data. *(pages 492–497)*

The chart shows the ages of various Presidents of the United States when they were inaugurated.

| | | |
|---|---|---|
| Washington 57 | Polk 49 | Hoover 54 |
| Jefferson 57 | Lincoln 52 | Truman 60 |
| Madison 57 | Grant 46 | Kennedy 43 |
| Jackson 61 | Arthur 50 | Nixon 56 |
| Tyler 51 | Taft 51 | Carter 52 |

**1.** Make a line plot of the data.

**2.** Make a stem-and-leaf plot of the data.

**3.** What is the lower extreme of the data?

Construct a circle graph. *(pages 498–499)*

**4.** Of 85 phone calls made one month, 52 were local, 28 were long distance, and 5 were international. Construct a circle graph showing the percent of the calls of each type. Round to the nearest percent.

Solve. Use a sample space. *(pages 502–507, 512–513)*

Robin has 2 coats (black and green) and 4 sweaters (green, red, brown, and orange).

**5.** In how many different ways can she wear a coat and a sweater?

**6.** What is the probability that if Robin picks a coat and sweater at random, she will select a black coat and red sweater?

Solve. *(pages 490–491, 510–511)*

**7.** The graph at right was used in an advertisement by Store B to compare its prices to Store A. What impression does the graph give about the comparison of prices?

**8.** Jackie has two holders with pens on her desk. One holder has 5 pens and the other has 4 pens. One pen in each holder is out of ink. What is the probability that Jackie will select a pen that is out of ink if she randomly picks a pen from either of the holders?

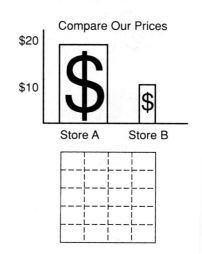

Compare Our Prices

## Statistical Claims

Statistics, like graphs, are frequently used in advertising to help convince consumers of a claim. All statistical claims ought to be examined, not only for their honesty and accuracy, but for their relevance to the claim being made. For example, you may read or hear that 90% of a car maker's automobiles sold within the past 10 years are still on the road. You may wonder what "still on the road" means and how this makes the cars reliable.

Work with a group. Each member should look for ads making statistical claims. Discuss each ad with the group, especially how the statistic being used helps support the claim?

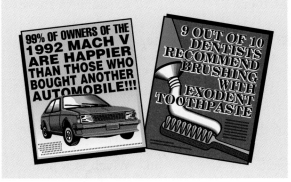

## *Palindromes*

*RADAR* is a palindrome. It is spelled the same forward and backward. Numbers can also be palindromes. The time, 10:01 is a palindrome; so is 234,432.

You can generate number palindromes. Take any number and add the reverse of the number to the number. If you don't get a palindrome keep going. Sometimes you get a palindrome right away; sometimes it takes a while.

Examples:

$$
\begin{array}{r}
123 \\
+\ 321 \\
\hline
444
\end{array}
\qquad
\begin{array}{r}
138 \\
+\ 831 \\
\hline
969
\end{array}
\qquad
\begin{array}{r}
372 \\
+\ 273 \\
\hline
645 \\
+\ 546 \\
\hline
1191 \\
+\ 1911 \\
\hline
3102 \\
+\ 2013 \\
\hline
5115
\end{array}
$$

## The Connection Game

Play with a partner. You'll need dot paper. Mark off the game area. Start with 5 dots by 5 dots.

Connect any 2 dots that are next to each other: above, below, or side-by-side. You may not connect more than 2 dots. The player who makes the last connection wins.

Find the answer.

**1.** 3 shirts
5 sweaters
number of outfits =
   **a.** 8
   **b.** 2
   **c.** 15
   **d.** none of these

**2.** 1 coat
4 shirts
number of outfits =
   **a.** 3
   **b.** 4
   **c.** 5
   **d.** none of these

**3.** 3 pants
3 shirts
number of outfits =
   **a.** 9
   **b.** 6
   **c.** 3
   **d.** none of these

**4.** $3.9 + 2.07 + 0.34$
   **a.** 2.80
   **b.** 6.31
   **c.** 28.0
   **d.** none of these

**5.** $8,000 - 784$
   **a.** 8,784
   **b.** 7,116
   **c.** 7,216
   **d.** none of these

**6.** $7 - 4.308$
   **a.** 3.308
   **b.** 11.308
   **c.** 2.692
   **d.** none of these

**7.** $28 \times 964$
   **a.** 26,992
   **b.** 26,492
   **c.** 9,140
   **d.** none of these

**8.** $402 \times 0.93$
   **a.** 3.7386
   **b.** 37.386
   **c.** 3,738.6
   **d.** none of these

**9.** $2.57 \times 0.08$
   **a.** 0.02056
   **b.** 0.2056
   **c.** 2.056
   **d.** none of these

**10.** $x - 13 = 2.5$
   **a.** 10.5
   **b.** 11.5
   **c.** 15.5
   **d.** none of these

**11.** $r + 7 = 23$
   **a.** 16
   **b.** 30
   **c.** 14
   **d.** none of these

**12.** $m + {}^-9 = {}^-2$
   **a.** ${}^-7$
   **b.** 7
   **c.** 11
   **d.** none of these

**13.** The prime factors of 72 are
   **a.** 2, 2, 2, 3, 3
   **b.** 2, 4, 3, 3
   **c.** 2, 2, 2, 9
   **d.** none of these

**14.** 75 is divisible by
   **a.** 2, 3
   **b.** 2, 3, 5
   **c.** 3, 5
   **d.** none of these

**15.** Which is a prime number?
   **a.** 57
   **b.** 77
   **c.** 91
   **d.** none of these

# PROBLEM SOLVING REVIEW

Remember the strategies and types of problems you've had so far. Solve.

- Making a table
- Working backward
- Multistep problems
- Using guess and check
- Using estimation
- Making a list
- Drawing a picture
- Using an equation

1. Gerald does not have a ruler, but he needs to measure some lengths. He does have strips of wood that he knows are 1 in., 2 in., 4 in., and 10 in. long.

   a. How long are the strips of wood that Gerald has?

   b. How can he measure a length of 7 in?

   c. What whole number lengths between 1 in. and 17 in. can he measure?

2. Jack rolled two cubes numbered 1 through 6 and added the face numbers. What fraction of the possible outcomes are prime numbers?

3. Jan is 5 yr older than Bob. Bob is 3 yr younger than Louise. List the friends from youngest to oldest.

4. Norma, Olive, and Petra study as a group. Each has a favorite subject: math, history, or English. Olive does not like math or history. Petra does not like history. What is each girl's favorite subject?

5. The Wright Brothers' first flight covered approximately 120 ft. There are 5,280 ft in one mi. Estimate the number of flights the Wright Brothers would have had to make to cover one mile.

6. Training for a 15 mi race, Karen ran 6 mi in 42 min. If she ran the entire 15 mi at the same pace, how long would it take her to complete the race?

7. Mrs. Roman takes one medicine every 2 h and another every 5 h. If she took both medicines at 11:00 A.M., when will she next take them together?

8. Danny has 5 kinds of juice. He wants to make a fruit drink by mixing 3 of them. How many different fruit drinks can Danny make?

9. Roberto's average on his first 4 tests was 92. After 5 tests his average dropped to 88. What was his grade on his fifth test?

10. Toward the end of a day, a letter carrier had 25 pieces of mail left. She had delivered 95% of the pieces she started with. With how many pieces of mail did she start?

## RETAKE!

Miss Rhodes has an unusual testing system in her math class. If the median *or* the mean of the lowest 6 scores on a quiz falls below 72, the whole class has to take the quiz again. Here are 5 of the lowest 6 scores.

73 60 81 75 69

If the class did not have to retake the quiz, what is the lowest possible missing score?

## DID YOU KNOW . . . ?

Juneau, Alaska, is the capital of our 49th state. With an area of 3,108 mi², it is the largest city in area in the United States.

If the area were in the shape of a square, between what two whole numbers would be the length of each side of the square?

## A PIECE OF THE PIE

In the computer activity *Pie Graphics*, you must estimate what percent of the circle each pie slice represents. This pencil-and-paper activity will help you develop skills estimating what percent of the pie a certain slice represents. Use these circles as guides.

12.5%     25%     37.5%     50%     62.5%     75%     87.5%

Estimate the percent of each circle that is shaded.

**1.**          **2.**          **3.**          **4.**

**5.**          **6.**          **7.**          **8.**

This section contains some games you can play at school or at home with your friends or family. You will need only a few simple materials to play most of these games. This list tells you what these items are and how you can substitute if you don't have them.

Number cubes (1–6) or numbered slips of paper in a box

A spinner (1–10) or numbered slips in a box

Different color markers, buttons, or small circles cut from paper

Small index cards or pieces of construction paper

# Find the Missing Number

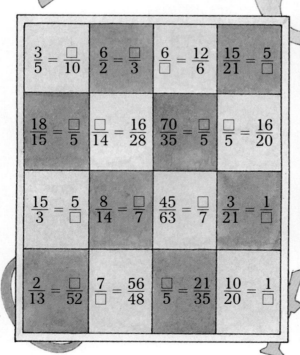

**Top left grid:**

| | | | |
|---|---|---|---|
| $\frac{6}{\square} = \frac{12}{6}$ | $\frac{6}{2} = \frac{\square}{3}$ | $\frac{\square}{5} = \frac{16}{20}$ | $\frac{10}{20} = \frac{1}{\square}$ |
| $\frac{\square}{5} = \frac{21}{35}$ | $\frac{2}{13} = \frac{\square}{52}$ | $\frac{15}{3} = \frac{5}{\square}$ | $\frac{7}{\square} = \frac{56}{48}$ |
| $\frac{3}{5} = \frac{\square}{10}$ | $\frac{6}{\square} = \frac{12}{6}$ | $\frac{10}{14} = \frac{\square}{7}$ | $\frac{\square}{14} = \frac{16}{28}$ |
| $\frac{70}{35} = \frac{\square}{5}$ | $\frac{18}{15} = \frac{\square}{5}$ | $\frac{\square}{25} = \frac{4}{10}$ | $\frac{45}{63} = \frac{\square}{7}$ |

**Top right grid:**

| | | | |
|---|---|---|---|
| $\frac{3}{4} = \frac{\square}{12}$ | $\frac{\square}{5} = \frac{21}{35}$ | $\frac{7}{\square} = \frac{56}{48}$ | $\frac{2}{13} = \frac{\square}{52}$ |
| $\frac{10}{20} = \frac{\square}{2}$ | $\frac{3}{21} = \frac{1}{\square}$ | $\frac{8}{14} = \frac{\square}{7}$ | $\frac{15}{3} = \frac{5}{\square}$ |
| $\frac{6}{2} = \frac{\square}{3}$ | $\frac{6}{\square} = \frac{12}{6}$ | $\frac{\square}{5} = \frac{16}{20}$ | $\frac{21}{6} = \frac{7}{\square}$ |
| $\frac{42}{84} = \frac{\square}{2}$ | $\frac{\square}{25} = \frac{4}{10}$ | $\frac{70}{35} = \frac{\square}{5}$ | $\frac{45}{63} = \frac{\square}{7}$ |

**Bottom left grid:**

| | | | |
|---|---|---|---|
| $\frac{3}{5} = \frac{\square}{10}$ | $\frac{6}{2} = \frac{\square}{3}$ | $\frac{6}{\square} = \frac{12}{6}$ | $\frac{15}{21} = \frac{5}{\square}$ |
| $\frac{18}{15} = \frac{\square}{5}$ | $\frac{\square}{14} = \frac{16}{28}$ | $\frac{70}{35} = \frac{\square}{5}$ | $\frac{\square}{5} = \frac{16}{20}$ |
| $\frac{15}{3} = \frac{5}{\square}$ | $\frac{8}{14} = \frac{\square}{7}$ | $\frac{45}{63} = \frac{\square}{7}$ | $\frac{3}{21} = \frac{1}{\square}$ |
| $\frac{2}{13} = \frac{\square}{52}$ | $\frac{7}{\square} = \frac{56}{48}$ | $\frac{\square}{5} = \frac{21}{35}$ | $\frac{10}{20} = \frac{1}{\square}$ |

**Bottom right grid:**

| | | | |
|---|---|---|---|
| $\frac{2}{13} = \frac{\square}{52}$ | $\frac{21}{6} = \frac{7}{\square}$ | $\frac{7}{\square} = \frac{56}{48}$ | $\frac{\square}{5} = \frac{21}{35}$ |
| $\frac{\square}{5} = \frac{16}{20}$ | $\frac{3}{21} = \frac{1}{\square}$ | $\frac{10}{14} = \frac{\square}{7}$ | $\frac{10}{20} = \frac{1}{\square}$ |
| $\frac{6}{12} = \frac{12}{\square}$ | $\frac{6}{2} = \frac{\square}{3}$ | $\frac{3}{5} = \frac{\square}{10}$ | $\frac{42}{84} = \frac{\square}{2}$ |
| $\frac{15}{3} = \frac{5}{\square}$ | $\frac{\square}{14} = \frac{16}{28}$ | $\frac{\square}{25} = \frac{4}{10}$ | $\frac{3}{4} = \frac{\square}{12}$ |

524

# *Find the Missing Number*

**Goal:** To cover all the squares in a row, column, or diagonal
**Number of Players:** 2–4
**Skills:** Chapters 5, 6, 7
**Materials:** Markers, a spinner (1–10)

**Rules**

1. Choose one of the missing number boards.

2. Take turns spinning the spinner.

3. If the number on the spinner is the answer to one of the problems on your board, place a marker on that square.

4. The player who covers all the squares in a row, column, or diagonal is the winner.

**Variations**

Make up your own missing number boards and use other spinners. Be sure to write problems whose answers will be one of the numbers on the spinner you use.

# Contact 7

| | | | | | | | |
|---|---|---|---|---|---|---|---|
| | | | | 0 | | | |
| 1 | 2 | 3 | 4 | 5 | 6 | 7 | 8 |
| 9 | 10 | 11 | 12 | 13 | 14 | 15 | 16 |
| 17 | 18 | 19 | 20 | 21 | 22 | 23 | 24 |
| 25 | 26 | 27 | 28 | 29 | 30 | 31 | 32 |
| 33 | 34 | 35 | 36 | 37 | 38 | 39 | 40 |
| 41 | 42 | 44 | 45 | 48 | 50 | 54 | 55 |
| 60 | 64 | 66 | 72 | 75 | 80 | 90 | 96 |
| 100 | 108 | 120 | 125 | 144 | 150 | 180 | 216 |

# Contact 7

**Goal:** To get the most points for touching boxes
**Number of Players:** 2 (or 1)
**Skills:** Chapters 2, 3, 4
**Materials:** 24 different color markers for each player, 3 number cubes

**Rules for Playing with a Partner**

1. Take turns rolling the 3 cubes. Make a number by adding, subtracting, multiplying, dividing, taking the square root of, or using as an exponent the numbers on the cubes. Put one of your markers on the box with your number, but don't cover another marker.

2. If the box you put the marker on touches other boxes with markers, you get a point for each box with a marker. The boxes may touch on a side or at a corner. After each turn, record the number of points you got on that turn.

3. Play until each player has had 8 turns.

4. The winner is the player who has more points. You may use a calculator to add your total points.

**Rules for Playing Alone**

1. Roll the 3 cubes. Make a number by adding, subtracting, multiplying, dividing, taking the square root of, or using as an exponent the numbers on the cubes. Put one of your markers on the box with your number, but don't cover another marker.

2. If the box you put the marker on touches other boxes with markers, you get a point for each box with a marker. The boxes may touch on a side or at a corner. After you put down a marker, record the number of points you got with that marker. Roll the cubes 8 times.

3. Find your total score. Use a calculator if you want. Play again. Try to get a higher total.

# Probability Bingo

| | | | |
|---|---|---|---|
| P(2) 11121 | P(odd) 2 4 6 8 5 | P(□) △○□△ | P(m) mom |
| P(even) 2 4 6 8 5 | P(vowel) house | P(e) abcd efgh | P(odd) 2 3 4 5 |
| P(T) THTT | P(Q) QQQQR | P(vowel) error | P(a) abc |
| P(△) △□□○□ | P(x) yxy yxy | P(T) TTT | P(r) drawer |

| | | | |
|---|---|---|---|
| P(even) 23478 | P(l) doll | P(T) TTHH | P(m or o) mom |
| P(l) parallel | P(even) 3 6 8 10 4 | P(p) poppy | P(H) HHHH |
| P(m) mom | P(△ or □) ○□○ ○□△ | P(○) △□□ ○△□ | P(e) abcd efgh |
| P(vowel) cage | P(not T) HHTH | P(not e) rattle | P(even) 2 4 6 8 5 |

| | | | |
|---|---|---|---|
| P(t) rattle | P(2) 11121 | P(△ or □) ○□○ ○□△ | P(odd) 2 3 4 5 |
| P(vowel) house | P(□) □□□ □□ | P(even) 2 4 6 8 5 | P(not T) HHTH |
| P(□) △○□△ | P(○) △□□ ○△□ | P(vowel) cage | P(e) abcd efgh |
| P(not e) rattle | P(H) HHHH | P(m) mom | P(T) TTHH |

| | | | |
|---|---|---|---|
| P(odd) 2 4 6 8 5 | P(l) doll | P(p) poppy | P(△) △□□○□ |
| P(even) 2 3 4 7 8 | P(T) TTT | P(m or o) mom | P(a) abc |
| P(H) HHHH | P(r) drawer | P(T) THTT | P(Q) QQQQR |
| P(x) yxy yxy | P(even) 3 6 8 10 4 | P(vowel) error | P(vowel) cookie |

## *Probability Bingo*

**Goal:** To cover all the squares in a row, column, or diagonal

**Number of Players:** 2–4

**Skills:** Chapter 12

**Materials:** Markers, 30 index cards marked in 2 sets with the following numbers: 0, 1, $\frac{1}{5}$, $\frac{2}{5}$, $\frac{3}{5}$, $\frac{4}{5}$, $\frac{1}{4}$, $\frac{1}{2}$, $\frac{3}{4}$, $\frac{1}{3}$, $\frac{2}{3}$, $\frac{1}{6}$, $\frac{5}{6}$, $\frac{1}{8}$, $\frac{3}{8}$, a number cube (1–6)

**Rules**

1. Mix up the cards and place them face down on the table.

2. Choose one of the bingo boards.

3. Take turns rolling the number cube. The player with the least number begins by turning over the top card.

4. If the number on the card shows the probability for one of the events on your board, place a marker on that square.

5. The next player turns over the next card, and play continues until someone covers all the squares in a row, column, or diagonal. That person is the winner.

# Shady Squares

**Goal:** To shade more of a given square than anyone else
**Number of Players:** 2–4
**Skills:** Chapters 10, 11
**Materials:** Graph paper, 10 pennies, paper cup

**Rules**

1. Each player draw a $10 \times 10$ square on a sheet of graph paper.

2. Players take turns putting the 10 pennies in the paper cup, shaking them, then spilling them onto the table.

3. After each toss, the player shades the percent of the square equal to either:

   a. the ratio of the number of heads to the number of tails
   b. the ratio of the number of tails to the number of heads
   c. the ratio of the number of heads to the total number of coins
   d. the ratio of the number of tails to the total number of coins

4. A player can decide to stop tossing coins and shading parts of the square before any turn. Play continues for 4 rounds. After 4 rounds, the player whose square is most completely filled in is the winner. A player who is forced to shade more than 100% of the square loses.

# Arithmetic Roundup

**Goal:** To make a problem with the desired goal
**Number of Players:** 2 or more
**Skills:** Chapter 3
**Materials:** Pencil and paper, 0–9 spinner

**Problem Forms**

| Greatest Product | Least Remainder |
|---|---|
| ___ . ___ ___ × ___ . ___ | ___ ___ ___ ÷ ___ ___ |

**Rules**

1. Choose a problem form. Each player draws the problem form on a sheet of paper. After you play with these problem forms, make up your own problem forms.

2. Take turns spinning a number. After each number is selected, write it in one of the blanks. Once you put a number in a blank, you can't move it.

3. After all the blanks have been filled in, the winner is the player closest to the goal. Use estimation to decide. Calculate the exact answers only if you can't tell by estimating.

4. The winner of each round gets 1 point. If there is a tie, each of those players gets 1 point.

# Make a Percent

**Goal:** To make fractions equal to a chosen percent
**Number of Players:** 2 or more
**Skills:** Chapters 10 and 11
**Materials:** Paper and pencil, 2 number cubes (1–6), 10 markers for each player

**Sample Game Form**

**Rules**

1. Each player makes a game form like the sample above.

2. Fill in each box with a percent. You may use the same percent more than once and you may used percents greater than 100%.

3. Take turns rolling the 2 cubes. On each roll, make a fraction. If the percent that is equivalent to the fraction is in your box, place a marker on that box. You may put only one marker on a box.

4. Play for 10 rounds. The winner is the player who has covered more boxes.

**Variations** Fill in the game form only with percents less than 100% or only with percents greater than 100%.

**Different Calculators**  Every calculator is different. Many of the keys that may appear on your calculator are pictured below, although the keys may be in different places. You should read the instructions for your calculator to learn how to use it.

**The Display**  A calculator usually does not show commas. Usually 8 digits is the most the display will show. A display never shows a dollar sign. You must press the decimal point key to show a decimal number. You press the clear key to return the display to zero.

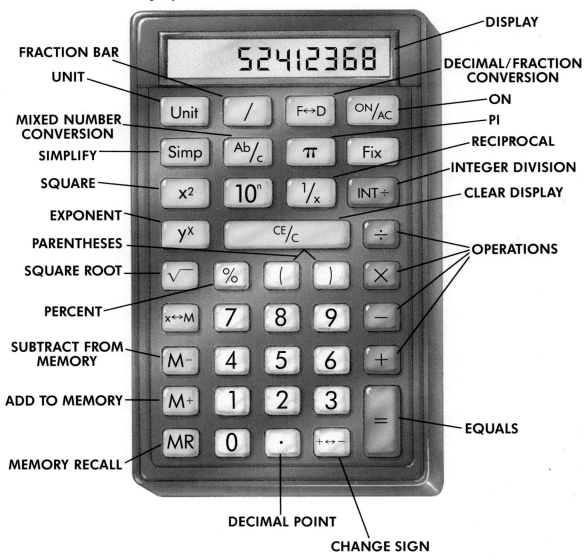

DISPLAY

FRACTION BAR

UNIT

DECIMAL/FRACTION CONVERSION

MIXED NUMBER CONVERSION

ON

PI

SIMPLIFY

RECIPROCAL

SQUARE

INTEGER DIVISION

EXPONENT

CLEAR DISPLAY

PARENTHESES

SQUARE ROOT

OPERATIONS

PERCENT

SUBTRACT FROM MEMORY

ADD TO MEMORY

EQUALS

MEMORY RECALL

DECIMAL POINT

CHANGE SIGN

**The Memory Feature**

[M+] stores the displayed number in the memory or adds the displayed number to the memory.

[M-] subtracts the displayed number from the memory.

[MR] displays the number stored in the memory.

If you wish to clear the memory, press [MR] followed by [M-]. This subtracts the numbers stored in the memory.

You can add a given number to several other numbers by using the memory feature. Add 36 to 9 and to 29.

**Press**      36 [M+] 9 [+] [MR] [=]

**Display**    36 M36    M9 M36 M45

**Press**      29 [+] [MR] [=]

**Display**     M29   M36 M65

So, 9 + 36 = 45, and 29 + 36 = 65.

**The Constant Feature**

On many calculators the [=] key can also be used to repeat an operation with the same number over and over again.

**Press**      10 [-] 2 [=] [=] [=] [=]

**Display**    10     2 8   6   4   2

The calculator subtracts 2 each time you press the [=] key.

**The Percent Key**

Many calculators have a percent key. You can use it to solve problems with percents. Find 50% of 80. On most calculators, enter 80 first.

**Press**      80 [×] 50 [%] [=]

**Display**    80      50 0.5 40

50% of 80 is 40.

534

**Operations Using Fractions and Mixed Numbers**

The keys discussed here enable you to use your calculator to perform operations with fractions. If your calculator does not have these keys, you will need to express fraction values as decimals before performing operations with them.

[Unit] enters the displayed value as the whole number portion of a mixed number.

[/] fraction bar.

[Ab/c] converts a mixed number to a fraction.

[F↔D] converts a fraction to a decimal or vice versa.

[Simp] simplifies a fraction. You can choose the factor by entering it after pressing the simplify key and then pressing the [=] key. If you do not enter a factor, the calculator will choose one when you press the [=] key.

Convert 1.75 to a fraction, and simplify the result.

**Press**    1 [.] 75 [F↔D] [Simp] [=] [Simp]   [=]

**Display**    1.75    1u 75/100   1u 15/20   1u 3/4

The result is $1\frac{3}{4}$.

Simplify $2\frac{9}{6}$, and convert it to a decimal.

**Press**    2 [Unit] 9 [/] 6 [Ab/c] [Simp]   [=]    [F↔D]

**Display**          2u 9/6    3u 3/6    3u 1/2   3.5

The result is 3.5.

Add $1\frac{4}{5}$ and $3\frac{7}{10}$, and express the sum in simplest form.

**Press**    1 [Unit] 4 [/] 5 [+] 3 [Unit] 7 [/] 10    [=]

**Display**     1u 4/5          3u 7/10     4u 15/10

**Press**    [Ab/c] [Simp]   [=]

**Display**    5u 5/10   5u 1/2

The result is $5\frac{1}{2}$.

**Integer Division**  Using the integer division key in place of the division key will give you your answer as a quotient and a remainder, instead of a decimal quotient. Find the quotient and remainder of $17 \div 3$.

**Press**     17 INT÷ 3 =

**Display**        17   3   Q5 R2

The quotient is 5 and the remainder is 2.

**The Exponent Key**  You can use an exponent key to raise a number to a power. Find $10^4$.

**Press**   10 $y^x$ 4 =

**Display**   10 4   10000

So, $10^4$ is 10,000.

**Other Keys**  There are a number of other keys you may find on your calculator.

$\pi$ enables you to calculate with a more precise value of $\pi$ than 3.14.

$1/x$ gives you the reciprocal of the number in the display.

$x^2$ gives you the square of the number in the display.

+↔− can be used to enter a negative number or to change the sign of a number in the display.

( ) are used to insert parentheses into a problem.

Find $2 + (20 \div 5)$.

**Press**     2 + ( 20 ÷ 5 ) =

**Display**   2         20    5 4   6

So, $2 + (20 \div 5) = 6$.

# GLOSSARY

## A

**absolute value** (p. 414) The distance an integer is from 0 on the number line.

**actual probability** (p. 396) The number of favorable outcomes divided by the total of possible outcomes.

**acute angle** (p. 234) An angle measuring less than 90°.

**acute triangle** (p. 244) A triangle with all acute angles.

**adjacent angles** (p. 236) Angles with a common vertex and side but no interior points in common.

**angle** (p. 233) Two rays with the same endpoint.

**angle bisector** (p. 458) A ray that divides an angle into two congruent parts.

**arc** (p. 456) A part of a circle.

**area** (p. 256) The measure of a surface of a plane figure.

**Associative Property** (pp. 36, 60) Changing the grouping of the addends (or factors) does not change the sum (or product).

**average** (p. 8) The quotient found by dividing the sum of a group of numbers by the number of addends.

## B

**base** [of a geometric shape] (p. 468) The face of a pyramid or a cone opposite the vertex. One of two congruent parallel faces of a prism or a cylinder.

**base** [of a power] (p. 4) One of equal factors in a product.

**basic counting principle** (p. 502) A principle that states that when you know the number of outcomes for each event you can multiply those numbers to find the number of outcomes in the sample space for the multiple events.

**bisector** (p. 458) A line that divides a line segment or an angle into two equal parts.

**box plot** (p. 496) A graphic display that divides the data into four parts, the middle two parts shown by a box from the lowest to highest quartile, the means and extremes shown by line segments.

**budget** (p. 339) A plan you make to be sure your income will cover your expenses.

## C

**capacity** (p. 22) The amount of fluid a container will hold.

**centimeter (cm)** (p. 20) A metric unit of length. 1 cm = 10 mm

**circle** (p. 254) The set of all points in a plane that are at the same distance from a point in the plane.

**circle graph** (p. 498) A circle divided into parts to show data.

**circumference** (p. 254) The distance around a circle.

**clustering** (p. 71) A process used to estimate a sum of numbers in close proximity by multiplying a representative addend by the number of addends.

**combinations** (p. 512) An arrangement of things in which the order does not matter.

**commission** (p. 354) A percent of the total sales a person makes.

**common factor** (p. 134) A number that is a factor of two or more numbers.

**Commutative Property** (pp. 36, 60) Changing the order of addends (or factors) does not change the sum (or product).

**compatible numbers** (p. 61) Numbers close to given numbers that make estimation easier.

**complementary angles** (p. 236) Angles the sum of whose measures is 90°.

**complementary events** (p. 507) Two events that together make up the sample space.

**composite number** (p. 132) A number that has more than two factors.

**cone** (p. 470) A space figure with one circular base and one vertex.

**congruent angles** (p. 236) Angles with the same measure.

**congruent figures** (p. 250) Figures that have the same size and shape.

**congruent line segments** (p. 232) Two line segments with the same length.

**congruent triangles** (p. 250) Triangles whose corresponding sides and angles are congruent.

**coordinate plane** (p. 436) A grid on a plane with two perpendicular number lines.

**coordinates** (p. 436) The numbers in an ordered pair associated with a point on a graph.

**corresponding angles** (p. 250) The angles at matching vertexes of congruent figures.

**corresponding sides** (p. 250) The matching sides of congruent figures.

**count on** (p. 43) A means of adding, by starting with one addend and counting up the amount of the next addend.

**cross products** (p. 280) Products used to check if two fractions are equivalent.

**cross section** (p. 472) The figure formed when a space figure is sliced by a plane.

**cubic centimeter** (**cm$^3$**) (p. 25) The amount of space contained in a cube with all edges 1 cm long.

**cylinder** (p. 470) A space figure with two parallel congruent circular bases.

# D

**data** (p. 129) Numbers that give information.

**degree** (p. 234) The unit of measure used to measure angles.

**degrees Celsius** (**°C**) (p. 416) the metric unit for measuring temperature.

**denominator** (p. 142) The bottom number in a fraction.

**dependent events** (p. 508) Two events in which the result of the first affects the result of the second.

**diagonal** (p. 245) A line segment that joins two vertexes of a polygon and is not a side of the polygon.

**diameter** (p. 254) The distance from the points on a circle through the center.

**discount** (p. 358) A decrease in the price of an item.

**discount rate** (p. 358) A reduction that is a percent of the original price.

**Distributive Property** (p. 60) The product of a factor and a sum is equal to the sum of the products.

**divisible** (p. 130) Capable of being divided evenly with a remainder.

**dodecahedron** (p. 462) A space figure made of 12 faces, each a regular pentagon.

**double bar graph** (p. 380) A graph that uses bars to compare two sets of data.

**double line graph** (p. 384) A graph that uses lines to compare the change over time of two sets of data.

# E

**edge** (p. 462) The intersection of two faces or two sides of a space figure.

**elapsed time** The time that passes between the start and end of an event.

**equation** (p. 34) A mathematical sentence stating that two quantities are equal.

**equally likely outcomes** (p. 394) When each result has the same chance of occurring.

**equilateral triangle** (p. 244) A triangle with all sides and angles congruent.

**equivalent fractions** (p. 144) Fractions that have the same value.

**estimate** (p. 16) A number close enough to an exact number that permits you to make a correct decision.

**evaluate** (p. 98) To substitute a number for each variable in an expression and then do the indicated arithmetic.

**expanded form** (p. 6) The representation of a number as the sum of products of each digit and a power of 10.

**experimental probability** (p. 396) The relative frequency of an outcome.

**exponent** (p. 4) The number showing how many times a base is used as a factor.

**exponential form** (p. 4) The form of a number written as a base with a power. The exponential form for 100 is $10^2$.

## F

**faces** (p. 462) The flat surfaces that form space figures.

**factors** (p. 4, 130) Any of two or more numbers that are multiplied to obtain a product.

**factor tree** (p. 133) A diagram showing the prime factorization of a number.

**fathom** (p. 70) Unit of water depth measuring 6 ft.

**formula** (p. 466) A short way of stating a rule.

**fraction** (p. 142) A number in the form $\frac{a}{b}$, where $b$ is not zero, that compares part of an object or a set with the whole.

**frequency** (p. 388) The number of times a given item appears in a set of data.

**front-end estimation.** (p. 42) An estimation method using the left digits of the numbers involved.

**function** (p. 114) A set of ordered pairs (x, y) such that for each value of x there is one and only one value of y.

**function rule** (p. 116) A rule that states how two variables are related to form a function.

## G

**geometric transformations** (p. 248) Changes in the position of a figure while the size and shape remain the same.

**gram** (g) (p. 24) A metric unit of mass. 1 g = 1,000 mg

**graph of a number** (p. 110) The point paired with a number on a number line.

**greatest common factor (GCF)** (p. 134) The greatest of the common factors of two or more numbers.

## H

**height (h)** (p. 256) The length of a segment that is perpendicular to the base.

**hypotenuse** (p. 454) The side opposite the right angle in a right triangle.

## I

**icosahedron** (p. 462) A space figure with 20 faces, all equilateral triangles.

**Identity Property** (p. 36, 60) The sum of any number and zero is that number; the product of one and any other number is that number.

**inequality** (p. 110) A number sentence that states two numbers or quantities are not equal.

**integers** (p. 414) The positive numbers 1, 2, 3, . . ., the negative numbers ⁻1, ⁻2, ⁻3, . . ., and zero.

**independent events** (p. 506) Events that have no effect on each other.

**interest** (p. 338) The money the bank charges you for a loan.

**interest rate** (p. 338) A percent of the principal you pay for a certain period of time.

**intersecting lines** (p. 233) Lines that cross each other.

**inverse operations** (p. 100) One operation that "undoes" the other.

**isosceles triangle** (p. 244) A triangle with two congruent sides and two congruent angles.

## K

**kilogram** (kg) (p. 24) A metric unit of mass. 1 kg = 1,000 g

**kilometer** (km) (p. 20) A metric unit of length. 1 km = 1,000 m

## L

**lattice** (p. 502) A chart with columns and rows used for listing all outcomes in the sample space.

**Law of Large Numbers** (p. 399) If you run a large number of experiments, the experimental probability you find will be close to the actual probability.

**least common denominator** (LCD) (p. 150) The LCM of two or more denominators.

**least common multiple** (LCM) (p. 136) The least of the common multiples of two nonzero numbers.

**legs of a right triangle** (p. 454) The sides of a right triangle that are not the hypotenuse.

**line** (p.232) A set of points that extends without end in opposite directions.

**line of reflection** (p. 248) The line over which a figure is reflected.

**line of symmetry** (p. 252) A line through a figure so that if the figure were folded on the line, the two parts of the figure would be congruent.

**line plot** (p. 492) A method of displaying a small set of data by showing the data along a segment and marking each frequency.

**line segment** (p. 232) A part of a line with two endpoints.

**liter (L)** (p. 22) A metric unit of capacity. 1 L = 1,000 mL

**lowest terms** (p. 146) A fraction is in lowest terms if the GCF of the numerator and the denominator is 1.

# M

**markup** (p. 359) An increase in the price of an item.

**mass** (p. 24) The quantity of matter in an object.

**mathematical expression** (p. 96) A combination of numbers, variables, and operation symbols.

**mean** (p. 382) The sum of the data items divided by the number of data items.

**median** (p. 382) The middle number in a set of data arranged in order.

**meter (m)** (p. 20) A metric unit of length. 1,000 m = 1 km

**milligram (mg)** (p. 24) A metric unit of mass. 1,000 mg = 1 g

**milliliter (mL)** (p. 22) A metric unit of capacity. 1,000 mL = 1 L

**millimeter (mm)** (p. 20) A metric unit of length. 1 mm = 0.1 cm

**mixed number** (p. 148) A number that has a whole number part and a fractional part.

**mode** (p. 380) The response or responses that appear most frequently in a set of data.

**multiple** (p. 136) The product of a given number and any whole number.

**multiplication principle** (p. 506) To find the probability of two independent events occurring at the same time, find the product of the individual probabilities.

# N

**negative numbers** (p. 414) Numbers less than zero.

**number line** (p. 8) A line in which numbers have been paired with points.

**numerator** (p. 142) The top number in a fraction.

# O

**obtuse angle** (p. 234) An angle that has a measure greater than 90° and less than 180°.

**obtuse triangle** (p. 244) A triangle with one obtuse angle.

**octahedron** (p. 462) A space figure with 8 faces, all equilateral triangles.

**opposites** (p. 414) Two numbers that are the same distance from 0 but on opposite sides of 0.

**ordered pair** (p. 436) A pair of numbers in which the order shows the location of a point on a grid. (4, 3) is an ordered pair.

**origin** (p. 436) The point where the $x$-axis and the $y$-axis meet.

**outcome** (p. 502) The result of a probability experiment.

**outlier** (p. 497) An extreme value compared to the other values.

# P

**parallel lines** (p. 233) Lines that never intersect and are in the same plane.

**parallelogram** (p. 240) A quadrilateral with opposite sides parallel.

**pentagon** (p. 240) A five-sided polygon.

**percent** (p. 310) The ratio of a number to 100. The symbol % means per hundred.

**percent of decrease** (p. 337) The ratio of the decrease to the original amount.

**percent of increase** (p. 336) The ratio of the increase to the original amount.

**percent of loss** (p. 337) The percent of decrease.

**percent of profit** (p. 337) The percent of increase.

**perimeter** (p. 16) The total distance around.

**permutation** (p. 512) An arrangement of things in which the order of the things is important.

**perpendicular** (p. 234) Two lines, line segments, or rays that form a right angle.

**perpendicular bisector** (p. 458) The bisector of a line segment that is also perpendicular to the line segment.

**pi (π)** (p. 254) The ratio of the circumference of a circle to its diameter.

**plane** (p. 232) A flat surface that goes on and on without end.

**point** (p. 232) An exact location.

**polygon** (p. 240) A closed, plane figure made from three or more line segments.

**population** (p. 378) The entire group about whom information is wanted.

**positive numbers** (p. 418) Numbers greater than zero.

**prime factorization** (p. 133) The product of prime factors that name a given number, such as $2 \times 2 \times 3 \times 5$ to name 60.

**prime number** (p. 132) A number that has exactly 2 factors, namely 1 and the number itself.

**principal** (p. 338) The amount of money you borrow.

**prism** (p. 468) A space figure with two bases that are congruent polygons and are on parallel planes.

**probability** (p. 392) A number describing the chance that an event will happen.

**proportion** (p. 277) Two equal ratios.

**pyramid** (p. 469) A space figure with only one base.

**Pythagorean theorem** (p. 455) If a triangle is a right triangle, the square of the hypotenuse is equal to the sum of the squares of the other two sides.

# Q

**quadrilateral** (p. 240) A four-sided polygon.

**quartiles** (p. 496) The values at the median, and at the median of the upper and lower half of the set of data.

# R

**radius (r)** (p. 254) The distance from the center to any point on a circle.

**random sample** (p. 378) A sampling made ensuring every member of the population has an equally likely chance of being selected.

**range** (p. 492) The difference between the greatest number and the least number in a list of data.

**rate** (p. 279) A ratio that compares two quantities of different kinds. A rate may be expressed as a ratio, a decimal, or a percent.

**ratio** (p. 274) A quotient of two numbers that is used to compare one quantity to another.

**ray** (p. 233) A part of a line with one endpoint.

**reciprocals** (p. 208) Two numbers whose product is one.

**rectangle** (p. 241) A parallelogram with all angles right angles.

**reflection** (p. 248) A geometric transformation that changes the position of a figure through the motion of a flip.

**reflection image** (p. 248) In a coordinate plane, the result of a reflection.

**regular polygon** (p. 240) A polygon in which all sides and angles are congruent.

**relative frequency** (p. 388) A ratio that compares a part to the whole.

**relative frequency table** (p. 388) A table that organizes information to enable one to find relative frequency.

**repeating decimals** (p. 154) A decimal in which the last digit or block of digits repeats without end.

**representative sample** (p. 378) A sample with characteristics similar to the population.

**rhombus** (p. 241) A parallelogram with all sides congruent.

**right angle** (p. 234) An angle with a measure of 90°.

**right triangle** (p. 244) A triangle with a right angle.

**rotation** (p. 248) A geometric transformation that changes the position of a figure through the motion of a turn.

## S

**sample** (p. 378) A part or subset of a population.

**sample space** (p. 502) List of all possible outcomes.

**scale** (p. 294) The ratio of the size of a drawing to the size of the actual object.

**scale drawing** (p. 294) A sketch of an object with all lengths in proportion to corresponding actual lengths.

**scalene triangle** (p. 244) A triangle with no congruent sides or angles.

**scientific notation** (p. 78) A way of naming numbers. There are two factors. One factor is a number greater than or equal to 1 but less than 10. The other factor is a power of 10.

**similar figures** (p. 291) Two figures whose corresponding angles are congruent and whose corresponding sides are in proportion.

**similar polygons** (p. 291) Polygons having the same shape, but not necessarily the same size.

**similar triangles** (p. 290) Triangles that have the same shape but not always the same size.

**solution** (p. 34) The number that replaces a variable to form a true equation.

**space figures** (p. 462) Figures that have 3 dimensions, length, width, and height.

**sphere** (p. 470) A space figure, all points on the surface of which are the same distance from the center.

**square** (p. 241) A parallelogram with all sides congruent and only right angles.

**square** (p. 452) The product of two equal factors.

**square root** (p. 452) One of two equal factors of a number.

**standard form** (p. 6) The usual, short form of a number. 573 is the standard form for 5 hundreds, 7 tens, 3 ones.

**standard unit** (p. 186) Units of measure that are the same everywhere.

**straight angle** (p. 234) An angle with a measure of 180°.

**substitution** (p. 98) To replace the variable with numbers.

**supplementary angles** (p. 236) Two angles whose measures add up to 180°.

**surface area** (p. 468) The sum of the areas of the faces of a space figure.

**symmetry** (p. 252) A property that a figure has when parts match on opposite sides of a line.

## T

**terminating decimal** (p. 154) A decimal with a limited number of nonzero digits.

**tessellation** (p. 249) Fills a plane with figures that touch but do not overlap.

**translation** (p. 249) A geometric transformation that changes the position of a figure through the motion of a slide.

**trapezoid** (p. 240) A quadrilateral with exactly one pair of parallel sides.

**tree diagram** (p. 502) A picture showing possible outcomes of an activity.

## U

**unit rate** (p. 279) The ratio of a quantity to 1.

**unit price** (p. 284) The cost per unit of a product.

## V

**variable** (p. 34) An unknown number.

**Venn diagram** (p. 238) A diagram that helps organize and classify numbers and objects. Usually made with ovals and circles.

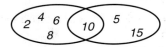

**vertex** (p. 233) The common endpoint of two rays or two segments.
**vertical angles** (p. 236) Opposite angles formed by two intersecting lines.
**volume** (p. 474) The amount of space inside a space figure.

# W

**word form** (p. 6) The long, written form for a number in words.

# X

**x-axis** (p. 436) The horizontal number line in a coordinate plane.

# Y

**y-axis** (p. 436) The vertical number line in a coordinate plane.

# Z

**Zero Property of Multiplication** (p. 60) The product of zero and any other number is zero.

# TABLE OF MEASURES

## Time

| | | | |
|---|---|---|---|
| 60 seconds (s) = 1 minute (min) | | 365 days ⎫ | |
| 60 minutes (min) = 1 hour (h) | | 52 weeks ⎬ = 1 year | |
| 24 hours = 1 day (d) | | 12 months ⎭ | |
| 7 days = 1 week | | 10 years = 1 decade | |
| | | 100 years = 1 century | |

---

## Metric

### LENGTH

10 millimeters (mm) = 1 centimeter (cm)

10 centimeters = 1 decimeter (dm)

10 decimeters ⎫
100 centimeters ⎭ = 1 meter

10 meters = 1 dekameter (dam)

10 dekameters = 1 hectometer (hm)

10 hectometers ⎫
1000 meters ⎭ = 1 kilometer (km)

### AREA

100 square millimeters = 1 square centimeter
(mm²)  (cm²)

10,000 square centimeters = 1 square meter (m²)

10,000 square meters = 1 hectare (ha)

### VOLUME

1000 cubic millimeters = 1 cubic centimeter
(mm³)  (cm³)

1,000,000 cubic centimeters = 1 cubic meter (m³)

### MASS

1000 milligrams (mg) = 1 gram (g)

1000 grams = 1 kilogram (kg)

### CAPACITY

1000 milliliters (mL) = 1 liter (L)

## United States Customary

### LENGTH

12 inches (in.) = 1 foot (ft)

3 feet ⎫
36 inches ⎭ = 1 yard (yd)

5280 feet ⎫
1760 yards ⎭ = 1 mile (mi)

### AREA

144 square inches (in.²) = 1 square foot (ft²)

9 square feet = 1 square yard (yd²)

4840 square yards = 1 acre (A)

### VOLUME

1728 cubic inches = 1 cubic foot (ft³)

27 cubic feet = 1 cubic yard (yd³)

### WEIGHT

16 ounces (oz) = 1 pound (lb)

2000 pounds = 1 ton (t)

### CAPACITY

8 fluid ounces (fl oz) = 1 cup (c)

2 cups = 1 pint (pt)

2 pints = 1 quart (qt)

4 quarts = 1 gallon (gal)

# INDEX

# Credits

**Series design**   Pronk & Associates

**Cover and title page design**   Sheaff Design, Inc.

**Cover and title page photography**   Schlowsky Photography

**Art production of openers**   Pronk & Associates

**Technical Art**   Pronk & Associates and Morgan Slade & Associates

ILLUSTRATIONS
Meg Kelleher Aubrey 165
Rudy Backart 57, 93 (top)
David Bathurst 1, 84, 85, 174, 175, 186, 187
Nancy Bernard 199, 373
Thach Bui 6, 7, 97, 432, 474, 475, 497, 506, 507, 508
Scott Cameron 104, 105
Ian Carr 16, 17, 190, 191, 207, 220
Doug Cushman 411
Chris Demerest 345
Greg Douglas 180, 181, 314, 315, 386, 452, 457, 467
Rodney Dunn 169
Catherine Farley 46, 48, 78, 79, 95
Ruth Flanigan 19 (right), 127
Raffeala Gal 188, 292, 293
Don Gauthier 392, 393, 440, 510
Bill Gilgannon 64, 65
Donna Gordon 282, 283, 296, 352, 358, 420
David Graves 31
Lois Green 502, 503
Chris Griffin 192
Walt Gunthardt 273, 418, 489
Tim Halstrom 375
Nancy Jackson 148, 149
Gary Lagendyk 349
Martyn Lengden Art and Illustration 34, 35, 138, 139, 150, 151, 161, 172, 173, 203, 231, 237, 274, 288, 403
Joe Lepiano 324
Scott MacNeill 93 (bottom), 109 (right), 519
Maryland CartoGraphics 479
Paul McCuster, 492, 493
Valerie McKeown 167
Jack McMaster 33, 70, 73, 102, 103, 146, 147
Susan Meddaugh 19 (left)
Margery Mintz 30, 91
Tomio Nitto 59
Cheryl Kirk Noll 55
Carol O'Malia 109 (left)
Diane Palmisciano 308, 487

Jun Park/Turning Point 42, 76, 77, 100, 101, 178, 309, 310, 353, 354, 401, 429, 459, 466, 468, 471
Carol Paton 222, 223, 262
Andrew Plewes 20, 26, 27, 62, 63, 116
Stephen Quinlan 36, 112, 113, 144, 145, 208, 209, 217, 318, 319, 335, 338, 416
Paul Rivoche xii–xv, 336, 504
Valerie Spain 125
Margo Stahl 8, 9, 24, 25, 39, 61, 152, 250, 260
Don Stuart 409
Craig Terlson 2, 3
Angela Vaculik 12, 13, 252, 294, 295, 301, 394, 395
Peter Venemen 472
Carl Wiens 422, 423, 491
Andreas Zaretzki 449
Paul Zwolak 120, 121

PHOTOGRAPHY
Ian Crysler 86, 87, 298, 299, 340, 364, 365, 384, 404, 480
Colin Ericson 134, 136, 137
Greg Holman 40, 41, 312
Keith Gabriel 210, 284, 332, 333, 362, 363, 380, 381, 396, 506, 508, 509
Birgitte Nielsen 498, 499
Dan Paul 66, 67, 80, 118, 119, 130, 142, 143, 185, 206, 214, 215, 218, 263, 276, 277, 280, 281, 301, 326, 327, 334, 376, 377, 378, 413, 456, 458, 476, 496

**4, 5** Dallas and John Heaton/Miller Comstock;   **10** David W. Hamilton/The Image Bank;   **14, 15** Buck Ennis/Stock Boston;   **22** Santi Vasalli/The Image Bank;   **39** Joseph Szkodzinski/The Image Bank;   **50, 51** M. Burgess/Miller Comstock;   **68, 69** Miller Comstock;   **73** Harald Sund/The Image Bank;   **75** Jas. Blank/The Stock Market;   **82** Derek Caron/Masterfile;   **83** Whitney Lane/The Image Bank;   **86** David William Hamil/The Image Bank; Melchior Digiacomo/The Image Bank;   **94** Jon Feingersh/The Stock Market;   **95** Gary Cralle/The Image Bank;   **96** Aram Gesar/The Image Bank;   **98** Steve Leonard/Masterfile;   **106, 107** Martha Swope Assoc./Carol Rose; **110** Guiliano Colliva/The Image Bank;   **114** Birgitte Nielsen;   **129** G. Fritz/H. Armstrong Roberts/Miller Comstock;   **141** Bryan Peterson/The Stock Market;   **156** (top) Johnson Wax Co./Ursula Charaf;   **156** IBM Corp/Thomas Way;   **157** (top) Johnson Wax Co./Ursula Charaf;   **157** 2) David Scharf, 1977 All rights reserved;   **158** NASA;   **159** Georg Gerster/Miller Comstock;   **160** Kul Bhatia/The Image Bank;   **161** Luis Padilla/The Image Bank;   **176** Viesti Associates Inc.;   **179** Stephen Marks/Stockphotos Inc.;   **183** Super-